Alliance Adrift

Yoichi Funabashi

COUNCIL ON FOREIGN RELATIONS PRESS
NEW YORK

Council on Foreign Relations Books are distributed by Brookings Institution Press (1-800-275-1447). For further information on Council publications, please write the Council on Foreign Relations, 58 East 68th Street, New York, NY 10021, or call the Director of Communications at (212) 434-9400. Or visit our website at www.foreignrelations.org.

Library of Congress Cataloging-in-Publication Data

Alliance Adrift / by Yoichi Funabashi
    p.   cm.
    Includes bibliographical references and index.
    ISBN 0-87609-251-2
       0-87609-248-2

Contents

Foreword

The U.S.-Japan alliance, the cornerstone of East Asia's evolving balance of power, has been shaped by broad political and economic trends over the past decade. After the end of the Cold War, economic and trade issues came to the fore while security issues were relegated to the background. As Washington became concerned about the growth of Chinese power, U.S.-Japanese security cooperation revived, culminating in the April 1996 agreement to enhance Japan's role within the alliance. However, with Sino-American ties warming and Japan apparently unable to play a leadership role in rescuing Asia from its economic difficulties, the pendulum may have once again begun to swing in the other direction. The alliance is now confronting the most critical stage since its birth in 1951, with the emergence of rising China, Japan's economic debilitation, Asia's economic meltdown, and Russia's free fall. Its viability as a "constant" is now being challenged in the changing political climate.

These broad transpacific current events are the result of the myriad actions and decisions of politicians, bureaucrats, and other individuals inside and outside the policy process, where history, geography, and political cultures are interwoven in the dynamics of security policy. In this insightful analysis, Yoichi Funabashi gives us a fly-on-the-wall account of the dynamics driving the alliance's evolution at a time when political realignment in Tokyo, nuclear crisis on the Korean peninsula, the rape of a Japanese schoolgirl in Okinawa, and tensions in the Taiwan straits have convulsed U.S.-Japanese relations. Funabashi takes us into the day-to-day world of the people and events that reshaped this indispensable alliance during the turbulent years of the mid-1990s.

Lawrence J. Korb
Director of Studies
Council on Foreign Relations

v

Preface

This book is an account of how the U.S. and Japanese governments attempted (or did not attempt) to "redefine" the U.S.-Japanese alliance.

Four case studies are presented: first, the serious impact of economic and trade frictions on the alliance; second, the question of how the alliance ought to function, as raised by the suspicion that North Korea was developing a nuclear weapons program and the resulting U.N. economic sanctions; third, the diverse protests against U.S. troops stationed in Japan that were triggered by the rape of an Okinawan girl by U.S. servicemen; and fourth, Chinese challenges to the alliance, particularly the strain in Sino-American relations caused by the issue of Taiwan and China's missile tests during the 1996 Taiwanese presidential election campaign, which caused the United States to dispatch an aircraft carrier to the region.

These events were all part of the "redefining" process, a process which continues to this day and is likely to continue. Thus this book is only a chapter in an ongoing story. Nevertheless, the four cases, which study events that occurred in the mid-1990s, share a common theme that must be considered when contemplating the future of the U.S.-Japan alliance.

To complete the unfinished task of redefinition, it is vital that both parties reflect on what has taken place, note where the "blind spot" in the relationship was, and identify what the problems are. I strongly believe that the U.S.-Japan alliance will continue to play a key role in maintaining stability and peace in the Asian-Pacific region as well as the world at large, and that the alliance is capable of providing a valuable framework for managing the future U.S.-Japan relationship.

Yet this is not to suggest that the existing alliance should be maintained in its current form, that its structure be set in concrete, or that it be encapsulated in a worn-out intellectual framework. Rather, the alliance must be rearranged to suit the new age, the mutually supportive roles of the two sides must be "redefined," and a framework must be created that will truly contribute to peace and stability in the 21st century.

Initiatives from both sides for an active intellectual dialogue are indispensable to achieve such changes. No tradition of such dynamic, intellectual dialogue between Japan and the United States exists, such ideas or thoughts having been "contained" during the Cold War. Furthermore, discussions of the U.S.-Japan security alliance have been either excessively ideological or overly emotional, whether conducted in Japan or the United States. Very few journalistic works based on in-depth research have dealt with the dramatic story of U.S.-Japan security.

Faced with this vacuum, I was determined to break free from the ideological, systemic, and psychological restraints and endeavor to distill the essence of the U.S.-Japan security alliance discourse.

Luckily, the current era has worked to my advantage. We are now living in an age when security alliances can be discussed freely.

In conducting my interviews, I paid careful attention to the many factors associated with each decision-making process and the reciprocity of those elements. Particular emphasis was placed on such elements as history, social psychology, political culture, and organizational theory.

Fortunately the interviewees were not only cooperative; they were also highly appealing people. And many were devoted public servants.

Another aim of this book was to remove the U.S.-Japan security alliance from a lofty stage where only "security pros" and "high priests" counted and to place it in an arena of free discussion where full participation from ordinary citizens was and could be expected. In other words, I wanted the issue to be taken down to a "civilian" level.

The U.S.-Japan alliance is not widely understood by the public. A major motive behind the book was my own urge to present the unadorned truth of the alliance to both the American and Japanese publics. This urge stems from my firm conviction that the U.S.-Japan alliance, one of the most successful bilateral relationships in the post–World War II era, may well be relegated to the "used" shelf unless a common ground for intellectual dialogue and a shared understanding of the challenges to the alliance's "mission and role" are developed in both countries.

While the use of the term "adrift" may strike some readers as overly "journalistic," that term, as is made clear in the book, was first used by U.S. security experts. Blessed with the keenest perceptions when it comes to U.S.-Japan security issues, these people came to feel that the alliance reached a critical moment during the mid-1990s. The term is merely an accurate reflection of their perception of that crisis. As I did my research, it became clear to me that the expression was not hyperbole, a sentiment I believe readers will come to share as they progress through the book.

I did not want to write a case study merely for the sake of writing a case study. What I have attempted to do is to focus on the moves made by the individual players, in order to extract concrete stories based on their words, their eyewitness accounts, and their recollections. Facts are the most important component of the book, but I have woven in historical and psychological aspects to present a multidimensional story.

I should note, however, that I did not begin with this approach. The interviewees not only told their stories in a very vivid fashion, but they also provided me with sharp psychological analyses of the other people involved. As my research continued, I increasingly felt the need to include these finer details in the main story. I also felt that this would aid readers in better understanding the material.

During my research I met a number of government officials, not only from the United States and Japan, but also from Korea, China, and Taiwan. The names of these officials are given in the list of persons interviewed.

I was able to interview some leaders, ministers, and other high-level officials on the record, but most would agree only to background interviews. Some of the Chinese and Taiwanese authorities did not wish even to be named on the interview list, and their names, of course, are therefore omitted. I am very grateful to all of these individuals who were so generous with their valuable time.

This book was initially written in Japanese after I completed my assignment as head of the *Asahi Shimbun* American General Bureau. I am particularly grateful for the cooperation of the publisher and editor of the *Asahi Shimbun,* who provided me with an invaluable sabbatical. During this sabbatical, my news assistant, Ben Goldberg, devoted himself to the project. Fluent in Japanese, he was always efficient in preparing the much-needed documentation in both English and Japanese. I am very thankful for all his work and effort.

This book was published in Japan in November 1997 by Iwanami Shoten under the title *Domei Hyohryu.* It was greeted with an unexpectedly positive response. In 1998, I was honored to receive the Shincho Arts and Sciences Award, one of the most prestigious prizes in Japan for a work in the humanities.

I am also highly honored that the English version of the book will be published by the Council on Foreign Relations. I am especially grateful for all the encouragement I received from Leslie Gelb, president of the Council. The publication of the book by the Council is all the more personally significant because President Gelb is one of the most prominent experts on issues of diplomacy and international security.

I would also like to express my sincere gratitude to Dr. Larry Korb, director of studies at the Council on Foreign Relations, for taking the lead in the actual publishing process and for providing indispensable assistance. I must also thank Professor Gary Hufbauer, formerly the Council's director of studies, who has been an ongoing source of intellectual stimulus since my time as a visiting fellow at the Institute for International Economics. I am very grateful and feel fortunate that he assumed a central role in publishing this book. Furthermore I benefited greatly from exceptional insights and support provided by Dr. Michael

Green, Olin Fellow at the Council on Foreign Relations, and Mr. Akihisa Nagashima, the research associate for the Council's Asia Security Studies program.

I received a generous grant for the English translation from the Global Foundation for Research and Scholarship (Tokyo) and the Nippon Foundation. The publication of *Alliance Adrift* in English is part of Project Alliance Tomorrow, a comparative study project on security alliances. I would like to express my deepest gratitude to the Global Foundation for Research and Scholarship for its support. I am also deeply appreciative of the partial grant endowed by the Ito Scholarship Foundation.

The translation was undertaken by Dr. Wendy Spinks, a professor at Josai International University in Japan. I am convinced that this book would not be here today were it not for her Herculean efforts, sharp insights, and prompt translation. I would like to express my most sincere gratitude for all her work, and I feel especially lucky that despite my missing many deadlines, her fuse was as slow as her work was quick.

I am also grateful to Mr. Takahiro Suzuki, acting administrative director of the Research Division at the Global Foundation for Research and Scholarship, and Kori Urayama, my research assistant, for their unstinting support in aiding the translation process and fact-checking.

Yoichi Funabashi
May 1998

Author's Note

In this publication, Chinese and Korean personal names are placed in the order that is traditional in those countries, that is, family name, followed by given name (e.g., Gong Ro-Myung, Yoo Chong Ha, where Gong and Yoo are family names). Other names, including Japanese ones, are placed with the given name followed by the family name (e.g., Ryutaro Hashimoto, William Perry).

MILITARY BASES IN OKINAWA

Kunigami village

Northern Training Area

Aha Training Area
(Japan-U.S. Status-of-Forces)
(Agreement 2-(-b)

Okuma Rest Center

Kesaji Communication Site

Higashi village

Henoko Ordnance
Ammunition Depot

Nago city

Ie-jima Auxiliary Airfield

Motobu town

Ie village

Yaedake Communication Site

Camp Schwab

Camp Hansen

Onna Communication Site

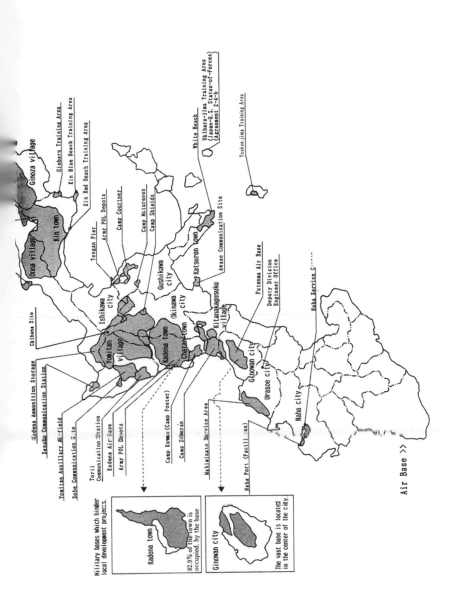

Kadena Ammunition Storage

Sennha Communication Station

Yositan Auxiliary Airfield

Sobe Communication Site

Torii Communication Station

Kadena Air Base

Army POL Depots

Camp Kuwae(Camp Foster)

Camp Zukeran

Makiminato Service Area

Naha Port (Facilities)

Chibana Site

Yomitan village

Kadena town

Chatan town

Ishikawa City

Gushikawa City

Okinawa City

Kitanakagusuku village

Ginowan city

Urasoe city

Naha city

Tengan Pier

Army POL Depots

Camp Courtney

Camp McTureous

Camp Shields

Katsuren town

Awase Communication Site

Futenma Air Base

Deputy Division
Engineer Office

Naha Service C------

Onna village

Kin town

Ginoza village

Ginbara Training Area

Kin Blue Beach Training Area

Kin Red Beach Training Area

White Beach

Ukibaru-Jima Training Area
(Japan-U.S. Status-of-Forces)
(Agreement 2-4-b)

Tsuken-Jima Training Area

Military bases which hinder
local development projects.

Kadena town

82.9% of the town is
occupied by the base

Ginowan city

The vast base is located
in the center of the city.

Air Base >>

I

Aerial view of Futenma Air Station.

Japanese Prime Minister Hiroshi Hashimoto and U.S. Ambassador Walter
Mondale announce the return of Futenma Air Station at a press conference
on April 12, 1996.

Chapter One

Futenma Air Station

"Does That Please You?"

Prime Minister Ryutaro Hashimoto punched the keys on the phone at his left with a practiced gesture. He was in his office. The setting sun filtering in from the courtyard suddenly waned. Outside the sky was already dark. It had just turned 6:00 P.M.

The prime minister was seated on the edge of a low table with his back to the courtyard. On his right was Foreign Minister Yukihiko Ikeda and Director-General of the Japan Defense Agency (JDA) Hideo Usui. To his left sat U.S. Ambassador to Japan Walter Mondale, Commander of the U.S. Forces in Japan Richard Meyers, and Deputy Chief of Mission at the U.S. Embassy in Japan Rust Deming.

Several high-ranking officials from the Ministry of Foreign Affairs (MOFA) and the Defense Agency as well as the PM's private secretaries were waiting. On the other end of the phone was the Governor of Okinawa Prefecture Masahide Ota. His voice could just be made out from the receiver. The waiting officials strained their ears to hear.

"I've secured the return of Futenma Air Station. But on condition that it's relocated somewhere else in Okinawa. Will you accept that? Does that please you?"

No one but Hashimoto could clearly catch the governor's reply, but they could hear him mumbling something. Deming, fluent in Japanese, was thinking to himself: *The PM sure didn't beat around the bush with the conditions.*

Usui was straining to catch the governor's answer. *He sounds a bit dubious. No, wait. Was that, "I'm not satisfied"?*

From his position, Deming could see a photo of former Prime Minister Eisaku Sato in the bookshelf behind the prime minister's desk. A long-haired shot. A white-haired shot. *I wonder when that was taken. He was exactly like Hashimoto when he was PM. Always short, lacquered hair. Maybe after he retired?* Under the photo hung a wooden sword and a bamboo sword.

"It's all right then, is it?"

The PM began to close. The governor seemed to be thanking him.

Did he say, "I appreciate it"? It sounded like he said, "It's a step forward." Usui concentrated every nerve in his body on the receiver in the PM's hand.

"Well, Ambassador Mondale is right here with me, so I'll hand you over to him. You studied in the States, so your English is good. Please thank him."

Having said that, Hashimoto thrust the phone at Ambassador Mondale. The ambassador looked nonplussed by the sudden move. His face turned red.

The ambassador and governor shared a few words. Mondale smiled at the "thank you" nuance. In possession of the receiver once again, Hashimoto more or less declared to the room, "Governor Ota was pleased. He's agreed."[1]

April 12, 1996.

The U.S. and Japanese governments agreed to the return to Japan of Futenma Air Station, the largest base relocation decision since the return of Okinawa to Japan in 1972.

Prime Minister Hashimoto and Ambassador Mondale held their last talks regarding the return of Futenma Air Station on that day. They were to hold a press conference that night at 8:00 P.M.

Hashimoto had spent all day at the Diet. In the morning he attended a meeting of the Budget Committee in the upper house, followed by a full session of the lower house at noon, then back to the budget session in the upper house in the afternoon. After returning to the PM's office, he was briefed by Masaki Orita, director-general of the North American Affairs Bureau at MOFA, and Masahiro Akiyama, director-general of the Bureau of Defense Policy, JDA. He then called in Ikeda and Usui, who had been waiting next door in the Cabinet's lounge. Finally, he called Mondale back into the room.

It was, in fact, on April 8 that Mondale had brought Hashimoto the official U.S. government decision to return Futenma Air Station. There were no last-minute details to discuss.

He probably just wants to let the Cabinet members know they did their bit too, Mondale was thinking. *Hashimoto wants to make this announcement himself. But there's nothing wrong with that. It is a Japanese issue after all. It's much better than having some Washington official come over and read out a statement.*[2]

The PM's office had let the press know that Hashimoto and Mondale wanted to hold a joint press conference that afternoon. Mondale immediately called U.S. Defense Secretary William Perry to get his opinion. Perry agreed that Hashimoto should have the spotlight.

After phoning Ota, the prime minister had one more call to make. That was to Takeshi Komura, general director of the Budget Bureau at the Ministry of Finance (MOF). Komura answered the phone.

"We got Futenma back." The prime minister's voice was upbeat. "It'll cost a bit, so I'm asking you to help us out on that."

Komura sounded as if he was resisting. The prime minister was a bit excited. "Look, this isn't about fiscal policy, you know. We'll be in deep trouble if you don't come through. Ambassador Mondale was here and it's been decided. I'm asking you. We'll set up an Okinawa Task Force. Give us someone from the Ministry of Finance. But it'll have to be someone who knows what's what, not some argumentative type."[3]

It was Hashimoto's one-man show. But he wasn't just starring in it. As one of the officials in the room later put it, Hashimoto "was the director, the star, the narrator, the scriptwriter and decided all the camera angles as well as who the audience was to be."

This is what the mass media dubbed "the PM play."

The PM Play

The PM play started on January 11 of that same year with the birth of the Hashimoto Cabinet. Hashimoto had decided in his heart of hearts that the first thing he had to do when prime minister was to meet the U.S. president.

Having received his political education at the hands of Eisaku Sato, Hashimoto had never wavered from the conservative mainstream. He also saw reviving the conservatives' fortunes as his duty. Just as the leader of the conservative mainstream in his time had done, Hashimoto felt no unease whatsoever about debuting as prime minister at a U.S.-Japan summit meeting. To the contrary, he thought it only natural to do so. It was the prevailing fashion, however, for the first encounter with the U.S. president to take place not in Washington but somewhere else, like Hosokawa's meeting with Clinton in New York.

The first thing Hashimoto did as prime minister was to call the U.S. president, Bill Clinton. On the morning after assuming his post, he telephoned Clinton and spoke with him for some 15 minutes, with Yayoi Matsuda, assistant division head in the Japan-U.S. Security Treaty Division at the Foreign Ministry's North American Affairs Bureau, acting as interpreter.

Clinton congratulated him on the prime ministry. He added, "There's a photo of you in your *kendo* outfit on the front page of the *New York Times*. Americans are scared of tough-guy Hashimoto."

"No, Ryutaro Hashimoto is really a gentle guy."

The conversation started with such banalities. Their conversation was mainly a greeting of a kind, but Hashimoto touched on "the suffering and anguish of the Okinawan people" (according to his subsequent press conference) and spoke of his "wish to work actively together towards the realignment, consolidation, and reduction of the bases." He closed by saying how much he was looking forward to President Clinton's scheduled visit to Japan in April, when they would discuss in depth the importance of the bilateral security structure.

Clinton had cancelled a visit to Japan the previous November. Clinton's Democratic White House had run head-on into Newt Gingrich's Republican Congress over cutting the fiscal deficit, and the federal government was brought to a standstill with federal payrolls delayed. In such circumstances Clinton had no choice but to cancel his visit.

The Japanese had sounded out the Americans about the possibility of Clinton visiting Japan in April 1996. But when asked, Ambassador Mondale had replied, "In the spring, maybe sometime in April." This was headlined in the U.S. dispatches as "Clinton's Japan Trip: 'Maybe April.'"[4]

It was almost a gibe or half in jest.

But it was not just Clinton's ephemeral presence that they were ridiculing. Japan's weakened state indicated by the phrase "Japan Passing" (as opposed to "Japan Bashing") could also be read into it.

Hashimoto said on the phone he was looking forward to Clinton's visit, but he really wanted to visit Clinton in the United States before then. The Ministry of Foreign Affairs was negative: "We're not sure it would be appropriate for you to visit first. They were the ones who cancelled. It's their turn to come here." Hashimoto, however, didn't care. And so it was arranged that Hashimoto's and Clinton's first meeting would take place at 8:00 P.M. on February 23 (10:00 A.M. on February 24, Japanese time) in Santa Monica, California.

The day prior to the summit, Hashimoto held a meeting on tactics in the small dining room at the PM's office. He asked how it would be if he asked Clinton directly for the return of Futenma Air Station. It was a kind of "royal query," Hashimoto saying he had his own ideas on the matter, but, be that as it may, he wanted to hear everyone else's opinion. Both the Ministry of Foreign Affairs and the Defense Agency were cautious.

"It has been concluded that it wouldn't be the right time to bring up Futenma." It was Sadajiro Furukawa, deputy Cabinet secretary, who summed up the ministry's and agency's opinion.

The bureaucrats had already debated the issue the previous day in Furukawa's office. Apart from Furukawa, the meeting was attended by Hiroshi Hirabayashi, chief Cabinet counselor for Foreign Affairs, Hitoshi Tanaka, deputy director-general at MOFA's North American

Affairs Bureau, and Masahiro Akiyama, director-general of the Bureau of Defense Policy at the JDA.

Hirabayashi made the point, "An early return of Futenma is a real possibility. If that's the case, how about bringing it up now? It'll earn points for the PM in the future. He won't win any points if he doesn't say anything. If it's all the same, why not let him take the initiative?"

His voice, however, was the exception. In the end, it was agreed that the PM shouldn't even mention the F-word (Futenma). In the session with the prime minister the next day, they restated their case. Hirabayashi held his tongue.

"You'll be touching America's most sensitive spot. Wouldn't that be too dangerous?"

"Isn't there a risk they won't perceive you as a statesman if you merely pass along the message that there's a strong desire along those lines in Okinawa?"

Although the language was polite, the bureaucrats were united in their opposition. If it was raised at the summit and rejected, it would inevitably have an adverse impact on future dialogue concerning the bases. And not just that. It would hurt U.S.-Japan relations just as a Liberal Democratic Party (LDP) prime minister was back in the saddle trying to set things right.

"But we just can't ignore Futenma, can we?" Hashimoto was not giving up easily. He believed that the return of Futenma was the key to solving the Okinawa base problem. He was worried that unless there was some clear progress made in either realigning or reducing the bases, the question of the bases as well as the U.S.-Japan Security Treaty would only become more difficult.

Even Hashimoto had no intention of turning his first summit meeting with Clinton into a negotiation over Futenma. He just wanted to sound out the waters and if possible set up a future direction for talks. But the opposition of his bureaucrats was much stronger than he anticipated.

He said, "Actually, I spent all last night thinking about it. And I decided I wouldn't bring it up. My reasons are a little different from yours, but my conclusion is the same."

The bureaucrats looked puzzled.

If you'd already decided, why did you force the issue?

You were intending to bring it up, but in the face of such strong opposition, are you covering up your embarrassment by saying that?

You thick-witted blockhead. You know all the issues involved. Do we have to spell it out in black-and-white so you'll get it?

The Hashimoto penchant was already making an appearance.[5]

The message Hashimoto was clearly trying to impart to the bureaucrats and to the central government machinery was, "I didn't decide after listening to you lot. I decided myself." Such an unfamiliar landlord at the PM's office was already making Kasumigaseki, the center of Japanese bureaucracy, uncomfortable.

"He's more like the director of the Political Research Committee than a prime minister."

"I'd like a talented assistant section chief like that working for me."

"He's a truly great squadron leader."

"It's Budget Bureau Officer Hashimoto's doing."

"The greatest crisis manager in the Cabinet."

Kasumigaseki's evaluation of Hashimoto became more twisted as time passed.

Hashimoto's manipulation of the Kasumigaseki cadres was fraught with tension. He seemed to believe: "Never show your full hand to the bureaucrats. That's the secret to manipulating them. The only way to move them is divide-and-rule."

No one can say for sure whether this wisdom was imparted to him by his mentor, Eisaku Sato, or if it was the product of his long years of survival in the LDP without his own faction but on wits and performance alone. Still, there's no doubt that, as Cabinet Secretary Seiroku Kajiyama put it around that time, he was "a master at creating tension."

Kajiyama's analysis of Hashimoto was, "He's not so good at multiple maneuvers, but he does his best work when his sights are set on one thing. So I wouldn't like to waste him fighting the rank and file."[6]

Kasumigaseki was forced to spend all its time guessing what Hashimoto was up to now, what his real intentions were. And Hashimoto seemed to enjoy every minute of it. His speech was either cloyingly sweet or infuriatingly vague. In short, he tended to be either over the top or too understated. At times, he spoke roughly, argumentatively, aggressively. Conversely, he could lay traps in sentences that went round and round. One high-ranking official at the Ministry of Foreign Affairs described his speech as "the politics of rhetoric and cant," and these turns of phrase were later to make the Kasumigaseki cadres a bundle of nerves.

Tough Guy

The White House was keeping a close eye on Hashimoto. The Clinton administration had only the vaguest idea of how solid the Hashimoto government was or of how long it would last. "The common wisdom of the analysts was that this could be short-termed and short-lived."[7]

The LDP revival wasn't genuine. The coalition with the Socialists (who changed their name to the Social Democrats in January 1996) was not likely to go well. Hashimoto had no strong support base within the LDP. The gainsayers went on and on. What's more, no one knew what Hashimoto's view vis-à-vis the United States was.

The analysis of a young Japanologist that "Hashimoto follows the Kishi-Nakasone line on U.S. relations whereas [Koichi] Kato [secretary general of the LDP and a PM contender from the same generation] adheres to the Yoshida-Miyazawa line" was discussed. The gist was that the Kishi-Nakasone line was more opportunistic and tactical.

The U.S. media wheeled out the old trade minister image of Hashimoto, writing, for example, "Japanese trade shogun Ryutaro Hashimoto wears his hair dramatically lacquered, shorter but similar to the style of sumo wrestlers and ancient samurai. The hairstyle could reflect his love of combat."[8] Another article found evidence of a Japanese superpower in his "debonair self-confidence and blunt talk that can border on brashness."[9]

The tough trade negotiations between Hashimoto, then minister of the Ministry of International Trade and Industry (MITI), and Mickey Kantor were well known. As national security adviser, Anthony Lake acknowledged Kantor's influence by saying, "Clinton was curious before to see [Hashimoto], because he heard so much about him from Mickey." Clinton's perception of Hashimoto depended to a large extent on Kantor's briefing.[10]

"Hashimoto never throws in the towel. He makes the competition do that because whoever throws in the towel has to make the first move the next time you sit down at the table. He really is a formidable negotiator."[11]

Kantor spoke jokingly of locking horns with Hashimoto as "trading swords for trading places," and both Clinton and Lake were amused. *Trading Places* was the title of the book by Clyde Prestowitz, himself once in charge of U.S. government trade negotiations with Japan as an adviser to the U.S. Department of Commerce.

Kantor took it upon himself to act as a kind of commentator on Hashimoto for the Clinton administration after Hashimoto became prime minister. Given that background, Clinton seemed to give weight to the Kantor-Hashimoto connection.

Indeed, there were those among Clinton's political advisers who wavered, wondering if a meeting with Hashimoto so close to a presidential election would be to the president's advantage. Their point was that foreign policy didn't win votes and Japan certainly didn't. They had had enough of Japan earning no votes domestically with the government of Tomiichi Murayama, the first Japanese Socialist head of government since 1947. They had plugged the considerable victories the United States had won in the bilateral trade negotiations for all they were worth, but media reaction was cool.

While the Clinton administration had maintained a certain relationship with the previous prime minister, Tomiichi Murayama, "Murayama was, after all, a Socialist."[12]

The Japanese side suspected that Clinton canceled his November 1995 visit because of the Murayama Cabinet, a suspicion that refused to go away. The White House denied it, saying "there was no such" consideration. "In fact, as I recall, my main concern was on the position towards Korea, and whether the Murayama government would be as clear in its views on Korea in regard to North Korea as his predecessors had been," said Anthony Lake later.[13]

Still, there were those in the White House who admitted that it would be a lie to say there wasn't an assessment that "there would be no political advantage whatsoever in going with Murayama at the helm."[14]

The U.S. side, however, did quietly sound out the possibility of visiting Japan at the beginning of 1996 to make amends for the November cancellation, but the Japanese refused in a roundabout way. Murayama had made it clear that he had no intention of having a summit. "There are all the court ceremonies in the New Year and we can't upset the court."

This was pretty straight talking for Murayama, especially going so far as to invoke the court. However, the Imperial Household Agency had already whispered to the Ministry of Foreign Affairs that "we'll manage something if it's the president of the United States who's coming."[15]

Hashimoto was leery of this un-Murayama-like conduct. *It would be a breach of etiquette to agree to a visit, to make the invitation, then resign just before he came. At the same time, it would also be extremely bad form to have him come and then resign immediately after as if nothing had happened. In his own way, Murayama must be doing some pretty hard thinking.* This was what went through Hashimoto's mind when he heard Murayama was hedging about Clinton's visit. And his instincts were right.[16]

On January 5, Murayama resigned.

Murayama's change of heart, his sense of responsibility and good intentions—Clinton first met with Murayama at the Naples summit in the summer of 1995, and responded warmly to Murayama's personal account of his life after the war and how he had been a part of building Japan's democracy through the labor movement, trying desperately to let the president see what he had in common with the United States—despite all this, the fact that Murayama could even become the Japanese prime minister was an indication of how the nature of the U.S.-Japan relationship had changed.

Washington Post columnist Jim Hoagland wrote, "Their [the Japanese] action also reflects an apparent feeling in the Diet that Japan had little to lose in its relations by choosing a Socialist as the nation's chief executive."[17] In the same vein, it may well have been "a reflection of an apparent U.S. feeling that the United States had little to lose in its relations with Japan even if it one-sidedly cancelled a presidential visit to Japan."

Indeed, the U.S. government could not achieve a consensus regarding whether Clinton should cancel right up to the last minute.

Lake looked back on the events of the time like this: "The State Department was especially strong in saying that he had to go to Japan and that it would be very damaging if he didn't. We [the National Security Council] all felt that way. But of course, every morning I would attend the 7:30 staff meetings, and it became evident to me towards the very end that with the government shutdown, it was just becoming extremely difficult for the president to go abroad. I concluded that it would be damaging not only here in the U.S., but also with our relations with Japan and in Asia if there was a public outcry here about the president at such a moment going abroad.

"We had laid to rest in 1992–93 concerns about the dangers of spending too much time on foreign policy at the expense of domestic policy. So in the end, as I recall, I agreed that he should stay at home. I didn't propose it, I wasn't happy about it by any means, but I thought it had become inevitable."[18]

The Japanese government learned of the cancellation in reports from the U.S. media. Takakazu Kuriyama, Japanese ambassador to the United States, had made a quick visit back to Japan before November 19 when Clinton's visit was scheduled. On November 13, in the car going to Dulles Airport, he read in the *Washington Post*, "Clinton's Visit to Japan Shortened." But he saw this as a consolation and boarded the plane. He learned of the postponement upon disembarking in Tokyo.[18]

Japan had hosted the Asia-Pacific Economic Cooperation (APEC) meeting in Osaka in 1995. The Japanese ambassador was called in with the other APEC ambassadors posted in Washington and told there of the cancellation. A high ranking official at the Ministry of Foreign Affairs was indignant. "The State Department should have given special consideration to Japan. Japan was the host, a summit between the two leaders had been scheduled, besides which Clinton was invited as a state guest."[20]

That was how little the Japanese presence, or rather Japan, mattered.

Hawk and Dove

The image of the tough guy in his *kendo* dress was soon to be amended. Stanley Roth, a presidential aide, had already given his provisional assessment of Hashimoto to the White House: "Even despite the Okinawan rape incident, Hashimoto was one of the few Japanese politi-

cians who spoke out on the importance of the U.S.-Japan relationship."
The view that "perhaps Hashimoto is a hawk on trade but a dove on
security" also started to circulate.

William Perry, secretary of defense, met Hashimoto in Tokyo in
November 1995. Hashimoto met Perry not in his capacity as trade minister but as chairman of the LDP. Perry passed on his opinion that
"Hashimoto has a sophisticated knowledge of security issues. I was
quite impressed."[21]

Hashimoto focused on security issues, stressing the importance of the
bilateral security relationship and what needed to be done to maintain it.
*Mickey Kantor has probably monopolized the field and is smugly telling Clinton
all about me. I need Clinton to get another picture of me. Perry can probably do
that and it would be better if that picture was seen through the security issue lens.*

Hashimoto was conscious of himself not as LDP chairman but as
apprentice PM. He said to Perry, "I'm apprehensive that the Japanese
have forgotten the role the U.S.-Japan Security Treaty plays. The treaty
should be just as important for America, not just Japan. How aware of
that are the American people? We need to discuss what each country
can do within the treaty framework.

"Almost all of Asia supported me when I stood firm against Mickey
Kantor's managed trade and numerical targets. There was a point when
I thought it didn't matter if the auto parts negotiations broke down. At
the same time, with one voice both Asia and the EC [European Commu-
nity] made a strong request 'not to destroy U.S-Japan relations.' When I
heard that, I was made acutely aware of how important a stable bilateral
relationship was and how necessary it was to global stability."[22]

Hashimoto was trying to change the tough-guy image into that of
someone who had learned the wisdom of survival under fire.
Hashimoto had stood for party chairmanship under the banner of
"LDPness" in the fall of the previous year. His views on foreign policy,
especially U.S.-Japan relations, after assuming the chairmanship were
colored by this LDPness. For example, in a speech titled "Becoming a
Party the People Can Entrust Their Future Dreams To," which he delivered at a celebration of the 40th anniversary of the party's foundation,
he made the following points:

> In modern history, our country has maintained stable international rela-
> tions whenever it has had friendly dealings with the United Kingdom
> and the United States of America, the two global leaders during this
> period. Based on that experience, I would like to emphasize anew the
> unchanging belief that there is no bilateral relationship which is more
> important to Japan than that with the United States.
>   The United States of America was an historically unprecedentedly
> generous victor in war towards the defeated Japan. We need to face up to
> the fact that both Japanese and Asian peace and stability have been main-
> tained by our security treaty with that America.[23]

Next, Hashimoto paid homage to three leaders in the 40-year history of the LDP (including its forerunner, the Liberal Party): Shigeru Yoshida, Nobusuke Kishi, and Eisaku Sato.

Yoshida "took the first steps towards Japanese independence by simultaneously signing the San Francisco Peace Treaty and the U.S.-Japan Security Treaty, bringing Japan peace and stability amid an escalating Cold War." As for Kishi, "He amended the security treaty, adding to the purely military terms of the old treaty the facilitation of economic cooperation for the promotion of economic activity between the two countries." Under Sato, "Amicability and trust in the bilateral relationship was strengthened with the reversion of Okinawa to Japan in 1972."

Hashimoto made doubly sure his point got home. "I strongly believe that we have reached a point where we must reacknowledge the importance of U.S.-Japan relations."

Hashimoto was not alone in his evaluation of Japan's alliances with the United States and the United Kingdom. The historical view that Japan must never repeat the folly of failing to maintain an alliance with those two countries was, in fact, the consensus of almost all the LDP leaders who had supported the bilateral alignment after the war.

"The U.K. was Japan's first window on a different civilization and a different standard of values. And it was a good partner to Japan. Friendship takes time to be built, but is easily broken."[24]

When Hashimoto whispers like this, he is expressing his determination not to repeat the fate of the 20-year-long alliance with the United Kingdom. It is a feeling reflected in his reply before the Diet to the effect that "I shudder to think of the nature of U.S.-Japan relations should the Japan-U.S. Security Treaty cease to function."[25]

Lake, who had visited Japan and met with Hashimoto in early February 1996, immediately reported his appraisal of Hashimoto to Clinton on his return. "He's changing now and transforming himself from tough negotiator to statesman."

Lake was impressed. "He was well aware of the tough-guy image he had in the States in the trade negotiations. That's why he was at pains to let the U.S. side know that he placed great store by the bilateral relationship. One thing that impressed me was that they were clearly making an effort to send a signal."[26]

The U.S. government was inwardly building its hopes that "just like Nixon could go to China because he was an anti-Communist, Hashimoto could be reasonable on trade because he was a tough negotiator."

Winston Lord, assistant secretary of state, held that view. "It gave us a sense of relief that, given that he was so tough with us on trade, it'd be all right to leave Japanese domestic affairs in his hands. So, conversely, we could probably be more rational, take a more flexible stance on future trade issues or anything. Most of us felt that this was good news, to have someone whose flank was already protected."[27]

As the February Santa Monica and April Tokyo summits came and went, the U.S. take on Hashimoto started to change. A White House aide was quoted after the April summit: "We used to say about John Kennedy that he was his own secretary of state. It can be said about Prime Minister Hashimoto that he is his own foreign minister and defense minister."[28]

Santa Monica

The U.S. side was also holding meetings in preparation for the Santa Monica summit. One was held in the Presidential Suite at the Sheraton Miramar Hotel on Wilshire Boulevard immediately prior to the summit. The summit was to be held in the suite.

Those who had gathered in Santa Monica were National Security Adviser Lake, White House Chief of Staff Leon Panetta, Assistant Secretary of State Lord, Deputy Assistant Secretary of Defense Kurt Campbell, and Ambassador Mondale.

Lake saw the summit as important. "He [Clinton] himself insisted on the Santa Monica meeting with a view towards a series of steps: first Santa Monica as an icebreaker to get acquainted, to lay the groundwork."[29]

The president had asked Lake to run matters this time. The White House had left Asian-Pacific affairs up to the State Department previously. This year, however, after Clinton's visit to Japan, it had to set up a summit meeting with China. Since it was also a presidential election year, the White House could not afford to make any foreign policy mistakes. At the very least, it had to make sure it called all the shots when Clinton was on the foreign policy stage.

The White House also wanted to shift the focus from just trade to security issues as well. The Japanese side had also sent a clear message that "the prime minister would like to speak mainly about security matters."

Fortunately, the Japanese had also conveyed "the prime minister's strong desire to keep the numbers small." In such a case, it would be possible to keep the top economic people out.

In the press briefing the day before the summit, White House Press Secretary Mike McCurry commented, "It's important to say at the outset that this will likely be one of the first meetings between a president of the United States and a Japanese prime minister that is not defined simply by the trade issue,"[30] indicating that the summit would cover foreign policy and security issues. Things were moving along as Lake had planned.

There were those before the summit who warned of the possibility that Japan might suddenly raise the question of the Futenma Air Station's return. They would have to avoid the prime minister making a direct appeal to Clinton and placing him on the spot. The opinion was voiced that the president should send a tough message to the prime minister before they met.

The U.S. side asked the Japanese about "Hashimoto's attitude on this question," but the Japanese were noncommittal. One minute they were saying, "Futenma is not an issue for the prime minister to bring up." Then the next they added, "This prime minister decides everything for himself, so we can't be 100 percent sure of anything."[31]

In the end, the White House decided not to send a tough message. It was, after all, the first meeting, and it didn't seem wise to harden Hashimoto's attitude by making the wrong move. It would be better to take a soft approach. Clinton liked the soft approach.

Initially "there was no plan for any defense officials to be at Santa Monica, then literally two days before the meeting the national security adviser, Anthony Lake, called Campbell and said 'Get on an airplane, you have got to come out and brief me and the president.'"[32] This was based on Lake's judgment that security issues and the question of the bases would almost certainly come up.

Campbell rented a car upon arrival at Los Angeles Airport. The line was really huge, which was frustrating. He waited in line for an hour, got the car, and streaked across town to a small hotel in the wealthy area of Malibu, where he met with Ambassador Mondale.

Mondale had been appointed ambassador to Japan in the spring of 1993. He had been Jimmy Carter's vice president. The Japanese government was happy with this "big shot" ambassador.

As soon as he took up office, however, U.S.-Japan trade friction broke out. In the negotiations over automobile parts, U.S. Trade Representative Mickey Kantor and MITI Minister Ryutaro Hashimoto were soon exchanging shots in their own version of *High Noon*. It was not an easy time to be ambassador.

When running in the 1984 presidential elections, Mondale made some Japan-bashing statements in a bid to win the labor vote. There were those in Japan who were alarmed and hoped that he wouldn't aggravate the trade issue, instead of acting as a brake on the U.S. government.

With the birth of the Clinton administration, Mondale actually wanted the job of ambassador to the United Nations. The Clinton White House, however, had earmarked that job for a woman. (Madeleine Albright was later appointed.[33])

Mondale was offered the ambassadorship to Russia, but he declined, letting it be known in a roundabout way that he wanted Japan.[33] In fact,

Richard Holbrooke, assistant secretary of state (East Asian affairs) in the Carter administration, was pushing hard for the post and had the support of Secretary of State Warren Christopher and Samuel Berger, number two in the National Security Council (NSC).[35]

Japan's Ministry of Foreign Affairs, however, was not well disposed towards Holbrooke. This stemmed from "doubts concerning his suitability" on the basis of his comments that the U.S. military would be forced to withdraw to a certain extent from the Asian-Pacific region in the future.[36] But the roots went even deeper. Feelings bordering on antagonism were to be heard within MOFA. The real story, which was "not for public consumption" but which trickled into the White House, ran along the lines of "he's rude," "he's too pushy," "he's a points earner," and "he'd be a drop in standards."

What with this and that, Holbrooke was switched over to Germany, and as a result Mondale got the Japan job. While Mondale was a political friend of Clinton's, they came from different generations, had different political beliefs, and tapped into different personal networks. Mondale was a traditional liberal and had strong ties with organized labor. He was different from the neo-liberal Clinton. In the Clinton administration, he was close to William Perry, the defense secretary, whom he found easy to talk to. In the 1970s, Carter had set up a special team to steer SALT (the U.S.-Soviet Strategic Arms Limitations Treaty) through the Senate, placing Vice President Mondale at the head. Mondale chose Perry as his deputy, and the two had been friends ever since.[37]

After being thrashed in the presidential election, Mondale had slipped out of the Washington mainstream, but ex–vice presidents still carried weight. Because Secretary of State Christopher was such a low-key presence and virtually invisible in Asia and the Pacific, Mondale naturally assumed the mantle of "Secretary of State for Asian Affairs."[38] After 1994, the State Department itself was being called on to reconsolidate the Clinton administration's Asia policies, especially to strengthen security relations.

At first being ambassador to Japan frustrated Mondale. Trade frictions exhausted him. He tried hard to make friends with the top leaders and not to make a deal with them on economic matters. He did not succeed much. He then found his man, Ryutaro Hashimoto. Unlike the strained relationship his predecessor, Michael Armacost, had had with Hashimoto,[39] Mondale set up with Hashimoto a behind-the-scenes pipeline for trade issues and strengthened their cooperation. With the formation of the Hashimoto government, Mondale proclaimed "the birth of a genuine administration" and urged that it "be treated with more care" all the more because of this relationship.

Kurt Campbell

Mondale saw Campbell as the point man for U.S.-Japan security issues. He highly praised Campbell's ability and vitality but also felt he was too young. Mondale had the impression that he was a bit dangerous, a young man in too much of a hurry.[40] He told Campbell, "I want you to work closely with the embassy. There are things that we can do too."

Mondale had advised the Japanese before the summit to exercise caution: "Aiming too high with the bases will have a negative impact on the relationship." Campbell had heard that and decided it was important to listen to Mondale's thoughts before he briefed the president. He knew he had to treat Mondale with due courtesy.

Mondale's greatest fear was the possibility that a reduction in the bases would lower the quality of the U.S. presence in the Asian-Pacific region. He added that he thought it best if this summit focused on security, not economics and trade. "That's what Japan seems to want too."

After the meeting ended, Campbell sped off towards Santa Monica. He had grown up in southern California and knew the territory. He had graduated from the University of California, San Diego, when Reagan was at his height. He thought he knew the roads around there, but things had changed a lot. He tried to follow Route 1 along the Pacific Coast, then cut through the elegant town of Pacific Palisades, but somewhere he took a wrong turn. His mind was working overtime.

While Campbell was studying at San Diego, he had gone to Erevan University in the capital of Armenia to study violin for a year. Fresno, Campbell's hometown, had one of the largest Armenian communities in the United States. The Armenians were famous for their musical talent. Although Campbell himself was not of Armenian descent, he was musically talented and was able to go to Erevan, thanks to the Armenian community's network.[41]

At the time, Armenia was still part of the Soviet Union. U.S.-Soviet relations were tense in the aftermath of the Soviet invasion of Afghanistan. Owing to the second oil shock, Armenia was not getting any oil from Iran and was suffering an energy crisis. Even in the university dormitories, the heaters were only turned on once a week. Campbell spent many nights curled up in his down jacket fighting off the bedbugs.

After San Diego, he went on to Brasenose College at Oxford. There he majored in international relations, earning a doctorate with his thesis on South Africa. At Brasenose, he rowed and played rugby in the first college teams. The tennis he had mastered as a child was evident at both San Diego and then Oxford. He had a college ranking and had played in professional tournaments. He had even played John McEnroe in a doubles match, although he lost.

Between 1988 and 1993 Campbell was associate professor at Harvard's John F. Kennedy School of Government. During that time, he was chosen as a White House Fellow for one year in 1992. This is a special program that chooses the best and the brightest of America's youth to serve as staff in the U.S. federal government for a year. Many of today's leaders have emerged from the program.

Campbell had been fortunate enough to work for Treasury Secretary Lloyd Bentsen. His outstanding work there got him head-hunted over to the North American Free Trade Agreement (NAFTA) team in the White House. And he had been on a roll ever since.

Moving over to the NSC, he became director of the Democracy Office. It was at this time that he first met Lake. He then switched to the Pentagon.

Campbell had had a connection with Joseph Nye, assistant secretary of defense, since his time at Harvard. Nye appointed him "counselor," akin to his chief of staff, but "the Pentagon is like a small country and there really is no chief of staff at the Pentagon."[42] After serving as counselor for a while, he was appointed deputy assistant secretary of defense for Asian and Pacific affairs in May 1995 at the tender age of 37.

Campbell had aced the course that so many young Americans with their sights set on Washington aspire to. He was energetic, always had a cool head on his shoulders, was highly creative, dynamic, and a loyal team player to boot.

Campbell's youthful élan, occasionally tinged with a puckish mischievousness, was revealed by Gayle Von Eckartsburg, staff member of the Japan Country Desk. She remembers how Campbell got her into a signing ceremony usually reserved for VIPs. Campbell simply burst into the Secret Service's office, said Secretary Christopher had lost the special pin he needed to get in to the event, and asked for another one, which he then gave to Von Eckartsburg.[43]

"Theodore Roosevelt used to be described as a steam engine in trousers, but that's Campbell to a T," said a Pentagon official.[44] "If an idea is interesting, he doesn't care if it comes from the Pentagon or from outside, it's no holds barred. He's an idea sponge. He always adopted and internalized good ideas." That's the kind of comment you heard.

Paul Giarra, who retired after serving as head of the Pentagon's Japan Division, spent the last days of a long career at the Pentagon working under Campbell. He looks back on those days as his most stimulating both intellectually and in terms of his work. "He always had some agendas. He always spoke first with a question. So, you always had to be prepared when you met him. You cannot beat something with nothing."[45]

His position and title as deputy assistant secretary was neither too high nor too low. In fact, it was perfect for an enterprising man. Campbell took full advantage of this, going all out for issues to tackle.

Nevertheless, he did appear to step on the toes of the assistant secretary class just above him. Campbell never forgot to maintain a humble demeanor in front of this group, and worked hard not to stand out, but the group just above him was overwhelmed by his intellectual prowess, his vitality, and his magnetism.

There were those who cautioned that Campbell was too aggressive. Warning signals were flashing at the State Department, at the White House, in the military, and at the all-important Pentagon.

Campbell was not without his own allies, however. The huge number of 30-somethings who accompanied Clinton into power were busy building their own lateral networks. More important, Campbell had won Perry's support. Perry had a high opinion of him. Lake liked him too.

Campbell headed to the Beverly Wilshire Hotel where the Japanese entourage was staying and spoke for 10 minutes with Director-General of North American Affairs Orita on Hashimoto's stance. Orita spoke "in vague generalities" from start to end, saying, "The prime minister may bring up Okinawa. But I have no idea of what he will actually do."

The time for the summit meeting was getting closer.

Campbell rushed over to the U.S. side's Sheraton Miramar and headed straight for Lake's room with Panetta. Lake was in the bathtub, but he wanted Campbell's report right away, so Campbell, through the closed door, recapped briefly the political situation surrounding Okinawa and Futenma and Mr. Hashimoto's disposition. When he finished, Lake suggested that Campbell plan on coming into the meeting.

Campbell was grateful for Lake's solicitation, but replied cautiously. "It's an honor for you to say so, sir. It's just that the Japanese are very strict about protocol and we have negotiated that there will be only four people in the meeting on each side. I don't think it's possible for me just to walk in."

Lake replied, "Let me take care of that." (In fact, immediately before the summit began, Lake walked out into the hallway, picked up a chair himself, then brought it in and put it down next to his and said to Campbell, "Come join me."[46])

That's Right, Futenma

Clinton was in a good mood.

He'd just played a round of golf at the famous course across the road from the Twentieth Century Fox studio, the Los Angeles Hillcrest Country Club. This classic course, opened in 1920, was built by Hollywood's wealthy Jewish residents, who were banned from playing on other courses because of the anti-Semitism of the day. Such big Hollywood stars as Groucho and Harpo Marx, Jack Benny, Danny Kaye, and Al

Jolson were members, and the club was still managed mainly by those of Jewish descent.

Clinton's score was good too. It was close to 80. Coming in under 80, a lifelong dream, seemed possible. (Clinton scored 79 at Coronado Island, just outside of San Diego on June 10 of that year.[47])

What's more, the Republican frontrunner, Bob Dole, had fared rather badly in the presidential preliminaries and the right-wing conservative Pat Buchanan was making inroads. Buchanan had beaten Dole in the Iowa party caucus a short while back. Dole was uninspiring. The opinion polls gave Clinton more than a 10 percentage point lead over Dole.

And it didn't end there. There was an exciting gathering after the summit was over. A movie showing and dinner were held at the mansion of music producer David Geffen, who was coordinating Clinton's Hollywood supporters.

California was the key to Clinton's reelection. He had already visited the state more than 20 times. (Clinton visited California a total of 27 times in the 48 months of his first presidency. As Henry Cisneros, housing and urban development secretary, put it, "The election of 1996 starts and ends with California.") Every time Clinton visited California, Hollywood superstars like Barbra Streisand, Tom Hanks, and Steven Spielberg helped push his ratings up.

Geffen was one of Hollywood's greatest power brokers. While still quite young, he had had success at the end of the 1960s representing Peter, Paul, and Mary and had grown into a driving force in the American music industry. In the 1992 presidential election, he donated $120,000 to the Clinton campaign and showed an unusual interest in politics. Having openly declared himself gay, he secured a public commitment from Clinton on the issue of gays in the armed forces.

He had an especially close relationship with the Hollywood lawyer who became the U.S. trade representative in Clinton's first administration, Mickey Kantor. Later, it was said that Kantor threatened trade sanctions against the Chinese over copyright issues and persisted with it out of loyalty to the U.S. music industry—or in short Geffen—which was losing the most from unlicensed CDs.

Geffen also helped raise the money for the documentary film *War Room*, which told the story of two staff advisers who were central figures in the 1992 election, James Carville and George Stephanopoulos.

MCA's Edgar Bronfman and film producer Steve Tisch would also show up on the night of the summit.[48] Both could easily write checks for $50,000 or $100,000.

Clinton had already arrived at the summit location. He ran a final check there with his aides. One said, "Hashimoto may raise some issues relating to Okinawa. It might even be better if he did. Let's draw him out and see what he has to say on it."[49]

Clinton nodded at the suggestion, and then, almost as if it had just crossed his mind, he turned to Lake. He was trying to remember the name of the base he had been briefed on earlier. "There's a base in Okinawa that's been in the news recently. What's it called again?"

As Lake was about to answer, Clinton preempted him. "That's right, Futenma." He wrote it down on a white card on the table and slipped it into his right chest pocket. Clinton was left-handed.

Extremely Difficult

It was Clinton who first broached the subject at the summit. "There are things we [the United States] can and can't do concerning the bases. We also can't afford to weaken the American presence in Asia, but I would welcome your frank thoughts on the matter."

Hashimoto was at a loss for words. He was tense. The high government officials with him were also pulled tight as a string. "I feel like I'm being tested by Mr. Clinton and everyone else." Hashimoto trotted out this apparently rehearsed joke and the Japanese officials laughed on cue.

One of the Americans was suspicious of "the asinine, nervous tittering of high-ranking Japanese officials at a summit meeting." It was such a contrast to the very relaxed Clinton. Clinton was there without any notes, but Hashimoto had placed a large stack of briefing papers on the table in front of him.

It was a very awkward moment. The prime minister seemed to have momentarily lost his tongue. He'd also turned slightly pale. After a brief pause, Hashimoto replied, "To tell you the truth, I'm in an awkward position myself. Were I to pass on the demands of the Okinawan people, it would be for the complete return of Futenma. However, bearing in mind the importance of U.S.-Japan security and maintaining the functionality of the U.S. armed forces, I realize that that is extremely difficult."

When the Japanese interpreter had finished translating into English, a perplexed Lake checked with the U.S. interpreter, Fumiko Gregg. "In short, did the prime minister ask for the return?"

Gregg explained, "No, the prime minister did not say he was asking for the return. He merely stated that this subject was of great concern in Okinawa."[50]

After the meeting, the aides huddled with Clinton. Lake, Lord, and Mondale, all three, couldn't make it out. "Why did Hashimoto say that? Did he say it knowing it wasn't possible? Why?" Someone said, "Let's tell them that Futenma isn't possible. If we don't, it'll be a muddle."

The Japanese interpreter, Yayoi Matsuda, had interpreted Hashimoto's last words as "extremely difficult." The Americans' interpretation was split between "he said it was impossible" and "he's saying in a Japanese way that this was something important."[51]

Both the Japanese Ministry of Foreign Affairs and the Defense Agency were in a flap because the prime minister had mentioned "Futenma" in a summit meeting. It was not in the script, and even worse, his phrasing had led to a misunderstanding.

The day after the Santa Monica summit, Hitoshi Tanaka and Takemasa Moriya had dinner with Campbell and Deming at the Watergate Hotel in Washington. Moriya was deputy director of the Defense Bureau at JDA.

Campbell set the ball rolling. "There is a majority opinion and a minority opinion in the U.S. government over Mr. Hashimoto's remarks. The majority view is that the prime minister expressed an understanding that returning Futenma was impossible. The minority view is that he expressed an interest that we should do it. Personally, I come down in the latter camp. Which exactly is it?"[52]

A Japanese official later recalled, "The damage control after the summit was something terrible. The U.S. believed that the statement indicated the prime minister's awareness of the difficulty of returning Futenma. So, they pressed us to say that that interpretation was right. In contrast, things weren't like that on our side. We parried, saying that the remark was a sign of the prime minister's great interest in the issue and should be taken seriously. It took us a week to convince the Americans to accept our case."[53]

Hashimoto's trip to Santa Monica had a "heart-stopping" aspect.[54]

Even on the flight over, Hashimoto felt like Hamlet: "to bring it up or not to bring it up." To borrow some classic Hashimoto hyperbole, "He was still in two minds when he arrived at the meeting."[55]

Hashimoto himself later confessed, "At the time, there were many people who thought it would be impossible to even mention the word 'Futenma.' I wasn't confident either. It was without any self-assurance that I raised the issue in my first meeting with President Clinton in Santa Monica. I think the Americans also took the issue in all seriousness."[56] "I, myself, didn't know what to do. What would happen if having raised an issue which had no clear prospects and the hopes of the residents excessively high, nothing happened? In the end, the Governor's face appeared in my mind's eye and I asked myself what was the main point for the Americans and so, I spoke of Futenma."[57]

The Buddhist Monk

After the meeting, Kurt Campbell phoned Defense Secretary William Perry and told him what had been said. He told him that Hashimoto had mentioned Futenma. Perry asked Campbell to fly back to Washington a bit early and instructed him to come to his house to report more fully. It was quite late at night when Campbell arrived at Perry's home in a quiet, leafy residential area of Virginia.

Campbell thought Perry looked like a Buddhist monk as he sat still listening with his chin resting on his locked fingers as if in prayer. *They usually apply the word "inscrutable" to Asians like the Japanese or Chinese, but it describes Perry to a T.*

Perry gave no instructions. He didn't say anything except to thank Campbell for coming over. Campbell almost had to excuse himself from the house, so engrossed in his thoughts was Perry on the sofa.[58]

Perry was contemplating the return of Futenma Air Station. He was also remembering his meeting with Hashimoto last November when he was in Japan. They met in Perry's suite at the Hotel Okura. It was late at night when Hashimoto turned up with an interpreter in tow. Taking some water out of the suite's fridge, he made himself a whisky and water, placed it on the table in front of him, and started talking effusively. It was all about U.S.-Japan security matters.

At the time, Hashimoto mentioned the Okinawan people's strong wish for the return of Futenma Air Station. But he spoke objectively, not as if it were a personal desire. After some 15 minutes, Hashimoto suddenly said, "I'm doing all the talking. I'm sorry. I'm sorry," and repeatedly urged Perry to speak.

Since then, Futenma Air Station had been on Perry's mind. No, it might be more correct to say that he was of two minds.

Both Democrat Mike Mansfield, a former ambassador to Japan, and Republican Richard Armitage, a former assistant deputy secretary of defense—two men Perry trusted—had been calling for the return of Futenma since immediately after the Okinawan rape incident in the fall of 1995. Mansfield had been stationed as a marine in China and the Philippines in the 1920s. He had a special attachment to the U.S. Marine Corps. After leaving the corps, he returned home to Montana. He worked as a coal miner and mining engineer for 10 years to support his family, then taught history at Montana University. Later he entered politics.

After World War II, when the marines faced the danger of dissolution, Mansfield worked desperately in Congress to keep the marines alive as an institution.

He also thought, however, that the Okinawan bases should be reduced, including the marine bases. He went on public record that "the U.S.-Japan treaty was crucial even in a post–Cold War era, but there is a need to change how it is applied."

During Mansfield's time as ambassador to Japan, he visited Okinawa three times. He even once traveled as far as the island of Iriomote. "I didn't see any cats."[59] He was referring to the indigenous wild cat, reputedly a living fossil.

Mansfield was a curious and ebullient man. That is probably one of the reasons he became the best-loved U.S. ambassador of the Japanese

people in the postwar era. Even after retiring from public life and open-
ing up an office in Washington, his visitors from Japan never dwindled.
And one of his most regular annual visitors was Okinawa Governor
Masahide Ota.

Ota spoke of the need to return Futenma Air Station each time they
met. Mansfield heard directly the voice of Okinawa from Ota on this
and other issues. He was also to learn about the reality of the bases from
the local mayors who accompanied Ota. He felt a righteous indignation
at the fact that even when Ota was in Washington he couldn't get an
appointment with the higher-ups at the State or Defense departments.
Mansfield gave him a warm reception.

Perry telephoned Mansfield that spring and asked to meet Mansfield somewhere quiet. Mansfield was only too happy to agree. Perry
had served in Asia in the rank and file as well. Mansfield had long
admired him.

Mansfield gave Perry a rundown of his conversations with Ota to
date. He also mentioned that Ota had specialized in journalism and history and had studied at Syracuse University. "Of course, the final decision will be made by the Japanese government. Nevertheless, Ota is the
head of the local government and is elected by the prefecture's people.
He should at least be listened to. Some of the higher-ups in the Defense
and State departments should receive him as a matter of courtesy."[60]

Mansfield also suggested that Perry look into the possibility of
returning Futenma Air Station. He felt that "Perry was in the process of
making up his mind." But Perry remained inscrutable.

Armitage was leaning towards the same position. Since the 1980s, his
voice carried weight as one of America's top experts on U.S.-Japan security matters. He had been in the navy and had served in Vietnam.

Armitage told a close friend, "The marines probably don't like what
either Campbell or I have to say. But I've served. That makes a difference. What stops as a policy criticism against me escalates into a personal attack in Campbell's case."

Armitage was a Republican. All the more reason why he was such a
reliable "brain trust" for Perry and Campbell. Someone said he was
"Perry and Campbell's talisman against the Republicans."

When asked his opinion by Perry in October 1995, Armitage urged
"returning Futenma as a first gesture of good faith towards the heavily
burdened Okinawan people and incorporating the marines' functions
into Kadena."

Armitage knew Futenma well. In the 1980s, he had served as assistant secretary at the Defense Department under Reagan. During that
time, Governor Ota's predecessor, Junji Nishime, visited Washington
twice in 1985 and 1988. Nishime had twice called for the return of

Futenma Air Station. Later in 1990, both governments had in effect shelved the issue, saying they would give it "further consideration."

Armitage was concerned that "without a large, symbolic return of a base this time, the bilateral security relationship would be torn out by its roots."[61] He reasoned that the return of Futenma Air Station could be a trump card for avoiding just such a scenario.

Friends of Japan in the United States started talking about returning Futenma. Both Republicans and Democrats were discussing it. A new wind had begun to blow.

But the armed forces, especially the marines, will put up one hell of a fight. The Buddhist monk meditated awhile longer.

Around the same time, Hashimoto was aboard the official airplane mid-Pacific on his way home. What he had said to Clinton kept coming back to him. "I don't think there'll be a return of Futenma unless we can come up with an alternative proposal. It's not my intention to hand you an ultimatum at this time. I want to see if we can't come up with some way of making it possible. I want you to try on your side and I'll try on mine."[62]

When I spoke my real mind, he replied in earnest. Hashimoto was relieved to be dealing with Clinton. But he was nervous and couldn't let it drop. *Which way would the dice tumble? It was a dangerous gamble. If the lucky numbers come up, where on earth can we shift the base?* Hashimoto racked his brain in search of candidates. A list of names and a map of Okinawa danced in his mind.

Notes

1. Interviews with Ryutaro Hashimoto, Hideo Usui, Masaki Orita, Masahiro Akiyama, and Walter Mondale.
2. Interview with Walter Mondale.
3. Interviews with Ryutaro Hashimoto, Hideo Usui, Masaki Orita, and Masahiro Akiyama.
4. *International Herald Tribune*, December 5, 1995.
5. Interviews with Ryutaro Hashimoto, Sadajiro Furukawa, Masaki Orita, Hiroshi Hirabayashi, and Masahiro Akiyama.
6. Interview with Seiroku Kajiyama.
7. Interview with a White House official.
8. *USA Today*, June 2, 1995, p. 4B.
9. *Los Angeles Times*, June 29, 1995, p. 8.
10. Interview with Anthony Lake.

11. Ibid.

12. Interview with a U.S. State Department official.

13. Interview with Anthony Lake.

14. Interview with a White House official.

15. Under the official rules of etiquette of the Ministry of Foreign Affairs, when heads of state visit Japan they are greeted in an official welcoming ceremony sponsored by the Imperial Court, normally in the form of a welcoming state dinner. Thus, the Imperial Household Agency is heavily involved whenever a state guest is to be expected.

16. Interviews with Ryutaro Hashimoto and Tomiichi Murayama.

17. Jim Hoagland, "There's No More American Premium," *Washington Post*, July 14, 1994, p. A23.

18. Interview with Anthony Lake.

19. Takakazu Kuriyama, *The Japan-U.S. Alliance: from Drift to Revitalization* (Tokyo: Nihon Keizai Shinbunsha, 1997, p. 236). (In Japanese.)

20. Interview with a high-ranking MOFA official.

21. Interview with William Perry.

22. Interview with Ryutaro Hashimoto.

23. Ryutaro Hashimoto, "Becoming a Party the People Can Entrust Their Future Dreams To," a speech presented at a party commemorating LDP's 40th anniversary, November 30, 1995. (In Japanese.)

24. Interview with Ryutaro Hashimoto.

25. Reply to the Budget Committee, House of Representatives, February 12, 1997.

26. Interview with Anthony Lake.

27. Interview with Winston Lord.

28. Interview with a high-ranking U.S. official.

29. Interview with a White House official.

30. Press briefing by Mike McCurry, February 22, 1996.

31. Interview with Masaki Orita.

32. Interview with Kurt Campbell.

33. Finlay Lewis, *Mondale: Portrait of an American Politician* (Tokyo: NHK Shuppan, 1994), pp. 352–354. (In Japanese.)

34. Ibid., p. 356.

35. Ibid., p. 358.

36. Ibid., p. 359.

37. Interview with William Perry.

38. Interview with a high-ranking Pentagon official.

39. Michael Armacost comments on his strained relationship with Ryutaro Hashimoto in his work *Friends or Rivals?*: "In our first meeting—a courtesy call in the spring of 1989—he seemed to have a chip on his shoulder. I particularly recall his assertion, 'The trouble with you Americans, Ambassador Armacost, is that you cannot forget that you won the war.'. . . I assured Hashimoto that since I was only eight years old and lived on the East Coast in 1945, the war with Japan had exerted little influence on my outlook. I expressed the hope that . . . we could overcome the unfortunate legacies of the past. But I left the meeting doubting we would become close. Subsequent events confirmed that intuition." Michael Armacost, *Friends or Rivals? The Insider's Account of U.S.-Japan Relations* (New York: Columbia University Press, 1996), p. 120.

40. Interview with Walter Mondale.

41. Interview with Kurt Campbell.

42. Ibid.

43. Interview with Gayle Von Eckartsburg.

44. Interview with Paul Giarra.

45. Ibid.

46. Interviews with Anthony Lake and Kurt Campbell.

47. *USA Today*, June 11, 1996, p. 1C.

48. *Los Angeles Times*, August 25, 1996, p. 1.

49. Interview with a high-ranking U.S. official.

50. Interview with Kurt Campbell.

51. Ibid.

52. Interviews with Kurt Campbell and Takemasa Moriya.

53. Interview with a high-ranking Japanese official.

54. Interview with Seiroku Kajiyama.

55. Interview with Ryutaro Hashimoto.

56. Reply to the Budget Committee, House of Representatives, April 3, 1997.

57. Reply to the Special Committee on Land Usage Accompanying the U.S.-Japan Security Treaty, House of Representatives, April 8, 1997.

58. Interview with Kurt Campbell.

59. Interview with Mike Mansfield.

60. Ibid.

61. Interview with Richard Armitage.

62. Interview with Ryutaro Hashimoto.

Chapter Two

———◆———

Tokyo

A Sense of Humility

Ryutaro Hashimoto officially assumed the office of prime minister on January 12, 1996.

Tomiichi Murayama had suddenly thrown in the towel. Relations with the United States, China, and Korea were all in disarray. Japanese diplomats "were bemoaning that the Chinese and Korean leaders weren't paying proper attention [to them]."[1] Murayama was referring to Chinese Chairman Jiang Zemin's behavior at the Sino-Japanese summit in Jakarta in 1994 and Korean president Kim Young Sam's actions at the U.N. annual general meeting in the fall of 1995. Nevertheless, Murayama didn't speak of the United States or China or Korea when he handed power over to Hashimoto. What he did deliver was Okinawa.

Murayama spoke slightly more formally on the subject with the three coalition party leaders and their secretary-generals. "Please keep the coalition government intact. Since I have promised to make a sincere effort to solve the Okinawan issue and set the wheels in motion, I would especially like you to keep that promise."[2]

For Murayama, this was tantamount to his dying wish.

On November 4, 1995, Governor Ota met with Murayama for the first time since the rape of the young Okinawan girl. Murayama had had his work cut out for him just arranging the meeting.

Hiroyuki Sonoda, a member of a coalition party, the New Party Sakigake, who served as deputy Cabinet secretary in the Murayama Cabinet, recollects: "We all thought that a Socialist government would be rather well equipped to deal with Okinawa, but that wasn't the case. It may offend the Socialists, but on the contrary, the Okinawa executive was extremely wary of them. It seemed strange to me, but we certainly had a lot of trouble there."[3]

Getting Ota "to come to the PM's office alone was not easy." Probably, "Ota wondered if this government could really take on the

Americans. And because the foreign ministry and the Cabinet secretary were both saying at the time that they couldn't review the Status of Forces Agreement, the Okinawans only grew all the more dubious."[4]

A meeting was finally set up, with Murayama and Ota finding some common ground to create a dialogue. Murayama was painfully aware that time was running out on the question of the bases, and he frankly told Ota as much. And yet, Murayama abandoned his Cabinet without fulfilling that responsibility. In his heart of hearts, he was ashamed. Murayama was also frightened that the good understanding he had so painstakingly established with Ota might change under an LDP government.

On leaving office, Murayama spoke one-on-one with Hashimoto. "Okinawa is my greatest regret. It's the only thing I ask of you."

"There's no need to even mention it. Solving the Okinawan affair is also my greatest concern."[5] Hashimoto probably didn't need the prompting. He had sworn to himself that he would make Okinawa the top priority of his government.

Hashimoto's feelings on Okinawa can be culled from the speech he gave as party chairman at the commemoration of the LDP's 40th anniversary: "The return of Okinawa was an historical achievement on which my mentor, Eisaku Sato, staked his political reputation. But I am truly humbled when I think of whether we as politicians have really striven to share the 23 years of suffering and sadness the people of Okinawa have gone through since that time; have we offered them encouragement and tried to ease their suffering? I would like to stress here that resolving the issue of the Okinawan bases is a duty laid upon us, the LDP, as the inheritors of Chairman Sato's achievement."[6]

Deep down, Hashimoto was thinking he would like to bring about the return of Futenma Air Station with his own hands if it was at all possible.

Okinawa Prefecture had already announced an action program for the return of all the U.S. bases by 2015, the return of Futenma by 2001 being included as the draw card for the first phase.

Shouldn't we rather be joining this move and pressing the United States? The Foreign Ministry will naturally say it's impossible. But we'd never do anything big if we followed their lead. They're under America's thumb. They were like spokesmen for the Americans when we got Okinawa back, saying a nuclear-free return couldn't be done, but Sato was right after all, wasn't he? Politicians are different from bureaucrats.

Hashimoto was telling himself it was time for a political decision just like Sato's.

How can we end the psychological suffering of the Okinawan people? If we don't approach this seriously, the whole security system will go awry. There'll be no point to a security alliance if all of Okinawa goes up in flames.

And if we don't do something with a big impact, no one will give us any credit for having set up the Special Action Committee Okinawa (SACO) with the United States and setting the bases realignment, consolidation, and reduction process in motion. They'll just see it as an extension of the base consolidation.

This is what Hashimoto was anxious about.[7]

The opinion polls were showing a sharp drop in support for the government now that the honeymoon period was over, but Hashimoto fretted over Okinawa.

Former Prime Minister Noboru Takeshita commented on a conversation with Hashimoto at the time. "I received a phone call when we were up to our ears in sorting out the housing finance companies. But he didn't mention that. He just went on and on about Futenma. After about 30 minutes, maybe he felt better and hung up. His wife (Mrs. Hashimoto) spoke to me first, saying by way of apology that he liked to call when he was frustrated."[8]

In the Diet, Hashimoto repeatedly gave diplomatic replies, such as "Under the fundamental direction of holding fast to the U.S.-Japan Security Treaty, I would like to respond realistically and sincerely in consultation with the U.S. concerning the realignment, consolidation and reduction of U.S. military facilities and areas in Okinawa, ensuring at the same time compatibility with the attainment of the same treaty's objectives."[9]

But there was a strong sense of anticipation in his heart.

The Ministry of Foreign Affairs

The Foreign Ministry was watching Hashimoto with dread.

Hashimoto had never served as foreign minister. He was extremely sensitive about this and often took on the ministry in a bravado fashion bordering on bluff: *I'll be damned if I'm going to let you make a fool out of me.* When something went wrong or there was a clash of opinion, he was "like a sulking boy."[10] The top echelon of the ministry was on guard against this awkward man, even though they thought deep down that "he's probably lonely," "he's just playing around."

Compared with the Ministry of International Trade and Industry (MITI) and the Ministry of Finance (MOF), Hashimoto's connections with the Ministry of Foreign Affairs (MOFA) were thin.

Hashimoto had a strong kind of "family consciousness." Once he belonged to and led a given organization, whether it was Azabu High, Keio University, or the *kendo* club, his sense of loyalty to it grew in leaps and bounds. It was a pugnacious sort of loyalty. As one government cadre who knew Hashimoto well put it, this may well have "been a habit which stemmed from his sense of responsibility as the head."[11] In any event, MOFA was not part of "the family," and he had never headed it.

In Kasumigaseki, he had already served as minister for health and welfare, transport, finance, and trade. His grasp of the central government bureaucracy rivaled that of Noboru Takeshita, former prime minister from the Tanaka faction. When Hashimoto was minister for health and welfare, he attended the funerals of even the noncareer civil servants. He even went so far as to find part-time work for a bereaved wife.

For some reason, he was effusive about "work-site operations," "subordinate work," and "thankless jobs" in the posts of such organizations like the Maritime Safety Agency and Customs.

When Hashimoto was finance minister, he spent a day at the Tokyo customs house. Masahiro Akiyama, director-general of the Japanese Defense Agency's (JDA) Bureau of Defense Policy, had been the head of the Tokyo customs house when he was still with MOF and he had Hashimoto come over. It was around the time when Hashimoto was the secretary-general of the Liberal Democratic Party (LDP) and had become finance minister, just after their huge defeat in the upper house elections. Hashimoto spent the whole day, Saturday, going over the place with a fine-tooth comb. He also visited the customs brokers' building, the packers' building, the warehouse custodians' building, the air freight clearing facility in Chiba Prefecture, and the drug-sniffer dog training center.

At MOFA, he tended to spotlight the specialists within its ranks rather than the elite. This could be said to be due to a sense of solidarity that Hashimoto, a mountain climber who climbed the Himalayas, had cultivated through contact with MOFA specialists working in the field in Nepal and elsewhere.

Vice Minister Sadayuki Hayashi was one of the few people at MOFA Hashimoto heeded. Hashimoto often said, "Saito and Hayashi aren't flashy, but they're men of integrity and can be relied upon."[12] Saito was Kunihiko Saito, Japanese ambassador to the United States.

But for Hayashi, his initial encounter with Hashimoto was a trial. At one of the Japanese government's morning briefing sessions at the Naples summit in the summer of 1994, Hashimoto, then trade minister, abused Hayashi from the outset, right in front of Prime Minister Murayama, Foreign Minister Yohei Kono, and Finance Minister Masayoshi Takemura.

He censured MOFA for not passing on to MITI a memorandum from Clinton to Japan's top leaders concerning the Clinton Round of trade liberalization initiatives. At the time, Hayashi was deputy minister for economic affairs at MOFA. He was a personal representative of the summit leaders, a so-called sherpa. The memorandum had been passed on to MOF, but not to MITI. It wasn't Hayashi's blunder but that of someone lower down the hierarchy, but Hashimoto didn't see it that way. MITI is always in an awkward, halfway-house position at the summits, where the foreign and finance ministers are official members of the delegation. That's why their people were always very sensitive about this kind of thing. Hashimoto had already rebuked Hayashi about it the previous evening. And then he brought it up again the next morning. He was hopping mad.

An "original experience" colored Hashimoto's criticism of MOFA. Not confined to this case alone, rather than being culled from a single conviction, Hashimoto's worldview tended to be formed on the basis of "original experientialism," burning impressions from diverse examples he had encountered crystallizing each time as "original experiences" into the nucleus of his perception of things. And his perception of MOFA was based on his "original experience" during the Gulf crisis.

At the time, Hashimoto was finance minister in Toshiki Kaifu's Cabinet. The United States asked the Japanese to provide air and sea lifts as a contribution to the multinational force and to provide transportation support for soldiers and goods. At the time, Minoru Tanba, then deputy director-general of the North American Affairs Bureau, MOFA, sent a heartfelt plea from Washington: "There is an extremely serious gap between what the Americans are thinking about Japan and what the Japanese government is planning to announce on the 29th [August 29, 1990].

"With regard to the air lift, no matter what they do the Americans are going to be 80 return flights short over the next three weeks. They're wondering if they can't ask Japan to handle 35 of those, but all the Japanese are offering is two flights. The navy wants to ask Japan to run 10 return trips in the next 8 weeks, but we haven't come up with anything. Every time Japan opens its mouth it mentions difficulties with the labor unions, but how do you explain the fact that right now there are 20 Japanese tankers in the Persian Gulf?

"If you don't set off some fireworks now, you'll only have more to lose later. What about taking the bull by the horns and chartering foreign planes and ships? The decision about to be taken in Tokyo today or tomorrow will determine the nature of U.S.-Japan relations for the next 10 or 20 years."

That was the gist of Tanba's "fireworks cable" (it was actually a fax).[13] Reading it persuaded Hashimoto. Having served as transport minister himself, Hashimoto thought, "Here's a job for me," and contacted the Transport Ministry. The Transport Ministry had already started amassing ships just in case, but what they needed to know most was what sort of shipping the Americans needed. Without that information, all the trouble of getting a convoy together would be futile.

But the all-important foreign policy cables were not being shared with the transport ministry. And when they finally did turn up after needling MOFA, sometimes all the information that didn't directly concern the transport ministry was blacked out. Junji Hayashi, vice minister of transport, said they couldn't cooperate without the proper information.

Hashimoto was receiving the cables as soon as they came in. Unlike the transport ministry, foreign policy cables were immediately sent directly to the chief officer of the Budget Bureau. While reading the cables, Hashimoto realized that what the Americans wanted were RORO (roll-on, roll-off) ships, not the vessels the transport ministry was readying.

Hashimoto had Takakazu Kuriyama, vice foreign minister, come to see him and urged that all cables dealing with this part of the Gulf crisis be immediately passed on to the transport ministry. Kuriyama avoided a direct answer, saying, "I'd like to take this matter up back at the ministry."

The next day after the Cabinet meeting, Prime Minister Kaifu said he wanted to see Hashimoto. Going along, Hashimoto found both Kuriyama and Foreign Minister Taro Nakayama waiting.

Kuriyama spoke. "As a result of consultation within the ministry, the conclusion has been reached that we cannot show them. The cables cover other issues, so we are unable to hand them over as is. We would be grateful if you would consent to us going there and providing them the pertinent information in person."

Hashimoto thought, "*You bastard*," but held his tongue.

"Well, that's what you have to do right away then, isn't it?"

"Yes."

"Fine."

Hashimoto backed off. He called Hayashi that afternoon and learned that Kuriyama had turned up, but had only talked in the most general of terms.

"Send an officer over to see me." Hashimoto hung up.

When the officer arrived at the minister's office, Hashimoto left the room, saying, "I have to step out to the toilet. The cables are over there, so have a look at them while I'm gone." When he came back, the officer's face was as white as a sheet.

"This is completely different. What we're getting ready is completely different."

"The Foreign Ministry is always like this. It's a question of loyalty!" Hashimoto's voice was shaking as he spoke to Sadayuki Hayashi.

Kono tried to intervene, but Hashimoto wouldn't listen. Murayama just sat there not uttering a word. After a while, Takemura tried to smooth things over with a "Will we move on then?" and Hashimoto finally calmed down.[14]

After the study session, Hashimoto met alone with Hiroyuki Sonoda, deputy Cabinet secretary. He said, "MOFA has always done things like this, all the way back. They sometimes don't even tell the prime minister what's going on but go ahead in secret. This time, it was just a small thing, but we're at the start of our administration and of our foreign policy. It's a crucial point in time. That's why I yelled at him."[15]

Hayashi was flexible but he had a core of steel. Originally, he had been an expert on the General Agreement on Tariff and Trade (GATT) and had been involved in many economic and trade negotiations. He believed that trade conflicts would be best solved under a multilateral trade system.

He had collided head on with Clinton's U.S. trade representative, Mickey Kantor. Kantor was pushing for numerical targets for U.S. imports into Japan. He wanted a backroom deal that would force U.S. products into the Japanese market.

Kantor seemed to suddenly erupt. He said, "That trade officer is so pigheaded he's causing us all kinds of trouble." This surprised Kono, but Hayashi was unfazed. He saw Kantor's "eruption" as a calculated tactic. It was obvious that he was trying to pressure Hayashi, who was there in the room with them.

When his wife was operated on for cancer, Hayashi told the doctor he was "ready to resign from the ministry at any time if my wife should need long-term care." Fortunately, the operation was a success and Hayashi did not have to leave the ministry, continuing on to become deputy minister, then vice minister.

All who knew him agreed that "his greatest asset is his lack of a big ego or self-promotion and his impartiality."[16]

Within MOFA, it was Hayashi who first proposed they look into the possibility of getting Futenma back. Shortly after he became vice minister, Hayashi called his bureau chiefs together and checked every outstanding problem one by one. At the time, he told them, "I want you to write down on a piece of paper and give to me the reasons why the U.S.-Japan Security Treaty is necessary."

His senior officers didn't hide their surprise. *What does he mean, write down on paper if the treaty is necessary or not? There must be something wrong with him.*

It was written all over their faces. When he had read what they had written, Hayashi thought: *Just as I suspected. This won't convince the populace. We'll have to start over with the treaty from scratch.*

Hayashi had never worked in any of the elite treaty, North American, or security areas that were the key to promotion in the postwar period. Most likely, Hayashi would not have made it to vice minister if the Cold War had continued. That's why his top staff were not only nonplussed when he asked them a question like that, they were also annoyed.

What are we going to do with a vice minister who doesn't understand the security treaty? Hayashi's commonsensical questioning of the basic premises appeared as a dare to them. The same could be said about the possibility of getting Futenma back. Hayashi was concerned that things couldn't be kept under control without a significant and symbolic return of a base. In his best amateur pose, Hayashi put the question to his top men, once again gathered in his office: "I don't suppose we could get Futenma Air Station back, could we?"

"They'll come back with some impossible condition if we ask them for something like that."

To the senior officer who said that, Hayashi calmly commented, "Why don't we find out just how impossible a condition they come up with?"[17] And to Hitoshi Tanaka, deputy director-general of the North American Affairs Bureau, he gave the special task of "finding out" what it would be.

The Hashimoto government was only a few days old.

Pressure Building

On January 5, 1996, Hitoshi Tanaka was appointed deputy director-general of the North American Bureau. It was the day the Murayama Cabinet resigned. Perhaps it was just mere coincidence, but Tanaka felt something inevitable about it. Possibly even a sense of purpose imbued with a feeling of wiping the slate clean.

Accompanied by his predecessor, Norimoto Takano, who was transferring to be minister at the embassy in Korea, Tanaka took special care in his courtesy calls on the people around the new prime minister, Hashimoto. Ken Moroi, adviser to Chichibu-Onoda Cement Company, was one of them.

Along with Jiro Ushio, chairman of Ushio Denki Company, Moroi was one of Governor Ota's brain trust. He was very up on Okinawan affairs. He was also a member of the Friends of Okinawa, a gathering of successful businessmen set up in 1990 to promote economic development in Okinawa by Sohei Nakayama, adviser to the Industrial Bank of Japan, and Hiroki Imasato, chairman of Nihon Seiko, with leading Okinawan businessmen Keiichi Inamine, chairman of the Ryuseki Corporation, and Meiki Kinjo, president of Orion

Beer. Some 50 businessmen from Okinawa and 50 more from the mainland were also members.

Taking advantage of the fact that they all had direct access to the top people in both the central and regional governments, they came forward to cooperate "in accurately ascertaining what both the prime minister and the governor were thinking and deepening their mutual understanding."

When speaking with Moroi, Tanaka felt something strange about a businessman extolling to him the importance of getting Futenma Air Station back. It would be an exaggeration to say it coincided with Hashimoto's intentions, but there was a certain affinity, and Tanaka felt some kind of pressure building.

Clinton is coming this spring. If the return of Futenma Air Station catches fire before that, the summit will be a shambles. We have to do something about Futenma, but it will be a painful blow if we try and it doesn't work out. I wonder what the PM thinks. Maybe he's privately aiming for the return of Futenma.[18]

Tanaka was nervous. What Moroi didn't tell Tanaka was that he was nursing a certain idea himself. *Hashimoto is the PM now. Things will finally start to move. The first thing we have to do is to get Hashimoto and Ota on the same wavelength. The Okinawa Group is ready to do what it takes.*

As Ushio was also chairman of the Keizai Doyukai, a leading business association, he was extremely busy. So Moroi flew to Okinawa as the mainland's forward scout. He met secretly with Ota, heard his real intentions, and conveyed them as faithfully as possible to Hashimoto. Akira Sakima, chairman of the Naha Chamber of Commerce and Industry and chairman of Ryukyu Bank, acted as the Okinawan's liaison, contacting Ota and arranging a secret meeting with Moroi. This was the game plan.

Sunday, February 8.
Tokyo had its heaviest snowfall in two years. Flights to Okinawa were delayed considerably. Moroi went straight to the hotel that was the venue for the clandestine rendezvous, the Palace on the Hill. He was already more than one hour late for the meeting, but Ota had come unaccompanied and was waiting by himself. They spoke together for about an hour and a half.

Moroi asked Ota, "If there is one thing you could ask of the prime minister, what would it be?"

Ota didn't hesitate. "The return of Futenma Air Station. There are three important items that have to be cleared up, but getting Futenma Air Station back is even more pressing."

The three important items were all issues deemed to be top priorities in the realignment, consolidation, and reduction of the Okinawan bases: the relocation of Naha Port, an end to the live artillery firing exercises over Prefectural Highway 104, and the relocation of parachute drop training at Yomitan Airfield.

Ota stuck to Futenma. "There are 16 schools in the vicinity of that air station. Helicopters have made crash landings on several occasions. There was a dreadful accident in 1959 at Miyamori Elementary School in Ishikawa when a jet crashed. If such a thing should ever happen again, there is a very real fear that things will spin out of control because everyone remembers Miyamori, even today."

The Miyamori Elementary School incident was a tragic accident in 1959. Just as the schoolchildren were receiving their milk, a jet crashed into the classrooms, killing 11 pupils and 6 residents, and injuring more than 200. The incident was etched into Ota's mind as the saddest, most painful event in the postwar period. Whenever he heard of Miyamori, it conjured up the faces of his pupils. Ota had taught there many years ago.

In 1946, Ota, who had just been released from an American prisoner of war camp, enrolled at Okinawa Teacher's College. Immediately after the war, Okinawa suffered an acute shortage of teachers. Many were either dead or had taken up other jobs to survive. A teacher training institute was therefore set up with six-month courses. That was the Okinawa Teacher's College.

Ota's first teaching post upon graduating was at Miyamori Elementary School. Although he only taught for a very short period, his pupils from those days still came to visit him.

Quite some time later, Ota became a professor at the University of the Ryukyus. At the time, one Kokichi Nakaya was studying in the history department of the faculty of humanities and sciences. He was a leader in the student movement and set forth his arguments mainly in the student newspaper at the university.

Nakaya scrupulously analyzed the Okinawan outlook of all the famous people who visited Okinawa and submitted a report to the effect that "they may be interested in Okinawan affairs, but they're not interested in the flesh and blood people who live here." It was a report well worth reading. At the time the reversion movement was at its height, but nevertheless Nakaya went off to Tokyo for 40 days as a student representative and fought with the national students' federation. This "experience on the mainland" provided him with a chance to see right through the "reversion to the mainland." He began criticizing the reversion movement, saying, "What's the good of reverting to a mainland like that?"

He mercilessly attacked Okinawa's lack of sense of self: "Everyone should have a name, and yet Okinawa has no face, no name." Every time he heard Nakaya speak, Ota felt his heart was being cut out.

Nakaya graduated from the university in 1966. He taught at a high school but two months later committed suicide in Chibanagusuku, central Okinawa. Teruo Hiyane (professor of political science at the University of the Ryukyus), who was at school with Nakaya, in 1972 published a posthumous collection of 31 of Nakaya's essays entitled *Name, Stand Up and Walk!* "The Death of a Niece" was one piece that was included.

> Thinking only of their own lives, the American pilots parachuted out of two planes which had run into engine trouble mid-flight. With no one at the helm, the unmanned planes zigzagged through the sky, crashing into a schoolyard.
>
> My niece, Sonoko, had just started grade one that March. She was reported missing by the newspapers at the time of the crash.
>
> On the evening of the second day, a body that they thought was Sonoko was discovered in the ashes. She was reduced to an unrecognizable bundle of sticks, a burnt body.
>
> The only thing that remained intact in her burnt away face was one dirty tooth sticking out from her lips. You couldn't see her middle tooth, still hidden in her gums. . . . About a month before, she had proudly shown her elder brother where she'd lost her tooth. For an instant that image of Sonoko pierced his brain.
>
> Sonoko's death was a turning point in his thinking. He was made to see the power external forces could exert on him.
>
> From that time on, he thought about the Okinawan reality. He felt in his bones that ethnic issues had lowered a dark veil with imperial powers coiled all around.

Ota knew that the death of his niece at Miyamori Elementary School was what had triggered Nakaya into taking time off from the university he had just enrolled in and getting involved in the student movement.

Ota told Moroi, "We've asked for it back before, but we've always been told 'no.' The mainland wasn't acting in good faith. Since the prime minister will be going to Santa Monica soon, I'd like him to directly ask Clinton for its return. I also want him to tell the newspapers that. Things will change a lot if Futenma is mentioned in the papers."[19]

Moroi had his secretary draw up a two-page memo the next day:

- Governor Ota is not anti-American. He is, rather, a sympathizer.
- He finds it intolerable that should the question of the bases not be dealt with appropriately, it might lead to a deterioration in the bilateral relationship.

- He regards the return of Futenma Air Station as the top priority in the bases issue.

- He expressed the desire that you call for the return of the air station at the Santa Monica summit and that you announce it to the press.

Armed with this memo, Moroi met with Hashimoto in the LDP chairman's office. He avoided the PM's office in a bid to maintain as low a profile as possible. With Kenji Eda, political secretary, also in attendance, Moroi briefly recounted his discussion with Ota and handed over the memo.

"This is what's been missing. We haven't had something like this before." Saying this, Hashimoto expressed his gratitude.[20]

The Resourceful General: Hitoshi Tanaka

The sensors Hitoshi Tanaka had placed around the PM's office faintly picked up Hashimoto's squirming.

We have to keep up with what's happening. He's a man who moves on his own accord. They say Eisaku Sato was his mentor, but he's different from Sato, who was a master at waiting politics. We have to make sure he doesn't shake us off.[21]

Like Hayashi, Tanaka was not a so-called treaty or security pro. He had served as the director of the Second North American Division in the North American Affairs Bureau, the head of the North East Asian Division in the Asian Affairs Bureau, and the director of the Policy Coordination Division in the Foreign Policy Bureau. He had close ties with the United Kingdom. He studied at Oxford immediately after joining the ministry. After joining senior management, he had been a research fellow at the International Institute for Strategic Studies (IISS) and had served as minister at the embassy in the United Kingdom. He had also been posted to Indonesia and knew a lot about Southeast Asia. He was an all-round player ready to tackle economics, Europe, America, Asia, you name it.

The head of the Japan-U.S. Security Treaty Division when Tanaka was director of the Second North American Division was Yukio Okamoto, later to handle Okinawan affairs as Hashimoto's special Cabinet representative. With two and a half years in his post and Okamoto three years in his, they were both men of presence.

Tanaka was a resourceful general. He was highly sensitive to the advantages of timing and place. This talent was brought to the fore when he was appointed the first director of the Policy Coordination Division of the newly established Foreign Policy Bureau in 1994 when dealing with the North Korean (Democratic People's Republic of Korea) nuclear crisis and again in 1995, the 50th anniversary of the end of World War II, when tackling "historical issues." He was praised as "one of the few policy oriented people at a ministry known for its coordination orientation."[22]

One of Tanaka's juniors at the Foreign Ministry describes him as "one of the ministry's three greatest strategic thinkers." The other two were Ryozo Kato, director-general of the Asian Affairs Bureau, and Koji Tsuruoka, director of the Second North American Division in the North American Affairs Bureau. His wife often told him, "It's not logic that moves people, dear. It's sensibility."

It was not as if Tanaka were lacking in the powers of manipulation. It was just that once he started building up a logic, a strategic logic, he was ruthless about discarding any irrelevant elements; to him they were like so many insects to be squashed.

Tanaka's strategic thinking was a breath of fresh air for the Americans. A high-ranking U.S. government official appraised Tanaka's qualities: "He was tougher, both with us and with his interlocutors, than I think people were comfortable with sometimes. I think his toughness showed through intellectually. He was very rigorous and he was relentless when he was making his arguments and making his assessments. He was thinking often on several planes at once. He thought strategically very well. And he was also a very good tactician. Generally speaking, my interlocutors in Japan are outstanding tacticians, the best tacticians I've ever worked with, but sometimes they don't combine it with the strategic vision. He had both."[23]

On the domestic front, some said, "Yes, he's incredibly good at foreign policy negotiations, but he hasn't gotten his hands dirty before, so he's a type the Okinawans don't like." Their point was, "He's unlucky that the main job of the North American Affairs Bureau has turned out to be Okinawa."[24.]

Tanaka himself was also aware of this. He later admitted that "I should have gone to Okinawa the very day I was appointed deputy director-general."

Tanaka set his net for the big fish but didn't chase after the minnows. He was seen as being "no good at laying the groundwork," "a bit high-handed." A top member of the Japan Defense Agency who worked with him in SACO was known to have whispered, "He's off doing things in places the rest of us run-of-the-mill officials have no way of knowing about. . . ." It was a description that combined a sense of alarm with a sense of admiration for "great deeds." He was oriented not towards the foreign policy of dots and lines but of whole surfaces. Tanaka seemed to be at his happiest when he could become the consummate spider spinning his conceptual web.

Tanaka believed that Japan should shrug off the treaty pros' "esoteric world of Diet treaty debate" at the earliest opportunity and pursue security policy as a strategy for Japan. He also spoke fervently within the ministry that "it is now possible domestically to debate the issue without any taboos. The need is now here for us administrators to stop merely explaining policy and to debate the thinking that lies behind that policy." An article Tanaka published in *Chuo Koron* (December 1996), "Considering the U.S.-Japan security system," is a good example of his thinking.

In that article, Tanaka expressed the view that "it is inconceivable that the security system will remain the same forever even when international relations and the domestic climate are changing." Based upon that, he made the following observations on the environmental changes at home and abroad:

1. It is widely acknowledged in America that the United States has a crucial interest in the Asian-Pacific region and that the forward deployment of troops in Japan is greatly beneficial to U.S. security. Moreover, there is no longer as great a "sense of guilt" among the Japanese as before for the security treaty not to be reciprocal.

2. Perceptions of security threats have changed and security issues are no longer viewed in the Cold War context of the U.S. and Soviet superpowers, but rather in terms of the Asia-Pacific region, especially the special conditions that prevail in the Far East. Central security issues have shifted to regional conditions that Japan itself may also be forced to become directly involved in.

3. It is no longer possible to debate the realignment, consolidation, and reduction of U.S. military bases without considering U.S. strategy and the bases' functions.

For Tanaka, the U.S.-Japanese security system was not something that could have as its "goal" the maintenance of or adherence to a given. It was more a useful "vehicle" for cooperating as allies in global and regional issues based on the security policies of each country. His was a much more functionalist, utilitarian position.

When discussing the U.S.-Japan treaty and its relevance to the United Nations with the Americans, Tanaka pounced on the U.S. side's "theory of predominance of the U.S.-Japan alliance," saying, "Japanese U.N. policy is not superseded by the U.S.-Japan treaty. It is a policy with its own worth. That's why we need to look into how the treaty can be applied from that perspective as well."

Middle management at the JDA took to calling him "Mr. National Interest." "Tanaka has this pet position that there's something more important than the security treaty, and that's Japan's national interest. That's why he's Mr. National Interest."[25]

Kurt Campbell reports, "He often begins his statements with, 'It is in Japanese national interests and this or that.' I don't necessarily think that what is in Japanese national interests and what is good for the U.S.-Japan security relationship are contrary. And I think Tanaka acknowledged that and that assessment illuminated his thinking."[26]

In a certain sense, the U.S.-Japan treaty became more relative in the face of the national interest. It was a stance which was gradually finding support among the Young Turks whether they were at MOFA or the JDA.

Some of the higher Americans pegged him as a "nationalist." A member of the Pentagon commented that "he's not anti-American, but he might be moving away."

And there were those Japan experts who interpreted the situation as "Tanaka's background was one of tough economic negotiations, confrontational stuff. That's his experience with the U.S. That's a major difference between him and Yukio Sato, Ryozo Kato, or Yukio Okamoto."[27] Yukio Sato (ambassador to Australia) was well known as the professional's professional when it came to security issues.

Slightly suspicious, the existing "high priests" of the Japanese-American security community like Richard Armitage, former assistant secretary of defense, began to keep a close eye on the Young Turks.

An Emotional Issue

Tanaka approached the Americans. His first sounding board was Rust Deming, deputy chief of mission at the U.S. Embassy. While Deming promised to sound out the State Department, he didn't sound too hopeful. Just as Tanaka thought, the answer was not favorable but just the hackneyed response that the U.S. military would never buy it.

In SACO as well, the Americans put forward a proposal for the partial transfer of Futenma's functions to Iwakuni Base. This concerned the relocation of the KC-130, a midair refueler. It was a proposal to shift the transport planes' apron.

The U.S. military was strongly opposed to returning Futenma Air Station. Noboru Hoshuyama, chief of the Defense Facilities Administration Agency, heard the marines commander say, "It'll only be returned when the security treaty is scrapped."

Hideo Usui, who was director-general of the JDA in Hashimoto's Cabinet, also thought returning Futenma Air Station was out of the question. "I thought Futenma, the marines' only base, would stay until the last because it was where the marines' Third Expeditionary Force was stationed in Okinawa for forward deployment. They were also very negative about Futenma as well."[28]

At the time, the JDA people judged the return of Futenma to be difficult not only because it functioned as a helicopter base for the marines but because of its wider functions. In fact, rather than being difficult, their assessment was that returning the base was closer to undesirable. Their reasons were as follows:

- its function as a base for the parts, equipment, and refueling that would be required for transportation in a time of crisis when a substantial number of U.S. forces would be deployed;

- its transportation function in moving those goods to the front;

- its assembly and servicing function for the large helicopters flown in from the U.S. mainland in transport planes; and

- its function as an emergency substitute air field for aircraft using Kadena if they could not use that field.

In other words, the U.S. Marine Corps had both air and land squadrons to carry out operations on land and sea. Consequently, the helicopter squadrons at the air wing's Futenma Air Station needed to be close to their land battalions because both had to carry out ongoing and closely coordinated training exercises. A long runway was also necessary in order to perform these diverse functions.

Adding this all together, there seemed to be no other suitable air field that could take Futenma's place. It was as if they were saying you can stand on your head but it won't come back.

In the middle of January, Tanaka met with Thomas Hubbard, deputy assistant secretary of state, and Kurt Campbell, deputy assistant secretary of defense, in San Francisco. The meeting was at a conference on U.S.-Japan security issues begun the previous year and cosponsored by the Pacific Forum CSIS, a research institute for security issues based in Hawaii, and the Japan Institute of International Affairs (chaired by Nobuo Matsunaga, a former Japanese ambassador to the United States), a think tank for Japan's foreign ministry. It was a closed forum that brought together both government officials and private sector researchers for intense, so-called track-two discussions.

All three had been invited. Rust Deming, deputy chief of mission at the U.S. Embassy in Tokyo, was also there.

Tanaka and Hubbard went way back. When Tanaka was director of the Second North American Division, Hubbard was head of the State Department's Japan Desk. When Tanaka was in charge of KEDO (Korean Energy Development Organization), which froze North Korea's nuclear development program and provided energy development aid, Hubbard was working on the same problem from the American end. At the time they averaged two phone calls a week.

While Tanaka was able to renew his friendship with Hubbard, his major coup was having a chance to speak at length with Kurt Campbell one-on-one. It was just small talk by way of self-introduction, but they both agreed that in order to make SACO meaningful, it was no good treating it as a negotiation between the United States and Japan. They had to work out some kind of a solution together and do something about the bases that had a symbolic impact.

Hubbard and Deming also endorsed this point. They decided to create the "Five of Us," adding Ichiro Fujisaki, minister at the Japanese Embassy. They were bound by an understanding to "share information between the five, to maintain confidentiality, and to be workmates."

An unofficial meeting of SACO was also held in parallel with the conference. Although launched the previous November, SACO had failed to make any headway. SACO finally started to take off after this meeting.

Option B

It was on February 28, three days after the meeting in Santa Monica, that U.S. Secretary of Defense William Perry called his top advisers into his office. Chairman of the Joint Chiefs of Staff John Shalikashvili, Secretary of the Army Togo West, Secretary of the Navy John Dalton, Secretary of the Air Force Sheila Widnall, and U.S. Marine Corps Commandant Charles Krulak were all present.

A large map of Okinawa was pinned up. Perry spoke quietly, saying, "There's one thing I'd like you to tell me. Would someone please explain to me why on an island the size of Okinawa the military needs two air bases?"[29]

Silence filled the room. No one attempted to answer. Perry locked his hands behind his head, and waited without breaking the silence.

The point Perry was trying to make was clear. He was, after all, a theoretician. If someone said one thing, three or four refutations would come flying back. And none of the military brass was confident that he or she could come up with a rebuttal to his rebuttal.

Even so, in the end it was Krulak who spoke up. He only put forward the general arguments of how key the U.S. Marine Corps base in Okinawa was, how much it contributed to regional security, and how maintaining their operations there was more important than ever.[30]

Perry said nothing. He just thanked everyone and ended the meeting.

It was immediately after this meeting that the return of Futenma Air Station appeared on the American and Japanese agendas. That day, a small meeting was held in Washington. Campbell and Tanaka were at the center of it. Campbell suggested to Tanaka that they consider two options: A and B.

Option A was relocating the KC-130s to Iwakuni.

Option B was the return of Futenma Air Station.

They did agree, however, that this had to be kept in the strictest confidence.

Notes

1. Interview with a high-ranking Japanese official.
2. Interview with Tomiichi Murayama.
3. Interview with Hiroyuki Sonoda.
4. Ibid.
5. Interview with Ryutaro Hashimoto.
6. Ryutaro Hashimoto, "Becoming a Party the People Can Entrust Their Future Dreams To," a speech presented at a party commemorating LDP's 40th anniversary, November 30, 1995. (In Japanese.)
7. Interview with Ryutaro Hashimoto.
8. Interview with Noboru Takeshita.
9. Budget Committee, House of Councilors, February 15, 1996.
10. Interview with a high-ranking MOFA official.
11. Interview with Kenji Eda.
12. Interview with Ryutaro Hashimoto.
13. Takeshige Kunimasa, "A Turning Point Called the Gulf War," *Sekai*, August 1997, p. 167.
14. Interviews with Ryutaro Hashimoto, Masayoshi Takemura, and Yohei Kono.
15. Interview with Hiroyuki Sonoda.
16. Interview with a high-ranking MOFA official.
17. Interview with Junji Hayashi.
18. Interview with Hitoshi Tanaka.
19. Interviews with Masahide Ota and Ken Moroi.
20. Interview with Ken Moroi.
21. Interview with Hitoshi Tanaka.
22. Interview with a high-ranking MOFA official.
23. Interview with Kurt Campbell.
24. Interview with an official in the PM's office.

25. Interview with a JDA official.

26. Interview with Kurt Campbell.

27. Interview with Michael Green.

28. Interview with Hideo Usui.

29. Interview with a high-ranking DOD official.

30. Ibid.

Chapter Three

Gulf Stream

Gulf Stream II

March 6, 1996.

All the U.S. and Japanese government members of the Special Action Committee on Okinawa (SACO) landed at Kadena Air Base in a Gulf Stream II jet. The day was clear but the wind was blustery.

They had departed early in the morning from Yokota Air Base. The aim was to see the U.S. bases in Okinawa together and be briefed on the bases' functions by the local commanders. It was the idea of Kurt Campbell, deputy assistant secretary of defense, and Thomas Hubbard, deputy assistant secretary of state. "The Foreign Ministry was a bit hesitant" but decided to go along for the ride.[1]

From Kadena, the entourage split up into three groups, boarded three different U.S. forces helicopters, and visited each base.

Thomas Hubbard, Kurt Campbell, Hitoshi Tanaka, and Takemasa Moriya of the Japanese Defense Agency (JDA) were on board the first helicopter. Peter Pace, deputy commander U.S. Forces Japan, Ichiro Fujizaki, minister at the Japanese Embassy in the United States, Kazuyoshi Umemoto, head of the Japan-U.S. Security Treaty Division at the Japanese Foreign Ministry, Robin Sakoda, head of the Japan Desk at the U.S. Defense Department, and Yoshiyuki Chibiki, head of the Planning Division at the Japanese Defense Facilities Administration Agency, were on board the second. The third helicopter carried the rest of the entourage.

First they visited Camp Courtney overlooking Kin Bay, which also doubled as the headquarters of the U.S. Marines' Third Expeditionary Force (III MEF). It was not a base for fighting troops but comprised the headquarters and residential facilities for the forces.

The III MEF was one of three MEFs and the only one in Okinawa, the first force being stationed at Camp Pendleton (California) and the second at Camp Lejeune (North Carolina).

They were briefed by Major General Wayne Rollings, commander of the Okinawa Marine Corps. On the table was documentation entitled "Special Action Committee Okinawa Brief 6 March 1996."

Why was the Pacific important to the U.S. forces and to the U.S. Marines?

"Economic growth in this region is six times greater than any other region."

"Trade in this region has quadrupled since 1980."

When speaking of the U.S. forces' overseas presence, the Americans always stress the economic importance. That day was no exception.

Why Okinawa?

"It's a strategic location."

"It is a location which covers from the east coast of Africa to Hawaii."

"You have a panoramic, commanding view of the Pacific Ocean, the Indian Ocean, the Persian Gulf, and Africa from Okinawa."

It's an unstable region.

"Russia, China, the Korean Peninsula, ASEAN [the Association of South East Asian Nations], Thailand, India all have their problems. For example, the Spratly Islands and Taiwan with China, the Straits of Malacca with ASEAN, and the U.S. presence with Thailand. . . ."

What are the U.S. objectives in this region?

"To prevent the emergence of a hostile, dominant power."

"To keep air and sea lines of communications open."

"To maintain economic and commercial access."

What is the mission of the III MEF?

"From humanitarian assistance, disaster relief, noncombatant evacuation operations [NEO] to peacekeeping activities and military operations."

It was stressed that the mission has a multifunction, multipurpose nature and that training exercises had to keep that point in mind. It was explained that an annual total of 70 training exercises and 35 firing exercises were scheduled.

What are the special feature of the marines in Okinawa?

"It is the only overseas forward deployment base, as well as a forward logistics base and a fuel base with 50 million gallons capacity. Five thousand individual pieces of equipment are stored in a total of 55,386 square feet of warehouse space."

According to Rollings, MCAS Futenma's First Marine Aircraft Wing's strategic requirements were:

"300 total aircraft: 70 in peacetime and 230 in times of contingency."

"Marine aviation logistics support; maintenance and repair of military aircraft."

"In other words, Futenma Air Station must provide support functions for the First Marine Aircraft Wing and other air units in times of peace and contingency in the Western Pacific."

The point he was trying to make was that Futenma was not used just by the marines but by other air force planes in times of emergency.

The entourage also visited both Kadena Air Base and Futenma Air Station.

At Kadena, the base for the 18th Wing of the air force, its commander, Brigadier General Tom Hobbins, spoke with them.

"The 18th Wing is the air force's largest combat force overseas in terms of the number of aircraft. In terms of population, it is the fourth largest in the world."

"At this base, we have 7,252 air force personnel and 10,984 members of family. We also have 594 staff members from the defense department here. 2,900 Japanese civilians and 3,000 Japanese construction workers also form the core of the Kadena team."

"The U.S. population on Okinawa is 54,000. 28,000 are active duty military personnel. Defense department staff total 1,414. 765 teachers and staff work at the American schools. 24,000 paramilitary personnel and family members reside here."

"We use 13 major installations. We lease them from 28,000 Okinawan families. The Japanese government leases on our behalf 90 percent of Kadena Air Base's 5,000 acres and 50 percent of its munitions area's 6,500 acres from some 10,000 Okinawan families."

"The U.S. forces in Okinawa contribute some two billion dollars to the prefectural economy. 55 percent of prefectural income comes from the Japanese government."[2]

They also received a brief talk at Futenma.

Futenma Air Station began in 1945 as a bomber base. The runway was lengthened to its current 9,000 feet (2,800 meters) during the early 1950s.

The air station is home to 3,500 marines and sailors. The air field is in constant use sixteen hours a day from 7 A.M. until 11 P.M. At present, it is used as a base for MAG-36, attached to the First Marine Aircraft Wing and some other squadrons. It is a U.N. facility and a divert base for other air force and naval aircraft operations in the vicinity of Okinawa.[3]

Headphones

Why is the American military so good at presentations?
Virtually all the members of the entourage were short of sleep.[4] Fatigued by the continuous stream of briefings, some of the Japanese were nevertheless impressed and quite absorbed. Some of them were recalling what a member of the U.S. military had once told them:

> "When the military give briefings, they're told to aim at elevator speeches. In other words, they are trained to give short, crisp briefings in the three minutes it takes an elevator to get where it's going. They're taught to focus not on what they know but on what their bosses need to know."[5]

> "Briefings are the key when you want to insert the necessary information into the heads of the top policymakers in Washington. So, to make it easier to grasp, you've got to be compact. The Pentagon is far better at this than the State Department. They write on and on. You'd better be visual too, use lots of tables and charts and maps. And finally, you have to be colorful and technical. That's the secret to surviving the information wars in this town."[6]

A question-and-answer session followed the briefing.

Moriya asked, "It's just a hypothetical question, but wouldn't it be possible to shift Futenma Air Station over to Kadena Air Base?" Moriya thought Kadena could respond a little more flexibly.

The American side responded with the nuance that "Both Futenma and Kadena are tied by the U.N. Status of Forces Agreement and it would be difficult for the U.S. to decide to return or unify bases on its own."

Of the U.S. military bases in Japan, seven were designated as "U.N. facilities": Yokota, Zama, Yokosuka, Sasebo, Kadena, Futenma, and White Beach. The Americans were referring to these bases.

The Yoshida-Acheson official communiqué of 1951 obligated Japan "to permit troops serving in U.N. activities in Korea to stay in Japan and to provide them with support" even after the signing of the San Francisco Peace Treaty. In accordance with this, a U.N. Status of Forces Agreement was signed. This same accord designates seven U.S. military facilities and areas in Japan as those which can be used by U.N. forces.

It was Kurt Campbell's fifth trip to Okinawa.

Before becoming deputy assistant secretary of defense, he knew nothing about Okinawa. In the summer of 1995, his first work in his new post was to meet with Okinawa Governor Masahide Ota.[7]

He asked Paul Giarra, Japan Desk officer, "Why am I meeting the governor of Okinawa?"

"Because there are bases there."

"I see."

That was how far his awareness went. But Campbell was shocked at how unfamiliar Okinawa was to the Japanese side as well. Tanaka confessed openly to Campbell that he'd been there "once about 25 years ago." He hadn't been since he went on a Self-Defense Force (SDF) jet as part of his orientation on joining the Foreign Ministry.

Catching sight from the helicopter of Futenma en route to the other bases, the base perimeters could be easily spotted as if carved out in the middle of a high-density housing area.

Futenma is situated right in the middle of Ginowan City. It accounts for a quarter of the city's surface area. Sixteen schools encircle it.

Campbell thought, *Why does a base have to be squeezed into such a small area?*

Tanaka was thinking the same thing.

Moriya was thinking something else. *Gee, the pilot's good. You don't have to worry about being on board. To tell the truth, it's pretty different from riding in a SDF helicopter.*

Moriya was totally impressed. "They fly in formation. Their timing at takeoff and touchdown was impeccable. The three of them came down, one, two, three without a moment's hesitation. Their logistics was perfect too, seamless. There was no gap."[8]

Moriya was even more surprised by the fact that the Futenma Air Station's commander had explained in minute detail the base's function and that the American side had answered all the Japanese questions thoroughly. This was something new.

Up until then, the Japanese had never asked the Americans about base functions. Even if they had, it's highly unlikely they would have received a proper answer.

Moriya had worked on the base question for two years when he was posted to the Defense Facilities Bureau in Osaka. He may have had more than one occasion to grind his teeth at the intransigence of the U.S. military. When the Americans and Japanese were jointly developing the FSX (a next-generation fighter), he was head of the aircraft section of the Outfitting Bureau. It was not just once or twice that he had been angered by American arrogance, even though it was Japan providing the money and technology.

After the rape of the young Okinawan girl by U.S. Marines, he warned that the base issue could spin out of control if things were left as is, but the Americans were at first almost patronizing.

Of course, there had never been a chance for the top foreign policy and defense officials on both sides to visit and learn about the bases together. The bases had at best been handled at the level of the U.S. Forces Japan. There had never been an occasion where they could visit in this form the Pacific forces (CINCPAC) or the joint command head-quarters, let alone the top of the Pentagon.

Despite the critical importance of the bases, especially the Okinawan bases, to the bilateral alliance, the U.S. government and the Japanese government had continuously avoided approaching the issue head on.

This is what the alliance should be like. This experience is a turning point that has changed the nature of U.S.-Japan security relations. Moriya was filled with emotion.

There are doubts that this visit to Okinawa was that significant. But it cannot be denied that it triggered off a kind of "chemical reaction" which set the scene for the return of Futenma Air Station and the "realignment, consolidation, reduction" of the U.S. military bases in Okinawa.

Hubbard was overwhelmed by the sheer size of Kadena Air Base. He later summed up his impressions. "That trip was a breakthrough. I started to think we had to give Futenma back when I actually saw just how big Kadena was. I came back and said please tell me why we (the marines) can't do these things on Kadena."[9]

The sound of the helicopter engines when they were visiting the bases in Okinawa was something else. It felt like your eardrums were going to burst. The sound was still reverberating in their ears as they laid back and headed for home in the Gulf Stream II.

Everyone was talking through his headphones aboard the helicopter. But despite this awkwardness, it was the best conversation they'd ever had in terms of understanding each other.

Back in Tokyo, Masahiro Akiyama, head of the Bureau of Defense Policy, hosted a dinner party at a Chinese restaurant. Everyone ate, drank, and made merry.

Somebody said, "There's a world of difference between seeing and not seeing." Everyone nodded.

Hashimoto's Master Stroke

It was easy enough to say that you would return Futenma, but where would you shift its functions; how many years would it take to shift them; how would you estimate the costs involved; who was going to pay; what would you do when the chips were down; and how would you reassess the strategic environment of the Asian-Pacific region when it was returned?

There was a huge amount of preparation that had to be done for considering Option B.

Between March 6 and March 20, the Americans were engaged in a kind of crash program. They came up with specific items, the Japanese would ask for some changes, and the Americans would then make amendments.

It was on March 21 that the Americans showed the Japanese a proposal for the return of Futenma. On that day both sides were at the U.S. Defense College working on a proposal for a joint declaration on U.S.-Japan security and the Agreement Concerning Reciprocal Provision of Logistic Support, Supplies, and Services (ACSA).

Only a very few gathered later in the Washington office of Thomas Hubbard, deputy assistant secretary of state, on the sixth floor of the State Department building. They chose the State Department because they thought they would be noticed if they met at the Defense Department. Almost a month had elapsed since the Santa Monica Summit.

On March 23, Tanaka proceeded to the prime minister's residence alone and handed Hashimoto the plan proposal.

Saturday. The prime minister's residence was quiet. Of the secretaries who had hung around Hashimoto like so many groupies since he became prime minister, only Hiroyasu Ando, seconded from the Foreign Ministry, was about on that day.

"Right, then. At last, eh?" Hashimoto was caught up in his emotions for a moment. But the problem was, where will we shift it? He knew that that was the next step, but he was worried. Besides, even assuming that they did relocate to an alternative base, what was to be done about the runway?

Hashimoto thought a slightly smaller runway would do, but the American proposal was likely to call for a fairly big one. Still, his main thought was that the Americans had done well to come this far.

The American proposal was reported to Yukihiko Ikeda, the foreign minister, the following Monday. Hashimoto had told them several times in the case of Futenma's return "don't even tell the minister about this," but the Foreign Ministry officers ignored him at least where the minister was concerned.[10]

During this period, the Defense Agency was completely out of the loop. Hideo Usui only learned about it on April 12 from the front page of the morning edition of the *Nihon Keizai Shimbun*. The headlines danced:

"Futenma Air Station to Be Returned within 5 Years"

"Japan and America Strike Basic Agreement"

"Functions Moved to Kadena"

"Realignment/Consolidation including Iwakuni"

"Early Withdrawal from Sobe Too"

[Washington, March 11 by Akihiko Miyamoto] It was made clear by American and Japanese sources on the 11th that the American and Japanese governments had reached a basic agreement on realizing the return of Futenma Air Station within five years, the focus of the realignment, consolidation, and reduction of U.S. military bases in Okinawa being discussed to coincide with President Clinton's visit to Japan.

In addition to transferring Futenma Air Station's function to Kadena Air Base, consolidation and reduction including Iwakuni base in Yamaguchi Prefecture will be implemented, thereby making it possible to reduce some of the U.S. Forces in Japan stationed in Okinawa. They also agreed to an early return of Sobe Communications Site, where the government is currently illegally using some land whose usage period has expired.[11]

Usui had to attend a budget session in the upper house that morning. He headed towards the Diet from the Akasaka accommodation quarters with his secretary, Tetsuro Kuroe, in tow.

Kuroe had read the morning edition at home and had immediately called Nobushige Takamizawa, the officer in charge of the Defense Policy Division. Takamizawa's initial reaction was, "That's not possible," but after a short pause he responded a little vaguely, "Gee, I don't know what to say. They may be up to something that we don't know about."

Kuroe reported that to Usui in the car. "Something's strange, isn't it?"

"Mmm, but life'd be a whole lot easier if we could achieve something like that."

Usui cocked his head, but didn't ask Kuroe to look into it further or anything. He found Masahiro Akiyama, head of the Bureau of Defense Policy, standing outside the government committee rooms at the Diet waiting for him.

Akiyama said, "There's a strange article in the papers. . . ."

Usui thought he would go on to say, "There's no truth to it," but Akiyama seemed to be having trouble following up. He was hesitating about saying something.

"The PM's office is moving in places we know nothing about, so perhaps the prime minister is thinking of something."

Kuroe thought: *He's not telling us everything.*

As the session came to a close, Usui got a memo from Kuroe. "The prime minister would like you to come to the PM's office this evening with the Cabinet secretary and the foreign minister. Ambassador Mondale will also be there apparently."

Usui nodded to show he had gotten the message.

Even today, Usui's face twists in bitterness when he speaks of that time. "It was not a very happy event for us, but we knew absolutely nothing about it. In fact, there was only one person each at the Defense Agency and the Foreign Ministry who knew what was going on. But they didn't even tell me about it. Some threatening directive seems to have been issued by the prime minister to the officer concerned to the effect that he'd kill him if he told anyone. A certain party told me so that same day, but I was still unconvinced."[12]

The "certain party" Usui was referring to was Bureau Chief Akiyama. But even Akiyama was kept outside the magic circle until very late. He was summoned to the PM's office on April 8 when Ambassador Mondale presented the prime minister with the official U.S. proposal on the return of the Futenma Air Station.

All the meetings, dialogue, promises, and decisions up to that point never left the unofficial arena. The fact that the Americans officially proposed the return of the Futenma Air Station was something totally different in nature from the maneuvering that had preceded it.

In order to iron out the last details, Hashimoto had called Masaki Orita of the North American Affairs Bureau and Akiyama to the PM 's office.

Mondale went home in fine spirits.

Hashimoto was excited. *Finally we've got the return of Futenma. Now all that remains is how the two governments will make the announcement. Let's think about that later.*

Repeating, "Thank you, thank you," Hashimoto went round the room giving everyone a two-handed shake in turn, pumping each hand vigorously.

Close to three weeks had passed since Hitoshi Tanaka made his top-secret report to Hashimoto.

Hashimoto was overwhelmed by emotion. *We did well to keep it a secret this long.*

There were times when Hashimoto himself had had an impulse to confide in someone. It was a thrilling moment. But he wrenched that impulse firmly back. There was something about that that felt good too.

Hashimoto had, in fact, spoken of it only twice. The first time was on March 30. He had traveled by car to Yamanashi to attend the wake of Shin Kanemaru, backroom power broker of the LDP. He was alone with Kenji Eda, his political affairs aide, and they had three hours there, then three hours back in the car. On long trips, Hashimoto normally brought along a book to read or slept. That day, he couldn't stop talking.

On the way back, he told Eda, "If I was the American president, I'd give Futenma back."

He asked Eda his reaction. Eda countered with a "what?"

"But I'd have some conditions." He paused here. "I'd probably ask for a proper search for a substitute base as well as a proper destination for the Harriers. In exchange, I'd want us to think more seriously about the bilateral security mechanism. If we did all that, I'd let us have it back. I have a feeling that he'll give it back to us."

"It'd be OK to use the semiconductors or insurance or anything for the deal if we were really going to get Futenma back, wouldn't it?"

"Uh huh, but I have my doubts. I don't think we'll have to do that."[13]

Eda had no way of knowing what was happening behind the scenes.

The second time was on April 11, the day before the joint press conference with Mondale at the prime minister's cherry blossom viewing party at Shinjuku Gyoen, when Hashimoto spotted Takeo Fukuchi, the previous Maritime Self-Defense Force's chief of staff, whom he'd studied with at Azabu Junior and Senior High. Hashimoto waded through the sea of people trying to get closer to Fukuchi, but the going was rough. There were more than 10,000 guests. So, Hashimoto waved at Fukuchi from a distance and shouted out loud, "Hey, I did it."

Fukuchi didn't know what he was talking about. He nodded on the following day when he heard the news about Futenma's return: "So, that's what it was."[14]

On the night of April 12, Prime Minister Hashimoto and Ambassador Mondale's joint press conference was over.

Hashimoto was with Sadajiro Furukawa, the deputy cabinet secretary, and their secretaries in the prime minister's working office.

"Let me have a whiskey and water today." Hashimoto wanted to wet his whistle first.

When everyone had a drink in his hand, Furukawa spoke formally to Hashimoto. "Mr. Prime Minister, you have shown us what politics is all about."

"Now you're being political!"

"No, sir, it was your politics."

"No, no, you're just being political."

They kept up this repartee several times, chatting over their glasses.

Furukawa thought to himself, *I will never forget Hashimoto's indescribable expression of knowing deep down he has really achieved something as long as he lived.*[15]

Akiyama accompanied the director-general back in the car to the defense agency from the PM's office. Akiyama apologized, saying, "I didn't tell you, sir, because I was told by the prime minister not to leak it to even the foreign minister or the director-general."

It was a shock to Usui that the U.S. military had agreed to the return of Futenma. *Then what was all that about that it can't be done, it's impossible?*

On the other hand, he was relieved. *Futenma is coming back. It's really an epoch-making event.*

But a sensation of overwhelming fatigue was winning the day. He left his office at the agency to go back to the accommodation quarters.

Speaking to his aide, Kuroe, who accompanied him from the minister's office to the front door, Usui said, "Well, we were truly outfenced by the Hashimoto master stroke today."[16]

Ryutaro Hashimoto, *kendo* fencer of the fifth rank, master instructor: touché. Hideo Usui, *kendo* fencer of the fifth rank, instructor: caught off balance.

Top Down

It was at the end of February that Defense Secretary Perry decided to return Futenma Air Station.[17]

Perry remembers informing Campbell of his decision. He says, "It was about a month before. I probably had told him earlier than that that I thought that we were making progress and that I was optimistic, but I really didn't know until about a month before that we had the basic agreements. Before that, the important issues, particularly Futenma, were still up in the air."[18] He told Campbell he would let Anthony Lake know later.[19]

Perry further recalls, "I worked [on the Okinawan crisis] primarily and Tony Lake was informed on it, but Secretary Christopher was the one who was more deeply involved in that, and I had many one-on-one discussions with him about Okinawa."[20]

The more important a decision was, the more Perry used a top-down approach. He was not a committee man. This time, too, he made the decision himself. His stance was, let's see how far Campbell and his team can take things now.

Perry had taken considerable pains to maintain secrecy. Apart from Campbell, he told only a very few people at the State Department and the White House of the decision to return Futenma.

Information management on the Japanese side was more thorough. Until Tanaka, who was shown the U.S. proposal in Hubbard's office, passed the information on to Prime Minister Hashimoto immediately after his return to Japan on March 23, only Vice Minister Hayashi knew about it. Tanaka, too, was very careful how he handled the information. This later left sour feelings.

There was no pacifying people at the Defense Agency.

They were brimming with indignation that just when a different dialogue on bilateral security matters had been started with SACO and they thought they were in the driver's seat, they had once again been shunted into the backseat.

Usui later said, "Information always leaks out and trips you up when you use the down-up method. There are those who say the prime minister went over the head of the agency just to make himself shine, but I think it was rather to better control the information. I think it couldn't be helped."[21] Usui spoke almost as if trying to convince himself.

Akiyama was also placed in a difficult position. Not only did Usui not know, but he also ignored Naoaki Murata, vice-head of the JDA.

Akiyama reported to both Usui and Murata on the same day, April 12. "You knew it, didn't you?"

Murata's tone was hostile.

He was cut to the quick by the criticism that information would leak out from the agency. He himself was aware that, compared with the information management at his old haunt, the Finance Ministry, their handling of information was somewhat lacking perhaps due to the tendency to decide everything by consensus. He had also heard that the Foreign Ministry and the PM's office had no trust in the agency on this point. Akiyama had his suspicions that this may have been why the Pentagon had also cut the JDA out of the loop.

All the more reason why Akiyama was desperate to keep the issue confidential.

Tanaka was attacked directly by a high-ranking official at the agency. "What do you mean by using us for all the data on the bases and military requirements and then keeping us in the dark about the most important things? That's just not right."[22]

Tanaka felt as if he were being pierced right through, but he endured it in silence. He thought, *I did something irregular. That's not right, you know.* He may have used a "forbidden trick," something that just wasn't allowed if you were going to live in Kasumigaseki. He also thought, *The boys over at the JDA will never forgive me.*[23]

However, he also thought, *But what else was there I could do? It had to be done to get the job done.* He also tried thinking that it was an "emergency shelter" type of measure. *This is not an issue for people lower than Perry to bring together. We won't be able to keep things quiet at home unless he's in charge. So, there was no other way of doing it.*

He also told himself this in an effort to convince himself.

There was no chance for the decision to be politically possible in the United States unless Perry and Campbell made it top-down. To that end, the Japanese had to use the American top-down policy decision-making approach in tandem.

Hashimoto was perfect for that approach. He was typecast for it. It was what he himself desired and played out. His unprecedented joint press conference with Ambassador Mondale was nothing more than a top-down, prime minister–led political performance engineered by the PM's office.

The bottom-up system of consensus and sanction, the very foundation of the Kasumigaseki bureaucracy, had started to creak.

SACO's Interim Report

The American and Japanese governments released an interim report on their realignment, consolidation, and reduction policy on April 15, 1996. It was completed to coincide with President Clinton's visit to Japan the next day.

The interim report cited the return of a total of 11 facilities, including the complete return of Futenma Air Station within five to seven years:

- Return Yomitan Auxiliary Airfield. Relocate parachute drop training (to Ie-jima).
- Return most of Camp Kuwae. Relocate the Naval Hospital and other facilities there to other U.S. facilities and areas in Okinawa.
- Accelerate return of Naha Port. Build a new port at Urasoe to allow for the return of Naha Port.
- Return Gimbaru Training Area. Relocate facilities to other U.S. facilities and areas in Okinawa.
- Return Futenma Air Station within the next five to seven years; functions to be relocated to Iwakuni and Kadena air bases; a new heliport to be built in Okinawa.
- Return major portion of Northern Training Area. Return more than half.
- Return Sobe Communications Site. Return Sobe Communications Site once a new site is constructed at Camp Hansen
- Return significant portion of Camp Zukeran. Return land as a result of housing consolidation.
- Release U.S. joint use of Aha Training Area (land).
- Return portions of Makiminato Service Area. Return land adjacent to Route 58.[24]

In addition, "improvements in training and transportation" were announced including the relocation of the midair refueler KC-130 (Hercules) to Iwakuni in conjunction with the transfer of a similar number of AV-8 (Harrier) aircraft to the U.S. mainland; the termination and relocation to the Japanese mainland of live artillery firing training over Prefectural Highway 104; and the termination of conditioning hikes on public roads in Okinawa. "Operational improvements" in the Status of Forces Agreement, including measures concerning markings on U.S.

forces official vehicles and expanding education programs for voluntary automobile insurance, were also announced.

Both governments pointed out that these changes would amount to "approximately a 23 percent reduction" in the total area of the U.S. bases in Okinawa and stressed that the significance of this reduction was that "while maintaining the U.S. forces in Japan capability and an adequate response stance, it would alleviate the impact of U.S. military activity" on local community life in Okinawa Prefecture.

Apart from Futenma, of the bases targeted for reversion or consolidation in the interim report, a specific date of return was given only for Sobe Communications Site. The Japanese side was thinking, *Without specific dates, there's a danger that the Americans will do an about-face with a change of government. Let's make it as concrete as possible.*[25]

The Americans were thinking the same thing. *We had all absorbed the lessons of Naha Port. It has been scheduled for return almost 20 years now and still a substitute site hasn't been found. We all agreed that we had lost the trust of the Okinawan people. We didn't want to make the same mistake twice.*[26]

U.S. allies are always afraid of large-scale policy shifts when there is a change of administration with the presidential elections. In the 1976 presidential elections, President Jimmy Carter's policy to withdraw U.S. troops from Korea was a classic example. His election promise was rolled back in the end and never carried out (only 3,000 personnel were cut), but this policy flip-flop planted hard-to-eradicate roots of mistrust in both Japan and Korea regarding the Carter administration.

Japan had had its fair share of thrills in Okinawa as well.

In the process of Okinawan reversion in 1967, Prime Minister Sato, who was visiting Washington, and President Lyndon Johnson agreed to "set a date within two to three years" for the reversion of Okinawa to Japan. In the spring of the following year, however, Johnson suddenly announced he would not be running in the presidential elections that year, taking the world by surprise. Sato was the most surprised of all. He was afraid that the reversion date for Okinawa would be changed. True, Sato successfully wrapped up the negotiation for the reversion of Okinawa with the new Nixon administration. Five years after the Sato-Johnson meeting, in May 1972, Okinawa reverted to the Japanese mainland.

Concerning when Futenma would be returned, the Japanese pushed for five to seven years, the Americans for five to ten years. In the end, the Japanese proposal won out.

There is no doubt that there were physical reasons why relocation would take at least that much time. Hashimoto noted in a subsequent press conference and in replies before the Diet that "the date was set taking into consideration the time that would be needed to locate an alternative site and come to an accommodation with local residents, to conduct archaeological surveys and environmental assessments and to draw up plans on how to reuse the former base sites."

Initially however, the Defense Facilities Administration Agency (DFAA) frowned upon the five-to-seven-year framework, saying, "practically speaking, it wasn't feasible." Hashimoto roared at Masuo Morodomi, head of the DFAA, when he tried to explain the reasons why he "wasn't confident." Hashimoto stuck to his guns about the five to seven years.

The PM's office quickly caught the prime minister's displeasure with the DFAA, leading to the less than flattering opinion that "all they can do is focus on the punctuation." But from the agency's point of view, there were reasons for not meekly acquiescing with a "yes, right," just because it was a top-down decision.

The agency was not at all sure that it could win the local residents over. "Look at how long it took with Narita, a civilian airport! They still haven't started on the second runway. In the final analysis, it all comes back to whether you can get the locals to agree. We were not confident at all."[27]

When all was said and done, the reason why Naha Port had not been returned some 20 years after the agreement to do so was that they had not been able to achieve the "acceptance of the locals."

Behind this issue lay the question of the income generated by the bases. There were 3,000 landowners who would be affected should the Futenma facility be returned. Despite the enactment of the Special Measures Act Accompanying the Return of Military Land (July 1995), which ensured that land payments would not stop immediately when the base was returned but would be subsidized for a three-year period thereafter, the landowners' agitation was still considerable.

Another factor that may have been involved was that the agency "had a petty side to it" and that "there'd be no work left if they got going in a hurry."[28] It was a curious organization originally created for the purpose of administering the U.S. military bases. No bases, no work. In that sense, it was not unreasonable to say that the DFAA had a relationship of "coexistence" and "cosurvival" with the landowners.

But the dice had already been rolled. And it was Hashimoto's "voice from on high"[29] that had decided the outcome.

At the same time, both the Americans and the Japanese were concerned with changes in the international climate, namely, changes in the situation on the Korean Peninsula. An unspoken awareness was emerging that there would be no need for a presence like that of the current U.S. Marine Corps in Okinawa if these trends could be brought to a peaceful conclusion, or even if not so peaceful a conclusion, if the current military tension evaporated one way or another.

Japan proposed that changes in the situation on the Korean Peninsula be clearly stated as an "environment change." The Americans, however, countered that it would not be preferable to mention environmental changes when the issue was not environmental changes but maintaining capabilities, and so it was left out.

Hubbard explained, "If we specified a return once the North Korea threat had disappeared, what kind of signal would that send to the Koreans? We said, let's not talk about the change in the situation, let's talk about facilities and capability."[30]

The U.S. military opposed the return of other bases as well. Clouded though they were by the return of Futenma Air Station, problems pertaining to the return of other bases were exceedingly vexatious.

A senior U.S. government official reminisced: "In fact, 90 percent of our work was on the other issues surrounding SACO, which were extremely complicated. . . . There is only a small group of people who worked on Futenma, but there was a much larger group of people that were working on the deliverables as part of the SACO package."[31]

"They are all difficult. . . . What the Okinawans want so much is not sometimes so much the land back, they want to plan for what to do with the land, and they want a lot of money associated with that land, and they want to ensure the payments. When the land is returned to family or farmers, it is returned outright sometimes, and there are no more payments. Okinawans don't want that. They want the land back and they want the payments to continue even if you do need the land, right? Sometimes with the marines or the air force, they wanted to give away little slivers of land that were not useful. Third, [the] JDA sometimes . . . was less than supportive about giving certain pieces of land back, and ultimately, there was concern at the embassy as well about this sort of avalanche process."[32]

The Japanese side put forward their case, but American resistance was so strong that a lot of things never happened.

The U.S. bases occupied the best sites in densely populated Okinawa. That alone was enough to stir up local sentiment. Emotions came to the boil just looking at the military's private golf courses and beaches.

Okuma Rest Center, situated cheek by jowl to JAL's Okuma beach resort, was one such site. But the Americans came back with the argument that "recreational facilities were vital for maintaining Marine Corps readiness for extremely tense forward deployments. Without them, they'll snap psychologically," and talks on returning even one facility came to nothing.

The U.S. military, especially the air force and the marines, stubbornly resisted the reduction of bases.

But Perry persisted. When speaking alone with Campbell, Perry asked, "How much do you think we should be able to reduce the bases?"

When Campbell replied, "I think between 15 percent and 20 percent at most," Perry stated, "Let's try for 25 percent."[33]

Campbell was running around like a bulldozer. He laid the ground-work with the military brass, CINCPAC, and the U.S. forces in Japan.

It was expected that the relocation costs would be colossal, but nobody could quote a definite figure. Sums like 200 billion to 300 billion yen or 400 billion to 600 billion yen were bandied about in the newspapers, but they weren't able to boil it down at this stage. Even the length of the run-way had yet to be decided. The cost of the transfer, how it would be appropriated and handled, was fudged from beginning to end. Whether it was to come from the ordinary budget, from a "special earmarking" in defense expenditure, depended entirely on the interpretation.

That "the various expenses involved would be given priority consideration in the budget compilation process"[34] was determined at the time of the budget requests for fiscal 1997. But it was still unclear whether that would be under a special earmarking.[35]

The JDA was afraid that it would come out of defense expenditure, eating into the ordinary defense budget as a result. Hashimoto said from the start he would "get the Ministry of Finance to make a special [budget] appropriation for it," trying to allay the agency's worries, but the agency's nerves were on edge on that score. From the outset, the Ministry of Finance had indicated its basic position that "SACO-related items came strictly under defense-related expenditure" and took the stance that "there's been no agreement on a special earmarking."

The suspicion of Noboru Hoshuyama, director-general of the Defense Facilities Administration Agency (DFAA), that "special earmarking was all talk," was shared widely by the JDA. "We heard all about a special allocation for the land reclamation at Naha Port and the relocation to Iwakuni, but in the end cuts had to be made somewhere. There'll be one hell of a scramble by the ground, maritime, and air forces to protect their own budgets."[36]

In the meantime, Perry was wary that the military might take advantage of the situation to inflate its demands. He emphasized time and time again that these plans "are not gold-plated."[37]

The military always did some gold-plating whenever a base was consolidated or relocated. Citing the need for modernization of some such chestnut, it tried to build something better than before. That couldn't be allowed. The order was to strip the gold-plating and keep costs to a minimum.

This question was later to surface concerning the relocation of Sobe Communications Site. The relocation of the site was acknowledged to be "a political problem that just couldn't wait."

The fight put up by Shoichi Chibana, one of the landowners, was widely known both at home and abroad and had become a symbol of the opposition struggle against expropriation of land for bases. Both governments wanted to remove this thorn from their sides.

But it was not as if the facility could just be relocated anywhere. Communications sites come with "a peculiarity known as radio waves." In addition to having to catch the radio waves in the area, the relocation site had to be found on Okinawa. Those in the field argued that an alternative site could not have anything around it blocking the waves because it had to be able to receive the necessary transmissions.

A suitable site was not easy to find. Camp Hansen was finally settled on. But was that really the only reason? There was criticism that "the Americans agreed to relocating to Camp Hansen although the only opposing landowner was [Shoichi] Chibana, while the rest of them were happy enough to continue because they wanted to construct a new state-of-the-art communications base."

To this, the Americans put forward the argument that "communications facilities require constant modernization and upkeep."

The Japanese reaction was complicated. On the one hand, there was the view that it was inevitable that "realignment, consolidation, reduction, and modernization" would take place, not just "realignment, consolidation, and reduction." Their argument was that "we have to give the military the benefit of a certain amount of modernization to win them over" and "Sobe is such an old facility, modernizing it is only natural. It will be to our advantage too if we can share the information it picks up."

On the other hand, some thought they could smell the "gold-plating" Perry had mentioned. One of the SACO members confessed to "righteous indignation."

When putting together the SACO interim report, the bickering over Sobe continued right up to the very end.

A Difference of Culture

Why did the Americans agree to return Futenma, which they had opposed so strongly? In order to answer that question, one would have to examine closely why they were opposing it, where the opposition came from, and what was the nature of the opposition.

In the first place, each section of the military had its own interests, turf, face, and ego. A top-ranking official at the State Department dubbed this "a difference of culture." "The air force wants to keep its Kadena base. The marines want to keep their Futenma Air Station. You can't expect a three-star air force general any more than a three-star marine general to be happy with having a mix. It's two cultures. It's like putting gaimusho [MOFA] with tsusansho [MITI] and telling them to get on together."[38]

A senior White House source revealed: "It all boiled down to military egos. The marines and the air force opposed it because they didn't want to share. CINCPAC was also against it openly and behind the scenes. The U.S. forces in Japan were no different."[39]

Asked "when will the Okinawan question be solved?" a short time after the decision had been taken to return Futenma, Richard Meyers, commander of the U.S. forces in Japan, aroused criticism with his reply: "I don't think it will ever be solved. There was no solution when I arrived here and there isn't likely to be one either. No, there won't be a solution."[40] This feeling was the norm among the U.S. military at the time.

The military believed it would be extremely difficult to find an alternative site for Futenma. That is precisely why it opposed the return of the base. Even after it was decided, smoothing ruffled military feathers was no easy task.

The second argument was that return would impede performance when the need arose. This was the question of so-called surge capacity. If a contingency situation arose in a neighboring region, the military would need take-off and landing space for the helicopters. It would also need the capacity to store equipment and carry out repairs. That capacity was available at Futenma, not at Kadena. The marines argued forcefully, sublease from Kadena Air Base and we'll be caught out when something blows.

Discussion on just how much the runway should be lengthened at the relocation base was especially fraught with tension. Although the Americans managed to get a commitment from the marines that they would not insist on the same length as the Futenma runway (9,000 feet, or 2,800 meters), there was a violent clash between the Japanese and the Americans as to whether it should be 800 meters, 1,000 meters, or 1,300 meters.

Another argument was about the "drop in deterrent capability." In the preparations for the Santa Monica Summit, Ambassador Mondale pushed the deterrent capability argument strongly.

This was a very convincing argument. Not just the military, but the embassy and the State Department were very cautious about it in general.[41]

If Futenma were restored to Japan, it could affect the operational duties of the U.S. Marine Corps. If that occurred, there was a danger that there would be a drop in quality in the all-important U.S. military presence in the Asian-Pacific region and especially in northeast Asia. In short, the military's deterrent capability might be impaired. The upshot was along the lines of, if we give the bases back here, we won't be able to carry out adequate marine operations, our capability will fall, and if that happens, it may give North Korea some funny ideas.

Up until a certain point, Ambassador Mondale was cautious about returning Futenma.[42] He argued fervently that it might "look like we were retreating from the Pacific" or "send the wrong signals."

Mondale had his own bitter memories. He rued the fact that as vice president during the Carter administration, he had supported the U.S. military withdrawal from Korea proposed by Carter, and as a result had sent precisely the wrong signals to both North and South. Carter had made that election promise after the fall of Saigon, when the confidence of America's allies had hit rock bottom.

In an attempt to accelerate the U.S. withdrawal, North Korea's Chairman Kim Il Sung attacked with a peace play for "North-South dialogue." South Korea's President Park Chung Hee, on the other hand, started quietly considering the nuclear option. He brooded that the only way to win the survival game with North Korea after the U.S. withdrawal would be nuclear. It was also a "weak man's threat" to contain Carter's withdrawal plan.

Mondale experienced the frighteningly unpredictable "billiard ball" effects that came from perceptions of U.S. withdrawal. Many on the American side also knew that this is what lay behind Mondale's argument about wrong signals.

The fact that it was an election year also presented a problem. In presidential election years, the White House usually tries to avoid making any large decisions that might serve as ammunition for the opposition. The Clinton administration was especially trying to avoid any decision that would rub the military the wrong way.

Clinton's Democratic administration had to guard constantly against a Republican Congress criticizing its decision to return the bases as "spineless," "a withdrawal," or "picking on the military." Behind these arguments lay the readdressing of U.S. post–Cold War strategies and policy priorities as well as domestic and economic priorities.

The White House was extremely sensitive about these points. The American people were looking inward. An isolationist and protectionist like the Republican Pat Buchanan was getting support. The electorate was not impressed with presidential foreign policy and trips abroad that did nothing visible back home. President Bush had been tossed away with such considerations.

That's what they were saying.

Just before the Santa Monica Summit on March 22, a meeting of the top men in uniform was held at the Defense Department. This meeting is held regularly every Thursday. John Shalikashvili, chairman of the Joint Chiefs of Staff, chaired it.

Two public opinion polls were presented to the group. The first was on whether you supported security relations with America's allies. It was being presented because it had jumped more than 10 points in the past few weeks. The second poll was on whether you supported the overseas stationing of U.S. troops. Support for this was falling.

In other words, the polls could be read as the American people wanting "to keep the alliances minus troops abroad." This was to present the top brass, who wanted to keep the overseas presence, with a bit of a sticky problem.

But of all the resistance, that from the White House itself was the most formidable. Perry said he "never had trouble persuading the White House" and they were "always supportive."[43] Yet, while he must have had the covert blessing of National Security Adviser Lake, those lower down the totem pole refused to give him the nod.

The White House's main interest was not whether to return Futenma. Its only interest was making the president's upcoming April visit to Japan a success.

Perry would be visiting Japan before the president. The point was who was going to raise the question of the Okinawan bases. There was a danger that Perry, so zealous on the Okinawa issue, would put it in the spotlight. If that happened, then the overwhelming interest during the president's visit might be Okinawa alone. That would be all right if Okinawa could be solved before the president's visit, but if things didn't work out it could damage the trip.

That's why they couldn't afford to set their hopes too high.

Civilian Control

This was where the brick wall stood. In any event, however, it proved to be a wall that could be overcome.

Military egos could be immobilized by a decision from the White House and the civilian leaders.

In actual fact, this job was left up to Defense Secretary Perry. Indeed, there was a danger that military leaders would be so dissatisfied with the decision that they would run to Congress. But at this stage, things didn't go that far. (Later in July of that year, Benjamin Gilman [R-N.Y.], chairman of the Foreign Affairs Committee in the House, sent Secretary of State Christopher a note warning that the return of Futenma would not be approved unless the alternative site had a 5,100-feet [just under 1,600 meters] long helicopter runway built. It was clear that this was the work of the marines, who were unhappy with the short helicopter runway, but it was rolled back by the State Department civilians and never followed up.)

Perry enjoyed a very good relationship with Shalikashvili, and neither Perry nor Campbell was remiss in his consideration of the Republicans. Republican security pros like Armitage were in favor of returning Futenma; or rather, promoting the return was also to the Republicans' advantage in terms of countertactics.

As a senior official with the Defense Department put it, it all boiled down to the fact that "No matter how the military might resist, it was in the end a decision for the defense secretary." One of the marines officers expressed this as, "I guess that's what they mean by civilian control."[44]

It was nevertheless true that by raising Futenma at the Santa Monica meeting, Hashimoto provided the necessary kind of *gaiatsu* ("outer pressure") for Perry and Campbell to convince Congress. "Because they could use the phrase, the president has demonstrated his understanding on that point."[45]

And that more than anything else was the catalyst the Americans provided to the Japanese to start working on the return of Futenma. This paved the way for virtually the only leverage the Japanese had, namely, "the weight of the prime minister's word."

A high-ranking official at the Foreign Ministry later commented, "America is a country which gives weight to the political discussions of the top and the political importance thereof, not a bottom-up approach. That's why one word from the prime minister has more weight than ten thousand from the bureaucrats. Moreover, it was the first statement from the newly formed [Hashimoto] Cabinet on the U.S. visit. We were able to gently apply the pressure, what is your response to that, you have to make some proposal."[46]

As a consequence, three courses of action were confirmed by both sides: (1) Futenma's relocation on Okinawa; (2) the domino transfer from Futenma to Iwakuni, and Iwakuni to Alaska; and (3) the transfer of contingency functions to Kadena. This, in turn, created a foundation for boiling these courses down to more specific measures.

In a certain sense, the Japanese were able to grasp the opening for Futenma's return by reversing the Americans', and especially the military's, golden rule of "maintaining capability levels."

The U.S. Marines would bring 300 aircraft into play in the event of a contingency. They reasoned that this was why they couldn't let Futenma go. Hearing that, Hashimoto said to one of the Japanese team, "If that's the case, it means they can give it back as long as that function is maintained. How about it?"

This single exchange gave the Japanese some powerful ammunition. They were able to move forward on the board, saying: We'll provide a relocation site and cover the costs involved, so give us back Futenma.

Perry himself saw that "once we got the military judgment that we could find a way of doing Futenma without Futenma, there was really no turning back."[47]

There was no attempt to come up with a precise figure for the cost at that time, however. That was left until later. A high-ranking U.S. official said, "We heard from a variety of people in the prime minister's office, and indeed from MOFA, that cost wasn't a problem here; that Hashimoto had said that this was the highest priority."[48]

Perry was encouraged by this. He used the Santa Monica meeting as leverage here as well. A senior person at the Defense Department said, "After that meeting, we were able to tell the Japanese the operational requirements for this and this base and that their functions were a, b, c, and d."[49]

It was not as if all of the marines from top to bottom were dead set against cutting bases and personnel. The marines' commandant himself was "in private, extremely supportive. His biggest issue was wanting to be kept in the loop; he wanted to be kept informed."[50]

Yes, there was strong resistance to returning Futenma, but opinions were voiced on relocating training exercises elsewhere, to Australia for example. Such suggestions were based on the premise that the bases in Okinawa should be kept to the last as front-line bases. To do that, some form of "rationalization" was required. They should separate the accident-prone training function and shift it somewhere else.

The civilians suspected that these ideas might be no more than a "smokescreen" to protect Futenma Air Station. But more important, what was politically crucial at this time was "a tangible reduction in the bases" and in a "symbolic case." In short, it had to be Futenma; in the face of political demands, it was a moral issue.

The length of the substitute helicopter runway was finally set at 1,300 meters. (The facility would be 1,500 meters including the cordon area.) This length was decided on taking into account the fact that the marines needed a slightly longer runway for their planned "dream helicopter," the V-22 tilt rotor aircraft, which could also be fixed wing.

In fact, the question of the runway was tough going to the very last. The marines, who thought they had been ruthlessly pinned down from above in April, started resisting again in September. Congress also applied pressure on the government. The Office of the Secretary of Defense withstood this pressure, refusing to budge from 1,300 meters. (The truth of the matter was that the Defense Department had still not settled the runway question at the time of SACO's final report in December. The final decision was made immediately after the bilateral security discussions in Annapolis, in March 1997.)

The drop in deterrent capability was an issue that required the utmost caution. In the eyes of Hitoshi Tanaka, deputy director of the North American Affairs Bureau, this was "the most formidable" of all the arguments the Americans put forward.

To begin with, the Nye Initiative, which had been pursued bilaterally for almost a year and a half, had "strengthening deterrence capability" as its main aim. The fact that the Defense Department stuck to its widely criticized "100,000 force structure" was based on the evaluation that it would demonstrate the United States' firm resolve on an American presence in and commitment to this region. All the more reason to be extremely careful about cutting bases on Okinawa.

Behind this theory of stronger deterrent capability was a common apprehension in both Japan and the United States about the American people's tendency to look inward. It was not wise to underestimate the American people's inward-looking propensity. Both governments were fearful of the danger that, over the long run, this could cause a hollowing-out of the bilateral alliance. Besides, changes in domestic Japanese support for the bilateral security arrangement also required a close eye.

According to a joint survey conducted by the *Yomiuri Shimbun* and the U.S. Gallup, Inc., between October and November 1995, the number of Japanese citing "good" bilateral relations fell to just over 20 percent, the lowest figure since the survey started in 1978. Concerning the bilateral security treaty, 60 percent responded that it was "beneficial," but those answering that U.S. forces in Asia "should be reduced" topped 50 percent.[51] Even the number of respondents who said the treaty was "beneficial" was 14 points lower than in 1988 and 5 points lower than in 1994.

It was clear that Okinawa and the bases were factors. The Americans evaluated this as meaning there was still widespread support for the bilateral security structure in Japan but that the strength of that support was eroding.

Perry and Campbell turned the stronger deterrent capability argument to their own ends, supporting it but calling for a reduction in the bases from that stance. In other words, they argued that it would be easier to maintain a sounder alliance if they acted first and reduced the number of bases. A DOD official said, "If we leave the question of the bases as stands, opposition to them will increase, which may well in the end topple the security structure from below. Should that happen, we'll lose our all-important deterrent capability. So, we need some kind of base reduction as a symbolic political decision."[52]

There may also have been an intimation of insurance against future evaluations. "Supposing we don't return Futenma this time and tide things over with some other measure. If the same sort of incident should arise in the future over Futenma, if civilians are killed or injured by a plane crash, it will inevitably raise a question of responsibility for the current Pentagon leaders. We have to show that the current leadership did their utmost."[53]

Campbell later disclosed that of all the other considerations, "making the first move to keep the alliance" and "insuring against criticism" were the two factors which were given the most consideration.[54]

The difficulties imposed by an election year and White House resistance persisted but were not enough to make Perry change his mind.

Someone high up in the White House later confessed that with regard to Republican attacks, "we already had a 10-point lead on Dole around then, so we weren't too worried. But when taking the initiative, we tried to focus on less ambitious things that would earn us a few easy points."[55]

The American leaning toward keeping the alliances minus the troops abroad, so evident in the polls, was a double-edged sword. It was evidence of a long-term American propensity to introversion and could in the final analysis be read as the people's voice demanding an American withdrawal.

From the direction of domestic American politics, the reduction of overseas bases could well be an unavoidable, long-term trend.

Depending on the interpretation, however, it could also be used to justify the reduction of the marines and bases. It could be argued, for example, that the vector of "realignment, consolidation, and reduction" of Okinawan bases starting with the return of Futenma dovetailed with both Japanese and U.S. domestic opinion.

For Perry the most crucial point was for both governments, especially the American, to show that they were serious in tackling the question of the Okinawan bases. He regarded it as signaling civilian control over the military, as well as the dependability of American deterrence capability and a first step towards a sound alliance.

Perry said immediately after the announcement of the return of Futenma, "Up until a month or so ago, there was the idea that maybe the Futenma issue could be pushed off and decided in November. I really wanted to get that moved up front and do the most significant things right away in order to demonstrate we were really serious about this."[56]

In fact, there was a secret struggle going on within the administration not only about returning Futenma but about Perry's visit to Japan itself.

A Sudden Gust from the South

For the SACO group, which was quietly working towards the return of Futenma Air Station, a totally unexpected event was the China-Taiwan showdown between March 8 and 25.

In December of the previous year, China carried out a military exercise off the Taiwanese coast, but at the time neither the Americans nor the Japanese paid it much heed.

This time, however, was different. The United States deployed its aircraft carrier USS *Independence* in protest. Tension mounted slightly in the southern seas. A sudden gust was blowing in from the south.

The China-Taiwan showdown had complicated implications for the negotiation over the Okinawan bases. The SACO team initially was so engrossed in the base affair that they were late in responding to it. Campbell looked back, saying, "The Japanese government was consumed by Okinawa . . . we spent almost no time talking about Taiwan and China."[57]

Even Campbell was in Japan for SACO talks when the aircraft carrier *Nimitz* was deployed and had not been told of the decision taken on the night of March 9, Washington time.

It was the White House that responded sharply.

The view that the return of Futenma was undesirable, or at least that it should be postponed, trickled up. This same opinion could be heard at the State and Defense departments.

Anthony Lake, national security adviser, was also leaning towards a "decisive postponement," and Sandra Kristoff, senior director of East Asian affairs at the National Security Council (NSC), was in favor of caution concerning the return of Futenma until the very last. In her words, "I argued very strongly against it. I mean, the NSC argued strongly against it. And I think Tony was not convinced. I think many of us were convinced that we did not have to make that decision now."[58]

When the *Nihon Keizai Shimbun* ran its scoop on the agreement to return Futenma in its morning edition on April 12, Lake cheerlessly made the parting remark, "Well, now what?" to a White House staff person.[59] His guess was that the pro-Futenma returners had made the leak to press their advantage and create a fait accompli, thereby cutting the ground out from under the let's-wait-and-see voices of caution.

The China-Taiwan showdown turned out to be a fair wind for the voices of caution. Their argument that East Asia was still teeming with danger and that to return U.S. bases on Okinawa in a prominent way would send the wrong signals to all of Asia took on a more convincing note.

What this changed the most was Okinawa's "context of strategical location."[60] The strategic importance of the Okinawan bases, including the marines' function, had been stressed time and time again, but mainly in logistical terms with an eye to the Korean Peninsula. Now perhaps China would have to be included in the picture. Didn't the showdown between Taiwan and China demonstrate that? This kind of argument came to the fore.

Jesse Helms (R-N.C.), chairman of the Senate Foreign Relations Committee, emphasized that the China-Taiwan contingency made bilateral security and the Okinawan bases even more important. His fundamental concern was China's hegemonistic ambitions. China had to be contained. Bilateral security ties had to be reinforced in order to do that. Helms didn't hesitate to say, "If the United States leaves the Japanese to fend for themselves, I am convinced that they will go nuclear within ten years."[61]

The White House was alert to such views as well. It was worried that it would come in for the same sort of criticism from hawks if Futenma was returned now.

There were also those in Japan who said that the showdown between Taiwan and China demonstrated that the Okinawan base issue had to be reviewed from a strategic perspective. Former JDA Director-General Tokuichiro Tamazawa, a representative in the House of Representatives (LDP), put this question to the government in the Diet: "Looking at the current situation in the Taiwan Straits, I believe that the importance of bilateral security ties is becoming more important in the sense of ensuring peace and stability in the Asia-Pacific region. Considering the Okinawan bases from this vantage point, I cannot endorse an approach which maintains that it is good enough to merely reduce the number in an unprincipled fashion. I also believe that we must negotiate with the United States bearing in mind the crucial role the bases play."[62]

The Japanese side was wary of having Futenma Air Station, and the Okinawan bases in general, casually linked to developments in the Taiwan Straits.

How to broach Okinawa became even more difficult. Yoshio Omori, then head of the Cabinet Research and Information Office, recalls: "[The Japanese government] didn't broach the Taiwan Straits issue head on because of Okinawa. The showdown in the Taiwan Straits made everything much more difficult. That's why they kept quiet about its implications. It wouldn't do either to have the local Okinawans saying, gee, is it that much of a crisis?"[63]

There is also evidence that the very few people involved in moving ahead behind the scenes with Futenma's return tried to use this as camouflage to cover up Futenma. In particular, they spread the impression that "getting Futenma back would be hard." They did nothing to stop the perception circulating that "that base is too tough a nut to crack after all."

The single greatest impact the showdown had, however, was most probably that it strengthened Perry's voice in the U.S. administration. The deployment of the carriers, decided by Perry, who took an active lead at the time of the crisis, acted to raise domestic support for Clinton's foreign policy, eradicating in one fell swoop criticism of his "wimpish foreign policy." It was a perfect stage for Clinton to show his strength just as the presidential election was warming up.

This firmly established Perry's voice and influence within the administration. Backed by this increased gravitas, Perry was able to go ahead with the return of Futenma Air Station.

Notes

1. Interview with Kurt Campbell.
2. Long mission briefing, February 26, 1996.

3. *Marine Corps Air Station Futenma.*

4. Interview with Robin Sakoda.

5. Major General Perry M. Smith, *Assignment: Pentagon* (Washington: Brasseys, Inc., 1993), p. 23.

6. Interview with Carl Ford.

7. Interview with Kurt Campbell.

8. Interview with Takemasa Moriya.

9. Interview with Thomas Hubbard.

10. Interviews with Ryutaro Hashimoto and high-ranking Japanese government officials.

11. *Asahi Shimbun,* April 12, 1996.

12. Interview with Hideo Usui.

13. Interviews with Ryutaro Hashimoto and Kenji Eda.

14. Interview with Takeo Fukuchi.

15. Interview with Sadajiro Furukawa.

16. Interview with Hideo Usui.

17. Interview with Kurt Campbell.

18. Interview with William Perry.

19. Interview with Kurt Campbell.

20. Interview with William Perry.

21. Interview with Hideo Usui.

22. Interview with a high-ranking JDA official.

23. Interview with Hitoshi Tanaka.

24. *The SACO Interim Report,* April 15, 1996.

25. Interview with a high-ranking MOFA official.

26. Interview with a high-ranking DOD official.

27. Interview with Masuo Morodomi.

28. Interview with a senior JDA official.

29. Interview with Masuo Morodomi.

30. Interview with Thomas Hubbard.

31. Interview with a senior U.S. government official.

32. Ibid.

33. Interview with Kurt Campbell.

34. Cabinet decision, July 30, 1996.

35. Cabinet decision, June 3, 1997.

36. Interview with Noboru Hoshuyama.

37. Interview with Kurt Campbell.

38. Interview with a senior State Department official.

39. Interview with a White House official.

40. *Reuters,* May 7, 1996.

41. Interview with a senior State Department official.

42. Interview with Walter Mondale.

43. Interview with William Perry.

44. Interview with a mid-level marine officer.

45. Interview with a senior U.S. government official.

46. Interview with a senior MOFA official.

47. Interview with William Perry.

48. Interview with a high-ranking U.S. government official.

49. Interview with a DOD official at the Japan Desk.

50. Interview with a senior DOD official.

51. A poll taken by Gallup and *Yomiuri Shimbun,* October–November 1995.

52. Interview with a senior DOD official.

53. Ibid.

54. Interview with Kurt Campbell.

55. Interview with a senior White House official.

56. Interview with William Perry.

57. Interview with Kurt Campbell.

58. Interview with Sandra Kristoff.

59. Interview with a White House official.

60. Interview with a senior DOD official.

61. "Clinton Wants to Avoid Election-Year Disputes with Japan," *Japan Economic Newswire,* April 8, 1996.

62. Foreign Affairs Committee, House of Representatives, March 13, 1996.

63. Interview with Yoshio Omori.

Chapter Four

The Korean Peninsula

"Speckles"

Andrews Air Force Base was bathed in the rays of a glorious spring day. Only a few people were out and about. The VIP lounge was closed too.

This huge air force base, located in Maryland on the outskirts of Washington, was famous as the home of *Air Force One*, the presidential aircraft. Richard Nixon, vice president under Dwight Eisenhower, used the base constantly. John F. Kennedy, Lyndon B. Johnson, and Ronald Reagan had all departed from here onto the world's foreign policy stage. Not only home to *Air Force One*, it was also home to all the government and military VIP aircraft.

Andrews was etched in the minds of the American people as the place the Iran hostages returned to, the place both Nixon and Jimmy Carter left from in disappointment, the place the Vietnam POWs came home to, and the place to which the national ice hockey team returned triumphant.

10:00 A.M., April 13, 1996.

There were no TV cameras or newscasters there that day. *Air Force One* could be spotted over in a corner of the field.

One by one top officers from the Defense Department and the State Department as well as officers in uniform got out of their cars and went into the waiting room. Defense Secretary William Perry was visiting Japan and Korea. This was his entourage.

The departure was set for 12:30 P.M. The flight would last 15 hours. The party was small. Perry's special assistants, Robert Hall and Paul Kern; his confidential assistant, Melba Boling; Undersecretary of Defense Walter Slocombe; Deputy Assistant Secretary of Defense Kurt Campbell; Senior Japan Desk Officer Robin Sakoda; Assistant Secretary of Defense Kenneth Bacon; Deputy Assistant Secretary of State Thomas Hubbard; and flight surgeon Colonel Michael Pietrzak plus a few others. They were accompanied by four members of the press: AP's

Robert Burns; *USA Today*'s William Nichols; TBS TV's Jun Ogawa; and *Asahi Shimbun*'s Yoichi Funabashi.[1]

The name of the VIP military aircraft was the *Speckled Trout*.

It was the smallest of the Pentagon's VIP planes and the oldest. A converted KC135 transporter, it was usually used by the joint chiefs of staff, but Perry had borrowed his "Speckles" from John Shalikashvili this time.

The press received copies of a small booklet called "U.S.-Japan Special Action Committee on Okinawa Background." It was jam-packed with material including an itinerary, the individual resumes of the group, an introduction on the current status of bilateral security ties and the bases on Okinawa, and a map of the bases. There was also a "list of health precautions at your destination" from the flight surgeon.

It was announced that lunch, dinner, and a snack would be served. "The total cost will be $10. Receipts will be issued if required."

In Tokyo, Perry and his entourage would be staying at the Hotel Okura. A single room was $185 (the exchange rate $1 = 105 yen). The Japanese government would cover the costs for Slocombe, Bacon, Hall, Campbell, and Kahn. Below that, information was provided on the hotel accommodation on Cheju Island, Korea, which they would be visiting after Tokyo. A single room was $250 (the exchange rate $1 = 760 won).

The members of the press talked among themselves.

"That's pretty considerate."

"What is?"

"There's no way you can get a single room at the Okura for $185. That's some discount! Much cheaper than Korea."

"Yeah. Not to mention the Japanese are covering the tab for Perry and the other big wigs."

"I wonder if this comes out of the compassionate budget too."

Mid-air refueling took place over Alaska, but you couldn't tell it was happening. There wasn't a sound. Hubbard came back to the press section and went around saying, "they've started refueling mid-air. The refueler is stuck right on top of us. It's enthralling. Want to come and have a look?"

Everyone took a turn in the cockpit. Outside the window, a deep blue celestial sphere spread out to infinity, just like in a planetarium. Below were the Alaskan ranges. McKinley was covered in snow. You could just make out the shadow of the refueler above. It was all over in about 40 minutes.

Perry was talking with his assistants one after the other in the office section at the rear of the plane. He was dressed very casually in the flight jacket the plane's crew had given him and a pair of slippers.

The truth of the matter was that his trip to Japan had at long last come about. It was touch and go as to whether he would be able to go right up until two weeks before. A lot of grumbling could be heard at the White House and in the upper echelons of the Defense Department about the trip. Most of his advisers were telling him not to go, that his visit should be put off.[2] Their argument was that, whether it was the reduction of the bases on Okinawa, the mutual security declaration, the Agreement Concerning Reciprocal Provision of Logistic Support, Supplies, and Services (ACSA), or anything else, there were too many worries. Nobody knew if they could all be ironed out by the visit. It was too risky to go with things up in the air. He should wait a month or so.

Perry held a meeting on what should be done with just a handful of aides: Slocombe, Campbell, and the Joint Chiefs of Staff. Slocombe argued for postponing. Perry listened attentively. He then moved over to the table alone and started to read some material that was there.

It was a cable from Ambassador Mondale. The cable said, "You must come to Tokyo. You have a reputation now with the Japanese for delivering. Don't miss this opportunity."

It was more owing to political considerations that Mondale was so keen to get Perry to Japan. It wouldn't do for the president's visit to be just about Okinawa. He believed, therefore, that it was necessary for Perry to come before and clear the way for the president, let out some of the "Okinawa gas." Mondale was very clear on that point.

Perry returned to the sofa and continued the discussion. "We have to choose. Either we go or we don't. There's no middle way. It's no good postponing this time."

Then he turned to Campbell and asked him, "How dangerous would it be if we did go? Would it be counterproductive? How should we look at this?"

Campbell replied, "I can't say that there is no possibility of being counterproductive, but I don't believe that will happen. We should be able to prepare in time."

On hearing that, Perry stood up and said, "Right. We're going. Let's make sure we're ready," ending the discussion.[3]

The argument for putting the visit off was not merely because of insufficient preparation. Behind it lay fears that Perry's visit would overshadow the president's. The White House was especially sensitive about this point, which, in turn, played on the minds of the top people at the Pentagon.

Indeed, Perry himself was probably the most concerned about it. He issued a strong directive that his visit was not to overlap in any way with that of the president's. Perry's choice of the old-fashioned "Speckles" was part of his efforts to maintain a low profile. He could have taken a big flashy plane, but he said "Speckles" would be better.[4]

The number of journalists was also carefully narrowed down. He insisted that he wanted them to "write from the perspective of his role being strictly to assist the president."[5]

The U.S.-Japan Joint Declaration on Security

Perry and his entourage touched down at Haneda Airport on the afternoon of April 14. With a police escort, they headed straight to the Hotel Okura.

The Americans had put the finishing touches to the U.S. draft on board the plane. It covered the *Japan-U.S. Joint Declaration on Security: Alliance for the 21st Century*, SACO's interim report, ACSA, and the essential points of responses at press conferences.

Now they had to work on it with the Japanese. Hubbard and Campbell got straight down to it. Tanaka and Akiyama formed the nucleus of the Japanese team. A draft mutual declaration had already been prepared in November of the previous year. Clinton's visit was suddenly put off. As a result, the draft also stayed in the drawer. Both sides took it out once again and started to hammer out a joint version.

They began creating a new draft, checking each word as they went along. There were two main problems. The first was how to write in the numbers, namely how "100,000 forces" and "47,000 forces" should be handled.

The Americans demanded that the 100,000 U.S. forces in the Asian-Pacific region and the 47,000 U.S. forces in Japan be stated clearly as "an unshakable presence." Leaving aside the 100,000, the Japanese were opposed to mentioning the 47,000, their reasons being consideration of "Okinawan sentiment."

Following the release in the previous spring of the Nye Report, as the East Asia Strategic Report (EASR) was dubbed, the numbers had been the object of fierce opposition in Okinawa as "making the bases a permanent fixture," whether it was 100,000 or 47,000. In the end, while the figure 100,000 was clearly cited, they compromised on the scale of the U.S. forces in Japan as "maintaining the present scale."

At that time, the Japanese were successful in winning an important concession from the Americans. With regard to the force structure, it was agreed that there would be "consultation" and "adjustment" between the two countries. This was incorporated as "a tie-in" with the 100,000 and "maintaining the present scale."[6]

It was originally considered because "we wanted to make a clear statement that we weren't fixing the number" (top member of the Japanese Defense Agency, or JDA). The Japanese readied themselves for a strong onslaught from the Americans, but "we were caught off guard because there was no resistance. They just said, 'OK.'"[7] The Japanese were thinking that if they could have input on the force structure, they could use this to win the Okinawans over.

For those in the Foreign Ministry who had been involved in U.S.-Japan security issues for many years, this was absolutely epoch-making. "Prior consultation" with Japan was made obligatory concerning important changes in stationing, important changes in equipment, combat operations, and bringing nuclear weapons and powered vessels into Japan.

Important changes in stationing referred to bringing troops into Japan; withdrawing troops were not covered. The treaty was set up so that "even if we asked [the military] to leave them here, they could pull them out on their own say-so."[8] The Japanese had asked the Americans before for improvements, but they had never responded. This time, however, they did.

A top member of the Foreign Ministry interpreted this as "that's just how strong the relationship of trust had become between the two countries," an assessment which was echoed by a senior official in the U.S. Defense Department: "We're allies, not an occupation force. It is Japan that says it wants it very much, so how can we refuse?"[9] But that wasn't the whole story.

In fact, given the outlook on the Korean Peninsula, it is more likely that the Americans saw it as unavoidable that they consult with the Japanese because the very nature of the U.S. forces structure was deeply related to their relationship with Japan, especially the shape of the U.S. military presence in Japan. They judged it to be a necessary mechanism also for the process of reviewing the guidelines on bilateral military cooperation.

The other problem was what to do with China. It was not clear what sort of a regional presence China would become. Even so, wouldn't spelling that out in black and white only encourage the Chinese threat argument?

The first idea they came up with was to use the word "engagement." They all agreed that even if it was usually used in a positive sense, as long as China took exception to it, they shouldn't use it.

Well, how about China's "constructive role" then? As an expression, it was fine. But were the Chinese really doing that currently? If you believed they were, you needed to preface the term with a "the." If you didn't, but hoped they would in the future, an "a" needed to be added. But if you did add an "a," wouldn't you be stating that they weren't doing it now? It was finally decided to link it to the word "positive," thereby fudging the issue somewhat and adding an "a."

The fact that the United States had come on strong during the China-Taiwan showdown about the Chinese missile exercises, deploying its aircraft carriers, had subtle implications on how China should be handled. The Japanese argued that "the American action was more than sufficiently effective, so let's not incite them any further."

The Americans countered with, "It's precisely because U.S.-Japan security has teeth that it was effective. There's no need to feel bad about it."

Of course, even the Americans had no objection to bringing China into the international fold and coexisting with them. The Americans already had a scenario for normalizing Sino-American relations and did not want the joint security declaration with Japan to have a negative impact on that scenario.

The section dealing with China ended up like this: "The prime minister and the president emphasized that it is extremely important for the stability and prosperity of the region that China play a positive and constructive role and in this context stressed the interest of both countries in furthering cooperation with China."[10]

Prime Minister Hashimoto met with Defense Secretary Perry that day (April 14) at 7:00 P.M. in the PM's office. Hashimoto thanked Perry for his efforts and expressed his gratitude in the most glowing terms. He then elaborated on his own views. One concerned the guidelines.

First, there were legal limits to what Japan could and couldn't do. There was a legal interpretation that even if Japan could dispatch minesweepers to remove abandoned mines, they could not destroy mines because that amounted to a combat action. He cited a few examples like that to stress how these self-imposed restraints were no longer suited to the times.

At the same time, however, he also emphasized that Japan had no intention whatsoever of playing a large military role; that it was Japan's intention to do those kinds of things within the framework of the bilateral security ties and to strengthen its support of America.

Hashimoto then cited one by one possible ways of achieving that.[11]

1. The United States mustn't think "Japan is just going to come along as a silent partner."

2. More bilateral consultations were needed.

3. Japan would work bit by bit towards becoming more involved in U.N. activities including peacekeeping operations (PKO). There must be a wide range of ways in which we can cooperate with one another in these areas.

Perry was highly impressed with the logic of Hashimoto's explanation. Wishing to talk more with Hashimoto not just about Okinawa but about the "next topic" and "strategic issues," he brought up the guidelines. Perry believed that in order to strengthen the bilateral security structure, they needed to review the guidelines and give them more backbone. He had even said that "SACO was a kind of down payment for the guidelines."[12] Perry was thinking that the bases couldn't be left as is if they were to be able to move on to the next topic; they should work on the bases as a way of creating a fair wind for the guidelines.

Hashimoto, on the other hand, was painfully aware of the need to put together a Japanese structure in readiness for a contingency arising on the Korean Peninsula. He surmised that there was an urgent need to reassess how the bilateral security system would be applied at such a time, how they should support American action, and what the constitutional implications were. Furthermore, he wanted to make the Guidelines Review the cornerstone of that process.

When the original guideline was drawn up in 1978, it only stipulated in general terms that the SDF and the U.S. forces would take joint measures only in the event that Japan is attacked forcefully by other countries. The review of the 1978 guidelines, however, was to strengthen the U.S.-Japan military cooperation on a concretely operational level in times of contingency. Up until then, Japan had been cautious about expanding military cooperation with the United States because of domestic political factors and the constitutional restriction on collective defense. In 1982, for instance, although the two countries agreed to study ways to deal with security threats in the Far East, virtually nothing was done since Japan feared criticism that such a move was not compatible with the country's constitution banning a role abroad for its military.

A review of the guidelines was a key pillar of the Joint Declaration on Security that was to be announced three days later.

Campbell was pulling all-nighters. Halfway through, he crossed the road to the U.S. Embassy because he "needed some clean copy" and continued working there.

Preparing the Joint Declaration took much longer than originally anticipated. Thomas Hubbard, deputy assistant secretary of state, was being a stickler: "Can't we put some more nuance in there? Can't that be rephrased a little more sophisticatedly?"

Hubbard was shortly to be transferred to the Philippine Embassy. If only for that reason alone, he felt this presidential visit to Japan had special significance. He wanted to make it a splendid declaration. He checked each and every word several times over, finishing just as the sky began to grow light.

After grabbing some shut-eye, Campbell went to Slocombe's room. One by one he handed over the beautifully typed documents: this is the Joint Declaration, this is SACO, this is ACSA . . . .

Cheju Island

Prior to visiting Japan, President Clinton stopped off in Korea. Touching down on Cheju on the evening of April 15, he flew out after noon the following day.

During his 1993 visit to Korea, he had shown the American flag and gone to Panmunjom in the demilitarized zone. This time, however, apart from a stroll on the beach with Hillary, he secluded himself in the Shilla Hotel, the venue for his meeting with President Kim Young Sam.

The meeting with President Kim took place in a suite at the Shilla Hotel at 5:50 A.M. It was the same room where Soviet President Mikhail Gorbachev had met President Roh Tae Woo in 1991.

The major fruit of the meeting was their joint proposal for "totally unconditional and early" four-way talks between representatives of North and South Korea as well as America and China. This was rated as "the start to a process for realizing a permanent peace and cooperation treaty."

The statement released after the meeting made the following points:

The two leaders "confirmed their stance that South and North Korea should take the initiative in pursuing a permanent peace and cooperation treaty, and that the United States would not consider independent negotiations with North Korea pertaining to peace on the Korean Peninsula." President Kim "confirmed that the Republic of Korea is ready to meet with representatives from North Korea at a government level without conditions." President Clinton "made it clear that the United States is ready to play a positive and cooperative role in supporting these actions." And finally, both presidents "agreed that Chinese cooperation would be extremely helpful."[13]

Explaining the emergence of this initiative, White House Press Secretary Mike McCurry said the South Korean government had approached the United States about pushing for ways for the two Koreas to open a dialogue, and the United States had advocated China's involvement.[14]

The idea, however, was not a new one. In the summer of the previous year, when Kim Young Sam was visiting the United States, the Americans and Koreans were already working secretly on putting this proposal together.

In the United States to attend the dedication of a Korean War Memorial extolling the ties between the two countries since the Korean War, Kim Young Sam decided he wanted to revisit the States. He had informed the Americans that he wanted it to be an official visit this time.

The Americans hesitated. They had already welcomed him on an official visit. Kim Young Sam spent three days in Washington in November 1993 as a state guest. It was the Clinton administration's first official dinner. They had shown the "champion of democracy" the maximum respect possible. Almost too much in fact. And there was the question of balance . . . .

But in the face of Korea's forceful request, they conceded to "consider it if they had some meaningful proposal." What the Korean Foreign Ministry came up with in response was "2+2." The idea was that, first of all, the two Koreas would sign a permanent peace treaty to replace the cease-fire agreement, with the United States and China standing by as guarantors.

In this way, Kim's visit to Washington that summer was very high level with an address to Congress and a meeting with Clinton at the White House. In his meeting with Clinton, Kim came straight out with "I'd like to announce this on the 15th of August." August 15 would be the 50th anniversary of South Korea's "glorious return," a national holiday celebrating independence from Japanese colonization. Kim Young Sam was planning to call for this in his commemoration speech that day.

However, just before the planned day the North Koreans seized a fishing boat from the South. The anti–North Korea sentiment of the domestic hawks flared up, scuttling any plans for dialogue between the two Koreas or "2+2" talks. Kim quickly shelved the idea, one-sidedly sinking it without adequate prior consultation or explanation to the United States. The Americans were not amused.

The Koreans weighed in heavily about Clinton coming to Korea as well as going to Japan in April 1996, but Clinton didn't show much interest. The feeling at the White House was, "We've done enough for Kim." The State Department was also hesitant. "We didn't want in any way to take away from the focus on Japan . . . as our most important partner, but also because the trip had already been delayed since November, which made it even more sensitive to Japan."[15] But Kim Young Sam insisted.

General elections were set for April 11, just before the Japan visit. If Clinton didn't come, Kim would be politically disgraced. Kim Dae Jung, leader of the National Congress for New Politics, was angling to make political mileage out of the fact. James Laney, U.S. ambassador to South Korea, did some behind-the-scenes work, enticing the Blue House with the offer that it would be possible for Clinton to consider visiting Korea if the Koreans were ready to take the initiative once more for four-way talks. This broke the ice.

In the end, Assistant Secretary of State Winston Lord remembers, "We were determined that it not take place in Seoul, but it could be a quick stop on an island on the way to Tokyo,"[16] and so Cheju Island became the venue.

Anthony Lake, national security adviser, did the groundwork for the four-way talks. He also played an instrumental role in forging the new U.S. approach to northeast Asia. "I had become increasingly concerned over the previous year about the direction our China policy had taken. . . . Korea is an immensely difficult and even dangerous issue. . . . I had [also] become quite involved from the start on Japan."[17]

In late January, Lake went to Korea. He exchanged ideas with Korea's foreign minister, Gong Ro-Myung, on the four-way deal. Lake also met clandestinely with Yoo Chong Ha, President Kim's senior secretary for national security and foreign affairs, on Cheju. Yoo was a career diplomat who had been ambassador to the European Community, vice minister of foreign affairs, and ambassador to the United Nations. Since 1994 he had been in the Blue House working in the Presidential Secretariat.

The United States would not only come under immediate threat if it messed up on the question of the Korean Peninsula. Its relations with China, South Korea, and Japan would all become strained, greatly endangering U.S. foreign policy.

The first true foreign policy crisis the Clinton administration faced was the economic sanctions against North Korea's nuclear development program. The tension in both U.S.-Japan and U.S.-Korea relations jumped markedly. While that crisis was barely averted by a meeting between former President Jimmy Carter and Chairman Kim Il Sung, it was an experience that sent chills up and down the spine. In a presidential election year, the last thing the White House wanted was a crisis on the Korean Peninsula.

There was very little change in the content of the four-party talks proposal put forward this time. Whereas the idea in the previous year took the form of the United States endorsing a Korean proposal, this time it was presented as a joint initiative of both presidents.

Assuming the parties would move ahead with the four-way talks, how to treat Japan and Russia was a very delicate question.

Japan and Russia were closely involved in stability on the Korean Peninsula, both historically and geopolitically speaking. Each considered that if a framework for peace and stability was being set up, it had the right to a voice. In its heart of hearts, the United States really wished for six-way talks too.

Lake said, "The original idea for the four-party process came from the Koreans. We could have been very comfortable about including the Japanese and the Russians from the outset. But the four-way idea was originally Korea's and we couldn't allow North Korea to drive a wedge between the U.S. and South Korea, so we deferred to the Koreans' initiative."[18]

Above all, the United States made sure Japan knew what was going on. Americans knew the Japanese would be miffed by being excluded, because the peace process for the Korean Peninsula previously put forward by the Republican administration had been a six-way mechanism. Japan, therefore, received detailed reports on how the dialogue with the Koreans was progressing. After the joint U.S.-Korean proposal, Japan immediately sent off its response that "it welcomed the four-party talks and was ready to cooperate."

Contact with the Russians was inadequate. Lord said, "I think we were less careful with the Russians and maybe we should have been more."[19] They had always been pushing the six-power approach, so they weren't too impressed. In fact, they reacted quite negatively.

Concerning how to tell the Chinese, the Koreans stuck to their guns that they should talk to them first and the Americans should follow on. The American assessment was that "the South Koreans really wanted to be involved in talking to the Chinese" to improve their relations with them, and it seems that they were right.[20]

To the Chinese, the Koreans were trying to create the impression that they were the "stars." Gong Ro-Myung visited China late in March, handed Chairman Jiang Zemin a letter from President Kim containing the four-way initiative, and asked for their support. The Chinese response was "not negative, but cautious."

According to Lake, China was trying to respond with an extremely tactical end in view. "I think the Chinese were never anxious to reveal to us just how much trouble they were having with the North Koreans, because that is a general principle that would reduce their influence perhaps with us. But, secondly, I think they were always very careful not to tell us exactly what they were saying to the North Koreans, because if they did that, then we could say, no, we wish you had said something else."[21]

"Postunification"

North Korea did not immediately criticize the proposal. Chinese Chairman Jiang Zemin sent Kim Young Sam a letter two or three days after the U.S.-Korean proposal on Cheju, making clear their support for the initiative as well as suggesting a two-stage approach where "the two Koreas should take the lead with China and the U.S. joining in later."

The four-way talks were also the product of Korea's wariness towards the Americans and the Japanese as well as the Chinese. Korea suspected that the United States would try to cut a "deal" with the North Koreans by going over their heads. This was definitely what the North Koreans had in mind.

A cease-fire agreement had been signed in the Korean War (1950–53), but it was only a temporary truce. For the following almost half century, the two Koreas had been in a state of simmering tension astride the demilitarized zone (DMZ). In the lead-up to Clinton's Korea visit, North Korea infiltrated armed soldiers into the DMZ no fewer than three times, breaking the cease-fire agreement and testing the South Koreans' patience.

Arguing that South Korea had not been directly involved in the ratification of the cease-fire agreement and that at the time of the war the South's troops had been under U.S.-Korean allied command, the North said it held doubts about South Korea's "ability to act as a direct party" and that it wished to sign a peace treaty with the United States. If that was not immediately possible, it wanted to keep the cease-fire with a provisional agreement with the United States.

The North Koreans were contriving first to consolidate their relations with the United States and, having done that, move forward with the normalization of relations with Japan. Having then achieved some economic leverage, they would respond to the South Koreans. The South Koreans became increasingly suspicious that the Americans might fall for the North's strategy, making the North think even less of the South and becoming a catalyst for ignoring them completely.

Why did North Korea seize a South Korean fishing boat at this time?

Some analyses tried to find a hint in what happened in the immediate aftermath of the Chinese missile threat to Taiwan. Just as China had tried to influence the Taiwanese general elections by firing its missiles, perhaps North Korea was conducting military agitation with an eye on the South Korean elections.

An alternative interpretation was that by making these infringements on the cease-fire agreement, the North might be aiming at dragging the United States towards a new peace treaty between the United States and the North.

The Americans, for their part, almost tediously belabored the point that the four-way process did not damage the North-South initiative and that any moves towards peace and stability on the peninsula must revolve around the two Koreas.

During the Bush administration in 1991, the then secretary of state, James Baker, visited the South and proposed a "2+4" six-way dialogue out of the blue. The Korean response was less than effusive. Whenever one of the superpowers, whether it was the United States, Russia, China, or Japan, mentioned "a multilateral framework" for peace and stability on the Korean Peninsula, South Korea always girded its loins instinctively.

If the South Koreans thought the Americans were being a bit too enthusiastic in going ahead with their cooperation on Korean energy development in the North or discussing humanitarian aid, they always suspected that the Americans were trying to partition North and South. They surmised that the United States was afraid that it would become more difficult to maintain its military presence if the two were united.

Close to 70 percent of the South Koreans believed that the U.S. forces in Korea should be withdrawn, or at the very least reduced, after unification.[22]

As the possibility of an internal collapse in North Korea seemed to be more likely with the deepening internal political crisis, international political jockeying over a postunification Korean Peninsula intensified.

What would happen to the U.S. military presence then? Would the Americans shift to an alliance minus the U.S. forces in Korea? Would they shift the emphasis away from a land to a navy presence? If the alliance was to be maintained, what sort of threat or country would it be an alliance against?

Would China stand by North Korea to the bitter end? Or would it accept unification? If it did, on what conditions? Would a U.S.-Korea alliance be acceptable? Would the Chinese differentiate by refusing a Japan-Korea alliance? Or, having had the threat of the Korean Peninsula removed, would they demand that the U.S. military withdraw from the entire region? If the U.S.-Korea alliance was dissolved, what impact would that have on the U.S.-Japan alliance? If it was to be an alliance minus the military, what would be the impact then?

Would it trigger a national movement in Japan against the bases, starting with the withdrawal of the bases in Okinawa? Could a consensus be created in Japan that it would be the last and sole host of U.S. bases in the region? Or would there be a consolidation of their determination to keep the bases as "insurance," bearing in mind a future Chinese threat? Wouldn't there even be voices raised in Japan about pulling out all the troops in the region? Or, conversely, wouldn't a perception that the Chinese were trying to force the United States out of the region gain ground, strengthening support for a presence in Japan to counter that?

As Lake put it, at this juncture "we really just didn't decide that. I see no point in deciding that now. . . . And I am not sure that it's imminent enough to require specific timing."[23]

However, the sense of jockeying grew. The convoluted interests and plans surrounding the four-way process and the bogies that were raised between each country quickly brought a realistic hue to postunification and made each side wonder how it could position itself to the best advantage.

The United States, Japan, and Korea

There was something stilted about the U.S.-Korean summit. Right from the first arrangements, things didn't click. The White House wanted time on Cheju to play golf and to choreograph "a president relaxing." It wanted to send the message that despite the tensions on the 38th Parallel, the North wouldn't make any foolish move with the American presence; stability was being maintained.

The Blue House, however, was thinking about sending a different message: our president in deep discussion with Clinton; our president going shoulder to shoulder with Clinton; our president telling Clinton about the realities of the peninsula.

The South Koreans were unhappy that a Korean visit had not been included in the plans for Clinton's visit to Japan the previous November. They were not pleased with being bypassed during a U.S. president's trip to Asia.

That Japanese visit was cancelled. They lobbied frantically to be put on the itinerary. This visit to Korea was the fruit of those efforts. And yet the Koreans weren't satisfied. President Clinton wasn't even staying one day. His visit was too short. It would look like an afterthought to the Japanese visit. And he wants to play golf? If he's got time for that, let's have him spend more time in a meeting of leaders. The Blue House protested, "President Kim has forbidden his ministers to play golf. He can't very well go out and play a round with the American president himself." So, this complication made the Americans give up.

Lake recollects: "[The president] loves playing golf. He and the First Lady were very interested in just having an opportunity to relax a little. . . . And nobody was particularly anxious to tell the president he shouldn't do this, but since I used to be the one who would talk to him, it was going to be my job. . . . I went and recommended that he not play golf while he was on Cheju Island, and he agreed. . . . But he was not happy about it. . . . He would blame me for never allowing him any fun anywhere on any of his trips.

"So then when we got to Cheju Island, we got onto *Marine One* helicopter . . . and damned if they hadn't put a picture of people playing golf on a golf course there. My heart sank, because I could see him looking at it and then looking at me. And then when we flew, . . . and I don't know if this was a conspiracy or not, we just happened to fly over almost every golf course on Cheju Island and again I could see him looking out the window at the golf courses."[24]

There was already a feeling in the White House that South Korea was tough, that Kim Young Sam was difficult to deal with. One of the president's entourage on the visit to Korea related that "things were looking up with Japan, it was very upbeat. But with Korea, to say things were going downhill would be an exaggeration, but no matter what we did there was tension. It was a real contrast."[25]

Things got very tense with the South several times over KEDO and food aid to North Korea. Stories leaked from the White House that President Kim had raised his voice in a meeting with President Clinton, or that he had put his hand on Clinton's leg to prevent him from getting up when he was about to leave a meeting, as if to say, "now hold your horses, young fella," and drive home the point that he hadn't finished yet.

The White House found Kim unpredictable and came to be wary of his volatility. What was unpredictable about Kim Young Sam was not so much his content but his style of politics and foreign policy. As one U.S.

government official said, "[He yelled] apparently in one phone call [with the president] . . . and he got pretty direct in one of their conversations."[26]

The fact that Kim was the South's first president with populist backing created a new problem for the Americans. Kim quoted Korean opinion polls even in his meetings with Clinton. He was often heard saying, "How can I explain that to the people?" and, "That won't convince the electorate." What irritated Kim Young Sam was, in a word, the U.S. approach to the North.

In his inauguration ceremony in February 1993, Kim emerged on the scene demonstrating enthusiasm towards dialogue between the two Koreas, saying that no matter what type of alliance there was, nothing was stronger than the bonds of race. When the nuclear doubt later surfaced with the North, however, it became a key foreign policy issue for the Americans. The Clinton administration was leaning towards a deal with the North, where if the North demonstrated that it did not possess nuclear capability, the Americans would cancel the Team Spirit military exercises and agree to talks with the North concerning economic aid in the future.

Kim Young Sam perceived a real danger in this. In November 1993, on his visit to the United States, Kim repeatedly explained that U.S. dialogue with the North should follow a dialogue between the two Koreas. A meeting intended only as a courtesy call ran one hour and twenty minutes.

That occasion had the effect of bringing home to the Americans the peninsula's tricky political situation and historical background as well as the "dead space" in their awareness of it. Up until that point, the Americans' approach to the North's nuclear doubt leaned towards the functional approach of preventing nuclear proliferation mainly through the International Atomic Energy Agency (IAEA). In order to tackle the North Koreans, however, they were beginning to explore ways of applying a regional approach to peace and stability in northeast Asia.

There was also a historical background to Korean mistrust of the United States.

The Koreans admonished the Americans on just how wrong a signal the Carter administration's policy of withdrawing the U.S. forces in Korea had sent to North Korea. And more incriminating, they admonished that the words in 1950 of Dean Acheson, secretary of state under President Harry Truman, a Democrat, that "the Korean Peninsula is outside the U.S. defense perimeter" were one of the main causes of the Korean War. The implication was: It's the Democrats again, you'd better take care. It almost sounded as if they were daring Clinton, who had never served in the military: Can you make the tough decisions?

President Kim's sermonizing tone was also a manifestation of Korea's mistrust of an America that kept the South out of the loop. It was meant to check any U.S. rapprochement with the North.

Perry went ahead to Cheju and met immediately with Defense Minister Yi Yanho. It was there that Perry briefed him thoroughly on the significance of strengthening American and Japanese security ties. Not wishing to miss a single word, the pens of the Korean aides flew across their pages. The Americans explained in detail their joint security declaration with Japan and the question of the bases in Okinawa.

The Koreans raised no doubts about the Joint Declaration itself. Their concern was directed more at the guidelines than the declaration. They were worried about the possibility that, if a contingency arose on the Korean Peninsula, Japan, having adopted the guidelines, would send in troops, planes, and pilots and join the fighting.

"That sort of speculation doesn't help at all. Let me confirm right here and now that neither the U.S. nor Japan are entertaining any such thoughts," said a high-ranking DOD official.

"I am not a Japan expert, but the more I study about Japan the more I realize that the strongest trend in Japan from here on in will not be towards militarism but towards pacifism."[27]

The Americans found themselves forced almost into overkill mode.

The United States did its utmost behind the scenes to promote cooperation on defense between the Koreans and the Japanese. Campbell said that the key to northeast Asian security over the next 10 to 15 years was which direction Japan-Korea relations went.[28] But Japan-Korea relations were tense. In 1995, the 50th anniversary of the end of World War II, anti-Japanese sentiment in Korea became particularly strong.

There is a territorial dispute over the sovereignty of Dok-to Island (Takeshima) in the Sea of Japan between the Japanese and Koreans. A photo of President Kim Young Sam talking to the commander of the garrison he had sent to Dok-to was given extensive coverage in the Korean press. The territorial wrangle added fuel to the flames of anti-Japanese nationalism.

South Koreans did not hide their suspicion that behind the dialogue between the Japanese and the North Koreans was a policy to partition the two Koreas. President Kim was infuriated that the Japanese had gone over their heads by not consulting them sufficiently about providing the North with food aid. His relations with the LDP's Koichi Kato, who was seen as the culprit, deteriorated to the point where "not only would he not meet his eyes, he wouldn't even look his way."

Additionally, it came to light in the fall of 1995 that Takami Etoh, director-general of the Management and Coordination Agency, had said that Japan had done good things for Korea when Korea was a Japanese colony. Relations between the two countries, which were already tense over the interpretation of the 1910 Annexation Treaty between Japan and Korea, plummeted. The Korean government demanded that the Japanese government take "appropriate measures." Kim Young Sam criticized

Japan, saying that it must stop making inflammatory remarks that distort history, that Japan went over South Korea's head on the rice negotiations and was taking an obstructive stance on unification.

With the birth of the Hashimoto government in January 1996, normalizing relations with Korea was a top Japanese priority. Japan was apprehensive about having a meeting with President Kim at the Asia-Europe Meeting (ASEM) held in Bangkok in March. Hashimoto secretly sent Yoshio Omori, head of the Cabinet Research and Information Office, to Korea to speak directly with his counterpart at the Blue House. He wasn't taking any chances.

The meeting between Hashimoto and Kim did take place, setting the bilateral relationship on the road to recovery, but things were still anything but smooth. The United States was worried because as relations between the Japanese and the Koreans deteriorated, China, taking advantage of the schism, had started making overtures to the South.

Anthony Lake: "A part of [our strategic overview] was the importance of stability . . . and stability came in one sense through the American presence, because if we were to withdraw from northeast Asia, you would then . . . inevitably begin . . . a triangular arms race among South Korea, China, and Japan. . . . And especially as South Korea begins to deepen its relationships with China, there is every potential for a triangular relationship that can either be cooperative or competitive, and I think our presence helps to keep it cooperative, or to make it as cooperative as possible."[29]

A top official with the Defense Department said, "China was the most wary of the Japan-U.S. Joint Declaration on Security. There are some things which point to China trying to plant the same doubts and suspicions in the minds of the Koreans. But we were able to eradicate most of their misunderstandings and worries through our close consultation with one another."[30]

To quote a senior U.S. official, in the final analysis, Korean insecurity "stemmed from their own insecurity. They're not sure who on earth their friends are. And from Kim Young Sam's own unpredictability."[31] Rather than being a personality problem, Kim's unpredictability was more the product of the historical and geopolitical situation Korea was placed in.

The United States tried to bundle U.S.-Japan and U.S.-Korea relations into a three-way cooperative partnership on security among the United States, Japan, and Korea. As the significance of the alliance evolved, it was becoming increasingly difficult to maintain a bilateral alliance. That was what lay behind the move. At the same time, China was testing America's bilateral alliances. Three-way cooperation would also act as protection against that.

Clinton headed straight for Japan as soon as the meeting was over. Perry didn't stop off in Japan. It wouldn't do to steal the president's limelight. He boarded *Speckled Trout* once more.

Notes

1. Memorandum for Secretary of Defense Perry's Party, April 10, 1996.
2. Interview with a senior DOD official.
3. Ibid.
4. Interview with Gayle Von Eckartsburg.
5. Interview with Kurt Campbell.
6. Interview with a senior MOFA official.
7. Ibid.
8. Interview with a senior MOFA official.
9. Interview with a senior DOD official.
10. "Japan-U.S. Joint Declaration on Security—Alliance for the 21st Century," April 1996.
11. Interview with Ryutaro Hashimoto.
12. Interview with a senior DOD official.
13. "U.S.-Korea Mutual Statement," July 1993.
14. "U.S. Backs Talks on Korea Peace; Clinton, Kim Propose Role for China," *Washington Post*, April 16, 1996, p. A1.
15. Interview with Winston Lord.
16. Ibid.
17. Interview with Anthony Lake.
18. Ibid.
19. Interview with Winston Lord.
20. Interview with Anthony Lake.
21. Ibid.
22. According to a poll in the October 28, 1996, edition of *Chung An Ilbo*, "annulment of the US-Korea alliance," "no need for stationing troops," and "reduction in scale of stationing" combined to account for 67.4 percent.
23. Interview with Anthony Lake.
24. Ibid.
25. Interview with a senior State Department official.
26. Ibid.
27. Interview with a senior DOD official.
28. Interview with Kurt Campbell.
29. Interview with Anthony Lake.
30. Interview with a senior DOD official.
31. Interview with a senior State Department official.

Chapter Five

Independence

The U.S.-Japan Summit

The U.S.-Japan summit took place at the Akasaka Palace in Moto Akasaka. It began at 11:00 A.M. on April 17.

A small meeting was held first with National Security Adviser Anthony Lake, Ambassador to Japan Walter Mondale, Secretary of State Warren Christopher, and Senior Director of the National Security Council's East Asia Bureau Sandra Kristoff on the U.S. side; and Foreign Minister Yukihiko Ikeda, Ambassador to the United States Kunihiko Saito, Director-General of the North American Affairs Bureau Masaki Orita, Director of the First North American Division Masaharu Kono, and Secretary for the Prime Minister Hiroyasu Ando on the Japanese side.

In the room set aside for the general session next door, the seats had been arranged in two parallel lines, and there was no room to place papers on the tables in front.

Winston Lord, assistant secretary of state, and Kurt Campbell, deputy assistant secretary of defense, were waiting behind the top economic and trade people, including U.S. Trade Representative Mickey Kantor, National Economic Council Chair Laura Tyson, and Undersecretary of the Treasury Lawrence Summers.

On the Japanese side, Finance Minister Wataru Kubo, Ministry of International Trade and Industry (MITI) Minister Shunpei Tsukahara, Japan Defense Agency (JDA) Chief Hideo Usui, Economic Planning Agency Chief Shusei Tanaka, as well as Shunji Yanai, vice-minister for foreign affairs, and Masahiro Akiyama, director-general of the Bureau of Defense Policy, were all lined up.

Usui had been instructed to come only the day before. It was the first time since the agency's creation in 1954 that a JDA chief would be attending a U.S.-Japan summit. Akiyama was there in his capacity as Usui's assistant.

The first U.S.-Japan summit in the postwar era was between Shigeru Yoshida and Harry Truman in September 1951. This was followed by a summit between Yoshida and Dwight Eisenhower in November 1954 and the Nobusuke Kishi–Eisenhower meeting in June 1957. The familiar Ron-Yasu sessions between Ronald Reagan and Yasuhiro Nakasone were to be held three or four times a year in the 1980s.

The Hashimoto-Clinton summit of April 1996 was the 67th. (Hashimoto upped the pace thereafter, meeting with Clinton in June and July 1996 and April and June 1997.) Since the start of the Clinton administration, there had been 11 U.S.-Japan summits.

The Americans had to respond to the never-ending stream of new Japanese prime ministers. It was Masaharu Kono, director of the First North American Division, who was in charge of virtually all of the summits during this period. At the first meeting of Clinton and Hashimoto, in Santa Monica the previous February, the two leaders had just agreed to call each other Bill and Ryu. But when the meeting was over, President Clinton came over to where Kono was sitting and said in a friendly way, "So, we meet again." From Clinton's point of view, Kono was the only familiar face he could say "hi" to on the Japanese side.

More than an hour had passed. The "extras" next door had long since run out of innocuous chitchat. And then the doors opened.

Hashimoto and Clinton emerged smiling from the room next door together. Hashimoto was completely at ease, a different man from Santa Monica. One of the Americans thought, *Clinton looks much more relaxed than I've ever seen him with any other Asian leader.*[1]

Hashimoto turned to the task of chairing the general session. He brought it to a close a scant 15 minutes later, as if to say, "Clinton and I've had our talk, the rest is just icing." They had discussed a wide variety of subjects, including bilateral issues as well as the international situation.

CHINA

Hashimoto said that it was important that China be given a strong message that the United States and Japan as well as the international community wanted a peaceful settlement of the Taiwanese issue. Clinton stated that America's basic policy was for "one China" and that there was a need to watch closely to ensure that the unification of China was a peaceful process.

The memory of the crisis in the Taiwan Straits still lingered on, leading both countries to push for a peaceful solution.

Compared to Hashimoto's positive attitude on an early acceptance of China into the World Trade Organization (WTO), Clinton was lukewarm. Hashimoto pressed Clinton, saying it would be best if a solution could be reached by the time Hong Kong reverted to China on July 1, 1997. He added that it would be a sign of respect for the Chinese leadership and would also be beneficial in terms of real interests.

But Clinton merely commented that while he "basically supported" its membership, it was important that China meet certain commercial conditions. Clinton had to take into account trends in Congress, especially those of the anti-China trade hawks like Congressman Richard Gephardt (D-Mo.).

Clinton said, "All China has to do is pitch us something that will make it easier to convince the American public, but they keep throwing us curve balls," gesturing as if to say it was too much. He also said he wanted to let China know America's true intentions, his own intentions, and to ask them to make it easier for him to convince the people back home.

THE KOREAN PENINSULA

Hashimoto reiterated his support for the joint U.S.-Korea call for four-party talks. Japan had been very quick off the mark in supporting it when it was first announced during Clinton's visit to Korea.

Japan and America had already confirmed with the Korean Energy Development Organization (KEDO) that they would continue to consult closely with South Korea. All three shared a common interest in preventing the North from going nuclear.

Hashimoto noted that Japan's relations with the North were only at the stage of unofficial contacts and that they were not in a position to begin genuine negotiations. Japan's relations with South Korea had "been delicate for a time," but had been repaired at the summit between the two leaders held at the Asia-Europe Meeting (ASEM) in March.

Other topics included the former Yugoslavia, Russia, and the Middle East peace process. Despite having sold the summit as a "security summit," Hashimoto and Clinton also managed to get down to brass tacks on economic and trade issues as well.

Since Clinton mentioned opening up the insurance, semiconductor, aviation, and film markets, Hashimoto rebutted each one by one. Confronted by "the ghost of Mickey Kantor's adversary,"[2] Clinton refrained from pursuing the matter further.[3]

A Symbol of the Japanese People's Unity

At their joint press conference, the two leaders signed the *Japan-U.S. Joint Declaration on Security: Alliance for the 21st Century.*

The key points of the declaration were:

- Bilateral security, which was based on the U.S.-Japan Security Treaty, was the foundation for maintaining peace and prosperity in the region into the 21st century.

- The most effective framework for Japanese defense was close defense cooperation between the two countries. America's deterrent capability based on the Security Treaty was the linchpin of Japanese security.

- The United States would maintain some 100,000 forward deployment troops in the Asian-Pacific region, virtually at their current level.

- In response to changing international situations, close consultations on military matters would be carried out, including bilateral defense policy and the structure of U.S. forces in Japan.

- They would begin a review of the Guidelines on U.S.-Japan Defense Cooperation. They would examine bilateral cooperation in times of contingency in the Japanese vicinity.

- Regarding Okinawa with its concentration of U.S. military bases, realignment, consolidation, and reduction thereof would be implemented, ensuring at the same time compatibility with the objectives of the Security Treaty.

- It was important for the region's stability and prosperity that China play a positive and constructive role. The United States and Japan would deepen their cooperation with China.

- Stability on the Korean Peninsula was extremely important for both countries. They would strive to this end, cooperating closely with South Korea.

- They would continue to work together to develop multilateral dialogue and cooperation on regional security in such forums as ASEAN.

The two leaders took the attitude that the Okinawa issue had already been dealt with during Defense Secretary Perry's visit. The leaders had reaffirmed the basic policy direction of realignment, consolidation, and reduction. They were satisfied with the important progress which had already been made in the Special Action Committee on Okinawa (SACO) and welcomed the broad-ranging measures indicated in its interim report of April 15, 1996. It was further revealed that the two leaders had made a firm commitment to bring SACO's work to a successful conclusion by November 1996.

Prior to the summit, the Clintons had met with Japan's emperor and empress at the Imperial Palace. It was the president's third meeting with the emperor, the Clintons having received the royal couple at the White House in June two years before. During a photo session with the four, the empress stood two paces behind the emperor. Seeing that, Hillary had also moved back. The Clintons' hospitality and consideration for their guests from faraway came across spontaneously, and both the emperor and empress held fond memories of the visit.

The emperor had visited Washington in the fall of 1960 as crown prince to attend a commemoration of 100 years of U.S.-Japanese friendship. He stayed at Blair House, the official residence for visiting VIPs on Pennsylvania Avenue just across from the White House. White birches stood outside the window. He brought back a few seeds and planted them in the garden at the Imperial Palace in a prayer that his first son, six-month-old Hironomiya, would grow up strong and healthy. He told the First Family the story of the white birches, saying, "They've grown up into fine, large trees." Hillary's eyes shone as she said, "How romantic." It was warm as a midsummer's day.

The emperor mentioned Okinawa that day. "I hope that we can move towards a solution with the careful cooperation of both governments and bearing in mind the feelings of the Okinawan people."

Clinton responded politely. "I believe I have a good understanding of how the Okinawan people feel. America values its friendship with the Japanese people, including the Okinawan people."

The emperor had his own special feelings about Okinawa. One thing his father, Emperor Hirohito, had left undone was paying respects to those who had fallen in the Battle of Okinawa. Emperor Akihito regarded this as his job.

He did not allow any official appointments on June 23, Okinawa's memorial day for the fallen. He had designated August 6 (Hiroshima), August 9 (Nagasaki), August 15 (the end of the war), and this day as "days of abstinence." When Okinawa held its minute of silence, he sat alone in his room observing his own silence. This he did each year without fail. When overseas visiting the United States in June 1994, he was in San Francisco on that day. He observed the silence where he was staying.

He visited Okinawa five times as crown prince. Accompanied by Princess Michiko on his first visit in 1975 as honorary chairman of the Okinawa Marine Exposition, he was attacked by radicals armed with Molotov cocktails at the memorial to the members of the Himeyuri Corps, young high-school girls who committed suicide or were killed in the waning days of the war.

After ascending the throne, he had visited a national planting ceremony in Itoman City in 1993 and made a "trip to pay homage to the souls of the dead" in 1995, the 50th anniversary of the end of the war.

During this time, the emperor was thinking and troubled about "what should be done to ease the hearts of the Okinawan people."[4] He went out of his way at official garden parties to speak to guests from Okinawa. He learned and recited traditional Okinawan poetry. In his study, a dictionary of the Okinawan language was always within reach.

In February 1997, on the death of Okinawa's first governor, Chobyo Yara, after its reversion to the Japanese mainland, the emperor sent a wreath in both his and the empress's name. It was his own idea.

One of his aides has remarked that apart from the "deep personal feeling" the emperor had towards Okinawa, he was acutely aware of and felt a responsibility as a symbolic emperor. "I believe it came from his unshakable faith in the Japanese constitution. The constitution's first article states that 'the emperor is the symbol of Japan, the symbol of its unity.' I believe he senses a danger, that having left Okinawa alone to bear such sacrifices, the very unity of the Japanese people may be endangered."[5]

Clinton was extremely moved by "such a complete oasis right in the heart of Tokyo" and "the sense of tradition." But he was most impressed by the emperor's words on Okinawa. He felt as if he were being transported back to the Okinawan issue, which had only been touched on in passing in the summit.

According to Ambassador Mondale, the emperor "approached the Okinawa issue as an environmental protectionist. He mentioned where and what sort of rare flora and fauna existed on Okinawa. He also spoke on the importance of protecting that environment."[6]

"I hope that we can move towards a solution with the careful cooperation of both governments and bearing in mind the feelings of the Okinawan people." This was the emperor's statement, conveyed by Makoto Watanabe, Imperial Household Agency Chamberlain, at the press briefing following the meeting. But, in reality, the emperor spoke to Clinton "in much stronger words, in a more forceful turn of phrase."[7]

A Quiet Power

The signing of the Japan-U.S. Joint Declaration on Security took place at the State Guest House during the press conference.

Clinton then visited the aircraft carrier USS *Independence*, which had put in to Yokosuka.

Clinton touched down on the deck in a helicopter just before 3:00 P.M. The First Lady and Secretary Christopher were also on board. There Clinton spoke to a large group of nearly 5,000 American crew and their families. A lot of schoolchildren from the elementary school at Yokosuka base were also there.

"The First Lady and I are delighted to be here, along with the secretary of state. I should tell you that this is a particularly emotional moment for the secretary of state because 51 years ago this September he came here to this very harbor as a 19-year-old ensign. So think what you might have ahead of you all in the navy. You may be secretary of state some day."

The crowd applauded enthusiastically.

"Way back in 1959, when the *Indy* slipped down the ways, the Cold War was at its peak. But because the *Indy* was there, along with millions of brave men and women, we won that long Cold War struggle.

"In the Cuban missile crisis, *Indy* was there. In Vietnam and Lebanon and Grenada, *Indy* was there. When Iraq invaded Kuwait, you were the first carrier on the scene."

Clinton went on to praise their deployment at the time of the show-down between China and Taiwan. "Your last deployment off Taiwan helped to calm a rising storm. Without firing a single shot, you reassured nations all around the Pacific. With the quiet power of your example, you gave the world another example of America's power."

The quiet power of presence.

"Without you, the stability and prosperity of Asia could be in danger, and, therefore, so could America's. Old rivalries could break out again. But with you here, Asia is more secure, and so is America."[8]

Japanese faces mingled among the officers who were listening.

Clad in uniform, officers of the Maritime Self-Defense Force (MSDF) for Yokosuka were on board, including the commander in chief of the Self-Defense Fleet, the commandant of Yokosuka District, and the commander of the Fleet Escort Force. The mayor of Yokosuka had also been invited.

It had been arranged that the Japanese navy escort *Myoko* would welcome *Indy* carrying the commander in chief, Clinton, on board. The problem here had been that *Indy*'s freeboard was so high that the president would end up looking down at the salute from the Japanese deck. So *Myoko,* the Maritime SDF's biggest ship with the exception of the icebreaker *Shirase,* had been chosen to do the honors. She was a Kongo-model escort ship (standard displacement of 7,250 tons). Despite such efforts, the president still ended up looking down; just less.

Another consideration was probably that the *Myoko* had the AEGIS-system as well. No doubt, they were using it as an opportunity to demonstrate the high-tech alliance between the two countries.

The *Myoko*'s entire crew lined up on deck to give the welcoming salute.

The political and campaign pros in the White House had long decided that Clinton would deliver a speech from *Indy*'s deck. They argued that it was a unique opportunity for the president to show the American people that America's naval presence was still crucial, that he valued the military, and that he was an excellent commander in chief.

A White House official recalled, "The public image people and the people that organized these Kodak moments are very clever, and . . . once the *Independence* went through the straits, there was no doubt in anyone's mind that we were going to the *Independence.* . . . Every one of us went out of our way to get a hat, an *Independence* hat."[9]

But there were those in the State Department and elsewhere who were a bit leery that including the *Myoko* might be overdoing it. Japan's Foreign Ministry wasn't too keen either. A Defense Department official remembered, "The question would be, immediately after the Taiwan Straits, whether we were doing too much by going onto the *Independence* itself and looking at a Japanese warship at the time that we were signing the security declaration. There was some nervousness about sending a wrong signal of hostility to China."[10] But the White House PR boys won out. The Defense Department also thought it was a chance to deliver a powerful performance for bilateral security.

A lively exchange of greetings was taking place in the reception area on the flight deck. One of the Japanese in uniform approached Campbell. "You know, we don't ever get to have this kind of ceremony; we do it privately. . . . But to be paid respects meant a tremendous amount."[11] Campbell could see how moved he was from these few words. There were even a few with tears in their eyes. The same thing had happened at the end of the summit at the Akasaka Palace. Akiyama had come over to Campbell, bowed very graciously, and said, "I just want to thank you."

It took Campbell completely by surprise. "For what?"

"The JDA has been in existence for many, many years, and we have never ever had any role in a summit. This is the first time that the director-general and myself, representing JDA, have ever been included, so that was nice; that made me feel good."[12]

Even though it was a pointless exercise, Campbell could not stop himself from dwelling on the complicated circumstances of the Defense Agency and Self-Defense Forces' "birth," their "legacy," their "environment." He felt gratitude to Perry once more. Perry had mentioned to Clinton that since this was a security summit, it was important that the security people be included.

The day before the summit with Japan, Perry and Campbell had flown into Cheju Island for the U.S.-Korea summit. Clinton hadn't arrived yet. Perry took Campbell aside and said it had been one of the highlights of his time as defense secretary. He also said he had made sure Campbell would be included in the president's party, that he wanted him to go in his place.[13]

Usui rated an invite to a "security summit." With Campbell in the president's party, Akiyama also rated one.

Blue Chip

The Defense Agency was elated. They'd been out in the wilderness for so long. In the face of public indifference, or even hostility, they had learned to duck.

The Defense Agency was established some 10 years later than the other ministries, after the war. The U.S. military was in charge along with the Foreign Ministry and the Procurement Agency. The Procurement Agency was subsequently absorbed into the Defense Facilities

Administration Agency, but for a long time it was the Foreign Ministry
that decided policy, the JDA acting as subcontractor. The Status of Forces
Agreement was the Foreign Ministry's fief; the Defense Facilities
Administration Agency was in charge of its actual implementation.

With the strengthening of the U.S.-Japan security dialogue in the fall
of 1994, in what was dubbed the Nye Initiative, and the bases issue, and
the China-Taiwan showdown, the role of the JDA had expanded to the
point where its director-general and defense policy bureau chief were
included in the summit. In a word, it meant that the JDA had taken its
first step as a policy agency.

Charles Freeman, assistant secretary of defense, and Joseph Nye's
predecessor, recalled that he had thought about talking policy with the
JDA when he was at the Pentagon but had given up in the end because
the JDA was neither used to nor had the intellectual capacity to talk policy; it was much more effective talking with MOFA. This weakness of
the JDA could hardly be expected to change overnight, but there was at
the very least a strong desire to participate in policy dialogue and to
become a policy agency.

It was Seiki Nishihiro who tirelessly expounded the need for ongoing security dialogue and for their own sources of intelligence with the
overseas security community. Nishihiro was a defense bureaucrat who
had made it to number two in the agency. A brilliant strategist, he still
wielded significant influence even after his retirement. On his own he
had sown the seeds of a future vision for an open Defense Agency and
SDF where they would create and promote policy, gather and evaluate
intelligence, incorporate it into policy, and take the floor.

This vision of Nishihiro's was shared by Hajime Hatakeyama,
deputy director-general of the JDA, but Hatakeyama passed away in
June 1995, followed by Nishihiro in December of the same year. It was
Masahiro Akiyama, appointed head of the Defense Policy Bureau in
April 1995, who took over their work.

Akiyama had been seconded from the Ministry of Finance. That fact
in itself indicated that the JDA was still a long way from being an
autonomous organization. Some of those seconded to the JDA fitted in
well and spoke out on the agency's position in Kasumigaseki, the
agency itself having need of such services.

A top man in uniform said that Hatakeyama and Akiyama had none
of the standoffishness so commonly seen among the born and bred
civilians, namely that "we white-collars aren't going to hang out with
you blue-collar guys."

The Finance Ministry explained self-servingly that officers from the
Budget Bureau were best suited to the Defense Agency, since, being
essentially an agency in charge of the national interest, they were skilled
in guiding the "national interest."

According to Masaharu Gotoda, a former minister of justice with experience in home affairs and police matters and who himself had been seconded to the Defense Agency as its inaugural Defense Division chief, this amounted to nothing more than grandstanding by the Finance Ministry. He seemed to find their self-serving logic absurd: *Who is the Finance Ministry to talk about statecraft? We don't need your budget officers to teach us about security matters, thank you very much.* Nevertheless, the ministry itself seemed to be convinced that it was charged with protecting the national interest.

An officer high up in the Finance Ministry said, "We try to look for affable types to send to the JDA, likable types. All the better if he's versed in both the pen and the sword."[14] Akiyama was their ideal man. He ran marathons and his sportsmanlike character was one of his attractions. He had a wide range of job experience, having been posted to the Japanese Embassy in Ottawa when still quite young and also being the first MOF career bureaucrat to serve as a chief of prefectural police (Nara) on secondment. He had also been in the budget area for a long time.

However, his experience was mainly in the areas of foreign affairs and trade; he had never been in charge of defense. Compared with Hatakeyama, who had been budget officer for defense, he was an amateur when he moved to the JDA in 1991 as deputy director-general. "Is it enough for the JDA to simply draw up defense plans or service plans with only the SDF (Self-Defense Forces) in mind? The agency needs to get involved now in coming up with trust-building measures for foreign policy too. So, I intend to work on security policy, intelligence, and international relations."[15]

Declaring this, Akiyama set about drawing pictures on a blank sheet. Some of those pictures included closer consultation with the Americans on security policy, a defense dialogue with China, and defense consultations with other Asia-Pacific countries. Military interlocution with Russia and South Korea were there too.

In the so-called Nye Initiative from 1994, which set its sights on strengthening the U.S.-Japan security dialogue, he worked with Joseph Nye, assistant secretary of defense, discussing the post–Cold War nature of bilateral security ties and putting in place a course for incorporating that into policy. During that process, the JDA's presence grew stronger. Robin Sakoda, director of the Japan Desk at the Defense Department, said, "It shouldn't have been called the 'Nye Initiative'; that was a misnomer. It should have been called the 'Nye-Akiyama Initiative.'"[16]

Grafted on to the Nye Initiative was SACO. This was followed by the task of revising the Agreement Concerning Reciprocal Provision of Logistic Support, Supplies, and Services (ACSA) and the guidelines. U.S.-Japan dialogue on security was becoming an area increasingly difficult to discuss without first-hand knowledge of the defense field. Voices at the JDA and SDF gradually came to be heard more and more.

A key senior official at the JDA recollects that "the Americans started treating us differently; it felt as if we'd finally made it as a blue-chip company." Behind this change was the shift in international conditions surrounding Japan since the start of the 1990s and the shift in Japanese perceptions of security.

First was the shock of the Gulf War. The Japanese people were made painfully aware of how unprepared Japan was for dealing with crises. People joked about Big Shot Japan, now behaving just like a huge "cash dispenser." Opinion polls, at first hesitant on sending the SDF on peacekeeping missions, slowly started to endorse the policy. They had learned that peace couldn't be bought with money alone. The Kobe earthquake and the sarin gas terrorist attack also brought home the need to constantly strengthen crisis management systems.

Hand in hand with this greater awareness, interest in and support for the roles and missions of the JDA and the SDF spread little by little. The climate was slowly ripening for the agency to play a greater role.

Despite this, however, the emergence of the JDA at this juncture was linked to hard-to-fathom changes in the U.S. policy decision-making process, especially in the balance of power between the agencies in charge of policy on Japan. It signified a drop in the importance of the State Department.

In addition to Secretary of State Warren Christopher's lack of political acumen, the State Department was no longer certain of being in the driver's seat on all international issues accompanying the Clinton administration's "reshuffling of post–Cold War priorities" and the greater emphasis being placed on domestic and economic issues. The end of the Cold War also saw calls for rationalizing the Defense Department, but it had successfully made the transition to the new era by flying the flag of its high-tech industrial policies and its power of procurement, not to mention the clout wielded by its two huge domestic political support bases, the veterans and its military bases (providing employment) at home.

The sinking fortunes of the State Department put its Japanese counterpart, the Foreign Ministry (MOFA), on the defensive. The State Department had lost the initiative on Japan policy to the economic instruments of government. It couldn't and didn't move when the Foreign Ministry tried to put bilateral security on the agenda. In fact, in chorus with the economic agencies, it was busy conveying trade and economic demands to Japan.

The Pentagon, especially Nye, struck at this chink in its armor. They staged a rear attack: *well, if that's the case, then, let's pursue our own security agenda, just the Pentagon and the JDA.*

The eruption of the Okinawan base issue, Hashimoto's making Okinawa his top priority, both pushed the JDA to the fore. And since this didn't stop at the bilateral Security Treaty or the Status of Forces Agreement, but progressed on to the realignment, consolidation, and reduction of the bases as well as the structure of the American forces and operational requirements, the JDA with its military expertise and knowledge of Okinawa was popping up more frequently.

This didn't change the fact, however, that the Defense Facilities Administration Agency, which was directly in charge of base administration, had more than its fair share of thankless tasks. Hence the epithet the "Native Lackeys."

"The game will all be up if it turns into a fiasco like Narita. We had that trouble at Sunagawa and know we were in the wrong there. That's why we don't want to force the issue. But if you try to settle it with money, you're accused of slapping the bills in their faces. You're completely on your own. There's nobody on your side," said Masuo Morodomi, director-general of the Defense Facilities Administration Agency.[17]

(The Sunagawa incident he referred to was a clash that took place in 1955–57 in opposition to the expansion of the U.S. Tachikawa Base in western Tokyo. The government arrested the workers and students who had infiltrated the base and charged seven with criminal infringement of the U.S.-Japan Security Treaty. The Regional Tokyo Court handed down a verdict of not guilty, deeming that the stationing of U.S. bases was unconstitutional [the Date Verdict], but the Supreme Court rescinded this and sent the case back down.)

Nevertheless, as it became no longer possible to ignore Okinawa Prefecture or the local municipalities around the bases, the position of the JDA, with its Defense Facilities Administration Bureau in Naha City, grew stronger.

Chided by Seiroku Kajiyama, Cabinet secretary, the Foreign Ministry decided to post a special minister plenipotentiary for Okinawan affairs on Okinawa permanently, appointing Hideki Harashima, ambassador to Tunisia, as its inaugural representative. Okinawan mistrust of the Foreign Ministry, however, was intense.

The headlines in the *Okinawa Times* (September 22, 1995) after the rape of a young Okinawan schoolgirl by U.S. servicemen, when it was learned that the Foreign Ministry had confirmed with the U.S. Embassy that there was no need for a review of the Status of Forces Agreement, were "Foreign Ministry Turns Its Back on Public Opinion"; "Just Like an Outpost of the U.S. Government"; "Anger Voiced against Cowardly Government."

Even the Foreign Ministry didn't think it could solve the whole Okinawan problem on its own. Nor did it want to. "It was such a crucial issue that we left it up to the Cabinet as a whole." They also felt cornered. "Up until then, it was only the Security Division chief who got down to the nitty-gritty on Okinawa working with the JDA and the Defense Facilities Administration Agency. But things couldn't be left like that anymore." There was almost assuredly a calculation that they needed some insurance, they weren't going to have all the responsibility shunted onto them.[18]

The position of Hashimoto and Kajiyama probably caused a subtle shift in the balance of power between the Foreign Ministry and the Defense Agency. For instance, Kajiyama chastised the young officer seconded from the MOFA to the Cabinet's foreign affairs advisory office, saying that if they had the time to draw up all that paperwork, why didn't they go down to Okinawa and convince the small landowners?

This Foreign Ministry bashing could be read as part of a larger groundswell of criticism directed at the bureaucrats, but in the case of Hashimoto and Kajiyama, there was another factor, namely MITI and the Ministry of Finance (MOF) beefs. Hashimoto had served as minister in both institutions and had many contacts there, while Kajiyama, having long reigned as the don of the commerce lobby, had close ties with the MITI men.

That point worked to Akiyama's advantage. Akiyama knew Hashimoto from his time at the Ministry of Finance. They were acquainted since the 1980s when Hashimoto was chairman of the LDP's Administration Research Committee. Hashimoto called Akiyama by his nickname, Akichan, a practice he didn't change even when he took up residence in the PM's office. (An aide revealed, however, that during a period of about six months when the Defense Agency was pushing for the consolidation of Kadena Air Force Base and the floating heliport was delayed, Hashimoto didn't call him Akichan. Hashimoto tended to run hot and cold on nicknames depending on the situation.[19])

The Intelligence Wars

The Defense Agency's Achilles' heel was intelligence. It was not told of the informal decision to return Futenma right until the very end. The agency was aggrieved.

Akiyama, who had been invited to a dinner party at the official residence of U.S. Embassy Deputy Chief of Mission Rust Deming in the spring of 1997, confronted the other guest that day, Deputy Assistant Secretary of Defense Kurt Campbell, and said, "On what sort of intelligence does the Pentagon base its decisions? I'm talking about why the JDA was kept out of the Okinawan and marines questions at the most important time."

The other people at the table were surprised by the viciousness of the tone but were given a graphic illustration, albeit late in the day, of just how sensitive the JDA was.

The JDA's mistrust of the Foreign Ministry over intelligence was striking inwards. There was intense unhappiness within the JDA that the Foreign Ministry was not passing on all of the intelligence from its overseas posts. And when it did pass information on, the JDA suspected it was using "flextime." The agency was exasperated that even information sent in by military officers stationed overseas failed to reach the all-important JDA and Joint Staff Council in a timely fashion due to "slip-ups" at MOFA.

The Foreign Ministry had the "prerogative of official cables," which meant it had a monopoly on the official cables covering foreign policy intelligence. Staff seconded from other ministries to overseas posts were forbidden from communicating independently with their own agencies. This rule stemmed from a desire never to repeat the mistake of two-tiered foreign policy, which had dragged Japan into World War II, the military firing off its own intelligence reports through unofficial channels to the ministry at home before the war. As foreign policy has become more multifaceted and specialized, however, each ministry has become increasingly responsible for negotiating directly with its counterparts overseas. And the reality was that the more powerful ministries like MOF and MITI did, in fact, use their own independent communication channels for gathering and conveying information.

But with defense intelligence, the Foreign Ministry kept strict control. If only for that reason alone, the JDA suspected that MOFA was sometimes manipulating information, especially during U.N. peacekeeping operations (PKO).

In order to achieve its burning ambition for a permanent seat for Japan on the U.N. Security Council, MOFA tended to tone down reports of any sign of local unrest. The JDA suspected it of manipulating information when the Japanese were sent as part of the PKO mission to help the Rwandan refugees by not properly informing the PM's office of the deterioration in public order. The Foreign Ministry was frightened that Prime Minister Murayama would withdraw the PKO force at any sign of trouble. A high official in the JDA who was in charge of the PKO mission at the time revealed that the Foreign Ministry even went so far as to instruct its people not to put "public order in Rwanda bad" in the official cables.

This manipulation of information by MOFA was even debated in the Diet. It was Masao Akamatsu, a member of the House of Representatives (New Frontier Party), who asked the question. "For example, a book I recently read called *Information Never Reaches the PM* explains in great and graphic detail how information from SDF officers posted overseas takes forever to reach the JDA proper. Has that sort of thing actually happened, and if it has, what have you assessed to be the cause of such delays?"

Information Never Reaches the PM—The Tragedy of an Intelligence Vacuum in Japan, by Iku Aso, documents the structural faults in the information function of the Murayama government at the time of the death of North Korea's Kim Il Sung, the Kobe earthquake, the sarin gas terrorist attack, and the PKO mission to Rwanda.

Defense Policy Bureau Director Akiyama's response can only be described as "fraught with meaning." "At present, I do not believe that the conveyance of information was so delayed as to create substantial hindrance, but we sometimes do experience what you so rightly point out. As for ourselves, it is our intention to give this matter the proper consideration and consult constantly with the Foreign Ministry to ensure that such a situation does not arise."[20]

The JDA and SDF felt they were discriminated against when serving overseas as well. At a farewell party held in the spring of 1996 for a certain military officer being posted overseas, his farewell speech raised a few eyebrows. "If, begrudging the outlay of ranks, emoluments, and a hundred pieces of gold, a commander does not know the enemy's situation, his is the height of inhumanity. Such a person is no man's commander, no ruler's counsellor, and no master of victory."

It was a quote from Sun-Tzu's *The Art of Warfare* on the use of spies and was a direct appeal to the top officials to improve the treatment of officers posted overseas to make sure they had the information they needed in times of crisis. The top civilian officials were flustered, one of them admitting he had instructed the officer in question to watch what he said, but the officer's appeal was welcomed by his colleagues. "JDA and SDF staff only made it to counsellor at the embassies. While the police ranked an ambassador, the JDA couldn't even make it to minister. In other leading countries, military officers ranked third after the ambassador and DCM, but in the Japanese legations we don't even make it into the top ten."

The departing officer was only voicing the strong dissatisfaction of all the other internationally minded men in uniform.

A high-ranking officer in the Foreign Ministry had tried to upgrade the status of military officers abroad when he was head of the personnel division but admitted that the JDA put it on hold, saying that an equilibrium had to be maintained with the civilians—a balance between uniforms and suits.

He recollected, "Military officers are often found next to the ambassador at official receptions. They often come up with key items of information through their networking with other military officers. So, I thought raising their status would also strengthen their intelligence-gathering capability. But I was quite surprised when I was told by none other than the JDA that there would be no need for that!"[21]

The JDA's newfound supersensitivity on intelligence was not unrelated to the "information fever" of the occupant of the PM's office himself. Prime Minister Ryutaro Hashimoto was extremely savvy about information. Of all the Japanese prime ministers, he was the first prime minister to meet openly and in public with the head of the CIA. In October 1996, CIA Director John Deutch visited Japan and had dinner with Hashimoto at the MOFA's Iikura reception facility, a good indication of Hashimoto's unusual interest in information.

The struggle between the Foreign Ministry and the JDA was a fight about what information would be conveyed to the prime minister as well as how and when. Success in the intelligence wars would determine their respective fates. The Foreign Ministry, the Defense Agency, the Cabinet Research and Information Office, the Cabinet Security Office and the National Policy Agency all scrambled over each other in their race to be first to the prime minister. The Cabinet Research and Information Office (CRIO) was the only information institution directly attached to the Cabinet. It was under the command of the Cabinet secretary, but it was standard procedure for the director to personally brief the prime minister, the Cabinet secretary, and the deputy Cabinet secretary. This access was CRIO's greatest weapon, but its job was to gather information, nothing more. On the other hand, accompanying the 1986 transformation of the National Defense Council into the Cabinet Security Council (comprising the prime minister and the seven other ministers with security-related portfolios), the Cabinet Security Office was established as its secretariat. It was in charge of drawing up defense guidelines and policy responses to security contingencies and crisis management. More often than not, the head of the CSO was seconded from the Defense Agency.

Whether it was information on the No Dong missile tests by North Korea, the U.S. government's reprisals against Iraq, the hostages in the Japanese Embassy in Peru, or Chinese military movements during the showdown with Taiwan, Hashimoto wanted information "as fast as possible, as close to the truth as possible, and as reliable as possible."

In the fall of 1996, at precisely the moment a high-ranking officer of the Foreign Ministry was briefing the prime minister on the possibility of an imminent attack on Iraq by the United States, a high ranking officer from the JDA burst into the PM's office to inform him that they were going to attack in one to two hours. Hashimoto turned to the MOFA official and remarked caustically, "Now that's the sort of information you should be bringing me."

During the Peruvian hostage crisis, Hashimoto was impressed by U.S. information on the Peruvian government's secret tunnel but felt he had missed out on the crucial piece of information on the decision to move in due to poor follow-up.

Hashimoto shared his philosophy with his aides. "Information's a living thing. It's got to be information we can use. It's much more useful when you have to take a decision to have relatively fresh information littered with question marks than to be handed something that has been all neatly arranged and ordered but is much too late."[22]

Hashimoto wanted it up-to-the minute, or at least warm. He complained more than once or twice about the intelligence-gathering capabilities of the Foreign Ministry. This criticism was strong grounds for the argument in favor of reforming the Foreign Ministry raised in government talks on administrative reform in the summer of 1997.

Deep down, the Foreign Ministry found a prime ministry that would pounce on snippets of information distressing. One of the Foreign Ministry intelligence analyst pros said, "There's no tribe who worships live information more than the Japanese politicians. It probably has something to do with the fact that they are so appallingly indifferent to doctrine and ideas. They've no conception that the value of information lies in assessing it."[23]

Another high-ranking officer was heard to grumble, "[The PM's office] squeals out for fresh information, but when they get conflicting reports they can't judge for themselves and come running to us to ask which is right. If they're going to clamor for the fresh stuff, they should at least learn how to assess it for themselves."[24]

It was not as if Hashimoto was satisfied with what he was getting from the Defense Agency either. He felt it had been slow in the China-Taiwan showdown. He was frustrated and chagrined that the information was probably there, but it just wasn't getting to him. In a roundabout way, this feeling of the prime minister's was made known to the JDA top brass.

Most likely, this feeling referred to the fact that the JDA had been slower in relaying to Hashimoto the deployment of the *Nimitz* than the CRIO. But the JDA had its own case to put.

In the exchange of information with the U.S. military, the JDA was extremely sensitive about information on the U.S. Navy, especially the movements of aircraft carriers. It had to pay the utmost respect to maintaining the confidentiality of top-secret information like that which the Japanese had been given as allies. It also had to exercise caution in how the information was conveyed upstairs. More times than not, this information was not passed on in raw form but as material for assessment.

Intelligence HQ

It was at the end of the 1980s that the JDA started lobbying for its own intelligence headquarters. Seiki Nishihiro was behind the attempt to break free of the Foreign Ministry's stranglehold on information and create its own intelligence structure.

Behind this lay the shock received during the KAL 007 incident. Korean Air flight 007 was shot down by Soviet military aircraft after having wandered off course into Soviet airspace, causing many deaths.

Secretary of State George Shultz released a strongly worded statement on the Soviets some 20 hours later. Since the Soviets still refused to admit to the shooting down, the U.S. government released a communication log in an attempt to confront them with "incontrovertible proof" in the U.N. Security Council.

It was a decisive victory against the Soviets for Reagan's hard-line foreign policy. The problem was that the communication record had been intercepted.

The communication had been intercepted by the Wakkanai detachment of the Second Division of the Ground SDF's surveillance outfit. Rather than being conveyed to the PM's office, or even the Defense Agency, it had gone straight to the U.S. National Security Agency (NSA).

The Japanese government was in a flap when informed by the U.S. government it was going public with the information. The Defense Agency opposed this fiercely, saying releasing the information would reveal its communication interception channels, but it was already too late. The Japanese government released a summary of the communication log just before the Americans did. It was portrayed as "an excellent opportunity to demonstrate the steadfastness of the U.S. and Japan against the Soviets," but the truth of the matter was that the government had no other choice.

This incident highlighted many problems in information management. The Japanese government learned that their state secrets were being told to the Americans before them. What was happening with their "information sovereignty"?

The PM's office had been informed very early on about the shooting, but it had no idea that the communication log had been passed on to U.S. intelligence. What was worse, after learning that the Americans had it and despite asking the JDA to pass the information on up, the office was kept waiting quite some time. Masaharu Gotoda, cabinet secretary at the time, recalls being ready to let the top heads at the agency roll if they dragged their feet any longer.

At the time those at the top of the JDA said they didn't know that information was being passed directly on from SDF in the field to U.S. intelligence. If that was true, then that in itself was a problem. But Gotoda had his suspicions that they really did know; if, despite knowing it all along, they had pretended not to, that was an even more serious problem.

During all this, the Foreign Ministry was completely out of the loop. "Contact between the Foreign Ministry and the JDA was completely cut. Neither trusted the other. The Foreign Ministry held the JDA in contempt and the JDA was worried that the information would be leaked if they told the Foreign Ministry."[25]

What was going on with Japan's information management, crisis management, and foreign policy?

As if Japan had no proprietary rights over the information whatsoever, the Americans used it in a one-sided propaganda war against the Soviets. Gotoda and the other government leaders "only found out later that U.S. soldiers were working alongside the SDF in the Wakkanai communications site." Gotoda further attests that "we only found out later that the communications site had been transferred from the U.S. military to the SDF."

A top official at the JDA at the time commented, "With cutbacks in the Pentagon budget and troop reduction, the Americans could no longer maintain the interception facility on their base. So, they left it to us, saying the SDF could use it but they wanted us to share any information we got." In short, the SDF personnel working there were "nothing much more than local labor."[26]

Having the Soviets learn of Japan's interception channel was a blow in terms of intelligence gathering. In terms of foreign policy and security as well, a vital case turned on the judgment of a single, low-ranking SDF officer. What was to be made of the yawning gap between the lip service paid to the alliance and the actual operational aspects thereof? And where was the civilian control at the time?

After World War II, the intelligence function of the SDF was deliberately carved up. Once again, this was a reaction to the "prewar monopoly the military had on intelligence and the distorted political machinations which stemmed from that."[27] And yet, although the monopoly and its distortions had been broken by this carve-up, it was replaced by a system of irresponsibility, with SDF in the field acting as virtual subcontractors to the U.S. military and U.S. intelligence without the knowledge of their superiors. This was not only detrimental to the pursuit of a sound defense policy, it was also detrimental to the building of a sound security alliance.

This sort of problem convinced Seiki Nishihiro that the JDA needed to create an intelligence headquarters. At that time, he had in mind something along the lines of the U.S. Defense Intelligence Agency (DIA).

Nishihiro attended the U.S.-Japan security talks held in Hawaii in 1985. At the time, he was director of the Defense Policy Bureau. John Sloane from the DIA also attended. To those in the know, Sloane was a top military intelligence man, a real professional. He was then in charge of Japan. At an outdoor party held at the residence of CINCPAC, Nishihiro talked at length with Sloane, inundating Sloane with questions through an interpreter.

Without their noticing, the sun had already gone down. The other guests had all gone home leaving just themselves. Not knowing where the exit was, it took them some time to find their way out and when they did, the drivers had all gone home. Arriving back where he was staying, Nishihiro found his staff in a panic: "The director's missing!" Many years later, Nishihiro admitted that he had received a lot of practical suggestions from Sloane that night.

(In the summer of 1997, Policy Director Sloane, now number three in the DIA, visited Japan for consultation between the DIA and the Japan Defense Intelligence Headquarters [JDIH]. Sloane visited Nishihiro's home in Tokyo to pay his respects to the departed.)

In a certain sense, the establishment of the intelligence headquarters resembled that of the JDA in that it came about because America needed it. As a former high-ranking official at the JDA pointed out, with the cuts in the U.S. defense budget and the trend towards fewer troops stationed in Japan, creating the headquarters hitched a ride on U.S. pressure for Japan to assume radio intelligence capabilities.

The other person Nishihiro conferred with was Masaharu Gotoda. Gotoda placed only one condition on Nishihiro's request for an intelligence HQ. "You have to ensure organizational and management liaison between the PM's office and the JDA. I won't allow it unless you do."

Gotoda later revealed that "politics in Japan doesn't have enough backbone. That's why I was worried about the uniforms using their intelligence as leverage for taking control of everything. I was apprehensive about the dangers of military intelligence being dressed up as political intelligence and being used to sway the Cabinet."[28]

In the spring of 1996, a bill for the partial amendment of the Defense Agency Act of Establishment to allow the establishment of an intelligence headquarters was tabled in the Diet. Representatives from the LDP and the New Frontier Party took the floor at question time, but there was no real debate.

Masao Akamatsu of the New Frontier Party asked, "What specific route for conveying the information gathered by the intelligence headquarters to the PM's office is being contemplated?" and "Who would determine if information was to be conveyed or not?"

Masahiro Akiyama, director of the Defense Policy Bureau, responded: "We would like to make our contact with the cabinet and the PM's office even closer than previously. In organizational terms, our contact with the Cabinet Research and Information Office will be maintained at the present level or even closer." With regard to who would determine what information was to be conveyed, "the assessment of the head and deputy head of the intelligence headquarters would be considerable" while "an intelligence committee would be established within the Defense Agency chaired by the deputy director-general to debate and direct the running of the headquarters and contact structures."[29]

A few representatives called for the establishment of the intelligence headquarters to improve not only the intelligence capabilities of the JDA but also the Cabinet as a whole. The LDP's Tomoharu Yoda pointed out that the infrastructural issue of how to link directly the intelligence headquarters to the PM's office as well as the exchange of staff from the Defense Agency, the Cabinet, the Foreign Ministry, and other agencies was an extremely important one. In response to this, Director Akiyama replied that the establishment of an intelligence headquarters would not stop at upgrading the intelligence functions of the Defense Agency, but, as a matter of course, would make an active contribution to strengthening the intelligence functions of the Cabinet and the government as a whole.

While those representatives in favor of establishing the intelligence headquarters voiced the opinion that Japan should have its own reconnaissance satellite, Director Akiyama refuted this, saying that while the JDA had heretofore been interested in reconnaissance satellites as a valuable means of gathering intelligence, there was currently no idea or plan to possess one.[30] His response that they would like to explore that possibility should a specific problem occur in the future, however, left some room to maneuver.[31]

Problems such as the implications of a stronger intelligence structure on U.S.-Japan security, how sharing intelligence with the United States affected collective self-defense rights, what was the appropriate approach in terms of civilian control—these and other important questions were hardly touched on in the debate.

As part of the coalition government, the Socialists voted for the amendment. Telling Akiyama he wouldn't be holding his tongue if he was in opposition, Shun Oide in the House of Representatives ran around creating a party consensus and working hard for the bill's passage. Akiyama was grateful to Oide, but having prepared and carefully checked a huge amount of documentation for his responses, he was disappointed by the overly understanding hearing in the Diet.

The Defense Intelligence Headquarters (JDIH) was launched in January 1997. The inaugural director was General Masahiro Kunimi and the deputy-director Takemasa Moriya, counselor to the Bureau of Defense.

The following is a list of the JDIH's organizational and operational objectives.

- To bring the disparate intelligence functions of the Defense Agency's Bureau, the Joint Staff Council, and the ground, air, and maritime commands under one roof and pursue the effective analysis of strategic intelligence. The Second Research Division attached to the Bureau of Defense, the Joint Staff Council's Second Staff Office, the Research Divisions under each command, and the First Research Division in the ground forces command were all incorporated. This last specialized in radio waves and communications (signals intelligence).

- The JDIH was to be placed under the command of the Joint Staff Council and its director would be a uniformed (SDF) officer. The deputy director would be a civilian (JDA) and serve concurrently as counselor to the Bureau of Defense. There would be a mix of civilians and military all the way down from the top to the division chief level. There had been no such systematic opportunity for senior JDA and SDF staff to work alongside each other. In particular, it was the first time the top military had had civilians working under them. Up until that point, forums for the military and civilians to work together were in the Joint Staff Council Secretariat, the Foreign Ministry's Japan-U.S. Security Treaty Division in the North American Affairs Bureau, and in the JDA's Defense Policy Division, its Public Relations Division, training at the military academy, and in overseas legations. But most of the top military brass retired from the service never having worked in the same place as civilians. One of the goals was to try and change that.

- The JDIH was divided into five areas: general affairs, planning, analysis, visuals, and radio with some 25 divisions and a total staff of 1,600, of which 1,000 were stationed at six different communication sites around the country. 1,300 were assigned to radio intelligence, namely tracking military movements by radio and communications in the vicinity.

Deciding whether to incorporate this section into the JDIH was touch and go within the government until the last minute. The National Police Agency (NPA) and MOFA were alarmed that it would concentrate enormous power in the hands of the agency and the Joint Staff Council if it was included. Akiyama, however, bulldozed it through, saying an intelligence headquarters without radio intelligence was unthinkable.

Akiyama remarked, "Up until then it hadn't been clear who was in charge of the radio intelligence, tucked away in separate rooms all over the place. People didn't know what they were up to. We needed to bring all that intelligence together."[32]

With the start-up of the JDIH, fears began to be voiced within the government concerning the JDA's upgraded intelligence capability and the leverage it might have on the PM's office:

"The intelligence channels of the ground, air, and maritime forces are totally disconnected. We're getting intelligence from the ground forces just because their man happens to be at the top, but the air and maritime forces are looking the other way. There's been no consolidation of intelligence that we can see."

"Because the JDIH director reports on intelligence to the uniforms' chairman of the Joint Staff Council, the Defense Policy Bureau's director may be compromised in terms of intelligence. The bureau's intelligence capabilities have already fallen off."

Akiyama rebutted these voices, saying, "The three forces may never share all their intelligence, but they're definitely making progress on sharing. Moreover, the intelligence from the JDIH to the director of the Defense Policy Bureau has improved out of sight both in terms of quantity and quality. The relationship between the two is also fine. That's precisely why the counselor for the Bureau of Defense is in there as the JDIH's number two."[33]

Akiyama also commented that the flow of intelligence between the JDA and the PM's office was much closer that it had ever been before. They were trying to respond to Gotoda's pithy insistence on close "organizational and management" links between the JDA and the prime minister by strengthening interaction with the Cabinet Research and Information Office. It was just that the CRIO felt it still wasn't enough and its nature was unclear.

A high-ranking official at the Foreign Ministry revealed that this sense of caution towards the JDA and the JDIH on the part of the Foreign Ministry, the CRIO, and the National Police Agency was due to "the singular Japanese fear of sectionalism."[34]

The very fact that the JDIH had been placed under the Joint Staff Council was the result of the civilians being pushed aside by the military. Nishihiro and Hatakeyama had initially envisioned it being placed under the Defense Agency, but each command, especially the ground forces with their radio intelligence specialists, refused to budge in its opposition. No one was thrilled at the prospect of their intelligence being "siphoned off" to the Joint Staff Council!

The military could only be swayed, and just barely then, by putting a soldier at the top and placing the HQ under the Joint Staff Council. The reality of the matter was that "it was a child of compromise between the JDA and the SDF."[35]

On the other hand, neither the Foreign Ministry nor the NPA knew how to overcome its own sectionalism. The Foreign Ministry was all nerves about the CRIO strengthening ties and sharing intelligence with the CIA on the situation in North Korea, and the JDA was fearful of the NPA using the CRIO to divert JDIH intelligence. There were even those within the JDA who regarded Gotoda, who was keeping a sharp eye on the civilian control of the JDA and SDF, as a spokesman for the "police family's" interests.

As if there weren't enough of that already, the launch of the JDIH only added fuel to the fires of intergovernmental rivalry and sectionalism.

The Men in Uniform

Hashimoto tried to cheer up the military. It was not unusual for him to invite mere officers from the SDF to listen to their opinions. At first, some of the soldiers were puzzled. One of the top brass was heard to say, "I was grateful, but I thought he misunderstood a little because he seemed to think that we were weak and being picked on by the agency."

That was probably not Hashimoto's intention. The soldiers were, however, ultra-sensitive to how they were juxtaposed in the prevailing "suits versus uniforms" framework, and how they were treated and listened to within a framework that presumed there was tension between the two. This sort of remark in itself could be said to indicate the military's instincts for self-preservation.

Soon after he became prime minister, Hashimoto met with the top brass from the Joint Staff Council at the PM's office. It was a courtesy meeting as the chairman and chiefs of staff of the three forces were all to be alternated. They were to meet in the Cabinet reception room next to the prime minister's working office. Hashimoto suggested they should come to the office after 5:30 P.M. His secretary made an appointment for 5:30. At this hour, the "office boys," the civilians, would officially be gone.

After the formalities were over in the Cabinet reception room, Hashimoto invited Chairman Tetsuya Nishimoto and Maritime Chief of Staff Takeo Fukuchi, both of whom were retiring, to join him next door in his office for a drink.

Hashimoto opened a new bottle of Yamazaki, 18-year-old malt whiskey, mixed it with hot water, pressing it on to the two men. After they had enjoyed their drinks for a while, Fukuchi got up his nerve to speak.

"May I say something to you, Mr. Prime Minister?"

"What is it?"

"On the occasion of my retirement, there are two things which make me extremely happy. I have worked my heart out sharpening my weapons for more than thirty years to protect the safety of this country. My greatest joy is to be able to retire in a peaceful Japan without ever having had to use any of them. The other is that today, for the first time ever, I have been allowed into the PM's office without any of the administrators in attendance. I would never have imagined that I would find myself in the prime minister's office drinking with the prime minister himself!"

Fukuchi became more emotional as he spoke, his voice choking. He had been to school with Hashimoto at Azabu Junior and Senior High. That probably had something to do with his letting his guard down. Hashimoto asked Nishimoto if that was true. He replied that it was; that it was the first time he had ever been in the prime minister's personal office.[36]

In April 1997, when John Shalikashvili, chairman of the Joint Chiefs of Staff, visited Japan, Hashimoto invited him to the PM's office for dinner. That the prime minister would invite America's top military man to the PM's office for a meal was in itself totally unprecedented.

Ralph Eberhardt, commander of the U.S. forces in Japan, Shigeru Sugiyama, chairman of the Joint Staff Council, Nobutoshi Watanabe, chief of staff of the Ground SDF, Kazuya Natsukawa, chief of staff of the Maritime SDF, and Koji Muraki, chief of staff of the Air SDF, were also invited. Apart from the interpreter, Yayoi Matsuda, and barring the prime minister, everyone was in uniform.

Hashimoto took Shalikashvili by surprise telling him he had read almost all of Tom Clancy's books. He added that he was always telling the younger politicians to read Tom Clancy and brush up their military knowledge.

Hashimoto had an interest in history and he was not averse to strutting his stuff. He could answer pat any sudden question in the Diet about whether the marines were an attack force or a defense force, for instance: "I believe the marines were a defense force during the Boxer Uprising. In the landing at Tripoli they were in the vanguard, but were almost tragically wiped out. In World War II as well, there are many cases when they were used not only as attack troops in the European front lines but as defense troops as well. In the Pacific War, the marines displayed their ability in counteroffensives for the U.S., so it is my understanding that they were attacking troops at that time. In the Korean War, they suffered several defeats and stuck to the defensive, but I believe they also carried out some landing operations."[37]

The postwar political and social constraints and taboos towards the uniforms were starting to melt. Torkel Patterson, a graduate of the U.S. Naval Academy and a former staff member at the White House, disclosed his impression in the spring of 1997. "The other day when I went to Yokosuka after quite a long absence, men of the Maritime SDF were walking around town in their uniforms. It really made me realize that Japan had changed."[38]

In the review of the Guidelines on U.S.-Japan Defense Cooperation, which commenced in the spring of 1996, the military was involved right from the very first and in an official capacity. When the guidelines were being drawn up in 1978, the JDA director-general at the time, Michita Sakata, emphasized civilian awareness of duty and responsibility by pointing out the inappropriateness of the previous approach when the chiefs of staff on both sides looked into the matter. He added that leaving it all up to the military was not good. This led to attempts to push the civilians to the forefront. The military was involved in the task but was confined to the wings.

This time, however, things were different. A top man at the JDA said, "Civilians and uniforms worked side by side." Another high-ranking official with the JDA noted that "before it was top-down, but this time it was bottom-up." Much of the bottom consisted of uniforms.

The fact that the guidelines closely impinged on the military's field of expertise was, of course, a factor. But so too was the fact that many of those in uniform had studied and lived in the United States; they spoke good English and could express themselves well. Given that it was a joint job with the Americans, those sorts of skills were needed.

And yet, Hashimoto felt that the military was not getting the recognition and respect it deserved in Japanese society, or worse, it wasn't even getting it at the Defense Agency. There were those in the JDA who saw Hashimoto's thoughtfulness towards the military as "fawning to the SDF." There was resentment about the removal of civilians in particular. Even some of the LDP elders said he was "too soft" on them, concern being voiced that "he didn't know how to keep a hold on them because he'd never fought." Hashimoto knew these complaints were out there. Knowing it, he was still eager to finish what he'd started.

The political acumen of previous prime ministers had been tested by the matter of how to maintain their distance from the military. Too close a relationship with the uniforms and it would work to your political disadvantage. But you still had to show consideration as the SDF's commander-in-chief. Noboru Takeshita remarked that he would like to give the military a chance to come to the PM's office if only once and hosted a buffet reception for more than 100 officers in the ground-floor great hall on the SDF's memorial day. They all came in uniform.

In Kiichi Miyazawa's case, he invited the chairman of the Joint Staff Council as well as the three chiefs of staff to the PM's office and dined with them in the small dining room. It was set up by his thoughtful staff so that the dove, Miyazawa, would not be seen as being "standoffish towards the SDF." The permanent deputy director-general of the JDA also attended.

Hashimoto had long considered it to be "inappropriate for there to be a distance between the prime minister and the uniforms, as long as the PM was the commander-in-chief."

Citing such examples as Toshiki Kaifu, who when inundated with visits from senior JDA officials and SDF officers during the Gulf War and the passage of the PKO bill through the Diet, issued orders that "the uniforms be kept away"; or Morihiro Hosokawa, who turned up at the SDF's memorial day in an ordinary suit (criticized as "kind of like going to a wedding in your pajamas"); or Tomiichi Murayama, who never seemed to be able to speak frankly with the military, Hashimoto was convinced that these episodes had scarred the hearts of the people in uniform. He was heard to mumble that he wanted to make a conscious change.

There is an amusing story about Kaifu. After the Gulf War, Kaifu had refused a request from the JDA to see off the Maritime SDF minesweepers that were being deployed to the Persian Gulf by the Japanese government at the port at Yokosuka. He watched it instead on TV.

Later, he had a secretary send a memo to the JDA saying that he had seen the departure on TV and that there was something that bothered him: What did they think they were doing sending them off with that military march music? Wasn't the ensign at the stern the old imperial flag of the rising sun? There was something strange about the ships all lined up as they sailed out, and so on.

The JDA replied that the song was a world-renowned song of the sea and that it had not been played on its own but as part of a medley; that the flag of the rising sun flown as the ensign of the Maritime SDF vessels had been decided by the Yoshida Cabinet and if he had any objections to it being flown, it would take an act of Cabinet to change it; and that leaving port with the ships lining up in a row was the safest way of sailing out. But "ole Sunday Toshiki still took a good bite out of us."[39] That memory did not easily fade from the people in the field at the JDA and the SDF. ("Sunday Toshiki" was a nickname Kaifu was given during the Gulf crisis, because he would call the top staff at the JDA and SDF to meet him not on weekdays but on Sundays, and what's more, not at the PM's office but at the Hotel Okura!)

"Of course, we can't let the uniforms into the PM's office more than necessary. We've got to keep the rules. Exercise moderation. But we need to create an atmosphere where the uniforms can come if they have some business. It's bizarre that the commander-in-chief won't meet with the uniforms unless he's got a bureaucrat with him.

"Even when they hold a security meeting or something, the only one in uniform is the chairman of the Joint Staff Council and they don't even let him speak. They get the head of the Defense Policy Bureau to talk instead. It's crazy. There must be times when they want a professional opinion. There must be times when they need a professional to answer. That's why they need the three chiefs of staff in there.

"Uniforms should be posted to the JDA. They should be used at division chief level or whatever. One of the counsellor posts should go to a uniform as well."

This is what Hashimoto was saying to his private secretary after he entered the PM's office.[40]

Notes

1. Interview with a senior U.S. administration official.

2. Interview with a senior White House official.

3. The depiction of the exchanges between Clinton and Hashimoto is based on interviews with Ryutaro Hashimoto and other participants.

4. Interview with an aide to the Emperor.

5. Ibid.

6. Interview with Walter Mondale.

7. Ibid.

8. Remarks by the president to U.S. military personnel on board the USS *Independence*, Yokosuka, Japan, Office of the Press Secretary, the White House, April 16, 1996.

9. Interview with a White House official.

10. Interview with a senior DOD official.

11. Interview with Kurt Campbell.

12. Ibid.

13. Ibid.

14. Interview with a senior MOF official.

15. Interview with Masahiro Akiyama.

16. Interview with Robin Sakoda.

17. Interview with Masuo Morodomi.

18. Interview with a senior MOFA official.

19. Interview with the private secretary to Ryutaro Hashimoto.

20. Security Committee, House of Representatives, April 11, 1996.

21. Interview with a senior MOFA official.

22. Interview with Ryutaro Hashimoto.

23. Interview with a senior MOFA official.

24. Ibid.

25. Interview with Masaharu Gotoda.

26. Interview with a former senior JDA official.

27. Interview with Masaharu Gotoda.

28. Ibid.

29. Security Committee, House of Representatives, April 11, 1996.

30. The Japanese government, however, decided on November 6, 1998, to develop and introduce intelligence satellites in an attempt to strengthen its

own intelligence capability, following North Korea's test launch of a Tae-podong ballistic missile that flew over Japan on August 31, 1998. The government announced its intention to develop and manufacture intelligence satellites in Japan and launch four satellites in 2002. Total costs for developing and making the four satellites and operating them for five years were estimated at 200 billion yen.

31.   Before the Cabinet Committee, House of Councilors, May 21, 1996.

32.   Interview with Masahiro Akiyama.

33.   Ibid.

34.   Interview with a senior MOFA official.

35.   Interview with a former senior JDA official.

36.   Interviews with Ryutaro Hashimoto and Takeo Fukuchi.

37.   Response to the Special Committee on Land Use Accompanying the Implementation of the U.S.-Japan Security Treaty, House of Councilors, April 10, 1997.

38.   Interview with Torkel Patterson.

39.   Interview with the then high-ranking JDA official.

40.   Interview with Ryutaro Hashimoto.

II

Conceptual diagram of the floating heliport.

April 18, 1996. President Bill Clinton speaks with Governor
Masao Ota of Okinawa Prefecture.

Chapter Six

Okinawa

Just in Passing

Masahide Ota, governor of Okinawa, had sworn to himself that come hell or high water, he wanted to state his case directly to the U.S. president, Bill Clinton. There would never be another chance like the president's visit this time.

This wish of the governor's had reached the PM's office in November of the previous year. That visit had been cancelled, but this time the president was coming to Japan.

Ota wrote a letter to Richard Meyers, commander of the U.S. forces in Japan, saying he wished to invite the president to Okinawa and asking his help in this matter. But Meyers only sent back a polite reply to the effect that "unfortunately, the Japanese government is in charge of determining the entire schedule for the visit and there is nothing I can do. I'm sorry."

Hearing that, Ota appealed directly to Prime Minister Hashimoto. Hashimoto replied that he would look into whether he could introduce the idea or not.

Upon the prime minister's instructions, the Foreign Ministry (MOFA) broached the Americans about a joint meeting between Clinton and Ota. They approached Ambassador Walter Mondale about the possibility, saying there were those in Japan who wanted Clinton to visit Okinawa. Mondale thought it would be difficult, however. Yet he thought that Ota paying Clinton a courtesy call was "desirable in the sense of showing due respect to the governor."[1] Mondale was eager, so both the Foreign Ministry and the U.S. State Department began laying the groundwork. The Foreign Ministry prepared a room next to where the summit was to be held in the Akasaka Palace. If things went well, the Japanese thought they could manage a meeting for some 20 minutes, or at the very least 5 minutes.

The White House, however, did not give them the nod. It didn't change its tune that Okinawa was essentially a Japanese problem, one for the central government of Japan to resolve.

After the White House entourage arrived in Japan, Ambassador Mondale suggested to National Security Adviser Anthony Lake that the president meet with Ota. But Lake refused point blank, saying that there was no need for the head of state of one country to hold an official meeting with the governor of another. And even if he did meet with him, he had no intention of saying anything but social pleasantries. In the words of a high-ranking official at the State Department, "Being a big fish himself, Mondale wasn't used to being told no and he was hopping mad," but there was nothing he could do but back down in the face of White House unwillingness.[2]

A top White House official later explained this reluctance. "Bringing in the governor directly into a meeting or some sort of formal setting was almost, in my mind looking back, an attempt for Tokyo to mediate between the two. Let the U.S. solve the problems with Okinawa, as though it were not a Japan problem. I would certainly concur with the philosophy that the president should not have seen Governor Ota."[3]

So there was no choice but to look for some social venue. The Foreign Ministry reported to the PM's office that the best that it could do would be to invite Governor Ota to the president's reception banquet scheduled for April 18 at the Hotel New Otani in downtown Tokyo and have them exchange courtesies.

The outlook on the bases was still unclear at this time. Ota, therefore, also avoided making a commitment on the invitation to lunch. On the evening of April 12, however, Futenma's return was announced, which made Ota decide to accept the invitation.

With the help of the Americans, the Japanese hastily decided to be somewhat inventive with the social side of the lunch. In short, they decided to have "the two of them pass by each other on the way out," as Masaharu Kono, director of the First North American Affairs Division, put it. Kono seated Ota on the route the president would take as he was leaving, thereby choreographing a "chance meeting."

Clinton's address to the gathering was short. He praised the close contacts between Japan and the United States, citing the case of the Los Angeles Dodgers' "tornado" Hideo Nomo and the Yakult Swallows' "big man" Terry Bross. "We see it in your great gift to American baseball, Hideo Nomo, and in Americans like Terry Bross, who come to Japan to play baseball."

The lunch reception was a lively affair with 300 guests. Mariko Terasaki Miller from Wyoming also there. Her father was Hidenari Terasaki, famous for acting as Emperor Hirohito's and General MacArthur's interpreter. Her mother was an American named Gwen.

Terasaki was the first secretary at the Japanese Embassy in Washington from March 1941 until December, when the war broke out. The name "Mariko" was used as the code word for the U.S. stance between the Japanese Embassy and the Foreign Ministry back home. Mariko was the first guest to speak.

At Ota's table were the mayors of Hiroshima and Nagasaki. The table diagonally opposite was occupied by the military from both countries: Byron Tobin, commander of the U.S. Navy in Japan, Admiral Archie Clemens, commander of the Seventh Fleet, Major General Peter Pace, deputy commander of the U.S. forces in Japan, and Shigeru Sugiyama, chairman of the Joint Staff Council. They were all in uniform.

Meyers admits that Ota greeted him with a "hi," Meyers himself making a friendly response. Ota felt Meyers was a good-mannered soldier and thought well of him.

One guest after another stood to speak, but everyone kept talking imperturbably at his own table.

Kurt Campbell's table was occupied by the security policy team plus one other person, the sumo wrestler Musashimaru. Musashimaru was seated next to Campbell. The conversation flowed on to American football and wrestling, this and that. Akebono, another American sumo wrestler and grand champion, came over to Musashimaru, told him some joke, then went back to his own seat.

As Campbell was sitting there listening to the speeches and not touching his dessert, Musashimaru leaned over and asked him in a longing tone, "Are you going to eat that?" Thinking now if ever was the time to grin and bear it, Campbell said "no" and as quick as a flash, Musashimaru said, "I'll have it then," and ate it in one fell swoop. Musashimaru told Campbell that he got invited to these kinds of ceremonial suppers all the time, and he sometimes felt like an ornament, and he never got enough to eat.

About when coffee was being served, Sadao Watanabe started playing saxophone. Right out of the blue he started playing a medley of American songs from his seat, then moved up on to the stage. As the prime minister's wife, Kumiko Hashimoto, was explaining to Clinton, the president nodded knowingly, saying, "Oh, Nabe Sada." He stressed the Sada part.

Watanabe played "Take the A Train" first, then "Homecoming." Clinton started to mark the rhythm.

Finally, the last speech was given by Tom Foley, former Speaker of the House of Representatives. The reception finished after 2:00 P.M.

The TV cameramen went after the celebrities, Hikaru Nishida, Yu Hayami, and Judy Ong. Kono had bragged before that "one or two showbiz people gets you much better TV coverage," and it seemed his calculation was dead right.

Another line of cameras focused on Clinton on his way out. As he left the head table, Ambassador Mondale moved quickly out in front, called "Governor! Governor!" and brought the two men together.

Ota thanked the president for his efforts in returning the base. And then he popped the question: "I would like you to visit Okinawa and see for yourself the situation with the bases."

Clinton said a word or two in response. "Thank you for your commitment to making a good home for the troops." He spoke softly and it was hard to catch what he said.

Mondale mentioned as a kind of amplification how the president was thinking a great deal about Okinawa.

Clinton looked a little tense, but the First Lady kept smiling all the while. She had a nice smile.

But there was no time to be dazzled, and Ota was jostled by the crowd as he watched Clinton's large back recede into the distance.

The Heart of Okinawa

Hashimoto and Ota met at the PM's office a scant two weeks after Hashimoto entered office. It was mainly to get acquainted.

But even then, Ota made a strong request for a plan that would show some visible progress on the realignment, consolidation, and reduction of the American bases. Saying that the core of the problem was the sense of inequality that the Okinawans felt with the mainland, he cited the example of the noise control regulations that had been enacted on the mainland but not on Okinawa as weighing heavily on local sentiment.

He also asked that any clear reference to the number of U.S. troops to be stationed in Japan as 47,000 be omitted from the Joint Declaration on Security scheduled for the April summit. Hashimoto merely replied that he would look closely into the matter. Ota felt that Hashimoto was intentionally avoiding getting in too deep, so he didn't pursue it any further.

After the meeting, Hashimoto took out a copy of Ota's book, *Czar of Okinawa: The U.S. High Commissioner* (Asahi Shimbunsha), saying he had meant to read it over New Year's. He asked Ota to sign it, which the governor did.

Hashimoto presented himself to the press after the talk. "At the outset, I began by offering the governor my apologies. My reason for doing so was that I thought I had had more to do with Okinawa than other people because I had been involved in the House of Representatives Standing Committee on Social and Labor Affairs with solving such questions as the compensation for children under six years of age and compensation for the *Tsushima-maru*, but there was so much I didn't know."

The *Tsushima-maru* incident took place in August 1944. It involved the sinking of an Okinawan evacuation vessel for children, the *Tsushima-maru*, off Akuseki Island in the Tokara Archipelago near the southern coast of Kagoshima, by a U.S. submarine torpedo with the loss of 1,484 lives.

Hashimoto was circumspect.

Ota told the reporters that he feared a life-threatening accident and that he wanted an end to the live artillery-firing exercises across Prefectural Highway 104 and the early return of Futenma Air Station, located as it was right in the middle of town.

Ota was upbeat. He looked calm as he reported that he had been able to speak with Hashimoto in the same good atmosphere as formerly with former Prime Minister Murayama and that he expected to be able to reassure the Okinawans about the prime minister.

During the Diet session on the failed housing finance corporations, Hashimoto was kept busy from morning to night with the deliberations, but he was reading Ota's book whenever he found a spare moment. Hashimoto was perfectly serious when he said that he could understand why the people of Okinawa were so angry when he read what the book had to say about the expropriation process.

Their second meeting was on March 22, when they had a meal together at a Chinese restaurant, Rogairo, in Roppongi. Just a stone's throw from Hashimoto's home, it had been a favorite for almost 20 years.

Hashimoto kept emptying his glass and pouring Ota very full glasses of Xiao Xin Jiu (Chinese wine). The competitive Ota raised his pitch, saying, "Well, well, a Jia Fan vintage? An excellent wine." The cuisine was Shanghai. On the table was shark's fin, sea cucumber, deep fried prawns, and crab. Both Hashimoto and Ota sucked on the Shanghai crabs.

Ota mentioned the fact that the former U.S. ambassador to Japan, Edwin Reischauer, had said that Okinawa is like a bone stuck in the throat of the bilateral relationship. Reischauer said if you didn't remove the bone, things wouldn't be normalized, and he looked for a solution during his time as ambassador. "I think there are still people like Reischauer among the Americans," said Ota.

Ota also mentioned that America was a diverse society. It wasn't as if everyone was arguing like the government and the military for holding fast to the 100,000 or the 47,000 line or the marines. There had to be someone who was thinking in more flexible, long-range terms.

Up until that point, Ota had entertained a certain image of Hashimoto. "Reading a lot of what had been written about him, I had the impression that he was high and mighty, and extremely egotistical." But "he was really very good-humored when you met him."[4]

Hashimoto and Ota continued to meet after that on a regular basis. Most of their meetings took place following landmarks in the security and bases question.

Hashimoto opened up to Ota to a remarkable degree. Hashimoto was good with policy, but rather than with policy, he tried to reach Ota via Okinawan sentiment.

He told him about his cousin, Genzaburo Hashimoto, a favorite cousin who had died in the war.

Told only that he was "not repatriated from the southwest islands," Hashimoto later learned from his father that the southwest islands actually referred to Okinawa. The cousin had been a navy pilot. "He treated me a little differently than my other cousins when I was down. He made me feel good. He used to come all the way out to visit me just on purpose. He probably thought he was going to die sometime. It would have been around April 1944. I would have just been starting first grade, and he used to pat me on my head and tell me he'd be coming back to the woods in Yasukuni, so I'd better come over and visit him. And don't forget to do what your mother tells you to. And that was it."[5]

Hashimoto's face changed to that of a young boy's when talking about Big Brother Genzaburo. His spirit is enshrined at the Yasukuni Shrine. They received the official notification of his death on October 16, 1944. Ever since, Hashimoto has treated that day as the anniversary of Big Brother Genzaburo's death.

Hashimoto also told Ota, "I've been to Okinawa 23 times, 3 times with my family." From time to time, the number of times he's visited Okinawa goes up or down a few, but there's no doubt that of all the Japanese prime ministers, he has visited Okinawa the most.

Mentor Eisaku Sato

Hashimoto's connections with Okinawa stem in large part from his mentor, Eisaku Sato, one of the most blue-blooded conservative politicians in postwar Japan.

When Prime Minister Sato came back from visiting Okinawa in 1965, he stirred up the young politicians, including Hashimoto, telling them to get down to Okinawa and get up on their soapboxes to let the Okinawans know the mainland hadn't forgotten them. He also told them to make sure they visited the Himeyuri Corps' memorial and to check out how noisy the U.S. planes were, how big the bases were, and how dependent the economy was on the bases.

The Himeyuri Memorial is dedicated to the souls of the 200 pupils and teachers of the No. 1 Girls' High School. After serving bravely in the war as nurses right until the very end, the Himeyuri Corps were killed by shells or gas bombs or took their own lives. The memorial is a grave for the unknown located at a battle site on the southern tip of Okinawa. Some 35,000 memorial pillars are dedicated there.

Led by Sosuke Uno, head of the LDP's youth section at the time of Sato's prompting, two groups of politicians visited not only the main island but other outlying islands including Miyako, Yaeyama, and Ishigaki.

Hashimoto gave a soapbox speech on Ishigaki. He remembers, "Wherever we went the trees were small. They'd only grown that much. I felt they were telling me how severe the fighting had been on Okinawa."[5]

Hashimoto had no idea how Sato was moving ahead with the negotiations on Okinawa's reversion. That belonged to the realm of diplomatic secrecy and there was no way he could know. But he had begun to learn a thing or two in the thrust and parry of the LDP's formidable factional wars, especially the one over the election of the LDP chairman in November 1968. Sato's vision for Okinawa—"nonnuclear, on a par with the mainland"—was part of it all.

Masayoshi Ohira, who was lobbying to stop Sato running a third time, was cool to Sato's idea, saying it was like "a cat trying to bite a whale," while Takeo Miki, not of the mainstream and who had also been campaigning under the banner of no third election, committed himself to the very same "nonnuclear, on a par with the mainland" platform when he himself ran for LDP chairman.

In any event, there is no doubt that both positions of "can't be done" and "what are you going to do if it can't?" were connected to factional rivalries. What's more, Miki was the foreign minister.

Sato, in the meantime, was exploring the possibility of a "nonnuclear, on a par with the mainland" reversion behind the scenes, while making statements in public that suggested a considerable backdown. Tactically, he was forced to resort to this kind of subterfuge.

For Hashimoto, politics began with Eisaku Sato. His father, Ryugo, who had lost out by belonging to a small faction, asked Sato to look out for his boy. Ryugo had served as minister for health and welfare as well as director-general of the Administrative Management Agency in the third Yoshida Cabinet. A former career bureaucrat at the Ministry of Finance, he shared both temperament and political ideas with Sato. He was part of the same study group Yoshida had put together for young bureaucrats from different ministries with political aspirations, and they were all elected together.

Sato was the head of his faction when the younger Hashimoto was elected, not to mention having been the formal go-between at Hashimoto's wedding. There would be no Hashimoto today if it hadn't been for Sato.

Hashimoto subsequently attached himself to the mainstream faction of Kakuei Tanaka and then to its successor, Noboru Takeshita's faction.

But as Seiroku Kajiyama points out, "He worshipped Sato as his mentor and acted as his follower. He doesn't think of himself as Tanaka's disciple."

Hashimoto always has a photo of Eisaku Sato in his office. When he holds public office, it comes along to his official office. It is a photo taken when Sato received the Nobel Peace Prize. The photo shows him in slight profile, with a happy, slightly plump face. And his hair is long.

Sato had let Hashimoto into a "very confidential matter": He wanted to grow his hair long but said it wouldn't do while he was still prime minister. It was about the time he was saying he wanted to be called "Ei-chan" to change his "aloof and cold" image.

But Hashimoto and Sato were miles apart both in age and status. They were not veteran campaigners who had been through the wars together. For Hashimoto, Sato was probably something like Mt. Fuji, a figure to be looked up to and worshipped from afar.

Even in *The Journals of Eisaku Sato* (Asahi Shimbunsha), there is no mention of Sato paying particular attention to Hashimoto's qualities or future potential. Rather, one finds sharp criticisms to the effect that Hashimoto was still a long way from being a politician worth his salt.[7] In Kakuei Tanaka and Takeo Fukuda's neck-and-neck battle for LDP chairman, Hashimoto went for Tanaka. This looked like "ingratitude" to Sato, who wanted "above everything else to make Fukuda prime minister."[8]

In the final analysis, Hashimoto was a self-made man.

Eisaku Sato's crowning achievement as prime minister was the reversion of Okinawa. And yet, Sato's reputation in Okinawa fluctuated.

Hashimoto believes Sato's exhaustion from Okinawa put Sato in an early grave. He may be right.

Okinawa's reversion was certainly a magnificent political and diplomatic achievement, but it also exacted a huge price. It has been pointed out that "threads" were exchanged for "a rope" in the Sato-Nixon summit of 1969. The argument is that Sato was forced to curb Japanese textile exports (the threads) to the United States in exchange for Okinawa's return (Okinawa means "rope in the offing" in Japanese).

Sato also had to announce that "South Korean security is of vital importance to Japanese security" and "maintaining peace and security in the area of Taiwan is also extremely important to Japanese security."

And finally, while the reversion of Okinawa was meant to be "non-nuclear, on a par with the mainland," there existed a secret agreement that in times of "grave emergency" the United States would be guaranteed the right to bring nuclear weapons in or transport them via Japan.

Will Sato's achievements stand up to historical scrutiny? It is difficult to say. But in spite of everything, Hashimoto's assessment of Sato's legacy in Okinawa was gentle. "If only Sato-san had lived a little longer,

Okinawa might be a little different today. Not anything glaring, but in his own unassuming way he might have been able to adjust the bases, to deal more skillfully with the local residents, and it might be a quieter kind of place."[9]

Sato was the first prime minister to visit Okinawa while in office. He did this on August 9, 1965. He declared, "Without the return of Okinawa to its homeland, the postwar period is not over for Japan." It is a phrase that has gone down in the annals of postwar Japanese politics.

But Sato could not carry out his promises to Okinawa. Promising Okinawa's economic development, he gave up office the very year of its reversion.

It was bad luck too that the following year Japan was hit by the oil shock.

I wish I could do something; it would also be repaying my mentor, Eisaku Sato. Hashimoto had the habit of seeing these kinds of bonds in terms of destiny.

Seiroku Kajiyama, Cabinet secretary, was also not afraid to voice publicly the view that he had found his place as a politician in the Okinawa question. Kajiyama was a powerful force within the LDP and was consolidating power in his position as Cabinet secretary for the coalition government.

The Hashimoto Cabinet was perched atop a very delicate power balance, and relations between Kajiyama and Hashimoto were at times a little tricky. Kajiyama felt Hashimoto was distant toward him, even though he was meant to be his right-hand man. He has no memory of the two of them spending time together in private. Seeing Hashimoto eating lunch with his private secretaries, Kajiyama didn't even try to hide his displeasure with "secretary politics." But the two were in step on Okinawa.

Hashimoto once told Ota something like this: "Cabinet Secretary Kajiyama and myself are doing our damn best on Okinawa. Can you imagine anything changing that? It's because the two of us are in on this together that I think we'll be able to muddle our way through." Ota felt the same.

In early April 1997, leaders of the LDP were trying to keep the three-way coalition among the LDP, the Socialists, and Sakigake together over the Special Measures Act on Expropriation of Land for U.S. Military Use. When the LDP leaders and people from the PM's office side, who were trying to get the bill passed by an overwhelming majority through a conservative alliance, all gathered together, Kajiyama yelled at Taku Yamazaki, chairman of the LDP's Policy Research Council: "I've staked my life on Okinawa. Don't stick your nose in! Are you prepared to take the responsibility if we can't get the Special Measures Act amended?"

When it came to Okinawa, Kajiyama's language was apt to harshen. Kajiyama lost his brother when he was a member of the Ibaragi Prefectural Assembly. His elder brother, Naoji, ran Joriku Marble, a company which processed stalagmites and stalactites into ornamental construction materials. He used coral from Okinawa. He had been to Okinawa many times during the Occupation. Kajiyama had often accompanied his brother, some 20 years older than him, to Okinawa.

Kajiyama had heard his brother say that it would be better if Okinawa didn't revert to the mainland; Okinawans might be happier if they got independence. His last wish was that Kajiyama did not forget Okinawa.

Kajiyama's feelings are expressed well in a memo called "U.S.-Japan Security and Okinawa": "It's late, but I can't get off to sleep thinking about this and that on Okinawa. I try to force myself to sleep by saying, right, I'll make a clean start on Okinawa tomorrow. And right on cue, an image of the Mabuni on Okinawa appears before my eyes. When I visited that hill, site of the last fierce battle of World War II and of so many deaths, I couldn't do anything to stop my tears. I think anyone who had been through the war like me would feel the same."

Ota was almost the same age as Kajiyama. Their relationship was close. "He knew from hard and bitter experience the misery of war. That's why I talk with Kajiyama-san about trying to make a society that's even just a tiny bit better for our children."[10]

Kajiyama was known as a bare-knuckles fighter, but there was a part of him that was pacifist. Every now and again, the pacifist spring or the nationalistic spring inside him would show up in his antagonism towards the U.S. military presence or the bases. He used to tell Ota to hang in there, you can say what we can't so stay in there.

Kajiyama's feelings on Okinawa vacillated. "If we just sold it [Futenma Air Station] off quietly, we wouldn't have to move it, but that would walk all over Okinawan feelings. At the same time, I feel ashamed deep down that all we've done is to make things more complicated by stirring up all this mud."[11]

Ota had decided there was nothing for it but to build up a relationship of trust with Hashimoto and Kajiyama and to bank on it.

Deputy Cabinet Secretary Sadajiro Furukawa was the person at the PM's office who kept in close communication with the top of the prefectural government in Okinawa. After having made it to permanent vice-minister for health and welfare (a career bureaucrat's post), he became deputy Cabinet secretary during the Murayama government. When the Hashimoto government was formed, he was asked by Hashimoto to stay on.

Unusual for a bureaucrat who had made it to the pinnacle of Kasumigaseki, Furukama was not a graduate of Tokyo University but of

Kyushu University and had worked in the Nagasaki prefectural government before joining the Ministry of Health and Welfare (MHW).

Furukawa joined the MHW in 1960, the year of the fierce anti–Security Treaty protests. Every day the streets of Kasumigaseki were filled with marching students and rang with slogans from their megaphones. His conscience pricked as he listened to them.

During his lunch break he joined one of the demonstrators' groups as they left Hibiya Park. Linking arms with the people on either side, he joined them in shouting slogans: "Down with the Security Treaty!" "Kishi Cabinet resign!"

He got as far as Ginza before he realized everyone else in the group was female. No wonder when he put his arms around them they were so small! It was a group of demonstrators from Noda Shoyu (Kikkoman today).

It was much later that Furukawa found himself spending time at the PM's office as counselor to the Cabinet. At the time of former Prime Minister Nobusuke Kishi's death, he was put in charge of the joint Cabinet and LDP funeral arrangements. He carefully read Kishi's works, tracing Kishi's political and strategic outlook at the time of the Security Treaty's amendment.

He felt he caught a glimpse of Kishi's philosophy on life. "If he thought something was necessary for the state, he didn't curry favor no matter how much the people criticized. Even if he was labeled a traitor, he was resigned as a politician to wait for history's verdict."

What music should Kishi be sent off with? Furukawa heard from someone who knew him well that Kishi often sang his high school song while taking a bath. He asked the New Japan Philharmonic to arrange "Our Cup Overflows with Flowers" as a funeral march.

Furukawa laughs now. "I paid my dues for opposing the Security Treaty by doing my best to arrange Kishi-san's funeral."[12]

The generation that joined the workforce or went on to postgraduate studies in the year of the Security Treaty amendment, 1960, was just reaching the top of the bureaucracy. Furukawa was one of them.

He was born into a farming family in Saga. In high school, he used to dig up *gobo*, a hardy vegetable with deep roots, dressed in just a singlet on winter mornings when the sleet came down. That may be where he learned the art of *nemawashi*, the consensus-building process in Japanese politics, applying a deft tug here, a sharp twist there.

Even today, there is an earthy smell to him. He has a small hobby farm in Kujukuri, Chiba, where he grows sweet potatoes, leeks, and Chinese watermelons. This is well known, and when he retired from the MHW, his juniors at the ministry bought him a small tractor as their farewell gift.

Furukawa had especially close relations with the vice-governor of Okinawa, Masanori Yoshimoto. Yoshimoto was a man of proven ability who had worked his way up from the labor movement.

Yoshimoto, who did not make friends easily but when he did he did so for life, hit it off with Furukawa. Furukawa and Yoshimoto were not afraid to admit they "felt a comradeship."

Yoshimoto was indispensable to Ota when he was negotiating with the central government. He was also indispensable to the PM's office when they were trying to decide something with Ota.

Both Kajiyama and Furukawa were greatly impressed with Yoshimoto's abilities. The PM's office was sometimes required to deal separately with "the idea man Ota" and "the practical man Yoshimoto."

On September 10, 1996, during a meeting between Hashimoto and Ota at the PM's office, when Ota was pushing for Hashimoto to visit Okinawa, Yoshimoto said somewhat cheekily, "I was at the head of the picketers when Sato-san came to Okinawa. I won't do that to you, sir."

Everyone burst out laughing. (Sato's historic visit to Okinawa actually met with huge demonstrations from hostile Okinawans.)

A week later, after Hashimoto's visit to Okinawa was over, Yoshimoto placed a call to Furukawa. "The prime minister has just this moment departed from the airport. He has left safely without a single stone being thrown."[13] Yoshimoto's tone was relieved but jaunty.

Public Notice and Inspection

It was, in fact, Prime Minister Tomiichi Murayama who invited Ota to the PM's office and gave him an unprecedentedly warm welcome. They met at the prime minister's residence on November 4, 1995.

On September 28 Ota had refused to sign the procedures for the expropriation of land for U.S. military use. The prefecture was being asked by the state to sign in place of those landowners who refused to sign the public notice and inspection papers, the arbitration application required when the government expropriated land from those who refused to provide their land for American military use. Ota had refused to do so.

Noboru Hoshuyama, director-general of the Defense Facilities Administration Agency, had flown to Okinawa in an attempt to change Ota's mind, but he went home having failed even to make contact with Ota. On October 21, a huge demonstration took place on Okinawa to protest the rape of a young Okinawan girl by U.S. soldiers.

Okinawa was making a "J'accuse" indictment.

In the meeting, Murayama apologized. "In your speech to the 100,000 people gathered to protest the rape, you apologized saying it was your fault for not being able to protect her virginity, but it is not your responsibility alone. I believe both the Cabinet and the prime minister are also at fault. Before, during, and after the war, how much have we really understood the suffering of the Okinawan people? We are made acutely aware of how much when we visit and look around, but back home we forget before we know it."

He went on, "You as the governor have the power of proxy. I realize that this was a difficult decision for you, that you must have thought long and hard. In light of Okinawan sentiment, it is not my intention to ask you to sign again. However, the provision of bases is an obligation under the U.S.-Japan Security Treaty. This time it is my turn to make a hard decision."[14]

The prefecture had made it clear that it would not cooperate in any way with the land use procedures applied to the U.S. base landowners without contracts, nor would it use its power of proxy. In response, the government decided to open talks with the prefecture in the Council on the Question of the U.S. Bases in Okinawa (tentative name); at the same time, with an eye on the expiration date of land usage for the bases, it was getting the paperwork ready to file suit on the performance of duties.

Murayama told Ota, "The government has no choice but to file suit."

Ota answered quietly, "I have no intention of fighting with the government."

President Clinton was scheduled to visit Japan on November 20. The leaders meant to reconfirm bilateral security ties at that time.

If the prefecture refused to sign the proxy papers, the government could do nothing but issue the order to sue the prefecture. If the prefecture still refused, the government would then sign in its place. Murayama wanted to let Ota know that things were moving in that direction. No legal blank could be permitted for the bases, not with Clinton coming. There was no time left.

Ota changed the subject. "Trouble with the bases is an everyday affair. But there is no framework on how we can discuss matters with the government or what procedures are to be followed."

Ota later said, "That being the case, we appealed directly to the Americans, but when we did, the Japanese government treated us coldly, telling us not to go sticking our noses into where we weren't invited."[15]

Murayama said that that wouldn't do, and promised he would get the Cabinet secretary to set up a vehicle for dialogue between the Japanese government and Okinawa Prefecture as soon as possible and to take an official decision in Cabinet on it.

In the beginning, relations between the PM's office and Okinawa Prefecture did not go smoothly.

Yoshimoto had made a confidential request to meet with Koken Nosaka, Murayama's chief Cabinet secretary, but Nosaka refused to see him one-on-one, saying, "He may well be the vice-governor of Okinawa, but a vice-governor is a vice-governor." Nosaka couldn't see why the Cabinet secretary had to meet a prefectural vice-governor; a Cabinet counselor could deal with it.

Yoshimoto was downcast, all the more so because with a Socialist government in power, as a seasoned labor union leader he had expected the Socialists' leaders to show a little more interest in Okinawa.

It was Hideyuki Maeshima, deputy secretary-general of the SDP, who stepped in to try to mediate between Yoshimoto and Nosaka. Maeshima knew Yoshimoto through the labor movement, having been in the All Japan Prefectural and Municipal Workers' Union himself.

Since Nozaka refused to give him the nod in spite of everything, Maeshima recommended Yoshimoto meet with Koichi Kato, secretary-general of the LDP, and arranged a meeting for them.[16]

Yoshimoto related to Kato in minute detail that Governor Ota had no intention of signing the papers, that there was a "high possibility that he was prepared to go to the wall saying no," and that this was his last resort after four years of being governor, because, in the final analysis, the central government wasn't serious about Okinawa at all.

Four years earlier, in 1991, Yoshimoto said that not a single one of the "Three Items" Yukihiko Ikeda, director-general of the JDA, had promised had been fulfilled. He pulled a scrap of paper out of his pocket with the three items on it and showed it to Kato. The first item was to work towards the return of the bases and to set up some sort of vehicle. Although a cross-ministry liaison council had been set up on how to use the base sites, nothing of any importance had been decided.

Ota was elected governor in December 1990. His first test came as soon as the new year. He was asked by the government to sign as proxy the public notice and inspection papers.

Ota initially looked like he would refuse. But if he did, it would inevitably have a huge impact on the Third Okinawa Economic Development Plan (1992–2001), Okinawa's economic lifeline. The government was already making sounds that it would sue over performance of duties, its trump card.

After agonizing for three months, Ota consented to sign. But then the government once again forgot all about Okinawa. Ota's mistrust of the central government grew deeper.

He was painfully aware that "he hadn't understood the politics." He had been taught the hard lesson that no matter how much they dealt with them in good faith, it was literally politics. Even if he did petition the central government, it was humiliating. He was "treated with contempt"; this "isn't a request or a petition. It's a solicitation." The stance of the central government was nothing more than "conceding a request."[17]

Neither the Kaifu Cabinet, nor the Miyazawa Cabinet, nor the Hosokawa Cabinet would listen to Ota's appeal. The very best Ota could do was speak at the National Prefectural Governors Association. Even there, he was always last on the bill. By that time, the prime minister had left. The director-general of the JDA or the Defense Facilities Administration Agency answered in his place, but they did nothing more than read out their prepared responses.

And yet, progress was made in some cases. Ota had recently been calling for the enactment of a Base Return Action Program (Law Containing Procedures Used in Returning Military Facilities and Promoting Utilization of Returned Land). This was a law requiring the government to pay the land rentals to owners of military sites returned, from the day following the return and for no longer than a period of three years.

In order to resolve the issue of the bases, the fears and anxieties of the landowners had to be alleviated. To that end, a system needed to be put in place where landowners' income would not fall to zero from day one of return and that would guarantee land rentals for a certain period even after the sites had been returned. It was an idea that had been originally put forward by Tatsuo Taira, who had been elected to the position of governor of Okinawa in 1950 and who had been instrumental in working for the reversion of Okinawa to Japan.

Ota requested this anew. Elected on his promise for the "base realignment and reduction," it was something he really wanted to achieve.

The proposal had been around for more than 10 years. The Okinawa Development Agency refused to budge. So, using legislation by House members in the Diet, it was introduced three times after 1980, but failed each time.

With the birth of the Murayama government, the atmosphere changed. Kosuke Uehara (SDP) and other members of the lower house from Okinawa took an active interest. The Special Measures bill passed in May 1995. "The LDP saved our face in a symbol of LDP-Socialist reconciliation," Uehara explained.[18]

The return of the Naha Seamen's Club, decided in 1993, was also the fruit of Ota's tenacious requests, petitions, and appeals. The Naha Seamen's Club, as the U.S. military called it, was a restaurant and entertainment facility for crews putting in to Naha Port. It shared the same no-tax preferential status as the bases, and it also had some Japanese members.

Ota campaigned that the location of the Naha Seamen's Club in a civilian area and its exemption from the food and drink tax was a holdover from the Occupation days. He said it should be relocated to a U.S. base.

The question had already been placed on the list of the 10 Facilities–18 Proposals for further consideration in the U.S.-Japan Joint Council, which was the vehicle for bilateral talks on the bases, but nothing had happened since.

Ota also made a direct request to Michael Armacost, the then U.S. ambassador to Japan. He had even asked the top embassy staff seated at his table when he was invited to the official lunch during President George Bush's visit to Japan.

He had made up his mind. *If the central bureaucracy is going to stay indifferent, then I have no option but to go over their heads and talk directly with the Americans.*

The central government had never once tried to deal with the Okinawan issue directly. There were huge obstacles in the way of realigning and/or reducing the bases. Every time an agenda for the return of the bases was announced there were fancy tags like 10 Facilities–18 Proposals or 23 Proposals or 3 Proposals, but they all disappeared into the night like so many fireworks.

Ota felt completely isolated. Following his 1990 decision to comply with the proxy signing, there was no subsequent impact whatsoever. The JDA's director-general's three items were thrown out like an old pair of shoes.

And then the rape incident occurred. There was no way the prefectural population would accept "compliance" this time. As Yoshimoto told Koichi Kato, Ota was prepared to "go to the wall saying no."

The Land and the Bases

Tomiichi Murayama was also fretting about Okinawa. Although the Socialists could go as far as saying they supported the treaty and that the Self-Defense Forces were constitutional, redefining bilateral security was too heavy a burden. Murayama couldn't let them split over security. But he was being inundated by a flood of momentous political events: the Kobe quake, the sarin gas attack, the Anti-Subversive Activities Act, the housing finance corporation scandal, the injection of public funds. The PM's office spent the days in a whirl and Murayama's concern over Okinawa fell into complete chaos.

Hideyuki Maeshima recollects, "They found themselves in government totally unprepared. The party top didn't really do much to follow up even the policy switch on security!"[19]

The Clinton visit was cancelled.

On November 19, Murayama met with President Clinton's stand-in, Vice President Al Gore, and revealed to him that they had decided to go ahead with filing the suit on performance of duties in order to get the proxy signature for the procedures to expropriate land for U.S. military use.

That night, Ota attended a very lively "Second World Uchinanchu ('Okinawans' in their own language) Congress," held in the Okinawa Convention Center in Ginowan City. He held a rushed press conference as soon as he learned what Murayama had said. Ota spat the words out: "What do they think Okinawa is? Really! Okinawa refuses to sacrifice its own human rights and a humane life for the happiness of the main-land. We had enough of that during the war."

With "is Okinawa Japan?" as his parting word, Ota stood up and left.[20] The alcohol from the party may have been doing some of the talking, but Ota was furious.

On November 21, Prime Minister Murayama issued Governor Ota an official warning to make the proxy signing for the land expropriation for military use.

On December 7, the prime minister filed suit against Governor Ota over his failure to perform duties regarding land expropriation for U.S. military sites.

On March 25, 1996, the verdict was handed down by the Naha branch of the Fukuoka High Court. "The Governor is instructed to sign the papers by proxy in the next three days." The Prefecture of Okinawa appealed immediately to the Supreme Court.

On March 29, 1996, Prime Minister Hashimoto signed the proxy papers. It was the fourth time expropriation had been applied under the Special Measures Act, but it was the first time the prime minister had signed.

The scene was set for an internecine struggle over the land and the bases. It was a clash between property rights and national interest. There was tension between the Constitution and the bilateral treaty. There was dissension among Okinawa, Japan, and the United States.

These contradictions reached their zenith from 1995 to 1996, at the time of the shift from the Murayama to the Hashimoto government.

Murayama entertained the thought that it was he who had to do it.

In the Diet, a Japan Communist Party member of the upper house went to the heart of the matter: The bilateral treaty had to be scrapped to be rid of base crimes and the review of the bilateral Status Agreement was a top priority. These were exactly the same arguments the Socialists, Murayama included, had made themselves until recently. Murayama replied, "Our premises are different."[21]

The house was in an uproar. Murayama followed up, "Taken comprehensively, the bilateral security structure, including its political significance in both countries, is extremely formidable."

Japan Communist Party member Hiroshi Kikunami parried with, "You said our stance is different, but I would like to point out that just until the other day, the Socialist Party took exactly the same position on scrapping the treaty. We won't accept any trumped-up answers about different positions!" While the Socialists were no longer hesitant about maintaining the Security Treaty, Okinawa was a different question.

It was precisely because there was a Socialist prime minister in office that they had to take this most difficult, toughest decision. Wouldn't that be better too for stopping Okinawa from becoming too radical?

I'll be the sacrificial lamb. Murayama seemed to find a certain pleasure in martyrdom.

But in the face of these contradictions and tension, Murayama's subjective thoughts just ran round in circles, and the Socialists were in utter disarray.

Yoshimoto said that Murayama had his own ideas but didn't know what to do with them,[22] but the same could be said of the SDP as a whole.

There was a time, early on, when the LDP set their hopes on a connection between the SDP and the reformist prefectural government. There was a keenness on the part of the Socialists as well to handle matters.

The LDP leadership, however, was aware that the only Socialist who could talk frankly with the Okinawa leadership was Hideyuki Maeshima.[23] And it was true that there were only a very few who could trace close ties to Yoshimoto through the labor movement. In the end, it was the LDP, and the Hashimoto government at that, that took over the Okinawan problem.

The LDP's assessment of Ota wavered with every turn. Even Hashimoto started to show irritation when he met with Ota at the height of the debate on the Special Measures Act in the spring of 1997. "He can't make up his mind on anything. Sitting on the fence again?" Sometimes he blew up with his private secretaries. Kajiyama said more than once or twice as if throwing in the towel, "Don't forget he's an academic!" Kajiyama used to say it was because Ota had pushed on Futenma's return that the PM had gone all out for it. That's why he wanted him to help on finding an alternative site. If he didn't, "It would be more than the PM could stand."[24]

The LDP was impatient with Ota, wondering why he didn't just cut off all his connections with the left-wing camp he came out of and become the "Chairman of the Prefectural People's Party."

There was something that the core of the administration had decided. Ota should not be made into some tragic hero. "If we made him into a tragic hero, Okinawa would be done for good. So would Japan. So we worked towards avoiding that at all costs." "He can't be a tragic hero now that we've come this far; he's in the same boat as the rest of us."[25] These were the whispers that could be heard in the heart of the administration.

All sorts of reproofs and noise could be heard back in Okinawa about Ota and Yoshimoto being so close to the PM's office. "The governor says he's built up a relationship of trust with the prime minister, but it's only the governor who's being sold out." "The governor's joined forces with the PM to push through their lying policies to keep Okinawa down."

Ota was not afraid to come out and say that he was placing his faith in his relationship of trust with Hashimoto. Ota was a man of frank disposition. Sometimes this guilelessness scared the living daylights out of those around him.

During the fall 1996 general elections, Ota came out in support of the Hashimoto government, eliciting quite a bit of talk. It was the first election under the new system of single-representative districts. Nobody knew how things were going to turn out. The opposition New Frontier Party was running a "Down-with-Hashimoto" campaign in Okayama, Hashimoto's homeground. Ota was worried that Hashimoto just might lose.

Ota was worrying about it so much, Yoshimoto reached the point where he felt like saying half jokingly, half teasingly, "Why don't you go off to Okayama then and join Hashimoto on his soapbox?"

But after a moment's thought, Ota turned around and said in all seriousness, "You go for me." Yoshimoto joked a little drolly, "No, it's no good if it's only the vice-governor. It has to be the governor, Governor."[26]

Afterwards they laughed about it.

The Lost and the Last

Ota learned of the end of World War II on October 23, 1945. More than two months had passed since the end of hostilities. He was on the southernmost tip of the main island at Mabuni Hill. He was 20 years old. He knew nothing about the emperor's radio broadcast or the unconditional surrender on board the USS *Missouri*.

A student at the Okinawa Teachers College, Ota was forcibly enlisted into the Blood and Iron Student Corps by the Okinawa Reserves Command. It was his job to take the Imperial Headquarters news to the locals in the evacuation shelters.

They were already completely surrounded. He didn't even know how to use a rifle properly. He was nothing more than a straggler, creeping up under cover of night to the tents of the American soldiers, throwing in grenades and making off with food.

Corpses blown up like balloons washed up onto the shore near Mabuni, where he was hiding, every day. As the days came and went, he was just staring at them absentmindedly.

Ota wrote about being a living corpse, both body and mind in pieces:

> Even though I felt a certain sense of guilt towards the teachers and friends I had seen die right before my eyes, I still couldn't help but be glad that I'd survived.
>
> At the same time, I found my "way of life" up until then inexpressibly sickening and I was incensed at the enormous power that was the state that had only allowed me to live that way. . . .
>
> Looking back, I started grade school the year of the Manchurian incident and when I graduated Japan was at war with China. When the Pacific War broke out, it was the year I entered the Okinawa Teachers

College. It was in this way that by the time I could understand what was going on around me, all of my education was literally "imperial" and "militaristic." As a result, I was immersed in passionate militarist ideology, both body and soul, and even a normal, shy boy like myself was skillfully transformed into a strapping "militant boy" by the time the Pacific War broke out.[27]

One day, he picked up some canned food and a copy of an American magazine. It was *Life*. Ota couldn't read English, but Corporal Usui, hiding out with him, could.

Corporal Usui said that his mother had raised him on her own. Ota didn't know his father either, because he had migrated to Brazil when Ota was one year old. That was part of the reason Ota was drawn to Usui and felt he was like a big brother.

Usui was a very kind person. He always carried with him a small *Webster*'s English dictionary. It never left his side even on the battlefield. That might have been why he never made it to officer but saw the war out as corporal. He said he had graduated from Tokyo University of Literature and Science (Tsukuba University today).

After a while, Corporal Usui put down the magazine and whispered to the young Ota, "Japan has surrendered."

Then he lowered his voice even further. "You mustn't tell anyone. We'll both be killed if you do."

Corporal Usui must have felt there was something to this young boy. "If we get out of this alive, go to Tokyo and learn English."[28]

How terrible it is to know nothing, not to be able to read. Ota smarted more at his own ignorance than at the news of Japan's defeat.

On October 23, Ota surrendered with a group of other prisoners. He was taken on a U.S. army truck to the Yaka POW camp in the township of Kin.

On the way, they approached a place called Hyakuna, where there was a camp for civilians. The civilians were let down off the truck. Corporal Usui said to Ota, "Get off! Get off! You're a civilian and you're a student here. Get off here. You shouldn't be put in a POW camp. Get off here and do something good for Okinawa's future."

He was a gentle man, but his words then were strong and intense.

But Ota didn't get off. He was dressed in uniform and was wearing a military cap. Even if he did get down, they'd take him for a soldier. "No, I'll go with everyone else." And so Ota went with them to the POW camp.

Ota had tried to find Corporal Usui several times after the war, but all traces had been lost and he never learned his friend's first name.

Very soon after the end of the war, Ota enlisted in a bomb disposal unit. They would ride around in jeeps, find an unexploded bomb, load it on the jeep, and drive along Prefectural Highway 104. "EXPLO-SIVE" was written all over the bombs, but at the time, he didn't know what it meant.

The Battle of Okinawa lasted three months, from April to June 1945. Bomb disposal has been going on for the past 50 years. Every year, bomb disposal is included in the prefectural budget (38 million yen in fiscal 1997; national treasury allocation for the same year, 313 million yen).

Ota comes originally from the island of Kume. His mother supported the family by cooking school meals, but the debts incurred to send his father overseas were heavy and life was tough. After graduating grade school, Ota had to work there as a janitor.

Ota entered Waseda University in 1950 when he was 25. His father came back when he was in his third year. Ota was at Waseda on a U.S. military scholarship. He then went to graduate school as an exchange student at Syracuse University in the United States.

When Ota was at Waseda, he and some others from Okinawa got a sculptor to sculpt a Peace Monument out of sheet copper. This was around the time of the Korean War, when you were labeled a Commie simply for using the word "peace." Ota was to go back to Okinawa to get ready for his trip to the United States. And he was going to take the Peace Memorial home.

Learning of his plans, his friends and teacher sent him letters and cables warning him that if he took the Peace Monument home hanging off his arm he might lose his trip to the United States; leave it at Nasada. But Ota went back to Okinawa with it in his arms. He was already marked by the Occupation Forces as "a deviant." So he topped it off with the Peace Monument. For a while his trip to the United States was doubtful.

The exchange students were to sail from White Beach, but come the night of the departure, Ota was left behind. Finally, at about 4:00 A.M., a U.S. Army jeep came to pick him up. Ota joined the rest of the exchange students, the U.S. soldiers, and base staff on the military boat and sailed for the United States via Taiwan.[30]

The Cornerstone of Peace

At Syracuse, Ota immersed himself in American democracy. He heard Martin Luther King's "I have a dream" speech and was deeply moved.[31] He also learned that baseball had a third base; people on Kume played with only two.[32]

He also went to debates on racial issues. His class heatedly debated for three days on how you should interpret the fact that while the media never wrote "white" when a white person committed a crime, it always included "black" when a black person was involved.

He was strongly impressed by the fact that "America is a place where they debate exhaustively the pros and cons of everything."

The conviction that "you had to debate everything to the very end" with the Americans; that you "had to state things clearly" with them was also born there. His trust in America, that it was all right to do that with America, grew, although "looking back today I was probably a bit too soft."[33]

After returning home, Ota became a professor at the Law Faculty of the University of the Ryukyus. He published a number of books, including *The Heart of Okinawa, The Ugly Japanese, Mass Consciousness in Okinawa,* and *Czar of Okinawa: The U.S. High Commissioner.*

He visited India in 1961. He wanted to follow in the footsteps of Gandhi. Gandhi's philosophy of passive resistance was a pacifist ideology that fascinated Ota throughout the postwar period. When he extracted the essence of his own experience of war, it led him to the same place.

Ota visited the Ganges where Gandhi had bathed. People were selling walking canes like the one Gandhi had used. Ota bought one.

India was appallingly poor. Ota was puzzled: "Why does a country which brought forth such a great leader have to suffer such misery?"

As he talked with people, however, he realized that they worshipped Gandhi as a saint and that his ideas were etched indelibly in their hearts.

India made him think about peace. "The shock it gave me changed my outlook on life." When thinking about peace, you had to think about what had to be protected from what and how. *What needs to be protected is not national identity or racial identity but human identity.*

What was human identity?

A memory of several naked U.S. soldiers during the war suddenly sprung to Ota's mind. They were sleeping naked. Ota was wearing a threadbare jacket thrown away by a Japanese officer. He was carrying a rifle. He was a soldier.

Ota raised the gun but he didn't shoot. He couldn't kill these naked, vulnerable men. "Some might be able to pull the trigger, but there are some who can't. Of course, I was terrified too. If I shot them and there was a counterattack, it'd be all up for me. But even so I just couldn't do it."

When he read in the papers that one of the guerrillas had hesitated and didn't shoot a hostage when the government troops stormed their way into the embassy during the Peru hostage crisis, what Ota remembered was himself at that time when he didn't shoot, when he couldn't shoot, and those naked, vulnerable men.

From a different angle, what about Okinawa? What about Japan?

The course of the people of Okinawa Prefecture over the last 100 years had been one of acquiring Japanese identity. "The key point for acquiring Japanese identity was to deny the Ryukyus' own traditions and culture and to imitate solely the language and customs of the other mainland prefectures."[34]

We have to have identities as Okinawans. But it can't be a passive identity where we join hands in despising and deploring discrimination from the mainland.

In March 1990, Ota concluded his last lecture at the University of the Ryukyus with this quote from Kunio Yanagida, one of the greatest humanists in modern Japan.

I want you to analyze minutely the discrimination towards Okinawa in the broader context of the structuralized discrimination throughout Japan; to gouge out its roots and to write a remedy for it. I want you to take the initiative. If you do, then the "light of learning" in Okinawa will overnight become a light for the whole country, a great hope starting, in turn, to grow for all humanity.

"It was with those words that Yanagida had urged his students on in their Okinawan studies." Ota's closing words were, "I hope in my heart to remain faithful to Kunio Yanagida's teachings." In other words, Ota would not be pursuing a search for national identity but for the basic conditions of human identity.[35]

Activism, Administration, Politics, and History

In 1990, Ota was "half dragged into politics," to use his own words.

He ran as the United Progressive candidate in the gubernatorial elections held in November. His campaign slogan was: "Peace, Coexistence, Autonomy." His two main campaign promises were getting rid of the bases and improving welfare and medical facilities for the elderly on outlying islands.

The Gulf crisis was taking place at the time. Military aircraft were taking off from the bases at a furious pace. Peace became a key issue in the election.

The incumbent, Governor Junji Nishime, was endorsed by the conservatives and had come out in favor of the PKO bill. Ota was against, which must have helped his cause because he beat Nishi by 30,000 votes.

He refused to use the headband or sash in his campaign, saying that it made him think of the war. No three cheers—*banzai, banzai, banzai*—were given either when he won.

In 1994, Ota was reelected overwhelmingly, easily defeating his challenger, a newcomer endorsed by the LDP. In the previous election, the contest between a conservative and progressive candidate was clear, but this time the policies of both candidates were not so far apart and the boundaries were blurred. Ota had a huge base of support, but rifts with the Socialists and Communists surfaced. Ota announced his plan to remove all the bases from Okinawan soil by 2015 and plans for a city of learning.

In 1995, the Cornerstone of Peace, a long-held dream of Ota's, was erected to commemorate the 50th anniversary of the end of the Pacific War and the Battle of Okinawa. The site of the last battle on Okinawa, Mabuni, was chosen as the location.

The names of all those who lost their lives in the Battle of Okinawa, regardless of their nationality, military or civilian status, age, or gender, were inscribed on the Cornerstone of Peace—in all, a total of 230,000 names.

However, virtually no progress was being made on reducing or eliminating the bases. To the contrary, there were moves in Washington and Tokyo to make them a permanent fixture.

Ota was shocked by the Nye Report of February 1995, which declared that U.S. forces in the Asian-Pacific region would be maintained at 100,000. If this was fixed for 10 or 20 years, there would be no movement on the realignment or reduction of the bases.

Ota began to attack the report vehemently. His attack was also prompted by an aversion to and mistrust of the one-sided handing down of an "edict from imperial headquarters" from the Pentagon's general staff in faraway Washington.

Ota said, "I saw during the war the tragic results of operations proposed at tables in the Imperial Army Headquarters hundreds of miles away from Okinawa. U.S. government thinking today bears a strong resemblance to that."[36]

At times like that, Ota even went so far as to bring up Staff Officer Jin. A staff officer of the 32nd Army in Okinawa, Naomichi Jin was a young major just over 30, who had been sent down from imperial headquarters. He was the envy of all the students. When asked, "Do you really think we can really repulse the American army when it comes?" he had no compunction in replying, "It will be nothing to Japan even if every last one of the million Okinawans dies an honorable death for the emperor (*gyokusai*)!" The militant young Ota admired him all the more.

Staff Officer Jin had been an officer in the air force. So he was in his element talking strategy, about how air force operations were the key to Okinawa, how we were going to blow the U.S. planes to smithereens when they arrived exhausted from their long flights, that's why we have to build airfields everywhere.

Ota and others were made to walk all night from Shuri to Yomitan, where an airfield was to be built, and work on its construction. They slept in tents and were laden down with straw baskets moving earth from dawn to dusk.

But after they had built the airfield, there were no planes. It didn't serve any purpose. Just the reverse, for when it got to the stage when the Americans were going to land, Jin barked that they had to destroy it fast.

"That's what I was most opposed to in the Nye Report." For Ota, not only the Nye Report but both the relocation and consolidation of the bases looked very much like the works of Staff Officer Jin and the decisions of the imperial headquarters at his rear.

(Naomichi Jin was ordered back to imperial headquarters a few days after the resounding defeat of the 32nd Army's comprehensive counteroffensive in May 1945 to make a direct appeal for planes to be sent to Okinawa. He left from Itoman with six fishermen in a five-meter-long dugout canoe. Slipping by the American patrol boats, he made it to Kagoshima. He made an impassioned appeal to the imperial headquarters but was told that they had already given up on Okinawa and were switching over to a battle for the mainland.)

Ota *is* Okinawa; he is the personification of its modern history of war and peace. Each of his words is plucked leaf by leaf from the tree of modern Okinawan history. If Ota has his contradictions, it is because Okinawa is itself one huge contradiction in the annals of modern Japanese history.

It is difficult to judge Ota by normal measures. Being an academic makes him too sharp as an activist. Being an activist gives him too strong a sense of responsibility as a top administrator. Being a top administrator, his political awareness is too finely honed. And being a politician, his historical awareness is too consummate.

It seems too that Ota is increasingly fascinated by the historical context of people who have left their mark either on ideology, the state, political parties, activism, or support organizations.

In a meeting with Murayama, he spoke of a book by Kei Wakaizumi. It is called *We Desire to Believe There Was No Other Choice* and was published in 1994 by Bungei Shunju. Wakaizumi was formerly a professor at the Kyoto Sangyo University. He was involved in the reversion of Okinawa as Prime Minister Sato's secret envoy.

In the book, Wakaizumi affirms that during the Sato-Nixon negotiations on returning Okinawa, "a secret pact on bringing nuclear weapons into Okinawa during times of emergency was signed by the two leaders."[37]

The existence of a secret pact on Okinawa had long been rumored since reversion. It was suspected that a pact had been signed in which "nonnuclear, on a par with the mainland" came with the following conditions: (1) the reintroduction into and the transit of nuclear weapons through Okinawa would be permitted in times of emergency;

and (2) the two governments would start secret negotiations on voluntary restraints on Japanese textile exports into America.

If this was true, it would be a serious betrayal by both governments.

It seems highly likely that Wakaizumi decided to publish the book
out of his "personal feelings of responsibility toward Okinawa."[38]

Ota told Murayama that there would be all hell to pay if this got out,
but his warning failed to resonate with Murayama, who replied merely
that he had had the Foreign Ministry look into it and that nothing like
it had taken place.

Wakaizumi became a famous mouthpiece for the conservatives
when still young, and Ota didn't think much of him and his American-
ized ways.

This is what made Wakaizumi's claim all the stranger.

Upon learning that Wakaizumi had considered committing suicide
in Okinawa, and that he visited Okinawa every June 23 to help gather
the remains of the still unknown dead, Ota thought to himself: *There's
no understanding people. Yes, they're definitely strange.* (Consumed by ter-
minal cancer, Wakaizumi died shortly thereafter in July 1996.)

Notes

1. Interview with Walter Mondale.

2. Interview with a high-ranking State Department official.

3. Interview with a senior White House official.

4. Interview with Masahide Ota.

5. Interview with Ryutaro Hashimoto.

6. Ryutaro Hashimoto's reply at a Diet session discussing amending the
   Special Measures Act of the Agreement under Article VI of the Treaty of
   Mutual Cooperation and Security between Japan and the United States of
   America, Regarding Facilities and Areas and the Status of United States
   Armed Forces in Japan, House of Councilors, April 11, 1997.

7. Takashi Ito (ed.), *The Journals of Eisaku Sato*, vol. 5 (Tokyo: Asahi Shimbunsha, 1997), p. 134.

8. Ibid., p. 131.

9. Interview with Ryutaro Hashimoto.

10. Interview with Masahide Ota.

11. Interview with Seiroku Kajiyama.

12. Interview with Sadajiro Furukawa.

13. Interview with Masanori Yoshimoto.

14. Interview with Tomiichi Murayama.

15. Interview with Masahide Ota.

16. Interview with Hideyuki Maeshima.

17. Interview with Masahide Ota.

18. Interview with Kosuke Uehara.

19. Interview with Hideyuki Maeshima.

20. Okinawa Times (ed.), *The Fiftieth Year Upheaval: The Complete Collection, Okinawa and the U.S. Bases* (Naha: Okinawa Times, 1996), p. 55.

21. Tomiichi Murayama, Budget Committee, House of Councilors, October 16, 1995.

22. Interview with Masanori Yoshimoto.

23. Interview with Koichi Kato.

24. Interview with Seiroku Kajiyama.

25. Interview with a senior official at the prime minister's office.

26. Interview with Masanori Yoshimoto.

27. Masahide Ota, *A Comprehensive History of the Battle of Okinawa* (Tokyo: Iwanami Shoten, 1982), preface. (In Japanese.)

28. Satoshi Kamata, "Anti-War Governor Works for Reduction of U.S. Bases," *Asahi Shimbun Weekly AERA,* January 15, 1991, p. 53. (In Japanese.)

29. Interview with Masahide Ota.

30. Ibid. See also Ota's *Okinawa: Cornerstone of Peace* (Tokyo: Iwanami Shoten, 1996), pp. 6–7. (In Japanese.)

31. Kamata, "Anti-War Governor," p. 56.

32. George Feifer, *Tennozan: The Battle of Okinawa and the Atomic Bomb* (New York: Tickner & Fields, 1992), p. 67.

33. Interview with Masahide Ota.

34. Masahide Ota, *Okinawa Refuses* (Tokyo: Kindai Bungeisha, 1996). (In Japanese.)

35. Ota, *Okinawa: Cornerstone of Peace*, p. 44.

36. Interview with Masahide Ota.

37. Kei Wakaizumi, *We Desire to Believe There Was No Other Choice* (Tokyo: Bungei Shunju, 1994). (In Japanese.)

38. Interview with Masahide Ota.

Chapter Seven

Washington

Ota Meets Perry

In June 1996, Masahide Ota, governor of Okinawa, visited Washington. He had been doing so almost every year since 1991. But this time was different.

The U.S. government could no longer ignore Ota. Defense Secretary William Perry was to see him. The meeting took place on the morning of June 17 in the defense secretary's office at the Department of Defense.

Ota brought with him Tatsuo Matayoshi, policy adviser to the governor, a few other senior members of the prefectural government, and local mayors, as well as reporters from the *Okinawa Times,* the *Ryukyu Shimpo,* and Television Ryukyu. He was accompanied by his old friend, Masao Nakachi, acting as aide and interpreter.

It was two months since the announcement of Futenma Air Station's return. In a press conference immediately after the announcement, Ota praised the decision as "a manifestation of the government's sincerity. We have to take things one step at a time."[1] Finding a relocation site on Okinawa was the condition for its return, but Governor Ota stated, "Given the severity of the current international situation, there can be no solution if we set our hearts on an unconditional return."

But in the Interim Report, much of the consolidation and/or reduction involved relocation within Okinawa, including the Yomitan parachute drop exercises and the Sobe Communications Site. Naturally, opposition was strong in the areas cited as potential candidates. Opposition from the municipalities around Kadena Air Base, said to be the most likely candidate for accepting Futenma, was fierce.

That is why, while Ota welcomed the move, he did not forget to spike it with the thorn that it was not necessarily acceptable to the people of Okinawa. In relation to the relocation of the transport unit to Iwakuni base, he also spoke of his distress in "shifting our own misery onto others."

When asked if relocation within Okinawa would split public opinion in two, his tone became rough. "That's the most distressing question. We've been doing our best for everyone. If what we're doing is wrong, then tell me what we should be doing."[2]

Whoever coined it, overnight the phrase "shuffling bases" was on everyone's lips. "Reducing the number of bases was just a phony slogan; the excessive burden lumped on Okinawa would never be alleviated." These and other comments were heard from deep within Ota's own political base. He had been elected as a progressive candidate.

Ota found himself forced to walk a tricky political tightrope. His visit to Washington came at a time when the Futenma shock was starting to wear off, and this sort of countersurge was swelling at home.

The meeting with Perry was businesslike. Ota listed individually the problems involved in the return of the base. "Building a new base with a 1,500-meter runway was unthinkable." He almost mentioned that 1,500 meters would hold the entire Koshien baseball field but stopped himself. He stressed how difficult it would be to find an alternative heliport for Futenma in the prefecture.

Tokushin Yamauchi, village mayor of Yomitan, was in Ota's entourage. Around that time, the papers had reported a plan to incorporate Futenma into the northern end of Kadena Air Base, at the old explosives depot. Yomitan was situated right next door to the old depot. Citing those articles, Yamauchi spread out a map and said, "You will find a resort here and a residential area here."

"It is completely inappropriate as an alternative site," Perry answered politely, saying that nothing had been decided yet.

The other point Ota stressed at this meeting was the economy. He also mentioned the cosmopolitan city concept for Okinawa. This was a point he emphasized particularly when he met Kurt Campbell after the meeting with Perry was concluded.

There were those on the American side, like Paul Giarra, former director of the Japan Desk at the Defense Department, who argued that the U.S. government should do more for the economic development of Okinawa. Giarra put forward the following case:

"Richard Gordon [mayor of Olongapo] performed a miracle bringing off the shift of Subic from military to civilian hands. America ought to be ashamed. Their minds are made up that a base means a bad economy. Their attitude then was what can we do for the Filipinos? Why didn't the miracle happen when the U.S. military was there? That's what we need to think about. And using that as a basis, we should be cooperating with economic development in Okinawa. If the Americans want to stay in Okinawa, that's what they have to do."[3] But this was a minority opinion and Giarra had already left the department.

The Americans were taken by surprise when Ota had tackled them on the economy. Ota went through the list of problems with Okinawa's economic development. The Americans wanted to know what his motives were in bringing economics so strongly into the picture.

What can the defense secretary do about economic issues? On the whole, the bases and the economy are two separate issues. If the bases do come back, it won't be enough to run around shouting opposition to the bases and calling for their removal; some realistic plans for how the sites are to be used will have to be floated. Is that what this change in the wind is all about? Vice-Governor Yoshimoto is strong on economics and has good ties with the business world. Is Ota trying to show us that he's good on it too?

Kurt Campbell and the others tried to figure out what was going on. As he listened, Campbell thought to himself, *Ota-san is doing his best to explain, but economics doesn't seem to be his strong point.*

Campbell spoke up. "Governor Ota, knowing you were coming to visit us, I ran a very close check on the past economic problems of Okinawa. I reached the conclusion that there is no connection between the bases and the Okinawa economy."[4]

Ota bristled with anger. He retorted harshly, "That's not true. Our economy can't develop because we have the bases."

"Ota Is Ungrateful"

There was, in fact, a different reason for what seemed to be Campbell's sudden challenge of Ota on economics. Campbell was unhappy. "Here we are having one hell of a time getting the bases back, not to mention going out of our way to set up a meeting with Perry, and Ota didn't say one word of thanks." What was more, "He even brought reporters along with him to the meeting with Perry! What's he trying to do? Impress them with how tough he is?"[5]

This was why Campbell felt he had to deliver Ota "another message" when there were no reporters there. The statement with the bases and the economy was his message.

Some of the Americans felt strongly that Ota was ungrateful. It was fairly common knowledge that the Americans were disappointed that even when Ota spoke with President Clinton, no word of thanks crossed his lips. This notion that Ota was an ingrate was to persist.

And Ota was to fight it just as tenaciously. To the American military man who told him, "They're all mad because you didn't thank the president for giving you back the bases," he retorted, "That's a little wrong. Isn't that like asking me to thank someone's who's invited themselves into my home when they give me back a little bit?"

There were people in Tokyo as well who found it a little unpalatable that Ota had pulled off an exclusive meeting with Perry in Washington.

The meeting took place on a Monday, but it was raised at the PM's office on the preceding Friday in a meeting with Ambassador Mondale and General Meyers, commander of the U.S. forces in Japan. Hashimoto expressed fears that there was a possibility that Ota's acting independently would "make things more complicated just as they looked like they were coming together. I need to proceed taking into full consideration Governor Ota's position. All it takes to keep my relations with the governor on an even keel is a small effort on my part. But when it comes to relations with the U.S. government, I'm not so confident."[6]

When Hashimoto told Mondale that, Mondale nodded. Mondale phoned Perry and told him, "Hashimoto is really opposed to this meeting. Would it be better if you didn't see Ota?"

Perry, however, disagreed, saying that in light of the critical nature of the Okinawan issue, it was important that he meet Governor Ota. "It's not as if we're going to take any decisions or negotiate anything."

Perry told his top staff, "Ota is already a political force that can't be ignored in Japanese politics. As long as that's true, there's a point to meeting him."

Mondale said that Ota should be left to O'Neill, but Perry didn't think so. Aloysius O'Neill was consul-general at the U.S. consulate in Naha.

"Perry paid no heed to the legalistic arguments that this kind of problem should be dealt with only with the Japanese government. The response was so like Perry. Even on a foggy night, if he thought he was on the right track he'd plow right ahead." So saying, Mondale later took off his hat to Perry.[7]

Both Perry and Campbell were confused. At the April summit between Clinton and Hashimoto, Hashimoto had asked that Ota meet the president, so why was he objecting now to this meeting with Defense Secretary Perry? *Has something happened between Hashimoto and Ota? Is something awkward happening with the relocation sites for the bases? Or does it have something to do with the land expropriation at Sobe Communications Site?*

They couldn't tell. The complicated relations among Japan, America, and Okinawa were casting their shadow.

Yes, Hashimoto instructed his staff to arrange a "dialogue" between Clinton and Ota, but it could not possibly be "equal." It could be nothing more than Hashimoto taking Ota over to Clinton for him to say "thank you" and "I hope we can continue to make progress in the future."

To Hashimoto, it was mortifying that Ota failed to express any thanks. *All he ever says is do this, do that. Never one word of thanks.*

This is what had been stuck in Hashimoto's throat ever since he made that call on April 23 telling Ota that Futenma was being returned. So, somewhere in Hashimoto's mind was the thought that by creating a situation where Ota had to thank Clinton, he could make him thank himself too.

Perry revealed no new directions or ideas in their meeting. And yet, his sincere approach was gratifying to Ota. Perry later recalled, "I think he was genuinely appreciative of what we were doing, but wanted more, and therefore did not want to seem too appreciative publicly. But in the private meeting, he was quite appreciative."[8]

Subtly, he stuck up for Ota, hinting that he was not the ingrate he was made out to be.

The Sapper

When his meeting with Ota was over, Perry admitted to Campbell, "If Clinton is reelected this fall, I'd like to go to Okinawa. I have to go to China too, but I'd like to go to Okinawa."[9] In the end, the visit to Okinawa did not happen.

Perry had special feelings about Okinawa. As an enlisted man, he had been stationed there after the war. From 1946 to 1947, he was in the Army Corps of Engineers.

He used to tell his visitors from Japan about his time in Okinawa. "I'll never forget the scene of devastation that I saw when our LST [Landing Ship Tank] landed at Naha. Not a building was intact where this last great battle of the Pacific was fought. The southern half of the island was stripped bare of vegetation and livestock. This was my personal exposure to the horrors of World War II, in which 50 million people died and tens of millions more were maimed, orphaned, or made homeless."

Perry's job in Okinawa was to map it. So, he literally walked it end to end. "Some of the men in my unit were married to Japanese women and others stayed on and became farmers. I have approached the Okinawa issue not just from this objective security concern, but I have indeed personal interest in Okinawa. I spent a very formative year in Okinawa. I was part of a team of engineers helping to build—rebuild—Okinawa, and I went there at a time when the country was devastated. And it's left a deep impression on me which lasts to this day."[10]

In fact, to his close, personal friends he was critical of the U.S. commanders in Okinawa immediately after the war. "That was the most miserable bunch of guys I had ever seen. These were all the guys . . . the cream of the crop were all sent home after the war; got home, got out, and got out early. And people that were left in Okinawa in 1946 were those who really didn't have anything better to do."[11]

A staff member at the Defense Department in charge of Asian-Pacific issues commented, "No matter how busy he was, if the subject was Okinawa he made time for it."

A staff member at Congress said that Perry knew more about Okinawa than any civilian or military person; his words carried real weight.

During his time as defense secretary, the Asian-Pacific region was relatively peaceful. That, however, was only the surface appearance, and Perry could feel strong undercurrents beginning to whirl.

Perry's strong affinities with Japan did not just stem from his Okinawan experience. He was highly interested in Japan in terms of technology and business as well. He visited Japan in 1993, when he was still deputy secretary of defense, and wanted to be taken "somewhere Japanese" for dinner. So he ended up in Roppongi, squeezed in among the Japanese salarymen, eating *yakitori* with his assistants.

The rape in Okinawa and the swift denouement that followed it made Perry acutely aware of the difficulties of the bilateral relationship. To convince the military, he used the argument that America would not be able to keep the bases if it intruded on people's lives, their day-to-day existence. In an interview in the *Asahi Shimbun* he said, "The most important measure is the intrusiveness, the noise levels, the footprint."[12]

In his meeting with Ota, Perry alluded to this position. Perry was fearful that "we have to do something about the onerous burden on Okinawa. If we don't, the bilateral security framework itself will come tumbling down."

After graduating from Vandergrift High in Pennsylvania, Perry went to Stanford University in California, going on to graduate school there as well. He majored in mathematics, earning his Ph.D. at Pennsylvania State. After leaving school, he worked for a firm in military electronics. In 1964, he set up his own high-tech company, ESL, Inc. This was his debut as an entrepreneur. At the same time, he was also involved in a Californian investment bank that specialized in high-tech firms.

Perry knew more about the Defense Department than any other defense secretary before him. From 1977 to 1981, during the Carter administration, he was undersecretary of defense for research and engineering. He was responsible for weapon systems procurement, communications, intelligence, and atomic energy.

Of all his work during this period, the one thing everyone still talks about is stealth technology. This was a challenge to develop material that could escape radar detection. Fixing on its future potential, Perry initiated a Stealth Plan within the department. He put forward the position that it was radar that had decided World War II and that beating radar would be the next revolution. Fifteen years later this idea bore fruit in the stealth aircraft that made a spectacular performance in the Gulf War.

After Carter lost the presidential election in 1980, Perry went back to Stanford. He formed a strategic research group and gave research his undivided attention. The license plate on his Mercedes at the time read "Hi-Tech."

With the birth of the Clinton administration, Perry returned to the Defense Department. This time he was number two, acting as deputy secretary to Defense Secretary Les Aspin. Aspin resigned at the end of 1993. The White House considered several successors, but in the end Perry got the job.

The media voiced their doubts. "Capable, but political influence questionable." "A technocrat, relations with Congress a drawback." "A big number-two man." In short, they saw him as a lightweight.

From the very outset, the Clinton administration's relations with the military were strained. The military in the field were vehemently against Clinton's policy of allowing gays into the forces. It was fraught with hostility to Clinton's "draft dodging" during the Vietnam War. Dissatisfaction with Perry's forerunner, Aspin, was also mounting. In other words, people resented the fact that this administration had no respect for the armed forces and weren't treating them properly.

Perry had also served commendably as a soldier. He was trained in artillery firing. Poor hearing in one ear was his legacy from that time. No one could fault Perry's military record. He could stand shoulder to shoulder with anyone.

But the Clinton administration as a whole was regarded as "antimilitary and antimilitaristic" by the Veterans' Association and others. It was precisely because of this considerable mistrust that Perry was judged to be too lightweight for the job. Perry's political senses, however, were sharply honed. More important, he knew the Washington bureaucracy like the back of his hand.

One tense problem followed another: containing the North Korean nuclear threat, the Haiti sanctions, the troop deployment to Bosnia. But Defense Secretary Perry was a consummate crisis manager.

The tone of the press started to change around that time: Perry is a mix between Lee Iacocca, Confucius, and Albert Schweitzer.[13]

As the days passed, Perry's relationship with Clinton became more solid. Clinton's confidence in Perry grew even stronger following the successful deployment of troops in Haiti in the fall of 1994. An aide reveals that sending troops to Bosnia in the fall of 1995 was "Perry's toughest decision," but he brought it off brilliantly.[14]

Perry was soon to be called "the greatest asset" of the Clinton administration. Congress was also impressed. But even Perry's nerves were frayed when he slipped up in his crisis management, especially the handling of the media, in the immediate wake of the terrorist bombing of the U.S. military facility in Saudi Arabia. Senator Arlen Specter (R-Pa.) called for his resignation. Other senators, however, were quick to support him.

Perry had the confidence of not only the governing Democrats but of the Republicans as well. Congressman Doug Bereuter (R-Neb.) did not stint his praise, saying he was one of the two best defense secretaries they had had in the past 20 years.[15] Dick Cheney, who had been President Bush's defense secretary, was the other.

Later, when looking back on his time as defense secretary, Perry praised himself, saying, "Those three years were the three years with the lowest number of those killed or injured in fighting in the history of the United States. The most important duty the defense secretary has is to make a firm military commitment, no matter how cautiously, when the time comes. It was the same for both Haiti and Bosnia."[16]

"Cooperative Security"

Perry seems to embrace a communication philosophy that people will understand if you talk to them.

Perry's secretary, Melba Boling, recalls, "I think Dr. Perry traveled as much as, maybe even a little bit more than, Frank [Carlucci]. . . . Dr. Perry simply felt that all the NATO countries and all the East European countries as well as all those in South America . . . he just felt, he had a policy of sitting down and talking with people and building a . . . I don't know what you would call it, not a coalition, but building a nucleus of people that you could trust and they could trust him. And you can only build those things by meeting with them one-on-one. And I think that is why [among all the Pentagon chiefs] he [and Secretary Carlucci] traveled [the most]."[17] Frank Carlucci had been defense secretary at the end of the Reagan administration. It was the last era of great foreign policy struggle in the dying stages of the Cold War.

Perry's thoughts are crystallized in a book published by the Brookings Institution before he became defense secretary, *A New Concept of Cooperative Security*. It was coauthored with Ashton Carter and John Steinbrunner. Perry argued for an end to the Cold War mentality and introduced the concept of "cooperative security" as the way forward on security in the post–Cold War era.[18]

He was questioning how the confrontational mentality of the Cold War, strategic concepts, policy development, budget allocations, organizational systems, external frameworks, and communication styles had to be changed into a more cooperative model.

Perry believed America's crowning diplomatic achievement was converting its former enemies, Japan and Germany (West Germany), into allies after World War II and building up a relationship of cooperation. He saw the seeds of a cooperative model of strategic policy in that example and believed that that relationship should not be perceived merely as the product of the Cold War.

He argued accordingly that there was a need to redefine who America's allies were in terms of cooperative security now that the Cold War was a thing of the past, and that if we didn't, Russia or China would be nervous about whether it was to be the next target—and whether they were to be the next targets.

When Perry joined the Defense Department, he didn't try to foist this new approach on the lower echelons of the organization. He did want to pursue it in individual cases, however, and was acutely aware of the need to switch from a confrontational stance to a cooperative one, especially where Russia and China were concerned. He stuck tenaciously to this position concerning Russian participation in the deployment of troops to Bosnia.

"The drive that he put into getting the Russians to participate in Bosnia, that was classic Perry. Real imagination. He is the best person I have ever seen at setting goals which are ambitious but attainable. I don't know how many trips he made, how many hours he spent with [Russian Defense Minister Pavel S.] Grachev, who is a difficult person to spend ten minutes with. And everyone told him a million reasons why it wouldn't work, but he kept pushing." That was how Walter Slocombe, undersecretary of defense, put it.[19]

Another example of "classic Perry" was his holding meetings with the defense ministers of Latin America. Up until that point, there was not a single multilateral forum for discussing security in the Western Hemisphere.

Another official said, "He believed that building a whole network of linkages could make everyone more secure and everyone stronger. I always used to call it his sort of World Wide Web of defense ministers."[20]

Perry was also exploring the possibility of holding a similar kind of meeting for the defense ministers of the Asia-Pacific region. At one stage he had even played with the possibility of expanding the Asia-Pacific Economic Cooperation (APEC) into a security forum, but creating a multilateral framework in the Asian-Pacific region, especially on cooperative security, was no easy task.

Perry himself later recalled that the three greatest crises during his time as defense secretary were the North Koreans' nuclear development program, the Okinawa rape, and the showdown between China and Taiwan.[21] True, he was kept busy with exigencies like Haiti and Bosnia, but they required more a crisis-management type of response. Perry recognized the urgency for America in the 21st century of building long-term relations of trust with the Chinese and developing the U.S.-Japan security relationship into something more befitting the post–Cold War era.

But the nuclear cloud over North Korea, the Okinawan bases, and the China-Taiwan showdown gave Perry no chance to move his preventive diplomacy and cooperative security forward. Apart from still dragging around the vestiges of the Cold War, the region lived cheek by jowl with the danger of a hot war involving the four powers of the United States, Japan, Russia, and China. What's more, mistrust of their neighbors was deeply rooted.

The suspicion that North Korea had gone nuclear and the U.N. economic sanctions that it triggered brought home to the United States, beyond any shadow of a doubt, that it had to be prepared to adopt measures of force if preventive diplomacy failed.

Perry entertained a certain romanticism about China. He was almost out of place in his strong pro-Chinese stance in the Clinton administration, which had come into power accusing the Republican candidate, George Bush, of "cuddling up to the despots in Beijing." In light of China's importance as an emerging superpower, he was working on a plan for military exchanges between the two countries.

His February 1994 visit to China was, in that way, a kind of intellectual "maiden voyage" to China. The Chinese gave him an extremely warm welcome. In the parade of honor before the People's Great Hall, the government of China honored him with a gun salute. Perry was pleased to see that the banquet in the Great Hall was attended by all the top Chinese government officials and strategists.

Perry, who normally didn't drink, went around each table, making toasts with old friends. But Sino-American relations took a turn for the worse in June 1995 when Taiwan's President Lee Teng-hui visited the United States. Two meetings with the Chinese defense minister, Chi Haotian, were called off. Perry, however, was a very patient man. In fact, patience was his motto: "Sir Michael Howard wisely observed that the last, best lesson we have to learn from the Cold War is patience."[22] He dealt with China patiently. Perry observed, "When it comes to strategic intentions, engagement is almost always better than ignorance. . . . In the best case, engaging China's military will allow us to have a positive influence on this important player in Chinese politics. At the very least, engagement . . . lower[s] the chances of a conflict arising from misunderstanding."[23]

"Don't blame Perry," says John Steinbrunner. "Blame the president and the people in the National Security Council. They have a lot to answer for here. Perry made a considerable attempt actually to embody these principles [of cooperation] in our relationship with China, and with Russia for that matter, without actually talking on these terms. In both cases, he was limited by the larger American political process, which has not yet come to terms with these ideas or applications."[24] Steinbrunner sees the cost of this policy failure being the confrontational diplomacy of sending aircraft carriers to the Taiwan Straits during the showdown.

Perry desired an intellectual dialogue with Japan. If possible, he wanted to be able to pick up the phone and talk with Japanese leaders as he could with those of other countries, but Japan was tricky. Perry's top-down approach of building up a relationship of trust through close personal contact didn't work well with Japan. During his time as defense secretary, he had six Japanese counterparts: Kazuo Aichi, Atsushi Kanda, Tokuichiro Tamazawa, Seishiro Eto, Hideo Usui, and Fumio Kyuma. It felt like he would get one business card at one meeting, then a new one the next time. The average time in office for JDA chiefs was a short nine months. Besides that, Japan's decision mechanism was a bottom-up system, not a top-down method. The norm was for the bureaucrats to make all the preliminary arrangements and the minister to stick to his script.

According to Robert Hall, "One of the most frustrating things for him in terms of working with Japan was the turnover of governments. And the turnover of the directors of the JDA. He would meet somebody and two weeks later, he would be out. It was so frustrating for him because he really believed in the personal connections."[25]

Perry also dreamed of a three-way security forum with the defense ministers of the United States, Japan, and China. He ran it past the JDA chief, whose response was less than enthusiastic. Talks broke off.

Every now and again Perry would grumble, "We can do it with the Latin Americans. We can do it with the Russians. But we can't do it with the Japanese. Communicating with the Japanese is really difficult."

Commodore Perry

In the meeting between Ota and Perry, Perry made a remark which greatly aroused the curiosity of those in the room. "It seems that I'm a distant relation to the famous Commodore Perry."

Perry had asked a genealogist to look into his family tree some two years prior. His mother had told him many times when he was a boy that his family was related to Commodore Perry, but he had never been shown any clear evidence. When he became defense secretary he decided to find out if it was really true and hired a genealogist.

He had no idea that genealogical searches took so much time. "They have to check each ancestral grave. It really is a lot of work."[26] Perry waited expectantly and received the initial results just before Ota's visit to the United States.

The evidence still wasn't 100 percent certain, but it seemed that the defense secretary was not the direct descendant of Commodore Perry but of his elder brother. Matthew Perry's older brother, Oliver Hazard, was the eldest son and nine years senior. Oliver Hazard was a hero in American naval history, having led a U.S. fleet during the War of 1812 with Britain. He attacked the British on Lake Erie and inflicted a humiliating defeat on the seemingly invincible British.

In the battle Oliver issued the order: "Don't give up the ship." This spirit is still revered today in the U.S. Navy. (In contrast, the old Imperial Japanese Navy discarded ships with gay abandon if they were bombed and could no longer be used.) At one time, the most numerous type of vessel in the U.S. Navy was called the Oliver Hazard Perry frigate.

Hall says, "People kept asking [William Perry] all the time. He always took great delight whenever we had one of these things where we were going to sell or do a loan or a gift of a Perry class frigate. He would always say, of course, this is the best kind of frigate. It's a Perry class. Very proud of his name."[27] It is an unusual episode in the life of a man who had very little affectation or arrogance.

"I had a genealogist look into it and it seems true," Perry told Ota. But Ota was surprisingly brusque, smiling but just commenting, "Is that right?" Perry expected a stronger reaction from Ota, who was after all a historian. The coolness knocked the wind out of Perry's sails somewhat and he refrained from any further personal comments.

Ota had a complicated attitude towards Commodore Perry. He remembered his shock when he read in the records of an American officer in the landing operations on Okinawa, "We've finally achieved Commodore Perry's dream."

Ota's view on Perry is given in detail in his book *Challenges of Okinawa*. He wrote:

> Under the banner of "liberating the people of the Ryukyus from Japanese oppression," when the chips were down [Perry] showed himself thoroughly to possess the callousness of the powerful in forcing his own ideas on others by letting his far superior firepower speak for him.[28]
>
> It cannot be denied that just like Imperial Japan, America was not interested in Okinawa for itself, but merely as a means to pursuing their policies, namely using Okinawa as a kind of political pawn.[29]
>
> Irrespective of the fact that the people of the Ryukyus were forced into accepting the Ryukuan-American Amity Commerce Treaty in the face of the Perry delegation's firepower . . . the U.S. occupation after the war dug up the Treaty of Amity to justify their occupation of Okinawa and use in their psychological battle with the local residents.
>
> Welcomed by some of the former local leaders, who were slaves to flunkeyism, the military authorities held a huge celebration for Perry's Centenary with colorful parades wending their way through the streets, a sight I still remember vividly.[30]

Ota states that "the postwar arrival of democracy in Japan [the mainland] was only made possible by the arrival of bases and the fortification of Okinawa." The statement captures the cruel reality that by keeping Okinawa under the thumb, the number of troops stationed on the mainland could be kept lower and the length of the soldiers' tour shorter and less expensive.

Commodore Matthew Perry laid anchor in Okinawa on May 26, 1853, well before putting in to Uraga. In other words, Perry landed in Okinawa before he landed in Japan. Perry understood the strategic value of the Ryukyus in the Pacific. In his attempt to open up Japan, he thought Okinawa should be pried open first, then used as a test case as well as as an advance camp for negotiating with the Japanese. He had his eye on the convoluted historical relations Japan had with the Ryukyus. The Americans would protect the Ryukyus by "liberating" them from the long yoke of Satsuma control and making them essentially a U.S. colony, and be praised, not criticized, for bringing to the islands the benefits of civilization under America's patronage.

Here Perry was following classic "threat of foreign enemy theory," saying that if the United States did not occupy the Ryukyus, then some other foreign power—Britain, Russia, or France—would. Brandishing this logic, he urged Washington to occupy the Ryukyus. Washington, however, sent him instructions that "only Congress is vested with the authority to declare war, so exercise extreme caution in the performance of your duties." Perry, in his eagerness for military exploits, warned of the use of force.

Commodore Perry visited Shuri Castle in June, leading a party of 200 marines. At 2,450 and 2,415 tons respectively, his flagship, the *Susquehanna,* and its sister ship, the *Pohatan,* were the largest warships in the world at the time. The largest ship the Japanese had was less than 100 tons. In addition to their imposing size, the warships boasted far superior firepower, carrying as they did a total crew of 1,951 and being armed with 128 cannons, both large and small. The reality was, therefore, that they demanded an audience.

One of the American sailors raped a Ryukyu woman in Naha. The enraged locals pelted him with stones and he drowned. Perry was absent at the time, but when he returned, instead of apologizing, he demanded the stone throwers be punished. The anger and pain of this incident still burns in the hearts of the people of Okinawa. "If there is any relationship of cause and effect between the September 1995 rape of the young Okinawan girl and that historical incident it has to be the structural nature of the insolence of troops serving in foreign shores."[31]

Perry's policy in the Ryukyus was a dress rehearsal for Japan. U.S.-Japan relations began on Okinawa with gunboat diplomacy.

It is wrong, however, to paint relations between Okinawa and the United States in only an anti-American vein. Okinawa's relations with America are, in a certain sense, both deeper and more important than its relations with Japan. Ota himself had been on exchange to the United States twice, at Syracuse University and the East-West Center in Hawaii. Leaders in all sectors in the 1950s and 1960s were sent to America, at the expense of the U.S. military. More than 1,000 studied at American universities. Even today, close to 400 residents of Okinawa Prefecture are studying at the Kadena campus of American universities.

Ota mentioned this in his meeting with Secretary Perry. "Before Okinawa reverted to Japan, there was a system of U.S. Defense Department and State Department scholarships, which made it possible for many young people to study in America. It has also done a lot to help us with our development. Since reversion, however, the U.S. government scholarship system for our young people has come to a standstill. Would it be possible to reinstate that program once more?"[32]

Okinawa has always been in an awkward position: during Edo times as well as after the Meiji Restoration when it was merged with Japan; after Japan's defeat in the war; after the occupation; after the mainland's independence; after its reversion. Its historical and geopolitical position makes it impossible for it to be free, forcing it to be caught up in a menage-à-trois with Japan and the United States.

The paths Governor Ota and Defense Secretary Perry had each taken after the war, as well as their encounter, were just one fateful, historical chance meeting among many between Japan and America in the postwar era.

Krulak

Just before Ota visited Washington, it was reported that Charles Krulak, commandant of the U.S. Marine Corps, was considering relocating the functions of the marines in Okinawa to Australia.

The *Defense News* reported, "Washington's top Marine Corps officer is seeking Pentagon and White House support for a plan to preserve U.S. military flexibility in East Asia by using Australia as an anchor for floating U.S. war depots and as a base for expanded military exercises."[33]

The move was timed because Australia's defense minister, Ian McLachlan, was shortly to visit Washington. Behind the announcement was also preparation for a scenario in which it would be difficult to keep the bases if antibase sentiment in Okinawa could not be curbed. It was also probably a reflection of the unhappiness of the marines in the front line. From where Krulak stood, he was speaking for those in the field who wanted to go to Australia where they would be more welcome, there was plenty of land, the cost of living was cheap, there were Western girls, and they could conduct exercises to their heart's content.

Perry and the other top brass at the Defense Department, however, were upset that Krulak had gone unilaterally public on this without their approval.

If you're going to make such a fuss, we don't mind getting out of Okinawa; don't come crying to us when the time comes; if you want to cut the bases that much, then how about Australia; just go ahead and try it. While perhaps not the best turn of phrase, Krulak's comments could be interpreted as "bare-assed defiance."

A top official at the Pentagon took this up directly, saying it was "negative in three ways. First, it had created a perception in Japan that a marine withdrawal was possible, which made it more difficult for us to go ahead with the base realignment, because it immediately raised the question that if you're going to move out anyway, why do we have to go through all of this fuss?

"Secondly, there was the impact on Australia, which didn't want the marines to be relocated there. Their idea was that they could accept the marines' exercises but that was all. It was a blow that they put a cross against us because how could they be expected to deal with the kind of marines corps commandant who went public on something as delicate as this without any prior consultation with Australia?

"And finally, there was China. His comments were quite capable of fanning Chinese paranoia that the transfer of U.S. Marines from Japan to Australia signaled they were finally getting ready to contain China."[34]

Krulak was the picture of a marine. He was a marine thoroughbred in terms of family as well. His father was General Victor Krulak, who had made it all the way to commanding U.S. Marine Forces Pacific. He served in both the Pacific and Korean wars. He was one of the first to preach the importance of landing craft for amphibious operations. Their effectiveness was proved in the Pacific War, especially at Guadalcanal, but their most dramatic success was at the Inchon landing in the Korean War.

Another achievement of Victor Krulak was the behind-the-scenes work he did in ensuring the passage of the National Security Act in 1947. The marines were trying to get the corps established as a separate service and at not less than three combat divisions. There was a growing fear that without such separate legislation, the marines would be disbanded. Marine sympathizers in the Congress, including Congressman Mike Mansfield, worked up a storm of support.

In fact, in his book *Marine*, Tom Clancy wrote that Victor Krulak's greatest achievement in life was bringing his son, Charles, "a warrior around whom they [the U.S. Marine Corps] could rally in time of need," into the world. Coming from an avid fan of the marines, this needs to be taken with quite a bit of salt, but Charles did better his father by one step in becoming U.S. Marine Corps commandant. So it is true that he excelled his father.[35]

Charles Krulak was an officer who had worked his way up from the infantry, not from the aviators. There is an unwritten rule in the marines that the commandant will be an infantry man. A graduate of Annapolis, he was, however, in the minority in the marines. He graduated Annapolis in 1964 and was sent straight to Vietnam to patrol villages for three months. Krulak had two lessons drummed into him there: Always clearly define the objectives of the fight before going into battle; and the only people who can protect the marines are the marines themselves.[36]

Krulak was stationed in Okinawa three times in the 1960s and 1970s (1965, 1970, and 1977).[37] Later, he served in the Operations Division, the nucleus of the U.S. Marine Corps, and then as assistant to Undersecretary of Defense Don Larson in charge of command, control, communication, and intelligence (C[3]I). He then got a long-awaited job in the White House. He worked in the National Security Council in the last year of the Reagan administration and the first year of the Bush administration.

He was in charge of logistics in Operation Desert Storm in the Gulf War. It was a huge job that involved providing a constant flow of troops and food supplies for the 90,000 marines deployed.

"The Gulf War was a true war of logistics. Because we won on logistics we also won the war. It's not an easy thing to admit or say for someone like myself who comes out of the infantry, but a fact's a fact."

Krulak's subsequent battles have not been in far distant jungles or deserts but in the political jungles and deserts of Washington. After the Gulf War, the Bush administration accelerated armament cuts and rationalization. It also cut the overseas U.S. presence. As part of this move, the White House and Pentagon civilians brought enormous pressure to bear for a reduction in marine troops as well.

The message was: cut your 198,000 to 159,000. The marines argued for 177,000. They came out in full force, waging a tremendous campaign on Congress. The smallest of the four services, they were the most powerful attackers when it came to tackling the Hill. The marines fought tenaciously, and, in the end, they were able to retain a level of 174,000, a number close enough to their initial demand.

On the basis of this work, Krulak was appointed commander of the U.S. Marine Forces Pacific in Hawaii. It was the highest position his father had held. And then on July 1, 1995, he succeeded Carl Mundy as U.S. Marine Corps commandant, a four-year post.

Iwo Jima

Krulak's appointment had, in fact, been announced much earlier at the ceremonies commemorating the 50th anniversary of the Battle of Iwo Jima held atop Mt. Suribachi, on the southern tip of the island.

The ceremony was attended by 800 marine veterans, survivors of the bloody 36-day battle, and their families. Walter Mondale, U.S. ambassador to Japan, was also there, looking somber.

The ceremonies were opened by Larry Snowden, U.S. Marine Corps lieutenant general (ret.) and chairman of the Reunion of Honor Committee, and the eldest daughter of the late Takeichi Nishi (army colonel). Yoshiko Komatsu. They were followed by Ambassador Mondale, with Navy Secretary John Dalton the last to speak. It was during this speech that Dalton announced Krulak's appointment to commandant.

Krulak had flow in from Marine Force Pacific Command at Camp H. M. Smith in Hawaii. Before the plane, which was carrying Commandant Mundy and his wife as well as Krulak and his wife, landed, it circled Mt. Suribachi at 5,000 feet. Mundy showed Krulak the paper with the announcement of his nomination.[38] Krulak was so moved he was speechless. Dalton made the announcement during the ceremonies on Mt. Suribachi.

"I was being told I was nominated for commandant at the exact same place where, some fifty years earlier, Navy Secretary James Forrestal had looked over at my godfather, General Holland M. Smith (who had led the assault on Iwo Jima), and, upon seeing the flag flying at the top of Mt. Suribachi, said, 'The raising of that flag . . . means a Marine Corps for the next five hundred years.'"[39]

Dalton solemnly noted, "There is no one more fitted to lead the glorious Marine Corps into the 21st century than Commandant Krulak."

Krulak's father, Victor, had fought in the Battle of Okinawa. Krulak's godfather was Holland M. Smith. Dalton was Krulak's best friend at Annapolis and pushed strongly for Krulak's nomination. It was a family.

The taking of Iwo Jima was a key battle in the United States' winning command of sea access to Japan. Seventy-five thousand marines were used. The Americans' plan in taking Iwo Jima was to ensure themselves of an emergency landing field for the strategic B-29 bombers out of Saipan and to build a valuable air and navy base for launching attacks on the Japanese mainland.

The Americans lost 6,821 men in the fighting. While this number was smaller than the 20,000 lost on the Japanese side, there was no other single battle in the history of the marines which resulted in more loss of life. Iwo Jima has a special meaning in the annals of the marines.

The battle was also an honorable one for the Japanese. Their supplies had been completely cut off. Their ammunition had run out. But the Japanese fought and died bravely. For a long time, this battle was recorded by the Americans as a fight between brave men on both sides.

Tadamichi Kuribayashi, commander of the reserve army, was a soldier in whom the emperor had the greatest confidence. When taking up his appointment as commander, he was called to the court and met with the emperor.

Kuribayashi had worked in the embassy in Washington as assistant military attaché for two years from 1928. During that time, he traveled all over the United States. In a letter he sent to his wife back home in Japan, he wrote, "The United States is the last country in the world Japan should fight. . . . One must never underestimate the Americans' fighting ability."[40]

Colonel Takeichi Nishi, head of the 26th Tank Division, also knew America well and spoke almost perfect English. He had participated in the 1932 Olympic Games in Los Angeles and won a gold medal in an equestrian event. His family was related to the imperial family and he was a baron. The handsome Baron Nishi was very popular at the Olympics. His conversation with Spencer Tracy and Mary Pickford in Hollywood was given extensive coverage in the *Los Angeles Times*. During the war, Nishi stopped his men from executing their marine prisoners.[41]

It is not known how either Kuribayashi or Nishi met their ends, but in the United States it is said that they faced the direction of the Imperial Palace and committed suicide.[42] Fifty years later both Kuribayashi's wife and Nishi's eldest daughter were there at the ceremony.

But it was easier to say "reunion" than to achieve it. Among some of the Japanese families of the fallen, there was no small suspicion that the Americans were going to turn it into some kind of festive victory parade. The senior member of the Iwo Jima Association warned that the Japanese side would refrain from attending if that was the case. A month before, Deputy Prime Minister and Foreign Minister Yohei Kono conveyed to Richard Mackey, commander of the Pacific Forces, his hope "it would not turn out to be anything untoward."

The Japanese had already learned how difficult it could be 10 years earlier. The Americans had requested they be permitted to hold a ceremony on the day of the Iwo Jima landing, February 19. Some of the Japanese families of the bereaved resisted. They also clashed over other dates, the Americans wishing to commemorate February 23, the day the U.S. flag was hoisted atop Mt. Suribachi, and the Japanese March 23, the day of "death with honor" (*gyokusai*).

Thus there was the chance that at the top of Mt. Suribachi at the site of the American victory memorial, the ceremonies might end once again in confrontation between the victors and the defeated. The decision to erect a memorial on a hill overlooking Okinahama on Iwo Jima's southern coast and to conduct an unveiling ceremony made it possible to have a reunion celebrating "peace and friendship."

It was Tsunezo Wachi, a former captain in the Imperial Japanese Navy and a survivor of Iwo Jima, who crystallized the symbolism of the Reunion with Honor without making the 40th anniversary reunion a commemoration of the U.S. victory. A detailed account of Wachi's life, how he had become a Buddhist monk after the war and had dedicated his life to gathering the remains of his comrades in arms and praying for their souls, is given in Fuyuko Kamisaka's *Still No Death in Honor on Iwo Jima*, but what interested Wachi the most was the thought of "reconciliation" between the two countries after the war and how it could be choreographed.

Still, overcoming history proved difficult. In 1968, when Iwo Jima reverted along with part of the Ogasawara Islands, it is said that the Americans requested that the Stars and Stripes still be flown even after they had gone, but the Japanese government refused. Wachi had requested a small statue of the Buddhist goddess of mercy be erected next to the huge bronze statue of the U.S. flag flying above Iwo Jima that stands near Arlington Cemetery in the Washington suburbs to ease the souls of the dead on both sides. The Americans turned him down.

The 50th anniversary of the end of hostilities, in 1995, turned out to be a difficult year. The Japanese government expressed its displeasure with the depiction of an atomic mushroom cloud being included in the commemorative stamps issued by the U.S. Postal Service, which led to the design being changed. The U.S. Veterans' Association criticized the Smithsonian's atomic bomb display for being "too sympathetic towards the Japanese," and the exhibition was eventually abandoned. The Japanese were reluctant to send the prime minister to the commemorative ceremony in Hawaii for the 50th anniversary of the war, which led to changes in plans to invite defense ministers. The name of the ceremony was also changed to "the end of hostilities."

The Japanese insistence that the site on Iwo Jima be a joint memorial for all those who had fallen in the battle was a manifestation of the same kind of feeling.

During the ceremony, the widow of General Kuribayashi, Yoshii Kuribayashi, read the eulogy:

> I would like to express my sincere gratitude to all those involved in this moving commemoration of the 50th anniversary of the fallen, both Japanese and American, in the Battle for Iwo Jima.
>
> Looking back, both Japanese and Americans, officers and enlisted men, were united together, giving their lives for their country and fighting a desperate fight.
>
> They fought gloriously, each and every man said to be a hero, the battle itself said to be the greatest of World War II.
>
> But when we think of how tragic their fight was and how they must have felt, we have nothing but tears.
>
> I believe this precious peace we have today was built for us by those who sacrificed themselves so selflessly.
>
> To the souls of the dear departed, please rest in peace.
>
> These are my words of eulogy on this memorial day.
>
> I pray for all your happiness.

Mark Lambert of the U.S. Embassy was there. Kuribayashi's voice was so small he had to strain to hear her. "The widow of the Japanese commander of the defense of Iwo Jima, she's almost 100 years old, she gave a speech that was so moving, and it made all these bombastic, long-winded speeches in the hot sun seem pretty trivial. It was so simple and to the point and her voice, you could just barely hear it."[43]

Notes

1. *Asahi Shimbun*, April 13, 1996.

2. Ibid.

3. Interview with Paul Giarra.

4. Interview with Kurt Campbell.

5. Ibid.

6. Interview with Ryutaro Hashimoto.

7. Interview with Walter Mondale.

8. Interview with William Perry.

9. Interview with Kurt Campbell.

10. Interview with William Perry.

11. Interview with a personal aide to William Perry who heard the conversation.

12. *Asahi Shimbun*, evening edition, April 15, 1996.

13. John Mintz, "Defense Titans on Perry: Focused, Brilliant, Gentle," *Washington Post*, January 26, 1994.

14. Interview with a senior DOD official.

15. Interview with Douglas Bereuter.

16. Interview with William Perry.

17. Interview with Melba Boling.

18. Ashton B. Carter, William J. Perry, and John D. Steinbrunner, *A New Concept of Cooperative Security*, Brookings Occasional Papers (Washington, D.C.: Brookings, 1992).

19. Interview with Walter Slocombe.

20. Interview with Robert Hall.

21. Interview with William Perry.

22. William Perry, "Preventive Defense," *Trilateral Note*, May 23, 1996, p. 9.

23. Ibid., p. 8.

24. Interview with John Steinbrunner.

25. Interview with Robert Hall.

26. Interview with William Perry.

27. Interview with Robert Hall.

28. Masahide Ota, *Challenges of Okinawa* (Tokyo: Kobunsha, 1990), p. 150. (In Japanese.)

29. Ibid., p. 147.

30. Ibid., p. 148.

31. Masao Nakachi in Kurayoshi Takara and Tomohiko Tamaki, *Perry and the Great Ryukyus* (Naha: Ryukyu Hoso, 1997). (In Japanese.)

32. Interview with Masahide Ota.

33. *Defense News,* June 10, 1996.

34. Interview with a high-ranking DOD official.

35. Tom Clancy, *Marine: A Guided Tour of a Marine Expeditionary Unit* (New York: Berkeley Books, 1996), p. 23.

36. Ibid., pp. 24–25.

37. Interview with Charles Krulak.

38. Ibid.

39. Ibid.

40. Bill D. Ross, *Iwo Jima: Legacy of Valor* (New York: Vintage Books, 1986), p. 20.

41. Ibid., pp. 346–347.

42. Ibid., p. 342.

43. Interview with Mark Lambert.

Chapter Eight

The Last Base

Shuffling Bases

When the Special Action Committee on Okinawa's (SACO) interim report was announced, Defense Secretary William Perry declared that 90 percent of its work was done. In response, top officials at the Japanese Defense Agency (JDA) said, "Now we have only 90 percent of the work left to do."[1]

There was a huge gap in the perceptions of the two sides. Particularly, where were the marines to go after Futenma? This was a headache right from the start. SACO's interim report of April 1996 didn't mention it, because no one had been able to make a decision. This thorn had to be extracted before Clinton arrived in Japan. SACO had to make haste.

Both the Japanese and the Americans were exploring whether Futenma could be split up. First, the Harrier jets at Iwakuni would be relocated to Alaska; they would be replaced by Futenma's midair KC-130 refuelers. Several functions would also be relocated to Kadena Air Base, and exercise functions would be shifted to Guam.

The Defense Department was quietly exploring ways to split Futenma between Korea and Guam. Opposition to American bases was mounting in Korea as well, however. Failure to reduce the concentration of bases there could well aggravate anti-American sentiment on the part of the Koreans. Strong resistance to relocating the base in Okinawa was foreseen. Korea was keeping a watchful eye on developments between Japan and the United States over the Status of Forces Agreement.

Of course, the rape in Okinawa was despicable. But there were rapes in Korea by U.S. soldiers, plus the Status of Forces Agreement (SOFA) with Korea was more unfavorable towards that host country. Korea was dissatisfied; the agreement should be adjusted; the Defense Department (DOD) had a pro-Japan bias.[2] So the Americans were certainly not in any position to talk about relocating Okinawan bases to Korea.

The Defense Department considered a partial relocation to Guam. Guam had been lobbying for a base. Legislators pushed for it too, saying that moving bases from Okinawa to Guam would be greatly welcomed. Kurt Campbell had many talks with the local legislators and other Guam representatives about the matter.[3]

But the marines refused to approve it. They were strongly opposed to splitting up their Okinawan facilities. While the talk of base relocation was couched in general terms, in the end, it came down to the marines.

The U.S. forces in Japan originally had three sites for building an alternative heliport to Futenma:

- the unutilized part of the explosives depot area at the northern end of Kadena Air Base (ASP-1);
- an area near the coast at Camp Hansen;
- at Camp Schwab.

The SACO team initially had its eye on the unused depot area, but if they were to build a runway there, they would have to carry out large-scale works including leveling half the mountain. It was a question of life and death for the neighboring towns and villages, which depended on the runoff from the mountain for irrigation. Opposition in the villages of Yomitan and Onna was especially vehement.

Strong resistance was also found among the local residents in the area near the coast at Camp Hansen. The cities, towns, and villages of Nago, Kin, Ginoza, and Onna all started opposition movements. The local assemblies all passed opposition resolutions.

The U.S. forces had tried to construct an urban exercise field there at the end of the 1980s but were prevented by local opposition and forced to amend their plans. The exercises envisioned involved a city battle where soldiers had to retake buildings occupied by the enemy using pistols and rifles, so the intention was to construct target buildings and a pistol range among others inside the base.

However, the locals resisted fiercely. So much so that having decided to go ahead with the exercise in May 1990, the army (First Special Unit) had to be transported by helicopter to avoid trouble with the residents.

In 1992, Vice President Dan Quayle, in Japan to celebrate the 20th anniversary of Okinawa's reversion to Japan, announced the termination of the urban exercises in Onna village and the removal of the facilities. The buildings and so on were, in fact, removed the next month.

This fierce local resistance to the bases becoming a permanent fixture needs to be seen in the singular historical context Okinawa found itself in after the war. In contrast to the U.S. bases on the Japanese mainland, the bases on Okinawa are located on forcibly seized land. This confiscation took place during the U.S. occupation of Okinawa from 1945, when the residents were still in holding camps. In comparison, on the mainland, the bases were built by taking over the former Imperial Army's bases.

The U.S. forces returned the people to their homes by the middle of 1947, but many of those who came from the center of the island, where the bases were concentrated, could not go back to where they lived because Kadena Air Base, Camp Kuwae, Camp Zukeran, and Futenma Air Station were there. They were forced to live in makeshift houses in small areas squeezed between the bases, and ended up staying there. Yomitan, Kadena, Chatan, Ginowan, Okinawa City, and Kitanaka-gusuku all grew up into residential areas in this way.

When war broke out in 1950 on the Korean Peninsula, the Americans started expanding the bases. American soldiers were mobilized under the provisions of the Compulsory Purchase of Land Act (Civilian Government Ordinance 109) to remove the stubbornly resisting farmers, and the land was expropriated. In Okinawa, this was referred to as expropriation by "rifles and bulldozers." Even after Okinawa's reversion to the mainland in 1972, the reality of the concentration of bases remained. Seventy-five percent of the U.S. bases in Japan were entrenched there.

The marines showed interest in Camp Schwab, a marine base on the Pacific side. They shared the Central Training Area, a huge exercise field, with Camp Hansen. In administrative terms, the training area straddled the village of Ginowan and Nago City.

Camp Schwab's key facility was the training area. It had a pistol range, a rifle range, a mortar range, and a large-bore tank firing range. There was also an LST landing ramp and a beach training area for amphibious landing operations.

It was a remote area about an hour and a half from Naha by car. It also went by the name of Fort Apache. There was concern that the married men (some 2,600) would object strongly to relocating Futenma to Camp Schwab. No wife wanted to live at Fort Apache.

But the marines thought it was worth considering if Camp Schwab was expanded through reclamation and the quality of life improved. Of the several Camp Schwab options, the reclamation option was called Schwab Heavy and the feeling was that the marines would go for it.

The decisive question at that juncture was whether they could get a long enough runway. The marines had indicated they would oppose any site, no matter where, if the runway was short.

Both the Okinawan government and residents were vehemently opposed to expanding Camp Schwab by land reclamation, claiming it would destroy the natural environment.

The Last Base: Kadena

The Prefecture of Okinawa had adopted a public stance of "not taking a stand on relocation sites." Vice-Governor Masanori Yoshimoto, however, was trying behind the scenes to push integration with Kadena.

The prefecture was alarmed that despite the several bases that were to be "returned" according to SACO, their return might well lead to "new construction" and "expansion." It was terrified that this would be seen as "run-around bases" or "shuffling bases."

It was no good adding that there had to be subtraction. On that point, the proposal to consolidate functions in Kadena evoked an image of an enormous vacuum cleaner sucking in the other bases. Yoshimoto thought they might just get away with this.

Even in the Okinawa development program for 2015 released by the prefecture, Kadena was slated to be the last base returned. So Yoshimoto's reckoning was that the populace would be able to stand it if the others were to be consolidated at "the last base." This was based on the assumption that the navy and the army would be the last U.S. presence to go.

The prefecture was pushing for "realignment, consolidation, and reduction" of the bases. But the governments of Japan and the United States were huge obstacles, and the best the prefecture could do was the three items.

Around that time, the government was talking about "realignment and consolidation." "Reduction" was not included. In November 1995 at the start of SACO, the Japanese government managed to slip in "reduction" along with "realignment and consolidation." Okinawa, on the other hand, inserted "consolidation" between "realignment and reduction." This meant that, finally, they both had the same position of "realignment, consolidation, and reduction."

This is why even in SACO, Okinawa Prefecture insisted on "opposition to a net increase in the bases," "opposition to the freezing of the bases," and "opposition to the perpetuation of the bases," while taking a slightly more flexible position on "approving provisional facilities," and saying so to the PM's office. Yoshimoto maintained, "It's OK, for example, to increase the land area that's returned by building multistoried apartment blocks or homes, but anything higher than three stories is perpetuation."[4]

Over the summer of 1996, the PM's office and the JDA had almost settled on the proposal to consolidate Kadena. Yoshimoto and Deputy Cabinet Secretary Sadajiro Furukawa were at the center of the arrangements. Hiroshi Hirabayashi, chief Cabinet counselor for external affairs, was involved too. Seiroku Kajiyama, Cabinet secretary, had also given it the thumbs up.

They all had their suspicions that "the fact that the marines are demanding a 1,500-meter runway proved they were not taking the issue seriously,"[5] Kajiyama being the most suspicious of the lot. He urged the Foreign Ministry to "push the Americans hard in the direction of consolidating Kadena."[6]

It was the JDA that was most in favor of the Kadena consolidation proposal. It believed the three sites were just "a smokescreen to save them from having to go to Kadena."[7]

"They'd already agreed to return ASP-1, so they probably thought it would be the easiest to relocate there. When I heard the proposal, it sounded very much like a desk-top theory by people who didn't know the area," said a JDA official shortly after it became known to the public.[8]

Checking with the prefecture along the way, the JDA was secretly exploring the Kadena consolidation proposal. JDA thinking was outlined in an internal document, "Regarding the Examination of the Relocation of Futenma Air Station," dated August 2, 1996. It was a position paper on how to explain the Kadena consolidation proposal to the Americans.

> While the proposal to integrate Futenma into Kadena Air Base is by no means a palatable one for the local residents, there is no other option if a phased reduction has to be condoned. This is because the residents of Okinawa, whose goal it is to have a "base-free Okinawa," believe that Kadena will be the last to go and that it will not be easy to get the Americans to return Kadena. Therefore, and precisely because this is so, they seem to think that the Kadena consolidation proposal would be acceptable.
>
> The land reclamation proposal for Camp Schwab involves construction in an "existing facility and area," but there is the possibility of protests in terms of protecting the mangroves and coral. It is thought that it would be totally unacceptable even should noise and safety objections be cleared, due to resistance stemming from the perception by the people of Okinawa that it would amount to a new base with the inherent fear of making the base a permanent fixture.
>
> Based on the opposition to relocating sites in Okinawa, it is imperative that we have the cooperation of the people of Okinawa and all levels of government from the governor down to local mayors as well as their assemblies if we are to successfully relocate Futenma air station.
>
> From this viewpoint, the Japanese side believes that examining thoroughly and pursuing the possibility of consolidating Futenma into Kadena Air Base, which the prefectural authorities have publicly supported, is the key to receiving the understanding of the prefecture and to Japan and America making the return of Futenma a reality.

The JDA found out that there were two sites in the United States where jet planes and helicopters shared the same airfield. It got hold of documentation showing that Hornet and transport helicopter squadrons had no trouble sharing facilities at the marines' Kaneohe Air Station in Hawaii.

The JDA "burned with a passion to clear up this question which had been hanging around for fifty years," according to a JDA official.[9] Japan had never had a say in running the treaty or the military structure, and it was as if the JDA wanted something tangible to show the public.

The JDA was ready to go for the Kadena consolidation proposal, but there were dissenters within the agency. Takehiko Shimaguchi, director of the Defense Facilities Administration Bureau in Naha City, was one. His main concern was the incredible noise an integrated base would generate, and he was very skeptical of the chances of winning the locals over.

Shimaguchi put his case to the agency, but the JDA's mind was already made up. The JDA expected resistance from the U.S. military, especially from the air force, to be intense. But they reckoned it to be a possibility, with people like Richard Armitage, former assistant secretary of defense and one of the first to talk about returning Futenma—an idea which had initially seemed improbable but then became real—putting their weight behind the consolidation proposal.

The JDA sent the Kadena consolidation proposal up to the PM's office in the middle of August. Masahiro Akiyama, director-general of the Defense Policy Bureau, and Shigeru Sugiyama, chairman of the Joint Staff Council, visited the PM's office and briefed Hashimoto on it.

They used a large-scale model made by the Joint Staff Council. They took into account differences in elevation, explaining that if Kadena was consolidated, the airfield would take on this form, the fighters would fly this route, the helicopters would use this runway, and so on.

It was a presentation based on their awareness that Hashimoto loved plastic models. Hashimoto leaned forward with a grin on his face to get a better look. His questions were exceedingly technical. What would happen to the already congested air traffic control at Kadena if Futenma was integrated? Wouldn't it break down? What had been done about that? "The airspace is congested enough as it is. Air traffic controllers will go mad if you throw a helicopter squadron in there as well."

And then he added, "When I was transport minister, I discussed returning air traffic control at Naha Airport back to Japan with the Americans, but they said they wanted it left with them because, although it might be all right during normal times, in the case of a contingency, there would be military operations involved. I even felt at times that this was something I shouldn't press them too hard on."[10]

Hashimoto didn't say he was against the Kadena proposal, but he didn't say he was for it either. He stuck firmly to his role of bystander from first to last.

The local residents came out in force against the Kadena consolidation proposal. The towns of Kadena-cho and Chatan joined forces with Okinawa City and lobbied furiously against it.

Kadena-cho, in particular, already had 83 percent of its area gobbled up by the base. The mayor, Tokujitsu Miyagi, spoke out saying that any further base density would be unbearable. "We had at long last got an agreement on noise prevention and thought that slightly quieter nights were coming. The relocation proposal just as that was about to happen was a thunderbolt out of the blue."[11] Kadena-cho's entire history was one of bolts out of the blue.

Miyagi let his unhappiness be known in an article in the *Okinawa Times*. "The locals were not told anything when the navy apron was relocated here from Naha after reversion. This time too, there was no notification whatsoever. When Special Unit 353 was stationed here temporarily from Clark Air Base in the Philippines, the government and the JDA asked us to lend them a place for a while, but they ended up being stationed here permanently."[12]

The local U.S. military also came out in opposition. They argued that they could not guarantee flight safety if the marine helicopters started using the already congested area. They feared the very existence of the bases would be threatened if there was an accident causing loss of Okinawan life. It is not as if the three-town alliance and the Kadena command were in cahoots, but they were, in fact, tacitly fighting the same battle.

Miyagi recalls, "The local military as well as Hobbins [commander, 18th Wing, Kadena] said [the Kadena proposal] was impossible. You couldn't just write something in Nagatacho, decide here and say, right, let's integrate with Kadena."[13]

Miyagi acted energetically. He and others made many demands for opposition to the Defense Administration Facilities Bureau in Naha. When Director Shimaguchi suggested they go and see the prefecture, given that it was the vice-governor who was mentioning Kadena, they replied that the top members refused to see them.

When Shimaguchi was in charge of the Defense Administration Facilities Agency's Facilities Planning Division, he ran into the proxy-signing procedural problem involved in the public notice and inspection. It was at the start of 1991.

He remembered that "Ota would come to Tokyo and say yes, then go back home and say no. He did that to me three times!"[14] Shimaguchi was not sure if the prefecture had the willingness and the power to join forces with the national government to negotiate with the local municipalities even though they themselves were leaning towards the Kadena proposal.

The Foreign Ministry was worried that the JDA was suddenly leaning towards the Kadena proposal. They were cautious about it. "We had information indicating that Kadena would be difficult and we believed it was pointless asking for something we couldn't get."[15] The ministry also worried that "the harder they pushed the Americans, who weren't keen on Kadena, the more [the pro-Kadena lobby of Kajiyama and Yoshimoto and the JDA began to believe that] it could be sold to the Okinawans." This was never stated explicitly, however.

As well as "being afraid that it would fall through if they did that," there was an argument for proceeding cautiously because of "the risk that information would be leaked if they consulted with the JDA."[16]

But no matter what they did, it is hard to believe that the Foreign Ministry could have gotten their way. They were in a very weak position with the PM's office, Okinawa, and the JDA all leaning towards the Kadena proposal.

Not a Second Futenma

But the Americans didn't budge. The U.S. Air Force was dug in deep, and it was around this time that the Foreign Ministry learned that the air force had started lobbying Congress. The rift between the U.S. Air Force and the U.S. Marine Corps was a hurdle. Things might have been different if they had decided to work something out together.

In early September of that year, a high-ranking official at the White House declared, "The Kadena proposal is no good. There's nothing we can do about the egos and rivalry in each of the services. If we forced the Kadena integration through in the face of military opposition, it would alienate the military completely."[17]

It was not just the air force that was against the Kadena consolidation proposal. The U.S. Embassy in Japan had conveyed its strong opposition to the State Department. The State Department was, therefore, cautious.

A State Department official who was opposed to the Kadena proposal throughout cited five reasons for caution:

1. If the marines were put on Kadena, you would increase the risk of accidents. Slow-moving helicopters and fast-moving fighter aircraft on the one base were not good for safety.

2. The marine presence there would take up space that would be needed in a contingency for bringing in C-5As and so on.

3. Kadena had pretty good relations with the surrounding communities, but if they put the marines in there, it would destroy all the good steps they had taken.

4. If you look down the road 20 years, Kadena is probably going to be the last facility in Okinawa, and the most important, so it shouldn't be loaded up and put at risk by seeking a short-term solution.

5. If you concentrated the main marine forces in Kadena, the leaders of the landowners and base protest movement could well use the intense local and national opposition to the marines to make Kadena the next target of large-scale protests. Kadena could not be made into the next political symbol.[18]

At the U.N. General Assembly in the fall of 1996, President Clinton met with Prime Minister Hashimoto in New York. At the meeting Clinton stated that Kadena must not be made into a second Futenma.

Prior to the meeting, there had been concern that Hashimoto would get into details in the meeting and come up with something the Americans could just not swallow. The Americans decided a clear message needed to be sent that it would be inappropriate for Hashimoto to mention Kadena.[19] A further message was probably sent that Kadena would be the last facility to go, so it required cautious handling.

At the beginning of August, a senior Defense Department official having lunch with a Japanese journalist at the Pentagon's Air Force Club looked around the room, lowered his voice, and said, "The Kadena option is still doable."[20] But by the end of August, it had sunk without a trace.

The selection of a relocation site was deadlocked. Even in the SACO meetings, the Americans said "no" to that, "no" to this, "no" to everything. Finally, one of the Japanese members asked, "What about Futenma, then?" For the first time in a long time, laughter was heard in a SACO meeting, although it was probably tinged with fatigue.

San Francisco

August 31, San Francisco.

The bilateral SACO team was holding its first meeting on the West Coast. The meeting had been requested by the Japanese. There was mounting uncertainty on the Japanese side, and especially at the JDA, that if SACO, which had been a joint effort to date, failed to proceed smoothly on Futenma's relocation, the Americans would make a unilateral decision in the end.

The JDA was frightened that the Americans were going to refuse the Kadena consolidation, the only remaining option. It wanted to give one more push to get the Americans to promise to leave Kadena as an option. Another objective was to convey to the Americans how things really stood with the Okinawa bases. A referendum was to be held in Okinawa on September 8. The prefecture was to vote on whether it was in favor of the bases staying.

The Foreign Ministry was worried that relations between the JDA, which was in favor of the Kadena consolidation, and the Defense Department, which was opposed, were on the verge of breaking down. It wanted to hold a meeting as soon as possible so that each side could state its frank opinion.

Walter Slocombe, undersecretary of defense, who had been in Japan in late June, had told the Japanese that Perry would come up with an alternative proposal by early September. So the Japanese thought there was a need to hold a SACO meeting before that and tell the Americans exactly what the Japanese position was.

The JDA had by then conducted a fairly thorough survey. It had had pilots from the Air SDF fly both fixed-wing aircraft and helicopters into the same airfield and had collated experimental data. It calculated that enough space for a helicopter runway could be generated by consolidating the housing sector.

In the meeting on September 23, the JDA gave an even more detailed briefing. Its arguments focused on the following two points:

- The consolidation of Kadena is achievable if we do this.

- As a relocation site, Camp Schwab has these problems.

The JDA claimed that a comprehensive appraisal led to the following conclusions:

- Deployment of marine air squadrons from the U.S. mainland would be smooth.

- A service apron for marshaling marine aircraft deployed from the U.S. mainland and repairing aircraft sent back from the front lines was readily available.

- Stationing marine air squadrons and high-stage service units (units with considerable expertise in engine maintenance, etc., referring to Futenma's helicopter servicing unit) in the same area would lead to more efficient aircraft servicing and rates of operation.

- There would be no constraints on the running of the V-22s scheduled to be introduced to the U.S. Marine Corps.

- It would facilitate the upgrading and modernization of Kadena Air Base.

- It was assured of a strong commitment by the Japanese government on the safe use of the base as a key strategic site.

For Kurt Campbell, this was a new argument, but he was not good with the technical aspects, so he asked the Japanese to talk with an expert from CINCPAC in Hawaii. Campbell picked up the phone there and then and called Hawaii. He said Nobushige Takamizawa, director of the JDA's Defense Operations Division, and Yayoi Matsuda, assistant director of MOFA's Japan-U.S. Security Treaty Division, were being sent over to CINCPAC and the people there were to cooperate fully, to listen to what they had to say. The two left immediately for Hawaii.

The San Francisco session of SACO was the last time the Japanese side pushed the Kadena proposal.

Looking back, it is difficult to understand why the JDA pushed the Kadena proposal so hard, marching straight towards "death with honor" (*gyokusai*).

There were those on the American side too, such as former Assistant Secretary of Defense Richard Armitage, who proposed integration with Kadena in the early stages. It was not as if the JDA alone was aiming at the wrong target.

The JDA are said to have failed to understand the Americans' true intentions. In fact, the JDA showed that it wasn't sufficiently aware of the real intentions of the all-important people of Okinawa.

The JDA ended up getting a bad rating from Prime Minister Hashimoto for "poor vision." The JDA had created friction in the SACO process as well as fermented mistrust on both sides.

Takemasa Moriya, counselor to the Bureau of Defense, however, coolly calculated from the outset that nothing else could have been done. Moriya confided to a very close friend just at the time they were trying to settle on the Kadena proposal, "In short, we couldn't move on to the next issue until we had tried everything, especially the Kadena consolidation proposal."

Moriya and the others always believed that they had a chance to pull off Kadena. At the same time, however, there was one other factor, dealing with Okinawa.

They had to give the Kadena proposal serious consideration as long as Vice-Governor Yoshimoto had raised it. They could not dismiss it out of hand if only because the perennially opposed Okinawans had brought it forward as a specific proposal. They had to make a sincere response. That is why, irrespective of whether Kadena was feasible or not, they had had to pursue the possibility to the very end.

One could call it a piece of *kabuki* if one liked, but the Americans didn't see it that way. Even if they had, they probably would have said they were not duty bound to keep the Japanese company in their domestic political games and flatly refused to have such a strategically important topic as Kadena used as bait.

"That typically Japanese, traditional way of doing things doesn't go down well with the Americans. I felt a kind of cultural gap that the very thought could be seriously entertained." That was how one of Moriya's colleagues, who respected him as a strategist, put it. "If there are strategists given to flights of fancy and those with their feet firmly on the ground, then Moriya is on the ground."[21]

Enter Yukio Okamoto

As the autumn winds began to blow, Campbell felt his misgivings mount. Both the proposal to integrate Kadena and that to expand Camp Schwab had met fierce resistance and were going nowhere.

Close to a year had passed since the rape of the young Okinawan schoolgirl. Five months had gone by since the decision to return Futenma. The two countries were scheduled to hold a "2+2" meeting between their respective Foreign Affairs ministers and Defense ministers. On September 24 the two leaders would meet in New York. They needed to come up with some general direction by then. There was no time. Campbell felt that "we were about to run into a brick wall at the '2+2' and we had nothing to show for it."[22]

It was during this time that Campbell met with Yukio Okamoto. Okamoto had moved to the private sector after serving as director of the First North American Affairs Division at the Foreign Ministry and had set up his own consultancy. Campbell knew Okamoto's name, having heard about him from Armitage. Armitage had suggested he meet Okamoto if he had the chance.

At the end of July when he was in Tokyo on business, Campbell invited Okamoto for a drink. They met for the first time in the bar at the Hotel Okura. Okamoto knew more about the bases on Okinawa than anybody else. Campbell remembers being strongly impressed by that. It was just that he was so up front about being opposed to the proposal to consolidate Kadena. That made an even stronger impression on Campbell. His argument was that "Kadena will become the next focus of the antibase movement, which is not desirable for the bilateral alliance."

Okamoto prevaricated on the nature of his relationship with the PM's office. But he spoke as if he knew exactly what was going on in its very heart. As he listened to what Okamoto had to say, Campbell began to feel, *Perhaps Hashimoto has some doubts about Kadena. I'd heard the PM's office was leaning towards the Kadena proposal, but perhaps things are more complicated than that.*

Okamoto was an impassioned diplomat. He was incredibly strong when the chips were down. He was a brave fighter in the storm trooper mold. His talents were given their best airing during the Gulf War. His all-round performance at that time is the stuff of legend in Kasumigaseki today. There are many Okamoto fans in other ministries as well.

An affable fellow, he was very careful to cultivate personal relations, particularly with his seniors and elders, which is why he was dubbed "Grandpa-Killer Extraordinaire." His inroads into political, business, and media circles were said to be just as impressive as that of his mentor and former director of the North American Affairs Bureau, Yukio Sato. This personality stood him in good stead as a consultant.

Entreated by the Hashimoto PM's office, he was later to handle Okinawan affairs as a special adviser to the prime minister. When setting up the position, Hashimoto asked Masahide Ota, Okinawa's governor, if he "had anyone in mind."

Ota replied, "Okamoto-san is extremely assertive and has the prefecture's trust. We would be grateful if you appointed him."[23] Hashimoto respected that wish.

Okamoto did not disappoint them. He built up a relation of trust with the mayors in the municipalities with bases, was the first to catch what they were thinking, and did his utmost to see that reflected in the measures on Okinawa.

There were some at the Foreign Ministry who were not pleased to see Okamoto sticking his nose into Okinawan affairs. One of them grumbled, "We helped him quite a bit when he set up on his own. He knows how we feel. And yet, butting in from the side like this could well scuttle things that look like they might soon be settled."[24]

Okamoto had no intention of compromising the SACO process. It was simply that he believed the only way to resolve the question of the bases was to wade into the local communities, synthesize their opinions, and voice them directly to the Americans.

Knowing full well that he was a nuisance, he ran every which way. What hurt him the most was the opposition from his old stomping ground at the Foreign Ministry. This was not just "village" mentality directed towards Okamoto, the individual, who had up and "left the village." He also felt "an inexpressible hostility towards a private citizen climbing up onto the stage of foreign affairs."[25]

Okamoto went to Washington in mid-August. He was on other business, but he met again with Campbell. He told Campbell that a committee on Okinawa (the Okinawa Problems Committee), chaired by Professor Haruo Shimada of Keio University, was soon to be launched as a private advisory body to the Cabinet secretary. The Japanese government's approach on economic development in Okinawa was set to become serious, and he wanted to help out with that.[26]

As he was taking his leave, Okamoto handed Campbell an aerial shot of Kadena-cho. It was a photo he had been given in June by the mayor, Tokujitsu Miyagi, and asked to show to "the right person on the American side."

The two huge runways at Kadena were smack in the middle, sitting pretty. Around them was the town, clinging like a shell to the perimeter of the base. It was a large, color shot taken from the air. After he had shown the photo to Campbell, Okamoto rolled it up, put it in a tube, and handed it to him. (Campbell later brought it to his appearance before Congress and showed it.) Campbell thought, *I'll need to stay in touch with this fellow. I'll just let MOFA know what's going on though the Japanese bureaucrats are almost abnormally touchy about private citizens getting involved. I'll have to be careful.*

Again it was Richard Armitage who gave Campbell a stimulus to explore a new venue. The two had been meeting on a monthly basis for opinion exchange. They met again in late August.

It was around this time that Armitage started talking about MOBs (mobile offshore bases); how the Americans had built floating bases in the Mekong Delta during the Vietnam War and attacked the Vietcong from them, how they had been used in the Persian Gulf in 1987 to out-flank Iranian mine operations. Armitage suggested strongly that the possibility be pursued.

Campbell took this idea home with him and immediately began gathering information from agencies such as the Strategy and Require-ment Office and the Acquisition and Technology Office. Campbell had heard of it before. After the SACO interim report was released in April, one of his staff members, Gayle Von Eckartsburg, had put it forward. Campbell did not show that much interest in it at the time.

What Eckartsburg had come up with was the concept for some sort of offshore floating facility originally proposed by Admiral William Owens, a navy supporter of high-tech strategy. Owens was so enam-ored with the idea that, when he was vice-chairman of the Joint Chiefs of Staff, he had a model about 8 feet wide and 10 feet long made and encased in glass, and kept next to his office.[27] The only problem was that there was resistance in the navy itself and among the Joint Chiefs of Staff, so it never got any further than the model. Campbell and oth-ers in a special team contacted Owens and worked around the clock on the concept.

In September, when the U.S. government had started exploring the MOB, Campbell felt the need to meet Okamoto again and brief him on the idea. *Tanaka [Hitoshi Tanaka, deputy director-general of the North Amer-ican Affairs Bureau at MOFA] is mediating for us with the PM's office. But he's always been cautious, and the JDA is fanatical about the Kadena proposal. I don't know how well our intentions are getting through to the PM. I'll get Okamoto to make doubly sure.*

Campbell sounded out the Japanese Embassy about meeting with Okamoto again. However, the diplomats sounded as if they didn't wel-come meeting with him. At this stage, they were intensely alarmed and averse to Okamoto getting involved in the bases.

"But Okamoto has the blessing of the PM's office. What do they mean, don't meet him? Perry has told me to keep an open door to as many ideas as possible."

This was Campbell's argument. But to avoid creating any "official" impression, he decided to meet Okamoto clandestinely and in San Francisco, not Washington. He was scheduled to attend a seminar at Stanford University on September 7. He would meet Okamoto then.

Notes

1. "SACO Base Accord Not Enough: Okinawa's Ota," *Jiji Press*, April 15, 1996.

2. Interview with a senior DOD official.

3. Interview with Robin Sakoda.

4. Interview with Masanori Yoshimoto.

5. Interview with Hiroshi Hirabayashi.

6. Interview with a senior MOFA official.

7. Interview with a senior JDA official.

8. Interview with a JDA official.

9. Ibid.

10. Interview with Ryutaro Hashimoto.

11. Interview with Tokujitsu Miyagi.

12. *Okinawa Times*, April 16, 1996.

13. Interview with Tokujitsu Miyagi.

14. Interview with Takehiko Shimaguchi.

15. Interview with a senior MOFA official.

16. Ibid.

17. Interview with a senior White House official.

18. Interview with a U.S. State Department official.

19. Interview with a White House official.

20. Author's conversation with a senior DOD official.

21. Interview with a JDA official.

22. Interview with Kurt Campbell.

23. Interview with Masahide Ota.

24. Based on the author's conversation with a senior MOFA official.

25. Interview with Yukio Okamoto.

26. Interview with Kurt Campbell.

27. Interview with William Owens.

Chapter Nine

—◆—

Floating at Sea

A Nonstarter

September 4.

A barbecue was held at the Azabu Nagasaka-cho residence of the deputy chief of mission at the U.S. Embassy, Rust Deming, in Tokyo. Many of the staff from the Japanese Ministry of Foreign Affairs' (MOFA) North American Affairs and Economic Affairs Bureaus attended the gathering. Deming had invited them to thank them for all they had done for the bilateral relationship. The MOFA staff mingled with the embassy staff, talking and laughing with cocktail glasses in hand.

Deming was one of the most knowledgeable people on Japan in the State Department. His father, Olcott, was America's second consul-general in Naha during the late 1950s. Deming used to go out to Okinawa during his summer vacations and made friends there, Okinawan friends, whom he still kept in touch with.[1]

When Masahide Ota, Okinawa's governor, was hunting for material on the U.S. occupation after the war, he came across a cable that had been sent to the State Department by Olcott Deming. At the time, the military was trying to shift from leasing land to buying it outright for permanent possession, but Deming senior was strongly opposed and had sent off a cable to that effect. The cable showed "a diplomat sincerely trying to convey to the State Department the truth, literally with Okinawa's best interests at heart." Ota was moved. He told Deming junior, "Your father was a benefactor for Okinawa." When Ota visited Washington, Deming senior always made sure to show up at Ota's reception party.[2]

The art deco residence was built by Shojiro Ishibashi, then president of the Bridgestone Tire and Rubber Company, before the war. During the war, the garden was used to grow vegetables, and an air raid shelter was built in the middle of the lawn. At the end of the war, it was the only house left standing in the immediate area.

After the war, the Ishibashis returned there from Karuizawa, where they had been evacuated, along with the Hatoyamas and other relatives. Prominent politicians such as Ichiro Hatoyama, Ichiro Kono, Bukichi Miki, and Tsuruhei Matsuno met there frequently. It was there that the Liberal Party, forerunner of today's Liberal Democratic Party, was formed (the LDP is the result of a 1955 merger between the Liberal Party and the Democratic Party). It was the start of the so-called 1955 system of Japanese postwar politics.

The building was bought by the U.S. government in 1952, the same year that Japan regained independence from the occupation and a year after the September 8 signing of the peace and security treaties. This history of the residence overlapped perfectly with the history of bilateral security.

Some of the younger staff were at the barbecue out in the garden; others were inside singing karaoke. Deming's wife joined in. She had a good voice and sang both Japanese and American songs.

They had hastily borrowed a karaoke set from the embassy for the occasion. A lot of the numbers were sentimental country and western tunes. Perhaps the Americans thought it would be rude if they didn't join in, but they immediately starting singing along. Before karaoke entered the English lexicon, it used to be translated as "sing along."

Hitoshi Tanaka, deputy director-general of the North American Affairs Bureau, was one of the guests. He received a message from Deming that there was an urgent call for him from Washington. "It's from Campbell."

Tanaka was shown to Deming's study on the second floor. He could still hear the karaoke singing, but it was possible to talk.

"Tanaka-san. Sorry to disturb your fun." *Why does Campbell keep switching from my first name to my family name? Does it mean something? Why is he using my family name tonight? Does he have something unpleasant to tell me?*

Tanaka waited for a bombshell as these thoughts raced through his mind.

"It's about Futenma's alternative heliport. An idea's come up that in addition to the Kadena consolidation proposal or relocating to Camp Schwab, a mobile offshore base [MOB] could be a useful option. I called you because I wanted to hear your thoughts on it first."

Tanaka told him straight out, "That'll never fly. It's a nonstarter. It's extremely risky setting all your hopes on a wild dream like that. And what's more, the minute you bring something like that up, we'll never be able to do Kadena or Camp Schwab."

"I know it sounds sudden, but don't say no right away. Give it some thought."[3] Campbell was insistent. He was scheduled to discuss this and other alternatives with Perry on September 6. Mondale would be there; nothing had been decided yet; it was still just an idea. And finally, he added, "At least take it to the prime minister. See what he thinks about it in private. Just keep it between the two of you."[4]

Tanaka reported to Masaki Orita, head of the North American Affairs Bureau, but his response was cautious too. "It's too risky betting on something we know nothing about."

"If we bring it up as an option, we'll never get back on land."

"Tabling something like that without even having done feasibility studies will just raise everyone's hopes and stir things up."[5]

Tanaka decided to tell Hashimoto about it after he found out the result of the meeting in Washington on the 6th.

September 8, Sunday.

Tanaka visited the PM's residence and briefed Hashimoto on the floating facility and the meeting in Washington. "I don't yet have a good idea of how serious it is. I think it's a possibility, but I'm concerned that we will lose our other options if it comes up. I think we should be cautious here."

Hashimoto, however, calmly replied, "No, let's look into it." He also said it would only be a slight step backwards in stance. He stretched out both arms, moved them up and down, then dropped them back to his side in a gesture of taking balance. "But don't kill the other two options."

Hashimoto emphasized the relationship with Okinawa, driving home the fact that it was important to start from what would be the best option for Okinawa. Environmental factors would have to be considered. And it had to be removable.

Hashimoto taunted Tanaka slightly. "It might deviate a little from the way bureaucrats think, but politicians love this sort of thing, you know."[6]

Tanaka felt uncomfortable with this tone of "I knew what was coming, I know everything that's going on." Still, given that the prime minister was keen on it, he had to swallow his negativist arguments. *That was true about Futenma too. Administrative arguments shouldn't hamper politics. It's probably his political instincts at work again.*

There was a call from Deming when he got back to the Foreign Ministry. He wanted to know the PM's reaction. In a slightly pugnacious tone, Tanaka told him the prime minister was keen.

"Campbell's been to a seminar at Stanford. He'll be on his way to San Francisco now. I'll call him with the news when he gets in." So saying, Deming hung up.

It was still Saturday the seventh in the United States.

Campbell and Okamoto had both flown into San Francisco airport that day and headed straight for the Hilton Hotel. When he had talked with Okamoto by phone earlier, Campbell told him of the offshore heliport. Okamoto didn't seem to know much and asked for pictures, drawings, things like that. Campbell handed him a package of material including a color photo of the model.

At the time, the image Campbell had in his mind was for a floating facility, something that could be moved anywhere after it was built.

"As you know," said Okamoto, "Japan has three weapons export principles. If this base was to be removed from Japan, it would cause problems in that connection."

"So, I think you'd better make an early decision that it will not be exported; it will not be mobile."

Halfway through, Campbell got a call from Tokyo. It was Deming.

"Hashimoto is keen on the floating facility idea. Tanaka's just let us know."

Campbell told Okamoto, passing on the message verbatim. Then he drained his glass of beer.

When the meeting was over, the two of them went straight back to the airport. Campbell called Perry from a pay phone in the airport lobby. When he looked up he found Okamoto calling someone on the next pay phone. Okamoto noticed too.

He had a friendly twinkle in his eyes. *Can he get Hashimoto directly? Or is he phoning Kajiyama? Maybe his wife? All the same, he came onto the scene with perfect timing. Must have theatrical talent!*

Okamoto found what Campbell had to say that day very different from their previous meeting. He could see Campbell perking up as he went along. *He likes new challenges. And he's certainly brave telling a private citizen like myself all that he does. But where does his mettle come from? His impassioned commitment to the alliance with Japan?*

They parted with a nod. They both felt as if some of the heavy weight they had been carrying around had been lifted.[7]

Slides

William Perry, secretary of defense, leaned forward to see the slides. Walter Mondale, U.S. ambassador to Japan, moved back.[8] Perry is near-sighted and Mondale is farsighted. They were looking at a huge image of the offshore heliport model.

It was Friday, September 6. The two had eaten breakfast together in the lounge next door to the defense secretary's office. After breakfast a briefing was held including the top military brass. "There were a lot of stars. All the uniformed guys were a minimum of three stars."[9]

They were roadblocked on the two proposed alternative sites for Futenma at that point, integration with Kadena or relocation to Camp Schwab. It was at this briefing that Deputy Assistant Secretary of Defense Campbell proposed the MOB. He had already started sounding it out within the Pentagon and resistance was strong.

"The first time I heard of it," Robin Sakoda said, "my reaction was the same reaction as 99 percent of the people that hear it for the first time, which is, 'come on! You have got to be kidding me!' This is too crazy, it's too wild an idea."[10]

The top brass weren't too enthusiastic either. Campbell's immediate superior, Assistant Secretary of Defense Franklin Kramer, came right out against it, saying it couldn't be done; we're not talking science fiction here! Caution was voiced about even including the slides of the offshore facility in the briefing that day. Campbell almost had to beg for the chance to show them.[11]

The navy leaders raised doubts about the semisub structure, saying the technology was not ready yet. They were alarmed at the possibility of the marines getting a huge floating facility like this.

Perry spoke. "Speaking as an engineer, there's nothing cutting-edge in terms of the technology. It's all 30 or 40 years old. The question is simply how to bring it all together."[12] Although the defense secretary avoided making a clear statement in the meeting, everyone in the room felt he was starting to show an uncommon interest in the concept. A DOD official said, "I think his response was really balanced. He is the 1 percent that is different. Remember that I said that 99 percent of the people that hear it, their initial reaction is 'you have gotta be crazy!' He is the 1 percent that was different. He is part of the 1 percent. He said, 'OK, I understand this, and I understand the things that we have to do in order to get there. And that is, we need to obviously examine it, but then figure out, if we don't have the technologies to do this now here in our lap right now, these are the things that we need to do to get there.'"[13]

Mondale showed his interest. "As a matter of principle, I liked it. I thought it would be less obtrusive to the citizens of Okinawa. It is not a pipe dream," as he explained later.[14]

Yet Mondale didn't make a direct endorsement of the offshore heliport either. Rather, he pointed out the extreme political difficulties entailed in the suggestions to date for both governments. He was especially negative about Kadena.

He did not want to do something that signaled to the region that the Americans were leaving. His point was that you cannot have an alliance without forward troops; you can't have an alliance without some inconvenience. The Japanese must confront the essential truth that if you want an alliance, you have to pay for it.[15]

He also mentioned that it did have the advantage of intruding less into the daily lives of the Okinawans. He immediately understood that it offered a potential way out of the serious political problems that confronted Prime Minister Hashimoto and Governor Ota. He then continued that it was an intriguing idea and should be considered.[16]

The briefing that day was only to consider the idea, not to select options. It was decided on the spot to dispatch Campbell to Japan to explain the concept after having sounded out the military, the White House, and finally Congress. The official U.S. government decision to include this as an option wasn't taken until the day after Campbell left, the night before his meeting with the Japanese on September 13.[17]

It was following this briefing that the U.S. government started tilting towards the mobile offshore base. Campbell was working out which aspect he should accentuate in order to get a better reception from the Japanese. As a result, he came up with a list of five advantages. He was never happy unless he had five arguments on an issue, and these had come to be known as Dr. Campbell's Five Points in Japanese officialdom.

- It matches both the requirements for the marines' contingency deployment and U.S. military presence.

- Noise would not be a problem if situated five miles offshore.

- It was not a permanent fixture.

- It would avoid environmental problems.

- It would be an opportunity to demonstrate to the world the prowess of joint technological cooperation between Japan and the United States.

A top U.S. government official at the time revealed to only a very few, close friends that "removability was the key element. The day will come when the two Koreas are united and the crucial duty of the marines will be over. You can't deny that possibility. When you think of that kind of scenario, it'd be better not to start large-scale construction on land."

Of course, that kind of statement was taboo in official settings.

The Second Futenma Shock

The morning of September 13.

The office of the director-general of the North American Affairs Bureau, the Japanese Ministry of Foreign Affairs. One of the Americans remembered, "It was a very quiet moment. . . . You could hear a pin drop."[18]

No one uttered a word after Deputy Assistant Secretary of Defense Campbell had spoken. Finally, Bureau of Defense Policy Director Masahiro Akiyama broke the silence.

"This is an American proposal, is it?"

"Yes. It is an official proposal from the government of the United States." Campbell answered Akiyama's question full of confidence.

Akiyama was extremely flustered. In an effort to hide the fact, he lowered his already normally high-pitched voice.

It was during a Special Action Committee on Okinawa (SACO) meeting that Campbell had asked for a special discussion with just a few of the Japanese, which was why they had moved from the meeting room at MOFA to this office.

The Japanese side consisted of Masaki Orita, director-general of the North American Affairs Bureau; Hitoshi Tanaka, deputy director-general of the North American Affairs Bureau; plus Akiyama and Takemasa Moriya, counselor to the Bureau of Defense. Apart from Campbell, the Americans comprised Charles Kartman, deputy assistant secretary of state, and Rust Deming.

Campbell dropped his bombshell when they were all seated at the table. "America would like to include an offshore heliport as an alternative to Futenma. That's what we're proposing."[19] He wasn't suggesting consolidation at Kadena or relocation to Camp Schwab but constructing a base offshore and moving the marine functions there.

To Akiyama, it was totally unexpected, but he had noticed a slight rustle in the air about a week ago. *Orita looks funny. He can't lie. Everything shows on his face. Was he up to something behind the scenes?*

Keen-eared Moriya had got information on "strange happenings at the PM's office."

Only a few days ago, Akiyama had received an inquiry via a third party from the acquaintance of a U.S. military person to the effect that they had heard Washington was considering an offshore heliport or something. Akiyama had responded, no, not at all, that he had heard nothing of it, but all the same he had been troubled by the query.

At MOF, Akiyama had served as the budget officer for the Ministry of Transport. He knew of the existence of this kind of concept. He had looked into floating construction and offshore airports at the time the Kansai International Airport was first mooted. He recalled that it had been dropped because of several problems with the mooring and welding technology.

The Japanese Defense Agency (JDA) had also looked into this construction method previously. There had been some discussion of building an offshore heliport and transferring U.S. Air Force night training flights at Atsugi base there. It never eventuated, however, because of American opposition; in the end, flights were transferred to Iwo Jima.

Masayuki Fujishima, counselor for facilities at the JDA, had in fact mentioned the idea and how interesting it was a few months ago. But Akiyama didn't make any move. He had a preconceived notion that it would be impossible. He certainly didn't expect to hear such a declaration from Campbell.

The higher-ups at MOFA seemed to have heard about it beforehand. They were staying pretty much out of the conversation. It was mainly Campbell and Akiyama who debated the pros and cons, with Akiyama asking the questions and Campbell answering them.

"That's right. When their job is over, it can be removed."

"If it was offshore, we could avoid a lot of the problems that are likely to happen with an onshore facility."

"You're quite right. There are many technical questions that still need to be sorted out. The proposal is that we work them out together, Japan and America."

When Akiyama got back to the JDA in Roppongi, he flew straight to the director-general's office. "This kind of thing is being discussed."

Akiyama spoke as if it didn't concern him, but he felt the anger welling up inside him as he gave a quick rundown on what had taken place. Frustration was probably more accurate. It was the same with the return of Futenma. This time too. The Defense Department and the Foreign Ministry had taken over and kept the JDA out of the loop.

"Does the prime minister know?"

"Well, who knows? I can't say when he learned of it, but I'm sure he has been briefed."

There was a message that Akiyama present himself at the PM's office after noon. Hashimoto was surrounded by his two Cabinet ministers, Foreign Minister Yukihiko Ikeda and JDA Director-General Usui, as well as Orita and Akiyama.

"The American proposal was to choose between consolidation at Kadena or relocating to Camp Schwab, but they would like to explore more comprehensive possibilities including this idea."

"The Americans seem serious about it. There's still a lot of details that have to be worked out including the design, location, how long it will take, and so on. The environmental implications will need to be checked out as well. It's good that it can be removed. Let's work on the assumption that we'll accept their proposal. Get them to consider it as one of the options."

Hashimoto was in good humor. "Going offshore would solve the noise problem, wouldn't it? It might be easier to go offshore than stay onshore. I get the picture. Let's tell Governor Ota as soon as we know there are no problems."

He called him himself. Ota was out. Hashimoto asked for a return call, but it was a long time coming. "A battle of wills with Ota-san, eh?"

And still no call came. "Oh, hang it. Let's do it later."

But he had lingering regrets. In an attempt to dissemble, Hashimoto altered his tone. "Don't let this get out! It can't be leaked no matter what!"[20]

Hashimoto wanted to announce the concept himself. He had decided the stage would be Okinawa.

Aggrieved Elements

Usui learned of the announcement in a one-page fax from the Defense Policy Section team at the Bureau of Defense Policy, which he received at the Hilton Hawaiian Village Hotel in Hawaii. He had stopped off there to pay a courtesy call on the U.S. Forces Pacific based in Hawaii en route to a "2+2" meeting of the two countries' foreign and defense ministers in New York on September 19.

On September 16 he met with Joseph Prueher, U.S. Navy commander-in-chief of the U.S. Pacific Command. Prueher's comment that they should keep as many relocation options open as possible was full of hidden connotations. Usui was hard-pressed to find an appropriate response. Hashimoto had sworn him to secrecy. Usui refrained from talking about it further.

The fax turned up later that night. By Japanese time, it was the evening of the following day. It was a fax of the entire speech made by Hashimoto that day in Okinawa. Usui's secretary, Tetsuro Kuroe, showed him the fax at breakfast. The section covering the offshore heliport was marked. Usui took out his glasses and started to read:

> Regarding the relocation site for the heliport, a condition for the return [of Futenma], it is well known that proposals for consolidating at Kadena and relocating to Schwab have been considered at a working level. This time, however, a new proposal has been put forward by the United States in bilateral talks.
>
> This concerns concentrating the technology in both countries to carry out research into the possibility of constructing a removable, offshore heliport.
>
> In fact, I have instructed the authorities involved to consider a wide range of options while at the same time looking into the matter myself to explore the feasibility of a removable offshore heliport that would not lead to environmental destruction.
>
> This current proposal suggested by the United States is in line with this thinking of mine and although there are many problems that need to be overcome, I believe it is worth considering as an option on its merits.
>
> Therefore, I would like to see this new proposal given serious consideration by the two countries along with the existing options, always consulting closely with Okinawan opinion.

Usui asked Tadahiko Furusawa, head of the Joint Staff Council Secretariat, what an offshore heliport was. Furusawa drew a picture to explain.

When Hashimoto told Kajiyama and Furukawa that he would go to Okinawa himself to make the announcement, the two of them cautioned him. Kajiyama said, "Won't they want everything to be put on floating docks?" but Hashimoto's mind was made up.

Furukawa contacted Masanori Yoshimoto, vice-governor of Okinawa Prefecture. If only because they had both worked so hard together to have Kadena settled, Furukawa felt he had to let him know as soon as possible. There were also several details that had to be worked out about Hashimoto's visit. Yoshimoto's response, however, was surprisingly low key. "Well, well. A floating dock, is it? There was talk of that a few years back."

The Defense Agency was not happy. Voices of intense displeasure leaked from the agency. Resentment towards the Foreign Ministry bubbled up.

"The Foreign Ministry was so busy reporting to the Americans. They went off to the United States, were told Kadena was difficult, came back home, went to the prime minister saying Kadena was impossible, and squashed it."

"No, the Americans used the Foreign Ministry to squash it."

Conversations like that were rife.

The movements of Yukio Okamoto also came in for a wide variety of speculation. From the very outset, the JDA had suspected he was just MOFA in another guise; MOFA had whispered to him its wishes and he had been used to squash the Kadena proposal. There were those at MOFA who suspected he'd been the one who had instigated talk on the floating facility. Both were wrong, but so thick was the veil among the PM's office, the Foreign Ministry, and the JDA that it gave rise to such wild conjectures.[21]

A senior official at the JDA in charge of SACO raised the following points about that time.

1. In pursuing the offshore heliport proposal, to what extent did the PM's office understand the military operational issues involved?

2. How serious was their consideration of the future key elements of bilateral defense cooperation?

3. Both the old explosives storage area at Kadena and Camp Schwab were scuttled by environmental constraints. Hadn't they overemphasized the arguments that sounded like they came from environmental activists?

4. Where did their confidence in the floating facility, especially the technology, come from?[22]

Criticism was even heard to the effect that the prime minister had been rash.

The Defense Facilities Administration Agency (DFAA) kept a sanguine eye on the floating facility proposal. Masuo Morodomi, director-general of the DFAA, was saying, "Being offshore doesn't make it easy. In terms of winning over the locals, it's just as tough. They still haven't been able to build Ishigaki airport and that's ten years! The locals won't agree and environmental activists have flocked there in droves from all around the world to protect the coral. That's how tough it is and there, we're talking about improving the locals' own transport access!"[23]

Akiyama was completely bowled over. He confided to a friend that it was a second Futenma shock. Just like with the return of Futenma, they'd been kept out of the loop.

I sweated my guts out all summer long. What was that all about? The DOD boys in Washington said they couldn't convince the military in the field, so we went all the way to Hawaii to engineer a persuasive case. Imagine what they must be thinking in the agency!

Akiyama knew the aggrieved elements were indignant with rage, and he knew only too well how they felt. *At least the prime minister was interested in the Kadena consolidation proposal. What made him change his mind so summarily? Was he worried about forcing it through in the face of such resistance from the U.S. military?*

Or . . . *In hindsight, perhaps the PM was thinking something else. And I was at fault for not picking it up. I have to shake this off right away.*[24]

Akiyama prided himself on being good at putting things behind him, both intellectually and emotionally. This time, however, convincing himself took a little longer than usual.

Surfacing

It took Deputy Assistant Secretary of Defense Campbell a full week to build a consensus within the government on presenting the proposal for the offshore heliport as an American proposal.

Prime Minister Hashimoto, who had learned of this American concept beforehand, was getting jittery because the official decision from the Americans was taking so long to arrive.

Fears abounded in the crucial marines that they would not be able to perform their duties in such a setting. The navy was alarmed that the base amounted to an aircraft carrier, and if so, it threatened their turf. If the Americans and the Japanese were to cooperate on technology, they certainly couldn't afford a replay of the trouble they had experienced with the FSX (next-generation fighter), which had escalated into a political issue. They had to get Congress' and the Commerce Department's support.

The biggest hurdle to deciding whether to consolidate at Kadena or relocate to Camp Schwab had been military egos. In either case, they had the ability to activate the air force lobby and the marine lobby in Congress, and in fact they did.

Come the fall and it would be the middle of the presidential election. The White House was edgy. There'd be hell to pay if things got complicated between America and Japan. And yet, there'd be trouble too if the

DOD pushed the military too hard and it started to squeal. But if Congress, and a Republican Congress at that, started to squeal there'd be even bigger trouble. Clinton's early days protesting the Vietnam War and dodging the draft had created tense relations between the White House and the military.

A high-placed official in the U.S. government recalls, "In a word, there was an unspoken pressure not to take military-related problems to the White House."[25] The White House was watching Futenma closely but wasn't touching. It was this kind of consideration that made the White House, when drafting a memorandum from President Clinton to Prime Minister Hashimoto in early September, contemplate inserting a request that the prime minister not go into "the details" of Futenma at the summit meeting. In the end, this concern was left out of the memorandum but instead conveyed by word of mouth to the Japanese by Ambassador Mondale.[26]

Futenma's return had run into difficulties, and there was the chance that the more the U.S. military flaunted its ego, the more doubts over U.S. military presence in Japan would mount. That was something the U.S. government feared, and it was watching Prime Minister Hashimoto's moves warily.

Hesitation and doubt over the Japanese government's approach to the Okinawan bases were beginning to emerge. Hadn't it announced a joint declaration on security at the April summit and reinforced the alliance? And yet, despite that, the Americans did not seem to have a good game plan with Okinawa. It looked like the alliance was being torn out by the roots. What was going on?

They could understand Okinawa's Governor Masahide Ota invoking Okinawan sentiment and putting forward issues based on Okinawa's "singular situation." But what was happening when even voices inside the LDP and the Foreign Ministry started calling for reductions in the bases and the American presence, especially a scaling back of the marines?

There was a growing tendency to unilaterally blow, or at least desire to blow, the return of Futenma up into an issue of the relocation, reduction, and, furthermore, the withdrawal of the marines, and to premise security debate on that. Not only was the Japanese government not doing anything to contradict that popular perception, wasn't it, rather, leaving it to its own designs?

Apparently, part of the background for this was the domestic emergence of a new political force where security was concerned. A high official in the U.S. government described this as a political game where everybody kicked the marines. The same official analyzed the new political force in the security arena as follows:

- The pro–Security Treaty lobby started arguing that "the security wouldn't hold if the number of marines stationed in Japan wasn't cut."
- The pro-treaty–minus-the-troops lobby was increasingly expecting a "first step on troop withdrawal."
- The scrap-the-treaty forces had started engineering "a hollowing-out of the security treaty by tapping into antimarine sentiment."
- The supporters of Japan as "a normal country" saw it as "a good opportunity to push Japan into shouldering more of the U.S. military burden."[27]

A high-ranking official in the State Department displayed his dissatisfaction with the statement read by Prime Minister Hashimoto on his visit to Okinawa on September 17, the very next day. "I thought he was more of a leader, but I was disappointed. Ninety percent was Okinawa and only 10 percent bilateral security. I wanted him to say more about the importance of the security relationship."[28]

Another high-ranking government official remarked, "I was worried that in his headlong pursuit of short-term domestic political goals, he would sacrifice America's long-term strategic requirements."[29]

The greatest source of U.S. fear was that the return of Futenma would fail to resolve the base question, which would then "spread like cancer cells."[30]

Mooring

However, calls for rationalizing the presence starting with a cut in the number of marines began being voiced in America, and by pro-treaty experts. Even Admiral William Owens (ret.), the father of the MOB concept and therefore the original source behind the current offshore heliport proposal, and Richard Armitage, former assistant secretary of defense, who had pushed strongly for it as an alternative to Futenma, both agreed that the future nature of the marines' presence would have to be rethought.

All through this, the United States' single greatest concern was ensuring the weight of the U.S. presence, and thereby American prestige. The heliport concept was, therefore, also a "status operation" to cover up wavering overseas confidence in U.S. leadership and U.S. domestic statesmen's lack of political power against the military.

They did not have the political power to force the respective services to consolidate the bases. The timing was bad too. If they couldn't keep the overseas bases in place, it would be interpreted as an American withdrawal. They didn't have the diplomatic power to convince people

that even if the bases were reduced, the U.S. presence and its commitment was rock solid. The offshore heliport was nothing more than the
product of such compromises.

It was not just a compromise between politics and the military. It was
also a compromise between politics and technology, "a technological
response to a political challenge."[31] At the same time, it also led to the prediction that the U.S. military presence in Japan would over the long run
gradually evolve into a navy and air force structure minus the marines.

An expert cooperating with the DOD from outside the government
remarked, "If there is any hidden agenda regarding the offshore heliport, that would be it." In this context, the need to "moor" the facility
until the contingency on the Korean Peninsula was over started to
become a distinct possibility. In other words, it was a stopgap.

No matter how much the marines stressed the global significance,
the real reason for them to be stationed in Okinawa was in case of a contingency on the Korean Peninsula. If the two Koreas headed towards a
reconciliation, that rationale would be fundamentally shaken. While it
was not something to be interwoven with political judgments, at this
point it did have to be kept at the back of the mind.

In fact, this was exactly what all the people pushing for the MOB concept had in mind. As will be explained later, the fact that both Owens
and Armitage, who were lobbying hard for the MOB, argued for a mov-
able offshore base as well as a reduction in the marines, bearing in mind
the possibility of situational changes on the Korean Peninsula, was an
indication of this hidden "mooring" intention.

In relation to the "longevity" of the offshore heliport, a high-ranking member of the U.S. government was heard to whisper, "Reunification of the two Koreas may come much earlier than we expect." He
thereby implied that the heliport would be a contingency measure
until that time.[32]

For those in favor of moving the bases offshore, making the marine
presence more functional and rationalizing the alliance, the offshore
heliport concept was deemed to be a first step in that direction.

It was no longer enough just to say that the U.S. military presence in
Japan is crucial to stability in the Asian-Pacific region. People in the
United States as well began to be frightened that unless the issues of
what sort of presence, how, against what, and with what requirements
were examined closely and explained persuasively, the United States
would be unable to maintain the bilateral alliance in the long run. And
these people were emerging from the ranks of those who had been in
favor of the bilateral security axis.

New approaches and efforts were starting up concerning the return of
Futenma and the offshore heliport, "reduction," "mooring," the nature
of the presence, and how it should be maintained. Some in the United
States also quietly joined the political game of kicking the marines.

Notes

1. Interview with Rust Deming.
2. Interview with Masahide Ota.
3. Interview with Hitoshi Tanaka.
4. Interview with Kurt Campbell.
5. Interview with Masaki Orita.
6. Interview with Ryutaro Hashimoto.
7. This section is based on interviews with Kurt Campbell and Yukio Okamoto.
8. Interview with Kurt Campbell.
9. Interview with Gayle Von Eckartsburg.
10. Interview with Robin Sakoda.
11. Interview with Kurt Campbell.
12. Interview with a senior DOD official.
13. Interview with Robin Sakoda.
14. Interview with Walter Mondale.
15. Interview with Kurt Campbell.
16. Interview with a senior DOD official.
17. Ibid.
18. Interview with Kurt Campbell.
19. Interviews with participants of the meeting.
20. Ibid.
21. Interview with a senior JDA official.
22. Interview with a senior JDA official.
23. Interview with Masuo Morodomi.
24. Interview with Masahiro Akiyama.
25. Interview with a senior U.S. administration official.
26. Interview with a White House official.
27. Interview with a senior U.S. administration official.
28. Interview with a senior State Department official.
29. Interview with a high-ranking U.S. government official.
30. Interview with a high-ranking U.S. government official.
31. Interview with Charles Freeman.
32. Interview with a senior U.S. administration official.

Chapter Ten

———◆———

The Balloon

Removability

In Japan, megafloat construction was being pursued not for military purposes but mainly by major shipbuilding and steel companies in the private sector. Japanese interest in it, therefore, to a large extent reflected the interests of these industries.

The visionary use of maritime technology spanned many fields, including major international airports, floating car parks, waste treatment facilities, sewage treatment facilities, power plants, liquid natural gas (LNG) storage, fishing bases, floating hotels, fishing parks, and leisure facilities. Each concept, however, was different from the others and complicated by different vested interests.

The technology, however, could be divided into two main types: facilities tethered by struts in the seabed and all-floating facilities.

The two main means of tethered construction were the quick installation platform method (QIP) and the gravity method (a gravity model of concrete-based maritime construction). The QIP method used a number of steel columns fixed to the seabed to support the platform, whereas the gravity method spread pilings in concrete all over the bottom and built the platform atop that. There was also a third means of construction called the jacket method, where the structure was built like a lookout tower.

Turning to the floating type, the two main means were the pontoon method and the semisubmersible method. In the pontoon method, a platform consisting of steel pontoon units was installed in calm sea protected by a breakwater. The floating units were then linked together. In the semisubmersible method, a platform at wave-free height was supported by the buoyancy of a lower structure submerged under the sea.

The technological feasibility of each of these methods had to be examined. First, how big would the platform be? At the very least, it had to have a 1,500-meter runway. An estimated 60 aircraft would be using the facility in normal times. Apart from the runway, the platform would need a control tower, hangars, etc. If it was located in waters 5 to 25 meters deep (500 meters to 2 kilometers from land), a connecting bridge would be required; if located in waters 50 to 100 meters deep (3 to 7 kilometers from land), it would require shipping access. In the first case, waves would be 5 to 14 meters high; in the second case, 15 meters high. The fact that this region was a typhoon area also had to be considered. And finally, the construction time would be seven years.

Each method had its advantages and disadvantages. While the Americans, and Campbell in particular, were getting data ready from the DOD Technology and Acquisition Office and U.S. companies like Brown & Root,[1] the Japanese were being briefed by staff from New Nippon Steel and IHI (Ishikawajima-Harima Heavy Industries).

What would the marines' reaction be to this idea? Both the Japanese and Americans exercised extreme care here. They were increasingly alarmed at how the marines kept knocking back requests in the process of identifying a suitable alternative for Futenma.

When the marines first heard of the offshore heliport concept, their immediate reaction was negative. There was a virtual emotional backlash. "They're trying to box us in somewhere." "They're trying to push us out into the ocean."

These fears of the marines had to be eradicated as much as possible. So, they went ahead with a technological feasibility study on the points of major concern to the marines: the length of the runway, the number of aircraft, the durability of the facility.

Prime Minister Ryutaro Hashimoto, however, was very excited about the offshore heliport proposal. And the biggest reason for this keenness was that it could be removed. Ever since the decision to return Futenma had been made, this was the one point Hashimoto consistently stressed. Although he did not have an offshore heliport in mind at the time, he underscored the point that it had to be removable to Ambassador Mondale even when the final details were being worked out. He had also said, "I'll try and win the local people over with the fact that it will be removable. I think that will be a convincing argument. Making the alternative removable is the only way."[2]

Hashimoto was also concerned about perceptions in the countries of the Asian-Pacific region. He believed that "we can't afford to create the impression that a new base is being created. A removable facility is also desirable to that end." It would not do to have people thinking that Japan was expanding militarily in this age of military contraction.[3]

In the Diet, he gave the following response. "As we were looking for ways to make the facility removable as well as avoiding danger, I myself recalled that we had used this type of construction at Okinotori Island. This happened to coincide with many people suggesting relocating to an offshore facility, some within the governments of both countries."[4]

Throughout, Okinawa did not change its opposition to the construction of new bases, base fixation, and functionary expansion. Removability became a key political symbol for creating an impression of base realignment, consolidation, and reduction, not "shuffling bases" or "passing the buck." Very little work, however, seems to have gone into thinking about what this word, removability, really meant.

What sort of situation would be a "removable" situation? Did it assume a situation where there was no longer any need for marines to be stationed in Okinawa? Supposing the marines were relocated to an offshore facility from Futenma; the facility would no longer be a base if the marines themselves withdrew. If that was so, whether the facility was removable or not would lose most of its meaning. If subsequent military use was a problem, all they had to do was think of another use, not make it expressly removable.

Nevertheless, whether an offshore facility or a removable base, both could be expected to have the psychological effect of "deflecting some of the glare of the military presence."[5] This rhetoric came to be used frequently as a kind of magic mantra to evoke an image that by isolating the military presence at sea, they could be moved offshore and someday would dissolve into the water and disappear into thin air.

In other words, the American presence, particularly the marines, was not an asset but a burden to Hashimoto. The offshore facility was significant because it represented a psychological watershed in Japanese political thinking.

A Trial Balloon

Now, when Campbell was quietly looking into the idea of an offshore facility, he received some information from the Japanese to the effect that Hashimoto himself seemed to be thinking along those lines. "We heard from several sources around the same time that Hashimoto had been thinking of an offshore facility from early on."[6] The message was that Hashimoto had been thinking about this idea for more than a year.

What on earth is going on? Hadn't the Japanese been pushing hard for Kadena's consolidation? Campbell instructed his staff to check out the background to the information. Some time later, the word got back to him.

"Hashimoto was interested in these kind of floating facilities when he was transport minister." "It looks like the Japanese shipbuilders and steel manufacturers are behind it." "The PM's office is collecting its own information without the JDA's or the Foreign Ministry's knowledge." "The Japanese manufacturers have been working on the U.S. Embassy for some time now."

When Campbell talked with Yukio Okamoto in mid-August, he was disconcerted when Okamoto suddenly came out with an unfamiliar term, QIP. *If it's coming from Okamoto, does that mean Hashimoto's interested?*

Campbell already had this information in early September, when he first sounded Tanaka out on it over the phone. That is why he was hopeful that as long as it was taken to the prime minister, Tanaka's cautious stance would change into something more positive. That is how Campbell interpreted the signal he received from Okamoto.

It is hard to know just when Okamoto thought up the offshore heliport proposal and when he decided to go for it. Information on the concept of an offshore floating facility had reached almost all of the related Japanese ministries at quite an early stage. It had not originated with Hashimoto.

It was Kenji Eda, political secretary for the prime minister, who pressed the idea in a specific manner on Hashimoto. Eda had become interested in the idea of a QIP floating facility around the end of July. He compiled documentation on it and in the middle of August briefed both Hashimoto and Kajiyama. "It uses the piling method. So it doesn't affect the sea currents. I think it has its advantages environmentally speaking as well."[7]

So, at the very latest, Hashimoto had already heard about floating facilities, albeit in QIP terms only, by the middle of August. The truth was that it was also Eda who had planted the QIP idea in Okamoto's mind.

Campbell was being nudged over to the offshore floating facility concept. When he heard the mobile offshore base (MOB) idea from Armitage, his greatest concern was the reaction from the Japanese side. However, it looked like the Japanese were ahead on this. What's more, if it was true that Hashimoto had already been interested in floating facilities, they might be able to push it through in a single stroke. Campbell knew the value of having Hashimoto interested, because his interest would spark a virtuous and self-reinforcing circle of interest on both sides of the Pacific.

Campbell also found out through his investigations that the Japanese were better at all the technologies involved. They did better floating options and were the best marine engineers in the world.[8] Campbell was in the habit of saying it was the Americans who had gotten men to the moon and he had never doubted U.S. technological hegemony, but in the marine area it looked like the Japanese were on top.

Given Hashimoto's enthusiasm, and the excellence of Japanese technology, Campbell and his team would have preferred for it to have been a joint proposal.[9] The Japanese, however, asked them to make it a U.S. proposal. Hideo Usui, director-general of the JDA, was later to comment that "we couldn't come forward pretentiously with a proposal where the technology was still not sufficiently established."[10] If that was the case, however, then the Americans shouldn't be able to propose it either because the technology was still missing there as well. And yet, why did the Americans put the proposal to the Japanese?

Was it because Hashimoto thought, what with the PM's office, the JDA, and Okinawa all pushing for consolidation with Kadena, that pressure from outside—gaiatsu—was the only way to change that trend?

Or was it because they were afraid of coming in for unwarranted suspicion, given the business implications, if they didn't make it an American proposal?

Did they want to make the Americans shoulder the burden of getting the military, especially the marines, to swallow this untried concept? If it was a U.S. proposal, the marines would curse not the Japanese government but the civilians at the DOD.

The Americans were hesitant, but in the end they decided to make it an American proposal. A senior DOD official conjectured about Japanese motives, "I think there was an assessment that there was a very good chance that this would fail. And this was what we would call a trial balloon. If the trial balloon fell, they would rather it be a U.S. trial balloon than a Hashimoto trial balloon."[11]

A senior official at the Japanese Foreign Ministry put it this way. "It was our way of confirming that they had cleared it all the way, otherwise they wouldn't propose it. It was no good coming up with a fireworks display. We wanted to be sure there was an inside commitment."[12] In short, by making the Americans propose it, the Japanese were asking the U.S. government and the military to make a united commitment on the idea, not just something sounded out by a few people on the American side.

By this time, a chilly breeze nipped at the Americans and Japanese in SACO (Special Action Committee on Okinawa), which had been begun with such fanfare.

The balloon bobbed and bounced in the breeze.

Marine Strategy in the 21st Century

Even though they were discussing a floating facility, there was a huge difference in the images of the two sides. The Japanese were approaching it from a commercial perspective, while the Americans were considering it from a military one.

The core of the American concept was the MOB put forward by Admiral William Owens. Owens predicted that naval operations in the future, say around 2021, would be radically different from what they were today. "Many of today's aircraft missions will probably be shared by aircraft carriers and MOBs."[13]

Owens's argument was that a combination of a sea-mobile base and two aircraft carriers would provide a much higher war-fighting capacity than that of five aircraft carriers and that it would be able to perform almost the same functions as aircraft carriers only at a lower cost. His summation was that they "could have an island anywhere we wanted one."

It was not the first time this concept had been mooted. During World War II, "The British built artificial islands in the English Channel to support the air defense of Great Britain."[14]

Owens also predicted that "there is no reason to assume that such bases would be exclusively naval. Indeed, the size of the assembled bases and the length of the runway on them would be capable of handling any service's aircraft."

It was precisely because of this potential that the military leaders feared that not only would such bases impinge on the turf of aircraft carriers, they would also eat into their construction budget. They tried to stop the move when Secretary Perry seemed to be leaning towards the floating facility proposal. The air force was also alarmed about losing out in a future turf war with the navy.

Owens revealed that "General Shalikashvili agreed with it. More significantly I think Secretary of Defense Perry was strongly in favor, and Dr. Deutch when he was the deputy secretary was favorable to it. . . . [But] at the high levels of the uniformed military in the services, this was not a popular concept. It was viewed in the navy as possibly taking away the need for as many carriers, and in the air force it seemed like the navy taking over their missions."[15]

Owens himself says that the concept was not a figment of military imagination. "With the deficit cuts, the military budget will probably continue to fall. The environmental movement is getting stronger everywhere. At our German bases, we can't move our tanks around on practice drills like we could 20 years ago. Whether it's the Middle East or the Far East, the bases are trammeled by complex political issues. Offshore bases can overcome all of these issues."[16]

Owens's attention was directed towards the outlook for the U.S. military presence in South Korea in the case of reconciliation between the two Koreas. "One would have to ask whether it would be possible to keep the 40,000 troops we have stationed in South Korea there. Where would they go? Where would be the best place for them? Would it be possible to put them in Japan? Probably very difficult. Would it be a better place to have some of them at least on a floating platform? Perhaps. . . . It could be that it is an element of a new way of looking at American presence in the Pacific."[17]

Richard Armitage, former assistant secretary of defense, who was also pushing the floating facility idea, spoke of a similar scenario. He thought, "If peace came to the Korean Peninsula, thereby putting an end to the marines' mission there, they could be withdrawn and stationed, say, in Australia."[18]

What lay behind this 21st-century vision was the possibility of fundamental change in the strategic climate on the Korean Peninsula and the accompanying change that would create in the role of the marines.

Owens spoke of his dream: "Wouldn't it be nice to have a Japanese and American flag together as a symbol of our friendship and our partnership and our willingness to be together?"[19]

Most important, they would be working together on a technological frontier. If this project was adopted, it would be on an unprecedented scale. Not only that. If it was successful, it might lead to a whole new nature of overseas military presence for the United States in the 21st century.

It is hard to remain a global power without bases in key locations around the globe. However, maintaining bases in the next century will become more difficult. The military will be forced to take a new approach at some point.

The DOD top officials thought it was too soon to be making those decisions but felt the time was right to at least start preparing for them. Owens's idea might show them one way. Moreover, Owens was thinking not just in defensive terms of alternative base sites but in terms of marine strategy, which would determine the rise and fall of power in the future.

They would be killing two birds with one stone if the idea could be made a reality using Japanese money and technology and if the United States could acquire the technological expertise from the Japanese.

Technological frontiers for security in the 21st century were definitely a factor as with theater missile defense (TMD). The problem was that previous technological cooperation between the two countries had always been dodgy, and the joint development of the FSX (next-generation fighter) had left a bad taste in mouths on both sides.

There was a danger that if the two nations forced the issue and became involved in joint development, they would be plagued once again by the sharp gap in their respective thinking: the United States fearing the exodus of their precious military technology, and the Japanese fearing the usurpation of their world-renowned civilian high-tech expertise. Campbell "exercised extreme caution in his preliminary sounding out of the Commerce Department and Congress to avoid a replay of the FSX."[20]

The Japanese were also in favor of using technological leverage to revitalize the bilateral alliance. This was easier said than done, however. Almost everyone wanted to avoid revisiting the "FSX nightmare."[21] Since the JDA was pushing hard on the Kadena consolidation proposal, it tended to be diffident about the floating facility initially. Even ignoring that, the majority opinion was for caution.

However, there were those who were trying to extract a more long-term significance. One of them disclosed that "if Japan was able to create an offshore facility like the one described, we would control 60 percent of the world's oceans. Supposing it was built in Okinawa, then Okinawa, including its marine area, would become the biggest part of Japan.

What's more, the facility would not just be for aircraft. It would have a wide range of maritime applications. Its base relocation function would not be restricted to the marines alone. If runways 2,000–3,000 meters long could be built, the air force would no longer need Kadena either."[22]

Both sides were projecting their respective visions onto the floating facility: their future power scenarios for the 21st century, the nature of their presence, and, in turn, the nature of the bilateral alliance.

But in the fall of 1996, such lofty strategic visions were alarming rather than acceptable. The Japanese knocked back Owens's offshore base idea for having "a different starting point." It was too military and did not sit well with Japan's civilian-based thinking. The Japanese viewed it as a kind of aircraft carrier, pointing out to the Americans it would be unpalatable if it caused alarm among Japan's neighbors.

A senior official at the Defense Department shook his head. "The Japanese mentioned how alarmist China was constantly, but we never heard anything like that from the Chinese themselves. The offshore heliport was different from a ship. It didn't move. Anyway, we had already explained clearly to the Chinese the goal of redefining the bilateral alliance."[23] He suspected that the Japanese were using Chinese alarm as an excuse to get "something that was not technologically interesting" like a QIP.

Another strong Japanese demand was "removability." They repeated time and again that being able to remove the facility when its job was done was "the prime minister's strong wish." "It doesn't have to be huge and we won't allow it to be mobile." The Japanese took what the Americans had initially been calling a "base" and turned it into a "facility."[24]

The Semisubmersible

The shipbuilders, steel manufacturers, general contractors, and trading companies were quick on their feet. They had started maneuvering and shouldering the concept almost 10 months before the government came up with the offshore heliport proposal. There had already been signs of collusion within the government sector during Murayama's term of office.

According to Takashi Imai, president of New Nippon Steel Company, events took the following course. "Around November 1995, we were approached by the government via the Floating Structures Association of Japan about whether a megafloat could be an alternative site for Futenma. At almost the same time, we were approached by the Research Group on Okinawa Maritime Space Usage Technology about QIP."[25]

The Floating Structures Association of Japan was a syndicate formed by shipbuilders and steel manufacturers to promote pontoon methods. The Research Group on Okinawa Maritime Space Usage Technology was a gathering of major trading companies led by Nissho Iwai that was pursuing the QIP method and the jacket method.

Syndicate officials said, "U.S. military interest in megafloats started to mount from the start of 1996. In February 1996, Mr. Tobin came to see the megafloats in Yokosuka, followed by Mr. Clemens in April."[26] Byron Tobin was commander of the U.S. Navy in Japan, and Admiral Archie Clemens was commander of the Seventh Fleet.

Clemens was originally a submariner. He was also a computer addict who would fire off e-mail at three in the morning. If he found any good Japanese technology, he wanted it. He was the first to set up a home page in the naval command in Japan. He showed exceptional interest in the megafloat.

Floating construction methods had been in the limelight since the industry had gone all out in its huge campaign for the Kansai airport, but they lost out that time to the general contractors and their reclamation method. Dreaming of this new business frontier, however, the shipbuilding and steel industry had been looking around for large-scale potential projects throughout the 1990s. The transport ministry and the Ministry of International Trade and Industry (MITI) were behind them too.

The single greatest factor in their failure to win the Kansai airport contract was "lack of a proven performance record." So, they went ahead and built a megafloat off Yokosuka, creating the Megafloat Technology Research Union in 1995 for that purpose.

The so-called QIP method had been previously utilized. It had been used for temporary wharves in the Vietnam War and for the preservation works on Okinotori Island.

Okinotori Island (part of the Ogasawara islands) was a coral atoll some 1,700 kilometers south of Tokyo and Japan's southernmost island. In the latter half of the 1980s, there was a danger that it would be submerged, Japan standing to lose some 400,000 square kilometers of territorial rights if it did. The government carried out "territorial preservation works" by building a steel wavebreak 50 meters in diameter and pouring it full of concrete to protect the rocks. The transport minister at the time was Ryutaro Hashimoto.

The QIP lobby was also pushing an offshore proposal for a relocation site for Naha Port. Despite being a key issue and one of the three items, the return of Naha Port was struggling in the face of local opposition from Urasoe, the proposed relocation site.

By the end of 1995, this group had revamped its report using the same material it had from Naha Port by sticking Futenma Air Station on the cover and had started lobbying the government to consider an offshore heliport as an alternative for Futenma. The Megafloat Technology Research Union, on the other hand, had started its construction of a megafloat for research purposes off the Yokosuka Bay.

(Construction was completed in June 1996.) It used the pontoon method.

Also by the end of 1995, it had prepared a detailed report on the technological feasibility of building an offshore heliport as a relocation site for Futenma. None other than a research officer in the Cabinet Research and Information Office had asked them to "look into floating construction methods" in November 1995 during the Murayama government. At the time, the research officer envisioned a small heliport.

An engineer at the Megafloat Technology Research Union told him, "It makes a huge difference if it's to go out in the open sea or in a protected bay. And this area is famous as the main typhoon corridor. You have to take that into consideration as well."

Upon hearing that, the officer just gave a noncommittal "is that so," and that was that. But a week later, he was back with more specifics. "I can't limit the possible area, but I'd like you to explore an offshore heliport with a 9000-feet [2,800-meter]-long runway." Going by the size of the runway, it was obvious that he was thinking about Futenma, and the officer confessed as much.

So the megafloat team rolled up their sleeves and a week later had their technological feasibility study report. Predicting that the site near Ginowan, home to Futenma, would be the most realistic choice, the feasibility study was based on seas 20 to 30 meters deep. Their quote for the entire project was a rough estimate of 480 billion yen.

The research officer whispered. "That means 120 billion yen a year over four years, or under 100 billion yen if we took it to five years."

"The government wanted some idea of cost."[27]

With President Clinton's visit looming (but, after all, cancelled), the government's nerve center was forced to think about the realignment, consolidation, and reduction of the Okinawa bases. Okinawa Prefecture was refusing the proxy signing of the public notice and inspection papers, and the resistance movement had developed into a prefecture-wide campaign. If the government didn't come up with something spectacular, relations with America and Okinawa would reach a total impasse.

In a meeting with Governor Masahide Ota and Vice-Governor Masanori Yoshimoto, those around Prime Minister Murayama learned just how important the return of Futenma was to them. Until that time, working on the assumption that the three items were the top priority, Murayama had requested they be resolved in his meeting with President Clinton in Washington at the start of the year. After the rape, however, that degree of base realignment, consolidation, and reduction was no longer enough.

Hiroyuki Sonoda, deputy Cabinet secretary, was more aware of that than anyone else. Hearing from Okinawan sources about the offshore heliport idea, Sonoda got Yoshio Omori, head of the Cabinet Research and Information office, to look into it quietly. Sonoda avoided disclosing who his Okinawan source was, but it was most likely Yoshimoto. Yoshimoto was interested in the idea and had been suggesting that the PM's office explore its feasibility. Immediately thereafter the research officer was dispatched to the marine float promotion group.

The hitch was that Koken Nosaka, chief Cabinet secretary, talked. Word got through to Okinawa and to Yoshimoto. Yoshimoto clammed up after that, reasoning to himself, *Well, if that's all they think of something this confidential, that's all right by me.* Also, at the end of the year, it was reported in the press that Seishiro Eto, director-general of the JDA, had said in a speech in Oita to his constituency, "I'd like to explore shifting Futenma offshore. This has come from the locals, so it's not the place of the government to say what's right or wrong."[28]

But this proved to be mere froth, bubbling up then disappearing without a trace. The offshore heliport proposal itself was semisubmerged for a while. Why didn't the Japanese government pursue the offshore heliport proposal any further at the time? Even after the birth of the Hashimoto government, Omori was still head of the Cabinet Research and Information Office, so the information was still there. Why didn't Prime Minister Hashimoto push the idea himself from the very first? In hindsight, these doubts remain.

"Perhaps he wasn't sure about how realistic it was."

"Maybe he yanked it back because he judged the climate to be totally wrong for making it a reality."

"Perhaps he wanted to see how things would shape up because his administration was new and events in Okinawa were developing at an alarming pace."

"Prime Minister Hashimoto is very proud, so perhaps he didn't want to take over one of the old Cabinet's ideas but to come up with his own vision instead, his own approach."

Speculation was rife in industrial circles. Omori cites the fact that "the handover between Cabinets didn't go smoothly." Later on in work by SACO, consolidation at Kadena and relocating to Camp Schwab emerged as the most promising options, so it is also conceivable that Hashimoto decided to wait and see how they developed.

The proposal for an offshore heliport emerged in the fall of 1996. When Omori saw it, he thought, "What's all this about then?"

SACO's Final Report

December 2, 1996.

Following the release of SACO's final report, the two governments held a reception in downtown Tokyo. Defense Secretary Perry gave a short speech. "When SACO started, everyone thought it would be impossible to reach an agreement. But we kept knocking on the door and finally, it opened. I am truly pleased to be able to sign a paper which will reduce the burden on the people of Okinawa."

The final report confirmed the complete or partial return of the 11 facilities and areas cited in the interim report. Approximately 21 percent, or some 5,000 hectares, of all U.S. facilities and areas in Okinawa would be returned.

The facilities and areas covered were Futenma Air Station, Northern Training Area, Aha Training Area, Gimbaru Training Area, Sobe Communication Site, Yomitan Auxiliary Airfield, Camp Kuwae, Senaha Communication Station, Makiminato Service Area, Naha Port, and housing consolidation (Camp Kuwae and Camp Zukeran). This was to be accompanied by the transfer of KC-130 Hercules aircraft to Iwakuni Air Base and the transfer of AV-8 Harrier aircraft from Iwakuni to the U.S. mainland.

Concerning a suitable substitute for Futenma Air Station, the report stated clearly that a sea-based facility (SBF) option would be pursued. "Compared to the other two options, the SBF is judged to be the best option in terms of enhanced safety and quality of life for the Okinawan people while maintaining operational capabilities of U.S. forces. In addition, the SBF can function as a fixed facility during its use as a military base and can also be removed when no longer necessary."[29]

Japan would provide the SBF in accordance with the Status of Forces Agreement. Three construction methods were said to be feasible: the pile-supported pier type, the pontoon type, and the semisubmersible type. It was also decided that a plan for implementation and the construction site be determined no later than the end of 1997.

Ryutaro Hashimoto was on his best behavior, saying that the SACO operations were over, but the work still remained. A close aide added the footnote, "The report is in, but the work has only turned the first page."

There were still a myriad of tasks that had to be completed.

Reaction in Okinawa was cool. An editorial in the *Okinawa Times* condemned the report. "The final report is nothing but a complete betrayal of Okinawan expectations. . . . It is nothing more than a new 'carving up' of Okinawa."[30] This, of course, was a reference to the Meiji government's high-handed incorporation of Okinawa into its administrative framework in the late 1800s.

"The vast majority of the facilities earmarked for return all stipulate relocation within Okinawa as a condition. Furthermore, approximately 80 percent of the land to be returned comes from the Northern Training Area, signaling no consideration whatsoever for the damage the populace has suffered from the bases. The pretense of having made a balanced return by returning a large tract of nonessential land makes a mockery of the people of Okinawa." In other words, the report was nothing more than a bean-counter's tract.

"We have always maintained that the U.S. bases are like a cancer on our attempts to promote development. From this perspective, relocating within the prefecture is akin to just moving the cancer from one part of the body to another."[31]

Governor Masahide Ota's appraisal was severe: "Even if everything is returned as promised, Okinawa will still be stuck with some 70 percent of the U.S. bases in Japan." While he did not go so far as equating relocation within Okinawa to cancer, he maintained his unbending opposition to it. More than anything else he fretted and suffered that relocation within the prefecture would pit Okinawan against Okinawan. Ota stuck to his position of being "primarily opposed to any base relocation within Okinawa." What would be the point of getting them returned if all it did was create rifts as bases were returned but shifted somewhere else?

Ota had remarked that there was no single position on the bases that encompassed all the prefectural populace. And quite rightly, for the residents, for the Prefectural People's Party, for prefectural awareness, there was no single stance that summed them all up, nor had such a unified position developed. Even supposing things proceeded as laid out in the report, the U.S. bases would still account for 8 percent of Okinawa Island's surface area, a figure exactly the same as immediately after World War II when the U.S. military first occupied Okinawa.

Not only Futenma, but all the other facilities and areas singled out for return in SACO had been decided from above. Not a single community was consulted about the return of the facility in their area. Dissatisfaction lingered over the Japanese government talking only to the prefecture; not enough had been done to see what people at the local municipal level wanted.

The decision to transfer Gimbaru Training Area to Blue Beach met with strong resistance from the local town of Kin. The town's mayor stood at the head of the demonstrators yelling, "Oppose the transfer to Blue Beach." Blue Beach was the town's only beautiful beach. Complaints welled up that once again, the decision showed a lack of adequate "reporting in the field."

One person involved in working on the question of the bases mentioned that "there are at least five relocation sites where the mayors will try to prevent it even physically if they have to." His grievance was that more should have been done to find out what people wanted at the local community level.

On this point, however, there was an aspect of "SACO respecting to a considerable extent the priorities laid out in Okinawa Prefecture's Action Program for the Return of the Bases."[32] The central government had decided that in its operations aimed at base realignment, consolidation, and reduction, SACO would not go over the head of the prefectural government to fix things directly with the local municipalities.

The 5,000 hectares to be returned corresponded to five airports the size of Narita or two air bases the size of Kadena. Over the next 5 to 7 years, several developments would have to be started. Was there enough time? Seiken Tobaru, mayor of Ginowan City—home to Futenma—estimated that they would never be ready by then. He was voicing the fear not that the return was too early, but that the transitionary phase was too short.

Even if the base was returned, it would take five years to create a consensus among the landowners and five years to put in water supply and drainage. It would take 10 years to prepare the site for other use, and there was the question, of course, of what would be built there. Tobaru's fears only deepened as time passed. SACO's rush to have something to show, the political top-down nature of the decision, were all quickly coming home to roost.

The runway on the SBF where Futenma was to relocate was set at 1,500 meters. This alone would make it as big as a local airport. But the all-important selection of a site had been put off and was to be determined sometime in 1997.

Government leaders were thinking of getting a private confirmation from the Okinawans by briefing them in advance of a bilateral agreement that it would be located off Camp Schwab, but the JDA's director-general Fumio Kyuma's statement that "the sea off Camp Schwab might be a strong candidate" triggered intense resistance in Okinawa, not least in the local city of Nago.

This, in turn, led to a decision to have a cooling-off period, leading to the putting off of selecting a site. It seems unlikely, in any event, that they would have been able to make a decision by the time of the final report even without the Kyuma remark.

Charles Krulak, U.S. Marine Corps commandant, asked the DOD to make its decision on the offshore heliport with "safety, quality of life, and long-term operational cost" as its key considerations.[33] He was warning them that if operational costs appeared to be too high, it would eat into the marines' budget, and if that happened, then the marines would have to think seriously.

Grumbling could still be heard among the marines in the field. If the sea-based facility was their only choice, they wanted a mobile one. The Japanese, however, were unwilling because of the weapons export implications and had settled on a fixed model. Mistrust towards Japan mounted even higher as calls for cutbacks in marines increased.

An article by Robert Hamilton in the *Marine Corps Gazette* is a good example of marine dissatisfaction over the SBF:

Any offshore facility adhering to U.S. Department of Defense safety, environmental, and security standards and meeting Marine Corps mission requirements will probably end up looking more like the giant offshore Kansai International Airport in Osaka, Japan, than what is currently being described as a modest and down-sized facility.

Anyone who has every [sic] experienced a major typhoon on Okinawa will realize the [sic] such a typhoon could turn Okinawa's first floating air facility into Okinawa's first underwater air facility, with the greatest sinking of U.S. military assets into the Pacific Ocean since Pearl Harbor.

Even if the engineering and environmental problems could be solved, a more basic policy problem remains. Currently on Okinawa, serious and committed young American men and women . . . are increasingly being viewed as mercenaries to be isolated and caged away from the local populace in peacetime and only set loose in times of military emergency.[34]

The article tweaked all of the Marine Corps' most sensitive nerves: budget issues (Kansai International Airport), quality of life (sinking), and honor (mercenaries).[35]

The Missing Piece of Ryukyu Lacquer Ware

The PM's office, the Foreign Ministry, the Defense Agency, everyone knew only too exasperatingly well how tough a job getting the bases returned was by the time SACO's final report was released. They were only reaping the bitter harvest of having done nothing about the concentration of bases in Okinawa for so long. It had been just one long succession of rushing to do something about the bases when the sites looked threatened, and then forgetting all about them when the crisis had passed.

A senior JDA official disclosed the three psychological stages the central government cadres handling Okinawan affairs always went through when fighting with Okinawa:

"The first stage is grasping Okinawa sentiment. They try to understand how they feel by reading books, studying the history, going out drinking together. The second stage is the reactionary phase. No matter what they do, things don't work out. Just as we thought, Okinawa is playing us for suckers. They blame themselves for expecting too much. And the final stage is feeling like Lao-tze and Chung-tze. No matter what they do, Okinawa will never change. Don't push too hard, take it easy, go with the flow."[36]

This predicament, however, affects the quality of security dialogue between Japan and the United States, the maturity of alliance management, and, in turn, the very nature of the alliance itself.

It is true that SACO attempted to identify a more fitting style of dialogue and consultation on bilateral security for the post–Cold War era. From its launch in November 1995 until the release of the final report in December 1996, more than 30 meetings were held at a pace of twice a month. There had never been this kind of close discussion between the two sides since the start of the Security Treaty. Members on both sides were aware of this and worked accordingly with great enthusiasm.

"It could well act as a prototype for future joint security operations between the two sides." "Okinawa and the bases forced us to look at things in the larger context of U.S. forward deployment in a post–Cold War world, Japan's burden-sharing role, and relations with neighboring countries."

There were those Japanese members who held great hopes. And that hope was right from the very start not to make SACO a negotiating venue. "Nothing would come of going around politely asking, 'and what would you like?' The Japanese side started tossing ideas around, like 'how about this?', including the return of Futenma. Things started to move from that process of running up against each other."[37]

This was something very new, especially for the JDA, and officials praised it highly. Nobushige Takamizawa, director of the JDA's Defense Operations Division, summed up the entire process, saying, "We had frank debates on everything including strategy. And that debate was based on military missions."[38] Takemasa Moriya, counselor at the Defense Bureau, disclosed that the talks were, in fact, so frank that "some of the Americans objected, asking why they had to go that far."[39]

Whether the talks really were so frank as to make the Americans huff and puff is another question, but it does appear certain that the Japanese attacked the talks aggressively but positively. And it was Secretary Perry who praised them for having raised the quality of the alliance. He praised SACO in a meeting with Director-General Kyuma: "The work over this past year has laid a foundation for the next decade of alliance."[40]

And yet, SACO was still not fully appreciated and still not put to full use. Keenness to make it a vehicle for dialogue, not negotiation, was good. Owing to the fact, however, that they didn't know what was being discussed with the Americans and that a clear Japanese stance was not visible—either to Japanese politicians or those around the prime minister, Cabinet Secretary Seiroku Kajiyama in particular—it looked like the Japanese, especially the Foreign Ministry, were not saying nearly enough to the Americans, whether it was on the Status of Forces Agreement, the bases, or marine cutbacks.

It was from this aspect that the Japanese side occasionally came in for criticism domestically. Sometimes it took the form of Foreign Ministry bashing. Criticism of the Foreign Ministry was especially strong in

March 1996, when it was unable to reveal the secret agreement to return Futenma.

"They give us all this fine talk about joint operations, but in the end, won't the Americans walk all over them?" "They're not negotiating properly, are they?" These and other gripes were heard not only from the Social Democrats but from the LDP as well.

The style of joint operations started to change into group bargaining around the beginning of fall 1996. As the JDA pushed the Kadena proposal strongly and the Americans resisted, SACO started to turn into a negotiation vehicle. The Foreign Ministry was inwardly very critical of this point, saying, "Things started going awry when the JDA laid in with their open diplomacy." As the debate was no longer dealt with within SACO but taken up outside, it quickly acquired the tone of public debate, group bargaining, and negotiation. The Defense Department bore the JDA a similar grudge. "They tried to pressure us by taking things public. That made our position much more difficult."[41]

In its approach to the bases, SACO tried to look for a solution in a broader context linking the bases, the force structure, and the international climate. There was at least a possibility that this might work, but there was not enough debate on these issues.

The Americans agreed to conduct bilateral consultations and adjustments on the structure of U.S. forces. However, when the Japanese started mentioning the nature of the force structure with an eye to domestic politics, the Americans became alarmed. A high-ranking DOD official did not hide his disappointment, saying, "The Japanese tend to look at the alliance not as a shared asset, but as a zero-sum game. Basically, they see the alliance in tactical terms."[42]

Some of the Japanese, on the other hand, were frustrated that having set up this framework for consultation and adjustment, they were unable to expand it into sustained, regular talks, with things reverting to normal. "How can we check all of their base functions if we don't know what they support, and how we can support the U.S. military?"

In the words of a high-ranking official at the Foreign Ministry, "In the proper order of things, defense cooperation should be top of the agenda. If defense cooperation comes first and we share some kind of operational plan or reciprocal cooperation plan, we can then talk jointly on whether we need this base or not. But talk of cutting the bases came in the absence of any common ground like that. From the Americans' point of view, they couldn't show us base cuts without some specific idea of what U.S.-Japan cooperation would look like."[41]

Amid the talk of strengthening the alliance, Japan failed to give a clear indication of what sort of alliance it wanted, how it would cooperate with the United States, what it could do, what it couldn't do. Without that, it was impossible to persuade those arguing strongly for maintaining the status quo in terms like "it was rational for the bases to exist" or "those in operation can be justified."

This was where the fundamental problem in the bilateral talks on the bases lay.

The piece of Ryukyu lacquer ware, which used to be on display in front of the office of the deputy assistant secretary of state, East Asian affairs, on the sixth floor of the State Department, disappeared sometime before Christmas. Governor Masahide Ota had brought it with him on his visit in June of that year as a gift for Thomas Hubbard. It was a deep vermilion lacquer tray made by Benbo, in the city of Naha.

Hubbard was being transferred to the Philippines Embassy in the summer. He told his secretary to display the tray not in his office but outside when he left to take up the new appointment. It didn't even take six months, however, for the now-ownerless vermilion piece of lacquer ware to end up in a cupboard.

"How long is it going to be Okinawa? SACO's over now." Voices imbued with a large measure of frustration started reverberating in Washington.

Notes

1. Interview with Robin Sakoda.
2. Interview with Ryutaro Hashimoto.
3. Ibid.
4. Response to the Special Committee on Land Usage Accompanying the Implementation of the Japan-U.S. Security Treaty, House of Representatives, April 8, 1997.
5. Interview with a senior Maritime SDF officer.
6. Interview with Kurt Campbell.
7. Interview with Kenji Eda.
8. Interview with Kurt Campbell.
9. Ibid.
10. Interview with Hideo Usui.
11. Interview with a senior DOD official
12. Interview with a senior MOFA official.
13. Interview with William Owens.
14. Ibid.
15. Ibid.

16. Ibid.

17. Interview with William Owens.

18. Interview with Richard Armitage.

19. Interview with William Owens.

20. Interview with a DOD official.

21. Interview with a senior JDA official.

22. Ibid.

23. Ibid.

24. Interview with a senior MOFA official.

25. Interview with Takashi Imai.

26. Interview with the Floating Structures Association of Japan officials.

27. Interview with a Marine Float manager.

28. "Offshore Relocation as an Axis of Discussion: Director-General Eto at Futenma Air Base," *Asahi Shimbun*, December 11, 1995.

29. *The SACO Final Report on Futenma Air Station*, p. 1.

30. *Okinawa Times*, December 2, 1996.

31. Ibid.

32. Interview with a senior JDA official.

33. Interview with Charles Krulak.

34. Robert V. Hamilton, "An Idea That Just Won't Float," *Marine Corps Gazette*, February 1997, p. 42.

35. Hamilton had been stationed on Okinawa as a U.S. Marine Corps artillery officer from 1982 to 1988.

36. Interview with a JDA official.

37. Ibid.

38. Interview with Nobushige Takamizawa.

39. Interview with Takemasa Moriya.

39. "Japan, U.S. Approve Okinawa Report: Futenma Station to Be Returned; Both Sides Hail Report as Historic Breakthrough," *Daily Yomiuri*, December 3, 1996, p. 1.

40. Interview with a senior DOD official.

41. Ibid.

42. Interview with a senior MOFA official.

III

October 29, 1994. Prime Minister Tomiichi Murayama reviews the
Self-Defense Forces.

June 17, 1994. Chairman Kim Il Sung of North Korea meets
Jimmy Carter, former U.S. president, in Pyongyang.

Chapter Eleven

———◆———

Confluence

Beckoned to the Pentagon

August 1994.

That summer, everything about the bilateral alliance looked adrift. Both in Washington and Tokyo, it suddenly became hard to read what the other side was thinking.

In Japan, the Murayama coalition government had taken office. Tomiichi Murayama, the head of the Japan Socialist Party (JSP), perennially opposed to the Security Treaty, was at the helm of the coalition. Ambassador Walter Mondale, who lost no time in meeting the new prime minister, worked to temper the shock, saying after his meeting that Murayama was an ordinary kind of fellow.

The Japan watchers in Washington looked on in alarm at the Asian fever enveloping Japan. *This is different from the emotional anti-Americanism of a short while ago. Might it be the start of a full-scale distancing from America?*[1]

Suspicion was rife. It still appeared as if the only thing the United States was interested in was foisting numerical trade targets onto the Japanese. Japan was concerned that the United States was tired of maintaining the sort of alliance relationship it had had up till then and was becoming more inward looking. Stories that the draft report of the advisory group on defense issues appointed by the previous prime minister, Morihiro Hosokawa, focused on the United Nations' peacekeeping operations (PKO) and Asian multilateral frameworks only enhanced these fears of the Japan watchers. One was heard to say, "Japan has lost touch with all this talk of the U.N. and Asia."[2]

Joseph Nye, chair of the National Intelligence Council (NIC), spent the summer not at his summer house in New Hampshire but in Washington. He was to take up the position of assistant secretary of defense at the DOD in September, but first his nomination had to be approved by Congress.

Nye was acquainted with several influential Republicans, and given his first-rate intellect, cultivation, vision, and experience, his confirmation should have been a mere formality, but there was always the possibility of some unforeseen pitfall. He devoted himself to the task of reviewing each area of responsibility, calling in the top staff at the Defense Department.

More than six months had passed since Defense Secretary William Perry and Deputy Secretary John Deutch had visited Nye to ask him if he would work with them as assistant secretary. Perry himself had only been in his job for a month or two. In fact, Perry's predecessor, Les Aspin, had also sent Nye an invitation to come on board as assistant secretary, but Nye had declined. Even a lesser person than Nye would have had second thoughts, given that Aspin was planning to double the number of assistant secretary posts in the name of organizational reform.

Nye accepted Perry's offer. He had already worked as deputy undersecretary of state in the Carter administration, so it was not his first time in Washington. Nevertheless, the Pentagon was quite a different proposition from Foggy Bottom. It had a daytime population of over 23,000. The famous five-sided building was a city in itself. It had 100,000 telephones, and the Defense Post Office handled over one million pieces of mail monthly.[3] Nye had visited the building many times and often got lost.

He would also have to get on well with the top brass in the army, navy, air force, and marine corps. It was especially important that he build up a good working relationship with the chairman of the Joint Chiefs of Staff, a huge section accounting for some 1,300 staff members. What floored him was how to read the different shoulder boards. One briefing was not enough to learn all the different ranks and uniforms.

It was at that time that Kurt Campbell gave Nye a copy of *Assignment: Pentagon*. Campbell had known Nye since his time as an associate professor at Harvard.

Assignment: Pentagon was subtitled *An Insider's Guide to the Puzzle Palace* and included a 13-page glossary of acronyms that began with AAW (anti-air warfare) and ended with WWMCCS (Worldwide Military Command and Control System).[4] There is no other branch of the U.S. government that abuses acronyms to the same extent as the Pentagon.

Essentially a how-to book for leading staff members, *Assignment: Pentagon* was full of practical and immediately useful tips.

> Don't eat your lunch at your desk. Use the lunch hour as a time to get together with people and find out what is happening outside your area.[5]
> Join the Pentagon Athletic Club [POAC]. . . . It is a great place to meet interesting people, to get rid of some of the frustrations of the job, and to stay in reasonably good shape.

> Take a speed reading course. . . . Speed reading and learning how to skim material with a practiced eye is really helpful.[6]
>
> Watch the first 10 minutes of the *MacNeil/Lehrer News Hour* (if you get home by 7:00 P.M.). This is now the best news broadcast on television. Since there are no commercials, you get your news faster and better than anywhere else. Tom Brokaw, Dan Rather, and Peter Jennings just can't compete with MacNeil/Lehrer as far as substantive news is concerned.[7]

Nye joined the POAC, as the athletics club is officially known, immediately. He liked working up a sweat on the squash court. As for the speed reading course, he didn't need it, having mastered it in his youth.

Nye had known Perry and Deutch a long time. Every summer for the past 10 years, they had worked on policy research together in the Aspen Strategy Group at the Aspen Institute in Colorado. He had been neighbors with Deutch back at Harvard, and their children were best friends.

Nye was a world-renowned international political scientist. His pioneering work on the implications of interdependence on international politics had left a significant mark in the field of international political research. Moreover, as his Harvard colleague Ezra Vogel acknowledged, "Nye was not only a superb academic, he was a superb administrator."[8]

Nye was unhappy about the Clinton administration's lack of interest in its relationship with Japan. He felt that despite the bilateral relationship being the linchpin of Asia-Pacific stability, the White House did not seem to be giving the relationship the attention it warranted.

He was diametrically opposed to the Japan-as-threat argument increasingly put forward by American revisionists since the end of the 1980s. The paper he wrote before joining the Clinton administration, "Coping with Japan,"[9] is a good illustration of that position. In it, Nye declared that the United States should adjust its relationship with Japan as it acquired world-power status and rebutted the "containing Japan" argument of James Fallows that the Japanese economic, financial, high-tech, and systemic challenge would demolish America's foundations as a global power. Nye argued that the problem was not containing Japan but the friction caused by economic troubles between the two countries. He called for "a strategy to advance the long-term interests of the American people [which] must go beyond 'jobs, jobs, jobs.'"[10]

"Jobs, jobs, jobs" was a slogan that President George Bush had come up with during the 1992 presidential election. It was a new way of assessing all U.S. foreign policy in terms of whether it would ensure or promote American employment and adjusting external relations accordingly.

Nye's paper was written as a critique of the Bush administration's Japanese policies, and even Nye himself probably never imagined it would apply just as well or more to the Clinton administration. But after the new administration's start, Japan bashing, instigated by U.S. Trade Representative Mickey Kantor, heated up and escalated into the coercive application of negotiations on managed trade, known as framework talks, with Japan. Bilateral relations rapidly deteriorated.

In the Hosokawa-Clinton summit held at the beginning of the year, trade talks collapsed when the two leaders were unable to reach an agreement. This was styled as the two countries now having entered "a mature relationship,"[11] but that was nothing more than a momentary face-saving cover-up.

Nye's fears had become a reality.

Confluence

Ezra Vogel, who was a senior analyst for East Asian affairs at the NIC, had set up an informal study group with Paul Giarra, head of DOD's Japan Desk; Michael Green, researcher with the Institute for Defense Analysis (IDA); and Patrick Cronin, a senior researcher at the Institute for National Strategic Studies (INSS), National Defense University. Based on their shared position that there was nothing "mature" about bilateral ties, that they were, in fact, "drifting," the men started honing their theoretical weapons and putting together a policy proposal reviewing U.S.-Japan policy.

Giarra, navy trained, had studied in Japan for a year at the National Defense College. He was genuinely concerned about a rift opening up in the relationship if nothing was done. He passed on a memo to that effect to his supervisor at the DOD, Deputy Assistant Secretary Kent Wiedemann, but Wiedemann shelved the proposal. He didn't like the term "drifting." Saying "how can you tell we are drifting?" he struck out the offending word.

Wiedemann was on loan from the State Department and belonged to the China school. That may have had something to do with it, but there were those in the State Department who were alarmed and saw this move at the Pentagon as an indirect criticism of them.

Green and Cronin both argued for strengthening bilateral security ties in the post–Cold War era. They coauthored a paper, "Redefining the U.S.-Japan Alliance,"[12] which expounded this position. They acknowledged that "in many ways this close relationship is only a superficial continuation of policy trajectories established during the Cold War. The reality is that today the U.S.-Japan alliance is on shakier ground than most will admit."[13] Then they sounded a warning: "One should not be misled by the fact that the Social Democratic Party (SDP) has ended its longstanding objection to the constitutionality of the alliance, and that U.S. trade negotiators are now careful to reassure everyone that economic friction with Japan is not intended to hurt the bilateral relationship. . . . However, there are growing signs in Japan's policy planning of renewed attention to the United Nations, to regional multilateral mechanisms, and to stronger independent capabilities as a means of hedging against possible U.S. withdrawal or fatigue."[14]

They took a very severe stance in particular on the report by the Higuchi Commission, the so-called Higuchi Report. "Although the report calls for U.S.-centered multilateralism, it does not explain how the alliance roles and missions will be related to the Japanese Self-Defense Forces' (SDF) new multilateral agenda. As it now stands, the report's recommendations suggest that multilateralism is a hedge against waning U.S. commitments to the alliance, and possibly even a distraction (in terms of political and financial resources) from bilateral defense cooperation."[15]

Cronin and Green's position on Japan was also influenced by discussions with leading members of the JDA—Chisato Yamauchi, Masayoshi Shinbo, Nobushige Takamizawa—who had been on exchange to the National Defense University (NDU) at Washington's Fort McNair as part of a personnel exchange program between Japan's Defense Agency and the NDU. Considerable doubts were voiced during those talks on the U.S. commitment to the Asian-Pacific region.

Ezra Vogel was keeping a close watch on how the enormous political changes in Japan brought about by the end of Liberal Democratic Party (LDP) domination and the emergence of "reformists" would impact on the bilateral relationship, especially bilateral security ties.

Famous for his book *Japan as Number One*, Vogel was originally a sociologist but had moved over to the position of senior analyst on the NIC at Nye's urging. Vogel's strengths were his fluency in Japanese and Chinese, his insights into the East Asian societies of Japan, China, and Korea, and his abundant personal contacts. Vogel had already visited Japan many times to meet with his old political acquaintances as well as government officials.

Vogel noted that new policy preparations were in the pipeline for both the midterm defense plan and the New Defense Program Outline (NDPO), so Japan would have to come up with ideas on cooperation with the United States. The Higuchi Report had already been released, sparking debate in Japan on post–Cold War security policy. The United States should not miss this chance to have input.

Vogel was convinced that the bilateral alliance must remain the building block of U.S. security ties in Asia. He judged the security alliance to be adrift; it was facing difficult challenges. His conclusion, however, was that Japanese political leaders were starting to support the alliance anew especially as leaders in Japanese security circles became increasingly willing to accept their share of an international effort to preserve global security, and as a new generation of Japanese politicians and government officials was increasingly prepared to address global security issues.

Vogel conveyed these thoughts in detail to Nye. "Ezra [Vogel] and I began talking in the spring of 1994. And Ezra said, 'You know, in the past, there has always been someone in the U.S. government who could work with the Japanese bureaucrats, and this provided a sense of re-assurance. And instead of that, what has happened is, there is really nobody that's paying attention to the security dimension. Everything is just focusing on the trade disputes.'"[16]

Nye sensed that Vogel thought this situation would hurt the U.S.-Japan security relationship and that the United States needed to do something to reinforce or strengthen the relationship. Nye had always respected Vogel's views, referring to him as his *sensei*, the Japanese word for teacher/mentor, in Asian affairs.

Nye was also receiving warnings and suggestions from Republican experts whom he knew personally, people like Richard Armitage, for-mer assistant secretary of defense, and Brent Scowcroft, former National Security Council adviser in the Bush administration.

Scowcroft had recently been to Japan and had just met with Seiki Nishihiro, JDA counselor. "I was beginning to worry about the U.S.-Japan Security Treaty and the number of people who were saying, 'well, you know, it's sort of outdated and we don't need it anymore.' It was my sense that the Security Treaty might even be more important in the post–Cold War period than it was before, because of the dynamic, rapidly changing character of the Asian scene. . . . I was happy to talk with what I thought to be a kindred spirit [Nishihiro]."[17]

Nishihiro stressed the need to get started quickly with a strategic dialogue between the two countries. Scowcroft passed this message along to Nye when he got back to Washington. While Nye was from a different party faction than Armitage and Scowcroft, they were think-ing almost the same thing.

The Giarra group, the Green-Cronin combination, the Fort McNair study group, the Harvard connection, Armitage associates—the views of a wide range of people converged here. Gayle Von Eckartsburg, a member of the Pentagon's Japan team and part of the Harvard connec-tion just like Nye, Vogel, and Campbell, put it this way: "I think it was a confluence of currents."[18]

The Higuchi Report

The Higuchi Report requires some explanation here.

The Advisory Group on Defense Issues (chaired by Hirotaro Higuchi, chairman of Asahi Breweries, Ltd.) was a private panel appointed by Prime Minister Morihiro Hosokawa in February 1994.

The result of a 20-meeting crash program to deliberate defense issues, its report *The Modality of the Security and Defense Capability of Japan: The Outlook for the 21st Century* was completed in August and delivered to Prime Minister Tomiichi Murayama. In the interim, the reins of government had passed from Hosokawa to Hata to Murayama.

The report said, "Japan should extricate itself from its security policy of the past that was, if anything, passive, and henceforth play an active role in shaping a new order. Indeed, Japan has the responsibility of playing such a role."[19]

So how was Japan going to create a security policy that was active and constructive?

First came "multilateral security cooperation," followed by "enhancing the functions of the Japan-U.S. security cooperative relationship." And then "maintenance and operation of highly reliable and efficient defense capability."

The report placed particular emphasis on multilateral cooperation under the umbrella of the United Nations, especially actively cooperating with peacekeeping operations, including peacekeeping forces (PKF). "Preventing the use of force as a means of settling international disputes is the intent of the United Nations Charter. That the international community will develop along these lines is extremely desirable for Japan in the light of its national interests, since the nation is engaged in economic activities around the globe and yet resolved not to tread the path to a major military power."[20]

It suggested establishing a specialist staff council on the same footing as the Land, Maritime, and Air Self-Defense Forces' Joint Staff Council. It called for "an early release of the freeze" on field PKF operations.

Field PKF operations referred to operations that did not lead to the use of arms, such as supervising cease-fires; supervising disarmament; stationing in and patrolling of demilitarized zones; collecting, storing, and disposing of surrendered weapons; and assisting in prisoner-of-war exchanges. Participating in all of these operations was frozen until release by a new law.

Based on "the common understanding that is recognized by the United Nations with regard to the use of arms," the report also called for a revision of one of the International Peace Cooperation Law's so-called Five PKO Principles[21] drawn up in keeping with "government constitutional interpretation and coordinated U.N. peacekeeping activities," namely, the provision stipulating that "the use of arms will be kept to a minimum and limited to the protection of the lives of those serving."

It deemed the bilateral security structure to be still "an indispensable precondition for the defense of Japan even in the post–Cold War security environment."[22] To that end, it proposed the enhancement of policy consultations and information exchange; promotion of the operational cooperation setup; improvement of the mutual cooperation setup in logistic support; promotion of mutual cooperation in equipment; and improvement of the support setup for U.S. forces.[23]

The report acknowledged that the U.N. Charter, the Japanese Constitution, and the Japan-U.S. Security Treaty formed the three written pillars of Japan's postwar security policies.

> When postwar Japan made a new start, we were given a new framework of basic national policies, externally by the United Nations Charter and internally by the Constitution. However, the idea of collective security upheld by a United Nations still in its infancy rapidly lost its basis for realization as it was exposed to the stern realities of international politics. Governments realized anew that self-defense capability was the best assurance of national security. Furthermore, the major nations were in a state of confrontation centering on the two superpowers, the United States and the Soviet Union, and realized they had no alternative but to ensure national security through an alliance of nations sharing common interests and values. Thus the Japan-U.S. Security Treaty was chosen as the realistic basis of postwar Japan's security policy.[24]

But now the Cold War was over. Japan should have a new security outlook; it should pursue a basis that dovetailed and gelled with the U.N. Charter and the Constitution. The realistic basis that had been thwarted by the Cold War was in sight. We shouldn't miss this opportunity.

The report stated that while U.N. peacekeeping activities "require in some cases that weapons be used to a certain extent,"[25] such activity did not correspond to the use of arms banned by Article 9 of the Japanese Constitution.[26] It also made clear its position that "in view of the purposes of the United Nations already described . . . it is natural that such use of arms should be permitted."[27]

The advisory group was a novel innovation. Instead of relying on the JDA and the rest of the bureaucracy to draw something up, Prime Minister Hosokawa had gathered a broad range of experts to approach the issue and help him formulate his basic stance on defense policy. Hosokawa asked them to discuss and come up with the foundations of a new defense outline to replace the existing NDPO. He was looking for a radical overhaul.

Hosokawa's politics were characterized by an emphasis on symbols, not only in substance but in style. Turning up at the SDF reviewing ceremony in civilian clothes was one example. "Just as I wanted to put a stop to going to the Imperial Palace in the formal attire of tails, I wanted to go before the SDF in my usual civilian style." (Opposition to his refusal to wear formal attire was so strong that he failed in that attempt. Hosokawa also tried to put a stop to the three heads of the legislature, the executive, and the judiciary all going out to Haneda airport to see the emperor off and welcome him home from overseas trips. He was successful in August 1993 when the emperor attended the funeral of the king of Belgium, but things reverted to normal thereafter.) Setting up the advisory group on defense issues was an illustration of his emphasis on style.

In practical terms, he intended to leave it in the hands of Nishihiro right from the very first. Hosokawa later commented that "of all the JDA old boys, Nishihiro was the most liberal, so I asked him to set it [the advisory group] up."[28]

Hosokawa said, "The number of Japan's land self-defense forces has hardly changed even though the Cold War is over. I thought we needed to cut back the land forces and switch to a defense structure centered on the maritime and air forces. That's why I had Nishihiro put the question at the start of the advisory group whether we couldn't cut the land division by half or a third."[29]

There were precedents for using a private advisory group of experts. Michita Sakada, director-general of the JDA, had set up a group to consider defense in 1957, as had Prime Minister Masayoshi Ohira on overall security.

The Advisory Group on Defense Issues, however, was going to draw up a blueprint for new Japanese security policy in the post–Cold War era and "after the collapse of the 1955 system" (namely, continuous LDP rule).

More than anything else, the timing was perfect.

The group's report became widely known as the Higuchi Report. Hirotaro Higuchi had made his name in the world of finance, but he had become something of a guru by turning Asahi Breweries into one of Japan's top companies with his outstanding business acumen. He was later selected as Harvard's Business Statesman for 1996. He was liberal and took a broad international view.

At the same time, he was well-known among the general populace as the chairman of a brewery. With his booming voice and smiling face, it was hoped that he would be able to put the bubbles back into the debate by taking flat defense issues and transforming them into sparkling security issues.

Ulterior Motives

When drawing up the Higuchi Report, the advisory group was successful in writing a draft without any intervention from the bureaucracy. However, the Cabinet Legislation Bureau did point out that the group's constitutional interpretation on peacekeeping activities did not necessarily match that of the bureau.

The Legislation Bureau's interpretation was based on that set forth by Atsuo Kudo, director-general of the Cabinet Legislation Bureau, in 1990 at the time of the Gulf crisis. Kudo stated that as the so-called U.N. forces differed according to their individual objectives and missions, the pros and cons of participating could not be debated arbitrarily. If the objective and mission of the U.N. forces in question, however, were accompanied by the use of arms, the Constitution would not allow for participation by the Self-Defense Forces. Conversely, if the objective and mission of the U.N. forces in question were not accompanied by the use of arms, then the Constitution did not expressly prohibit participation by the Self-Defense Forces, but given that the existing Self-Defense Forces Law did not stipulate that kind of mission for the SDF, their participation could not be allowed.

Debate pivoted here on one's interpretation of the nature of the "international disputes" stipulated in Article 9 of the Japanese Constitution. It said, "The Japanese people forever renounce war as a sovereign right of the nation, and the threat or use of force as means of settling international disputes."

If that referred only to disputes between sovereign states with no intervention by a collective security system, then participating in a collective security system, even if it involved the use of arms, would not be forbidden by the Constitution.

If that was so, a further problem was whether the present United Nations could be called a collective security system. If, in realistic terms, the United Nations could be classified as such, an interpretation allowing participation in actions sanctioned under Chapter 7 of the U.N. Charter based on a decision by the Security Council would be possible.

Those in favor of active and constructive participation in the United Nations came up with the position that "international security" equaled "collective security." The Advisory Group on Defense Issues drew up its blueprint, which basically adopted this stance.

Regarding the point made by the Cabinet Legislation Bureau, Professor Akio Watanabe of Aoyama Gakuin University, a key member, verifies that while the group "toned the expression down somewhat, we pushed our own case through."[30]

Another instance was when Prime Minister Tomiichi Murayama asked the members of the group before receiving the final report if they wouldn't give him a break on the section referring to "revising the constraints laid down in the International Peace Cooperation Law limiting the permissible use of arms to legitimate self-defense." Here they watered down the tone of the final draft considerably.

Indeed, PKO-related issues became the subject of Diet debate. Tokuichiro Tamazawa, JDA chief, responded, saying, "I have yet to make up my mind regarding field operations [by the SDF in PKO], and it is a matter which will probably have to be looked into in the future. Regarding PKF, I think we need to get more experience, we need more time regarding whether to release the [freeze], we don't have enough experience yet."[31]

The Murayama government seemed to be trying to put out the fires that were being fanned. The government was probably hampered by the need to maintain coalition stability among the LDP, the SDP, and the New Party Sakigake.

The advisory group came about originally from a discussion between JDA counselor Seiki Nishihiro and Chichibu-Onoda Cement Corporation Chairman Ken Moroi. They had the support of the JDA from Deputy Director-General Hajime Hatakeyama all the way. The JDA maintained a seemly distance. Watanabe says that they had complete freedom when writing the draft.

Hosokawa was apparently not happy with the report. He had wanted disarmament stressed, and he didn't feel that that point had come through enough. Feeling they could have been bolder in their proposals for force cutbacks, he couldn't approve it.[32]

Resistance from the SDF in the field was strong, however. Excessively radical comments were heard from leaders in the Land SDF: "We'll fight for our 180,000 to the last! If we don't get them we're ready to die the honorable death [*gyokusai*]!"

The report itself called for a 30,000 reduction in forces, centering mainly on the Land SDF, and collapsing part of the land divisions into a brigade, but Hosokawa thought it was all very cosmetic.

What was more, the authors had focused too much on PKO. Perhaps they were still suffering from the after effects of the Gulf War. . . . He also surmised that the fact that they were writing the report at a time when doubts over North Korea's nuclear program were escalating and the possibility of U.N. economic sanctions looked imminent had made it difficult to come up with any bold disarmament. If that was the case, however, the policy proposals in that area were weak.

The only catch was that Hosokawa was no longer prime minister when the report was finished.

If there was any meddling with the writing of the report, it came from Washington. Security experts in Washington condemned their neglect of the bilateral alliance.

Republican security pros like Richard Armitage, former assistant secretary of defense, and Carl Ford, former deputy assistant secretary of defense, both expressed alarm. They raised voices of concern about Japan's sudden tilt towards multilateralism.

Up until the Bush administration, the United States had taken an extremely cautious stance on multilateral frameworks in the Asian-Pacific region. Since the advent of the Clinton administration, however, a change had occurred. Clinton's people, especially in their early days, advocated an assertive multilateralism.

Since the end of the Cold War, the United Nations, which was no good for anything during the Cold War because of Soviet-American confrontation and the North-South rift, was experiencing a new lease on life. Positive feeling towards the United Nations jumped in the wake of the Gulf War. "Cooperative security" was even beginning to be the keyword of the day.

As a consequence, Watanabe viewed the criticism from Washington as "a hangover of the pro-treaty school's reasoning from the old days." There was probably something to that. Nye himself, a Democrat, did not see any problem with multilateral cooperation. "I read the Higuchi Report, but I couldn't see what the problem was. In fact, I was encouraged by Japan's new activism and the width of its global perspective and its positiveness. I was impressed by the PKO approach."[33]

The critical remarks from pro-alliance people were a surprise to the members of the advisory group. Watanabe and many of the other members were almost unanimous on the point that "the nature of post–Cold War security is shifting substantially towards cooperative security, multilateral cooperation, or the U.N. role. Bilateral security had to be debated in the light of that kind of historical sense. If it wasn't, we would never be rid of the bipolar confrontation between the cooperative security lobby and the bilateral security lobby."[34]

It was just that Nishihiro was sensitive to criticism in the United States, and the Foreign Ministry had also conveyed its concern. Halfway through the writing, Watanabe thought of switching the order around and placing the Japan-U.S. Security Treaty before multilateral cooperation, but after seeking the advice of a friend in the United States, he decided to leave it as it was.

In fact, there were various views on the Higuchi Report in the United States. For instance, a special report from the Pacific Forum CSIS was very positive.

Some U.S. officials and former officials view the Higuchi report as indicative of a trend away from close Japan-U.S. security cooperation toward greater independence through the modality of multilateralism. We view it as an effort to gain greater public consensus of peacekeeping operations (PKO) as a legitimate and appropriate mission for the Self-Defense

Forces. The report states that multilateral security cooperation is dependent upon United States leadership. . . .

Concerning force structure, the report calls for enhanced Command, Control, Communications, and Intelligence (C³I) capability, greater inter-service and Japan-U.S. military inter-operability, improved maneuverability and combat readiness, more effective and flexible use of limited personnel resources, and the development of a national ballistic missile defense capability. We agree with these priorities and see them as essential for the establishment of a solid defense capability.[35]

Perhaps some of the criticism from Washington was aimed at the U.S. government. Seeing a clear trend away from the United States by Japan in the report, critics came up with the argument that this was the result of the United States' bashing and neglect of Japan. It was part of a campaign to get the American government to give up its overwhelming preoccupation with economics and switch to something new. They were looking for material that would support their argument. It just happened to be the Higuchi Report.

A senior JDA official who looked after the advisory group behind the scenes recalled, "The criticism in Washington had a certain aspect of shock therapy, of trying to make the government bureaucrats show some interest in Japan again."[36] In short, there were ulterior motives lurking behind U.S. reactions.

Takemasa Moriya, counselor at the Defense Bureau, was another who found something strange in the Washington air around that time. Nevertheless, he hoped that the criticism would act as a catalyst to get the U.S. government moving. "Everywhere you went in Washington, you got exactly the same reaction. They all started reciting in chorus that we had the order back to front; that you couldn't have multilateral cooperation without solid bilateral security and self-defense capability first. And that's when Vogel and Nye started to move. That's what changes Washington. We flatter ourselves that it was the Higuchi Report which extracted the Nye report."[37]

The Nye Report referred to the Defense Department's East Asia Strategy Report, released the following February. In it, the United States once more tightened its commitment to the Asian-Pacific region.

It is certain that of the three pillars of multilateral cooperation, Japan-U.S. security, and self-defense capability, the Higuchi Report placed the most stress on multilateral cooperation. The report made it the first pillar, which undeniably created the impression in terms of format of playing down Japan-U.S. security. It was not, however, the hedging against a weakening American commitment or the retreat from bilateral military cooperation that critics like Cronin and Green portrayed it to be. Japan had not changed its larger framework of pursuing a security policy founded on the bilateral alliance in the post–Cold War world.

The very fact that this kind of criticism emerged from the United States in this form at this time was a clear indication of the paltry nature of bilateral policy talks, the dearth of political dialogue, the instability of bilateral relations—in a word, how far adrift the two countries were.

"Where Should I Phone?"

Joseph Nye took up his position as assistant secretary of defense on September 15. The Pentagon was in a state of extreme tension over whether troops would be ordered into Haiti (they moved in on September 19). His first order of business was a breakfast with Hajime Hatakeyama, deputy director-general of the JDA.

The breakfast actually took place in early September at the Madison Hotel in downtown Washington, immediately before Nye officially took up his post. Hatakeyama was an old friend of Carl Ford, who had set up the meeting with Nye. In addition to Thomas Hubbard, deputy assistant secretary of state for East Asian affairs, and Stanley Roth, senior director of the NSC's East Asian Bureau, the meeting was also attended by Giarra, Armitage, and Ford. The main aim, however, was to have Nye and Hatakeyama get acquainted.

Hatakeyama's trip to the United States came about at the suggestion of Seiki Nishihiro, Hatakeyama's predecessor at the JDA. Nishihiro was worried about the severe criticism that the Higuchi Report had come in for from American bilateral security experts. Armitage, who had just been to Japan, had also conveyed to him the general feeling in the United States. Nishihiro himself was intimately involved with the report, having been a member of the advisory group. So he asked Hatakeyama to go to Washington and explain things.

Hatakeyama expressed his concern, saying, "I don't know whom I should call in Washington. Where on earth should I phone?" He didn't beat about the bush; he wanted to know who in the Clinton administration was in charge of U.S.-Japan security issues; who his counterpart was. "We will soon be starting to draw up the National Defense Program Outline. We want to be able to do that in close consultation with America. As things stand at the moment, though, we can't get through." Nye assured him that he would always be available, that he shouldn't hesitate to call him up whenever he needed to.[38]

This is the "telephone breakfast" that was said to have initiated the process that later became known as the Nye Initiative. Looking back, Nye recalled, "Hatakeyama asserted that the bilateral security relationship, which had become completely regulated during the Cold War, needed to be reconfirmed and reactivated now in the post–Cold War era. It was an impressive meeting. And later, after I had become assistant secretary of defense, I decided Japan would be the first place I went."[39]

One of the Americans at the meeting noticed that Hatakeyama didn't eat much breakfast and just nibbled at his food. By then Hatakeyama was suffering from cancer, although even he didn't know it yet.

Hatakeyama also met with Walter Slocombe, undersecretary of defense, on this trip. Although they agreed to conducting joint research on theater missile defense (TMD), the meeting was probably more of a courtesy call, but it did produce a useful by-product. Slocombe, after listening to Hatakeyama's exhortation on the importance of strengthening the bilateral security relationship, realized how completely Japan had slipped out of view in the administration's diplomacy and security policies. He immediately raised the issue with Defense Secretary Perry. Perry decided to place more emphasis on Japan in his upcoming trip to Asia. He also decided that the first assignment for his newly appointed assistant secretary, Nye, would be to accompany him.

Hatakeyama didn't say a word all the way from Narita airport to his home in Kawasaki. The scowl on his face didn't disappear.

His secretary, Yuji Dochin, had never seen Hatakeyama like this. *But he loves talking and making provocative arguments to his staff. Something's wrong.*

Dochin was troubled by something Hatakeyama had said to him that summer when he came home from tennis. "My throat feels like it's blocked. The timing's wrong when I have a glass of water." It was two weeks later that Hatakeyama was told he had cancer of the esophagus.

But Hatakeyama's taciturnity on the way back from the airport was not only due to the sharp pains in his chest that often afflicted him. He was in disagreement with Tokuichiro Tamazawa, JDA director-general, over whether his successor should be Naoaki Murata, director of the Defense Bureau, or Noboru Hoshuyama, director-general of the Defense Facilities Administration Agency. The bad blood between them was still there. He had to do something about it when he got home.

The matter weighed heavily on him. Hatakeyama wanted Murata, but Tamazawa clung to Hoshuyama. He liked the affable and upright Hoshuyama.

Tamazawa suspected that the JDA as a whole had shifted over to the New Renewal Party (which changed its name to the New Frontier Party at the end of 1994) after the birth of the Hosokawa government in the summer of the previous year. Both the LDP and the New Renewal Party had just started a turf battle in Kasumigaseki, checking up on who was for which party or faction. The JDA and the SDF were not exempted from this struggle.

It was a very tense time for Deputy Director-General Hatakeyama. Tamazawa was not pleased by Hatakeyama's September trip to the United States. *He's just a deputy. Who does he think he is going off to America without checking properly with me?* He was even suspicious about the agreement Hatakeyama had reached with Slocombe on the TMD research. *Is there something behind it? Has he meddled somewhere uncalled for?* Nor did he try to hide those feelings.

In early October, Hatakeyama had to be hospitalized. When he went to inform Tamazawa, he was shocked to hear him say, "Haven't you done enough anyway?" *Is he so uncomfortable with me as his deputy?*

Hatakeyama left the room, but not before checking Tamazawa with, "I want Murata to be the next deputy director-general."

The day before he went to the hospital, Hatakeyama heard at a party at the Hotel Okura that Hoshuyama was threatening to resign. Okinawa was up in arms about Hoshuyama's comment in mid-September that he wanted Okinawa to change in the direction of coexisting with the bases. The SDP even called in Cabinet for "a complete retraction of the statement." The Okinawa branch of the SDP called for his resignation or dismissal. The LDP and the JDA, however, were jockeying to get away with a partial retraction, arguing that a complete retraction would amount to a denial of the bilateral security structure. It was at this time that Hoshuyama suddenly threatened to resign his post.

"What a mess!"

Hatakeyama had to go back to the office again at night. While he was in the deputy director-general's office with his deputies seeing what they could do by way of damage control, there was a phone call from Mrs. Hatakeyama. She was furious and screamed at his secretary. "He's being admitted to the hospital tomorrow. How can you keep him at the agency this late? Enough is enough!"

So prompted, Hatakeyama left the room. (Hoshuyama had criticized Prime Minister Tomiichi Murayama, saying that he should sign the proxy papers if Okinawa's governor, Masahide Ota, had refused to do so. He later went as far as saying, "This is what happens when you have a stupid prime minister." The incident escalated into a political issue, and he was fired on October 19.)

Hatakeyama was in and out of the hospital after that. He resigned on April 21, 1995. At 11:00 A.M., he went to the director-general's office where Tamazawa accepted his resignation. He was seen off, and walked out the front entrance of the building.

Hatakeyama had refused a sendoff with band and guard of honor. There was no traditional rendering of "Auld Lang Syne" for a departing deputy director-general either. Staff were lined up between the different services' buildings to see him off. Hatakeyama acknowledged them with a nod and walked towards the main gate.

He had told Dochin to be standing by with a car; he would raise his arm if he couldn't make it to the gate on his own. The car followed behind him, a little off to the side, at a sedate pace.

Just in front of the entrance to the Air SDF's building, he raised his arm. Boarding the car, he traveled the 50 meters or so to the main gate. Returning the guard's salute, he got out of the car and accepted a bouquet from a female secretary. He could hardly stay on his feet.

On the way to the National Cancer Center in Tsukiji, he looked back, saying, "I'm glad I got out at the end. That was good." Hatakeyama passed away soon thereafter.[40]

Preestablished Deterrent Harmony

Hatakeyama was one of the ex–Ministry of Finance men who had been transferred to the JDA. He had followed the well-trodden course of Defense Bureau director, head of the Personnel Bureau, head of the Finance Bureau, head of the Defense Bureau, and deputy director-general of the agency. During that time, he promoted Japanese involvement in international security, especially the United Nations' PKO.

In April 1991, after the end of the Gulf War, Japan participated in the minesweeping operations in the Persian Gulf. Commanded by Taosa Ochiai, there were 511 Maritime SDF personnel in the Persian Gulf Minesweeping Expeditionary Unit. Four timber minesweepers spent six months in the difficult, shallow, sludge-infested seas, destroying a total of 34 mines.

The personnel who landed at the port of Rasht in the United Arab Emirates city of Dubai were shocked to see people wearing T-shirts emblazoned with "Thanks to the Countries That Have Contributed to Restoring the Gulf." There was no Japanese flag among the flags of the countries that had helped. Hadn't Japan contributed some $9 billion?

By July, however, the Japanese flag was there on the T-shirts with the rest of them. The people of Kuwait had learned that the Japanese minesweepers were out there silently cleaning up the seas.

"It's not money, but sweat!" Hatakeyama couldn't count how many times he had uttered those lines. When sending the PKO unit to Cambodia, he said he would go before the troops to have a look around and flew off to Phnom Penh.

Hatakeyama had moved to the JDA at the strong insistence of Nishihiro. Nishihiro was the JDA's first true-born deputy director-general (the top bureaucratic post). In the 40 years until his retirement in 1990, he had worked on defense policy at the agency.

Nishihiro undeniably had a huge wealth of expertise as a defense cadre as well as a deeply cultivated mind and a very balanced common sense that was strengthened by his wide circle of friends. He spoke no English, but he had the insight, the powers of expression, and the international sense that made professionals abroad trust him.

Hatakeyama followed Nishihiro's internationalist security line. For the nationalists within the agency, the Nishihiro line erred on the side of deterrence theory and on the side of bilateral security. He did not assume a specific threat and prepare defense capability to meet that. He built up defense capability centered on the powers of deterrence. Making the bilateral security relationship Japan's central axis was Nishihiro's basic defense ideology and that of the Nishihiro line.

The nationalists weren't comfortable with this. Whether "nationalists" was an accurate label is also questionable. It was not as if they formed a single school or had a united theory or single leader. They were similar, however, in terms of temperament, feeling, and thinking. For example, they argued the following:

First, *mission.* "The mission of the SDF is, and always will be, the essential defense of the nation." Disaster rescue and PKO were heresy. Following the lead of other ministries they would "forget their spirit." Therefore, equipment systems, tanks, and fighter planes were not to be neglected.

Second, *area policing* was a job for the military in any country, not something to be done at the request of the police. Interministerial cooperation, especially requests from the police, should be kept to a bare minimum.

Finally, *civilian control* was to be guaranteed by the suits in the agency controlling the SDF. In such instances, they would unfailingly drag out the Defense Agency Establishment Law. Article 4 of the law reads, "The Defense Agency will have as its objective the protection of Japan's peace and independence, and to this end its mission is to control and manage the Land Self-Defense Force, the Maritime Self-Defense Force, and the Air Self-Defense Force, and perform the related administrative affairs." They tried to use the narrowest definition possible.

Those bureaucrats with this kind of orientation were also called "the civvy-control suit brigade." The work of JDA officials began and ended with controlling the uniforms; the upshot was that they saw the Defense Agency as the "SDF control agency" and tended to believe that that was what civilian control was all about.

They also resisted Nishihiro's post–Cold War impassioned rationalization of the SDF, the so-called compactification. Nishihiro left the service without even getting started on this; Hatakeyama was the one who actually tackled it. While opposition from the Land SDF was naturally fierce, it was nothing compared to that of the Maritime SDF, but he stuck to the Nishihiro line.

There were, however, very subtle differences in the thinking of Nishihiro and Hatakeyama. For example, in 1987 an incident occurred when the Soviet Union's electronic surveillance plane *Badger* penetrated Japanese airspace twice over Okinawa. An SDF aircraft fired several lightballs from its 20-millimeter machine guns in warning. This sparked a controversy over whether it amounted to a "warning" or "the use of arms"; was it "legitimate self-defense" or an "emergency evacuation?"

The pilot in the SDF aircraft was told, "You can't shoot in the case of simple airspace incursion; however, you can fire in the case of legitimate self-defense or emergency evacuation." The pilot, however, was given no clear criteria for what was a simple airspace incursion or what was legitimate self-defense or emergency evacuation.

In the Diet, debate focused on whether shooting down an aircraft in this case was legally permissible. Seiki Nishihiro, at the time head of the Defense Bureau, said in effect that "there is no law for shooting down [a plane]"; "the existing legal framework is lacking. We will look into it."

Nishihiro, however, did nothing to close the loophole. He believed that "a country that said, 'it's an incursion of airspace, shoot them down every time even in peacetime,' was not a democratic state. Legally, there's nothing more that can be done. Thinking about that is a job for the politicians."[41]

It could also be said that he thought it was impossible to think that far ahead if they were only going to presuppose a contingency when deterrence broke down.

Hatakeyama had his doubts on this position. *What should we do when deterrence did break down? We can't go on saying we'll work to prevent fires but won't put them out if they start!*

He argued that they needed a manual on what to do in such a case. Hatakeyama encountered Keiji Omori, then a deputy of Nishihiro's. Omori said, "One shot at the Marco Polo Bridge thrust this country into misery. That's why we can't afford to create a manual for hypothetical contingencies."

"If that's the case, shouldn't you be stating that clearly to the Diet? Shouldn't you be saying, in the historical light of one shot at the Marco Polo Bridge plunging this country into misery, we shouldn't draw up such a manual? Where's the civilian control if we tell the Diet one thing and go ahead and do something else?"

Civilian control should take place in the Diet and was the politicians' responsibility. It was not the suits in the agency controlling the uniforms. He was in the habit of saying that's the director-general's job. This was the starting point of Hatakeyama's thinking, from where his basic ideas stemmed.

Obviously, we have no way of asking the deceased Hatakeyama how this ideology linked up to his passion in his student days when he shouted "Down with the Treaty"—how it developed, how it was synthesized, how it was sublimated. Hatakeyama's best friend from his student days at the education faculty of Tokyo University, Ryuichi Nagao, now a professor at Tokyo University, writes that in 1960, the year of the treaty demonstrations, Hatakeyama was right in the thick of things.[42] It seemed that Hatakeyama really believed that the Kishi Cabinet represented the return of Japanese fascism. That was the prevailing spirit on the campus of Tokyo University.

Three years after Hatakeyama joined the Ministry of Finance, he met Nagao at the ministry. They could see the demonstrators outside the window. Hatakeyama mumbled almost to himself, "Is it right that I'm here doing this?" Much later, at a class reunion after Hatakeyama had become deputy director-general at the JDA, he told his old classmates, most probably helped by the informality of the occasion, that "Japan will never make war. Why? Because the minister is from MOF, the deputy director-general is from MOF, and the Defense Bureau director is from MOF, everyone is from MOF. And MOF is in the business of not spending money. It's a tightwad ministry. So, we'll be all right."[43]

The JDA director-general when Hatakeyama was head of the Defense Bureau was Yukihiko Ikeda and the deputy director-general was Akira Hiyoshi. Both, like Hatakeyama, were ex-MOF men. Ikeda and Hatakeyama were also in the same year together at Tokyo University.

Perhaps Hatakeyama was trying to convince himself that peace could be bought with money, or rather that peace could be valued in monetary terms. On that point, it seems that peace logic and budget logic, or even MOF logic, formed a preestablished harmony. In front of the same classmates he had probably argued passionately about peace with, Hatakeyama appeared to have found the perfect ideological hiding place. There may have been something comfortable about a preestablished harmony of deterrence—or should that be a preestablished deterrent harmony?—under the umbrella of the bilateral alliance.

Sweat, Not Money

Hatakeyama's final ideological resting place, however, was sweat, not money. It was a new international security thinking born from tackling PKO in the field, and it was crystallized in the deputy director-general's charge delivered at the briefing for senior SDF members held immediately after his return from the United States.

First, the Cold War between East and West was over, and domestic party politics had entered an era of coalition building, so let's forget about precedent and respond positively and on the basis of our own independent judgement. "Up until now, the JDA and the SDF have come in for sharp criticism from the Diet and the mass media for our tilt towards peace-at-any-price, our always following precedented suit, driving safely, our red-tapeism. But the situation both inside and outside the country has changed dramatically today. New, positive responses are required free from the trammels of precedent within the framework of firmly upholding the Constitution, defense-only security policy, and three nonnuclear principles."

Second, global peace and stability are prerequisites for Japan's security. Let's have policies on the broad internal and external issues of security. "As an organization with units actively serving in the PKO, a means for contributing to global peace and stability, having our own policy is, in fact, the responsibility of the JDA and SDF. We need to dispatch units on the basis of JDA and SDF policy, not because someone tells us to go. In order to do that, we need intelligence gathering, analysis, and assessment functions second to none."

Third, let's push ahead on internationalization. "First, we need to increase opportunities for positive dialogue. And we need to be able to speak clearly in the first person, not responding in hypothetical question-and-answer formats. We also need to formulate our own ideas on Japan's mid- to long-term security and test them out on non-Japanese minds."

"Where should I phone?"

In Washington, on what was to be Hatakeyama's last trip overseas, this direct query, with which he had challenged Japan's allies, quietly but firmly implied a more fundamental question. Nye was greatly taken aback. And he was convinced that his fears had not been misplaced.

In early October, Nye made his first overseas trip as assistant secretary of defense. Japan was his first stop. He had wanted to see Hatakeyama but had been told that he was in the hospital.

Hatakeyama never made any calls to Washington.

Notes

1. Author's conversation with Michael Green and Patrick Cronin in the summer of 1994.

2. Conversation with Michael Green.

3. Interview with Kurt Campbell.

4. Perry M. Smith, *Assignment: Pentagon* (Washington: Brassey's, 1993).

5. Ibid., p. 21.

6. Ibid., p. 18.

7. Ibid., p. 31.

8. Interview with Ezra Vogel.

9. Joseph Nye, "Coping with Japan," *Foreign Policy,* no. 89 (Winter 1992–93), pp. 96–115.

10. Ibid., p. 97.

11. Gwen Ifill, "A 'Mature' Relationship: Japan and U.S. Agree That They Can't Agree, and Trade Talks Collapse," *New York Times,* February 13, 1994, Section 4, p. 2.

12. Patrick Cronin and Michael Green, "Redefining the U.S.-Japan Alliance: Tokyo's National Defense Program," Institute for National Strategic Studies, McNair Paper 31, National Defense University, November 1994.

13. Ibid., pp. 1–2.

14. Ibid., p. 2.

15. Ibid., p. 9.

16. Interview with Joseph Nye.

17. Interview with Brent Scowcroft.

18. Interview with Gayle Von Eckartsburg.

19. *The Modality of the Security and Defense Capability of Japan: The Outlook for the 21st Century,* as quoted in Appendix B of Torkel Patterson, James A. Kelly, and Ralph A. Cossa, "Strategy and Force Structure Response of Japan and the United States to the New Security Environment in Northeast Asia," Pacific Forum CSIS Special Report, June 1995, p. 94.

20. Ibid., p. 94.

21. Ibid., p. 106.

22. Ibid., p. 108.

23. Ibid., pp. 109–110.

24. Ibid., p. 85.

25. Ibid., p. 104.

26. Ibid., p. 95.

27. Ibid., p. 104.

28. Interview with Morihiro Hosokawa.

29. Ibid.

30. Interview with Akio Watanabe.

31. Response to Tokuichiro Tamazawa, director-general of JDA, to the Standing Committee on Audit, House of Councilors, September 2, 1994.

32. Interview with Morihiro Hosokawa.

33. Interview with Joseph Nye.

34. Interview with Akio Watanabe.

35. Patterson, Kelly, and Cossa, "Strategy and Force Structure Responses of Japan and the United States to the New Security Environments in Northeast Asia," pp. 22–23.

36. Interview with a senior JDA official.

37. Interview with Takemasa Moriya.

38. Interview with Joseph Nye.

39. Ibid.

40. This section is based on the author's interviews with Masahiro Akiyama, Akira Hiyoshi, and Yuji Dochin.

41. An account from Keiji Omori.

42. Ryuichi Nagao, *The Setting of the American Century* (Tokyo: PHP Institute, 1992), afterword. (In Japanese.)

43. Interview with Ryuichi Nagao.

Chapter Twelve

The Nye Initiative

Oxygen

Assistant Secretary of Defense Joseph Nye set his first sights on creating the East Asian Strategy Report (EASR), later to be dubbed the Nye Report. It was released by the Department of Defense in February 1995.

A member of the DOD said that Nye had made up his mind to release this report on his first day at the department. "Because he came on strong about February as the deadline, we were run off our feet. It was released right at the end of February, on the 28th."

In the preface, Defense Secretary William Perry indicated a change in direction, stating that "two previous Department of Defense strategy reports, in 1990 and 1992, envisioned post–Cold War troop reductions continuing in the region through the end of the decade. This year's report, by contrast, reaffirms our commitment to maintain a stable forward presence in the region, at the existing level of about 100,000 troops, for the foreseeable future."[1]

The report described this U.S. presence as "oxygen." "Security is like oxygen: you do not tend to notice until you begin to lose it."[2]

U.S. forces stationed in the Asian-Pacific region had fallen from 130,000 in 1990 to 100,000 in 1994. During the Bush administration, rapid cuts were made in U.S. troops stationed overseas. The 1992 strategy report spoke of reducing them to 90,000.

Perry and Nye judged there was a need to stop this move. Perry observed, "The United States has committed the mistake of unilateral and hasty withdrawal of its troops four times in this century."[3] Its rapid withdrawal of forces after World War I, World War II, the Korean War, and the Vietnam War all resulted in global instability. He was most emphatic that this time, with the end of the Cold War, the United States should not repeat that history.

Nye endorsed this position. According to him, "we had to be able to fight and win two major regional conflicts at the same time. They were never named as such, but the two were very clearly the Persian Gulf and Korea."[4] He realized that the 90,000-troop strength envisioned by the Bush administration would not be enough and arrived at 100,000 as the lowest feasible figure.

Around that period, apprehension was mounting, mainly in Singapore, that the Americans might pull out of Asia. Japan and Korea felt increasingly threatened by North Korea's nuclear weapons development. Even during the Bush administration, Defense Secretary Dick Cheney responded to this "Northern Threat," temporarily freezing the planned troop cutbacks. However, the prevailing opinion was that this did not represent any change in the United States' long-term plans for troop withdrawal.

Paul Giarra: "The difficulty was that nobody believed that the U.S. was serious about holding the line in Asia. I believe that the perception was then, and frankly still is, that the U.S. cannot withstand the budgetary pressures, the U.S. is tired of what it's been doing, the U.S. doesn't have the will or the continuity or the foresight to maintain a force structure."[5]

At the beginning of the 1990s, there was not as much talk about the peace dividend in the Asian-Pacific region as there was in Europe. Asia differed from Europe in that the Cold War was not completely over there. The structure of the Cold War there was also different from that of Europe. During the Cold War era, two hot wars had broken out in Asia: Korea and Vietnam. Even after the end of the Cold War, the menace of a nuclear-armed North Korea was on the rise and there was a widening perception of, and growing concern about, U.S. withdrawal with the closure of Clark and Subic bases in the Philippines.

The reduction in troop strength put forward in the East Asia Strategy Initiative (EASI) announced by the Bush administration in 1990 invited such misgivings. It planned a 10 to 12 percent reduction in troops over the following three years. And, in fact, in keeping with this plan, 6,000 of the troops stationed in Japan were withdrawn, mainly from Okinawa.

Michael Armacost said the East Asia Strategy Initiative was aimed at "preempting haphazard congressional cuts through a process of controlled reductions."[6]

The difference between the EASR and the EASI that Perry emphasized in the preface of the Nye Report was not just a question of cutting or maintaining. Its audience was fundamentally different. The EASI was clearly addressed to a domestic audience, and Congress at that. Its main aim was to show the Democratic Congress that the United States was pulling back this far. In contrast, the EASR aimed at showing the Asia-Pacific countries the U.S. commitment to not pulling back any more than this.

From the stance of a Pentagon officer in charge of Asia-Pacific policy like Giarra, however, the fact that withdrawal from Asia had been held to a much slower pace than Europe, when the post–Cold War trend was for drastic troop reduction, was a great success.

The 400,000 troops in Europe were sliced quickly to 100,000, while the 135,000 in Asia were also cut to 100,000, placing American troop strength in both hemispheres around the same level. It made for a neatly "balanced commitment" for the global, two-ocean power.

Andrew Bennett, currently an associate professor at Georgetown University who was involved in drafting the report, related that "apart from being on a par now with Europe, the number itself, 100,000, was easy to remember!"[7] From the U.S. point of view, having the same numbers in Europe and Asia suggested no priority tilt in either direction, and it could also be portrayed as "a psychological defense line in the sand" indicating that "withdrawal and reductions stopped here."[8]

Nor was Perry oblivious to the symbolism involved. "There was a symbolic value to committing to a number. . . . It was both the military judgment that 100,000 was the right amount plus the geopolitical significance of maintaining a level commitment."[9]

However, many issues surfaced during the discussion process. How to correlate the concepts of commitment and forward deployment with force structure, for example. Or, how to position domestic troop strength, especially on Hawaii, Guam, the West Coast, and Alaska. Adding these troops to the count would mean 500,000 troops in the Asian-Pacific region. It was possible to argue that shifting the forward deployment troops slightly back would not damage the U.S. commitment.

Hawaiian Governor Benjamin Caetano had made clear his willingness to accept the U.S. marines stationed in Okinawa if they were transferred to Hawaii. After the Okinawan rape, he said, "We would be glad to take those troops" and even wrote to the president. Caetano later commented that all he obtained from the White House was notification that his letter had been received and a request to appreciate the complicated nature of the matter.[10]

Nye, however, placed great store on forward deployment and decided to confine the figures to U.S. troop strength overseas. He believed that without this, the countries of Asia would not be convinced of the U.S. commitment and presence.

The grumbling came rather from domestic quarters. The military in the field were apprehensive and critical: they didn't want fixed figures; that would have to be adjusted according to tactics; what was important wasn't the numbers, but capability; coming up with numbers just wasn't appropriate. So "there was a little friction" between the uniforms and the civilians.[11]

Military leaders felt that they would like to buy the latest weapons with any money saved by cuts in troops stationed overseas. It seems that the air force was the most vehemently opposed to fixed numbers.

The air force was a fiend for high tech, and they wanted to use any cuts in troop strength to go even more high tech. The civilians incorporated into the EASR words to the effect that "adjustments will be made from time to time due to changing security environments, technological advancements, and reorganizations required by changes in overall force structure" in an attempt to allay the military's fears.[12]

Finally, Nye had a chat with Wesley Clark, the Joint Chiefs of Staff's head of strategic planning policy, getting his approval for "approximately 100,000." There was an assessment in certain parts of the military that having a fixed figure could be politically useful at a time of strong pressure for public spending cuts. If they had an external public commitment, it would be easy to rebuff congressional demands for reductions. So it could be to their advantage to cooperate. This political judgment most likely gave Nye some added momentum.

Magic Number

The figure of approximately 100,000, however, quickly took on a life of its own as if it were some kind of magic number. Before anyone knew what was happening, it started drawing attacks from such people as Chalmers Johnson, president of the Japan Policy Research Institute and a renowned Japanologist, for being fixed for the next 20 years.[13]

Even in Japan the figure was taken too literally. After stating that "the U.S. intended to maintain that strength for a minimum of 20 years, with Secretary of State Christopher even talking of 50 years or indefinitely," Okinawa's Governor Masahide Ota wrote, "If America maintains 100,000 troops there is very little likelihood of any base realignment, consolidation, or reduction in Okinawa."[14]

The criticisms put forward by the Pentagon's military experts can be summarized as follows:

- There was no clear, rational reason for fixing troop strength at 100,000. In short, it was difficult to specify a scenario where it would be necessary. The biggest issue here was whether the United States could maintain its two-conflicts strategy in the future. It was predicted that criticism of this strategy, which assumed an overseas presence, would mount together with pressure for military budget cuts. Even Perry stated that America might have no choice but to abandon the two-conflicts strategy if cost reductions through base closures and improved procurement weren't achieved over the next two to three years.[15]

- No persuasive arguments had been given that the "foreseeable future" was considerably long term. Unification of the two Koreas might happen earlier than expected. Michael McDavitt, former head of CINCPAC planning, predicted that with "either a peace treaty or actual unification [of the two Koreas, there would be a] change in the total number of U.S. forces in East Asia from the 100,000. I don't know what it would change to, but I think it would change in ways that could impact on the air force at Misawa."[16]

- It was unwise to discuss fighting strength in terms of troops. It was generally accepted that fighting strength could only be expressed in manpower terms for the army and ground troops. While highly praising the Nye Initiative, William Pendley, deputy assistant secretary of defense in the Bush administration, said, "They shouldn't have presented numbers; they should have presented capability."[17]

- It underestimated the fiscal deficit pressures. According to a special report by the Pacific Forum CSIS, authored by Torkel Patterson, James Kelly, and Ralph Cossa, "The EASR should be viewed (absent hostilities) as a ceiling for U.S. forward deployed force structure and not as a floor." The report cited mounting budget pressures in the future as the main reason.[18]

- It did not sufficiently incorporate assessments on rapidly advancing technological breakthroughs that might change the nature of the U.S. presence. Doug Paal, National Security Council (NSC) official for East Asian affairs in the Bush administration, pointed out that it was quite conceivable that technological advances would markedly increase air coverage, making it more than possible for aircraft transferred from Kadena to Alaska, for example, to fulfill their air defense duties.

Nye, himself, was flexible. "Suppose that in five years' time, Kim Il Jong is gone and Korea [is] peacefully unified. Then we don't need 100,000 troops. I would think you could make major drawbacks. On the other hand, suppose that 5 years from now, or 10 years from now . . . the Russians start threatening in the area so you feel threatened about Hokkaido or something. We may need more than 100,000 troops. So the idea [was] that 100,000 was a marker for now, but it was not a number that was locked in concrete."[19] He reiterated that 100,000 should not be regarded as or made into a magic number.

Most difficult to predict and a very volatile beast was the mood of the American public. A staff member of Senator Sam Nunn (D-Ga.) and a specialist on military affairs remarked that the figure of 100,000 in Europe and 100,000 in Asia would not be fixed forever. Then there was bound to be pressure for a revision in the future. His personal view was that he couldn't imagine that troops would not be pulled out from the Korean Peninsula and Okinawa in the next 10 years.[20]

That was the general atmosphere on the Hill. The staff member said, "A Republican congressman elected in Georgia in the landslide gains made by the Republicans in the 1994 election called for a withdrawal from NATO, but while it hadn't swung to that extent, public feeling in the U.S. was becoming increasingly inward-looking, with back home sentiment on the rise. If it got any stronger, there was every chance that pressure to pull the troops out of the Asia-Pacific, including Japan, would escalate."[21]

The rape incident in Okinawa in September 1995 further complicated debate on the 100,000-troops structure. It was Paul Giarra who said that American officials feared the incident might create cracks in bilateral security cooperation and led to their insisting on the 100,000 figure. On the other hand, Japanese government officials found themselves in a political situation where it was difficult to assert that not a single U.S. soldier would be removed from Japan.[22]

Giarra had left the Pentagon at the end of 1995 with only one regret. He had wanted to incorporate the 100,000 figure into the Joint Security Declaration, which was to have been made on the occasion of Clinton's November visit to Japan (which was ultimately postponed). The Japanese, however, were not very enthusiastic.

The Americans insisted that "while it might not be necessary to mention U.S. troop strength in Japan at 47,000, the 100,000 in Asia should be made known." The Japanese resisted. A high-ranking official at the Pentagon noted that the Japanese were privately very supportive of the 100,000 but realized that with the Okinawan incident it would not be a good tactical moment to say so.[23]

There existed within the Japanese government a subtle slant on this point. It had to take into account the strong backlash in Okinawa against the Nye Report, fearing it meant making the bases a permanent fixture. The fall of 1995, when the government was working hard to put together the draft Joint Security Declaration, followed the rape incident, which made it an extremely politically sensitive issue. And yet, as the same high-ranking official at the Pentagon pointed out, the Japanese Foreign Ministry (MOFA) welcomed the Nye Report's figure of 100,000, a stance which did not alter.

Masaki Orita, head of the North American Affairs Bureau at MOFA, endorsed that view, saying, "They did a good job getting that far. America was turning inward. Putting an end to that was a tremendous achievement. If it hadn't been successful, U.S. withdrawal would have snowballed."[24]

The blueprint for long-term strategic objectives in the bilateral relationship and the nature of that vision, the original aim of the Nye Initiative, were obscured as debate heated up on the 100,000 structure. Whereas the Nye Initiative was originally intended to spark policy debate between the two countries, "It ended up becoming a synonym for the status quo," as Michael Green, a young, leading U.S. researcher on Japan, put it.[25]

His point was that what should have been a chance to redefine the nature of bilateral security degenerated as diplomats on both sides of the Pacific, bent on upholding the status quo, merely went through the motions of reaffirmation. From the very start, the 100,000 structure was nothing more than a political and psychological presence mixing fact and fiction. Its value lay in its ambiguity.

However, it was the psychological gap between the United States and Japan—and between the United States and Asia for that matter—the political vacuum as well as the absence of strong leadership, that combined to create a situation where nothing but jointly reckoned figures could be trusted. There was no similar debate in NATO over numbers.

It was as if the magic number was a psychological Maginot Line. The policymakers wanted to demonstrate the presence with an ostentatious show of numbers. But it was also an intimation of America's apprehension as well as a by-product of the absence of trust between the United States and the countries of the Asian-Pacific region.

The China Factor

The background of the Nye Initiative, actually, goes back to the end of the 1980s. As the Cold War was about to end, bringing to a close the era of unambiguous enemies and threats, there was a growing trend in both the United States and Japan toward reassessing security policies. Seiki Nishihiro, at the time number two in the Japanese Defense Agency (JDA), was one such person.

During the Bush administration, Nishihiro approached Brent Scowcroft, NSC presidential aide, about joint strategy talks, but nothing ever came of it. Nishihiro's idea was to coordinate bilateral security policy with a view to the Soviet Union, China, the Korean Peninsula, and the Middle East.

Scowcroft didn't take up this offer. He said, "China is not the kind of country to listen to what anybody else has to say."[26] His decision may well have been affected by the Bush administration's position on China; Bush, the first U.S. liaison chief in Beijing since normalization, was alleged to be the United States' leading China expert.

More than that, however, the United States probably did not see the matter as being that urgent. From the collapse of the Berlin Wall to Germany's unification, U.S. diplomatic focus was riveted on Europe. After that, it was absorbed with the crisis in Kuwait and the Gulf War. As far as the Bush administration was concerned, the Asian-Pacific region was truly pacific.

Following the crackdown in Tiananmen Square, China had no choice but to stay quiet. The only thorn in the U.S. side was the North Korean nuclear development issue.

Scowcroft seemed to be bothered by that. When Nye visited Japan in November 1994 and met with Nishihiro, among others, a letter from Scowcroft had arrived on Nishihiro's desk around the same time. Scowcroft said, "I regret that we could not initiate a new security dialogue at that time. However, I feel very much encouraged to see the Nye Initiative right now."[27]

Nye was interested in Nishihiro's central theme of the China factor. In fact, Nye himself was preoccupied with the question of how Japan and the United States should respond to the emergence of China, how that factor should be positioned in the U.S. global strategy.

Following the change to the Clinton administration, relations with China were anything but smooth. Human rights, China's most-favored-nation status, its missile exports, the trade imbalance, intellectual property rights, the World Trade Organization, and the Taiwan issue: There was no end to the bickering.

The United States' single greatest concern, however, was not dealing with these individual problems but determining what sort of long-term strategy it should come up with for a China that was emerging as a military and economic power. At least, that was Nye's perception.

Nye's basic conviction was that it was crucial that China not be cast as an enemy. China was not to be contained but engaged. China, however, proved to be precisely "the kind of country that didn't listen to what anybody else had to say." That is why redefining the U.S.-Japan alliance, how to rearrange the alliance into something new and more lasting, became an issue.

Nye himself described the bilateral alliance's rationale as follows: "I think we have a policy of engagement towards China, but it's much better if the U.S. and Japan work together to engage China rather than letting China play off Japan against the U.S. In other words, if Chinese power is going to increase, which it will, and the Chinese then play off the U.S. against Japan, it will make friction in U.S.-Japan relations, but it also will mean that China will not have to be as responsible a power as it would be."[28]

The Pentagon's best Asia people, like Paul Giarra of the Japan Desk, were keenly aware of the need to create a long-term Asia-Pacific strategy, especially a strong U.S.-Japan alliance, that faced up to the challenge of China. "Everyone's interests coincide in maintaining stability. And as long as we can make sure that the Chinese understand that, then we are going to be OK."[29]

Giarra used to expound his China view as, "China had to be made to understand that the U.S. was not withdrawing from this region. In order to make sure China got that message, America had to continue to engage it, to show leadership, and to provide regional and global political cohesion. If we wanted China to take us seriously, we had to deal realistically with it, because there is a side to a country like China that doesn't treat people as people."[30]

Both "containment" and "engagement" could be interpreted in many ways. In the process of drawing up the first installment of the Nye Initiative, the East Asian Strategy Report, opinion was divided. Andrew Bennett acknowledged that "the hardest part was the language on some of the issues that, today, are still the most troubling ones; how to address China's evolving role, trying to discuss what the new basis for the alliance with Japan was and give the rationale for that."[31]

The Clinton administration's basic foreign policy stance was one of "engagement and enlargement." It was a concept put forward by Anthony Lake, national security adviser, and based on his conviction that it was in the U.S. national interest that the sole world superpower remain engaged to enlarge human rights and democracy.

Engagement was not something copyrighted by Nye but simply the basic foreign policy line of the administration. It was Nye, however, who clearly placed the redefinition of the U.S.-Japan alliance within the new context of this challenge. This also answered the question of "why do we need an alliance now that the Cold War is over?"[32]

For Nye, the redefinition of the U.S.-Japan alliance was none other than a redefinition in the face of the China challenge.

Carbon Dioxide

Depending on your outlook, the Nye Initiative could be said to be the harbinger of the U.S. Asia-Pacific strategy in the 21st century. Nye believed that the United States was the only "Pacific nation capable of developing military power on a global scale."[33] The United States, however, had to accept the simultaneous challenge of Japan and China shoulder-to-shoulder in the Asian-Pacific region. The initiative was an attempt to respond directly to the long-term strategic issues of how to respond to that, what kind of relationship should be established with each.

There was a very strong tendency here to view both Japan and China as challengers of the existing order. As the architect of that order, the United States had to engage them. In the words of the Nye Report, the U.S. presence in this region acted as "oxygen." In such a blueprint, Japan and China were nothing more than possible sources of carbon dioxide. The Nye strategy was to join forces with Japan to create a basic framework for approaching China.

Just as George Kennan had conceived the strategy of containment of the U.S.S.R. by the West in the Cold War, Joseph Nye can be said to have been looking for a policy of engagement with China via the U.S.-Japan alliance in the post–Cold War era. Nye often spoke of the possible dangers of an emerging China by alluding to the rise and fall of Athens and

Sparta in Ancient Greece. "It is important to realize that periods of rise and fall of great powers are often periods of instability. The explanation of the Peloponnesian War, for example, was the rise of power of Athens and the fear it created in Sparta."[34]

When he visited Japan in November 1994, Nye went with his Foreign Ministry counterparts to a private club where they had a very free-ranging brainstorming session. Nye respected the professional sophistication of the Japanese diplomats, and the comments of one diplomat that night made a deep impression.

Sumio Tarui, head of the MOFA's China division, put the following questions to Nye: "Will you play off China versus Japan? . . . If the Chinese market gets bigger will you forget Japan? And why aren't you just going to balance power in China versus Japan?" And so forth.[35]

Nye felt, "That was a good question to ask. And I think what we had to do was answer that we are willing to reaffirm the U.S.-Japan relationship so that the two of us can coordinate our policies to work together on these questions. So that's the type of discussion that gets at the most basic fears."[36]

The initiative was not intended to cast China as the enemy. Ezra Vogel, advanced analyst with the NIC, was given the job of assuring them on that point.

Using his personal connections with the senior embassy staff at the Chinese Embassy in Washington, Vogel conveyed this message at every opportunity. Nye also visited China in November 1995, and met with Chinese Defense Minister Chi Haotian and the top military leaders.

The purpose of this trip to China was to find a way to reopen military exchanges between the United States and China, which had been suspended following the visit of Taiwanese President Lee Teng-hui to Washington. Nye also intended to brief the Chinese on the Nye Initiative, given the timing of President Clinton's visit to Japan and the scheduled Joint Security Declaration. He certainly had no intention of discussing the content of the declaration with the Chinese because that was something confidential between America and Japan.[37] What he did explain to the Chinese was that the United States and Japan intended to cooperate in encouraging Chinese participation in the international community, that this intention would be articulated in the Joint Declaration, and that the United States was not interested in containing China but pursuing a basic policy of engagement.

"We are going to have many points of friction—over human rights, over Taiwan, over WTO—but do not read that as a policy of containment. If we wanted containment, we would treat you the way we treated the Soviet Union during the Cold War. It means no contact, no trade, trying to isolate you at every point. That's not what we are interested in."[38]

The Chinese government appears to have understood. Nye recounted that "there was really no complaint." In fact, Defense Minister Chi said he had read Nye's testimony in congressional hearings in October and was pleased by it.[39] The Chinese were, however, concerned about how Congress would act.

During this visit to China, Nye was also lectured by Chi and others on the revival of Japanese militarism. "When I was in Beijing last November, meeting with the Chinese defense minister, he was objecting even to the idea of Japanese Self-Defense Forces participating in U.N. humanitarian operations. And I asked why, and he said because of Japanese militarism. And I said, you know, I have been to Japan dozens of times, and I don't see any Japanese militarism, and I don't think it's there; it's not a problem. And he said, you've forgotten the 1930s."[40]

Their standard response was, "Well, you don't see it now," but then they'd go and talk about the 1930s again.[41] Nye was learning the hard way about China's fears of a possible resurgence of militarism in Japan.

Just as China could not throw off its fears about Japan in the future, Japanese fears about a future China were mounting. China's repeated nuclear tests only aggravated anti-Chinese feeling in Japan, and its threatening military actions in the South China Sea and the Taiwan Straits filled a maritime nation like Japan with a strong sense of foreboding.

Japan's domestic pro-China forces, who had maintained a certain level of political influence ever since the 1972 normalization of Sino-Japanese relations, found their star waning in both political and business circles. Even the mass media, which had avidly been pro-China, changed after Tiananmen Square and became critical.

In the fall of 1995, Vogel was surprised when meeting top political and government leaders in Japan at the substantial shift in their perceptions of China. "China began to be much tougher on Japan with the 50th anniversary speeches. Japanese opinion has grown much more concerned about China. And I think that has strengthened the public support for the [U.S.-Japan] security relationship. Up until Secretary of Defense Perry's visit to Japan, Japanese leaders had been very concerned about the ascendancy of China."[42]

There was very little awareness by U.S. government officials of the tensions building between China and Taiwan in the fall of 1994 when the Nye Initiative started gathering momentum. "There wasn't a lot of discussion of Taiwan when we started. . . . We spent more time on Korea than we did on Taiwan."[43]

A year later when Nye visited China, however, the China factor could no longer be ignored. The Chinese themselves had their own doubts: the Americans and Japanese were overhauling their alliance from a totally new angle; the theater missile defense (TMD) they were discussing might reach as far as Taiwan when it was installed. Some of the Chinese diplomats suspected that America and Japan had manipulated publicity on tensions between China and Taiwan in an attempt to deflect public interest away from the redefinition work on U.S.-Japan security, which was increasingly shaky following the rape of a young Okinawan girl by U.S. servicemen.

On hearing this far-fetched interpretation, a high-ranking official at the U.S. State Department laughed. "It certainly gives you a good picture of how self-centered their worldview is!"[44]

After Nye's resignation at the end of 1995, China's challenging of this redefinition of U.S.-Japan security escalated sharply every step of the way, starting with the U.S.-Japan summit in the following April, the Japan-U.S. Joint Security Declaration, and the guidelines review.

The Three-Legged Stool

The Nye Initiative was not attempted as a laboratory experiment. Nor was it a new idea created in a vacuum. It was steered through the dense political mists of Washington, great care being taken to ensure it did not fall victim to bureaucratic pitfalls and to establish a clear vantage point.

The Clinton administration had made the economy and trade policy its top priorities. Having ridden into Washington with the slogan "it's the economy, stupid," it made economic policy the "star of the show."

The newly established National Economic Council (NEC), the U.S. Trade Representative (USTR), and the Treasury became the new power centers. Much attention was directed to the trade rivalry with Japan, and a very tough style of trade negotiation was adopted. Although the outward position was to focus on coordinating the "three legs" of security, economics and trade, and a common global agenda, the administration's sights were really set on economics and trade.

Nye recalls, "The administration had a metaphor, they called it a three-legged stool ... saying that the relationship with Japan had three legs: one was economic, the other leg was the political-military leg, the third leg was other global issues. But if you look carefully at this stool during the first two years of the Clinton administration, the stool was primarily resting on one leg, the economic leg, and the other two were, I think, gravely neglected. Ezra [Vogel] and I would go to meetings at the White House and come back and shake our heads together about all this."[45]

Nye tried to introduce an agenda for security policy on Japan, but both the National Security Council and the State Department hesitated. Extreme caution had to be exercised.

When Perry had invited him to join the Pentagon, Nye had expressed his desire to do something about strengthening security ties with Japan, the implication being that he would come if he were given a free hand to do that. Perry recalls, "I told him [Nye] then that one of the principal things that I wanted him to do was make this initiative a reality. So, there was a congruence of thinking between myself and Joe. . . . And I believe the opportunity to pursue the Nye Initiative was one of the factors which led him to accept the job of my assistant secretary, and he undertook that with a lot of enthusiasm."[46]

Perry also gave Nye the credit for sharpening the security debate and helping identify "the correct answer, namely that whatever the level of competition between the U.S. and Japan in economic matters, both countries had a transcendental interest in the security relations, and that we had to keep the security relations strong, not hold it hostage to economic[s]."[47]

Nye arrived ready to take on all comers. According to Kurt Campbell, soon to be Nye's top assistant in the fall of 1994, "Joe met with Secretary Perry extensively at the outset. . . . Secretary Perry was extremely supportive, had seen some of the same things himself, and essentially gave Joe Nye carte blanche to begin this process. Secretary Perry carried the water at the White House, made sure that he was given the responsibility. . . . Winston Lord obviously supported [the initiative] and there was a very good partnership between him and Nye."[48]

Things, however, did not go that smoothly. As a high-ranking Pentagon official explained, "To say you need a Japan initiative—the Nye Initiative—means that something is wrong. And to say something is wrong is to say that the State Department is not doing its job. So, they wanted to defend themselves." Thomas Hubbard, deputy assistant secretary of state, also admitted that "there was some friction on the working level between the Japan Desk at the State Department and the Pentagon. However, on the whole, the Department of Defense, the State Department, and the White House NSC were able to form cooperative working relationships."[49]

Stanley Roth, national security adviser for East Asian affairs, remarked, "about 80 percent the Pentagon initiated. Somebody had to take the initiative. Bilateral security dialogue had to be moved one way or another."[50] Hubbard states that "the State Department helped launch the Nye Initiative. There was no turf battle. It was like a seamless connection between the White House, the State Department, and the Pentagon."[51]

A breakthrough came in October 1994 when Nye accompanied Perry on his first *nemawashi* ("groundwork-building") trip. In Tokyo he had a chance to talk with Lord and Roth. At that time, Lord came out in favor of Nye's attempt to strengthen security dialogue between Japan and the United States. Roth also agreed that the issue should be left in Nye's hands.

On that occasion Nye also met with Mondale, who was encouraging. "Japan's political leaders are always saying they want someone in the Clinton administration like [Richard] Armitage. I think they're right. I want you to play that role, to become the Clinton administration's Rick Armitage."[52]

The relationship between Nye and Lord was smooth. Lord was very frustrated with the slippage in U.S.-Japan policy as well as U.S.-China policy less than six months after Clinton's highly successful hosting of the Asian-Pacific Economic Cooperation (APEC) summit in Seattle in 1993. Lord's feelings were well expressed in a private memo he sent to Secretary of State Warren Christopher. It was dubbed the "Malaise Memo." In it he sounded a warning about what he saw as the malaise in U.S. Asian diplomacy.[53]

It was in this context that Lord inwardly cried "Eureka!" when the Nye Initiative emerged from the Pentagon. It would have been too risky if the State Department had taken the lead, but if it was the Defense Department, Lord believed that the USTR and Commerce Department would not be able to obstruct it openly. He thought it would be a wise move for the State Department to hide behind the Pentagon and quietly and unobtrusively support the initiative.

Another reason for the Pentagon spearheading the initiative was the fact that it was their International Security Agency (ISA) that was invested with the major responsibility and authority for making policy proposals. Hubbard said, "It was completely normal that the Pentagon take the lead, because, no matter what anyone said, they had 47,000 U.S. troops stationed in Japan!"[54]

Nye himself was not grandstanding. According to Gayle von Eckartsburg "I think Joe Nye was uncomfortable with it being called the Nye Initiative, to tell you the truth, very much so. And none of our internal papers say 'Nye Initiative,' and we all sometimes put in parentheses 'otherwise called the Nye Initiative' just so people would know what we were talking about."[55]

Nor was Nye doing all the work by himself. In the words of a White House official, "It wasn't that the White House had just said to Joe Nye 'go do your thing.' He did this with a lot of consultations here and in full cooperation with the rest of the U.S. government. It was referred to as the Nye Initiative, but I think it was, in fact, referred to in that way more in Japan that it was in the U.S., because, in fact, there were a lot of people who were involved in it and very supportive."[56]

The Trade Guys

The problem was the "trade guys." Since the inception of the Clinton administration, they had been pushing numerical target for exports to Japan.

A White House staff member in the first Clinton administration later confessed that "I can say this now, but that was a mistake on our part. That overweening pride so common to new administrations backfired on us."[57] In any event, this forced the U.S. administration into a fierce and unproductive battle of attrition in negotiations with Japan.

At the time, the trade guys wielded enormous political clout. One middle-ranking Pentagon official observed that "these guys are very political. Trade policy is strongly colored by political elements and they were very powerful politically speaking. We always had to keep it in mind that we would be going nowhere if they blocked us."[58]

The trade guys' hard-line stance on Japan, however, began to relax somewhat in the fall of 1994. In September, an agreement was reached on insurance and some other items in the bilateral trade talks. Finally there was some light in the bilateral economic relationship, which had been plunged into darkness ever since the agree-to-disagree Hosokawa-Clinton summit at the beginning of the year.

Ezra Vogel: "So at that point, the people working on economic issues were not so concerned about our making progress on security issues. So in a way, that was very fortunate too because it meant that the people concerned with economic issues would not stand in the way of advances on the Security Treaty."[59]

During the previous Bush administration, a fierce behind-the-scenes battle had been waged between the State Department and the Pentagon on the one hand, which both put the highest priority on maintaining the bilateral security relationship, and the USTR and the Commerce Department on the other hand, which were both pushing for tangible results in the trade and economic negotiations.

There was concern at the Defense Department that trade and economic disputes might adversely affect security ties. The Bush administration, however, was increasingly apprehensive that it would be impossible to maintain a favorable security relationship if trade and economic disputes went unchecked. In that respect, it did not differ significantly from its successor, the Clinton administration.

In his book, *Friends or Rivals?*, former U.S. Ambassador to Japan Michael Armacost wrote: "The Japanese had frequently argued that Washington's pressure for economic concessions might undermine Japanese public support for the alliance. They were now being told the reverse: failure to provide a greater measure of reciprocity could diminish support for the alliance in the United States."[60] This, however, was a new post–Cold War dynamic for both the Republicans and the Democrats.

According to Vogel, not one of the Clinton trade guys "said in a government meeting that it wouldn't matter if security was sacrificed to win points on the economic and trade fronts."[61] It was only from the spring to summer of 1995 when negotiations on auto parts had "visibility zero" that some "tension" arose. "There were probably some people at that time who didn't want too much progress on security because it might take the pressure off the auto issue."[62]

Finding some sort of equilibrium between trade and security ties plagued the Clinton administration from first to last. In the section on ties with Japan, the East Asia-Pacific Strategy Report warned, "We must not allow trade friction to undermine our security alliance" but did not neglect immediately to drive home the point that "if public support for the relationship is to be maintained over the long term, progress must continue to be made by both sides in addressing fundamental economic issues."[63]

The "oxygen" concept, which had become the key idea in the Nye Report, graphically emphasized the importance of security and economic-related links. As well as being a link that anchored security in the economic development of the Asian-Pacific region and the U.S. presence, it was a concept that touched on the link between U.S. national economic interests and national military interests. This "theory of linking the economy and security based on the oxygen theory"[64] was beginning to form the nexus of America's post–Cold War diplomacy.

Nye believed "there was no need to strategically link it every step of the way; having a strategic link in your head was enough,"[65] but how were you meant to look at the relationship, how were you meant to receive it? Did it mean don't engage in trade negotiations that shake up the security relationship? Or solve the trade issues if you want to preserve the security ties? Or perhaps it was a warning: If you, Japan, don't make trade concessions, we can't keep the security relationship. Or yet a threat: If you don't give us trade concessions, we'll have to think twice about the security relationship.

One of these interpretations could be seen in the remarks of Michael McCurry, White House press secretary, after talks on auto parts stalled. McCurry said that if there was no progress on economic and trade negotiations, it would have a bad influence on the security relationship. This was swiftly met by complaints from both the State Department and the Pentagon.

As a high-ranking official at the Pentagon put it, "The problem was that they had treated trade and security as trade-off relationships. In any event, the little flurry at the time did not later become serious."[66]

The Nye Initiative represented a unique case in which one individual—not the president, nor the White House security adviser, nor the secretary of state, nor the secretary of defense, but an assistant secretary of defense—developed a strategy for bilateral security, did the groundwork personally with officials in Japan and the United States, and developed a final and finished national policy. Perry's assessment was,

"What's that word you have in Japanese? *Newamashi!* That's what it was. We did that one almost like the Japanese government in terms of reaching a consensus before putting it to a decision. The U.S. government doesn't often operate that way, and in this case, they did, and I think Joe Nye gets a lot of credit for that."[67]

There was more to it than that, apparently. Vogel said, "The ideal pattern is for the president or the White House to work out strategy in broad outline, but this was a unique case, beginning at a much lower level and moving up to the top without encountering opposition from above."[68]

This point was another indication of the economics and trade orientation of the Clinton administration and its low priority on security policy for Japan. Had it been a high-priority issue, it would not have been left to create a life of its own under the name of an individual assistant defense secretary. And yet, it was precisely this low status that allowed it to escape raising undue apprehension on the part of the trade guys and to survive. In the words of a USTR official, "It was because it was a policy initiative by an assistant secretary that we didn't pay it much interest or attention."[69]

Brent Scowcroft, presidential aide in the Bush administration, had high praise for the Nye Initiative. "Well, I like to think we would have done something of the same thing, because . . . with the end of the Cold War, it was important to sit down and have a defense dialogue as well as a diplomatic dialogue on how the relationship . . . needed to be adjusted and modified and reinvigorated to deal with the new set of circumstances." He went on, "[Under Bush] it would have been a unified administration on how to proceed, starting from the president."[70] In other words, it would have been a Bush Initiative.

Hop, Skip, Jump

Nye thought of implementing the initiative in a hop-skip-jump fashion. The hop would be the EASR release in February 1995, the skip would be the Japanese government's new National Defense Program Outline (NDPO), and the jump a joint declaration to be issued at a Japan-U.S. summit. His approach was extremely cerebral, aiming at working on redefining bilateral security starting with the paper-writing process. He felt that the two countries ought to cooperate not only on policy talks but in the actual process itself. He said there could be no alliance without policy talks.

The first attempt was when the Americans showed the Japanese the EASR draft at the end of 1994 and asked for their comments. This was to show them that the policy talks with Japan were serious. So much so that they were chastised by the uniforms for "showing it to the Japanese before us."[71] Although an alliance in name, there had been almost no policy coordination by the Americans and Japanese up until that point. Nye wanted to change that. He wanted the initiative to take the form of "a coupler."

"We thought it very necessary to change that *sempai-kohai* relationship into a more equal relationship,"[72] said Andrew Bennett, a member of the Nye team, using the Japanese words for "senior" and "junior." The Americans hoped the Japanese would do the same thing they had done with the EASR with their own NDPO.

"It was not that we Americans told the Japanese to put X, Y, Z in their NDPO over the next five years, but that we did it together,"[73] said Vogel. An exchange of opinions was taking place at the initial drafting stage.

The Japanese were able to prepare their defense outline with the EASR draft in hand, and the Americans were able to finish the EASR with a rough idea of what the Japanese outline would look like. Nye's idea was to imbue each paper with a common spirit, a shared direction. He even had Michael Green, a Japan specialist, go over the drafts of both papers.

The NDPO provides the basic direction for long-term Japanese defense capability. Twenty years had passed since the first NDPO in 1976, during which time the Cold War had become a thing of the past. Japan needed a new outline. The basic tenet of the new NDPO was "the concept of a basic and standard defense capability, defined as possessing the minimum necessary defense capability for an independent nation so that it would not become a source of instability in the surrounding region by creating a vacuum of power rather than building a capability directly linked to a military threat to Japan."

The new outline also stated unequivocally that Japan-U.S. security arrangements "are indispensable to Japan's security and will also continue to play a key role in achieving peace and stability in the surrounding region of Japan and establishing a more stable security environment."

It stressed over and over again the value of the alliance not just to Japan's security but to "peace and stability in the surrounding region." Based on this fundamental awareness, it deemed greater policy consultations, joint studies, mutual exchange of equipment and technology, and the facilitation of smooth and effective stationing of U.S. forces in Japan necessary "to enhance the credibility of the Japan-U.S. Security Arrangements and ensure their effective implementation."

In addition to national defense, the outline was clear on the new functions of large-scale disaster response, terrorism response, international peacekeeping activities, and contributing to the creation of a more stable security environment. A key policy development was incorporated into the section on disaster response: reviewing the guidelines on bilateral defense cooperation.

"Should a situation arise in the areas surrounding Japan, which will have an important influence on national peace and security, [Japan will] take appropriate response in accordance with the Constitution and relevant laws and regulations, for example, by properly supporting the [*sic*] U.N. activities when needed, and by ensuring the smooth and effective implementation of the Japan-U.S. Security Arrangements."

The NDPO expressed whiffs of Japanese "independence" and "propensity for autonomy" in references to strengthening a priori intelligence functions and so on, but very few voices at the Pentagon mentioned them. With the head of the Japanese Socialists, Tomiichi Murayama, as prime minister, some in the U.S. government worried about Japan distancing itself from the United States, but the finished NDPO satisfied the Americans. As one Pentagon official put it, "To be honest, I didn't think the Japanese would go this far."[74]

It is probably closer to the truth to say that it was precisely because it was the Murayama government, with Socialists in the Cabinet, that the Japanese were able to produce such a forthright outline. Being in government themselves, the Socialists could no longer play their perennial game of objecting for objection's sake.

The Pentagon was impressed with the NDPO, particularly in that it made the centrality of the alliance to Japan's security policy much clearer than ever before. Not only was it true that "in the previous NDPO, the whole document referred to the U.S.-Japan alliance only two times, yet in this new one there were thirteen instances";[75] but the new outline also earned high points for its clear stance on using bilateral security to create stability throughout the Asian-Pacific region.

The Pentagon did not just show the EASR to Japan alone. It also briefed the governments of South Korea, Australia, and the Philippines. Consultations with Japan were the most thorough, however. Chuck Downs, currently an American Enterprise Institute research staff member who has long been involved in policy planning at the Pentagon and who also played a leading role in the EASR, recounts that Japan and South Korea both raised questions about each other's military doctrine and intentions. Perceptions on those matters made a big difference in their reactions. He also heard many varying views concerning China's military capabilities and intentions, as well as many requests for changes in wording.[76]

The Americans were not totally satisfied with the talks on policy. They had hoped that the Nye Initiative would kindle a security debate within Japan. They especially wanted the politicians to get involved early and broaden the debate. The Japanese side, notably the Foreign Ministry, were cautious, however. They said the Murayama coalition was like "walking on eggs" when it came to security issues and asked the Americans not to "rock the boat."

Vogel said, "The Japanese bureaucrats reminded us not to meet with Japanese politicians directly. They were nervous about Murayama's reaction if and when the redefinition of the U.S.-Japan alliance began. They were also nervous about Murayama's reaction if and when the redefinition of the U.S.-Japan alliance was publicly debated, which might make Murayama more cautious and would lead to a slowing down of the whole discussion of redefining the alliance between the U.S. and Japan."[77] Using his extensive personal contacts in Japan, Vogel nevertheless tried to meet and talk with politicians whenever he was there.

There was only a limited effort to secure political support within the United States. The Pentagon managed to get the support of internationalists like Republican Doug Bereuter of Nebraska, chairman of the Asia and Pacific Subcommittee of the House Foreign Relations Committee, and Lee Hamilton, the ranking minority member, as well as some others, but little consensus building with the Democrats took place.

Japan's response to the Pentagon's initiative came mainly from the Foreign Ministry. Policy dialogue between the DOD and the JDA, however, had advanced considerably, as demonstrated by the draft cooperation on the EASR and the NDPO. A member of the Pentagon said that "compared to the Foreign Ministry, which was determined to maintain the status quo, the Defense Agency, especially the middle ranks, seemed to have a more sensible and growing inclination to cooperate with the United States."[78]

The JDA was very keen to have the new NDPO announced in conjunction with the Japan-U.S. Joint Security Declaration in November 1995. The Joint Declaration would be released on the occasion of Clinton's visit, and then the agency would announce the NDPO, the underlying calculation being that in that way the agency could ward off a lot of criticism. So much so that even when the November visit fell through, there were still those in the agency insisting that the Joint Declaration be made first.

In fact, objections were raised by the Foreign Ministry. A high-ranking official at the ministry remembers thinking, "The right way to go about it was first to consolidate domestic consensus, next to draw up the outline, and then have a joint Japan-U.S. declaration, not trying to slip the NDPO in under cover of the summit and the Joint Declaration."

The JDA accused the Foreign Ministry of taking advantage of *gaiatsu* ("foreign pressure") from the U.S. State Department for its own ends, but the JDA shared the same tendency of relying on State Department *gaiatsu* to move its own agenda along.

In any event, Perry's conclusion on the summit was that "the Okinawan tragedy opened up a fundamental and very deep discussion within the Japanese government as to what their real alternatives were."[79]

As for the Nye Initiative, it ended up just being the Nye Initiative. It never developed into a Clinton Initiative. Tony Lake, Clinton's national security adviser, was later to say, "It can't be called the Nye Initiative forever. It's about time we let Clinton win a few points."[80] This was in the spring of 1996 when the White House was making preparations for Clinton's visit to Japan.

For Clinton's first three years, the White House invested very little of its political capital in Asia-Pacific policy. In 1996, the last year of his first term in office, however, there was a flurry of activity in the policy areas of Japan, China, and Korea. While there was an aspect of crisis management to this, preventing something from blowing up in this election year, another factor was containing criticism that this administration was very enthusiastic about peripheral issues and peripheral areas like Haiti and Bosnia, but ran away from the big, central issues.

The Nye Initiative could certainly be sold as earning points on that score, but they wouldn't be points for the president because the initiative carried someone else's name. That is what Lake was saying.

Redefinition or Reaffirmation?

The Nye Initiative aimed at reconstructing the bilateral security relationship in the post–Cold War era. How successful was it in achieving that?

First, it was designed to eradicate both Japanese and Asian-Pacific fears of an eventual American withdrawal from the region. On this count, it was fairly successful. All those who supported the Nye Initiative agreed that the "100,000 troop strength" had made a contribution there. Stanley Roth said, "Japan's concern also came perhaps from the advent of a Democratic administration. The Carter administration's abrupt call for the withdrawal of American troops in South Korea was remembered throughout Asian capitals. When Clinton came to power, the overlap of policymakers in the two administrations perhaps may have generated some concerns." Roth's assessment was that "against this backdrop, it is even more successful; the fact that we were able to get rid of this unnecessary fear was perhaps the most successful part of the Nye Initiative."[81]

It is true that the fatalistic perceptions on U.S. troop withdrawals once widely held throughout Asia did diminish. Nevertheless, strong uneasiness persisted among Asia-Pacific countries regarding whether the United States, having its hands tied by domestic affairs, especially the budget—as amply demonstrated by the postponement of President Clinton's November 1995 visit to Japan—was going unilaterally to "realign and rationalize" its commitment to and presence in the region. The China factor unmistakably came into play here. A Pentagon official quipped, "It's quite true that fears of a U.S. withdrawal have receded, more thanks to China than anyone else."[82]

China's faith in its military power, as seen from its actions during the showdown with Taiwan, had made the countries in the Asian-Pacific region even more jittery and raised their expectations for the U.S. presence. Japan's NDPO agreed on the "oxygen theory"—that the U.S. presence and its bases in Japan contributed to the region's stability and peace—and lauded its merits highly. A member of the Pentagon pointed out that "the NDPO was much clearer on that point than the Higuchi report."[83] The oxygen theory also found basic support throughout Asia, except in China.

There were some reservations voiced, however, in both Japan and the United States along the lines that the closure of the U.S. bases in the Philippines had not made the region any more unstable, or that U.S. forces had already been cut from 135,000 in 1990 to 100,000 in 1994 without any resulting problems.

In response to these arguments, Andrew Bennett countered, "If the U.S. had not had a military presence, then what would have happened to the North Korean nuclear negotiations? How nervous would Japan have been about China's missile test near the Taiwan Straits? How would the disputes and tensions between Japan and Korea over the Takeshima/Dok-to islands have developed?"[84]

Were Japan and America successful in creating a shared long-term vision and policy for engaging China? Andrew Bennett believes that the two countries were able to deal calmly and in an organized fashion with the threat of China's "missile diplomacy" in the days of the Taiwanese presidential election because working together on the Nye Initiative had helped prepare them psychologically. But this would be overrating the initiative.

As Nye states it, the reality was that "the first step towards restoring long-term relations was about to be taken at the summit between Clinton and Jiang Zemin in the fall of 1995, but everything was set back by the showdown with Taiwan."[85] It was easy to speak of the bilateral alliance "engaging" China, but the most decisive factor there was the state of Sino-American relations.

The Nye Initiative's attitude to China was based on power politics to the very last. It regarded both Japan and China as two simultaneously emerging powers; of the two, it sought to constrain China's hegemonic bent by joining forces with Japan. This position was supported by the American assessment that apprehension over China was mounting in Japan, and interest in U.S.-Japan security would grow in such a context. It was a view shared by Ezra Vogel.

What was Nye's position? "The U.S. is good, as an open society, at maintaining long-term relationships; it's not very good at flicking back and forth like a light switch, depending on instantaneous advantages. . . . My feeling is that the appropriate strategy in Asia was not to switch back and forth between China and Japan but to solidify the alliance with Japan, and then work with the Japanese to engage China, and try to bring China into the world system as a responsible power."[86]

"On the question of China becoming democratic, would there be less value in the U.S.-Japan security relationship? I think it would be less. China as a democratic country would be less of a concern, and I don't think it would mean that we would have no U.S.-Japan relationship, but I think the number of troops would be considerably less . . . but we should be that lucky!"[87] His was always a long-term vision of the alliance with an eye on China.

It was just that, depending on place and time, Nye's strategy of "engaging" China could run perilously close to being "containment." In such a case, there was a strong risk of tension between Japanese and U.S. China policy given Japan's different geographical, historical, and cultural relationship with that country.

A Japanese official, who had been involved in the Nye Initiative from first to last, revealed, "There are differences in approach between the U.S. and Japan with regard to China policy. When we talk about 'engagement,' the Japanese emphasis is closer to the true meaning of engagement. If China misbehaves, then we have no option but containment, but we would like to keep it discreet."[88]

In the final analysis, the Americans painted a vision of stabilizing Japan-U.S.-China relations in terms of power politics in the Nye Initiative, but there were many fine points that remained unanswered.

The relationship between security and economics would no doubt continue to be a tricky topic. The Nye Initiative assuredly had the effect of dampening some of the predominance of economic and trade items advocated by the trade guys. It would be dangerous, however, to overestimate that aspect. U.S. emphasis on economic and trade policy was a long-term trend, and the inward-looking orientation of the American people should still be seen as strong. It would be difficult to create healthy security ties without also creating healthy relations in the area of economic and trade issues.

During the U.S.-Japan summit held in Santa Monica in February 1996, Prime Minister Ryutaro Hashimoto commented that there were specific trade issues pending between the two countries, but they should not be allowed to undermine the entire relationship, implying that the security leverage should be used to contain economic and trade issues. Clinton, however, drove home the importance of resolving economic and trade matters. He had been elected, and reelected, on the economy. It was still "the economy, stupid."

In Clinton's second term, however, the situation changed and a certain leeway emerged. The emphasis on the economy and trade was still there, but the policy balance was changing.

For the presidential briefing aboard *Air Force One* en route to Japan in April 1996, Anthony Lake and the rest of the NSC staff were thinking they would like to focus on security issues. Clinton, however, showed a singular interest in economic and trade issues. A high-ranking U.S. official later recollected, "Mickey Kantor was still there, but interestingly enough, even though a lot of the briefing covered [economics], the points that the president left in his statement, and the points he emphasized with Hashimoto, and the way he addressed the economics issues with Hashimoto, made it quite clear that the president had heard what Tony Lake was saying. . . . In the April meeting [Hashimoto rebutted each economic argument], but it was those kinds of rebuttals that you have to say . . . and they were not intended to engage the other person in debate. It was very much, OK, we have some trade issues, OK, now that you have said that, let me say this. . . . [That was] the last hurrah [for Mickey Kantor]. And I think it was not only the last hurrah, I don't think it went very well then."[89]

Did the Nye Initiative contribute to building understanding among the American people for security policy in the post–Cold War era? Nye's theory of linking economics and security was also a theory for rebuilding the domestic political support base indispensable for a sustained security relationship in the post–Cold War era. Dazzled only by the all too rapid and dramatic geopolitical changes caused by the end of the Cold War, security policy that failed to take into account the huge political, economic, and social changes under way in the United States itself ran the risk of running counter to the current of domestic politics and being swept away. Bearing that in mind, the intent was to raise interest in security issues by linking them to the economy, which was easy to understand and had the interest of the American people.

Major currents in the American domestic scene included a sense of employment downsizing, a rocky sense of security, an inward-looking orientation, the rise of economic nationalism, and the hollowing out of two-party politics. On the Japanese side, they included loss of confidence and sense of direction regarding the course of an economic superpower; anti-American, anti-Chinese, and anti-Korean nationalism; an anti-American, pro-Asia leaning; chronic political instability; and a lack of political leadership.

In a way, the Nye Initiative was a defensive action against these two sets of domestic trends that were hurting the bilateral relationship. The initiative cannot be said, however, to have strengthened either the domestic political support base or the new nature of the post–Cold War order. Initially, it was an engagement between a very small number of diplomatic and defense mandarins. Its bureaucratic approach was quite conspicuous, although it eventually involved the press and politicians. Still, there was very little evidence of broad political backing.

Was this, in reality, a "redefinition" of the alliance or a "reaffirmation"? Redefining alliances is a risky enough business, all the more so if the alliance in question has been functioning smoothly to date. Although the term "redefinition" was bandied about a lot, there was not a lot of rejustifying the alliance from scratch.

While the Japan-U.S. Joint Declaration on security, assumed to be the goal of the Nye Initiative, was said to represent a "security revision," there was no such plan or intent. True, interest in and a direction for reviewing the guidelines and responding to contingencies in the vicinity of Japan could be found in both the Joint Declaration and the new NDPO, but that only represented an extension and strengthening of existing bilateral security cooperation, not a shift or a change. Rather, the authors could be said to have taken a gradualist approach.

As demonstrated by the chorus of "don't open up Pandora's box" that rang forth simultaneously from the security guys in both countries when debate surfaced on reviewing the Status of Forces Agreement, the bureaucrats formulating security policy on both sides of the Pacific were for the status quo and leaned strongly towards both political and psychological inertia.

It was a high official in both the Reagan and Bush administrations who said, "It's not worth going to all the trouble of giving it a name like the Nye Initiative. There's nothing that new about it. Five years earlier, simply maintaining the alliance for its own sake would have sufficed. But what were [then] matters of routine today seem to require some kind of special celebration."[90]

For those who worked on it, the Nye Initiative was a redefinition and a reaffirmation. A high-ranking Pentagon official said that it was both. "It has a reaffirming aspect because both [countries] decided to harness the best and the finest part of the alliance in the future. At the same time, it had a redefining aspect because we both would utilize untapped and unexplored resources in the future."[91]

A Japanese diplomat described it as "somewhere in the middle of redefinition and reaffirmation. It can be called a redefinition because we started building a more flexible rationale for the security structure from a zero base. It's just that when you use the word 'redefinition' in Japan, it might be mistaken for revision of the Constitution. We lost the bilateral security direction with the Gulf War and economic friction, so we tried to get a new fix on it. I'm in the processing of trying to find a word that isn't redefinition or reaffirmation."[92]

Another problem with redefinition was that it is likely to stir up suspicion in other countries. Since Japan and the United States had been allies for so long, it would have been enough, one would think, to make minor adjustments quietly without all the redefinition fanfare. This, in fact, was what worried some senior South Korean Foreign Ministry officials. They said the initiative should have been discussed more discreetly in order not to arouse unnecessary suspicion.[93]

Both China and Korea were watching the redefinition operation warily. Some U.S. officials believed that the United States should make an attempt to strengthen its dialogue with Korea in tandem with its move towards Japan. Vogel visited South Korea in the fall of 1994 to explore that possibility. The Koreans were interested, but the State Department was cautious, so nothing came of it. Vogel revealed that "the State Department was in charge of Korean Peninsula issues, so I think they did not want the Pentagon to meddle with those issues. Lord in particular was cautious."[94]

Takakazu Kuriyama, former Japanese ambassador to the United States, argued that the initiative was reaffirmation and redefinition. He wrote, "The Joint Declaration 'reaffirmed' the commitment of both countries to the security structure, and, at the same time, 'redefined' its significance."[95]

It was most unlikely that the initiative would end in just reaffirmation because both countries had to explain to their respective publics why the Security Treaty was still necessary despite the end of the Cold War. The new dangers were "instability" and "uncertainty." Feeling itself unfairly treated as a security threat, China expressed skepticism.

The truth of the matter was, even with the knowledge that the initiative would cause a certain amount of apprehension in other countries, the need to prop up the alliance was so urgent that top officials had no choice but to come up with redefinition.

Japan, the United States, and Asia

The Nye Initiative was pursued at a time of unprecedented growth and development in the Asian-Pacific region. The oxygen theory would not have been tenable without that backdrop and context. The Nye Report was a declaration that the United States would remain a central power in the region. "Oxygen" was clever copy to make the U.S. presence seem to be a "common good," having almost magical powers of evocation.

The U.S.-Japan alliance was deemed to be an indispensable part of that image. Prime Minister Ryutaro Hashimoto, in fact, categorized the U.S.-Japan security structure as "a framework to ensure U.S. presence" and defined it as "playing the role of a kind of common good" in a speech on his January 1997 tour of Southeast Asia. This rhetoric emphasized that it was "not aimed at any given country." It was unclear, however, whether the U.S.-Japan alliance itself was perceived as a "common good" in the Asian-Pacific region.

A new relationship between the U.S.-Japan alliance and the Asian-Pacific region was needed as well as a redefinition of Japan's relations with the region. During the Cold War, U.S.-Japan security was viewed as a part of the larger mosaic of the Soviet-American nuclear "balance of terror," and the region assumed the aspect of a dispensable "calculated security."[96] When the Cold War ended, this "calculated" aspect faded to be replaced by "content"; in short, the region's instability and uncertainty were exposed.

There were three issues involved here. The first concerned the Far East clause of Article 6 in the U.S.-Japan Security Treaty (which later became connected with "Contingencies in Japan's Vicinity"). The second concerned the application of collective defense to regional security. And the third concerned what to do about the relationship of the U.S.-Japan alliance to multilateral regional security in the Asian-Pacific region.

Through the coordination of the EASR and the NDPO, the Americans thought the Japanese had shown a more maneuverable response not only to the Security Treaty's Article 5 situations (Japanese contingencies), but also to Article 6 situations (Far East contingencies). The U.S. government had consistently shown an interest in conducting joint Article 6 operations within the framework of the bilateral security structure.

The Japanese government had always been cautious, fearing that involvement in Article 6 contingencies and "being ensnared in American conflicts" would trigger domestic unrest and defiance. Bilateral security cooperation had always emphasized the Article 5 aspect of defending Japan proper.

In the process of the Nye Initiative, however, the Japanese started to show a greater interest in Article 6 (vicinity) contingencies. "The relationship between Articles 5 and 6 has always been flexible, but more importance came to be attached to Article 6 rather than Article 5."[97]

Many approaches were possible and did indeed materialize, including shifting Article 6 into Article 5 and dealing with it there, or pushing Article 5 over into Article 6 and dealing with that there. What became apparent in this process, however, was the move to apply bilateral security more effectively and smoothly to contingencies arising in Japan's vicinity. The focus had to be revised from the "Far East," a legal concept of the treaty's contingency conditions, to "vicinity," a security concept.

With regard to the guidelines revision as well, there are many cooperative items being considered by both countries that are in conflict with collective defense, a public consensus about which has yet to emerge in Japan.

Both Nye and Vogel gave weight to the "political effect" of the Nye Initiative. Vogel said, "We placed greater emphasis on the large political aspects rather than the more military aspects of contingency and what have you. You could talk all you like about contingency cooperation but it wouldn't last if you didn't have a domestic support base."[98]

Regarding the relationship between multilateral security frameworks and bilateral alliances, the EASR says nothing more than that the multilateral regional framework should "supplement" not "supplant" bilateral alliances. These issues were never settled, but basically put off until a future date. The process ended without a clear redefinition of them.

An alliance must be seen as having balanced advantages and burdens and be supported by both countries if it is to last. How was that requirement met? A feature of the U.S.-Japan alliance after the Cold War is that both sides became sharply conscious of the burdens involved. In the future, political pressure towards a "lighter alliance," "a burdenless alliance" is likely to grow in both countries. There is a very good chance that the perception of "imbalance" would increase in the event of a contingency on the Korean Peninsula. There is also a high risk, depending on the nature of Japan's commitment, that the perception will lead to an explosion of accusations of Japan being a free rider, a cash dispenser, making the U.S. troops seem like mercenaries.

The trump card Nye used in the United States was Japan's "compassionate budget" (some $5 billion a year in host-nation support). He said, "It is cheaper to base troops in Japan than to keep them in California. But even more important, it means that when you are testifying before congressional committees and the congressman says, 'Why are we paying for these troops in Japan when we are closing bases in my home state of California? I demand you close the bases in Japan first and open the base in my district, where people vote. . . . Japan never does anything; it doesn't pay its own share; it's not like Germany or the NATO countries with its own contribution to defense,' you say, 'Congressman, Japan is doing more than any other country in terms of host nation support.'"[99]

Doug Bereuter remarked, "Japan pays more host nation support than any other country. We are now asking Germany and Korea to share burdens on a par with Japan."[100]

Thanks to this kind of exchange, Senator John McCain (R-Ariz.), an expert on foreign policy and the Asian-Pacific region, pointed out that Japan is no longer criticized in Congress for taking a free ride on security. "Congress supports a U.S. troop strength of 100,000 in the Asia-Pacific, but their main reason is the fact that the Japanese government and the people of Japan shoulder a great burden for the U.S. presence."[101]

At the same time, it cannot be denied that there is a growing awareness in the United States of how important the alliance with Japan is in keeping America a world power. Carl Ford, a former deputy assistant secretary of defense, makes no bones about it. He said, "Without the U.S.-Japan alliance, the U.S. would not be able to remain a global power."[102] If it were not for the alliance, the costs for maintaining U.S. forward deployment would "reach an unsustainable level." It is only with the bases in Japan that U.S. forward deployment strategy is viable and effective.

That is not all. There is a new consciousness of the value of the alliance with Japan for America's Asia-Pacific strategy. Secretary Perry has commented that "we believe in the centrality, the critical importance, of the Asia-Pacific to the United States; the centrality of the U.S.-Japan security alliance to that relationship. . . . This was a strong foundation . . . it is the foundation on which all else is built."[103]

Kurt Campbell, deputy assistant secretary of defense, commented. "It's often thought that the U.S.-Japan security relationship gives Japan a greater flexibility to act in Asia, and I think that's well understood. What's not as well understood is that it also anchors the United States in Asia and the Pacific. . . . It improves American ability to operate and to act as an Asian nation, having this relationship with Japan."[104]

His point is that the alliance is a useful springboard for both nations into the Asian-Pacific region. It is too early to say whether these recent developments will lead to a closing of the yawning gap in perceptions held by the two countries on the alliance. In the United States, an alliance is a relationship between independent nations that "come to each other's aid when the need arises." Under the current treaty, the U.S.-Japan alliance is a one-sided one, however, in which the United States is required to defend Japan but Japan is not obliged to defend America.

Criticism and dissatisfaction over this state of affairs still abounds, and is likely to be a dilemma that remains to the bitter end. And yet, as James Auer, former head of the Pentagon's Japan Desk, pointed out, "While placing great store on independence themselves, the Americans probably don't want to see Japan on an equal footing."[104]

Will America and Japan be able to take their relationship from an alliance which assumes both partners' independence to an alliance based on the spirit of mutual dependence? In other words, will they be able to achieve a stable relationship in which each supports the other according to its respective capabilities and role sharing? The attempt to reconstruct the alliance that went by the name of the Nye Initiative was a challenge to create and share precisely that kind of a dynamic alliance.

Notes

1. U.S. Department of Defense, *United States Security Strategy for the East Asia–Pacific Region*, February 1995, preface.

2. Ibid., p. 1.

3. Interview with William Perry.

4. Interview with Joseph Nye.

5. Interview with Paul Giarra.

6. Michael Armacost, *Friends or Rivals? The Insider's Account of U.S.-Japan Relations* (New York: Columbia University Press, 1996), p. 85.

7. Interview with Andrew Bennett.

8. Interview with Paul Giarra.

9. Interview with William Perry.

10. Interview with Benjamin Caetano.

11. Interview with Joseph Nye.

12. *United States Security Strategy for the East Asia–Pacific Region,* p. 23.

13. Chalmers Johnson and E. B. Keehn, "The Pentagon's Ossified Strategy," *Foreign Affairs,* vol. 74, no. 4 (July/August 1995), p. 112.

14. Masahide Ota, "The Bases Can't Be Left until the 21st Century," *Sekai,* December 1995. (In Japanese.)

15. David Fulghum, "Two-War Strategy May Be Abandoned," *Aviation Week and Space Technology,* January 29, 1996, p. 40.

16. Interview with Michael McDavitt.

17. Interview with William Pendley.

18. Torkel Patterson, James A. Kelly, and Ralph A. Cossa, "Strategy and Force Structure Responses of Japan and the United States to the New Security Environments in Northeast Asia," *Pacific Forum CSIS Special Report,* pp. 12–13.

19. Interview with Joseph Nye.

20. Interview with a staff member of Sam Nunn.

21. Ibid.

22. Interview with Paul Giarra.

23. Interview with a senior DOD official.

24. Interview with Masaki Orita.

25. Based on the author's conversation with Michael Green.

26. Interview with Brent Scowcroft.

27. Ibid.

28. Interview with Joseph Nye.

29. Interview with Paul Giarra.

30. Ibid.

31. Interview with Andrew Bennett.

32. Interview with Joseph Nye.

33. Ibid.

34. Ibid.

35. Interview with Sumio Tarui.

36. Interview with Joseph Nye.

37. Ibid.

38. Ibid.

39. Ibid.

40. Ibid.

41. Ibid.

42. Interview with Ezra Vogel.

43. Interview with Joseph Nye.

44. Conversation with a high-ranking State Department official.

45. Ibid.

46. Interview with William Perry.

47. Ibid.

48. Interview with Kurt Campbell.

49. Interview with Thomas Hubbard.

50. Interview with Stanley Roth.

51. Interview with Thomas Hubbard.

52. Interview with Rust Deming.

53. Daniel Williams, Clay Chander, "U.S. Aide Sees Relations With Asia in Peril," *Washington Post*, May 5, 1994.

54. Interview with Thomas Hubbard.

55. Interview with Gayle Von Eckartsburg.

56. Interview with a White House official.

57. Ibid.

58. Interview with Gayle Von Eckartsburg.

59. Interview with Ezra Vogel.

60. Armacost, *Friends or Rivals?* p. 85.

61. Interview with Ezra Vogel.

62. Ibid.

63. *United States Security Strategy for the East Asia–Pacific Region*, p. 10.

64. Interview with William Perry.

65. Interview with Joseph Nye.

66. Interview with a senior DOD official.

67. Interview with William Perry.

68. Interview with Ezra Vogel.

69. Based on author's conversation with a USTR official.

70. Interview with Brent Scowcroft.

71. Interview with a senior DOD official.

72. Interview with Andrew Bennett.

73. Interview with Ezra Vogel.

74. Interview with a DOD official.

75. Interview with Michael Green.

76. Interview with Chuck Downs.

77. Interview with Ezra Vogel.

78. Author's conversation with a DOD official.

79. Interview with William Perry.

80. Author's conversation with a White House official.

81. Interview with Stanley Roth.

82. Interview with a DOD official.

83. Ibid.

84. Interview with Andrew Bennett.

85. Interview with Joseph Nye.

86. Ibid.

87. Ibid.

88. Interview with a MOFA official.

89. Interview with a senior White House official.

90. Author's conversation with Richard Armitage.

91. Interview with a high-ranking DOD official.

92. Interview with Kazuyoshi Umemoto.

93. Interview with a high-ranking South Korean Foreign Ministry official.

94. Interview with Ezra Vogel.

95. Takakazu Kuriyama, *The Japan U.S. Alliance: From Drift to Revitalization* (Tokyo: Nihon Keizai Shimbunsha, 1997), pp. 258–259. (In Japanese.)

96. Interview with a high-ranking MOFA official.

97. Ibid.

98. Interview with Ezra Vogel.

99. Interview with Joseph Nye.

100. Interview with Doug Bereuter.

101. Interview with John McCain.

102. Interview with Carl Ford.

103. Interview with William Perry.

104. Interview with Kurt Campbell.

105. Interview with James Auer.

Chapter Thirteen

◀━━━▶

The Nuclear Crisis

Wrapping Paper

From the spring to the summer of 1994, the greatest fear of the people who had attended the "telephone breakfast" held at the Madison Hotel, the first meeting between Hajime Hatakeyama, deputy director-general of the Japanese Defense Agency (JDA), and Joseph Nye, assistant secretary for defense, was the crisis on the Korean Peninsula. As head of the U.S. National Intelligence Council (NIC), Nye was kept up to the minute on developments and knew how grave the Korean crisis was. He was also painfully aware of how precarious U.S.-Japan relations would be in the wake of the crisis.

"North Korea is very weak right now economically and having a lot of trouble. But sometimes people think that aggression in international affairs only happens when a country is strong; it can actually happen when a country is weak. . . . If you are on the top of a 12-story building, and the building is on fire and you look over the edge and you say, 'If I jump off this building, there is only one chance in 10 that I will survive the jump. But if I stand here on the building, there is a 100 percent chance that I will die,' then you will probably jump. North Korea is like that."[1]

Nye was not exaggerating in his use of such an analogy. He argued forcefully that the North Korean threat should not be underestimated. "The guidelines that are now being discussed between the U.S. and Japan, and between Hashimoto and Clinton, are essential to me because the idea that the American Congress would send U.S. troops to die in Korea and the Japanese would not provide food or fuel or support is out of the question. I mean, that would quickly break up the alliance."[2]

Nye was not alone in thinking along these lines. Thomas Hubbard shared his stance. "I remember during the Vietnam War, for example, we were flying battle wounded practically off the battlefield in Vietnam into U.S. military hospitals in Japan. It wasn't very widely known, but we don't have those hospitals anymore. If there were a war in Korea, to what extent could we use Japanese medical facilities, airports, and the like, that's what you ought to be talking about."[3]

The crisis, which had its origins in suspicions that North Korea was building nuclear weapons, swiftly turned much graver when a proposal for economic sanctions was tabled in the United Nations, and North Korea declared it regarded any such action as "a declaration of war." Secretary William Perry later recalled that Northeast Asia came as dangerously close to war as it ever had since the Korean War.[4]

The nuclear suspicions developed into a crisis from 1993 to 1995. In February 1993, when the International Atomic Energy Agency (IAEA) asked for a special inspection of two facilities that the North Koreans had not put on the inspection list, North Korea refused and stated it would leave the Nonproliferation Treaty (NPT) in March.

In response, the American-led move for U.N. economic sanctions on North Korea became more vigorous. Using the economic sanctions as leverage, the United States brought pressure to bear on North Korea to withdraw its secession from the NPT and accept the inspections. Although this brought the North Koreans to the negotiating table, they still refused to give up the nuclear option. In the March 1994 talks between the two Koreas, the chief North Korean delegate declared, "Seoul will turn into a sea of fire," and walked out.[5]

Perry, preparing for the worst by sending Patriot missiles to South Korea, also recognized "the policies and strategies we invoke today will have a certain risk. . . . I'd rather face that risk than face the risk of even greater catastrophe two or three years from now."[6] Some in the Pentagon were all for a so-called surgical operation, i.e., using air strikes to knock out North Korea's Yongbyon reactor.

Perry took a serious view of the situation. He was especially worried about North Korea reinforcing its forces along the border, particularly its artillery forces.[7] He was also cautious, however. He believed that if they were forced to set in motion such a plan of action (i.e., a surgical air strike to destroy nuclear facilities), the North Koreans would most certainly wage total warfare.

The Pentagon started examining in the strictest confidence "if it does come to war" contingency scenarios. Basing estimates on the Vietnam War and the Gulf War, planners expected the first 90 days of total warfare would result in 52,000 U.S. troop casualties, killed and wounded, and 490,000 South Korean. The war itself would cause one million deaths, of which 80,000 to 100,000 would be Americans.

The United States entered a state of readiness in mid-June 1994. The Joint Chiefs of Staff looked at three options:

Option I: To send 2,000 emergency deployment units to South Korea.

Option II: To add fighters, including the F-117 Stealth bomber, to the forces at the front; later to reinforce artillery forces; and in addition to the aircraft carrier already deployed, to send a second aircraft carrier mobile unit. This would add 10,000 troops to the current 37,000 U.S. troop strength.

Option III: To inject further several tens of thousands of army and marine troops in the case of protracted total warfare.

Perry leaned towards the second option. They could send two aircraft carriers and stare the North Koreans down. What worried Perry was that the North Koreans might stage a surprise attack before the U.S. troops could be reinforced. "They're not stupid. They could well make a move before we could reinforce. . . . Saddam Hussein's biggest mistake was letting the U.S. build up its troops willy nilly for a period of six months. The North Koreans have probably studied that case exhaustively."[8]

On June 15, the United States presented its draft Security Council resolution on North Korean sanctions to the other council members. On June 16, General Gary Luck, commander in chief of U.S. forces in Korea, met clandestinely with James Laney, U.S. ambassador to South Korea. They decided to implement the withdrawal of Americans in South Korea. Raney made arrangements to have his daughter and her three children, who just happened to be visiting, out of the country by Sunday, July 19, in other words, in three days' time.[9]

Perry later stated that three alternatives to increase U.S. military forces in Korea were proposed in June. President Clinton was poised to authorize one of these when the briefing was interrupted by a telephone call from former President Carter reporting that North Korea had agreed to stop all nuclear reprocessing action and negotiate an agreement to freeze its nuclear program.[10] A few months later, North Korea signed the Agreement Framework, which froze its nuclear program and drew the region back from the brink of conflict.

How would Japan be involved when U.S. forces in Japan took action during a contingency on the Korean Peninsula? This was a grave issue that impacted directly on Japan's own defense. There was no alliance between Japan and South Korea, nor was there any framework or agreement on crisis prevention or crisis management among the United States, Japan, and Korea or including China. The region was a naked jungle, Japan's only prop being its alliance with the United States.

Starting in the spring of 1993, the U.S. forces in Japan began to inform Japan's Joint Staff Council about things U.S. troops would need in the case of an emergency on the Korean Peninsula. As the requests kept coming in dribs and drabs, the Japanese asked for them to be put into one comprehensive list, only to receive a list of requests in the spring of 1994 some 1,900 items long!

The requests ranged from things like simplifying customs procedures for U.S. military staff at Narita Airport to letting the U.S. military share civilian airports to asking for tugboat services when U.S. military ships broke down. Many of the requests involved uses of collective self-defense rights that the Japanese government said infringed the Japanese Constitution. This was not a matter for the Joint Staff, nor was it something that could be answered on the spot.

The Americans were increasingly exasperated with explanations that repeatedly cited "Japan's domestic circumstances." Their feeling was, "Hey! Aren't these talks about protecting Japan? Doesn't a contingency on the Korean Peninsula directly affect your own defense? Aren't we allies?"[11]

In April 1992, the commander of the Seventh Pacific Fleet approached the JDA about the possibility of deploying Maritime Self-Defense Forces (SDF) minesweepers in the case of a Korean emergency. The U.S. military only had two minesweepers in Sasebo, but Japan had more than 30. Moreover, Japan's minesweeping capability was extremely high. The United States counted on it.

When the JDA responded that using Japanese minesweepers was impossible because it corresponded to the use of collective self-defense rights and was not constitutionally permissible, the Americans asked the question again, saying, "[Dealing with contingencies on the Korean Peninsula] is defending Japan, so isn't it possible?" The JDA explained that it "couldn't get domestic political support" and that was that.[12]

What could Japan and the United States do together during an emergency on the Korean Peninsula? Both countries had been allied for a long time without deciding that question. It was no exaggeration to say that bilateral security was an empty "alliance" wrapper devoid of any "joint operations" content.

The first attempt to inject some content was the guidelines approved by the Cabinet and the Committee on U.S.-Japan Security Talks in November 1978. The official name of the guidelines was "Guidelines for U.S. Japan Defense Cooperation" and its objective was to lay down a response framework for Article 5 (Japan contingencies) and Article 6 (Far East contingencies) conditions in the U.S.-Japan Security Treaty. They contained three points:

1. Arrangements for preventing invasion;

2. Responding to an armed attack on Japan (Japan contingencies); and

3. Responding to conditions in the Far East other than Japan with a significant impact on Japanese security (Far East contingencies).[13]

The principal object of the joint study at that time was joint responses to Japan contingencies and affording facilities to U.S. forces in a Far East contingency.

Regarding the work on Far East contingencies, however, it was thought that it would be possible to approach it within the confines of Japan's individual self-defense rights permitted by the constitution. Putting together operations plans (code-named 50–52), the United States expressed its desire to discuss the subject with the Japanese.[14]

The Americans later drew up a joint U.S. and South Korea operations plan (code-named 50–27) for a contingency on the Korean Peninsula that regarded Japan as an integral part of the operations plan. The joint operations plan for Japan, however, remained a blank.

Contingency

The New Frontier Party's Tsutomu Hata was foreign minister in the Hosokawa Cabinet. He had a chance to meet George Mitchell (D-Maine), then majority leader of the Senate, and several other influential senators on a visit to Washington in the spring of 1994 thanks to the help of his old friend Senator Bob Dole (R-Kans.). Mitchell asked him what Japan intended to do if something happened on the Korean Peninsula.

Hata, who had squeezed in this trip to Washington between being constantly grilled in the Diet, hadn't yet shaken off his Diet rhetoric and replied almost reflexively, "What we can do within the constraints of the constitution." Mitchell just stared in amazement at a loss for words. It was as though he was thinking, *What do you mean within the constraints of the Constitution when something is happening in the country next door, in your seas? And what exactly are you going to do within those constraints?*

Another senator followed up. "America sends off its young to a distant place, exposing them to danger, and Japan does nothing. That's just not acceptable. It's Japan that's in danger, that's being threatened. What do you mean by not doing anything?"

Hata could feel the wave of disbelief in the room, but he was not in an easy position. He had to bear in mind the Socialists who formed part of the coalition. The Japan Socialist Party (JSP) was extremely sensitive about North Korea. Carelessly setting off a debate could well provoke the North. So, for the time being, he would stop "Diet debate" and "public debate." Instead, Hata instructed the Foreign Ministry (MOFA) to make an exhaustive study on what exactly Japan could do if worse came to worst; and what procedures were needed for doing what they had to do but weren't allowed to.[15]

Shigeru Ito of the JSP was Hosokawa's transport minister. During his time in office, it was the U.N. sanctions on North Korea that caused him the most distress. As transport minister he was also the minister responsible for supervising the Maritime Safety Agency (MSA), which patrolled Japan's coasts. He received many confidential instructions from both the PM's office and the Foreign Ministry and had very involved discussions one-on-one with the director-general of the MSA.

The MSA had to be ready for anything, including deploying coast guard boats to rescue Japanese nationals and borrowing metal detectors from the police in preparation for seajacks. In the case of large-scale sea landings by refugees from North Korea, however, they would have to resort to emergency legislation or extrajurisdictional measures.

Why on earth has this country ended up like this? Is it really because the existence of the Socialists, strong but in perennial opposition, made it impossible to do anything on constitutional debate? All Ito could do was smile grimly.

It was none other than his party, the Socialists, that had opposed proposed amendments to the Self-Defense Forces Act that would allow government aircraft to be flown to rescue Japanese nationals, forcing the amendments to be carried over to the next Diet session. There was no other way except dispatching MSA patrol boats or civilian ships and planes.

There were two lessons Ito learned here. The first was that diplomatic efforts had to be strengthened so that things didn't get so far out of hand. The second was that even then, the possibility of a contingency occurring was not zero. That being the case, Japan as a nation had to be prepared.

He and the director-general of the MSA decided that they would take full responsibility for the actions of the MSA staff; they would not make the staff responsible. "The official stance in the PKO bill may well be that it's up to the individual soldier to decide whether to shoot, that the officers won't give that order, but let's not have that here."

Leaders at the MSA had confirmed that "we can't just send those in the field off into dangerous waters. If the worst comes to the worst, let's have some staff from the agency headquarters on board too."[16]

North Korea was now saying that if the U.N. sanctions went into force, it would make not only Seoul but Japan a "sea of fire." There was a very good chance that if something did happen, it would be disastrous.

Prime Minister Hosokawa attests to being woken up twice in the middle of the night by calls from his aides on North Korean military developments. The first time was the news that North Korea's tanks had started moving towards the border. The next time was the news that North Korea had started setting the sights of its long-range guns on Seoul. Neither case led to a "sea of fire," but it was certain that North Korea was upping the provocation stakes.[17]

In May of the previous year, 1993, North Korea fired its No Dong 1 medium-range trajectory missile into the Sea of Japan. The experiment was successful, which meant that in addition to South Korea, the western half of Japan was now within firing range of North Korea.

"North Korea is firing missiles and hitting fairly accurately targets 500 kilometers off. If they had nuclear heads, they could mount an attack several hundred times stronger than Hiroshima." So did Nobuo Ishihara, deputy Cabinet secretary, leak confidential information he had received from the JDA to the press a little later. "It was an action prompted by political conviction."[18] In other words, Ishihara suspected that the political leaders of the coalition government wanted to keep it a secret out of a fear of a hypersensitive reaction from the Japanese public, which, in turn, could provoke the North Koreans as well as cause damage to the coalition government itself. Ishihara judged that keeping the news a secret for such a shortsighted reason would do no good for the Japanese public.

Ishihara and the others felt the time was ripe for rousing public opinion.

A Close Call

In June 1993, Japanese politics were undergoing a huge transition, the kind that happens only every few decades. The Liberal Democratic Party (LDP), which had ruled undisputed for 38 years, was on the brink of collapse. Both politics and political parties had suddenly started to slide. It was in this context that the Hosokawa Cabinet emerged. No headway was made, however, in the instability and murkiness of the political situation, and the focus of politics was reform, not crisis management.

Even so, Ishihara started a secret gathering of bureaucrats at the beginning of fall 1993, called the Four-Way Forum. Led by the Cabinet Office of Security, the group also comprised high-ranking officials from the Foreign Ministry, the JDA, and the National Policy Agency. It was not merely a forum for exchanging information but also a venue for examining worst-case scenario policy responses, especially cross-ministry types of policies.

Hosokawa was made increasingly aware of the seriousness of the situation by both the United States and South Korea at the Asia-Pacific Economic Cooperation (APEC) summit held in Seattle in November 1993. Clinton said that if things came to that, the United States would have to use the U.S. bases in Okinawa and asked for Japan to ready its domestic structure. A yellow light flashed on in Hosokawa's mind.

At the summit the following February, Hosokawa's sense of crisis grew. "He had been told the summit would only be about the economic initiative, but, in fact, the Korean Peninsula took up half the agenda."[19] Clinton once again emphasized the serious nature of the situation and tried to wake Japan up. The yellow light was now red. The day after Hosokawa went back home, he called Ishihara in and instructed him to study the Korean contingency.[20]

The first issue on the agenda was deciding their reaction if the United Nations called for sanctions. Recommendations of a kind came in from the Foreign Ministry, the JDA, and elsewhere: a freeze on official visits, trade, and remittances; maritime searches and preventive action; rescue of Japanese nationals; domestic and coast patrols to protect domestic facilities from North Korean terrorism or surprise attacks; U.S. force support; refugee countermeasures.

North Korea had declared that it would regard the implementation of U.N. sanctions as a declaration of war. There was a very grave danger that things would escalate into war. By the spring of 1994, voices started emerging from the U.S. government that a military solution could not be ruled out. The research went on at a frantic pace on what could be done under existing law about cooperating with U.S. forces should war break out; deploying the SDF to guard key facilities such as nuclear power plants; rescuing Japanese nationals; transporting international refugees. What could be partially done? What would require legal amendments? And what would require new legislation?

There were 9,000 Japanese nationals in South Korea. As long as the SDF could not go to pick them up, there was no choice but to rely on U.S. forces. The United States, however, was asking Japan not only to rescue its own nationals but to contribute to the rescue of all foreign nationals. The number of refugees could well exceed two million in a worst-case scenario. In such a situation, it was conceivable that several tens of thousands would end up in Japan. Japan had absolutely no holding capability for war refugees.

The trickiest issue was ensuring the safety of Japan's nuclear power plants and deploying the minesweepers. Japan had 25 nuclear power plants on its Sea of Japan coast, and it was possible that special guerrilla units from North Korea would try to destroy them. The police, however, took the position that they could not respond to subversive actions by special units. What was to be done then? Nothing for it but to deploy the Self-Defense Forces. And if that was so, then the law had to be amended.

Although there might be some debate, there would be no problem with deploying minesweepers to remove floating mines that might endanger Japanese shipping from the open seas. But what if they were asked to sweep for mines in areas close to the Korean Peninsula or in the vicinity of the implementation line of a naval blockade? That would be difficult because it raised constitutional questions over collective self-defense rights.

We have to get the contingency legislation ready. In that case, time-limited legislation would be best.[21]

That was Ishihara's judgment, but this was not a job for the bureaucrats. The politicians had to make the decision. Hosokawa, however, abruptly resigned from office. Looking back on events, Ishihara said,

"From April 8 when Hosokawa announced his resignation until April 25 when the Hata Cabinet was formed, the political vacuum reached a nadir. And that period overlapped with a period of rapid escalation in the North Korean crisis."[22] The political vacuum continued thereafter and the decisiveness of the politicians was just as lacking. The Hata Cabinet did not even last two months.

Japan underwent another political upheaval in June 1994. The fragile Hata coalition Cabinet began collapsing. On June 17, the LDP decided to table a motion of no confidence in the Hata Cabinet in the Diet. They would wait until after the budget bill for fiscal 1994 had passed the following week, then put the motion straightaway. The Socialists were expected to go along with this. On the day in question, President Jimmy Carter signed an agreement with North Korean chairman Kim Il Sung in Pyongyang for a freeze in the North Korean nuclear development program and a moratorium on the U.N. sanctions.

It had been a close call, but hostilities on the Korean Peninsula had been averted. Ito said he could still remember his feeling of relief as if it were only yesterday. But it was not only Ito who felt that way. It had also been a close call for Japan and the U.S.-Japan alliance.

Traumatized

The U.S. government was once again made acutely aware of just how fragile its alliance with Japan was. There was a growing sense of foreboding that they would not be able to work together in the case of a contingency. The Japanese were also painfully aware of the fragility. The North Korean crisis itself was one issue, but one false move and it could well set off a crisis in the U.S.-Japan security relationship. That was an even more frightening prospect.

This sense of crisis can be seen, for example, in the writings of Hitoshi Tanaka, who was then director of the Foreign Policy Coordination Division in MOFA. "Japan would be directly threatened were North Korea to possess nuclear weapons. Should chaos reign on the Korean Peninsula, Japan would inevitably be embroiled. In the circumstances of a contingency on the Korean Peninsula, Japan's security would be forced to rely to a great degree on America. Should Japan be unable to provide America with adequate support, however, would America consider Japan a country worth protecting?"[23]

Japan had bitter memories from the Gulf War. Always one step behind everyone else, everything it did was woeful and pathetic. It lost a great deal of its credibility in the international community. Its "checkbook diplomacy" and "cash dispenser" response was a huge shock to its American ally as well. Nothing more was ever heard of the

"U.S.-Japan global partnership" that the Bush administration had initially been pursuing with the Kaifu government, and Secretary of State James Baker never took Japan seriously again.

There were people at the Japan Desk in the Pentagon who greatly mistrusted Japan. This mistrust ran along the lines that Japan was hypocritical when it came to making selfish demands for equal treatment, prior consultations, and base cuts without fighting itself.

It was after that period that Michael Powell, then a special staff member of the Office of the Secretary of Defense for Bilateral Security Affairs, started mentioning the "three myths of U.S.-Japan security": the myth of alliance, the myth that economics and security could be dealt with separately, and the myth that the alliance stopped Japan from becoming a military superpower.[24]

That is a view of Japan perhaps highly colored by revisionist theory but more likely an expression of a sense of betrayal at the fecklessness of Japan's response at the time of the Gulf War. The root of the problem was the one-sided nature of the alliance's burden. In the face of crisis this was perceived as unfair.

In 1955, when Mamoru Shigemitsu, Japan's foreign minister, broached the question of making the Security Treaty more reciprocal, his U.S. counterpart, Secretary of State John Foster Dulles, rejected the idea on the grounds that Japan was neither ready nor had the power to conclude a mutual defense treaty. Dulles pointed out that Article 9 of the Japanese Constitution prohibited Japan from dispatching troops overseas, thereby making it impossible for Japan to protect a U.S. territory such as Guam, and that Japan did not even possess sufficient military capability to protect its own territory.[25] Politically, it has been finessed as a nonissue, yet it remains potentially explosive. Every time there was a crisis, a chorus of American voices was suddenly shouting, "Why should we sacrifice the young of our nation while Japan looks on? You call that an alliance?" Even the U.S. media were starting to write articles titled "If War Comes to Korea, Japan May Not Back U.S."[26]

From the spring to the summer of 1994, when the United Nations was considering sanctions against North Korea, criticism of Japan as a good-for-nothing, irresponsible country trying to buy peace with money was growing. What's more, this time if something happened, it would hit Japan directly, and casualties to U.S. forces in Korea would be vastly higher than in the Gulf War.

The sense of crisis may have been even more acute, however, among Japan's diplomats and JDA staff. For them, the sense of ineffectualness and fretfulness at the time of the Gulf War had left deep scars, not only at a policy level, but on a personal, psychological level. They were traumatized.

The view of the Japanese people on security issues was greatly affected by the Gulf experience. Japanese debate on security matters changed fundamentally, as did views on PKO. The passage of the International Peace Cooperation Law in 1992 and the deployment of a PKO force to Cambodia are good indications of this change in national awareness. According to a June 1993 survey by the *Yomiuri* newspaper, 56 percent of the populace was in favor of PKO participation. And yet, old habits die hard.

Crisis Management

That was not all. With the Hanshin earthquake, the sarin gas attack, and the hostages in Peru, the Japanese government found itself taxed to the limit in dealing with one crisis after another. Threats were becoming more diverse, more of a daily occurrence, making problems more real, more in the ordinary course of events. Crisis management, patrolling territorial waters, countering terrorism were all becoming key policy issues. Once again, however, there was virtually no structural or legal framework in place. It was the Hanshin earthquake that exposed this to the public eye.

Japan was totally vulnerable to internal threats, let alone external threats and contingencies. The illusion that it was progressive not to use the SDF, that it was pacifist to keep them contained, was widely embraced.

Takemasa Moriya, counselor at the Bureau of Defense, had faced a similar case before. VIPs from around the globe converged on Tokyo for the funeral of Emperor Hirohito on February 24, 1989. Some 9,800 guests from 163 countries, of whom 700 were VIPs, were coming. What was to be done about their protection? The government's greatest concern was ensuring their safety. At the time, Moriya was director of the Defense Bureau's Operations Division and was made part of the government's funeral security team.

VIP crafts were touching down one after the other at Haneda and Narita airports. The problem was how to protect the crafts from then on. The police came to the JDA saying they wouldn't be able to keep up using the standard security procedure of traveling in convoy along the Keiyo freeway; they would like the SDF to handle security from Narita to metropolitan Tokyo's limits, after which they would take over.

It turned out, however, that there were not enough heliports in Tokyo to handle the SDF flying the VIPs in. When Moriya suggested they use the metropolitan government-managed Tokyo Heliport in Shin Kiba, the police were reluctant, saying it was too far from central Tokyo. The next proposal was to use the old national rail freight yards at Shiodome, near Shimbashi, but still the police refused to agree, saying there were too many high-rise buildings in the vicinity and they feared snipers.

How about the Imperial Palace then?

"Oh no, that would be too disrespectful."

Well, what about the U.S. Forces Heliport at Hardy Barracks? This time it was the Foreign Ministry that opposed it as an affront to national prestige. As a last resort, Moriya thought of the State Guest House in Akasaka, but it turned out that Prime Minister Takeshita was going to be using it to conduct "condolence diplomacy" and it wouldn't do to have helicopters taking off and landing in the front garden as they were organizing the cavalcades, so that too was rejected.

If the front garden was no good, what about the heliport at the side? Was that no good?

"That hasn't been used for such a long time it's like a small copse now. Some of the trees have been planted by His Majesty himself, so we can't go and cut them down."

It can't be helped then. We'll have to let them down at the SDF garrison in Ichigaya. Will that do?

But no, this time it was the Imperial Household Agency that raised an objection. All foreign guests of state have to be welcomed by members of the imperial family. It certainly wouldn't do to have them going into SDF facilities. When Moriya replied along the lines of "Is that right? Well, the Defense Agency will have nothing more to do with it," Sadajiro Furukawa, deputy Cabinet secretary, addressed the problem, saying, "All right. I'll see that the State Guest House heliport can be used. Do it there." In the end, they cut down 200 trees, put the heliport back into service, and used that.[27]

Moriya had been witness to "the weird and tortuous impact of having shut the SDF out from anything and everything."[28] Moriya was once asked by Kurt Campbell why Japan had been unable to give a clear answer on joint operations with the United States at the time of the 1994 Korean crisis. It was just after Campbell had started as deputy assistant secretary of defense. Beginning with the Mitsuya operation that became a problem in the 1965 session of the Diet,[29] Moriya explained in detail the domestic conditions that prevented Japan not only from researching contingencies but almost from being able to carry out crisis management. He outlined the history of how political reasons had prevented the creation of a contingency law and a crisis management structure, and how officials meant to conduct joint research on contingencies outside Japan in the 1978 guidelines but that no headway had been made.

"Domestic conditions" corresponded to the various systemic leftovers of World War II and the political vacuum that had been a constant since 1993.

The vacuum made the Kasumigaseki bureaucrats jumpy and apprehensive. The reason Ishihara and the others had gone ahead with their clandestine research on a legal framework for contingencies, why they thought of making it a time-limited piece of legislation, was partly because of their own sense of emergency as those in charge of crisis management in a political vacuum.

Nothing will happen if we take it to the politicians. If we're not careful, giving it to them might spread the sense of crisis and prevent us from achieving what looks possible.[30]

Kasumigaseki's assessment remained virtually unchanged with the birth of the Murayama government. On July 8, 1994, with the death of Kim Il Sung, the North Korean chairman, Tokuichiro Tamazawa, director general of the JDA, sounded out Ishihara about opening a meeting of the Security Council, but Ishihara was cautious. Apart from the rule that the council can only be convened to deal with existing emergencies, he had to think of the downside of holding a meeting with the frail Murayama government.[31]

The new National Defense Program Outline (NDPO), which was released in November 1995 as the Japanese counterpart to the Nye Report of February 1995, mentioned the need to deal with contingencies in the vicinity of Japan. Nevertheless, the Foreign Ministry and JDA officials agreed with the Murayama Cabinet's course of not putting a review of the guidelines on the agenda because "if it was handled poorly and tampered with they would lose not only the bath water but the baby too."

There were those at the JDA who thought the director-general should mention the guidelines when announcing the new NDPO. The Foreign Ministry frowned on this, however. "Don't you think that would be a bit too tough, you know, what with it being the Murayama Cabinet. . . ."

"It'll create all sorts of trouble if this Cabinet starts debating all manner of things and puts the guidelines on the agenda."[32]

By the time the Hashimoto Cabinet took office, these pent-up concerns and leftover issues were piled mountain high. Hashimoto had worked on crisis management and the contingency structure as chairman of the LDP's Policy Research Council during the Hosokawa government when the LDP was in opposition. He was determined to make these matters a priority when he took office.

The LDP, on the other hand, had made Tsutomu Kawara, a former JDA director-general, chairman of its Research Commission on Security. Kawara had promised himself to inject new life into the commission, which had fallen into a state of hibernation.

Kawara said, "Up until that point, the Research Commission on Security had been open but idle. Being involved with it myself, I was gnashing my teeth. Talking about security or the SDF was like grasping at air when we weren't in control of the government." But its day had finally come. "Rather than linking it to war, what was needed was strengthening security in a changing international environment. . . . I thought it was a little premature talking of crisis response in security matters, but I decided to start with that in order to win public sympathy."[33]

As a result, the Research Commission on Security wrote two papers in March 1996, "The Significance of the Japan-U.S. Security Structure Today" and "Responding to Far East Contingencies." According to Shigenobu Tamura, special researcher with the LDP's Policy Research Council, who was in charge of drafting both papers, the reality was that the party took the lead with Hashimoto and Kawara coordinating later as "it wouldn't do if their ideas were different."[34]

Following this approach, the government put "joint cooperation between the United States and Japan on contingencies in the vicinity of Japan" into the Japan-U.S. Security Declaration of April 1996. After that, the revision of the guidelines went forward at a smart pace.

Responses were considered for each of five situations: "peacetime," "pre-crisis," "crisis (vicinity contingency)," "crisis overflow to Japan and the defense of Japan," and "postcrisis." An interim report was released in June 1997, which took a serious view of "conditions in the vicinity of Japan which have important repercussions on Japan's peace and security" and gave a list of 40 items to be considered as possible areas of bilateral cooperation. They covered humanitarian activities in disaster areas; activities to ensure the effectiveness of economic sanctions; evacuation activities for noncombatant personnel; rear regional support for U.S. military activities; minesweeping; and ongoing cooperation in PKO information exchange.

When he launched the Nye Initiative, Nye had in mind enhancing the guidelines. His real intention was: *With the current structure left as is, the alliance will be in shatters the minute a contingency occurs on the Korean Peninsula. That's why the guidelines are so crucial as evidence that Japan will support U.S. forces when a contingency arises and a war situation prevails.*[35]

For Nye, the guidelines were more than a military operational pledge for when things got bad. They were also a pledge for the survival of the alliance. Not confined to preparing for contingency, the guidelines were an ongoing preparation and also a political preparation. They were political insurance.

The 1996 and 1997 revision of the new guidelines, however, did not develop in a straight line from that kind of strategic or political approach. In a manner of speaking, it too was a "confluence": a redefinition and reaffirmation of U.S.-Japan security in the post–Cold War era by the Nye Initiative; the need for contingency responses and legal provisions under the pressure of the crisis on the Korean Peninsula; the severe public criticism of the government's crisis management structure and boosting that into systemic consolidation; a growing desire for broader, international security as seen in ever stronger public support for involvement in U.N. peacekeeping operations; and public approval for JDA and SDF activities in noncombatant areas and a growing pride in their professionalism. These were the strands that came together in an intricate weave to create the confluence.

Notes

1. Interview with Joseph Nye.
2. Ibid.
3. Interview with Thomas Hubbard.
4. Interview with William Perry.
5. "North Korea's 'Sea of Fire' Threat Shakes Seoul," *Financial Times,* March 22, 1994, p. 6.
6. R. Jeffrey Smith, "Perry Sharply Warns North Korea," *Washington Post,* March 31, 1994, p. A1.
7. Interview with William Perry.
8. Ibid.
9. Don Oberdofer gives a detailed account of these events in *The Two Koreas: A Contemporary History* (Boston: Addison-Wesley Publishing Company, 1997).
10. William Perry's speech to the Pacific Forum, March 18, 1997.
11. "U.S.-Japan Security Treaty: Confronting a Crisis Amidst the North Korean Nuclear Suspicions," *Asahi Shimbun,* December 24, 1996. (In Japanese.)
12. Ibid.
13. Akihiko Tanaka, *Security: Attempts during the Fifty Years since the War* (Tokyo: Yomiuri Shinbunsha, 1997), p. 284. (In Japanese.)
14. Interview with a senior DOD official.
15. Interview with Tsutomu Hata.
16. Interview with Shigeru Ito.
17. Interview with Morihiro Hosokawa.
18. Interview with a high-ranking JDA official.
19. Interview with Nobuo Ishihara.
20. Interview with Morihiro Hosokawa.
21. Interview with Nobuo Ishihara.
22. Ibid.
23. Hitoshi Tanaka, "An Examination of North Korean Nuclear Suspicions," *Gaiko Forum,* July 1994. (In Japanese.)
24. Interview with Michael Powell.

25. Kazuya Sakamoto, "Material/Personnel Cooperation and the Future of the U.S.-Japan Security Treaty," paper presented for the CSIS Conference, "U.S.-Japan Security Relations," May 2, 1996, p. 46.

26. David Williams, "If War Comes to Korea, Japan May Not Back U.S.," *Los Angeles Times,* June 12, 1994, p. 2.

27. This episode is based on interviews with Sadajiro Furukawa and Takemasa Moriya.

28. Interview with Takemasa Moriya.

29. In February 1965, Socialist parliamentarian Haruo Okada grilled the government of Prime Minister Eisaku Sato at a Diet session by revealing that a group of top officers in the Japanese Defense Agency had studied their own defense plan in preparation for a possible war. The plan, often referred to as the "Mitsuya Operation," examined how the SDF could be mobilized in case of an outbreak of war on the Korean Peninsula and its possible repercussions on Japan. The plan caused an uproar in Japan, as the public perceived the plan as being a JDA-led conspiracy to revive the prewar imperial army. After the incident, contingency-planning became a taboo within JDA for years to follow. For further details see Tanaka, *Security: Attempts during the Fifty Years since the War,* pp. 215–216.

30. Interview with Nobuo Ishihara.

31. Ibid.

32. Interviews with high-ranking officials at MOFA and JDA.

33. Interview with Tsutomu Kawara.

34. Interview with Shigenobu Tamura.

35. Interview with Joseph Nye.

Chapter Fourteen

——◆——

Rape

Labor Day

September 7, 1995.

Labor Day (September 4) had come and gone, but there was still a summer holiday mood at the U.S. Embassy in Tokyo. Early that morning, the telephone at Deputy Chief of Mission Rust Deming's residence rang shrilly. It was from the embassy.

"There's been a rape in Okinawa. Three marines have been arrested. We'll call again when we know more."

Ambassador Walter Mondale was not in Japan, having gone home to Minnesota for summer vacation. Deming rang him in Minnesota immediately. "The victim is a 12-year-old schoolgirl." Mondale seemed shocked. Before hanging up, Deming said, "But we still don't know much. I'll call back when we know more."[1]

The rape had occurred on Labor Day Monday. The navy's Criminal Investigation Division in conjunction with the Okinawan police had interrogated three marines, and they had been arrested that morning. The U.S. consul-general in Okinawa, Aloysius O'Neill, had notified the embassy in Tokyo, but since the Okinawa police had said they did not want to go public with the incident to protect the schoolgirl's identity, he couldn't make up his mind on the spot how it should be handled. On September 8, however, the *Ryukyu Shimpo* ran the story:

> On September 8th, the prefectural police had a warrant of arrest for the three marines on suspicion of abduction and rape. The three men were being held in custody by the Americans' Naval Criminal Investigation Service (NCIS). The rape had taken place during the evening of September 4, in the northern area of the main island. The three soldiers were suspected of forcing the schoolgirl into a car on her way home from shopping and taking her to a nearby beach and raping her. Following the incident, the prefectural police set up an emergency patrol to trace where the three men had fled in the car from the site of the crime. They identi-

fied the three men from the rental car used in the crime and followed up their investigation. The prefectural police had requested that the Americans hand the men over to Okinawan custody.[2]

Since it was now public, the incident required a public response. O'Neill spent the weekend working out how best to deal with the situation. On Monday, September 11, O'Neill visited Governor Masahide Ota at the Prefectural Offices to offer an apology. It was to be the first of many public U.S. apologies.

The Pentagon, September 8, 8:00 A.M.

Kurt Campbell, deputy assistant secretary of defense, took an urgent call from Tokyo. "Unit 1 of the Criminal Investigation Unit at the Okinawa Prefectural Police and Ishikawa Precinct have announced they have an arrest warrant for the three servicemen." Campbell immediately called an emergency meeting to discuss the appropriate response.

Paul Giarra's face still contorted in agony when recalling the event. "We were all repelled by what had happened, although it was early on in the process, and there hadn't been a trial yet. We knew that if there was any truth, and there probably was because these three men were in custody, that this was a black mark for the U.S.

"I remember feeling personally mortified because as a military officer, I knew that we did our best to put our best face forward, to be on our best behavior. But unfortunately, that didn't always happen, and it was a shame that the good, responsible, decent Americans, many of them very young Americans who were away from home under military discipline, would be tarred by this brush.

"My first instinct was to apologize. My next instinct was that someone from Washington needed to go immediately to Japan, and preferably to Okinawa, to apologize and to show that this was being taken very seriously."[3]

Assistant Secretary for Defense Joseph Nye was shaken utterly. A wave of fear ran through him that the Nye Initiative, so painstakingly put together over the past year, would shatter into pieces. He was later to say it was like a blow from a typhoon.

The press club at the Okinawa Prefectural Offices, September 11.

Suzuyo Takazato, a member of the Naha City Council who had been in Beijing to attend the nongovernmental organization (NGO) forum of the U.N. Fourth World Conference on Women, was holding a press conference. She had been handed a newspaper clipping about the rape virtually as she stepped off the plane in Naha on September 10. She was dumbstruck.

Takazato had attended the Beijing forum as a member of "NGO Beijing-Okinawa Unai." She had spoken there on how the military was a structural aggressor towards women, reporting that its essential nature led to so-called comfort women and to gang rape in war zones. She won the support of women from Vietnam, Cambodia, and the United States and their support was still fresh in her mind.

During her press conference, Takazato made the following appeal:

"The question of the bases has been approached from peace, land, and the environment. But has it ever been approached from the human rights of women? It is extremely difficult to know what exactly is going on with sex offenses by U.S. soldiers. There have been cases to date which have been hushed up. The rape of this young schoolgirl is a violation of the human rights of all the women of Okinawa."[4]

As she spoke, her voice cracked and the tears rolled uncontrollably down her cheeks. Many of the people who were watching the live television broadcast were touched.

If there was an accident involving U.S. aircraft, it was always front-page news. The Prefectural Assembly discussed it. When it was a woman victim of sexual assault by a U.S. soldier, however, it only made the social section.

Prior to the schoolgirl rape, an incident had taken place in May in Naha City in which a 24-year-old Okinawan woman had been hammered to death by a U.S. soldier. The newspapers pigeonholed it as a "love triangle gone wrong," writing that the woman had been divorced—as if that had anything to do with it. Takazato cited that example and called for a change in journalists' attitudes. Takazato had worked for many years as a women's counselor. She had seen many of the victims of rapes perpetrated by U.S. servicemen. Unable to tell anyone and with no one's help, the victims bore huge psychological scars.

Takazato continued, "In this rape, the perpetrators say they discussed first going to a brothel on the side of the base. But they decided not to because it was poor and dirty and reminded them of home. So they rented a car, drove a long way out and committed the rape. American economic power is not as strong as it once was and the areas around the bases are some of the poorest, the American soldiers now prowling about residential areas demanding free sex. The housing area is totally vulnerable without any fencing. The whole of Okinawa is exposed to the sexual violence of the bases."[5]

By posing the violation of human rights derived from the structural violence of the military as the "base question," Takazato challenged the equation by changing it from one of "peace" and "land" and "accidents" to one of "human rights" and "women's rights."

Clause 5, Article 17, of the Status of Forces Agreement

The three servicemen were being held at Camp Hansen, and the Japanese investigation authorities were not able to take custody of them.

Demonstrations were immediately staged: What do you think the people of Okinawa are? Isn't Japan a constitutional state?

It was stipulated in Clause 5, Article 17, of the Status of Forces Agreement (SOFA), that "the custody of an accused member of the United States armed forces or the civilian component over whom Japan is to exercise jurisdiction shall, if he is in the hands of the United States, remain with the United States until he is charged by Japan."

Denunciation was fierce. The Girard case,[6] which took place almost 40 years ago, immediately flashed in people's minds. Why couldn't they be handed over to the Japanese when they were arrested? Article 17 had been criticized as an "unequal provision" ever since SOFA had come into force in 1960. There had been more than 4,500 U.S. military-related crimes since Okinawa's reversion in 1972, including 12 murders. Each time there had been trouble with handing the suspects over into Japanese custody and compensation for the victims.

With the suspects held in custody inside the bases, if they escaped back to the United States, there was nothing the Japanese authorities could do. Additionally, jurisdiction depended on whether the crime had been committed "on duty" or "off duty." If it had been committed on duty, then the Americans had primary right to exercise jurisdiction; if it was off duty, then the Japanese had primary right. However, whether it was on or off duty was determined by whether the commander of the U.S. armed forces issued a testimonial to that effect.

The 1974 shooting at the Iejima firing range led to a joint U.S.-Japan committee to discuss SOFA-related issues. The Japanese government, however, told the Americans that "they would place first priority on American-Japanese friendship and relinquish their right of jurisdiction."

Mistrust towards both the U.S. armed forces and the Japanese government was strong. People started calling for a complete review of SOFA, not just Article 17. While those on the Japanese mainland had only the vaguest idea of what it meant, for the people of Okinawa it was an affair that provoked misgivings, uneasiness, and apprehension on an everyday basis. For example, the following privileges, preferences, and exemptive measures were all based on SOFA: U.S. military vehicles are exempt from tolls on all toll roads; members of the U.S. armed forces can enter and leave Japan without visa or passport; they can drive without taking a driving test if they possess an American driver's license; U.S. armed forces' imports of daily necessaries are not subject to customs tariffs; business, property, and golf usage taxes are not levied on U.S. armed forces' facilities; damages from accidents occurring in the course of U.S. armed forces duty are partly paid by the Japanese; losses to the fishing industry through the destruction of fishing nets, etc., during U.S. armed forces exercises are compensated by Japan.

There was also a strong backlash over training marches through civilian areas. These especially worried the residents of the communities bordering on the Camp Hansen training area, Kin, and Ginoza. Several hundred U.S. soldiers in full combat dress with small automatic weapons slung across their shoulders would march by. This was permitted under Article 5 of SOFA as "movement between facilities." There was a time when the U.S. armed forces insisted that the "marches" through civilian areas were "training." This was switched to "movement between facilities" when it was counterargued that "if training outside the facilities is permitted, then what's the point of providing all those training areas?"

SOFA was signed in 1960. In the more than 30 years since then, Japanese awareness of human rights had grown, Japan itself had developed into an economic power, and urbanization and conversion of farm lands into residential areas had proceeded apace. Despite that, the Japanese were still forced to accept SOFA's "unequal provisions." Unhappiness was not confined to Okinawa alone. It went beyond political stances and was an affront to the self-respect of the Japanese as a people.

The U.S.-Japan agreement was also attacked for being much more discriminatory than agreements signed with NATO countries. Regarding the delivery of criminals in custody, the SOFA signed between what was then West Germany and NATO (the 1959 Bonn Agreement) stated that "favorable consideration will be given to requests from the German authorities for transfer of custody."

Limits were also put on land usage by stationed troops. "Bearing in mind our shared defense obligations, if there is a clear case of benefit to be gained by use of the land by the German side, the armed forces will respond appropriately to requests to vacate." Why was what was permitted to the Germans not allowed for Japan? The demands started to become more strident, more exacting.

Mark Lambert of the U.S. Embassy in Tokyo was appointed to handle the protest groups that kept turning up on the doorstep. He recalls, "[They were] from all sorts of groups, mainly affiliated either with Okinawa, the teachers' union . . . [or] Christian groups who came through, and we would rotate—there were three of us from the political and military section. We would rotate meetings with them, accept their petitions, having them translated, making sure Ambassador Mondale saw them, and forwarding them to Washington. . . . One thing that has always struck me about Japanese protesters is how polite they are. I had served in Bogotá, Colombia, before Tokyo, and they're not quite as polite there."[7]

When the protest groups were asked what was needed the most right then, they would all say that SOFA needed to be changed. When pressed on which part of SOFA needed to be revised, they were not so clear. It was obvious that they hadn't read it. After a couple of weeks, however, this changed. The Japanese newspapers started running articles comparing in detail Japan's SOFA with that of European countries. The protesters turning up at the embassy started to base their demands on that comparison. If the truth be known, there were not that many experts who could compare the Japanese and European cases with confidence on the American side either.

A little later, demands to reduce or close the bases came to the fore. And then came the demand for the withdrawal of the marines. Lambert said, "I remember one woman, very well spoken, I believe she was with a Christian group, saying we just don't need the marines anymore. Perhaps we needed you during the Korean War, or shortly afterwards, but we don't need you anymore. Asia is at peace. Very soft spoken, very eloquent. . . . But the organized stuff came later. I remember pins, a map of Okinawa that says 'No Base, No Rape.'"[8]

Apology

On September 13, Mondale was back on the job. A thick pile of briefing material from Deputy Chief of Mission Rust Deming awaited him. It detailed developments since the rape. Reading the file in the car, Mondale realized that the political implications were much more serious that he had first thought.[9] One reporter with the *Okinawa Times* had said that the rape case was symbolic as it occurred on the 50th anniversary of the end of the war with the United States.[10]

As soon as he reached the embassy, Mondale told Deming that the incident made him feel sick; it was inexcusable; first we have to make an apology; everything else can wait. Mondale was not slow to move. He started by phoning Yohei Kono, Japan's foreign minister, and met with him on September 21.

During the meeting, Mondale exploded: "It's inhuman. They're just animals." The Foreign Ministry (MOFA) actually briefed the press that Mondale had used that term, "animals."[11] There was no stronger word.

Mondale met with Governor Masahide Ota, who had arrived in Tokyo a little earlier. "Please accept my heartfelt apologies to the victim, her family, and the Okinawan people."[12] Ota accepted the words in the spirit in which they were offered. Responding to Ota's remark that there had been 4,500 criminal incidents involving U.S. servicemen, including 12 murders, since reversion, Mondale bowed his head, saying it had been their intention to do all they could to avoid this kind of occurrence and that he was overwhelmed with shame.[13]

President Clinton also expressed deep regret in a radio address on September 21. He said, "We will not allow any injustice to the Japanese people to be taken so lightly."[14] Campbell and Giarra felt there was a need for action as well as words. They decided to order a "stand-down" of the U.S. troops in Okinawa (i.e., no training and no exercises) and a day of reflection. The idea did not come from the marines or the uniformed services, but mainly from the Office of the Secretary of Defense. On September 27, Perry announced in a press conference in New York following U.S.-Japan "2+2" security talks a stand-down of the marine Third Expeditionary Force in Okinawa for a day of reflection.

The marines resisted. When Consul-General O'Neill had visited Governor Ota at the prefectural offices to apologize, the prefecture had really been looking for an apology from Okinawa marines commander Wayne Rollings. Rollings, however, did not show up. All that did was a single note of apology from the Okinawa marines' press section.

Perry took a very serious view of the situation, saying the incident was so outrageous, a fundamental review had to be made; it was going to be a problem not just in Okinawa or Japan but in the United States as well; something had to be done. Perry asked for improvements in base operations in Okinawa, but the kind of report he got back "was not much more than business as usual."[15]

All it said was that the American military had suggested solutions for the bases many times in the past to the Japanese government, but it was the Japanese who had been unwilling to make the changes, either to put up the money that was necessary or to accept the redeployment to other islands; it was going to be difficult to maintain operational readiness if we made major moves; and so on. "[It] was a very discouraging report. [It] was not acceptable."[16] Perry asked the armed forces to come up with something better.

Right until just before the "2+2", there were sections of the services that were still refusing to cooperate with the stand-down. "There was a fear that they would be manipulated by political forces that were hostile to the alliance."[17]

Before the press conference Perry had boarded a plane bound for New York with Joseph Nye, the assistant secretary of defense. During the flight, he called Admiral Richard Mackey of CINCPAC in Hawaii because he had heard Mackey was opposing the stand-down.[18]

Sending a special envoy to apologize never happened. No one could think of the right person. Jim Auer, former director of the Japan Desk at the Pentagon, suggested that First Lady Hillary Clinton go to Okinawa to "personalize American empathy for the suffering of the victim."[19] The idea was quietly sounded out with the Japanese, who showed no interest.

There was undeniably the possibility of a backlash being triggered in America by "excessive apology." There was also a risk of emotional outbursts along the lines of, "If we have to go to these lengths even though we've been there protecting Japan all along, then let's pull out the troops."

Rapid developments in the situation also made it difficult to determine what sort of apology should be extended. Moreover, any envoy sent ran the risk of not being received by Governor Ota. There was also the assessment that being used in the Okinawan's political game of rejecting a visit was not what the Americans needed.[20]

"Isn't Japan Still an Independent Nation?"

Neither government was eager to revise SOFA. Mondale's meeting with Foreign Minister Kono focused first on this issue. Mondale clearly expressed his opposition to any review. "I understand well the feeling of the Okinawan people, but I can't agree to what's being said." Kono agreed that "it would take at least one or two years to revise SOFA. What's important is resolving this case to Okinawa's satisfaction as quickly as possible."[21]

Kono informed Mondale, however, that the prefectural police were complaining it could not carry out a satisfactory investigation. Mondale looked surprised. "That's strange. That can't be right. Investigate where and when you like around the clock." Kono replied, "Let's set up a forum where the two countries can settle this question of custody properly. And if we don't do it immediately, domestic opinion won't hold."

"All right, I'll make the military agree. And I won't leave this room until they do say 'yes.'" Mondale instructed David Shear, head of the U.S. Embassy's Security Division, who had accompanied him to the meeting, to call U.S. forces in Japan. Shear borrowed the room next door to the foreign minister's office to make the call.[22] (After this episode, the Americans agreed to late-night questioning of the suspects, which helped speed up the evidence-gathering process. The three servicemen were charged by the Naha district attorney on September 29, eight days after the papers had been forwarded from the prefectural police. The three were handed over into Japanese custody the same day.)

Kono had met with Governor Masahide Ota of Okinawa at the Foreign Ministry two days before. Their conversation was curt.

Ota: "The Americans talk about making sure it doesn't happen again, but incidents keep happening. I understand the government stressing the importance of the Security Treaty, but I won't stand for Okinawa taking the brunt."

Kono: "I hear that the investigations are proceeding unhindered. All this talk about revising SOFA is going too far."

On his way back in the car, Ota whispered to himself, "Going too far, you say? You have no other choice!"[23] Okinawa was on the verge of erupting over the Foreign Ministry's obstinate stance on revising SOFA.

It was later widely accepted that that stance had caused the protests to escalate. Kono, however, knew in his own way that they had no other choice.

This incident is certainly outrageous. It's quite right that something has to be done about the bases. But it would be better not to have all of Japan yelling "Get out, American forces." Mightn't we get away with nimbly handling SOFA in terms of content, not principle? If I don't speak up, who will?[24]

Kono felt something close to a sense of mission. When the Murayama Cabinet was formed, Murayama asked Kono to take on either the finance portfolio or foreign affairs. Kono sought the advice of his mentor and former prime minister, Kiichi Miyazawa. In a most un-Miyazawa-like biting turn of phrase, Miyazawa told him that as long as things stood they way they did, he had to take on the job of foreign minister. Kono took Miyazawa's words as a lamentation for the state of U.S.-Japan relations. He set his mind to building a relationship of trust with his U.S. counterpart, Secretary of State Warren Christopher, starting with his diplomatic debut at the Naples Summit in the summer of 1994.

So when the Okinawan rape incident occurred, Kono told himself that it was his job to do his utmost to ensure the bilateral relationship did not suffer. "We'll be all done for if even the foreign minister starts bending to the wind." There was also the question of his dignity as general secretary of the Liberal Democratic Party (LDP).[25]

Prime Minister Tomiichi Murayama refrained from commenting, saying it came under the jurisdiction of the foreign minister. He did not come out for or against a revision of SOFA, but Kono saw through that and knew that, deep down, Murayama would have liked to have seen a revision. But Murayama could never act as a political backstop.

Kono was afraid that there would be a showdown between the United States and Japan over a revision of SOFA, but he was even more afraid, in fact, that if they set off in the direction of reviewing the agreement, it might lead to domestic pressure for a revision of the treaty itself. Here he was in agreement with the MOFA bureaucrats.[26]

Debate had already started on the nature of U.S. troop stationing. Kono believed that the Americans would not leave troops where they weren't welcome; the Philippines showed that. If the Japanese forced a SOFA revision on them, the Americans would think their troops weren't welcome. He was concerned that this would have significant repercussions on the future stationing of troops.

Kono, however, was on his own. At the government level, the Cabinet agreed in its meeting on October 19 not to review SOFA, but things were not so easy at the party level. All three parties in the coalition called for revision. Kono came under heavy fire during a meeting of the coalition party leaders. "What are you going to do if you're that weak-kneed? If they don't want to have the revision, then let the Americans say so! Why do we have to worry about how they feel and drop it without a word? It's unbearable in terms of national sentiment. The government has to be ready to get involved." Kono was showered with tongue lashings by even his LDP colleagues.

Wataru Kubo, general secretary of the Socialists, was particularly severe. "It's just like the Occupation when the agreement prevents the use of Japanese judicial powers. We want to revise SOFA. Why can't the Japanese government say that? All of Okinawa is up in arms calling for a revision. If we knock it back, resolving the bases will only be more difficult. Why can't you see something as simple as that?"[27]

Unusually, Kono became hot under the collar. "Isn't it more important to get the suspects handed over as quickly as possible? That doesn't take a revision of the agreement, just a change in how it's run. Whatever do you think we'll get out of forcing a clash between the two countries on this?[28]

Kubo was worked up too. "That means that the Japanese people will never be able to protect themselves in their own courts from U.S. armed forces' crimes! What on earth will happen to the law?" As general secretary of the Socialist Party, he had to have his full say. The Socialists had consistently called for a revision of the agreement. Their day had come.[29]

Things weren't over yet. Even members of that bastion of pro-treaty support, the LDP's Defense Caucus (chaired by Kudoku Ono), were calling for a revision of SOFA. One of them posed the question: "Is it right for us to keep quiet, even though we've just agreed to increasing host nation support for the American troops in Japan?" He was referring to the decision taken the previous year to increase the so-called compassionate budget.

Finance Minister Masayoshi Takemura, leader of the New Party Sakigake and coalition partner, remarked at a press conference in Taira on Okinawa, "Isn't [Japan] still an independent nation?"[30] Displeasure with the Americans in each party was not easily quashed.

In late October, the matter was finally settled in the form of operational reforms, but this led to a second outburst of indignation. Attending a liaison meeting of coalition party leaders at the Hotel New Ohtani on the evening of November 2, Kono was emotionally drained and physically exhausted. Dinner was already over. Kono, who had come late, tried to eat his meal, but he was so inundated with questions that he couldn't get a bite in. His stand-in until he arrived, Vice-Minister for Foreign Affairs Sadayuki Hayashi, "was being attacked like a punching bag."[31]

Once again, Kubo attacked Kono and the Foreign Ministry. It was Ryutaro Hashimoto, who arrived halfway through, who put an end to the increasingly vitriolic exchange. He had been listening to the two argue with a frown on his face, when he suddenly broke in smiling.

"I've been mediated many times before, but I've never mediated myself. It's not my style, but I'll mediate for you today. I understand Kubo-san's point. But in this case, I think what Kono-san is saying is more correct."[32]

Hashimoto had just taken over the LDP leadership a month earlier. That night he played mediator as the general secretary of the LDP. He clearly sensed that his day was coming.

The U.S. government did not change its firm opposition to a revision of SOFA one iota. Nye was firm on this. "We will not touch one letter of the text. We will deal with it as a question of Article 17 interpretation and implementation."

Nye insisted that they not open what could be a Pandora's box. "The Japanese SOFA itself is probably the best from the point of view of the host nation of any SOFAs we have. . . . We hand over to Japan more than two-thirds of the cases and in Germany it has been one-tenth of one percent, and in the last year, not at all. . . . We think Japan will provide a fair trial." Nye repeated that the existing SOFA was not disadvantageous to Japan. He said revising SOFA "raises the prospect [that] all the bureaucrats and lawyers will start tinkering with everything."[33]

"Don't open Pandora's box" subsequently became the slogan of the State Department and the Foreign Ministry. There was also strong opposition to a revision from the military in the field. It was only natural to afford certain privileges and prerogatives to young people serving in far-off lands who never knew when they would be sent off to fight or die in the pursuit of duty. The military also had doubts about how much respect foreign legal authorities would pay to the human rights of U.S. servicemen.

Another issue was the question of balance with other countries. If the United States reviewed Japan's SOFA, then they would have to review the others. They were especially nervous about the implications for Korea, because the Koreans had already been voicing dissatisfaction with their own SOFA. They had called more than once for a revision, claiming it was much more disadvantageous than the Japanese SOFA. Politicians in the National Assembly in Seoul were unanimous on this point regardless of their party affiliations. The Korean government had to be seen as being tough on the issue. The United States therefore had to tread carefully with South Korea. It did not want to upset U.S.-Korean relations in the face of the North Korean threat.

When visiting Washington in the spring of the following year, Gong Ro-Myung, Korea's foreign minister, devoted almost all of his meeting with Defense Secretary Perry to the SOFA question. Perry, who had been expecting a discussion on North Korea, was amazed. He expressed his reluctance to take up the issue, and no progress was made on that occasion. It was a good illustration of Korean tenacity on the issue.

Someone high up in the U.S. government remarked that "there is great confidence in the Japanese judicial system. Frankly, in Korea this would have been very difficult."[34] Nevertheless, there was no guarantee that this American distrust of Asian human rights and democracy was not also directed towards Japan. Rather, the Okinawan people felt that it still existed, as did some politicians in the central government.

Action

Objections voiced in the protests in Okinawa quickly gained widespread support throughout Japan. Both governments were slow to catch on to this. Seishiro Eto, former Japanese Defense Agency (JDA) director-general, later confessed, "To be honest, I did not expect things to get so big. I didn't think it would go as far as the bases."[35] A senior official in the U.S. forces who was working in Japan at the time said, "Both sides were slow to realize the political implications. And the Socialists and Governor Ota were very quick to realize the political implications. . . . Governor Ota [could] trot out and say . . . you don't have [license plates] on the vehicles on Okinawa . . . relating that to this criminal activity. . . . The Socialist Party across the board was all but dead. . . . The Okinawa prefectural government by itself revived [it] and the Socialist causes."[36]

Both governments seemed to think they could deal with the issue on a SOFA implementation level. But as protest action by the Okinawan people flared up and the LDP's own Research Commission on Security was saying the treaty would be placed at risk if things were left as is, there was a growing consensus that a comprehensive approach to the bases was required. At the same time, the brunt of the criticism was being directed at the Foreign Ministry and the JDA, because they were viewed as the two bureaucracies who had opposed the SOFA review.

A Foreign Ministry official has attested that Kono was not swayed. Kono firmly believed in keeping SOFA and acted accordingly. Moreover, if SOFA was revised, it would be a matter for the Treaties Bureau, which was well known for its very conservative stance.[37]

In the JDA, however, there were those who saw the risks. Masahiro Akiyama, director-general of the Defense Bureau, and Takemasa Moriya, then director of the Defense Policy division, among others, shared a deepening apprehension that the bilateral security structure could well be scuttled from below if something wasn't done about the Okinawa bases. They thought the issue also had grave implications for the proxy signing over of land use that Governor Ota had refused. They were concerned that the Murayama government, egged on by the Socialists, might well ruin the security relationship.

Moriya criticized the lack of concern about Okinawa in the central bureaucracy. He said, "What would you do if U.S. troops marched right through the middle of Kasumigaseki in full combat dress? That happens every day on Okinawa!"[38] Akiyama believed there was a need to work jointly with the Pentagon on a new initiative. In the manner that Hatakeyama had met with Assistant Secretary of Defense Joseph Nye the previous year and set the Nye Initiative in motion, Akiyama's assessment was that both defense authorities had to work together once more. He decided to place a direct call to Nye.

Akiyama was impressed with Nye's long-term strategic vision and the fact that "Dr. Nye's English was easy to understand because he explained things like he was speaking to his students."[39] In mid-October, in the middle of the night Japan time, he called Nye to the phone.

"I'm just on my way to the White House. I'm having lunch with the president and some other people." Nye's tone was bright. Akiyama told Nye that the situation in Okinawa was very volatile; that he was very worried. Nye said he would hurry the review of SOFA implementation along in an effort to quiet things down that way.

"That won't be nearly enough. Governor Ota is out on full offensive. It's already escalated into how to get the bases back. So we need to set up some sort of joint commission on returning the bases."

A mass meeting on Okinawa was scheduled for October 21. "Wouldn't an announcement of an implementation review quiet things down?"

"No, in fact, I'd rather have you announce it later."[40]

Akiyama was concerned that in the present antibase mood any announcement of a token SOFA review would add fuel to the fire. In the end, the implementation review of SOFA was decided on in a U.S.-Japan meeting in Tokyo on October 25. It was agreed that in the case of violent crimes such as murder and rape, "the United States will consider favorably any request for the transfer of suspects into Japanese custody before charging."

The focus now shifted to the bases. Nye at first seemed hesitant about taking up the base question. That was partly why Akiyama suddenly decided to dispatch his counselor, Katsuei Hirasawa, to Washington. The aim was to tell the Americans just how urgent things were in Japan and to ascertain the Pentagon's real feelings.

Hirasawa reported back on his meeting with Kurt Campbell, deputy assistant secretary of defense. "They're taking it seriously. I get the feeling that they realize that just a SOFA implementation review won't do the trick; that they'll have to tackle the bases as well. The problem is the State Department and our Foreign Ministry."[41]

After consulting internally about a new forum to discuss the bases, Nye had a draft proposal drawn up and passed it on to Perry. Perry had some requests. "First of all, it designated a bilateral group, Japanese, American, civilian, and military, to work on the problem. Secondly, what they were charged to come up with was not an analysis but an action plan. . . . And third, it had to have a deadline."[42]

Perry's insistence on calling the group an Action Committee squared with Akiyama's intention. He also thought a deadline was required. Without it, he believed that the S in SACO (Special Action Committee on Okinawa) would come to mean "Stalling."

For the past two years Perry had been ordering the armed forces to make improvements in the base situation on Okinawa but to no avail. He remembers, "Every time we would meet with the Defense Ministry [*sic*], either here or in Tokyo, and we had specific proposals for changes to be made, the resistance, on the one hand, of our military forces, whose responsibility is maintaining operational readiness, and on the other hand, the Japanese government, who was resisting the idea of making very considerable expenses, frustrated every proposal that came along. And so, the rape incident was just outrageous enough that it was the catalyst; it caused people to sort of rise above the detailed arguing that they had had, and say, 'Let's rise above that and find a way to finally solve this.'"[43]

The establishment of SACO was officially announced in November 1995 by Prime Minister Murayama and Vice President Al Gore, standing in for President Clinton. It was positioned under the bilateral foreign policy and defense ministers' Security Committee (2+2) and its brief was to examine not only the realignment and reduction of the U.S. bases, but SOFA as well. For the time being, SACO would work vigorously on the question of conditions for returning the bases that the Japanese had been requesting since 1990, and expanding the scope of facilities to be returned.

SACO was not welcomed by everyone, however. There were those in the Foreign Ministry who were lukewarm about the idea, saying they already had a forum for discussing the base problems, so what was the point of gilding the cage? The Foreign Ministry had been afraid from the very first that SOFA would be transmuted into the bases. The reason why Kono "sweated blood, enough to make him want to quit,"[44] was because he believed he had to try to stop it at the water's edge before it escalated into an issue of the bases, of U.S. troop stationing, of the bilateral security structure. He was at a loss somewhat because SACO was doing nothing but taking up the very question of the bases.

Many high-ranking officials at the Defense Agency were wary. The "realignment-consolidation-reduction" slogan sounded good, but it was their job to actually go out there and convince the landowners. It would be difficult enough finding relocation sites. The three items already decided on were not making any headway. They would be less than happy to have a further list thrust in front of them.

The JDA had no rights or say in SOFA. It came completely under the jurisdiction of the Foreign Ministry. Hirasawa was the first of many who criticized MOFA about SOFA, saying, "You couldn't tell which side they were on by what they were saying."[45] Hirasawa and others resented the fact that "MOFA tried to wrap everything up" in the SOFA implementation review on October 25. The truth of the matter was, however, that the JDA was also playing catch-up, responding to developments rather than creating them. There were those within the agency who argued that the bases were, after all, a matter for the Foreign Ministry and the Defense Facilities Administration Agency, so the JDA shouldn't get itself involved.

Looking back, a high-ranking official at the Defense Department remembered thinking that the JDA was not positive about resolving the base issue. Its main concern was whether SACO would go further than revising the implementation of SOFA and escalate into demanding a reduction of the bases or of the U.S. armed forces' presence.[46]

In all-important Okinawa, people were also very cool in a sort of show-us-what-you've-got stance. Even at the first meeting between Prime Minister Murayama and Governor Ota, which took place at the beginning of February 1995, Vice-Governor Masanori Yoshimoto, also present, spoke out. He remarked: "I suppose it's better than nothing." Deputy Cabinet Secretary Hiroyuki Sonoda was riled at this and countered, "I won't stand for being told something like it's better than nothing!"

Sonoda recollects that "the Foreign Ministry was initially not so interested, nor were the Americans. But there was no way the Okinawans were going to be satisfied if it didn't look like something was going to be done about it and fast. If only because we had tried to make an exception, I wanted to tell him [Yoshimoto] that he'd gone too far. After all, old Murayama couldn't say it."[47]

The agreement to "realign-consolidate-reduce" the bases had also been made out of consideration for Okinawa. It was a point that Seishiro Eto, JDA director-general, had insisted upon. Up until then, the government was for realignment and reduction. Okinawa was for consolidation and reduction. Eto also suggested no change to the overall U.S. troop strength, however.[48]

The joint press release by Eto and Defense Secretary Perry, who visited Japan in November 1995, added "reduction" to create "realignment, consolidation, and reduction." It also stressed at the same time that U.S. troop strength in the Asian-Pacific region would remain at 100,000 with 47,000 in Japan. This was the only time that the Japanese figure of 47,000 was unambiguously stated. It was a declaration of the two leaders' intention to make it clear that a "reduction in the bases" did not mean a "reduction in troop strength."

However, the base issue did not end with SOFA and "realignment, consolidation, and reduction." The fact was that the basis for providing the U.S. armed forces with the bases themselves, the very foundation of the bilateral security structure, and the land itself, were starting to shake.

The Elephant's Cage

The Sobe Communications Site in Yomitan, which usually went by the name of the Elephant's Cage, suddenly pops up out of the cane fields. One of a number of U.S. navy communications facilities watching nuclear submarine and warship movements, its job is listening in to coded transmissions from military facilities in neighboring countries. Few people are there, just a huge cylindrical shape swallowing the beams of the Okinawan sun.

Inside the perimeter is a small piece of privately owned land, some 236 meters square, stuck in the throats of both governments because its owner, Shoichi Chibana, has refused to renew the lease.

At zero hundred hours on April 1, 1996, the government's lease on the land expired. The lonely rebellion of Shoichi Chibana put the U.S. armed forces in the position of "illegal occupation." It was an action fraught with political overtones, making the U.S. armed forces no longer a guest but a trespasser, and the Japanese government its accomplice.

Behind the protests against the bases, which had exploded following the Okinawan schoolgirl rape, was another battle over land. It reverberated deep and low like a Ryukyu drum in an organ point of base politics and base diplomacy. The bases were a blend of problems. There were the U.S. servicemen's crimes and the accidents; the public morals question; the human rights and environmental issues. Finally, the bases were to get the attention they deserved by being linked to the question of peace, put forward in the form of an antibase struggle. Yet the most knotty issue remained the land.

Many of the sites had been confiscated by the U.S. armed forces immediately after the war. Some of them were also later incorporated into the bases during the Korean War by "rifles and bulldozers." The grudge against the bases was also a grudge about land. The land for bases had been a precious source of income for poor Okinawa. The land payments all had to be paid by the Japanese government. Okinawa became a classic land payments economy, giving birth in the process to rigid vested interests between the Defense Facilities Administration Agency and the landowners.

The Japanese government was obliged to guarantee unhindered use for the U.S. armed forces. In order to do so, the government enacted a law (the Special Measures Act on Expropriation of Land for U.S. Military Use) that stipulated procedures for enforced use of land belonging to landowners opposed to providing military sites. The law required the prefecture to sign as proxy the necessary arbitration forms for enforced land use known as "public notice and inspection." As has already been mentioned, Ota refused to sign in September 1995.

Ota was not prompted to make that decision by the rape of the Okinawan schoolgirl. According to him, the catalyst for the decision was his shock upon reading the *East Asia Strategy Report,* the so-called Nye Report, released by the Pentagon the previous February. He remembers starting to believe when the Nye Report came out that it was all over; there was nothing for it but to have the government rethink the proxy-signing situation.

The report smacked of browbeating, complete with its figure of 100,000 U.S. troops in the Asian-Pacific region, as if trying to clamp down on Okinawa's demands for realignment and reduction of the bases. The rape in September definitely acted as a trigger for the ensuing antibase protests in Okinawa. It is also certain that it made Ota's refusal to sign the public notice and inspection papers inevitable. Nor is there any room for doubt that his refusal was an indictment of the government's lack of sincerity up until that time.

In his first meeting with Murayama in November 1995, Ota vented his mistrust of the central government by saying, "I signed as proxy five years ago (1990) on the condition that an improvement would be made on the bases. Despite that, there has been virtually no progress on realignment or reduction."[49] He discussed the question of the bases in relation to the nature of a new, post–Cold War security framework in the Asian-Pacific region. He had a notion that a solution for the bases could be found in a more flexible U.S. troop structure in the area. If U.S. troop strength was fixed at 100,000, then that approach would no longer be open to him. That is why he reacted so sensitively to the Nye Report.[50]

The only card left to Ota was to refuse the proxy signing, and it was a powerful one. By refusing to sign, thereby placing the U.S. armed forces in the position of unlawful occupation, he markedly weakened the Japanese government's bargaining power with the United States. This was central government's Achilles' heel in dealing with the bases.

On April 1, when the site entered a legal vacuum, Cabinet Secretary Seiroku Kajiyama announced the government's position that "it couldn't immediately be called a violation." While the government could have claimed under civil law the right to manage a site with an expired lease, it decided it would be impossible to defend that right given the landowner's clear intention to fight for a return to its lawful owner. The problem was that if that happened, the government would no longer be able to say that continued use by the U.S. armed forces was in keeping with the law. It would also mean that entry to the site by the lawful owner "couldn't immediately be called a violation."[51]

What about the U.S. forces? Article 3 of the Japan-U.S. SOFA stipulated U.S. administrative rights in the following terms: "Within the facilities and areas, the United States may take all the measures necessary for their establishment, operation, safeguarding and control." Therefore, the Japanese government judged that "the U.S. armed forces, which have the right of administration, can prevent entry into sites at their own discretion."

In other words, if the United States was going to administer the sites by itself, it should feel free to prevent entry, and if it did so, well, that was a matter for its own judgment. However, since the Japanese government was unable to claim right of administration, it was not in a position to refuse anything. If the United States refused entry but the lawful owner forced entry anyway, then it would be possible to apply SOFA's special criminal measures and/or Japanese criminal law (breaking and entering, interference with a government official in the execution of his duties).

Or to paraphrase more freely, Japan did not know what to do, having rented a cottage as a "host" from a different landlord to put up a "guest," when the landlord decided to force entry into the cottage. It was tantamount to saying to the guest, if you prevent the landlord's entry and you want us to call the police, we'll telephone. In short, it's all up to you.

On May 11, 1996, the Okinawa Prefectural Committee on Expropriation (a seven-person committee chaired by Kenji Miki) decided not to permit the six-month emergency extension that the Naha Bureau of the Defense Facilities Administration Agency had applied for. It rejected the government's case completely, saying, "The government failed to explain adequately the urgency and obstacles which would pertain if the site could not be used." The matter was reconciled by a provisional ruling from the Naha District Court, where Shoichi Chibana had filed suit against the government to allow him entry to the site.

On May 14, Shoichi Chibana and his family and supporters entered the base. For some two hours he was able finally to set foot, and barefoot at that, on his land. Chibana, his wife, his children, and singer Shokichi Kina sat in a circle, played the banjolike *sanshin*, sang, danced, and drank. Their first tune was a song of celebration in the Kagiyade style. "How to express the happiness of this day. The dew is falling on the flowers' buds, which look ready to blossom at any moment." There were five playing the *sanshin*, including Chibana.

After the war, there were no pythons or water buffalo left. People made "rattle sanshin" from empty cans and parachute string. Life couldn't go on without the *sanshin*.

The voices grew livelier. Kina sang his best-known song, "Hana" ("A Flower in Every Heart"), and everyone clapped in time. They then went over to part of the "remains of the house" and prayed to the spirits of their ancestors, sprinkling offerings of the local *awamori* brandy all over.

When Chibana was a child, the site had been a vegetable plot. He remembers playing there. He had never been there since. The government pays 676 yen per day for the use of the site, which the Defense Facilities Administration Agency sends annually in a lump sum. Since filing suit against the government for the return of the land, Chibana has not accepted the payments.

Upon entering the Elephant's Cage, Chibana had removed his shoes as if to make sure he was really on his land. The U.S. servicemen inside the cage stared on from a distance as if looking at some strange beast.[52]

Cabinet Secretary Kajiyama had now changed his tune to "we can no longer say that it can't immediately be called a violation." There was the possibility that the unlawful occupation might turn out to be long term. Kajiyama's statement was taken to mean that the government was considering new legislation.

One year later, on May 14, 1997, leases with 3,000 landowners for 12 bases, including Kadena, were due to expire. Look at what was happening with just one landowner, Shoichi Chibana; the government wouldn't stand a chance if 3,000 did the same! The sense of crisis was acute.

The land question, the question of forced usage, rumbled on all through 1996. The piece of theater called SACO was still being played on stage, but behind the scenes a struggle was being fought with an eye to May 14. The government made many approaches to the prefecture. The discussion between Hashimoto and Ota in June 1996 showed just how alarmed the government was. Hashimoto asked Ota if he couldn't hurry along the Okinawa Prefectural Committee on Expropriation's decision. Hashimoto said, almost as if to himself, "The question is whether there isn't something the governor can do." Ota responded that the committee was an independent institution, no one should intervene in it, this was a time for caution. Conversely he made a request of Hashimoto: "I want you to avoid at all costs any law that applies only to Okinawa, any sort of law that could be interpreted as discriminatory." Hashimoto responded that he understood the prefecture's requests, but he pressed Ota once again for action. "Isn't there something that can be done to speed up the Expropriation Committee?"[53]

It was about this time that attacks on the top members of the prefectural government by the PM's office started to escalate. Ota and Yoshimoto both toughed it out, however, flatly refusing to interfere with the committee's workings.

National feeling towards the bases were also becoming problematical. Why was some of small Japan's prime real estate encircled by huge

U.S. military fences? You didn't have to live in Kadena or Yokota to wonder about this. At the same time, the bases were increasingly regarded as a new outpost of prosperous Japan. This image was underpinned by the discontent and uneasiness of Japanese citizens about an economic superpower in which the state might be well off but the people remained poor. The base was increasingly being approached in terms of human rights, the environment, women's issues, urban development, regional government autonomy. . . . This was accompanied by the budding of a new school of thought on political power. Antibase sentiment, buttressed by pacifism and nationalism, remained strong.

Kajiyama had at one time spoken his real thoughts on the question of the bases. "We let something build up for 50 years and turned it into a monster."[54] Part of the central problem was the government's failure to devise a policy for coping with the bases. The real problem was that the government had not come up with any solution.

The bureaucrats in charge of the base issue were often overcome by a feeling of ineffectualness. One of the Foreign Ministry officials involved in the whole SACO process confessed, "I believed that the hardest part of maintaining the bilateral security structure was, in the end, the bases. It's completely my own personal opinion, but a large part of the problem was Japan's failure to do something about land issues.

"Because, you take Yokota or Atsugi. After the war they were all just paddies or vegetable plots, so bases weren't a problem. If we had had proper land policies in place then, and had built parks or golf courses around them, the problem wouldn't be so acute. As the local population increased, the bases should have been moved in a planned fashion to depopulated areas.

"But Japan couldn't do that. They still only have one runway at Narita Airport. The metropolitan freeway has only two lanes. Even the Tomei freeway [linking Tokyo and Nagoya] has only three. And all because of the same problem. They have trouble with bases in Germany too, but they can be dealt with within the realm of the bases. In Japan, though, the question of the bases immediately becomes an issue about the whole security thing."[55]

Point of Intolerance

The U.S. government was watching with some apprehension the changes in the Japanese political scene. Americans were concerned that the introduction of the single-representative electoral system would strengthen the antibase drive. Nye's predecessor, Assistant Secretary of Defense Charles Freeman, had warned when he was still in that post that "the change to a single-representative electoral system will strengthen the hand of the governor. The central government's voice on the bases and its voice towards the governor is likely to weaken. It will be more difficult from now on to maintain the status quo on the bases." Freeman had discussed this matter with Ambassador Mondale in Tokyo but "didn't have any bright ideas on what should be done."[56]

When Nye moved to consolidate security ties between America and Japan, Ezra Vogel, senior analyst with the National Intelligence Council (NIC), among others, concurred with Freeman's analysis and spoke of the importance of Nye's endeavor.[57] The question of the bases, however, slipped right out of the Nye Initiative. A member of the Pentagon revealed that this was largely due to the Foreign Ministry's "skepticism on the initiative being the right place to discuss the bases. The Foreign Ministry being negative automatically made the State Department negative."[58]

There were also those in the U.S. government who, in a cross between analysis and conjecture, saw the Foreign Ministry's negativism stemming from the fact that the bases were Japan's largest bargaining chip in bilateral security discussions.

The single greatest hurdle, however, was that having clearly stated a troop strength of 100,000 in the Nye Report, Nye himself was reluctant to pursue at the same time a reduction in bases that might lower that figure. He wanted to reassure Japan that U.S. force levels would remain constant.

In fact, it is not as if both governments had never discussed the bases. When Prime Minister Murayama visited Washington in January 1995, Clinton himself raised the "three Okinawan issues" and showed his desire to resolve the situation, saying he had instructed Ambassador Mondale to that effect. The three issues he was referring to were the return of Naha Port, an end to the parachute drop exercises at Yomitan Auxiliary Airfield and the return of the same facility, and an end to the live artillery firing exercises over Prefectural Highway 104. These had been requested of Defense Secretary Perry by Kazuo Aichi, JDA director-general, in April of the preceding year and been placed on the bilateral talks agenda.

Very little headway was made until the abduction and rape of the Okinawan schoolgirl. Everyone spoke of the radical changes in the international situation following the end of the Cold War and expounded the need for injecting new meaning into the alliance. Nye was convinced of the urgency from that point of view and took the lead. Virtually no one, however, showed the way in preparing or finding remedies for the impact that the upheavals in domestic politics in both countries would have on the alliance.

An exception was a closed session held in San Francisco in spring 1995 by a joint group of government and private-sector security experts cosponsored by the Pacific Forum and the Japan Institute of International Affairs (JIIA). The group released an appeal on the need to deal seriously with Okinawan issues. In its report, the forum warned that "for both its conservatives and hawks, Japan's compassionate budget had reached a point of intolerance."[57] It argued further that "in order to win the support of the Japanese public, interest had to be shown in the bases, including a reduction in the bases on Okinawa."[60]

SACO was meant precisely to be a mechanism for responding to that issue. It was the price both sides had to pay for their dilatory dealing with the bases. The Japanese first put the ball in the Americans' court by conveying the demands from Okinawa, then the Americans hit it right back by demanding the Japanese come up with relocation sites on the Japanese mainland in exchange for realigning or reducing the bases in Okinawa. What had been clearly missing from the debate up until then was a joint U.S.-Japan discussion on the mission and role of the U.S. forces' bases in Okinawa in the post–Cold War era. To begin with, what was the objective of the Marine Third Expeditionary Force, which was stationed in Okinawa? In order to fulfill that objective, where did it need bases and how many? SACO was the first venue for dialogue about those kinds of operational requirements.

U.S. participants in SACO came from the State Department, the Defense Department, the Joint Chiefs of Staff, the Pacific forces, and the high command of the U.S. forces in Japan. A senior official with the Foreign Ministry, who had worked for a reduction in bases on the 20th anniversary of Okinawa's reversion to Japan, pointed out, "If you compare the realignment-consolidation-reduction process at the time with SACO's, the U.S. forces in Japan were everything then, but this time it was the Pentagon calling the shots. That was the decisive difference."[61]

The U.S.-Japan Security Consultation Committee (SCC) upgraded its U.S. members in 1990 from the U.S. ambassador in Japan and the commander of the Pacific forces to the secretaries of state and defense (the Japanese members were the foreign minister and the director-general of the JDA), but these top members were very rarely all in attendance at the same time.

The debate had also matured. Takemasa Moriya, counselor for the Defense Bureau and a key SACO member, remarked, "The discussion was much more sophisticated than before. With Futenma, for instance, we got right into its operational aspects and how the U.S. forces would use it in a contingency. Each individual function of the base was critically examined, then calculated back. It's an oversimplification, but before that we used to just say we'll let you use the bases, so go right ahead and do what you want. This was a significant change."[62]

The Okinawa rape had the effect of turning a bilateral security dialogue that had largely been an intellectual exercise into a joint security matter. Through the rape incident, the issues of security and the bases finally received the attention they deserved in the White House, especially at the presidential level. Andrew Bennett, who had been involved with Nye in writing the Nye Report, recalled that "of course the terrible incident in Okinawa raised a lot of problems for the relationship. On the other hand, you could look at it and say how much better we were able to weather the crisis because we had put so much time into the relationship. What would have happened if we hadn't been building for a year on the EASR report, Joe's trips and all the rest, then it really would have been a serious crisis."[63]

Nye himself said, "We learned about thinking ahead from that tragic incident. It forced us to think ahead about the possibility of Korean unification and its implications for Okinawa's force structure and possible force reduction."[64] A high official in the Foreign Ministry disclosed an even stronger impression. "The Nye Initiative was in the right direction and had good intentions. But it still didn't drive at the hardcore issues until the incident. That confronted us with more basic problems. It made the Americans sit up and realize that things could go dreadfully wrong and gave more scope and depth to the discussions."[65]

The Alarm

And still, rather than solving the problem, SACO ended up placing where the problem lay into sharp relief. Sterile bureaucratic government, which undermined the Japanese policymaking process, also interfered with the Cabinet tackling this issue head on. Insisting that the bases were a matter for SOFA, the Foreign Ministry did not want the JDA to become involved. It saw the issue as coming under its own jurisdiction and that of the Defense Facilities Administration Agency. Former JDA Chief Noboru Hoshuyama, criticized this stance. "The Japanese government had no conception of asking for a return. All they're concerned with is how to manage them. Asking for the bases back should be the job of the Foreign Ministry, but they don't do it. But the minute the defense agency says, well, if you're not going to we will, they act like their authority has been violated."[66]

On the contrary, the Foreign Ministry felt the fact that the JDA's Defense Bureau, which was not well informed on the bases, had come to the forefront lay behind unnecessary tensions such as the "battle to the death" over the consolidation of Kadena. "In the SACO process, it was not the Defense Facilities Administration Agency, which had always been involved in the base question, but the JDA proper's Defense Bureau. It was a different process from before. But the Defense Bureau is not directly involved in handling the base question and never has been."[67]

The Foreign Ministry thought that there was "dead ground" there. From the JDA's viewpoint, however, a critical problem was that discussion based on operational functions had been left up in the air because the Foreign Ministry and the Defense Facilities Administration Agency had been handling the base question since Okinawa's reversion. Even if Okinawa called for realignment or reduction of the bases, those agencies were unable to assess the operational functions and incorporate them into demands of the United States as a realistic proposal. They were unhappy that "they talk about an alliance, but Japan knows nothing about the functions or running of the U.S. forces' bases and America has never told us." The JDA deemed SACO to be a very important step forward in that regard.[68]

The director-general of the Defense Bureau and the chairman of the Joint Staff Council became official members of SACO. This meant that the director-general of the Defense Bureau and the head of the Joint Staff Council's Secretariat were also included in the official members of the joint U.S-Japan committee. This raised the JDA's say on the bases.

In the eyes of the JDA, the Foreign Ministry was incapable of coming up with any alternative proposals for, say, a relocation for Futenma; it merely could criticize or act as the Americans' messenger boy. SACO was an opportunity to amend the existing relationship between the Foreign Ministry and the JDA.

The existing division of duties was maintained. The Foreign Ministry remained the main government body in charge of security policy because it presided over the Japan-U.S. Security Treaty and SOFA, and the JDA was left in charge of defense policy. Since the bases, force structure, and the international environment all had to be tabled in SACO, however, it was a chance for the two institutions to create a new, cooperative relationship. That did not happen, however.

Beginning with the Foreign Ministry, there were voices in the central government that said, "The trouble was that from first to last [Okinawa Prefecture] couldn't make up its mind on anything. That was our biggest miscalculation."[69] Futenma's relocation was a graphic illustration. A high-ranking official at the Foreign Ministry disclosed that the single, greatest problem about SACO was Governor Ota's politics. "The prefecture was opposed to relocation and stayed aloof from the issue all the way along. It also came in angling for a cutback in the marines."[70]

Top officials of the Foreign Ministry criticized the prefecture for trying to make a political issue out of the bases by holding the public notice and inspection process hostage. "Sobe Communications Site was not included in the first phase of the prefecture's action program, and yet they refused the [public notice and inspection] proxy signing. What else were we meant to think but they were harassing us?"[71]

Criticism of Ota in some American circles was even more biting. "Ota betrayed. . . . The DOD owes him nothing. . . . Ota left SACO hanging, he backed away. . . . He just used it and didn't follow through on any commitments. . . . Ota had a chance, and he blew it," said one senior analyst close to the Pentagon Japan Desk.[72]

And yet, it was none other than Ota who had sounded the alarm and who did not flatly reject SACO out of hand, although he was opposed to relocating the bases within Okinawa. His stubborn stance had to have been a trump card for the Japanese when negotiating with the United States.

SACO was a discussion and decision process to get things moving on the bases, transcending the routine that had existed up until then. As Perry indicated, it was an attempt to confine the process to bilateral action between the United States and Japan, and to avoid as much as possible getting into the SOFA domain, which would require "consideration of other countries." Perry had even thought of "numerical targets" on reductions. Moreover, the JDA was included in the process from the outset. There was the hope that this would help the DFAA overcome its "professional negativism," which, if all went well, could be used to pressure the U.S. military. By using the agency's expertise, SACO might have been able to come up with counterassessments of the "operational specifications" claimed by the U.S. military.

SACO also exerted a subtle influence on relations between the Japanese government and Okinawa prefecture. Because it was premised on the return of the bases, it undermined, in a certain sense, the position of the traditional base supporters. The base lobby's conviction was that with the collapse of the Soviet Union, there was no choice but to amend the "northern" orientation of the security structure "accompanied by an increase in the geopolitical weight of the Okinawan bases."[73] That assessment remained the same even after the Okinawan rape incident. Tsutomu Kawara, chairman of the LDP Research Commission on Security, commented that "the loudest voices were saying that in order to establish trust in bilateral security ties, they should have been thinking in a context of the bases staying rather than clamoring for their return."[74]

When Taro Nakayama, member of the Diet's lower house and of the LDP's Research Commission on Foreign Policy, visited the United States to request the return of the bases from the Americans, he was sharply rebuked by Seishiro Eto, former JDA director-general. "I'd prefer it if he didn't go around flippantly mentioning 'return,' 'return.' I mean, that'd be a denial of the U.S. 100,000 presence, wouldn't it? He should get a better grip on the international conditions surrounding Japan before he opens his mouth."[75]

However, the lobby's position weakened when the decision was taken to return Futenma, symbol of the U.S. presence. The logic that "lightening the burden of the bases would serve to maintain the security relationship" ended up beating the logic that "maintaining the base presence was the secret to maintaining the security relationship." As a natural result, the pro-security lobby hedged after that, deciding to get some insurance.

Viewed from Ota's line of "consolidation and/or reductions" of Okinawan bases, the line of resistance on the mainland softened. In the spring of 1997, when everyone on the mainland was calling for cuts in marine strength, it looked for a moment like a frontal breakthrough might be made. On the other hand, SACO had the magnetism to pull Okinawa into the process of return as a direct and responsible party. As it became clearer that the returns were basically in the same direction as the consolidation and reduction called for by the prefecture, Okinawa distanced itself from SACO, trying to stand outside in an effort to avoid its thrall. However, Perry at least envisioned involving Okinawa as a responsible player. That was one of the reasons why he brushed off Hashimoto's and Mondale's attempts to prevent him from meeting with Ota.

Or perhaps that was precisely why Ota and Yoshimoto felt wary of SACO from the outset. They were afraid of becoming embroiled.

Notes

1. Interviews with Walter Mondale and Rust Deming.

2. "Okinawa Rape Case Spurs Revision of Base Accords," *Asahi News Service*, September 20, 1995.

3. Interview with Paul Giarra.

4. "Rage: Rape Case by U.S. Servicemen," *Okinawa Times*, September 15, 1995. (In Japanese.)

5. Interview with Suzuyo Takazato.

6. The Girard case took place on January 30, 1957, just before the start of the Kishi administration, in Gunma Prefecture. Specialist Third Class soldier William Girard, who was on guard at a U.S. military firing range in Somagahara, grew annoyed at impoverished Japanese "brass-pickers" who were scavenging nearby for empty shell casings that they might sell for scrap. After having tossed out a few empty shell cases to lure the brass-pickers, he suddenly fired an empty shell case from his rifle-grenade launcher towards the people, killing a woman named Naka Sakai. The case rocked the foundations of U.S.-Japan bilateral ties and caused an intense confrontation between the two nations. Girard eventually went to trial at the Maebashi District Court in the prefecture, was found guilty, and was sentenced in November 1957 to three years in prison. He was suspended for four years and went back to the United States in December 1957. See Akihiko Tanaka, *Security: Attempts during the Fifty Years since the War*, p. 170.

7. Interview with Mark Lambert.

8. Ibid.

9. Interview with Walter Mondale.

10. "Okinawans' Anger Mounts Ahead of New Japan-U.S. Base Accord," *Agence France Presse,* September 27, 1995.

11. *Los Angeles Times,* October 28, 1995, p. 1.

12. "Mondale Apologizes to Okinawa Governor over Rape Case," *Mainichi Daily News,* September 20, 1995, p. 1.

13. Interview with Masahide Ota.

14. "Clinton Offers Apology in Girl's Rape," *Associated Press,* September 22, 1995.

15. Interview with William Perry.

16. Ibid.

17. Interview with Rust Deming.

18. Interview with a DOD official.

19. James Auer, "Crisis over the Okinawa Rape: A High Level Visit Might Help," *Japan Digest Forum,* October 12, 1995.

20. Interview with Paul Giarra.

21. Interview with Yohei Kono.

22. Interview with Walter Mondale.

23. Interview with Masahide Ota.

24. Interview with Yohei Kono.

25. Ibid.

26. Ibid.

27. Interview with Wataru Kubo.

28. Interview with Yohei Kono.

29. Interview with Wataru Kubo.

30. *Asahi Shimbun,* September 24, 1995.

31. Interview with Yohei Kono.

32. Interviews with Yohei Kono and Wataru Kubo.

33. Interview with Joseph Nye.

34. Interview with a senior U.S. administration official.

35. Interview with Seishiro Eto.

36. Interview with a senior White House official.

37. Interview with Tadamichi Yamamoto.

38. Interview with Takemasa Moriya.

39. Interview with Masahiro Akiyama.

40. Ibid.

41. Interview with Katsuei Hirasawa.

42. Interview with William Perry.

43. Ibid.

44. Interview with Tadamichi Yamamoto.

45. Interview with Katsuei Hirasawa.

46. Interview with a senior DOD official.

47. Interview with Hiroyuki Sonoda.

48. Interview with Seishiro Eto.

49. Interview with Masahide Ota.

50. Ibid.

51. "Continued U.S. Use of Okinawa Land Not Illegal: Kajiyama," *Japan Policy & Politics*, April 1, 1996.

52. Interview with Shoichi Chibana.

53. Interview with Masahide Ota.

54. Interview with Seiroku Kajiyama.

55. Interview with a MOFA official in charge of U.S. base issues.

56. Interview with Charles Freeman.

57. Interview with Ezra Vogel.

58. Interview with a senior DOD official.

59. Ralph Cossa, "Change and Renewal: The United States–Japan Security Relationship into the 21st Century—A Conference Summary," from Pacific Forum CSIS Special Report, *Change and Renewal: The United States–Japan Security Relationship into the 21st Century*, March 1995, p. 13.

60. Joseph Nye Jr., "American Security Strategy for East Asia and the U.S.-Japan Security Alliance," from Pacific Forum CSIS Special Report, *The United States-Japan Security Relationship into the 21st Century*, p. 30.

61. Interview with a high-ranking MOFA official.

62. Interview with Takemasa Moriya.

63. Interview with Andrew Bennett.

64. Interview with Joseph Nye.

65. Interview with a senior MOFA official.

66. Interview with Noboru Hoshuyama.

67. Interview with a senior MOFA official.

68. Author's conversation with a senior JDA official.

69. Interview with a high-ranking official in the PM's office.

70. Interview with a high-ranking MOFA official.

71. Conversation with a JDA official.

72. Author's conversation with a senior analyst close to the Pentagon Japan Desk.

73. Interview with Tsutomu Kawara.

74. Ibid.

75. Interview with Seishiro Eto.

Chapter Fifteen

The Marines

Advocating a Marine Withdrawal

The most controversial part of the Nye Initiative was the 100,000-troop strength commitment. As already mentioned, criticism of this was loud and diverse. But the controversy also had an unexpected by-product; it led to debate on the rationale for the marines stationed in Japan. Arguments calling for a withdrawal of the marines began to be heard.

The 100,000 figure was not to be taken as a fixed number. In the case of major developments towards a peaceful reconciliation on the Korean Peninsula, U.S. forces in Korea would no longer be necessary. Nor would marines in Okinawa. Why not? Because the main mission of the marines in Okinawa was to stand by in readiness for a flare-up on the Korean Peninsula.

Frequently, the debate went like this: Of the 28,000 U.S. troops stationed in Okinawa, 18,000 were marines. But why wait for peace on the Korean Peninsula? The marines in Okinawa didn't shoulder any of the readiness role for a contingency on the peninsula. The bases were merely forward supply, training, and waiting stations. Accordingly, there was no incontrovertible need for marines to be stationed in Okinawa. If you concentrated all those troublesome marines in Okinawa, the whole bilateral security relationship could go awry. It would be much better to pull them out right now.

One of the first to advocate withdrawing the marines was Mike Mochizuki of the Washington-based Brookings Institution. His field of expertise was Japanese politics and security. Mochizuki pointed out that "despite their location, the Marines on Okinawa are poorly suited to make rapid deployments to places such as South Korea. The . . . U.S. amphibious ships homeported nearby in Sasebo, Japan, have only enough capacity for about 3,000 troops and associated equipment; any additional Marine ships would have to come from the United States, defeating much of the benefit of forward basing."[1] His proposal was that the marines should be returned to Hawaii.

Defense of Japan was not the top priority of the marines in Okinawa. This fact was clear from the congressional testimony by the then secretary of defense, Caspar Weinberger, in April 1982. Before the Senate Appropriations Subcommittee, Weinberger spoke to the effect that the marines in Okinawa are not allocated to defense duties for Japan and that they are a conforming force of the Seventh Fleet, which can be posted anywhere in the Seventh Fleet's normal area of operations such as the West Pacific and the Indian Ocean.[2]

There were four amphibious ships in Sasebo that only the 2,000 troops of the 31st Marine Expeditionary Force (31 MEF) could use. The main force, the Third Expeditionary Force (III MEF) had no ships, so they could not be immediately dispatched. In an emergency, the First Expeditionary Force in California would board amphibious ships in San Diego.

Satoshi Morimoto, a senior researcher at the Nomura Research Institute, endorsed Mochizuki's position: "If that's the case, there's no need to have [the marines] in Okinawa." Morimoto had been the director of the Foreign Ministry's (MOFA) National Security Policy Division. "It is highly unlikely that the marines would be used in the Straits of Taiwan or the vicinity of China, and even if they were deployed to the Middle East or the Gulf, there is no necessity strategically speaking for them to be stationed in Okinawa. The role of the marines in Okinawa is rather to accept incoming troops from the American mainland or other areas in the Asia-Pacific, to train them and maintain operational readiness. There is no need for them to be stationed permanently in Okinawa for that."[3]

From a completely different angle, Charles Freeman, former assistant secretary of defense, insisted that the marines in Okinawa should be transferred to Korea. "After unification, it is likely that the U.S. forces in Korea will be pulled out. It would be undesirable for a void to occur there, however. That's why the marines in Okinawa should be sent there to fill the gap."[4] Much of this discussion assumed that the U.S. military presence would be mainly an air and navy one in the future, not the marines.

The Nye Report maintained that "United States forces in Japan are committed to and prepared for not only the defense of Japan and other nearby United States interests, but to the preservation of peace and security in the entire Far East region."[5] Korea was naturally included in the Far East.

When the initiative was launched, the question of "what would happen to the marines in Okinawa and the bases in the event of a peaceful unification of the two Koreas?" was not considered to be a very realistic one. Memories of the North Korean nuclear crisis were still fresh.

The Pentagon leadership regarded readiness for a contingency on the Korean Peninsula as the mission of the marines in Okinawa. Carl Ford, former deputy assistant secretary of defense, commented that "probably half of the marines in Okinawa were there for Korea,"[6] but Nye thought "the number was higher, more like three quarters."[7] Advocates of this school leaned towards assuming a withdrawal of the marines after the unification of the two Koreas. The problem was, however, that they did not attempt to separate the marines from the navy and army and focused on checking and defining only the marines' rationale for being on Okinawa. They argued that there was very little military significance in singling out just the marines. Generally speaking, their position was that the mere presence of the U.S. forces acted as a deterrent. While it was clear that they were also thinking about what would happen when the deterrent failed, they did not want to be drawn into a debate on specific threats.

Presidential aide Stanley Roth disclosed that "I thought we had to create a new rationale incorporating all elements in the Nye Initiative's redefinition of security in order to ensure that it didn't lead to a perception that the bases and the bilateral security treaty would no longer be required after the unification of the two Koreas."[8] This meant taking a far-ranging, flexible approach on the role of the military and their presence, or, in other words, a theory of "diffusion."

The marines also stressed this theory of diffusion. Thomas Linn, chief officer for strategic concepts at the marines' headquarters in Washington, explained, "If the threat in Korea goes away, that doesn't really affect us, in our opinion. We still see U.S. Marines in Okinawa playing an important role in doing whatever comes up in the East Asian littoral, be it humanitarian assistance, be it the evacuation of noncombatants, be it disaster relief, be it a lesser conflict that might occur. When you take a look at some of the other disputes that might come up, Korea is just one, and there are going to be other places that you might use marines, be it in the Malacca Straits or the Spratlys, you name it. U.S. bases in Japan also ensure that we protect the sea lines of communications (SLOCs) from Saudi Arabia to Japan."[9] He added a footnote to the theory of a navy-and-air-centered presence in the future, saying, "these advocates also include the marines in their talk of the navy, meaning a balanced naval power including the marines."

The argument for withdrawing the marines, which was triggered by the debate on the 100,000-troop level, developed into a hot political slogan in the wake of the Okinawan rape incident. In the spring of 1997, it created tension within the bilateral relationship.

A Change in Washington

Washington at the beginning of 1997 was a completely different world from the Washington of one year earlier. In contrast to the many snowfalls the previous year, the winter was a warm one. More important, the political weather map was all new. Foreign policy interests and priorities in the Asian-Pacific region had shifted away from Japan to China.

In the spring of 1996, Washington had been trying to construct an East Asian foreign policy with Clinton's visit to Japan as the axis. Using a reinforced alliance with Japan as leverage, the dynamics of trying to rebuild relations with Asia and China were at work. The plan in the spring of 1997 was to improve relations with China premised on the strengthening of the U.S.-Japan alliance. Consideration towards Japan's particular domestic political problems was overshadowed by and increasingly pinned down by strategic considerations regarding China. It would not do to have Japan's particular domestic political problems, for instance the Okinawa bases, drawn into the process of improving relations with China.

The administration's lineup had also changed radically. More than 3,000 officials are usually reshuffled in every change of administration. The second Clinton administration had many shuffles. It was a different ball game from the first term in office, and the changes impacted on U.S.-Japan relations.

William Perry resigned as defense secretary and went back to Stanford. Ambassador to Japan Walter Mondale also went back home to Minnesota and returned to practicing law. Winston Lord, assistant secretary of state, was holed up in his Park Avenue home in New York, busy redecorating and rearranging his antique Chinese furniture. His East Asia portfolio at the State Department remained unfilled. (Stanley Roth was later appointed to the post in August 1997.)

Perry believed it wouldn't matter if they reduced the number of marines in Okinawa a little. *The important thing is the marines' presence, not the numbers. Theoretically it would be possible to cut the numbers with contingency stationing in advance integrated facilities in Okinawa and by allowing joint U.S.-Japan use of the bases. It was preferable for the question of troop cuts to be considered in conjunction with the guidelines.*[10]

"If we cut the troops by about 5,000, would it be seen as a one-time political, peacetime gesture, or as a down payment?" This was how one high-ranking official at the Pentagon phrased the question to his Japanese friend.[11]

Republican security experts, including Richard Armitage, former assistant secretary of defense, and Torkel Patterson, former director of the Pentagon's Japan Desk, made comments that could be interpreted as favoring the withdrawal of the marines.[12] Both attached certain conditions and were full of nuance, but they were seen as having a certain realism when viewed in the context of the quadrennial defense review (QDR) that the U.S. government was scheduled to release in May 1997. This encouraged the Japanese proponents of cuts in the marines.

Up until then, the American advocates of marine cutbacks tended to be of the liberal Democrat school, but here now were some hard-headed Republican conservatives arguing the same thing. The impact was quite different. Voices in Okinawa had been calling for a reduction in the number of marines from the previous year. Governor Masahide Ota as well as Vice Governor Masanori Yoshimoto stressed the point. Acting in concert with the leadership of the Democratic Party of Japan, Yoshimoto put forward a proposal for linking marine cutbacks to the contingency stationing argument.[13]

Ever since a floating facility became a promising candidate for Futenma's relocation, Yoshimoto saw it as "a first step to withdrawing the marines." He elaborated that "this will open the way to a marines withdrawal from Okinawa and Japan. We'll need to bring forward our planning on the assumption of a withdrawal in 5 to 10 years."[14]

The centrist political parties, including the Socialists, the Democrats, and the New Frontier Party, also started arguing for a marine withdrawal. Certain sections of the Liberal Democratic Party (LDP) also argued the same point.

More tellingly, the same kind of voices leaked out even from the PM's office. In particular, Cabinet Secretary Seiroku Kajiyama was not afraid to say, "I find the very fact that the U.S. forces are in Okinawa unbearable." He lashed out at the Foreign Ministry, saying, "How about bringing the Americans over to our side instead of always dancing to their tune?" He wondered why the ministry couldn't use the withdraw-the-marines argument starting to be voiced in the United States a little more adroitly to entice the Americans over to Japan's position and expressed his frustration by asking, "Just which way is the Foreign Ministry facing?" He wouldn't press for cuts, but wanted to know why it wasn't able to get the Americans to transfer their training functions back to the United States. He also asked Yukio Okamoto, special adviser to the prime minister on Okinawa affairs, "Can't you get a little something more [concessions] from America?"[15]

The Leopard Changes His Spots

Hashimoto was covering his tracks. His responses in the Diet on this question were without fail exemplary. "When I consider the circumstances surrounding our country at the present juncture, I do not believe that the marines are in a situation where they are no longer required. I believe that the stationing of marines is a significant factor in maintaining the stability of this region both tangibly and intangibly. That is also the view of the Americans."[16]

It is not that Hashimoto was not aware of Okinawan sentiment. The United States was unyielding and wouldn't budge. He even intimated to Okinawa that he was chagrined about that. Hashimoto replied to a question in the Diet from Hajime Ishii (New Frontier Party) in the lower house: "It has been conveyed to Japan by those responsible that America has no intention of changing the U.S. military presence in Okinawa. In light of such circumstances, I am sure that I feel just as strong a sense of acute apology to the people of Okinawa as you."[17]

Hashimoto met with Okinawa Governor Masahide Ota on February 17, 1997, and clearly expressed how difficult it would be for "the government to help in reducing the marines" as requested by Ota. Hashimoto's public stance that "we will not demand marine cutbacks" never wavered. He believed that "at the very least it's not something Japan should bring up," and he was convinced that he himself should not raise it. He had also said, "If you're going to say that, are you prepared to fill the hole the marines leave with the Special Defense Forces [SDF]? If you're not, then it's irresponsible."[18]

The truth was, however, that Hashimoto was considering whether it was possible. It seems that he was also wondering if the Japanese couldn't talk the problem over in one way or another with the Americans. In the September 9, 1996, "Prime Minister's Remarks on Okinawa," he even stated, "As is clear from the Joint Security Declaration I made with President Clinton in April this year, we will continue to strive through diplomatic means for stability in the Asian situation and maintain consultations with the United States to discuss military readiness including U.S. military force composition." This section was inserted out of consideration for Okinawan demands.

Hashimoto also showed an inclination in that direction in the Diet. "I am not considering calling for their withdrawal at present. Speaking in the long run, however, I have made it clear on many occasions that there will be bilateral consultation on diverse issues with an eye to changes in the region's situation."[19] He wanted to explore the possibility by "sounding out America's true intentions." He never showed his hand, however, and did not miss a trick in setting up his alibi. From Washington, it was hard to know what he was thinking.

Was he placing bets both ways? A high-ranking official at the White House had his suspicions. "It appeared that during this period of time, very senior Japanese officials—like you can imagine who—were sending out two messages at once. One was, see if you can get the U.S. to move on this [a symbolic marine cutback], and at the same time, telling another group, I am very comfortable, I don't want to see reductions."[20]

Such conflicting signals created confusion downstream, making all those involved feel more wary, more exposed, and more tense.

As mentioned previously, President Clinton had intimated in the preparations for the New York summit in September of the previous year that they should be careful not to create a second Futenma. Explaining, a high White House official said that what the president meant was that he wanted the Japanese to be careful not to create the impression that they were arguing for a reduction in the marines, or further, that they would welcome the withdrawal of U.S. troops. The White House was concerned about the "Prime Minister's Remarks" released on September 10, "parts of which might be interpreted as welcoming withdrawal."[21] That is why they insisted at every opportunity on maintaining the 100,000 U.S. troop strength in Asia.

Clinton touched on this even at the November meeting of the Asia-Pacific Economic Cooperation (APEC) in the Philippines. This made the U.S. government only watch more closely to see what position Hashimoto would take in the midst of the calls for marine cutbacks that were being made in Japan. Had it been earlier, this kind of innuendo would probably have been seen as catering to special domestic political demands, especially the "special circumstances" of the Okinawa question, and the United States might well have understood that and gone along with the charade. This time, however, that didn't happen.

Madeleine Albright, the new secretary of state, was a true believer in American power and was known for her "macho" style. She was convinced that the United States should maintain a maximum overseas presence and that it was precisely due to that presence that American foreign policy was trusted in Asia. Albright was the first member of the new administration to visit Japan, meeting with Foreign Minister Yukihiko Ikeda on February 23 and Prime Minister Hashimoto the following day. Prior to her visit, she told Secretary of Defense William Cohen that Japan had to be given the message that the United States would not budge an inch concerning its military presence in Japan and she was going to Japan to reinforce that idea.

Hashimoto had the feeling that perhaps MOFA had not adequately passed on the United States' true intentions; perhaps MOFA had not crossed swords with America. He told his aides in a briefing session just before meeting Albright, "Things went well with Okinawa because Perry and Mondale were there. But both of them have gone. We'll have to get Albright to go the full mile on this one." What would be the best way of broaching the marine cutback? Hashimoto remarked, "I guess there's no other way but to go for broke."[22]

During the meeting, Albright's tone was full of meaning. She listened to Hashimoto in silence when he said, "Bearing in mind changes in the international situation, we would like to hold joint consultations in the medium to long term on a number of questions, including troop levels and structures. That has been clearly stated in the Japan-U.S. Joint Declaration on Security."[23]

Albright did not forget the message Japan had to be given, however, and reminded Hashimoto. "I realize that there are many aspects to the Okinawan question. I also understand that it needs to be paid special attention. Our ultimate objective, however, is how to best build and manage bilateral security. Let neither of us forget that."[24]

According to Kajiyama, during the meeting Hashimoto and Albright "both spoke their minds." A high-ranking member of the government revealed, however, that even here "sounding out [the Americans on] the possibility" of the "withdraw-the-marines argument" was "squashed superbly."[25]

Hashimoto was not slow to change. A senior member of the government said he was amazed at how quickly the prime minister changed his spots.

The Slack

MOFA was opposed to the withdraw-the-marines line. First and foremost, it judged withdrawal to be a remote possibility. It was concerned about the danger of sending the "wrong signal" overseas, especially to North Korea. It was aware, however, that this consideration also existed in the United States and that the top-down method made untoward developments a political possibility. Depending on which way the QDR went, the possibility existed that marine cutbacks could suddenly emerge. There was a sense of fear: "We were most worried about being left up a tree without a ladder if that happened; we wouldn't be able to look anyone in the eye if we were left standing by the wayside."[26]

So the ministry came up with a way of dealing with it, even in briefing sessions at the PM's office, by saying, "There are both domestic and overseas proponents for a reduction in the marines, but it is not an immediate question. We should consult with the United States in response to changes that could or should occur."[27]

The marines' presence will remain unchanged for all eternity; is that all we have to say? Mention cutbacks and "you'll send the wrong signal"; is that all we have to say? Won't we back ourselves into a corner if we keep saying that and then a reduction actually happens?[28]

Sadayuki Hayashi, vice-minister of foreign affairs, was among those leaning towards the position that MOFA should not dismiss the withdraw-the-marines argument out of hand; if only for that reason, there was a need for joint talks on the U.S. force structure and a process for adjustment. MOFA's concern was not the cutback itself, but whether it couldn't use this to create a reason for joint talks on U.S. troop structure. A high-ranking MOFA official remarked, "Prior consultation is required when America brings troops in, but the Americans are one-sided when it comes to pulling them out; we wanted to do something to change that situation."[29]

The United States, however, did not come to the party. At one stage, the Foreign Ministry even dragged out the quotas on future U.S. troop strengths from the old bottom-up review and considered talks on the "disparity" of 2,000 to 3,000 that existed between the quotas and the existing level. The ministry was thinking of the "slack" between the quota and the actual number of personnel. In other words, given that the actual numbers were lower than the quota, might not it be possible to have a cutback by lowering the quota to match the level of the actual number of personnel? MOFA even considered raising the possibility of reducing the marines' civilian component in Okinawa.

The Defense Agency (JDA) viewed the mounting advocacy for withdrawing the marines in Japan with a deepening sense of crisis. It was also concerned about the growing marines-as-bad-guys thesis. It had no objection to the Foreign Ministry's talks on force structure per se but did not think the timing was right to bring it up. The situation with North Korea, for one, was proof that it was not the right time. Resistance was especially strong to any approach that targeted the slack. "That kind of cheap trick is in pretty poor taste. It's the kind of approach the LDP takes during budget compilation. It's not the sort of thing that works with international reasoning. Start doing something like that and the much-awaited talks process would degenerate into a lobby for marine cutbacks, reduction talks. We'd be hounded [by Okinawa and the opposition parties] all year round and have to come up with something. No, it's not a good idea at all."[30]

Defending the Marines

The Defense Agency's counteroffensive started from the top. At the end of February, Chairman of the Joint Staff Council Shigeru Sugiyama and Director-General of the Defense Bureau Masahiro Akiyama visited the PM's office and briefed the prime minister.

They pointed out the military problems with the withdraw-the-marines thesis. The marines consisted of three groups: the maritime wing, the ground force, and the training group. The latter two were stationed in Okinawa. The ground group had to be ready to move out at a moment's notice. In order to do that, there had to be an airfield and port nearby. The training group had to conduct live artillery practice and amphibious landings in typical Asian topography. They needed to be located only a few miles distant.

It was also best to have the marine presence in "a forward and the safest possible" location. They had to be out of enemy air and missile range but close enough to be the first on the scene. And that place was not the Philippines, Malaysia, or Guam. It was Okinawa. The first echelon required a marine expeditionary force. To split them up would not make military sense. Therefore it would not be advisable to change and decentralize them.

This amounted to an outright defense of the marines. Broadly speaking, this argument asserted that "the 18,000 marines currently stationed in Okinawa is the minimum unit and cannot be divided any further. Calling for further division was equivalent to asking the question: will we keep them or not?"

Hashimoto listened in silence. But after hearing them out, he commented only, "I see your point." (Visiting Japan in April of that year, John Shalikashvili, chairman of the Joint Chiefs of Staff, thanked Sugiyama for his briefing of the prime minister at that time.[31])

It was Noboru Yamaguchi, a colonel in the SDF and deputy chief of the Ground Staff Office's Defense Planning Division, and other middle-rank soldiers familiar with the United States who developed the JDA's and Joint Staff Council's defend-the-marines argument in greater detail. At the start of the year, Yamaguchi had presented a paper on "Why Should Marines Remain in Okinawa? A Military Perspective."[32] The paper asserted:

- Should a Korean contingency occur, Okinawa will . . . serve to restore the situation. This is the exact factor to deter such a contingency.[33]

- In [the] case of Korean contingency, . . . 250 90-minute-flights from Okinawa to Korea can bring a combat unit composed of an infantry regiment augmented by artillery pieces, tanks, combat engineers, helicopters and fixed-wing aircraft, and supporting elements with 30-days-supply if the MPF [Maritime Pre-Positioning Force] squadron is properly positioned.[34]

- The 31st Marine Expeditionary Unit (Special Operation Capable) . . . stationed in Okinawa, supported by a four-ship amphibious squadron homeported at Sasebo, can serve as a ready landing team whenever necessary.

- If we think about the situation in the future, particularly after the reunification of Korea, it would be difficult to see a continued U.S. Army presence in the peninsula. Under a situation where we do not see the presence of the U.S. Army in the Korean Peninsula, the marines on Okinawa, who will be the only land force presence in the region, will play a far more important role to assure U.S. commitment to the region.[35]

- The marines have played an important peacetime role besides fighting wars. For example, III MEF in Okinawa played [a] central role in the disaster relief operations in Bangladesh in 1992 and provided engineer support for the Kobe earthquake in 1995. . . . marines' unique capabilities have also been utilized for regional confidence building. . . . The 31st Marine Expeditionary Force based in Okinawa sailed to Vladivostok and conducted a joint disaster relief and humanitarian assistance exercise with the Russians. . . . Military contribution for confidence building of this kind will become more and more important for regional stability.[36]

Yamaguchi saw relocating marines to Australia, Southeast Asia, or Hawaii as one option, as well as technological breakthroughs such as "drastic improvement in airlift capabilities or high-speed sealift capabilities that may enable marines to do the same job from the U.S. mainland."[37]

Yamaguchi pointed out that as long as the main force of the Seventh Fleet, which acted with the marines, was homeported in Japan, stationing the marines at a distance from the fleet would trigger operational problems. Sugiyama's and Akiyama's briefing of the prime minister had argued the same point.

The JDA's counteroffensive was not carried out in concert with the Americans, but the Pentagon tried to check the structure talks attack from MOFA by joining forces with the JDA. A senior official at the Pentagon remarked, "Compared to MOFA, which around January-February was totally caught up in and using all its energy on domestic tactics, we were able to have a much more strategic and constructive dialogue with the JDA. We were even able to add greater depth to the three-way talks between the U.S., Japanese, and Korean defense authorities on strategic questions concerning North Korea."[38]

Korea was the key to the marines and an ultimate rationale for the marine presence in Okinawa.

Organized Defense

The defend-the-marines position required considerable courage since the marines had been thoroughly made out to be the bad guys in Japan. Antimarine sentiment was rife. That was just how strong an image the rape incident had planted in the minds of the Japanese people. In his everything-you-ever-wanted to know about *Marine*, Tom Clancy wrote, "The Corps has had its share of members it would like to forget; Lee Harvey Oswald and the idiots who raped a young girl in Okinawa in 1995 come to mind."[39] Lee Harvey Oswald, President Kennedy's assassin, had been a marine, and the three marines who had raped the Okinawan schoolgirl were equally despicable.

Perry was also having his share of trouble with the marines. Marine response after the rape had been slow and took the position of belittling the significance of the incident. Because CINCPAC Richard Mackey was uncooperative, problems that should have been handled at a lower level kept coming up to Perry to deal with. Perry made his move after Admiral Mackey's offensive statement following the rape of the young girl that "if they had the money to rent a car, why didn't they just go out and buy themselves a woman?"

The first thing Perry did was read the transcript of the statement very carefully. *How insensitive not just to the specific situation, but to the Japanese government, the political environment in which he had to work. He seemed to have not a scrap of consideration for that. How did he expect to remain effective in Japan saying something like that? How could he show his face when he went back? They will have no respect for him.*[40]

Having come to that conclusion, Perry acted on the management principle: If you decide that you are going to make a change, don't linger; do it immediately. He called Mackey, who happened to be in Washington, that same day. They spoke one-on-one in the secretary's office. "I have great respect for the job that you have done up to this point, but this is unacceptable. I'm sorry but the conclusion I've reached is that it will diminish your ability to be effective in the job in the future."[41]

Mackey said he was sorry. He recognized it was a mistake; it had just sort of slipped out. He was not as convinced, however, that it was going to be a problem for him in Japan. The decision, however, was Perry's. Mackey fell silent for a moment, then agreed to tender his resignation.

Before Perry met with Mackey he had met with chairman of the Joint Chiefs of Staff and with the chief of Naval Operations to hear their opinions. Both concurred with his judgment. The next phone call he made was to President Clinton. When the president heard what Mackey had said, he was shocked and said he couldn't understand it. He was reluctant to lose Mackey's services but saw and accepted Perry's point.[42]

In the words of one of Perry's lieutenants, "Admiral Mackey, who had a fine career as a naval aviator, left his job with a serious cloud hanging over him. . . . It's not often that history gives you the opportunity at a second chance, and what is tragic . . . is that Mackey failed both times. He failed initially to respond quickly, but then failed the second time by not reflecting sensitively in his discussions what a tragedy Okinawa was."[43]

With the young girl's rape, Futenma's return, and the floating facility, the Okinawa bases turned into a marine issue. During this period, relations between the leadership in the Pentagon and the U.S. Marine Corps were often tense. Perry praised Charles Krulak, marine commandant, for his cooperation, but the sort of mentality reflected in Mackey's remark was still strong in the field. A former U.S. Navy officer pointed out that in their involvement with Japan, "The [marines'] experience on Iwo Jima was their starting point, and they seemed to think that since they had paid for the bases in their own blood, it was only natural for them to be stationed in Japan. Their approach was exploitative with very little sense of being a guest."[44]

The more the marines were bashed, the more they tended to stick together and cover for each other. At the time of the Okinawa rape incident, Okinawa Rengo, a union coalition, called for the resignation of the Okinawa marines commander, Wayne Rollings. In response, the top brass in the corps were stubbornly determined to keep him. As a military specialist and an ex-marine working for Congress described it, "Since they are the smallest of the four services, there is a very strong obsession that the big guys will swallow them if they don't keep making an effort to assert themselves. Their sense of victimization is also the strongest of the lot."[45]

When honoring their successive commandants, apart from military achievements abroad, their achievements at home—that is, how well they have fought to preserve the corps' current troop level—earned a special mention. Commandant Krulak had already earned several medals with his "organized defense" in the 1993 bottom-up review and the 1997 QDR.

The general American image of the marines, however, was more favorable than that of the other three services. The presidential helicopter was *Marine One*. In his memoirs *The Politics of Diplomacy,* James Baker, a former secretary of state, writes proudly of joining the marines after graduating from Princeton.[46] George Shultz, another former secretary of state, often mentioned when he was in office the fact that he had been in the marines.[47] Hollywood also never seemed to tire of the brave, tough-guy marine image in movies like *Independence Day.* Congress was also generally favorable towards the marines. A U.S. Navy officer remarked that they were perceived as being honest; when they didn't need money they said so, and if any money was left over, they said so too. So they were trusted.

On the ground, at sea, and in the air in postmodern warfare, no matter where, it was an age of computer games and Tomahawk cruise missiles. The air force competed for the most sophisticated technology and the navy was perceived as a diplomatic weapon. In this context, the marines might be lowtech, but they were proud of the fact that they were the ones risking their lives on the battlefield. That pride had been fostered by a number of myths and even legacies, many of which were born of marine bravery in the fierce battle for Iwo Jima. In many Americans' minds, the photo by the Associated Press' Joe Rosenthal of the marines raising the American flag atop Mount Suribachi was the most evocative scene of the Pacific War, or even the entire Second World War. The marines were America's brightest icon.

Having a law that required that the U.S. Marine Corps maintain three expeditionary forces, one of which was to be stationed on Okinawa, was a special consideration to ensure their continued existence. Were the entire III MEF to be withdrawn from Okinawa, it would require an amendment to that law.[48]

As early as 1992, before becoming commandant, Charles Krulak had written that the challenge for the marines was to redefine their force structure to accomplish their role as effectively as possible within the constraints imposed by shrinking defense budgets.[49] In the same report, he added, "the Third FSSG [force service support group] on Okinawa will retain all functions of combat service support, but they will need to be accomplished by company-sized units rather than battalions."[50]

The marines fought back against the withdrawal and reduction advocates, arguing that their role in the Asian-Pacific region would become only more important in the future. Charles Krulak said, "During the Cold War, marines were called upon to protect our nation's and our allies' interests on an average of once every 15 weeks. Since 1990, marines have responded to this call on average once every five weeks—an increase in taskings by a factor of three. As a result, the enduring requirement for a ready, air-ground force, operating forward from the sea and possessing unimpeded access to potential trouble spots around the world, became readily apparent during the QDR. III MEF marines on Okinawa are an integral part of the regional security apparatus. It is through their presence that we maintain stability in the region. . . . I believe the critical role that the United States plays in the region through our presence will grow exponentially in the next century; this will be particularly true for the role of the naval forces in the region."[51]

The marines were included in this reference to naval forces. Krulak was pursuing closer coexistence with the navy. "The Marine Corps has always been inextricably linked to the navy. We always will be."[52] This was all part of the marines' survival game.

Krulak also stressed another future role for the marines in the region, namely, acting as a deterrent to China. "The role of the Marine Corps throughout the region is one of deterrence of these types of scenarios [crises in China, Taiwan, the South China Sea, Korea]."[53] The top brass in Japan's SDF were struck by his strong interest in this topic, wondering if he was trying to play the China card against the withdraw-the-marines advocates. There was some head shaking on the Japanese side, but Krulak earnestly pointed at the map of the Chinese littoral zone and spoke of many possible scenarios where the marines might be called upon.[54]

Annapolis

The Clinton administration was watching the growing advocacy for marine cutbacks apprehensively. The Americans had conveyed the message that the QDR included no reductions for U.S. forces in Japan in a communiqué from the Pentagon's number-two official, John White, to MOFA's top mandarin, Vice-Minister Sadayuki Hayashi. But there was no stopping the reduce-the-marines argument inside Japan. If anything, it seemed to have grown stronger following Albright's trip to Japan.

The administration would have to keep sending even clearer messages to Japan.

Of particular concern was the Washington summit scheduled for April. It would be disastrous if Japan raised the issue there. The White House assessment was that whatever else, the possibility had to be nipped in the bud before then. An exasperated White House official recalled a little later that "this was a point in time when we were first getting over the effects of heightened tensions on the Korean Peninsula with regard to submarine incidents, the negotiations to get the statement of regret [about a high-level North Korean's defection to the South], trying to get the four-party process on track, the U.N. world food program . . . speculation as to whether or not Kim Jung Il was centrally in power . . . so it was a great period of uncertainty with respect to the Korean Peninsula, and this was neither the right time, nor politically the right signal to be sending to the North Koreans, that the U.S. and Japan were beginning to talk about reductions in troops; it just didn't make any sense at all."[55]

In the preparations for the summit, trips to Japan were scheduled for Vice President Al Gore in late March and Secretary of Defense William Cohen in early April. There was a need to maximize both these opportunities and send Japan an unequivocal message. However, even prior to that, talks between high-ranking security officials from both sides were scheduled to be held at the Naval Academy in Annapolis, Maryland, on March 3. They were to have a day-long session of talks. So it was decided in a meeting between President Clinton and Secretary Cohen the preceding day that they would set the ball rolling by having the U.S. government representatives convey a unmistakable signal.

Kurt Campbell, deputy assistant secretary of defense, opened the talks. He declared in his penetrating baritone that there was something he would like to say first. "We are not going to reduce our forces . . . and . . . let's remember that the last year we have spent 70 to 80 percent of our time on [local issues] and that there are larger strategic issues: the rise of China, tremendous uncertainty on the Korean Peninsula. . . . We [have] to focus more attention on those issues of strategic importance to the U.S. and Japan."[56]

As if intimidated, none of the Japanese said anything right away. Then Hitoshi Tanaka, deputy director of the North American Affairs Bureau, spoke up. "Okinawa is not a local issue nor a tactical one. MOFA's Japan-U.S. Security Treaty Division receives 30 to 40 inquiries every day on Okinawa from the Diet. It is a national issue."[57]

The Americans weren't satisfied with this reply.

Here we have gone to all this trouble with SACO to work on the Okinawa bases. Why does Japan choose right now, when we've already released our final report, to start talking about reducing the marines at this stage? North Korea

is extremely unstable. Isn't that one more reason we should be moving enthu-
siastically ahead with revising the guidelines?[58]

The Americans were not convinced. They were worried that most of
the Japanese political parties were clamoring for a reduction in the
marines just as the vote on amending the Special Measures Act on
Expropriation of Land for U.S. Military Use was about to come before
the Diet. The backlash was strong: Were they going to sacrifice the bilateral alliance for the sake of short-term political considerations?

The Americans countered the Japanese demands for consultation
and adjustments. "If you're going to say that, let's wait until we hear the
sound of hammers on Futenma's replacement." Or, "Let's listen to what
you have to say if there is still dissatisfaction in Okinawa after all of
SACO has been implemented. It's a bit odd to be bringing up the next
issue when this process is just beginning!"[59]

It looked like the "exploratory" team on security and Okinawa, centered around Campbell and Tanaka, was no longer functioning. One
member of the Japanese side had the impression that the marines were
making sure that Campbell and Tanaka didn't meet one-on-one. *There's*
usually only one marine in these meetings, but this time there are two and they
seem to be flanking Campbell. I wonder if they're worried that the two authors
of Futenma's return might be cutting a secret deal again on marine cutbacks.[60]

This reaction seems to have been a little overwrought, but the atmosphere surrounding the topic was tense enough for the Japanese side to
receive such an impression.

Campbell was no longer under Perry's patronage, and these were
unsettling times for him. He had to be extremely careful that he wasn't
stabbed in the back by the marines. Perhaps in reaction to having been
kept down until then, the marines were waging a relentless attack to
quash Japanese advocacy for marine cutbacks. He needed to take into
consideration the change in the weathervane at the top of the Pentagon.
We'll be in for a chewing out from inside the Pentagon if this time, after we've
just put the finishing touches to SACO, the Japanese start brandishing the
reduce-the-marines argument. They'll wonder what SACO was ever about,
hadn't it served any purpose? This time it'll be me on the stand, no two ways
about it.[61]

Campbell was engaged in another fight at the same time over the
QDR. There were internal gripes over a 100,000-strong presence in the
Asian-Pacific region. While all the other areas had generally experienced
cutbacks, Campbell prided himself that he had fought long and hard to
keep the same level for the Asian-Pacific region. If Japan started advocating reductions in the marines, however, it would fuel the U.S. critics.

The support base for the U.S. presence in the Asian-Pacific Region is falling.
We're the ones holding it up, but MOFA doesn't understand that.[62]

The critics were not only domestic. Strong apprehension from South Korea and elsewhere on reductions in the U.S. forces in Japan had started to circulate. On March 20, Kim Dong Jin, the South Korean defense minister, told his visitors, a delegation of policy officials from the LDP, the Social Democratic Party (SDP), and Sakigake, that the existence of the marines in Okinawa was valuable in terms of rapid response capabilities in times of contingency. "It has a whole different meaning from sending reinforcements from Honolulu or Guam. Japan is a one-state pacifist, but do you really believe that everything is fine as long as Japan is at peace, even if a conflict breaks out right next door?"[63]

The Americans were getting edgy. "In the new year, MOFA started asking if we couldn't trim the marines in Okinawa a bit. They wanted to know if we couldn't move them to Hawaii or somewhere. It was something we couldn't agree to because the marines function as units. We told them very clearly that it was impossible. Then the next approach was to try . . . that there would be reductions immediately after changes on the Korean Peninsula, and we tried to point out that it is hard to predict how those changes would occur, what we would commit to is that once there were those changes that we would consult. . . . and then there was the question of whether we should have a formal consultation mechanism to discuss troop reductions, or maybe a biannual, or some sort of security review, and we thought that sounded quite artificial."[64]

The Special Measures Act

In early March, the PM's office decided to call a cease-fire. Hashimoto started telling people around him, "We've probably said as much as we can get away with." On March 14, Yukio Okamoto, special adviser to the prime minister on Okinawa affairs, touched on "the possibility of marine cuts" in the LDP's Research Commission on Security, and his remarks were given wide press coverage. Seiroku Kajiyama took Okamoto roundly to task. A close aide of the prime minister confided that "the prime minister and Kaji [Chief Cabinet Secretary Kajiyama] might have seen things differently, but the issue was settled until he stirred things up. He [Okamoto] didn't consider that fact sufficiently. It's all well and good having him do things clandestinely, but he slipped up there."[65]

Okamoto was scheduled to go to the United States shortly but cancelled the trip. Kajiyama later remarked, "If he went off to America, Okinawa would only raise its hopes. I didn't think it was right that we should fan their hopes too much, not when the Japanese mainland wasn't prepared to accept any of the bases."[66]

There were two hitches. The first was Hashimoto's trip to the United States. The other was the amendment to the Special Measures

Act on Expropriation of Land for U.S. Military Use. The two were closely linked.

Hashimoto would be meeting President Clinton in Washington in late April. He would lose his credibility if he could not provide "a certain answer" on the use of U.S. military sites. Hashimoto was anxious about that. The leases for sites at 12 U.S. bases currently under enforced usage would expire on May 14. If this turned into a situation of "unlawful occupation" once again, he wouldn't be able to look Clinton in the eye. On Clinton's visit to Japan the previous year, part of the Sobe Communications Site belonging to a private landowner had fallen into a state of unlawful occupation. That sort of thing couldn't be repeated.

Hashimoto was so worried he even told a meeting of the LDP leadership that he wouldn't be able to go to the United States if the amendment didn't pass. The Special Measures amendment was aimed at allowing the continued use of land under enforced usage even after lease expiration. It stipulated that the existing lease relationship would remain while the prefectural expropriation committee was deliberating arbitration requests. It was a so-called emergency measure, but at least they could avoid the legal void.

Governor Masahide Ota and the Okinawans, however, were vehemently opposed to the Special Measures Act. Ota had also started a campaign that packaged opposition to the Special Measures Act with the reduce-the-marines argument. He was saying, "Seventy percent of the troops stationed in Okinawa are marines, so a cutback in their number is the surest way to reduce the bases." He repeated, "Perhaps the government can't mention troop cuts, but Okinawa can't afford to say, oh really, and just back down. We are placed in danger every day, so we don't have that luxury."[67]

The Socialists had also come out in opposition. The SDP executive came up with a proposal linking the Special Measures amendment to a marines cutback. In government party talks on the amendment, which commenced at the start of March, the SDP executive conveyed to the LDP executive that "we can find some sort of common ground if we get a favorable response on the marines issue. We may not be able to endorse [the amendment], but we can probably avoid an official party ruling against it."[68]

The reduce-the-marines argument was being used very much as a pawn in domestic politics. Hashimoto insisted that "debate on the Special Measures Act should not be linked to marine cutbacks." At the same time, the prime minister's entourage pressed the Foreign Ministry to find out if the Americans couldn't come up with some common ground. Kajiyama quietly instructed MOFA and the JDA to sound this out, saying, "Can't we extract some kind of concession from America on marine cutbacks so we can bring the SDP in? If cuts aren't possible, a forum for consultation, anything will do."[69]

The biggest fear of the Foreign Ministry was that the LDP and SDP would cut a deal for passing the amendment involving a reduction in the marines. This was so because, in a certain sense, it was a deal between "unlawful occupation by U.S. forces" and "U.S. forces go home." The Special Measures amendment would prevent unlawful occupation, but we'll make the U.S. forces leave. Let's promise that. Oh, they can't do that? Well, then, we'll just have to let them stay. But it's not our problem then if they fall into unlawful occupation.

The Foreign Ministry was seriously afraid that if Japan's political parties made a deal that "touched America's most sensitive nerve,"[70] they would never be able to repair the damage done to the bilateral relationship. As it turned out, the Okinawa branch of the SDP opposed any conditions being made, so the SDP could not push it any more than they already had. In the end, the SDP executive had no option but to back down, keeping its hopes alive in the form of "consultation and adjustment of troop levels." The following question—or rather, monologue—put to Foreign Minister Yukihiko Ikeda in the Diet by Shigeru Ito, general secretary of the SDP, is an excellent illustration of the difficult position the SDP found itself in as a coalition partner and responsible political party:

"I think it is odd to go out walking on a stormy day without any protection. It is also abnormal to go out on a sunny day wrapped up in a raincoat and coat, clad in rain boots, and holding an umbrella. It is perfectly normal that what type of [U.S. forces] presence is required is determined by the surrounding environment. In such a scenario, efforts should be made in a better direction, not a bad one. . . . Determining how to make efforts towards creating a consensus, a harmony in that area is probably my job. I happened to raise the pros and cons on the question of the Special Measures Act, but I do not believe for a moment that it would be acceptable to oppose it, so I am thinking that we have to fulfill our important political responsibilities."[71]

After exchanging pats on the backs with Ito and saying, "I am basically in agreement with what the committee member has just stated," Ikeda gave what amounted to a verbal high-five. He continued, "The Joint Declaration [on Security, which stipulates consultation and adjustment] is not just words; we have told [the Americans] we'll be doing it." This provided welcome political ammunition for Ito, who was being severely attacked on the issue by more leftist colleagues. The SDP could make no further assertions on marine cuts. The LDP would work energetically for "consultation and amendment." There was no doubt that this was a set piece by the coalition partners.

The support for a reduction of the marines and the Special Measures Act were tangled up in mounting confrontation and discord over future visions of political realignments and the base of support of the Hashimoto government at the time. True, there was a small flickering flame over different perceptions of national policy, but the wick was a fiery ball of unadulterated power struggle.

The clash between the conservative league and the LDP-SDP-Sakigake coalition league was setting off sparks. The three-party lobby was trying politically to massage the SDP, who had been pushing hard for a reduction in the marines, and the Democrats, who were advocating contingency stationing. In contrast, the conservative grouping of Yasuhiro Nakasone and Ichiro Ozawa, strongman of the New Frontier Party, was trying to prevent that. Kajiyama learned to his own chagrin just how firm the U.S. position was and judged that a compromise with the Socialists, so obstinate on this point, would be difficult. So they decided to join forces with the New Frontier Party and force the amendment through with an overwhelming majority.

Both the Japanese and the Americans started to misread each other. The Foreign Ministry couldn't get a handle on the direction of the new U.S. administration. Campbell's interpretation in hindsight was that it "coincided at the same time that we were having the initial stages of the Quadrennial Defense Review, and we had a new secretary of defense, and there was tremendous uncertainty here about what our position would be. . . . I think that some of our MOFA interlocutors believed that this was a hint that we were ready to make decisions to downgrade our presence."[72]

A member of the Foreign Ministry confessed that losing Perry and Mondale really hurt them. The Americans strongly resisted Japanese requests for policy consultations, which was unexpected.[73] Only a year earlier, the Japanese had been astounded by the fact that the Americans had "so surprisingly and so easily accepted" their proposal for the same.[74] They were very understanding, saying "We're not an occupying force. Japan does so much for us. How could we refuse that?"[75]

Campbell later revealed that "Tanaka-san [Hitoshi Tanaka, deputy director, North American Affairs Bureau, MOFA] argued that it was no longer acceptable for the U.S. to unilaterally make decisions about force levels that relate to Japanese security, and . . . I thought that was an extremely persuasive argument. . . . He could make arguments like that in a way that was extremely compelling and often more aggressively than normal Japanese bureaucrats. I had no problem with that kind of argument. . . . For those of us who truly wanted a true partnership, that kind of approach seems simple."[76]

And yet in the spring of 1997 the Americans obdurately resisted that approach. They were frightened that it might send the wrong signal to North Korea; there was a danger that it might raise hopes in Okinawa and among advocates for marine cutbacks; and it would fan arguments for troop cuts in America. Michael Green, a U.S.-Japan security specialist involved in the process, remarked, "The notion that Japan is pressing the U.S. . . . would be the Philippine model. Just creating any image of that is so dangerous. . . . South Koreans say, we don't want an Acheson statement. . . . [The Clinton administration] were very clear on Okinawa. It was good."[77] After all, "the timing was just too bad," as one of the Americans put it.

Throughout this period, Campbell's responses on this question turned into "daily policy consultations.""I would say I pass information and have diplomatic exchanges with the embassy of Japan or directly to MOFA or JDA 20 to 30 times a week personally. My office, probably 200 to 300 times. . . . We are not talking about occasional discussions. . . . On every issue, Iran, Iraq, developments in China, Cambodia . . . we talk constantly. . . . The level of contact and trust and exchange is much higher than is widely perceived."[78]

Another problem with the reduce-the-marines argument was that it targeted only the marines without trying to consult or adjust on the total troop structure of the U.S. forces. On March 11, the U.S. House of Representatives endorsed a resolution to thank the Okinawans "for their contributions towards ensuring the treaty's implementation and regional peace and stability," which was passed with 403 votes in favor, 16 against, and 15 abstentions.[79] Five Republicans among the congressmen who opposed the motion, including Floyd Spence (South Carolina), chairman of the National Security Committee, had visited Okinawa in January. They had heard many complaints and much criticism of Japan from the U.S. Marines in Okinawa. They got the impression that all the political parties in Japan were in cahoots on marine bashing.

Political considerations, where a reduction in the marines was a given, raced too far ahead in Japanese policymakers' mad rush to match the numbers for "marine cutbacks" and to create a "consultation forum." They forgot to debate the fundamental issues of what to do about troop strength, how to look at the rationale for them being there, how to read the quality of future challenges and scenarios.

An even greater miscalculation by MOFA, however, was perhaps the "drastic changes in Japan's domestic politics," as one high-ranking MOFA official put it.[80] A Japanese diplomat in charge of negotiations during this period confessed that he was "made painfully aware of just how fragile the level of support for the security relationship was in Japan, just like a piece of chipboard, despite all the pro-alliance avowals."[81]

A life-and-death issue for the alliance like stationed troop strength was treated as if it were an object for speculation. Security was just a political tool or even worse, a political toy. All discussions were viewed in the domestic context of "countermeasures for Okinawa." And that is the kind of tinted glasses through which the Americans started looking at Japan. Around this time, a MOFA official was heard to mutter, "No matter what we say, it will only be taken as a political statement."[82]

Notes

1. Mike Mochizuki and Michael O'Hanlon, "We Don't Need Okinawa," *Washington Times*, December 27, 1995, p. A15.

2. From congressional testimony by Casper Weinberger before the Senate Appropriations Subcommittee, April 21, 1982.

3. Satoshi Morimoto, "U.S. Marine Corps Should Withdraw from Okinawa," *Asahi Shimbun*, September 13, 1996.

4. Interview with Charles Freeman.

5. *East Asia Strategy Report*, U.S. Department of Defense, February 1995, p. 25.

6. Interview with Carl Ford.

7. Interview with Joseph Nye.

8. Interview with Stanley Roth.

9. Interview with Thomas Linn.

10. Author's conversation with a senior DOD official who conversed with William Perry.

11. Author's conversation with a senior DOD official.

12. Author's conversations with Richard Armitage and Torkel Patterson.

13. Interview with Masanori Yoshimoto.

14. Ibid.

15. Interview with Seiroku Kajiyama.

16. Response to the House of Representatives' Standing Committee on the Budget, February 3, 1997.

17. Response to the House of Representatives' Standing Committee on the Budget, January 27, 1997.

18. Interview with a private secretary to Ryutaro Hashimoto.

19. Response to the House of Representatives' Standing Committee on the Budget, January 31, 1997.

20. Interview with a senior White House official.

21. Interview with a senior State Department official.

22. Interview with a senior JDA official.

23. Interview with a senior MOFA official.

24. Ibid.

25. Interview with a senior JDA official.

26. Interview with a senior MOFA official.

27. Ibid.

28. Interview with Sadayuki Hayashi.

29. Interview with a senior MOFA official.

30. Interview with a senior JDA official.

31. Ibid.

32. At the Tokyo Conference on "U.S.-Japan Security Relations," January 12, 1997.

33. Noboru Yamaguchi, *Why Should Marines Remain in Okinawa? A Military Perspective*, January 1997, p. 3.

34. Ibid., p. 5.

35. Ibid., p. 7.

36. Ibid., pp. 8–9.

37. Ibid., p. 10.

38. Interview with a senior DOD official.

39. Tom Clancy, *Marine: A Guided Tour of a Marine Expeditionary Unit* (New York: Berkeley Publishing Group, 1996), p. 44.

40. Interview with William Perry.

41. Ibid.

42. Ibid.

43. Interview with one of Perry's aides.

44. Author's conversation with a former U.S. Navy officer.

45. Interview with an assistant to Sam Nunn.

46. James Baker, *The Politics of Diplomacy* (New York: G.P. Putnam, 1995), p. 368.

47. George P. Shultz, *Turmoil and Triumph: My Years as Secretary of State* (New York: Scribner's, 1993), p. 26.

48. The United States Code Title 10 Section 5063 (a) states the composition of the Marine Corps as follows: "The Marine Corps, within the Department of the Navy, shall be so organized as to include not less than three combat divisions and three air wings, and such other land combat, aviation, and other services as may be organic therein." Even though this statement leaves the law open to broad interpretation regarding specific manpower levels, it explicitly declares the number of MEF as being no less than three. In case of transfer, reassignment, consolidation, or abolition of any function, power, or duty, the secretary of defense, according to U.S. Code Title 10 Section 125, ". . . shall take appropriate action to provide more effective, efficient, and economical administration and operation, and to eliminate duplication, in the Department of Defense," which is subject to Section 2 of the National Security Act of 1947 (50 U.S.C. 401). However, except as provided by subsections (b) and (c) of Section 125, ". . . a function, power, or duty vested in the Department of Defense . . . by law may not be substantially transferred, reassigned, consolidated, or abolished."

49. Charles Krulak, "A Corps of Marines for the Future: Relevant, Ready, Capable," *Marine Corps Gazette,* June 1992, p. 14.

50. Ibid., p. 17.

51. Interview with Charles Krulak.

52. Ibid.

53. Ibid.

54. Author's conversation with a top SDF official.

55. Interview with a high-level White House official.

56. Interview with Kurt Campbell.

57. Interview with Hitoshi Tanaka.

58. Interview with one of the American participants in the meeting.

59. Author's conversation with a DOD official.

60. Author's conversation with a Japanese participant.

61. Interview with Kurt Campbell.

62. Ibid.

63. *Asahi Shimbun,* March 21, 1997.

64. Interview with a senior U.S. government official.

65. Interview with Kenji Eda.

66. Interview with Seiroku Kajiyama.

67. Interview with Masahide Ota.

68. *Foresight,* April 1997, p. 125.

69. Interview with Seiroku Kajiyama.

70. Interview with a senior MOFA official.

71. Standing Committee on Foreign Affairs, House of Representatives, April 16, 1997.

72. Interview with Kurt Campbell.

73. Interview with a MOFA official.

74. Interview with a top MOFA official.

75. Interview with a senior DOD official.

76. Interview with Kurt Campbell.

77. Interview with Michael Green.

78. Interview with Kurt Campbell.

79. "U.S. House Adopts Resolution Thanking Okinawa People," *Kyodo News International,* March 11, 1997.

80. Interview with a senior MOFA official.

81. Ibid.

82. Interview with a senior MOFA official.

IV

U.S. nuclear aircraft carrier USS *Nimitz*.

China's Defense Minister Chi Haotian and U.S. Secretary of Defense William Perry in front of the Department of Defense on December 9, 1996.

Chapter Sixteen

The China-Taiwan Crisis

Yonaguni Island

It was not as if anyone had told them to, but some people on Yonaguni-cho in Yaeyama District, Okinawa Prefecture, headed out to Irizaki, the island's westernmost point, while others headed for the beach at Nantahama. They squinted and stared out to the west in the direction of the Straits of Taiwan. All there was was a haze. On a clear day, you could see Taiwan, and every now and then the sunlight would flash on the car windows on the opposite shore like sparks. That day, there were no flashes.

Thirty kilometers off to the west were several fishing grounds known as the Suou Shoals, Aino Shoals, and Mekura Shoals. Sea bream, Japanese bluefish, kinmedai, and, in the right season, walleye pollack could be caught. The locals were pole-and-line fishermen from way back. Fishing this way for tuna was a heroic business. You had to spear the tuna with a harpoon from a dugout boat called a *sabani*. The tuna, weighing at least 100 kilos, would then do its damnedest to escape at 100 kilometers per hour. It was a life-and-death struggle between fisherman and fish.

Yonaguni, Japan's westernmost island, was situated almost halfway between Ishigaki Island and Taiwan. An officer from the Maritime Safety Agency (MSA) came from Ishigaki Island on 7 to 10 day stints. That day, the locals had received this announcement from the officer:

> Xinhua News Agency has announced that from March 8 to 15, 1996, the Chinese People's Liberation Army will conduct naval and air force exercises with live ammunition. The announcement stated, "For the sake of safety, the Chinese government requests the governments of relevant countries and the authorities of relevant regions to notify ships and aircraft of their countries and regions not to enter the said sea area and air space during this period."

351

Attaching a notification that the announcement had been forwarded by the Ishigaki branch of the MSA dated March 5, 1996, Yonaguni-cho's mayor, Seizo Irinaka, pinned it up without further comment outside the town hall.

In the early hours of March 8, 1996, true to the warning, China fired three missiles into the sea off Taiwan. One of them flew right over Keelung and landed in the sea off Hualien, a scant 60 kilometers from Yonaguni.

From there to the south was a fishing ground for himedai and ara. An extremely remote outlying island like Yonaguni could not market fish outside the prefecture unless the fish were highly prized delicacies.

The town's population was 1,800. It had neither hospital nor bookstore. Schooling on the island only went as far as junior high. A living was eked out from fishing, raising cattle, and tourism. The town's fishing cooperative had 174 members concentrated mainly in and around the Kubura district. Fishing was the only source of income for 54 of them. Now they could not put their boats out to sea.

Mayor Irinaka had just come back from Hualien and Keelung at the end of February to ask for an end to military exercises by Taiwan. Taiwan had repeatedly conducted military exercises in an area covering some 43 kilometers east-west and 56 kilometers north-south in the open seas between Taiwan and Yonaguni from 1994. In June 1994 and January 1995, fishing boats from Yonaguni had twice been photographed by a Taiwanese guardship. The fishermen were indignant, all the more so because the incidents had taken place in Japanese waters. It was becoming more difficult and dangerous to put out to sea. Their catch was also falling. What awaited Irinaka after he came home from Taiwan was the warning about Chinese military exercises.

Relations between China and Taiwan grew tense. Since the summer of the previous year, the Taiwanese conducted exercises after the Chinese had done so in the seas off Taiwan. The Taiwanese gave advance warning of one month for their exercises, but unscheduled exercises were also on the increase as the situation with China deteriorated. It was a one-two punch for Yonaguni-cho.

From April 11 to April 15, Mayor Seizo Irinaka led a "petitioning delegation," including the head of the town council, Kazuo Niizato, which put its case to Okinawa Prefecture and the Japanese government. The delegation visited the Okinawa Prefectural Assembly and the prefectural government offices on April 11. Vice-Governor Masanori Yoshimoto came from Yonaguni-cho, which probably had something to do with his willingness to help out.[1]

"The governor has instructed me to consolidate our approach. The matter has also been discussed in the Assembly, so we are looking into what the prefecture can do. The prefecture will lobby for this irrespective of whether we have diplomatic relations or not, or formally/informally. Our relations with Fujian Province in China have been growing stronger, so we'd like to create some setting for mutual understanding."[2]

On April 12, the delegation visited the Diet, the PM's office, and the Foreign Ministry, among others places. It handed its petition addressed to Prime Minister Hashimoto to Deputy Cabinet Secretary Yoshizo Watanabe. The petition ran as follows:

> Yonaguni-cho strongly petitions the government to take the appropriate measures and maintain a resolute diplomatic stance towards the Chinese government and the Taiwanese authorities, to ensure that no military exercises whatsoever are conducted in the neighboring waters of Yonaguni Island so as to protect the lives, bodies, and assets of the people of Yonaguni-cho as Japanese nationals and ensure the safe operation of the fishing industry.

The Japanese government seemed to have forgotten that this was its own territory. At least, that was the impression Irinaka had. Irinaka and the people appealed. "It's because there are humans on outlying islands like this, who live there, that the country is maintained, that it remains Japan." They learned just how hard it was to get their compatriots to understand how things stood in a remote town.[3]

It was not, however, as if the country did nothing for them. The 11th District of the MSA had sent its patrol boat *Teruzuki* to patrol the waters north of Yonaguni. The Ishigaki branch of the MSA was also broadcasting warnings twice a day in Japanese and English for ships not to enter the Chinese military exercise area. It was not until more than a month after that, on April 28, however, that the government official in charge came to the area. Transport Minister Yoshiyuki Kamei and Taku Yamazaki, head of the Liberal Democratic Party's (LDP) Policy Research Council, flew in from Naha on an MSA YS-11 aircraft. They were accompanied by the director-general of the MSA, Yutaka Hatano.

When the aircraft was just over the Senkaku Islands, they radioed a message to the crew on board the 11th District's boat patrolling the area. "We are depending on you to patrol the Senkaku Islands around the clock." Tokyo's attention seemed more focused on the Senkaku Islands than on Yonaguni.

The residents of Yonaguni came up with many interpretations of this action. *Are the uninhabited Senkaku Islands more important to the state than little Yonaguni? Or did they do it because it was a matter of face for the state?*[4]

Yonaguni and Taiwan had shared close ties since before the war. Taiwan was a Japanese colony, but its living standards were higher than westernmost Japan. Taiwanese currency was used in Yonaguni, and the annual school trip was always to Taiwan. Taiwan was where the children of the island first set eyes on a modern department store. When people fell seriously ill, they were taken to Taiwan Medical College.

After the war, Taiwan gained independence from Japan and the ties diminished. Contact revived again in the 1980s. Yonaguni-cho established a sister-city relationship with Taiwan's Hualien on the opposite shore. Visits by high school students and community choirs took place. The television in the airport lobby picked up programs from Taiwan. Mobile phones could also be used, provided they were made in Taiwan. The scene was typical of peaceful maritime Asia.

This was shattered by the roar of Chinese missiles and the ominous tremors of approaching aircraft carriers. The peaceful southern seas were suddenly transformed into a geopolitical puzzle. The area was a sea route between the Pacific Ocean and the East China Sea. Yonaguni was located at a crossroads of currents and cultures. On that day, Yonaguni was in the middle of an enormous cultural eddy comprising China and the United States.

Responding to a newspaper interview after the Chinese military exercises were over, Irinaka said, "If only because of its sheer size, I had thought China was a magnanimous country, but it seems to have become quite a trouble spot. Using these fearsome weapons to threaten people, it's not human. I want them to be stopped from ever doing it again. Okinawa Prefecture seems to be totally engrossed in the bases, however."[5]

In the same interview, the mayor of Hualien, Chen Quingshui, said, "We hope that Japan and the United States will advise and persuade China to let Taiwan go forward with a smooth election [sic]. . . . We hope that the U.S. and Japan can help convince China . . . that the only way to solve the problem is through peaceful means. . . . From a personal view as a private citizen, I hope the Americans maintain a presence on Okinawa just in case China ever does attack. Americans could then help prevent such an attack, serving as a buffer, a balance, or a deterrent for military action. . . . If China really wanted to go to war with the U.S., it would win in the long run. Just think about Vietnam and what happened to the U.S. ground troops. If the U.S. were to get involved they could only maintain superiority in the short run. But it would be so difficult to maintain supplies for so long. America is so far away from Taiwan."[6]

Tongfeng (East Wind)

The missiles were targeted politically at Taiwan's president, Lee Tenghui. A general election was scheduled for March 23, with Lee running as the candidate of the Kuomintang (KMT). Beijing suspected him of being a "hidden advocate of independence." In June of the previous year, the Clinton administration, bowing to congressional pressure, had issued Lee a visa so he could give an address at Cornell University, his alma mater. China was infuriated. Since that time, relations between the United States and China had been extremely strained and China-Taiwan relations were also very rocky.

The Chinese leadership had several reasons to be apprehensive. If Lee won the election, Taiwan could well move quickly in the direction of independence. If the opposition Democratic Progressive Party (DPP) did well, the pro-independence movement might gain even greater momentum. If that happened, U.S. and Japanese supporters of Taiwan's independence would be encouraged. This, in turn, might have repercussions on Hong Kong, which was scheduled to revert to China in July 1997. That was not all. The separatist movement in the autonomous district of Xinjiang Uighur and the movement for Tibetan independence would be strengthened. That was what the military exercises and missile tests were really all about.

In early February, one month before the tests, the 150,000-strong People's Liberation Army (PLA) started massing on the Chinese coast opposite Taiwan. Known as "Express 60," which apparently referred to the 60-hour time frame for mobilization, it was the largest movement of troops since the Sino-Vietnamese War of 1979.

"Strait 961," a contingency scenario of an invasion to liberate Taiwan, had been finalized by the Chinese Central Military Commission in 1994. It was a three-phase operation. Phase I was a strategic missile strike to take out air force bases, radar bases, and communications systems; Phase II was gaining air superiority with joint air and naval operations; and Phase III was a landing invasion in which the army, supported by the navy and airforce, would cross the Strait of Taiwan and invade. Strait 961 could be considered the grand finale to the invasion-of-Taiwan exercises carried out intermittently from July of the previous year to protest Lee's visit to the United States.

The exercises also had three parts. The first part was set for March 8 to March 15. A total of four missiles were launched, three on March 8 and one on March 13. They were fired from Haitan in Fujian Province by the PLA's Second Artillery (strategic rocket forces). The missiles were Tongfeng-15s, or what were called M-9s in the West. The Tongfeng-15 was a mobile short-range ballistic missile. It used rocket propulsion fuel and could be transported on trucks or freight cars. It had a range of 600 kilometers.

The Tongfeng-15 had originally been developed for export use by China, which had noted the role played by the Soviet-manufactured SCUD missiles in the Iran-Iraq War. If fired from Fujian Province, the missiles could cover the entire land area of Taiwan and only take five to six minutes to get there. Taiwan did not have the capability to shoot them down.

The target areas were set at some 30 kilometers from Keelung in the north and approximately 50 kilometers from Kaohsiung in the south. These were Taiwan's two largest ports, and both had naval bases. That wasn't all. With only a minor adjustment to the sights away from Keelung, Taipei could become a target. Kaohsiung was the south's largest city. It meant that China could wreak devastation anywhere in Taiwan. The fact that this was "intimidation" was painfully obvious.

The second part of the exercises, as if making a partial strike with Phase I action, commenced at noon on March 12 and finished on March 20. It was carried out at the southern end of the Taiwan Straits near Dongshan (Fujian) and Nan'ao (Guangdong) Islands. It comprised joint air-navy surface and sea attacks using live artillery.

Weather was poor on March 12, so the exercise was scaled down to 10 aircraft and 10 ships. On March 13 more than 40 aircraft and 10 ships participated, then 20 aircraft and 40 ships on March 14. The aircraft included fighter planes and bombers capable of attacking vessels at sea. It was an operation aimed at gaining air superiority. The sea elements participating were diverse and included a nuclear attack submarine, diesel submarines, guided missile destroyers, and guided missile escorts. Su-27 FLANKER aircraft acquired from Russia were also there to conduct air-to-air attack drills.

The third part of the exercises overlapped with the second. It began on March 18 and finished on March 25. The exercise area consisted of the sea area and air space in the vicinity of China's Haitan Island, Fujian Province, at the northern end of the strait. The island was apparently chosen because of its topographical resemblance to Taiwan. It was only 10 nautical miles from the Taiwanese territory of Mazu's Dong Guang and Uqiu. What is more, the eastern tip of the exercise's area was very close to the official boundary line down the middle of the Taiwan Straits. Another calculated attempt to raise the psychological impact.

This concluding part involved the three services of land, sea, and air. The plan was for the army and navy to secure a beachhead on Haitan with air backup support and the deployment of helicopters. Consistently poor weather conditions, however, meant that very little of this part was carried out according to plan: just bombing exercises for helicopters, a small-scale amphibious landing rehearsal, and simulated operations. China's president, Jiang Zemin, was scheduled to visit the area on March 19, probably to witness the "moment of landing," but this too was cancelled, perhaps due to adverse weather.

If Strait 961 had the political aim of curbing Taiwan's tilt towards independence, it could probably be deemed a success. The DPP failed to gain its expected share of the vote. During a campaign speech given on March 8, the day of the first missile launch, Lee Teng-hui remarked, "Communist China should not conduct any exercises whatsoever in the vicinity of Taiwan. Communist China is most afraid of freedom, democracy, and me."[7] It is also true, however, that the people of Taiwan were afraid of China and Chinese missiles.

When China announced its military exercises, military authorities in the United States, Taiwan, and Japan were alarmed that "feigning exercises, China was actually going to invade." During the Gulf crisis, the troops Saddam Hussein mobilized near the Kuwaiti border were there in the guise of "exercises."[8]

Any military professional would instinctively think exercises are dangerous, but the Chinese exercises were ultimately extremely political in nature. The Office of Naval Intelligence's report *Chinese Exercise Strait 961: 8–25 March 1996* made the following assessment:

> There was a clear political objective in choosing the timing, scope, thrust, and location of this exercise: China sought to influence Taiwan's upcoming election process. It successfully met this objective. . . . The military objective of the exercise was less clear. . . . [It] provided an excellent opportunity for realistic training . . . and for testing the current state of its newly evolving, joint operations. . . . [It] reflected another stage in implementation of a new military strategy for carrying out a high-tech war, including integration of new tactics and logistics support capabilities."[9]

It was, however, unclear whether the political objective was thoroughly fulfilled. The exercises dampened fervor for independence among voters. At the same time, it stiffened antiunification sentiment across the board.

Liu Huaqiu Visits the United States

If the essence of diplomacy is timing, the March 1996 visit to America by Liu Huaqiu, director at the Chinese State Council's Office of Foreign Affairs, was consummate diplomacy. He arrived in Washington immediately after China's announcement of the military exercises in the Taiwan Straits. Because Sino-American relations had taken a sharp turn for the worse following Lee Teng-hui's trip, the number of Chinese VIPs visiting Washington had dropped appreciably. Even the Sino-American summit held on the occasion of the U.N. General Assembly's 50th anniversary had failed to patch up the rift caused by Lee's visit. The issues to be dealt with had piled up and prevented any next step from being taken.

Trade, missile exports, Tibet, Taiwan, human rights—especially Taiwan and human rights—were thorny issues. China maintained that Lee should not have been allowed to visit the United States. In his speech to the United Nations immediately prior to the summit, President Jiang Zemin did not forget to criticize America. "Certain big powers, often under the cover of 'freedom,' 'democracy,' and 'human rights,' set out to encroach upon the sovereignty of other countries, interfere in their internal affairs, and undermine their national unity and ethnic harmony."[10]

Even setting up the summit itself had been an awkward process. The Chinese asked the Americans to create an opportunity for Jiang Zemin to make an official visit to Washington before the U.N. General Assembly meeting, but the Clinton administration refused circuitously. Administration leaders knew full well that Congress would be down on them like a ton of bricks if they accepted Jiang as an official state guest at this juncture. The summit was initially going to be held at the New York Public Library, but the day before the Chinese asked for a change of location. Their reason was that the library was not suitable since it was holding an exhibit of protest panels against the Tiananmen incident. The location was switched to the Lincoln Center. In fact, the Lincoln Center had just finished showing a BBC documentary on the demonstrators at Tiananmen Square ("The Gate of Heavenly Peace").[11]

This was the third meeting between Clinton and Jiang, but it was very stilted. Both leaders read their respective "talking points." They had to start afresh somewhere. The White House set its sights on creating closer contacts with the Chinese Office of Foreign Affairs, which came under the direct jurisdiction of the State Council. The main task of the State Council was to make plans for overseas visits by Chinese VIPs as well as for visits by official state guests to China.

Not only was it a small organization with a mere 20 or so staff members, but almost everyone was either seconded from the Chinese Foreign Ministry or held positions in both places, which made it appear to be an outpost of the ministry. Their work was bureaucratic and clerical. However, because they were in charge of the "information" and "assessment" of people's comings and goings, they were a hidden source of power. It was during Chen Yi's time as foreign minister that this double-portfolio practice began.

Liu Huaqiu held the post of vice minister of foreign affairs (United States and Europe). It was in his position as senior officer at the Office of Foreign Affairs, however, that he reported directly to Premier Li Peng. This direct link was a strength. Liu Huaqiu was also a candidate for the Communist Party's Central Committee and served as Li Peng's right-hand man as the director of the Central Committee's Central Foreign Affairs Leading Group, which Li Peng headed.

Liu Huaqiu hailed from Guangdong and was still, in his mid-50s, in his prime. He was unquestionably energetic and a fast thinker. In both physique and thinking, there was something about him that resembled the Deng Xiaoping of old. The diplomats in China saw him as more of a politician than a cadre. Americans saw him and Zeng

Qinghong, senior officer in the Central Committee's General Office, as "shadow leaders" and watched them closely.

The ostensible purpose of Liu's visit to the United States was to attend the Chinese government's internal country briefing held at their embassy in Washington. It was March 5. The Chinese had announced they would begin their military exercises on March 8.

The White House was wondering if it couldn't profit from Liu Huaqiu's visit. In order to do that, Washington had to have him come before the exercises started on March 8. Then the U.S. government would have a chance to convey its position regarding the exercises issue in advance. Samuel Berger, the number-two man on the National Security Council (NSC), described these as "boulders in the stream."[12] They told the Chinese that Anthony Lake was willing to meet them. They also hinted that if things went well, they might also be able to see the president.

The State Department was cautious. Some worried that something like this might undermine the official diplomatic channels between Secretary Warren Christopher and Minister Qian Qichen. Others had doubts as to whether Liu Huaqiu was really Lake's counterpart; wasn't he perhaps lower even than their number two, Samuel Berger? Another factor was that they had not granted Jiang Zemin his wish to visit the White House. How could you justify saying "no" to Jiang but "yes" to Liu?[13]

Liu Huaqiu spoke good English and was well acquainted with America. It was just that there were some China hands in the State Department who felt he wasn't as talented a diplomat as Qian Qichen; he could be quite acerbic.[14] There still was the fact, however, that he reported directly to Li Peng. His relations with the Chinese Foreign Ministry were also firm. If he wasn't good enough, just who was a satisfactory counterpart for Lake? Winston Lord, assistant secretary of state, who played a part in normalizing Sino-American relations in the early 1970s, supported Lake's meeting Liu Huaqiu as "a natural reinforcement of the Christopher channel."[15]

It was the White House's intention to have Liu meet Clinton. Lake was also contemplating making a visit to China to mirror Liu Huaqiu's visit to the United States. Lake's plan was for Liu's visit to the United States and his reciprocal visit to China to be the hop and skip, which would then culminate in a "jump to normalization" with a meeting between Clinton and Jiang Zemin at the Asia-Pacific Economic Cooperation (APEC) conference scheduled for Manila in the fall. This was why he was very keen to meet with Jiang on his own visit to China. Having Liu Huaqiu meet Clinton beforehand was "a sort of preemptive"[16] to make sure that Lake would have the access he wanted; in other words, it was bait. (Lake actually visited Beijing in July and met not only with Liu Huaqiu but also in quick succession with President Jiang, Premier Li Peng, Vice Premier and Foreign Minister Qian Qichen, and Defense Minister Chi Haotian.[17])

There was a desire on the American side to try something different from merely reading out talking points, which was apt to happen in discussions with China. They had to make progress in restoring relations with China; they wanted a forum for a more honest exchange of ideas and thoughts and wondered if they might not be able to create that sort of relationship with the Chinese. Lake believed the real reason why they were in their current situation was because there wasn't enough communication between the two sides, because both sides had been laboring under misunderstandings.

Liu Huaqiu arrived in Washington March 8, Eastern Standard Time. Actually, when Liu had arrived at New York's JFK Airport the previous day, he had called the White House in an attempt to get Lake directly on the line. Lake at the time was in his office in the West Wing talking with a group of aides. They had just received the news that China had fired its first missile into the waters off Taiwan. Lake was holding an emergency conference to discuss that news.[18]

"I just arrived at Kennedy Airport and am looking forward to our meeting. Thank you for the invitation to the state dinner. That's quite an honor. I am also looking forward to meeting Secretary Perry and Secretary Christopher." Liu sounded very happy. Lake waited for him to finish his set piece, then jumped right in. "Well, I think we have a bit of a problem here. China has just launched a missile."

Liu Huaqiu went dead silent. There was nothing. It seemed for a moment he didn't quite understand what was being said. Before he could respond, Lake said, "Just a moment. We've just received a report that another missile has gone off." Lake was vaunting the U.S. real-time prowess in intelligence gathering. The AEGIS-equipped USS *Bunker Hill*, in the southern end of the Taiwan Straits, was capable of tracking the Chinese missiles from the moment they were launched until the moment of impact. That information was fed immediately into the White House, and Lake was making full use of it.[19]

"This Is Not a Bluff"

The Americans dined with Liu on the night of March 8 in the Madison Room on the eighth floor of the State Department building. Perhaps grilled would be a better word than dined. Lake set the ball rolling.

"You have a reputation for being tough, and I know that the Chinese government thinks I have a reputation for being very strong in some of my views. I think this is a good thing because we can speak directly and do business together."[20] Right from the very start there was no beating about the bush.

Christopher made the criticism that the Chinese action was "unnecessarily risky" and "unnecessarily reckless."[21] Defense Secretary Perry was merciless. "Your statements that these are routine military exercises are not credible. As an old artillery officer, I understand very well, and the PLA understands very well, the symbolism of bracketing a target. Your actions will be counterproductive, particularly if you repeat your launches [that is, your action will actually increase votes for President Lee]. You cannot follow up with the threat implied by your action [inadequate lift capability]. You have underestimated the political will of [the] U.S. The U.S. has vital national security interests in the Western Pacific which these actions threaten. You have not taken adequate consideration of the correlation of forces in the region. The U.S. has more than enough military capability to protect its interests in the region and is prepared to demonstrate that. For all of these reasons . . . your missile firings, particularly if repeated, will be a political failure, and will come to be seen as such, even in China."[22]

The Americans also warned Liu that if things escalated, there would be "grave consequences" should China attack Taiwan—"words not spoken to China since the countries established diplomatic ties, and universally understood as code for a military response."[23] Liu Huaqiu countered along the lines that Taiwan was an internal issue, not an international one; responsibility for this situation lies totally with the leaders in Taiwan; China's exercises do not violate international law; as long as it is independent, every country has the right to use force.[24]

The U.S. government's assessment was that China would not invade Taiwan.[25] But no matter what the situation, China would never clearly state that it would not make an attack on Taiwan. The Americans judged that China would never cut a deal with them on Taiwan. Liu Huaqiu didn't show the slightest wavering on that point. So the United States had to stand by militarily in readiness for a worst-case scenario and had already begun to do so. There was the risk, however, that China would misread and overreact to this U.S. move. It was important to send the Chinese a clear message to ensure that they didn't.

Lake had breakfasted with Charles Freeman, former assistant secretary of defense, at the beginning of the new year. Freeman was well known as an expert on China. He had recently returned from a series of discussions with top Chinese leaders.

Freeman reported in detail that the Chinese had put the finishing touches to their military plans for an attack on Taiwan and were in a position to put that plan in motion at any time.[26] "The PLA have drawn up plans to attack Taiwan with regular missiles once a day for thirty days, plans to block the Taiwan Straits, and plans to make a landing assault on some of Taiwan's smaller islands."[27]

China had threatened that if the United States tried to defend Taiwan, "We'll rain nuclear bombs on Los Angeles."[28] This story had been in the press. It was clearly disinformation for the purpose of psychological warfare, but it created a strong anti-Chinese backlash in certain American circles. Lake mentioned this "rain nuclear bombs" statement, which he had heard via Freeman, to Liu Huaqiu. He drove home the point that "that kind of talk is not acceptable, either to the American government or to me personally."[29] Liu used the defense that it was not an official statement by the Chinese government.

The Americans sent an unequivocal message to China in the March 8 dinner meeting. The message was that the United States was not going to stand by in the face of this missile intimidation; it would make a military response to any military action by China. Perry said quietly that this was not a bluff.[30] They had already decided to deploy the USS *Independence* to the straits. If, however, China was willing to exercise self-restraint and limit military action to exercises, the U.S. response would also be limited accordingly. Once again the U.S. position was made quite clear: the United States would not provoke China militarily.

In response to this, the Chinese repeated that China's action was only a military exercise. In short, as a senior staff member at the White House described it, this was a meeting "for both sides to make sure that the other side did not misread the other's intentions and overreact. America made it very clear what it would do, how it would do it, and what it wouldn't do. We told them this was not about choosing sides, China or Taiwan. U.S. national interests were at stake here and if they were threatened, then we would be forced to take action. So we drove home the point that whenever China conducted any kind of military exercise, it had to remember to consider the U.S. element."[31]

"We Have No Kissinger in Our Government"

During this crisis, the Americans kept their communications with Taiwan wide open. They would let the Taiwanese know what they were thinking. They would not, however, conduct in-depth talks on policy. That was intentional. This was an international issue, an issue affecting all of the Asian-Pacific region, as well as an issue with grave implications for U.S. national interests. It was not simply a Taiwan issue.

There was another reason why they had to be careful that Taiwan did not get too cocky. They could not give China the impression that Taiwan and the United States were ganging up on them. The Americans exercised extreme caution here. Before the Chinese exercise, the White House called for informal talks with Taiwan at the senior official level. Samuel Berger met clandestinely with Ding Mou-shih, secretary-general of Taiwan's National Security Council. He had served the previous six years as head of Taiwan's Coordination Council for North American Affairs in the Taipei Economic and Cultural Representative Office in Washington. He was, in effect, Taiwan's ambassador to the United States. A high-ranking official at the White House remarked, "For too long our discussions with Taipei had happened through too many intermediaries, and too many ears, and too many mouths translating. . . . We trusted [Ding] . . . because he was a career foreign service person."[32]

During their meeting, Berger cautioned against being spurred on by election fever into provoking China. He especially hoped that Taiwan would be careful not to give China the impression that it was tilting towards independence. Intensifying that sort of impression would place the United States in a difficult position. Berger made doubly sure by reiterating that the United States did not want to be forced into such a position.

Later on in Taiwan, people started reciting the tale of the China-Taiwan crisis. It went something like this: Deploying U.S. aircraft carriers was just a show cooked up by America and China. It had strengthened Jiang Zemin's position against the Chinese military. The United States was secretly trying to prop up Jiang Zemin. The aircraft carriers were a gift.

The narrative continued. The United States had stopped sending the USS *Nimitz* through the straits. This was because China had promised not to conduct any more missile-launching exercises. America had secretly told Taiwan about this deal.[33] A high official in the Pentagon snorted at this "complete utter rubbish." He then added, "First of all, the Chinese would never ever ever do a deal on Taiwan. [It's] a non-negotiable. Secondly, our relationship is not at that level, and remember, we are at a period of time when there is very little interaction at the highest levels. Who would cut such a deal? We have no Henry Kissinger in our government."[34]

Just how much meaning Liu Huaqiu's visit to the United States had is a matter for speculation. China went on with its planned military exercise including its missile launches. China demonstrated anew via the missile launches its unbending principle that it would use force if Taiwan declared independence, while the United States reaffirmed its position via its aircraft carrier deployment that it would not tolerate unification of Taiwan with the mainland by force. Whether Liu Huaqiu went to Washington or stayed home, nothing seemed to have changed.

A White House official, however, looking back, said, "That meeting with Liu Huaqiu . . . had the effect of reinforcing the point that this is a serious president. . . . If you try to go back and look at, for example, what the result would have been had there not been a Liu Huaqiu–Anthony Lake meeting at the same time as the demonstration of force in the strait, I think you have to conclude that the result would have been much different."[35]

Perry said about the meeting with Liu Huaqiu: "I do think that meeting, that dinner meeting with him, was very important not because of what it affected at the time, but because [of] how it would be seen in China in retrospect, looking back at the events. They could look at that and say, my lord, here the Americans were warning us and telling us. We thought they were bluffing, but they were not. We better take that seriously."[36]

Lake and Liu Huaqiu met a second time on March 9. They spent the whole day in discussion in Middleburg, Virginia, at a farm which was the country retreat of Pamela Harriman, U.S. ambassador to France. Wanting "to get away from the telephones and have an uninterrupted conversation,"[37] Lake had asked her if they could use the farm. After first marrying Winston Churchill's son, Pamela Harriman had married Averell Harriman, heir to the Harriman fortune and former ambassador to the Soviet Union. She was a very influential Democrat and star of the Washington social circuit. In the 1992 election, she was one of the first to support Clinton and contributed a sizable sum of money to his campaign.

The Americans at the meeting were Lake, Lord, and Robert Suettinger, who was in charge of the Chinese and Korean issue in the NSC, among others. On the Chinese side, apart from Liu Huaqiu, were Vice-Minister of the Foreign Ministry Yang Jieci, Deputy Chief of the Foreign Ministry's Asia-Oceania Bureau Liu Xiaoming, and Ambassador to the U.S. Lidaoyu. Lake did not think it was a good thing to shut the State Department out and pursue White House diplomacy. That is why he had Assistant Secretary of State Lord at his side in the meeting.

Compared with the previous night's meeting at the State Department, which had concentrated mainly on tensions in the Taiwan Straits, this day they spoke broadly about the entire Sino-American relationship. According to a high-placed White House official, "The whole purpose of the discussions between Lake and Liu was to give us some framework within which we could handle issues, that we were not just careening from one issue to another . . . and that we somehow needed to grab hold of all of that and put it inside a conceptual package that would make it so that not every time we talked about an issue, the whole relationship got blown up. And that was the purpose of the strategic dialogue."[38]

Lord described it as "a strategic discussion, the kind of thing that Kissinger and all those are always saying we ought to be doing." In other words, they talked "about the next century and where our two countries fit, and how we can cooperate, and then we got some of the tough issues in that context."[39]

Anthony Lake added this dimension to the picture: "I think the Chinese, if we are going to be in the region, wanted us to be serious. . . . I think they like to deal with an American government that is clear and serious about the protection of its interests, because they can see that and then take it into their calculations. Serious governments hate uncertainty about others' policies more than anything else."[40]

Notes

1. Interview with Seizo Irinaka.

2. Interview with Masanori Yoshimoto.

3. Interview with Seizo Irinaka.

4. Author's conversations with Seizo Irinaka and Nagayoshi Arazaki.

5. *Asahi Shimbun,* March 29, 1996.

6. Ibid.

7. "Politics Shall Be Learned from Taipei," *Asahi Shimbun,* March 18, 1996.

8. Author's conversation with SDF officials.

9. *Chinese Exercise Strait 961:* March 8–25, 1996, Office of Naval Intelligence, 1996.

10. Quoted in "Clinton and Jiang Meet, Try to Mend Fences; U.S.-China Talks Center on Trade, Human Rights," *Chicago Tribune,* October 25, 1995, p. 3.

11. Elaine Sciolino, "The U.N. at 50: Clinton and Jiang; Library's Rights Exhibit Hits a Raw Chinese Nerve," *New York Times,* October 24, 1995.

12. Interview with a White House official.

13. Author's conversation with a State Department official.

14. Interview with a senior State Department official.

15. Interview with Winston Lord.

16. Interview with a senior White House official.

17. "Chinese President Meets U.S. President assistant," Xinhua News Agency, July 9, 1996.

18. Interview with a senior White House official.

19. Interview with Anthony Lake.

20. Ibid.

21. "Clinton Orders Warships to Taiwan Area; U.S. Warns China about Its Ongoing Military Exercises," *Houston Chronicle,* March 11, 1996, p. 1.

22. Interview with William Perry.

23. Barton Gellman, "U.S. and China Nearly Came to Blows in, '96; Tension over Taiwan Prompted Repair of Ties," *Washington Post,* June 21, 1998, p. A1.

24. Interview with a participant in the meeting.

25. Interview with William Perry.

26. Interview with Charles Freeman.

27. Ibid.

28. "U.S. Carrier off Taiwan Trails Analysts' Worries in Its Wake," *Los Angeles Times,* March 19, 1996, p. A3.

29. Interview with Anthony Lake.

30. Interview with William Perry.

31. Interview with a senior White House official.

32. Ibid.

33. *Yomiuri Shimbun* (evening edition), March 22, 1996, quoted in Hidenori Ijiri, *The Structure of the China-Taiwan Crisis* (Tokyo: Keiso Shobo, 1997) p. 222. (In Japanese.)

34. Interview with a senior DOD official.

35. Interview with a White House official.

36. Interview with William Perry.

37. Interview with a White House official.

38. Interview with a senior White House official.

39. Interview with Winston Lord.

40. Interview with Anthony Lake.

Chapter Seventeen

—◆—

The Navy

"The Best Damned Navy in the World"

Friday, March 8, 1996.

The number of pizzas ordered by the Pentagon over the weekend showed a huge increase. The Domino's vans—"30 minutes guaranteed"—kept coming in a steady stream. On a normal weekday, the Pentagon orders 300 Domino's pizzas, but on these two weekend days orders topped 600. Frank Meeks, Domino's Washington, D.C., manager, thought to himself, *Something big must be happening. They've got to be holding a lot of emergency meetings.*[1]

Domino's keeps track of how many pizzas are ordered by important centers of government in Washington, D.C., in what is called the "pizza-meter." The pizza-meter had shown its infallibility during the Gulf War. Between 10:00 P.M. and 2:00 A.M. on the night before the January 16, 1991, attack on Iraq by the multilateral troops, 55 pizzas were delivered to the White House, 75 to the State Department, and 125 to the Pentagon. Ever since Domino's publicity about its "pizza-meter" statistics, the CIA has completely stopped ordering from Domino's in order to maintain its secrecy in crisis and contingency cases.[2]

It was not only Domino's that noticed the abnormally high jump in pizza orders by the Pentagon that weekend. The Washington office of Mitsubishi Corporation had sent an emergency report to its Tokyo headquarters: "The DOD has entered a state of alert." One of the "signs" it cited was the pizza orders.[3]

The day the Americans deployed the USS *Independence* was March 5, the same day of the morning broadcast on Chinese government TV about the missiles exercise on March 8. They did not dally. The very next day, the USS *Independence* had already left Manila on its way to Taiwan.[4] It was Defense Secretary William Perry's call. He consulted first with the chairman of the Joint Chiefs of Staff, John Shalikashvili, then made the decision. This was towards the end of February, before the Chinese had announced the missile launchings.

From analyzing various kinds of intelligence, the Pentagon top people had all agreed that it was likely that there would be missile tests. They knew the Chinese communications people were on the move; they had seen the movement of the mobile missiles. Perry issued a "tethering order" for the USS *Independence,* which meant that it had to be able to be in the vicinity within less than a day.[5] The length of the tether was 180 kilometers from Taiwan. Thanks to these preparations, the aircraft carrier was on the move the minute the Chinese government made its announcement and was on station within 18 hours of sailing.

Perry first proposed the action to Tony Lake, National Security Council (NSC) adviser at the White House, and then spoke with Secretary of State Warren Christopher. Both agreed that it was the right decision. Lake went to the president, who agreed with "no hesitation at all."[6] So the decision was mainly a Pentagon initiative, not a White House one.

Perry wondered if the Chinese might not be misreading America's concerns and interests in the Taiwan Straits. *Perhaps they think America is going to pull out of the Asian-Pacific region one day. They probably think they're testing our resolve. They might just be underrating us, thinking that the Clinton administration will pull in its horns if they pressure it. If that's the case, America has to show its determination here.*[7]

Perry decided that "we have to show China how important security in the Western Pacific is to America's national interest. The only way to do that is to deploy our aircraft carriers."[8] Perry fell into the habit of saying, "It's time for the best damn navy in the world."[9]

On the night of March 9, the U.S. government decided to deploy the USS *Nimitz* as well as the the USS *Independence.* Once again, this was Perry's decision. Consulting with even fewer people than about the USS *Independence,* he sought President Clinton's approval.[10]

A very small crisis team had been put together with people from the White House, the Pentagon, and the State Department. From the DOD, General Ronald Fogelman, air force chief of staff, and from the White House, Sandra Kristoff, senior director of the NSC's East Asian Bureau, were part of the team. They discussed the possible scenarios: How could and should the United States respond to a Chinese attack, a sea blockade, a missile hit, active movements of forces on sea, or a land invasion?

If there was an attack and a sea blockade, the United States would probably have to defend Taiwan because the word "blockade" is used in the Taiwan Relations Act. That probability was extremely low, however. But what about the other scenarios? They tried to look at all the angles by placing the different cases in a matrix.

Perry said the reason "we dispatched two carrier battle groups to Taiwan [was] not because we expected they were going to be involved in a military conflict, but to demonstrate we had the military power. Now, two is, I think, quite sufficient to make that point. Two would have been a formidable military force."[11]

The United States did not normally keep two carrier battle groups in the western Pacific. So the leaders had to choose between bringing in the USS *Carl Vinson*, from the West Coast, which had just finished a training exercise, or the USS *Nimitz*, which was in the Persian Gulf. Perry chose the USS *Nimitz*, and the carrier set sail for Taiwan a few days after the decision had been taken.[12]

This was the largest massing of U.S. military force in the western Pacific since the Vietnam War. Carriers were capable of carrying 110 to 130 fighters. They also carried 200 Tomahawk missiles. Battle groups were accompanied by several nuclear submarines. The USS *Independence* was deployed in a battle group which included the AEGIS-equipped USS *Bunker Hill*, the Hawkeye electronic surveillance plane, and two nuclear submarines.

The USS *Nimitz* carrier battle group was even more befitting the best damned navy in the world. The USS *Nimitz* itself was so long that it was like a horizontal Empire State Building at sea. Its hull-to-mast height was equivalent to a 24-story building. It was capable of round-the-clock tracking of all targets within a several thousand mile radius, whether in the air, on the sea, or beneath it. It carried a crew of 6,000, over 3,000 of whom belonged to air units. Its fighter planes were supersonic, and its missiles could travel at twice the speed of sound. The carrier itself could cover 500 miles in a day. Being nuclear powered, it could keep on running indefinitely.

Eighty-five percent of the earth's land and 95 percent of its population was within reach of U.S. aircraft carriers, which ruled the waves. America had 12 such aircraft carriers. It cost about $4 billion to build one and $44 million annually to keep it afloat. The USS *Nimitz* was the largest of the 12 carriers and had the most destructive power. It was the undisputed champion of the best damned navy in the world.

The next choice that had to be made was whether to send the USS *Nimitz* through the straits as a demonstration of U.S. concern. It had already sailed through the straits in December 1995, the first time since 1979, the year America recognized China and severed diplomatic ties with Taiwan. Should the USS *Nimitz* be sent through again?

They had to ask that Taiwan restrain itself at all costs. On no account was it to make a unilateral declaration of independence. The Americans were secretly in touch with Taiwan. The Taiwanese national defense authorities were taking a wary stance. They wanted the Americans to hold back on sending a carrier through the straits. "China does not want things to get out of hand. They don't want to create a military conflict. We must exercise extreme caution here."[13]

The Pentagon was impressed by this restrained stance from the Taiwanese national defense authorities.[14] Having confirmed this approach, they decided to sell Taiwan the anti-air Stinger missile. Due to its limited range, the Stinger could not be used to attack China. If, however, China attacked Taiwan, the Stinger, hidden in valleys and mountains, would be effective against low-flying Chinese fighters and helicopters. The Pentagon judged that this corresponded to "the export of weapons necessary to enable Taiwan to maintain a sufficient capability" stipulated in the Taiwan Relations Act.[15]

If the option to send a carrier through the straits was exercised, it would incur the wrath of China. China issued a warning. On March 17, Premier Li Peng checked the United States in a news conference in the Great Hall of the People, saying, "If some foreign force makes a show of force in the Taiwan Straits, that will not be helpful but will make the situation all the more complicated."[16]

Opinion within the U.S. government was split between hard-liners and soft-liners. Those who urged caution asserted that it would be better not to deploy aircraft carriers in dangerous areas. There was a chance that the Chinese missiles would go off track and enter Taiwanese territorial waters. If that happened, it could lead to unforeseen contingencies. There was apparently some fear of this kind of contingency within the Chinese leadership as well.

Chinese hard-liners might use the deployment of U.S. aircraft carriers to create a crisis. The United States had sent carriers to the straits to check the Chinese in 1959 under President Eisenhower, when the Chinese had tried to attack the two islands of Quemoy and Matsu. Then the Chinese had been forced to abandon the attack, but the episode had endured as an affront to the Chinese. If only for that reason alone, prudence was required this time. Any action that could be taken as a provocation had to be avoided. Conversely, self-restraint on the part of America could encourage pro-restraint forces within China.

In the end, the United States did not send its carriers through the straits. Additionally, in order to ensure the "nonexpansion" of the Chinese military exercises, the USS *Nimitz's* sailing speed was reduced to superslow to give China adequate time to respond should the need arise. The United States took a stare-down-China approach, by deploying the two carriers USS *Independence* and USS *Nimitz* to the waters off Taiwan and having them stand by there. Of the several options that the president was briefed on, "The least option, understand, the least option was the one we took."[17]

"We Were Surprised That They Were Surprised"

Apparently, China was not expecting the United States to deploy its aircraft carriers. "They were surprised when we sent those two carriers in. They should not have been surprised; the fact that they were surprised means that they were misreading how seriously we took this." Perry almost seemed to be saying "we were surprised that they were surprised!"[18]

Although it seems a little hard to believe that the Chinese had not foreseen the deployment of U.S. aircraft carriers, every U.S. government official forced into crisis management mode by developments in the Straits of Taiwan during this time swore China hadn't seen this coming. Perry disclosed that "there was some evidence, which I am not free to discuss, but . . . I am satisfied from the discussions I have had with some fairly high-level Chinese officials that they were not expecting that to happen."[19] Perry's allusion is probably based on electronic intelligence on communications between the Chinese military in the field.

Some of the Chinese diplomats were heard to mumble that "we had expected the USS *Independence* but not the USS *Nimitz*." Such statements, however, are less than reliable. They were "too neat an explanation."[20] Even mentioning the very word "surprise" was an insult to the Chinese. First, it would mean that they had misread U.S. intentions. This risked raising the question of why they insisted on going ahead and ignoring the extremely clear warning the Americans had given Liu Huaqiu. Even more incriminating, they would have had absolutely no face if they left the impression that they had turned tail in the face of America's overwhelming military power. If not properly handled, this might have gone all the way to the top and become a question of prestige for the Chinese leadership.

Even if China had "misread" the situation, they should not have been blamed for their seemingly sheer incompetence. In July of the previous year, when China conducted its missile exercises in the Taiwan Straits to protest Lee Teng-hui's trip to the United States, the Americans made absolutely no response. It would, therefore, not be strange for the Chinese to think they would do nothing this time too. That is precisely why the United States was so sensitive. As an official at the White House put it, "We had responded fairly mildly at that time, and didn't believe we could respond mildly again."[21]

The deployment of the carriers found strong support at home. Even Republican presidential candidate Bob Dole released a statement saying "I support sending a strong signal to China." Dole had been personally involved in shaping the Taiwan Relations Act. He did not, however, forget to take a swipe at Clinton's "back and forth, yo-yo foreign policy"and to remark that he looked forward to a proper policy toward China.[22]

Republican Doug Bereuter, chairman of the House Committee on International Relations' Subcommittee on Asia-Pacific Affairs, said that the carriers should have been sent earlier.[23] Although Washington had fairly accurate information on the Chinese military exercises, analysts were not sure until the last minute whether the Chinese were actually going to launch the missiles. This, therefore, made an earlier deployment of the carriers difficult.

Reactions by the countries of the Asia-Pacific region were also complicated and hard to evaluate. The military response of sending in the carriers was played up too much; America's diplomatic efforts were inadequate. That was probably one reason for Asian confusion. While the White House was enthusiastic in communicating with Liu Huaqiu, it showed hardly any interest in sharing thoughts and coordinating policy with its all-important allies.

Of all the countries in the Asia-Pacific region, only Japan and Australia voiced criticism of the missile exercise. Lee Kuan Yew, senior minister of Singapore, also issued a warning to China later that "if it attacks Taiwan, then China's hopes of becoming an industrial nation in 25 years will suffer a major setback."[24] A White House official perhaps reflects a more widespread skepticism when he says, "I was quite struck at the time by how mild the reaction was by everybody. There was a quiet 'attaboy' from pretty much all over ASEAN."[25]

However, many countries behind the scenes supported the deployment of the carriers. Perry attested that "most of the other countries in the region made private statements to us that they not only supported but strongly supported and applauded the action . . . nearly every nation in the region."[26] A very senior member of the Defense Department, however, looking back on events, said, "We failed to win firm support from the countries of Asia because of the State Department's weak diplomatic efforts. We have given China the wrong impression."[27] Mike Mansfield, former ambassador to Japan, remarked, "When China fired missiles offshore of Taiwan, the secretary of state was in Syria. In my view he should have been in Asia. . . . I think that [dispatching two aircraft carriers] is certainly a symbol of brute force, [it] was very essential, but we needed words from top officials in a much more effective way."[28]

But to have made too strong a diplomatic assault would have run the risk of creating an impression of containing China, which would have hurt China's prestige more. The U.S. government had to take that point into consideration as well.

Among themselves, the Taiwanese welcomed the deployment of the carriers enthusiastically. The Taiwan military, however, was in general very restrained. In addition to pleas from the Americans urging restraint, they probably did not want to provoke China seriously. Taiwan was scheduled to get 150 F-16 fighters and 60 Mirage fighters from the United States in addition to 130 domestic versions of the F-16 by the year 2000. The planes would make it more difficult for China to have air superiority. Right now, though, the Taiwanese were in a weak position. They did not want to rock the boat.

These military considerations were a factor, but there were also political considerations. During the general election campaign, the opposition New Party had criticized meddling by foreign powers. In a full-page advertisement the New Party had placed in the *Lian He Bao (United Daily News)*, "Where Will Our Dignity Be if U.S. Forces Come?" the party asserted that "as long as the United States refuses to sign a joint defense treaty with Taiwan guaranteeing mutual defense, in other words, if the United States is merely using Taiwan as a pawn, this will only increase tensions on both sides of the Straits. If their arrival brings no result, or they just turn around and sail away again, then they might as well not come."[29]

Irrespective of political affiliations, all the parties were thumping themselves on the chest: We should solve our own problems ourselves; we should not entertain too high hopes of the United States.

Behind all of this, however, was surely a cool calculation that if they welcomed the carriers with open arms, there was a very strong likelihood of an emotional backlash from China; nor were the Taiwanese likely to be too keen about an American display of compassion. As Masatake Wakabayashi, a professor at Tokyo University and a leading authority on Taiwan, pointed out, Taiwan "had learned a lot from the Israelis' reaction during the Gulf War when they exercised restraint and did not lash back even when Iraq fired missiles into their country." Taiwan "played the victim very well."[30]

"An Obsessive Interest"

Perry did not hesitate to say that "deploying the carriers was a great success." This was because "above all else, it had contributed to making China's missile intimidation a political failure."[31] After sending the carriers, the Chinese suddenly started sending the Americans signals that "this was only a military exercise; we have no intention of attacking or invading Taiwan." Mike Doubleday, a Pentagon spokesman, told reporters on March 14 that "in public and private conversations, the United States has been assured that the Chinese do not intend to take any military action against Taiwan."[32]

The signals they sent were diverse. They clearly conveyed when the missile launches would begin and end; they were clear about the target areas; and they left their radio communications on the same frequency so they could be heard. In all, they fired four missiles in the exercises that spring. One of the Pentagon's China experts remembers, "We had information that China had initially planned to fire 10 missiles. Mightn't they have only fired the four because America sent the carriers? That is another piece of information we received."[33]

Another U.S. official said, "I think it made our position towards Jiang Zemin and the military section of the Chinese Foreign Ministry stronger.

Jiang and the Foreign Ministry seemed to have been saying internally that it shouldn't assume that the U.S. would do nothing, so their voices were probably strengthened by the fact that we came out so resolutely."[34]

Perry's view on this point was "I do believe that they were prepared to launch more than four. And I don't have ways of knowing whether they stopped at four because of the carriers, or whether they stopped at four because the first four were successful, in some technical sense of the word. . . . I don't think they were launching those missiles for technical reasons to begin with; I think they were launching them for political reasons. . . . My interpretation . . . is that they stopped because of the carriers, but that is an inference."[35]

Another U.S. government official and China expert said, "The approach . . . 'because we think it's so, therefore it will be so,' was exposed to the harsh light of reality and didn't hold very well, and they backed away from it. We have deliberately chosen to downplay that. We have never made any effort to try and overstate the importance of what we did, because, on the one hand, we didn't want to mislead Taiwan into thinking we were going to come to their defense . . . every time they make an error of one sort or another. But I mean there's this sort of subjective will that was always a part of Mao's thinking, that if we're united in our belief we can make anything happen. They can't. And I think that was clear to them."[36]

His point was, in short, that the Chinese military were forced to hesitate when confronted by two carriers. Subjectivity and good intentions stood for nothing in such a situation. In order to make them realize that, however, the Americans could not turn it into a political point of contention. To do that would be playing right into the hands of the military hardliners: What do you mean sending your carriers in here? It would only fuel nationalism: We're not going to stand for America insulting us! That would not be to America's advantage either.

Some of the U.S. strategic issues experts tended to be apprehensive that dispatching the carriers might backfire, as the naval blockade had done during the Cuban crisis. That action was a serious affront to the Soviet military, teaching them the lesson that no matter how many nuclear warheads and missiles you had, you could not be a superpower without maritime power. This in turn led to the Soviet program of strengthening of submarine capability and larger warships in what was known as the "Gorshkov Naval Strategy." Sergei Gorshkov was commander of the Soviet Navy and the driving force behind this increase of naval power.

There was a sense of alarm about China's "obsessive interest in carriers," said Eric McVadon, a retired admiral and navy attaché to China in the early 1990s.[37] At that time, China could not afford to have its own aircraft carriers. McVadon's assessment was that this was why the Chinese were so interested in anticarrier attack capability that would make the United States think twice before deploying its carriers. Regarding China's purchase from Russia of two Sovremeny-class destroyers equipped with Sunburn antiship missiles, the U.S. government took the attitude in public that "there's nothing that we [the U.S. government] see that contravenes international law or our own law," but privately it was not amused because the deal corresponded to nothing less than anticarrier attack capability.[38]

One of the Pentagon's top China experts remarked, "Perhaps they are thinking about using them in a Taiwan scenario. . . . It seems that their objective is to create enough conventional military capability to be able to inflict a high enough casualty rate or cost on the U.S. that would make us reconsider, or at least keep us out of the zone around Taiwan."[39] If only for that reason, the Americans had to be very careful not to damage Chinese face.

Walter Slocombe, however, did not subscribe to the Cuban crisis analogy. "I don't believe it. There is no question that China intends to modernize its military [but] for all of China's size and growing wealth, and vast population and so forth, it is not anywhere near the military power one could say. . . . So I think it's inevitable that China will want to add to its military capability. And they also, I think, understand that there are very real limits to their capacity to project power; I think they understand . . . that there is some political cost to pay if they were to embark on what would appear to be a major effort to build a world-class capacity to project power. . . . A naval race between the U.S. and China is not something which we look upon with any trepidation; it would be foolish for it to happen."[40]

As Perry said, the deployment of the carriers had been a success to the extent that they clearly demonstrated the U.S. commitment not to withdraw from the region. This was, however, a form of shock therapy that the United States had been forced to adopt because of the failure of the Clinton administration's Chinese diplomacy.

Perry's decision to deploy the carriers assured him of even greater confidence and popularity among the military and reinforced his political standing at home. At the same time, it also meant that the friendly approach to China he had been pursuing up until then was put on hold. China's launching of missiles also brought about an escalation in the rhetoric of the anti-Chinese hawks. Instead of praising Perry, the most right-wing reactionaries upbraided him. In an article entitled "The Peking Pentagon; China's Military Loves Bill Perry," he was criticized for being too soft on China.[41]

In this thrust and parry, Perry's decision unintentionally took on domestic political implications.

Defending Home Waters: A Deep-Sea Navy

China had commenced military exercises for Taiwan contingency scenarios in the previous summer. The first foray was in July 1995 when the positions of President Jiang Zemin and Vice-Premier/Foreign Minister Qian Qichen deteriorated after Lee Teng-hui's trip to the United States. "It's because you're too soft that this kind of unnecessary thing happens." The main source of the criticism was the military. Reports had been received that the two men had been forced to perform self-criticism.

The July 1995 missile tests were of great significance to China, for it was the first time China fired its ballistic missiles at a sea area conspicuously adjacent to Taiwan. The United States, despite its commitment to Taiwan's security as outlined in the Taiwan Relations Act, took no action against China.[42] Specifically, section 2(b)6 of the act states that the United States would maintain the capacity "to resist any resort to force or other forms of coercion that would jeopardize the security, the social or economic system, of the people of Taiwan." Furthermore, section 2(b)4 declares "boycotts and embargoes" as among the "other than peaceful means" that would pose a grave threat to the peace and security of the region.[43]

The second round of military exercises was in December and was timed to overlap with Taiwan's parliamentary elections. Shortly thereafter, America's aircraft carrier, the USS *Nimitz*, "just happened to" sail through the Taiwan Straits. Perry confirms that "that was a routine deployment."[44] The Pentagon may have preferred to utilize clearer and less ambiguous signals to China, but the divergent outlooks between the Pentagon and the State Department hampered such signals from taking place.[45]

The U.S. administration did not inform the Taiwan authorities of the carriers' passage, and the press in Taiwan kicked up a huge fuss when they found out about it. As a senior White House official reveals, "there was no protest" from China, which was not even aware that the USS *Nimitz* had gone through the straits. The truth of the matter was that the Chinese only learned about it because the Taiwanese newspapers had played it up as "America shows its intent to China."[46]

Among the China experts at the State Department, the dominant view was that Jiang Zemin had yet to consolidate his power base and the military was trying to fill the void. While Deng Xiaoping was still physically alive, politically China was in a post-Deng phase of flux. Taiwan was in the process of becoming a litmus test of Jiang's leadership and the focus of the succession struggle.

Jiang had been pushing for a soft approach on the peaceful unification of the two Chinas with the so-called Eight Items Proposal he put forward in January 1995. Democratic elections for Taiwan's national parliament and the presidency were scheduled in 1995–96. Lee Teng-hui's plan was to face up to China backed up by the will of the Taiwanese people, and he did not make much of Jiang's proposal. Jiang lost face. And to add insult to injury, there was Lee Teng-hui's trip to the United States. Jiang's position vis-à-vis the military was weakened. The military argued for exercises focused on Taiwan and had gone ahead with them in the wake of Lee's visit to the United States.

In December 1995, Charles Freeman, former assistant secretary of defense, visited China and got the following "inside scoop" from key Chinese military personnel: "The Chinese had decided, and they told many people including me, to conduct six military maneuvers; these maneuvers would culminate around the time of the Taiwan presidential election, which at that time had not yet been fixed. There was no specific date set, although it was known to be probably March, and by October many of the details of these military maneuvers were known, including plans for missile firings and the like, although unfortunately very few people took these plans seriously."[47]

With minor amendments these plans were implemented mainly at the behest of the People's Liberation Army (PLA). Jiang Zemin joined in. Although his visit to the site of the exercise ceremony failed to eventuate, he was involved far enough to have a visit scheduled for March 19. The exercises were carried out with the party's blessing.

The party's Central Committee Military Commission was in charge of the Taiwan issue, but it was really the jurisdiction of the party's Central Committee Foreign Affairs Commission, which was controlled by Li Peng. Jiang Zemin had no choice but to join forces with Li Peng on Taiwan policy and confront the military. Jiang's position was once again very delicate.

A senior member of the White House revealed, "We were aware by that time that the whole Taiwan issue, and responding to the Li Teng-hui visit to Cornell was a very controversial issue within the leadership, that President Jiang had been criticized as had Foreign Minister Qian, and we had a perception that military influence on China's policy had risen, but again it wasn't anything that we could substantiate. But it was something that we were concerned about, but again just sort of background."[48]

The Americans were trying to figure out how they should respond to the rise of the PLA. Secretary Perry's efforts to bring about Sino-American military exchanges was partly spurred by this concern. If Americans didn't understand the military, they would never understand China. If they couldn't get through to the military, they wouldn't be able to talk with China. If they could create a relationship of trust with the military, it would then be possible to coordinate policy with China.

However, the PLA, like the rest of China, was undergoing huge changes. While relations between the party and the army were still founded on the inviolate principle of "the military would serve the party," it was all very complicated. Post-Deng jockeying cast a long shadow here as well. The PLA had substantially overhauled its military doctrine at the end of the 1980s. Formerly, its main adversary was the Soviet Union, so its defense was focused on the north and the army had the leading role. It needed cooperation from the United States and Japan on the international front.

The collapse of the Soviet Union changed all that. The Chinese would not have to worry about their northern border for at least the next 20 to 30 years. The military leaders boasted that "China has never been in a safer security environment for 50 years."

It was in 1985, shortly after Soviet leader Mikhail Gorbachev's rise, that the Chinese Central Committee issued an internal communiqué to the effect that they need no longer prepare and train for "early and large-scale nuclear warfare." Their reaction was quick. From now on, their main target would not be large-scale warfare with the Soviet Union nor would their tactics be aimed at a possible "early, major, and nuclear war"; instead they would prepare for local, limited war (*jubu zhanzheng*) on neighboring borders, especially to ensure that their sovereignty in the southern seas was not threatened or violated.[49] In the view of Beijing policymakers, the possibility of global warfare had been eliminated due to the changing global power balance between the United States and Russia.

The Chinese had switched from north to south, a 180-degree about-face. Liu Huaqing, vice president of the Central Committee who had served as navy commander from 1982 until 1988, instructed the navy to draw up a comprehensive strategy for defending the southern seas. Up until that point, the Chinese Navy had concentrated its efforts on guarding the coast; in other words, "defending home waters." This had to be changed into defending home oceans, which meant extending the line of defense 200 to 400 nautical miles from the coast. They would have to think up a special structure for the South China Sea, where China had territorial disputes with several Southeast Asian countries. The new structure for defending home oceans was to be in place by the year 2000. After that, China would start building a deep-sea navy for 2050.

China's military, however, had an Achilles' heel; their equipment was old-fashioned and their technology outdated. In the modernization program begun in the 1980s, the economy was seen as the greatest key to state unity. Even in the Four Modernizations, modernization of the military was last on the list. The military went ahead with personnel cutbacks. Its budget also came under pressure. Updating equipment was not easy. The military found itself forced to go into business.

They were unhappy, but it was Deng Xiaoping himself who had made the call; there was nothing they could do. Deng had the charisma and the credibility to force the military to put up with things. During the 1992 U.S. presidential campaign, the Bush administration, in its desire to win the Texas vote, signed a contract with General Dynamics, headquartered in Fort Worth, Texas, to export 150 F-16 fighter planes to Taiwan. The Chinese grumbled but restrained themselves. Deng Xiaoping had told the military to be patient. The Gulf War, however, knocked the military leaders right off their feet. The generals were blown away by the destructive power of the U.S. super-high-tech weaponry, which they saw in all its glory every day on CNN.

A Clinton administration official specializing in China outlined the development of China's military modernization as follows: "In 1992, we started to see the first evidence in China of a clear shift in the way it approaches its doctrine, its military modernization . . . then in March of 1996, it's almost a graduation exercise of about four to five years of intensive work that they have been doing. . . . They need purchases of everything. . . . The important purchase, or experimental doctrine . . . is when they buy squadrons, you know, they start to create operational units. And in that area, their purchase of the SU-27s, their continuing purchase of Kilo-class submarines, their purchase of Sovremeny destroyers were important."[50]

In 1993, Liu Huaqing declared that he was going to turn the "short-armed, slow-footed" Chinese military into a high-tech force. The Chinese stepped up their purchase of modern Russian weapons. Still, a military doctrine had to be adopted to decide what the high-tech focus was going to be, what they were going to set their sights on.

In 1994, a new military doctrine targeted at Taiwan emerged. In order to upgrade their Taiwan invasion capability, the Chinese acquired short-range land-to-land missiles (Tongfeng), state-of-the-art fighters (Sukhoi), and submarines (Kilo class). The culmination of this process was the three-part military exercises of March 1996.

The Geopolitics of Taiwan

The Sino-American relationship under the Clinton administration "flip-flopped like a yo-yo," as Republican Senator Bob Dole put it.

At first the administration treated the Chinese leadership as if it were in the same class as Saddam Hussein. Inviting 40 Chinese dissidents and Tibetan activists to the White House, Clinton declared, "Starting today, the United States will speak with one voice on China."[51] The policy was to pressure China by linking extension of its most-favored-nation (MFN) status to human rights issues. One year later, there had been a complete reversal.

Human rights and the MFN status were unbundled as the result of fierce lobbying from American big business. (Business leaders may once again have impressed upon the Chinese Karl Marx's lesson that when looking at things in the United States under capitalism the politics of the "superstructure" is determined by the economics of the "substructure," and told themselves that "America is the epitome of a capitalist country.")

In 1994, Lee Teng-hui asked to spend one night in the United States on his way to Costa Rica, but the administration refused. His plane did land in Hawaii where it had been given permission to refuel, but Lee refused to take one step outside the plane in protest. It had also been decided not to issue a visa for Lee to participate in the graduation ceremony at his alma mater, Cornell University. Taiwan's foreign minister, Frederick Chien, castigated the Americans as "a bunch of spineless jellyfish."[52] One year later, there had been a complete reversal here as well.

Congress placed pressure on Clinton by passing a nonbinding resolution supporting Lee's visit to Cornell by 360 to 0 in the House and 97 to 1 in the Senate. The White House bowed to this pressure and decided to issue the visa at the last moment. This reversal took place less than a week after Secretary of State Christopher had adamantly confirmed to the Chinese foreign minister, Qian Qichen, that "no visa would be issued."

The Clinton administration was the first, truly post–Cold War government in the United States. Diplomacy was seen as inferior to economics, and the grass-roots agenda was projected, unadulterated, on the diplomatic screen. Until around the summer of 1993, the administration took the position that even meeting with high-level Chinese officials, who "ignored human rights," was "indecent." In his Senate confirmation hearings in January 1993 after being appointed secretary of state, Warren Christopher stated, "The objective of our China policy is to work for a peaceful revolution from communism to democracy."[53] This was a so-called peaceful evolution.

Nevertheless, the administration could not ignore China forever. First of all, it needed Chinese cooperation on the North Korean nuclear development problem. China had a special relationship with North Korea. Besides, it was also a permanent member of the U.N. Security Council.

It was in September 1994 that the Clinton administration came up with its policy of "engaging" China. Perry led the way on this. He had been thinking from the very first that they needed to build up a more practical relationship with China. In order to do that, he put promoting military exchanges between the two countries on his agenda. Perry himself went to China in November 1994 to put his finger on the pulse. He had received an informal assurance that, returning the compliment, China's defense minister, Chi Haotian, would visit the United States. In protest at Lee Teng-hui's trip to the United States, however, China cancelled Chi Haotian's visit. Just when things had settled down and Perry was about to invite Chi Haotian again, along came the China-Taiwan crisis. This time, it was the United States that had to withdraw its invitation. Definitely a lot of flip-flops.

While it is clear that many of these contradictions in the Sino-American relationship stemmed from the internal contradiction in U.S.

politics, the United States had a tendency to view China's own internal contradiction as a "primary contradiction." Americans judged the Chinese situation to be fluid and unstable. They tried to read what the intentions and motives of its Taiwan policy were:

- China is involved in a post–Deng Xiaoping struggle for succession. No matter who emerges, the new leadership will not be stable without the support of the military. The military are very aggressive on Taiwan and suspect that Jiang Zemin is too soft. Jiang cannot risk taking too dovelike a stance at this time.

- China has serious political, economic, social, and ideological problems. Of these, the issue of Taiwan may be used to stir up nationalism, to unite national debate, and create social solidarity. Playing up the Taiwan issue and bashing the United States creates one kind of "false sense of menace," which is a convenient way of binding the nation closer together. (According to an internal poll conducted by the Chinese government, at the beginning of 1996, 90 percent of those surveyed responded that "China should be hard on Taiwan." In another survey conducted by the *Chinese Youth Daily* in the summer of 1995, more than 70 percent of the "young opinion leaders" said that "of all the countries in the world, America is the most hostile to China.")

- Chinese relations with Asian countries have never been so good. Its economy is also developing. In contrast, U.S. relations with Japan and Europe are very shaky. If China plays hardball with Taiwan, no one but the United States is likely to come to Taiwan's aid. This differs significantly from the time of the Korean War, when China was faced by a united front. At least, that is probably how China sees it. In short, China thinks time is on its side. It undoubtedly believes that its best course of action would be not to invade Taiwan in one fell swoop but to use a gradual, water-torture approach and to wear Taiwan down psychologically and continually test America's resolve.

- In military terms, Taiwan still does not have the capability to strike back at China. This situation may well change when Taiwan takes delivery of its F-16s. Until that time, Taiwan needs to be taught a lesson. Moreover, its political parties are totally engrossed in factional in-fighting. China probably sees the timing as perfect for creating a psychological impact.

Back in the United States, however, China's diplomacy of intimidation by missiles was coming to be perceived as the first signs of its emergence as a military superpower. Administration leaders warned that

China's intimidation of Taiwan should not only be interpreted as an operation to divert interest from domestic Chinese factors, especially social problems and the distinctive tremors that accompany any change in leadership, to external issues. Rather, they deemed this as being aimed at preventing Taiwan from forming an alliance that might view China as the enemy when China emerged on the scene as a military superpower in the 21st century.

This amounted to a "rediscovery" of Taiwan's geopolitical and strategic position. As China's economic relations with other East Asian countries deepened, China would put more effort into "home ocean defense" in the southern seas. As its interest in oil lanes grew as it evolved into a huge oil importer itself, China would come to have its own deep-sea navy. In short, it would begin to cast a military shadow over the open seas. At such a time, Taiwan would become not only a crucial political but a military cornerstone. The Chinese military had to be eyeing Taiwan in that light.

Chinese leaders had traditionally displayed this perspective. Deng Xiaoping once explained to a delegation of Hong Kong drafters of legislation in 1987: "Without unification, Taiwan will be unable to maintain its status, because if it doesn't do this [unite], it is likely to be swallowed up by some other country, America or Japan, for instance."[54]

This statement was startlingly similar in both concept and tenor to a statement made by Shi Lang in the Qing Dynasty (1644–1912). Shi Lang was a general who emphasized Taiwan's strategic value. "Taiwan is a small island, but it provides protection for many of our provinces. If it be abandoned, it does not matter whether it is handed over to the barbarians or becomes the possession of traitors to the state. But it matters if this plays into the hands of the Dutch." His statement expresses the sense of threat that if Taiwan was not united with China, it would end up in the hands of countries hostile to China, thereby threatening China's national security.

The fears of China's leaders, however, could not all be dealt with as mere paranoia. Historically speaking, the "Western Powers" had always viewed Taiwan in this light as well. Commodore Matthew Perry believed that Taiwan was the key to controlling all of southern China as well as access to the East China Sea.

Tsuyoshi Inoue, father of Meiji Japan's judiciary and education systems, stressed to Prime Minister Hirobumi Ito in 1894 before the Sino-Japanese War, "If this large island fell into the hands of others, Japan's Okinawa Islands will be unable to sleep soundly at night. Should we miss this opportunity, one of the great powers will most definitely possess Taiwan two or three years hence."[55]

The U.S. and Chinese strategy game with a view to the 21st century had started like a chess game between their respective strategists. Should

China build itself a deep-sea navy and foray out into the open seas, the Americans would become even more sensitive to the strategic value of Taiwan and any threat towards it.

The intellectual radar of the Americans was picking up Chinese ambitions. Not having Taiwan under its own control would feel like a dagger at China's throat. There was a very strong possibility that at such a time, China's policy of patience would reach its limit and be replaced by a policy of force.

Meanwhile, the intellectual radar of China was picking up a U.S. plot. America intended to use its powerful aircraft carriers to check China's deep-sea strategy. The United States did not want China to become part of the order-making apparatus in the Asia-Pacific region. Therefore, it would probably create strife in this region to fan apprehension of China by its neighbors and anti-Chinese sentiment on China's borders. Americans wanted to use this strife to make an appeal for the significance and value of their presence.

Taiwan had emerged as a geopolitical strategic factor. Were the missile launches an indication of that? Did they herald the start of a new Cold War in Asia? What moves would Japan make? And what moves would the U.S.-Japan alliance make?

Notes

1. Interview with Frank Meeks.
2. "Pizza Index Up Under Clinton," *Knight-Ridder Newspapers*, December 20, 1993.
3. Author's conversation with Sumio Takeichi, Mitsubishi's representative in Washington, D.C.
4. Interview with a senior DOD official.
5. Ibid.
6. Interview with William Perry.
7. Ibid.
8. Ibid.
9. William Perry's remarks at the Pacific Forum CSIS, March 1997.
10. Interview with William Perry.
11. "Remarks by William Perry at Georgetown University," *Federal News Service*, April 18, 1996.
12. *Federal News Service*, April 18, 1996.
13. Interview with a Taiwanese top government leader.
14. Interview with a senior DOD official.
15. Ibid.

16. "China Tells U.S. to Keep Out of Strait; Li Says Warships Will Muddle Affair," *Houston Chronicle*, March 18, 1996, p. 1.

17. Interview with a senior U.S. government official.

18. Interview with William Perry.

19. Ibid.

20. Interview with a high-level White House official.

21. Interview with a White House official.

22. Brian Knowlton, "Beijing Warns the U.S. on Taiwan Intervention, Second Carrier is Sent by U.S. as 'Precaution,'" *International Herald Tribune*, March 12, 1996.

23. Interview with Doug Bereuter.

24. "Suicide? War on Taiwan Could Sink China's Economy," *Dallas Morning News*, March 12, 1996, p. 15A.

25. Interview with a White House official.

26. Interview with William Perry.

27. Interview with a senior DOD official.

28. Interview with Mike Mansfield.

29. Masatake Wakabayashi, *Taiwan's Taiwanese Speakers, Chinese Speakers, and Japanese Speakers* (Tokyo: Asahi Shimbunsha, 1997), p. 337. (In Japanese.)

30. Ibid., p. 341.

31. Interview with William Perry.

32. "China Says It Will End Maneuvers as Planned," *Los Angeles Times*, March 15, 1996, p. 1.

33. Interview with a DOD official.

34. Interview with a senior State Department official.

35. Interview with William Perry.

36. Interview with a White House official.

37. Interview with Eric McVadon.

38. Bill Gertz, "U.S. Not Against Russia-China Deal; But Arms Treaties Must Be Observed," *Washington Times*, January 11, 1997.

39. Interview with a DOD official.

40. Interview with Walter Slocombe.

41. *American Spectator*, April 1996.

42. John Garver, *Face Off: China, the United States, and Taiwan's Democratization* (Seattle: University of Washington Press, 1997), p. 74.

43. Ibid., p. 77. (The text of the act is in Robert Downen, *The Taiwan Pawn in the China Game,* Washington, D.C.: Georgetown University, Center for Strategic and International Studies, 1981.)

44. Interview with William Perry.

45. Garver, *Face Off,* p. 87.

46. Interview with a senior White House official.

47. Interview with Charles Freeman.

48. Interview with a White House official.

49. Paul Godwin, "Technology, Strategy, and Operations: The PLA's Continuing Dilemma," a paper prepared for the SIPRI Workshop "Military Technology and Offensive Capability in Southern Asia," Solna, Sweden, September 22–24, 1995, p. 4.

50. Interview with a DOD official.

51. "China Called Clinton's Bluff on Human Rights," *Los Angeles Times,* September 10, 1996, p. A1.

52. *Los Angeles Times,* September 9, 1996.

53. Warren Christopher's statement from his confirmation hearing.

54. A statement made during a press conference, April 16, 1987.

55. The author is grateful to Professor Masatake Wakabayashi for this quote.

Chapter Eighteen

The U.S.-Japan Link

"I Can't Sleep at Night"

After the outbreak of the China-Taiwan crisis, there were days when Prime Minister Hashimoto couldn't sleep. He was tense and his smile had disappeared. A senior official at the PM's office almost every day disclosed, "I've never seen the prime minister look so exhausted."

"What course of action could Japan take if things exploded? What should they do for the U.S. forces and how?" He handed out the homework rapid fire. The first thing they had to make sure of was how the U.S.-Japan Security Treaty would be set in motion in the event of a China-Taiwan contingency.

"How about providing facility areas and other aid? What about resupplying at sea? That shouldn't involve any armed clashes. But it might happen. We need to push the envelope and check that out."

Hashimoto summoned officials from the Cabinet Security Office (CSO), the Foreign Ministry (MOFA), and the Defense Agency (JDA), stirring them up with questions like these.

There was something else that was keeping Hashimoto awake at night, and that was rescue operations for Japanese nationals in Taiwan should the need arise.

"How many airports are there in Taiwan? How many runways are there that can handle the official government aircraft? How many runways are there that the SDF's [Self-Defense Forces] C-130 transporters could use? Where are they located? If we ran a shuttle operation, how many shuttles would we need and how many people could they fly out? If we sent ships to rescue Japanese nationals, how many ports are there on the other side, not the Straits side, and how many ships can they hold?"

The questions came in rapid succession, but the answers couldn't keep up. The Cabinet Security Office was run off its feet. Even so, it had already started work on a "paper plan"[1] a little earlier with the help of the Foreign Ministry, the Defense Agency, and the transport ministry. Everything was hypothetical, so they had done it more or less as a kind of intellectual exercise.[2]

There were approximately 10,000 Japanese permanent residents and 10,000 Japanese tourists in Taiwan. The high number of tourists is unusual. The Japanese are now great travelers, covering the globe. Compared to former years, their number has jumped markedly, raising the risk of trouble somewhere, sometime.

Japanese rescue planes would use Naha, the closest airport to Taiwan. The shuttles would be flown from there. The officials would restrict travel to Taiwan. That would help them get the Japanese nationals out faster. They would also use ships, which, bearing in mind the need for safety, would use ports on the eastern coast, not the western coast near to China. They also looked into countermeasures in case armed guerrillas infiltrated any refugees from Taiwan.

Hashimoto instructed the CSO to examine more closely what sort of signal restricting travel to Taiwan would send to China and also how Taiwan would perceive it. The Ministry of Transport had restricted travel to the Philippines when the head of Mitsui Trading's Manila branch, Nobuyuki Wakaoji, was kidnapped. Hashimoto remembered that the Philippines government had expressed its displeasure.

The instructions Hashimoto issued at this time were later generalized into what was referred to as the "Four Crisis Management Instructions":

1. The rescue of Japanese nationals;
2. Measures for large-scale refugees;
3. Coast guards/terrorist measures;
4. Support for the United States.

Hashimoto told the bureaucrats that the scariest thing at times like this was a slip-up. "If the exercises go according to plan, no crisis should occur. We don't know how accurate their missiles are. If they miss their target and something happens, how will Taiwan react? That's why accidental factors might come into play on this side, too. That's what's scary."[3]

What would happen to oil transportation if the Taiwan Straits was blocked? What would be the impact on distribution to Southeast Asia? What would happen with trade to China? Hashimoto's "concerns about the impact on Japanese livelihood resembled those of a MITI minister."[4] He used a crisis management approach in responding to the China-Taiwan showdown. And he swore to himself that if Japan finds itself in a position where it has to take action, it mustn't repeat the shameful performance in the 1990–91 Gulf War and the 1994 crisis on the Korean

Peninsula. Nor is it right to have bureaucrats creeping around deciding emergency responses like in 1994. This is a job for the politicians.[5]

He told Masahiro Akiyama, director-general, Bureau of Defense Policy, JDA, after Akiyama had finished briefing him on China's intent with the exercises and the detailed military operations, "Listen, this is very important stuff, so please repeat what you've just told me to the head of the Cabinet Legislation Bureau [CLB]. They're the crisis management point men, politically speaking."[6] The CLB is well known for its strict interpretation of the constitution, which to many conservative politicians seems to block Japan from coping with contingencies more flexibly.

Akiyama was taken aback but contacted the CLB right away. He briefed the entire staff of the bureau. Akiyama felt he couldn't take military men along with him, so he explained the military background himself like "an old pro from J-5 at the Joint Staff Council."[7] J-5 at the Joint Staff Council was the section in charge of medium-to-long-term strategic issues and defense dialogue. It was also handling the review of the U.S.-Japan guidelines.

The crux of the matter involved Article 6 of the Security Treaty. Was the situation grave enough to influence Japanese security? And if so, what could Japan do and how far? At this juncture, however, the government did not attempt to answer these questions. "The prime minister may have been thinking about it, but the government as such did not discuss it, nor were any decisions made," testified a top Japanese government official.[8]

A Yellow Light

How did the Japanese government perceive the possibility of an armed conflict? Information was drawn together mainly from the Cabinet Research and Information Office (CRIO), Japanese legations abroad, the Foreign Ministry, and the Defense Agency. Convinced that "you never know, but an armed conflict might just happen," the CRIO was flashing a yellow light. "We've heard that they have activated their SU-27 fighters."

The SU-27 was the former Soviet Union's much-prized Suhoy fighter plane. China had bought 46 in 1992, later increasing them to a total of 72. They were originally bought to rival the F-16 fighters Taiwan had contracted from the United States. An analysis of their capability was conducted using a simulation of where China would move the SU-27s to and how they would fly them.

The CRIO also reported that China looked "poised" for an invasion. There was a possibility of small-scale forces landing on the Taiwanese islands in the vicinity of Quemoy and Matsu. The number of amphibious vessels in place, however, was limited, so that they would have had to employ "shuttle transport" for any assault. That was highly unlikely, so the probability of an invasion of Taiwan was considered low.

Elsewhere, the CRIO predicted that the United States would deploy not only the USS *Independence* but also the USS *Nimitz* to the area, and it was right. Hashimoto was impressed with CRIO's information. After the crisis was over, he revealed that "Omori had the most accurate information. Heads and shoulders above the rest."[9] Yoshio Omori was the director of the Cabinet Research and Information Office and a former police agency intelligence officer.

Criticism welled up within the government that it was risky passing on unadulterated CRIO information, including "speculation," to the top. Hashimoto paid no heed, however. He was more impressed by the sharp political sense Omori displayed in his presentations. For instance, Omori flavored his assessment with the perception that China, by using its missile intimidation to force Taiwan into declaring martial law, was aiming to destroy the legitimacy of the Taiwanese election itself, taking place as it would have to under martial law.

Omori said, "If China bombed or attacked one of the islands smaller than Quemoy and Matsu, Taiwan would probably be unable to hold out. If even one island was occupied, they would have to reintroduce the martial law that President Lee Teng-hui was so averse to. In that case, it would no longer be possible to conduct 'China's [Taiwan's] first-ever direct election of a leader by democratic vote,' reducing the election to one under martial law. I believed that there was, therefore, a very real chance of a limited offensive and that we had to be ready to respond to such a contingency."[10]

It was not only the CRIO that set yellow lights flashing. The Defense Agency reported to the PM's office that "there are at least 10,000 islands near Quemoy and Matsu. They may land on one of those." The agency immediately received word that Hashimoto wanted it to brief him in more detail.

On March 11, senior members of both the Foreign Ministry and the Defense Agency were called to the PM's office in quick succession. The JDA had prepared a one-page memo divided into three sections on "Chinese moves," "U.S. moves," and "Japanese responses":

- There is a possibility that China will land on one of Taiwan's small islands.
- The United States will deploy the USS *Nimitz*.
- As long as the United States deploys the USS *Nimitz*, there is no need for Japan to make a move.

The JDA had already briefed Hashimoto on a China-Taiwan crisis scenario before his late February summit with Clinton in Santa Monica:

- China is planning a large-scale military exercise around the time of Taiwan's upcoming presidential election.
- There is a high likelihood of landing drills.
- They plan missile launches.
- They may launch a new missile model at that time.

The new model of missile referred to was a long-range missile. In the end, the Chinese did not use it, but the Tongfeng-15, which had a range of 600 kilometers. "The Chinese used their most reliable missile. They couldn't afford any mistakes, so they gave themselves a wide safety margin."[11]

This March 11 prediction of the USS *Nimitz* deployment was not only early but accurate. The Chinese, however, did not land on islands near Quemoy and Matsu. The JDA information was wrong there. The Defense Agency had the Air SDF's early-warning aircraft, the E-2C, and the Maritime SDF's electronic surveillance aircraft, the EP-3, scouring the skies. Whereas the E-2C usually flew only one mission a week, now it was flying daily missions to strengthen surveillance. The EP-3 was in the air 24 hours a day.

The JDA was also ready to move its communications unit to Ishigaki Island but in the end did not, keeping to its usual Naha and Miyako radar site arrangements. A high-ranking SDF officer in charge of day-to-day command in the Joint Staff Council attested, "We were ready to move them if the order came from higher up, but the order never came. We did not change any of our unit positions."[12]

Radio waves and communications intelligence proved their worth. "We had early knowledge that the missile exercise had ended with four launches. You can tell from the radio waves. But the Chinese can tell what we're doing too."[13]

MOFA looked on bitterly at the yellow-light presentations by the CRIO and the JDA. A top MOFA official said, "It was just like the weather forecast. It doesn't matter so much if they call for rain and it shines, but they get into trouble when they say it will be fine and it rains. So they [the CRIO and JDA] tend to always predict rain."[14]

MOFA's assessment was that "armed conflict would not occur," which basically came down to "it should be dealt with calmly." Information from the Americans was also extremely subdued, indicating "it won't escalate into a contingency." Regarding the deployment of the USS *Nimitz* as well, MOFA emphasized the fact that the intentionally slow speed at which the ship sailed was a ploy to give the Chinese time for deescalation, in other words, to reduce the scale of the exercise. A senior member at the ministry described this as being "akin to a psychological, virtual positioning."[15]

These differences, in fact, also derived from each institution's respective missions.

A JDA official said, "I can well understand MOFA's position. But just like the Pentagon, the role of the JDA is to think about what to do if something happens. We shared their emphasis on the fact that the Chinese exercise was a restrained one."[16]

Dependence on U.S. Intelligence

Japanese intelligence was fragmented and patchy. Japan had no choice but to rely on the United States. Hashimoto was unhappy that the information he received from the United States was insufficient. The nightmare of the time of the Gulf War came back to haunt him. *America eulogizes its alliance with Japan so much but won't give us any information when the chips are down. Can you call that an alliance?*[17]

The White House was under constant attack. A senior member at the White House remembered that "I think State [the State Department] was pretty much out of the loop. [Ambassador Saito] had difficulty getting access to Lake. Not because we didn't want to give it to him, but just finding the time really. . . . I recollect he came in, I recollect that there were phone calls from him."[18]

Another staffer said, "I am not sure if that pressure was coming out of the prime minister's office, or if it was more at a couple of levels below. . . . Part of the problem from a Japanese point of view is a lack of real-time intelligence, independent intelligence. Your prime minister had to rely a great deal on what was being provided through the U.S., and having only bits and pieces of information that were brought together by Japanese sources probably made him less comfortable, given his own personal focus on what was going on."[19]

That was exactly right. The United States gave prior notification of its deployment of the aircraft carrier USS *Independence*. "It was not in the form of prior consultation or anything like that. It was more of a courtesy."[20] Ambassador Walter Mondale, however, was frustrated by the three-hour delay in reports from Washington, which meant that "reports to the Japanese government were also three hours late. Somebody in the huge Washington bureaucracy had probably forgotten about it, but that wasn't acceptable."[21]

Japan was completely out of the loop, however, on the deployment of USS *Nimitz*. Although the behind the scenes connection between the SDF and the U.S. military was working and the JDA received information on this at a fairly early stage, MOFA was given no notice. That was a shock for Japan. "The U.S. military had started a genuine restraining movement, and yet its ally received no by-your-leave, no consultation, no explanation, nothing." The Japanese lodged a complaint with the Americans: "We were extremely tense, as an ally."[22]

This decision was taken by only a handful people starting with Secretary William Perry. Neither Walter Slocombe, undersecretary of defense, nor Kurt Campbell, deputy assistant secretary of defense, were in the know.[23] Nor was the Japanese Embassy informed. Ambassador Walter Mondale was on the phone right away, complaining to Secretary Perry. "We are allies with Japan, so if we don't let Japan know at such a decisive time, Japan cannot support the U.S. government's decision. I want you to make sure this sort of thing doesn't happen again. I also want you to send me information on the China-Taiwan crisis more expeditiously. I will make sure the information gets to the Japanese government in better time."[24]

A White House National Security Council (NSC) official said, "Ambassador Mondale wanted to make sure that whatever actions that were taking place with regard to the Taiwan Straits were understood and shared. He thought that was very important. And, in fact, [he] made a request that more timely information, information in more detail, information that was more operational in nature, was shared with Japan, and at his request, that information was provided."[25]

The flow of information became smoother once the Mondale-Perry hotline was set up. So much so that the Americans were heard to say "that was the first time we had shared so much information with Japan."[26]

Immediately the Japanese were swamped with information from the Americans. The Japanese started receiving "deep briefs" like "they're building a grandstand for Chinese VIPs to watch the exercise" or "the PLA [People's Liberation Army] has just landed on a deserted island near Taiwan, but it is not near the Taiwanese possessions of Quemoy and Matsu."

All this information came from the U.S. specialty, its surveillance satellite. Japan was buying the satellite intelligence and analyzing it but not fast enough for this kind of situation.

Subliminal

The U.S. bases in Okinawa were not busy during the China-Taiwan showdown in the Taiwan Straits. An air force commander at Kadena Air Base recalled that "the navy obviously used a few facilities in support, but in terms of the 18th Wing, we did not have much other than the radar support. Almost all the rest of it was with the *Independence* and when the *Nimitz* came in."[27] He was referring to the fact that "the Japanese were provided with movements by the PLA which the U.S. surveillance planes had picked up on their radar, which had a far broader range than the Japanese surveillance planes."[28]

The marines did not neglect their readiness at this time. If China attempted a land assault on Taiwan, the marines would probably be forced to respond in some way. On March 15, a round-the-clock standby was issued for the 2,000 members of the 31st Marine Expeditionary Unit (31 MEU). The Harriers at Kadena, the artillery at Camp Hansen, and the helicopter squadron at Futenma were all placed on alert. The latter were kept busy servicing and checking the fuel for 24 helicopters.

On March 17, a supply ship for the USS *Independence* sailed out of port. It was carrying 5,200 meals, a daily ration of 7,800 bottles of water, and 28,000 hamburgers. A fuel supply ship carrying 4.5 million liters, or 10 days' supply, also headed out. In the end, the marines were not called upon. However, the crisis was still a manifestation of just how important the base in Okinawa was for U.S. military operations.

There was a growing perception among defense authorities on both sides that the Taiwan factor might change the role of the bases on Okinawa. A middle-echelon official at the JDA predicted around this time that "in the future, when considering the China factor, Okinawa's significance may change. The importance of the marines may also increase," although he put this forward as his "personal opinion."[29]

In particular, the marines started emphasizing that "the China-Taiwan crisis was an event which renewed the awareness of the U.S. Marines of Okinawa's strategic importance."[30] In fact, the foreign policy authorities in both countries intimated that this "fervency" on the part of the marines was a nuisance at the time. One highly placed MOFA official remarked that "the marines seemed to be thinking that it would be their time if China implemented a land assault on Quemoy and Matsu. And the Chinese probably started turning a wary eye on them in that light."[31]

Advocacy for a bilateral "reconsolidation" did not cease with the role of the Okinawan bases. Former Assistant Secretary of Defense Richard Armitage, former Japan Desk Director at the Pentagon James Auer, and other advocates of strengthening the bilateral alliance saw the crisis as a good chance for bolstering bilateral talks and shaking up Japan. It breathed life into a completely different camp.

There were those on the American side, especially in the White House, who began to see the crisis as an excuse for putting off Futenma's return. However, this was such a politically sensitive issue that Japan would never allow such an excuse. Such a transparent approach would only earn the deep mistrust of the Japanese and shake the foundations of the alliance. The Japanese would start suspecting that the United States was using Chinese intimidation as a means to sabotage resolution of the base issue and perpetuate the "cap in the bottle" presence.

It was as if the two sides just couldn't keep the China-Taiwan crisis separate from Futenma, from Okinawa's role, from the Joint Security Declaration, from the guidelines review, from the bilateral security structure, and from the Japanese constitution. "It's a pretty sensitive issue. . . . That series of events in the Taiwan Straits, I would say, had a subliminal effect on us," recalled a U.S. diplomat stationed in Japan.[32] It was there subtly in the background, it could be perceived, but there was no clear awareness of it.

Hashimoto repeatedly stressed the need to proceed with caution so as not to provoke China. Even as Yonaguni-cho at Okinawa's westernmost tip was being drenched in the spray of Chinese missiles as they plunged into the sea and calling for naval protection to be dispatched, Hashimoto was negative, saying "it would stand out too much if we sent the Maritime SDF."[33]

When Tokuichiro Tamazawa, Liberal Democratic Party (LDP) member of the House of Representatives, questioned Hashimoto in the Diet whether the visit of Chinese Foreign Minister Qian Qichen should be cancelled in protest, he stressed the need for "dialogue," saying, "I would, in fact, prefer to have him come earlier."[34]

Hashimoto wanted to avoid making Japan stand out with any criticism of China. He added they should consider "the effect of Japan making rash moves or statements on its own in an international climate where at present no other country but Japan and the United States has expressed concern [about China's missile exercises]."[35] He also pointed out that while the countries in the Asia-Pacific region had shown their support for the deployment of the U.S. aircraft carriers, their feelings on the issue were complicated. He added that moving criticism of China up an octave was not the best course for Japan.

Criticism of China and dissatisfaction with the government's handling of the matter, however, erupted in the Diet. One member said, "The quiet, peaceful days of our citizens have been threatened. . . . Japan's national interests have been violated. I believe that, as the right of a sovereign state, we must make a stern protest to China."[36]

Another remarked, "Only recently, the U.S. sent two aircraft carriers to guard the vicinity, which has acted, I believe, as a significant deterrent. . . . In sharp contrast, however, and despite the various comments of the government, our own country has taken an extremely weak and ambiguous stance. This is a military exercise being conducted on the open seas, so it is not against international law. The government has gone to the trouble of releasing comments similar to Chinese comments. It is pathetic. I am not asking for a show of resistance or for Japan to cover Taiwan, but how can you just sit there when someone is threatening you?"[37]

Many of the representatives were calling for "a resolute stance from the government." They said having the director-general of MOFA's Asian Affairs Bureau lodge a protest with the acting DCM at the Chinese Embassy in Japan was too low level; they wanted administrative talks on yen loans to China postponed or even placed under review. There were also expressions of dissatisfaction about bilateral security being in permanent hibernation.

"This last declaration [on joint U.S.-Japan security] touches on regional affairs. It uses a phrase like 'tension on the Korean Peninsula,' but there is no specific mention of problems in the Taiwan Straits between China and Taiwan. . . . Doesn't the fact that there is no such mention indicate that a crucial issue for bilateral security and Japan's safety in the future has been omitted, or intentionally left out? That is how it would appear to me."[38]

Concerning what had and had not been discussed between Japan and the United States during the crisis, Hashimoto stuck to his position that "I do not believe that I should answer expressly whether those kinds of topics were discussed or not."[39]

Commenting that "politics needs to constantly consider each and every possibility," Foreign Minister Yukihiko Ikeda remarked in an allusion to Zen philosophy that the connection between a Taiwan contingency and U.S.-Japan security was "akin to something which gravitates profoundly but looks like a vacuum."[40]

This strategy of ambiguity was shared by the U.S. administration. For example, Joseph Nye's response when asked by the Chinese how Washington would respond to a threat against Taiwan was, "We don't know what we would do, and you don't—because it's going to depend on the circumstances."[41]

Another important question was whether U.S. naval movements off Taiwan should be the subject of "prior consultation" as stipulated in the official exchange of documents based on Article 6 of the Japan-U.S. security treaty. A member asked, "Is not the deployment of the U.S. Navy . . . a clear case of operations action? If that is so, in such a case, the USS *Independence* is homeported in Yokosuka and even today's newspapers report 'U.S. Fleet Fighters, Overpowering Drills, Takeoff Every Five Minutes.' I believe that this obviously comes under the requirement for prior consultations, but I would like to hear the government's opinion."[42]

The government responded, "We understand the facts of the situation are that as tension has mounted in the Taiwan Straits, U.S. Navy warships, including the USS *Independence*, are maintaining a patrol by conducting routine exercises in the waters between Taiwan and Okinawa. It is our interpretation that this kind of action is not covered by the requirements for prior consultation."[43]

In other words, action by the USS *Independence* was not "operations action," but "patrol action" and therefore not subject to "prior consultation." The question of prior consultation, however, raised far more penetrating questions for both countries than simply whether action by the U.S. aircraft carriers warranted its invocation or not.

Prior Consultation

Not only did the Japanese government deem that the situation did not meet the conditions for invoking prior consultation, it was wary about even the step before that, namely, holding policy talks with the United States. "Japan had no intention of becoming a main player."[44]

Americans did not think the situation warranted prior consultation either. There was even the opinion at the White House that it might be politically smarter not to give Japan prior notice, let alone prior consultation. "We made a conscious effort to avoid joint operational action with Japan. This was because, in light of the domestic [Japanese] political situation with a coalition government in office, we deemed it would be to our disadvantage if we got embroiled in things and they said no to everything we suggested."[45]

In a subsequent interview with the *Sankei Shimbun*, former Prime Minister Kiichi Miyazawa mentioned the statement of a high U.S. government official that "there would probably be no prior consultation if tensions in the Taiwan Straits escalated into conflict." He added that the same official had also said, "The situation is complicated, but we would view it as a civil war and [U.S. military action] would most likely take the form of support from a humanitarian perspective."[46]

This gave a glimpse of the Americans' understanding that action by the U.S. forces in Japan in response to a China-Taiwan conflict would not lead directly to the invocation of the U.S.-Japan Security Treaty. Behind this lay a solid political consideration of two factors: a Chinese backlash that "U.S.-Japan security should be confined to Japan and America" and avoiding a domestic fuss in Japan should prior consultations take place.

Within Japan, there was a feeling that the deployment of the U.S. carriers during the China-Taiwan crisis was an action aimed largely at Japan. If the United States didn't deploy them, there was a risk that Japan would accuse the Americans of sacrificing bilateral security in their eagerness to mend relations with China. So the deployment was needed to prevent that. A high-ranking official at the Pentagon later added the footnote that "we did not deploy them specially for Japan. We were thinking of the entire Asian region."[47] Anthony Lake, NSC adviser, recalled that "[the message of sending the two carriers was delivered] definitely mostly to China. . . . You are stating publicly that the gravest issues or consequences would arise . . . beyond China, I don't think it was just Japan. We did discuss it, it was regional certainly, that we wanted to use this as an opportunity to send a message throughout the region."[48]

Japanese reaction must have been an important element, nevertheless. Japan would have been very skittish had the Americans done nothing. To the Americans, it was necessary to take into account the risk that Japan would wonder about the efficacy of bilateral security if the Americans just stood idly by and did nothing in a Taiwanese contingency. On the other hand, however, pressuring Japan into responding jointly with the United States to a Taiwanese contingency also had the potential of undermining the security relationship because Japan was not keen on such action.

During his 1995 visit to China, Charles Freeman, former assistant secretary of defense, asked the Chinese to exercise restraint in the use of force towards Taiwan, warning them that such action might lead to Japanese rearmament. "If we decide not to intervene, there will be many people in Japan who will see this as a default on American responsibility to manage the strategic perimeter of Japan, and there will be a lot of people and a lot of pressure demanding that Japan acquire the capability to do this by itself without the U.S. Conversely, if the U.S. decides to intervene, then we have to use bases in Japan to do it. This means that the Japanese government has to choose between good relations with China and its alliance with the U.S. I think any Japanese government would choose the U.S., but I also think that no Japanese government would be comfortable being put in this position by a foreigner, and there would also be pressure then for Japan to acquire its own independent military capabilities so that foreigners could not again put Japan in this kind of unfavorable position."[49]

This was a manifestation of a deep reticence, a desire to use Chinese fear of the risk of Japanese rearmament to solve inconsistencies between the United States and China over Taiwan, as well as inconsistencies between the United States and Japan, through Chinese self-restraint. It would be no skin off the Americans' noses if this could be pulled off. The Chinese, however, merely retorted that "Taiwan is a question of sovereignty for China, a question of national pride, and should Taiwan try to separate itself, we will have no choice but to prevent that by force."[50]

There is no doubt that at the bottom of all this U.S. caution on prior consultation lay the desire to maintain freedom of action by keeping the application of prior consultation to as narrowly defined a range as possible, to prevent its invocation.

In fact, there were many different opinions within the U.S. government. A high-ranking official at the Pentagon indicated he felt the problem was that it was precisely this kind of "painkiller statement" in the form of "consideration" of "Chinese sensibilities" and "domestic Japanese political circumstances" that hindered the maturity of U.S.-Japan security. "It is peculiar to say that it would have a negative impact in terms of domestic politics if something happened with Taiwan and Japan was consulted beforehand. Let's suppose something did happen in the Taiwan Straits. Wouldn't it be even more difficult for Japan if the Japanese prime minister and the Japanese government received no prior briefing whatsoever, no advance consultations?"[51]

In order to atone for not having informed Japan or conducting prior consultation at the time of the USS *Nimitz*'s deployment, the same official revealed that the U.S. government had "decided to consult beforehand with Japan on any and all U.S. military action in future crises in the Taiwan Straits." He added, "Up until then, America had tried to avoid doing that by citing Japanese limitations when they wanted to consult with it on something, or in the case of the Taiwan contingency, by expressing the view that that military action was not covered by the prior consultation in the U.S.-Japan Security Treaty."[52]

"Their judgment was that, that way, Japanese politics would go smoother and it was good for maintaining bilateral ties as well. I won't deny that that problem exists. But it also means that America had never treated Japan as an equal partner. That was no longer viable and couldn't go on."[53]

During the China-Taiwan showdown in the middle of March 1996, Japan and the United States conducted virtually no policy talks. The bilateral link was tenuous. In military terms, the links were nonexistent. The automatic information exchange between the U.S. forces and Japan's SDF, known as the Link 11 System, was not put into play. The exchange was a data-sharing system that allowed for information on hostile submarines picked up by Japanese ships, for example, to be automatically relayed to the U.S. AEGIS ships and vice versa. It operated on predetermined frequencies and codes. During the China-Taiwan crisis, however, it was not used. The U.S. Navy had decided on a course of "independent action."

Even in political terms, contact was insufficient. During the crisis, the two countries failed to work out how bilateral security would function, leaving the situation ambiguous. Rust Deming, deputy chief of mission at the U.S. Embassy in Tokyo, attested to the fact that "there were no discussions whatsoever during the China-Taiwan crisis on how the U.S.-Japan Security Treaty would be applied or how both countries would respond in terms of the treaty at that time."[54]

Kurt Campbell, deputy assistant secretary of defense, said, "We never saw any steps . . . other than the military exercises, and so we never had to get into a situation where we actually talked about contingencies. . . . We did not see any real possibility of conflict, and so we did not go in any way . . . into any detail about any potential operational responses."[55]

Each side depended mainly on calling for self-restraint by both China and Taiwan, as there was very little coordination of Taiwan policy. As the exercises were rapidly scaled back halfway through and self-restraint exercised, neither had to face up to the issue. The alliance did not face a head-on test. There was no need for prior consultation nor did Japan have to choose between the United States and China.

If you believe that China responded to America's carrier diplomacy with scaled-back exercises and self-restraint, then the carrier diplomacy would have to be termed a success in the sense that it defended the bilateral alliance. However, China struck later at the relationship between a Taiwan contingency and U.S.-Japan security, putting both the United States and Japan on the defensive. The interim report on the New Guidelines for U.S.-Japan Defense Cooperation, the so-called Guidelines Review, came in for repeated criticism from this viewpoint.

Did the "contingencies in the vicinity of Japan" covered by the guidelines include a contingency in the Taiwan Straits? Would the guidelines be applied if a conflict broke out there? China staged a diplomatic attack on both Japan and the United States aimed at testing their alliance. The United States and Japan were anxious and in disarray, which raised bogies on both sides, each suspecting the other of implying something different to China. The United States very quickly briefed China that "during the review of the guidelines, we never discussed with Japan responses to a contingency in the Taiwan Straits." The Japanese learned of this from the Chinese. What the Chinese had said was quite true, but Japan suspected the Americans had given the Chinese such a favorable answer without coordinating sufficiently with Japan in order to create a better impression with the Chinese. The Americans shared a similar sense of alarm towards the Japanese.

In Japan, this issue became embroiled in political jockeying. It led to a confrontation between Koichi Kato, Seiroku Kajiyama, and Yasuhiro Nakasone. Kato, general secretary of the LDP, commented during a visit to China that "the guidelines are not aimed at China. They are aimed at a contingency on the Korean Peninsula." Kajiyama, Cabinet secretary, asserted that "it is true that the Korean Peninsula is a problem, but it shouldn't be categorically stated that other regions are not a problem."[56] Nakasone, former prime minister, said, "It would be wrong to say that Taiwan is not included in the interpretation of the U.S.-Japan Security Treaty."

Kato's argument was seen as a political gesture of consideration to the SDP's long-standing position of "clearly stating the exclusion of a Taiwan contingency from the guidelines and opposition to an expansionist interpretation of the range of the 'Far East' in the U.S.-Japan Security Treaty." (In fact, according to Kato, he never mentioned "the exclusion of Taiwan from the guidelines" on his visit to China in July

1997. What he said was 1) the review of the guidelines was not being conducted on the assumption of a hostile China; and 2) the question of the Taiwan Straits was basically an issue for Sino-American relations, not Sino-Japanese relations.[57] The Chinese vice foreign minister, Tang Jiaxuan, expressed his dissatisfaction that although Kato had said "they didn't have China in mind, there was no clear explanation that Taiwan was not included."[58])

The LDP defense lobby came out in force against this, a move also deriving from the conservatives' alliance, to use this material to attack Kato. However, in the preparations for Prime Minister Hashimoto's September 1997 trip to China, Kajiyama and others, judging that the Chinese took Kato's statement as a pledge and would try to pin Hashimoto down on it, served to intentionally contrive to create the nuance that "it couldn't be said that Taiwan wasn't included." Most likely there was also a calculation to provide the prime minister with some room to maneuver so that he could tell the Chinese leaders "both arguments exist in Japan."[59] This conflict of opinions could not merely be attributed to a political dispute between the conservatives' alliance and the ruling three-party coalition.

The government was hard-pressed to maintain its basic stance that "vicinity contingencies do not assume specific areas" and "China is pursuing a peaceful resolution of the Taiwan question; we do not assume a Taiwan contingency." Given that the government was committed to supporting One China, and as long as China kept talking about a "peaceful resolution," its line of argument was that no contingency could be allowed there, and therefore there would be no contingency.

The China-Taiwan showdown was an unfamiliar kind of crisis for Japan. It was not that China was hegemonic, or that tensions between China and Taiwan had assumed a more intractable nature. It was because it posed a long-term and strategic challenge, a challenge over what choice Japan would make in the case of Sino-American conflict.

Despite Japanese fears and apprehension that a U.S. policy of reconciliation and U.S. consideration towards China might take place at the cost of U.S.-Japan relations, the gravest main contradiction in terms of security for Japan was antagonism in Sino-American relations. The Japanese experienced that fear in the showdown between China and the United States in the spring of 1996. It is not as if they became acutely aware of it, however. Once again, this awareness may never have left the subliminal domain.

Looking back on events, Yoshio Omori, who had served as CRIO director for four years from 1993, said, "The most serious crisis during that time was not Aum [a religious terrorist incident], or [the hostages in] Peru, but the China-Taiwan showdown." He went on, "That was our gravest moment at least in the sense that it exposed us to a kind of catalyst for confronting the question of what role Japan should play in the fabric of Asia and the world in the 21st century as it became entangled in Sino-American power politics."[60]

According to Omori, this crisis hid another dire situation. "But we couldn't say that it was serious. The Japanese government couldn't say it, nor did the United States use that turn of phrase. Especially if the Japanese government said, this is big trouble, it could be used as an excuse for the mainland attacking or the Taiwanese attacking, or it could trigger something like that, so we couldn't say anything. Conversely, it was also frustrating that we couldn't use this chance to make the Japanese people, including the media, aware of the seriousness of the matter."

The Senkaku Question

On October 3, 1996, Yukio Takeuchi, minister plenipotentiary at the Japanese Embassy in Washington, felt as if he had been slapped in the face when he learned what Nicholas Burns, a spokesman for the State Department, had said. In response to a reporter's question at a regular press briefing about whether the U.S.-Japan Security Treaty covered the disputed Diaoyu/Senkaku Islands and if the United States would be obligated to assist Japan if any military conflict broke out, Burns had said, "That would be a hypothetical situation, of course, and my policy is not to comment upon hypotheses. . . . I don't have the defense treaty in front of me. . . . I can't quote it."[61] Burns parried the question with "the United States has urged all the claimants to these islands to exercise peaceful means. And we are confident that they can resolve this issue through peaceful means."[62] No quotation, no answer.

The dispute between Japan and China over the Senkaku (or Diaoyu in Chinese) Islands had flared up again. If it escalated, what would the U.S. government do? Would the bilateral Security Treaty apply or not? A report for Congress provided the answer.

Larry Niksch, specialist in Asian affairs with the Congressional Research Service, had just written a report entitled "Senkaku (Diaoyu) Islands Dispute: The U.S. Legal Relationship and Obligations." After summarizing the history of the dispute and each country's competing claims as well as the U.S. stance hitherto, Niksch showed that the United States had always taken a "neutral position" on sovereign and territorial rights but that it had promised that the U.S.-Japan Security Treaty was "applicable" here. Niksch drew the following conclusion:

> In short, while maintaining neutrality on the competing claims, the United States agreed in the Okinawa Reversion Treaty to apply the Security Treaty to the treaty area, including the Senkaku (Diaoyu) islands. It

also should be noted that in ratifying the Treaty, the Senate did not act on the advice of several committee witnesses that it include in the instrument of ratification reservations concerning the Senkakus. Moreover, the Security Treaty itself declares in Article V that each party would act "in accordance with its constitutional provisions and processes" in response to "an armed attack . . . in the territories under the administration of Japan." "Administration" rather than "sovereignty" is the key distinction that applies to the islands. Since 1971, the United States and Japan have not altered the application of the Security Treaty to the islands.[63]

It wasn't only Burns who didn't have a statement. Assistant Secretary of State Winston Lord also responded to a question on whether the U.S.-Japan security agreement applied to the Senkakus with "I will not comment on hypothetical situations."

Even Walter Mondale, U.S. ambassador to Japan, was reported by the *New York Times* as saying, "American forces would not be compelled by the treaty to intervene in a dispute" over the Senkakus.[64] The Japanese suspected that the U.S. government had started orchestrating a campaign. Hadn't it come up with press guidelines that this issue was "hypothetical," and "couldn't be answered"? If spokesmen did answer, they were to say "America is neutral on the Senkakus."

A right-wing Japanese group had built a lighthouse on the islands in the summer and applied to the Maritime Safety Agency for approval. Saying there were no legal grounds for the removal of this structure, the Japanese government did nothing about it. The Chinese government criticized the Japanese government "authorities' nonintervention and inducement" and called for "immediate measures."

The *Liberation Army Daily*, the organ of the PLA, issued a warning: "We will not allow one scrap of land, not one drop of water to pass into others' hands."[65] Hong Kong and Taiwanese Chinese were demonstrating. On September 26, the *Bao Yu*, a freight vessel carrying Hong Kong activists from the Worldwide Alliance of Chinese Fishermen, approached within 12 nautical miles of the islands and was stopped by a Japanese patrol boat. Five of the passengers jumped overboard. One of them died. The incident was broadcast on Hong Kong television and triggered anti-Japanese feelings.

Less than one year away from its reversion to China on July 1, 1997, Hong Kong was suffering from countdown anxiety. The pro-democracy lobby was gradually being pushed into a corner. It needed some sort of action, some protest, and along came the Senkakus.

It was a perfect opportunity for some "patriotic action." The Chinese government couldn't complain about this. In fact, it would probably support it. The Chinese government could also use "patriotic action" as a card against Japan. What's more, it would also be an opportunity to show Beijing the mobilization capabilities of the democracy movement. A mixed psychology of ingratiation and wanting to earn thanks was at work.

In Taiwan, the New Party kicked up a fuss. It called President Lee Teng-hui a "hidden member of the pro-independence school" and parted company with the Kuomintang. The New Party did this to rattle Lee's power base. Seeing the Senkakus, if anything, as a decisive issue with which to split Japanese-Taiwan relations, the members thought they could back the highly cautious and prudent Lee Teng-hui into a corner. They could also take advantage of the feeling of unity with the mainland by appealing to patriotism. They were trying to leverage a different kind of Chinese nationalism from the Taiwanese nationalism of the Democratic Progressive Party (DPP). When the country's national athletic games were held in their stronghold of Kaoshsiung, the DPP had tried to send the torch-bearer to the Senkaku Islands. The party was in the forefront on this issue. The new party wanted to force both Lee Teng-hui and the opposition DPP onto the defensive.

On October 6, the Hong Kong activists joined up with the group from Taiwan's New Party. In the early hours of October 7, they moored alongside a reef just west of the island. Four people landed and raised the flags of both China and Taiwan. The Chinese flag drifted off and the Taiwanese flag was removed by an MSA officer and taken on board an MSA patrol boat. At the time, there were 41 boats violating Japanese territorial waters. By 1:00 P.M. that afternoon, they had all moved out.[66]

Politics, Not Logic

Burns's comment came just at that time. Minister Takeuchi told himself: *This is so different from their former statements. It's terrible. We need to wake them up and fast!*[67]

Takeuchi was an expert on treaties. A similar event had taken place in 1978. He was then in the Legal Affairs Division of MOFA's Treaties Bureau and had written a report on the Senkaku Islands. He asked the ministry in Tokyo to send him a copy urgently. The report was a systemic historical survey of the U.S. government's position and statements on this issue.

In June 1971, the Okinawa Reversion Treaty was signed between the United States and Japan. In November, the Chinese government issued a "Statement of the Ministry of Foreign Affairs of the People's Republic of China" that asserted officially for the first time the Chinese claim to the Senkaku Islands. In March 1972, the Japanese government released "The Basic View of the Ministry of Affairs on the Senkaku Islands." The text of the Chinese diplomatic statement ran as follows:

In the past few years, the Japanese Sato government, ignoring the historical facts and the strong opposition of the Chinese people, has repeatedly
claimed that Japan has the so-called "title to China" territory of the
Tiaoyu [Diaoyu] and other islands and, in collusion with U.S. imperial-
ism, has engaged in all kinds of activities to invade and annex the above-
mentioned islands. Not long ago, the U.S. Congress and the Japanese Diet
one after the other approved the agreeement [*sic*] on the "reversion" of
Okinawa. In this agreement, the governments of the United States and
Japan flagrantly included the Tiaoyu and other islands in the "area of
reversion." This is a gross encroachment upon China's territorial
integrity and sovereignty. The Chinese people absolutely will not tolerate
this! . . . The fraud of the "reversion" of Okinawa to Japan jointly con-
trived by the U.S. and Japanese governments is a new grave step to
strengthen U.S.-Japan military collusion and to accelerate the revival of
Japanese militarism. . . . After World War II, the Japanese government
illicitly handed over to the United States the Tiaoyu and other islands
appertaining to Taiwan, and the United States government unilaterally
declared that it enjoyed the so-called "administrative rights" over these
islands. This in itself was illegal. . . .[68]

The Japanese foreign ministry's "Basic View" ran as follows.

From 1885 on, surveys of the Senkaku Islands had been thoroughly made
by the Government of Japan through the agencies of Okinawa Prefecture
and by way of other methods. Through these surveys, it was confirmed
that the Senkaku Islands had been uninhabited and showed no trace of
having been under the control of China. Based on this confirmation, the
Government of Japan made a Cabinet Decision on 14 January 1895 to
erect a marker on the Islands to formally incorporate the Senkaku Islands
into the territory of Japan. . . . The Senkaku Islands are not included in the
territory which Japan renounced under Article II of the San Francisco
Peace Treaty. The Senkaku Islands have been placed under the administration of the United States of America as part of the Nansei Shoto
Islands, in accordance with Article III of the said treaty, and are included
in the area, the administrative rights over which are to revert to Japan in
accordance with the Agreement between Japan and the United States of
America Concerning the Ryukyu Islands and the Daito Islands signed on
17 June 1971. The facts outlined herein clearly indicate the status of the
Senkaku Islands being part of the territory of Japan.[69]

Neither the Japanese nor the Chinese government had changed its
position since then; only the U.S. government had.

During its occupation of Okinawa, the United States consistently
maintained that the "territorial rights were Japan's." The U.S. military
had used the Senkaku Islands during their occupation of Okinawa as a
firing range. Despite this fact, when the U.S. government called for the
Senate to ratify the Okinawa Reversion Treaty, it clearly demonstrated

its intention to maintain "neutrality" concerning the question of Japanese and Taiwanese territorial claims to the Senkaku Islands.

What had occurred was that, in order to ensure that the U.S. government's tilt toward Japan on the Senkaku dispute did not interfere with the restoration of Sino-American relations, the Nixon administration had strengthened its "rapprochement towards China." In a communiqué dated October 21, 1971, the State Department clearly stated its position that "the reversion of administrative rights over Okinawa by no means signifies a bias towards any of the demands of the parties involved. Having the administrative rights returned does not work to the advantage of the Japanese claims. Nor should it work to the disadvantage of any other country's claims."[70]

At the same time, however, the U.S. government had confirmed that all the treaties, accords, and agreements signed between itself and Japan, including the U.S.-Japan Security Treaty, applied equally to "Okinawa and the Senkaku Islands" as to the Japanese mainland. William Rogers, secretary of state at the time, attested before Congress that "the security treaty will apply to a reverted Okinawa."[71]

Burns's 1996 comment, however, muddled sovereignty and territorial rights with administrative rights and could well create an impression that the Security Treaty would not be applied. At the very least, it made the U.S. look as if it was reserving judgment. Takeuchi's earlier report included the press guidelines circulated by the State Department at the time. His own thoughts were: *Even so, this time they seem to have upped the extent of their "neutrality." On the whole, America as a country has poor institutional memory.*[72]

Whenever there was a change in administration in the United States, new political appointees were appointed. The incoming team always had its own agendas which it foisted onto the bureaucracy. While on the one hand, this generated a certain invigoration, on the other, it made for poor organizational transitions.

After checking back through all the old reports, Takeuchi put together a concise, easily comprehensible paper and quickly shot it off to the State Department.

Some private sector experts had already started to criticize the ambiguous attitude of the U.S. government, saying, "It is plain that the Security Treaty applies. If the U.S. government doesn't take a clear stance on this, it will damage the alliance." Some of the same talk could be heard within the U.S. government itself. In Mondale's case, it is probably true that he "didn't realize the seriousness of the matter until Hayashi [Sadayuki Hayashi, vice minister of foreign affairs] pointed it out." He later confessed that "[he] was misquoted but [it was] partly my fault. I should have realized earlier just how delicate an issue this was for Japan."[73]

A senior official at the State Department said about Burns's comment, "After the Burns comment, the State Department, especially the Japan Section, seemed to think he had blown it, but he'd already said it and [Secretary] Christopher liked him, so it was hard for them to ask him to amend what he'd said."[74] The same official added, "The initial reaction by the State Department was the wrong reaction, and it was done without considered thought. It was done in isolation, without thinking about the strategic alliance; it was done somewhat in isolation from a legalistic point of view, without the right people intervening early on. And once that mistake had been made, it was defended for a few days too long before the more correct interpretation and decision was made. And I can only have a degree of sympathy for the frustration and the irritation that *Gaimusho* [MOFA] had with regard to this."[75]

But there was more to it than that. A member of the White House staff revealed that "I asserted that we should immediately make it clearly known to Japan that our position was that Article V of the treaty applied, but it wasn't taken up."[76] This was not just a casual remark; it was imbued with political significance. True, Burns's comment may not have been "a sophisticated argument," as one MOFA person put it. Many of MOFA's treaty pros, including Takeuchi, were sure they'd won on logic. The only problem was that the Clinton administration was more interested in politics than logic. And the politics were, we have to get our relationship with China back on an even keel. We don't want any Sino-Japanese strife getting in the way. "With regard to the Senkakus . . . the Japanese government . . . wanted [a] black-and-white response quickly without having the sufficient amount of preparation and dialogue."[77] "China was taking steps to quell the disturbance. . . . If we said anything further about it . . . we would muddy the waters."[78] And the United States did not want to do that. Burns's off-the-cuff comment was a frank expression of what the heart of the U.S. administration was really thinking.

By the time the Pentagon started to think about a counterattack, it was already too late. "Many of the political appointees at the State Department . . . were unaware of the diplomatic record. They had not reviewed it closely, and that's unfortunate. So the initial comments, I think, caused some real concern among our Japanese friends. . . . We had some internal discussions with Secretary Perry and others about the . . . two separate issues involved here: the sovereignty question, and then there was the security question. The two kept getting mixed up. . . . I would like to say that there is ample coordination done in the interagency, but there is not."[79] So said one high-ranking Pentagon official.

Perry, Walter Slocombe, and Campbell all worked on this problem. Perry's assessment was that the Defense Department needed to make the position clear: "This is not an issue of interpretation . . . it's a statement of fact."[80] Perry gave Campbell permission to go to the press with this. "We [the U.S.] do not take a position on matters of sovereignty. The U.S.-Japan Security Treaty applies to this area. If Japan was involved in a conflict in which Japanese forces or Japanese personnel came under attack, then the United States would be obligated to support." Perry himself also quietly conveyed this stance in a meeting with the Japanese, during his visit to Japan in December 1996 to put the finishing touches on SACO's final report.[81]

Nationalism and Democracy

The Chinese government dealt with the situation calmly. It was watching to make sure that the "patriotic actions" of the Hong Kong and Taiwanese activists did not get too far out of hand. There was a fear that the democracy lobby in Hong Kong might use the issue as a cover to fuel nationalism inside China and accuse the Chinese government of "faintheartedness." Domestically, the Chinese government indicated very early on that it would not allow anti-Japanese demonstrations.

News of the September 26 death of a Hong Kong activist spread like wildfire in Beijing over the Internet. The Xinhua News Agency also reported the memorial service four days later.[82] The Chinese government stopped demonstrations from above. That was where China differed from Hong Kong and Taiwan. If the government decided to stop them, it could.

However, there were many claims whirling around inside China, which meant that the government was still subject to pressure from hard-liners. A Chinese diplomat revealed that "Japan is using its aid to China more and more as a diplomatic weapon. There was mounting internal criticism that in its desire for money, the Chinese government was conducting a diplomacy of kowtowing. And on top of that there was the question of Diaoyu [the Senkakus]. There was dissatisfaction that the government was being too soft on Japan on this too. We [the Chinese Ministry of Foreign Affairs] were under a lot of pressure at home."[83]

China was forced to walk a tightrope in order to keep the hard-liners under control. China sent two maritime survey vessels to the vicinity of the Senkaku Islands, not only to make a show of China's sovereignty but also as a demonstration to quell the hard-liners back home. In response, the Japanese sent two MSA vessels to tail the Chinese ships.

Later, in the Japanese Diet, the opposition criticized the government, saying, "The important thing was not removing some upstart activists from Hong Kong and Taiwan, but the removal and control of the Chinese government's maritime survey vessels which had violated Japanese territorial waters." The opposition also attacked the ambiguous U.S. stance. "If the U.S. troops stationed in Okinawa refuse to mobilize for Okinawa's sake, despite the fact that [the Senkaku Islands] are a part of Okinawa, are they not neglecting their obligation as laid down in the Joint Declaration of April 17 [1996] that both governments make every effort to gain a broad understanding from the Japanese people on the critical nature of the bases?"[84]

Sino-Japanese relations had been strained by the conflicting claims to the Senkakus before. The tension that fall, however, took place in several new contexts. Nationalism was on the rise in both Japan and China as both countries developed into greater world powers. Additionally, Hong Kong and Taiwan had caught the democracy bug.

In Japan, a general election was scheduled for October 20. This would be the first election held under the new electoral system of single-seat constituencies. The Liberal Democrats were plagued with doubts. At the end of September, the LDP went public with a clear campaign promise that "the Senkakus and Takeshima are Japanese territories."[85] Taku Yamazaki, chairman of the LDP's Policy Research Council, commented that "China has used intimidation and gunboat diplomacy. Japan will not do the same." He was referring to the missile exercises China had conducted in March of that year before Taiwan's general elections. A sense of discomfort towards China was spreading in Japan. It was evident that the LDP promise was a maneuver aimed at the elections, an attempt to show that the LDP was different from the other parties in its tough stance on the Senkakus.

The Japanese government had decided from the start that it "would not permit" the erection of the lighthouse. The domestic situation was such, however, that "we couldn't say domestically that we wouldn't allow it."[86]

Both nationalism and democracy complicated the affair. At the same time, however, there was probably an element of "show" involved. Politicians everywhere—Hong Kong, Taiwan, Japan, and the United States—were preoccupied with elections, and they tailored their comments and actions accordingly.

The general view in Washington was "running into the delicate election period, relations were tense enough with China."[87] In Japan, however, the suspicion was that "the U.S. is so cautious and afraid of a flare-up on this because of the presidential elections."

The Pro-Japan Lobby and the Pro-China Lobby

Another change was the growing impression that there was a pro-Japan lobby and a pro-China lobby within America's foreign policy and security groups. At times, this highlighted a Defense Department versus State Department motif. The Defense Department was the pro-Japan lobby while the State Department was the pro-China lobby.

Because the White House placed priority on improving relations with China with a view to the presidential elections, the State Department fortified its attitude of "don't provoke China too much." In contrast, the Pentagon had come up with a clearer emphasis on the importance of the U.S.-Japan alliance. It was still in the process of consolidating the bilateral security ties, a process set in motion two years before by the Nye Initiative and which had evolved into the Joint Security Declaration and SACO.

In addition, regarding policy towards China, there was a little bit of "if the State Department was employing a strategy of engagement, then the Pentagon had to create a strategy of hedging. This was unavoidable given the nature of our job."[88] In other words, it was the Pentagon's job to be prepared to confront China if the policy of engagement failed.

Having commenced military exchanges with China in the hope of improving relations, however, the Pentagon was, in fact, ahead of the State Department and working to reopen a dialogue with China. On his October visit to Japan, Campbell told LDP General Secretary Koichi Kato and other persons of influence that the islands issue came under Article V of the Security Treaty and stressed its extremely delicate diplomatic nature.

Elsewhere, many people in the State Department also made clear their view that "in private, the Japanese were exactly right." It was just that they did not want to be put into the position of being tested by both Japan and China. The State Department may also have been further subject to a certain pigheadedness: "We can't bow to pressure from the Defense Department and change a stand we were so adamant about initially."[89]

In truth, it was not so simple as neatly pitting the State Department against the Defense Department. And yet, more and more a view of Defense Department versus State Department, pro-Japan lobby versus pro-China lobby, was gaining credence. China was in the habit of viewing things in that light. Campbell ended up taking on the job of proclaiming that the Senkakus "are covered by Article V of the U.S.-Japan Security Treaty," which later caused a high-ranking Chinese government official to be very critical of him as a Japanese fop, "very critical, of me personally."[90]

China started to set its sights on the Pentagon. On October 16, a spokesman for the Chinese Ministry of Foreign Affairs made the remark that "Diaoyu [the Senkakus] is a Sino-Japanese issue and we will not permit any 'third country' to intervene. If the U.S.-Japan Security Treaty goes beyond a bilateral range, this will only introduce complicating factors into the regional security of Asia and raise not only alarm in China but throughout the region."[91]

The "Fearless Brigade" and the "Cheerless Brigade"

It was not only Washington that was experiencing a conflict of opinion. Washington was paying attention to the fact that "Tokyo seems to be divided on this question too."

According to one person in charge of Japanese affairs in the U.S. government, "there is tension between the traditional pro-American school in MOFA and the younger national-interest centered school, or more specifically a conflict of opinion between pro-American advocates like [Ryozo] Kato and the national-interest advocates like [Yukio] Takeuchi and [Hitoshi] Tanaka."[92]

Ryozo Kato, director-general of the Asian Affairs Bureau at MOFA, argued within the ministry that "we should not be pushing this question too hard and testing the loyalty of the Americans. It's not in our best interests to aggravate U.S.-Japan relations over this question." He said, "Think about the cost effect."

There has to be a limit to what we can gain by taking an openly hard-line tack. Don't they say tailor your pitch to your audience? Isn't it smarter not to get hot under the collar about something like Burns's comment but to take the diplomatic high road and quietly consolidate a common understanding?[93]

Yukio Takeuchi, minister plenipotentiary at the Japanese Embassy in Washington, and Hitoshi Tanaka, deputy director-general of the North American Affairs Bureau at MOFA, countered with "ambiguity in territorial questions is unforgivable" and "this goes to the very core of U.S.-Japan security."[94]

For the MOFA treaty pros, there was a feeling that "it would be no exaggeration to say that all of Japan's territorial issues came from American blunders." Everything was plain as plain could be in the San Francisco Peace Treaty, but the United States had vacillated, sowing the seeds for all this trouble. The MacArthur Line (later to be the Syngman Rhee Line) had been drawn artificially; Takeshima just happened to end up on the wrong side. (The MacArthur Line referred to the Japanese fishing area permitted by the United States during the Occupation. The line was redrawn three times, in 1945, 1946, and 1947. It was abolished in April 1952, just before the Peace Treaty with Japan went into effect.)

Takeuchi and the other treaty pros were still carrying around some emotional baggage from the early 1970s, when they believed the Senkaku Islands were sacrificed to the U.S. policy of rapprochement with China. That is why they were so incensed by the comments from Burns and Mondale. "Enough's enough!" There was an inward suspicion that "in other words, we ended up paying the bill for Kissinger's strong-arm diplomacy. [Winston] Lord was part of that."[95]

The JDA was gloomy too. A high-ranking official at the JDA later disclosed that the islands issue "created incredibly strong distrust towards
America. Skepticism towards the White House and the State Department was especially intense." The JDA took its pent-up frustrations
directly to the Pentagon, "since the Foreign Ministry never got anywhere no matter how much they tried."

"It makes things very difficult when you fudge the issue on the
Senkaku Islands and U.S.-Japan security. This isn't Okinawa, you
know! We want you to deal with this first. How are we meant to keep
the SDF under control with this sort of thing going on? There they are
defending a place like that. Any wonder if they're not thinking deep
down, who wants to rely on the Americans? We can do it ourselves!"[96]

It is not known on what grounds the JDA came forward so confi-
dently. One reason, however, may be that the JDA had acquired from an
American intelligence institution the results of a military simulation by
the Chinese forces. According to the simulation of a Sino-Japanese battle in the Senkaku Islands, China had no hope of winning with its current naval capability.

The U.S. assessment was that China was handling the matter so
calmly because it was aware of its military deficiencies. An intelligence
officer in a position to know these things said, "We have information
that the Chinese military have carried out this kind of internal examination twice in the past. The first time was in 1971 and this is the second
time. In both cases, they're said to have reached the conclusion that they
would lose. This is what has led to their rational conduct in not rocking
the boat."[97]

The JDA response to the Senkaku Islands was also influenced by the
tenor of the backlash inside Japan over China's actions in the China-
Taiwan showdown in the spring of that year. In the Diet, government
officials had been showered with shouts of "stand firm against China."
It was also around this time that there was talk, half in jest, within
MOFA of a division between the "fearless brigade" and "cheerless
brigade." It was a mournful description that divided those who wanted
Japan to "stand firm and resolute against China," from those who just
folded their arms and said glumly, "But it's not as if we can move out of
the neighborhood."

This also may have been a reflection of the mounting unease within
the ministry towards its China school, its expert China diplomats, who
tended to think and act as "agents" for China. There was also probably an
agreement of sorts with the argument that the U.S.-Japan relationship
should not be strained over the Senkakus nor should Sino-Japanese relations be strained any further. But it was not easy to get the logic accepted
that since we shouldn't aggravate our relationship with China, we should
tone down what we say to the United States. It was much more promis-

ing in terms of "cost effect" to use the hook that we shouldn't aggravate our relationship with the United States, so let's tone down what we're saying to China as well.

Sino-Japanese relations were that difficult. In an opinion poll conducted by the PM's office at the end of 1996, 51.3 percent of those surveyed said they "felt no strong affinity with China," while 45.1 percent said they did. In a similar survey the previous year, both figures were level at 48.4 percent. The results meant that more than half of the Japanese disliked China.[98]

On the other hand, the same sort of phenomenon could be seen in China. The number of Japan-haters was on the increase. In the best-selling *A China That Can Say No,* Japan was pilloried right alongside the United States. The book did not pull any punches on Japanese treachery, saying that "although China relinquished of its own free will demands for war redemptions [from Japan], Japan is trying to freeze soft yen loans to China citing China's nuclear tests as the reason"; or "Japan is not entitled to a permanent seat on the U.N. Security Council."[99]

That summer, a Chinese diplomat stationed overseas commented, "I was amazed when I was home for summer vacation to find all of my son's high school friends reading *A China That Can Say No*. It was being widely read even in Guang Xi and Shen Xi Provinces." He then went on to say, "In a word, China is unhappy that Japan does whatever the United States tells it to do. They're unhappy that they can't discuss Asian questions with Japan. There's also the problem that students who go to Japan to study all come back unfavorably disposed towards Japan. Have Japan's leaders ever invited Chinese exchange students to tea?"[100]

According to the results of a survey on young people's attitudes towards Japan, reported in the February 15, 1997, edition of the *China Youth Daily*, only 14.5 percent had a favorable impression of Japan, with 41.5 percent claiming an unfavorable impression.[101]

The Maritime Safety Agency

Cabinet Secretary Seiroku Kajiyama's say on the Senkaku Islands was significant. He pronounced to MOFA, "This is a question of Japanese territory, so it has to be dealt with properly. Arrest anyone who enters Japanese territory. Send a list of questions to the Chinese government. Are they ordering demonstrations or supporting them?"[102]

The office of the Chief Cabinet Counselor for External Affairs had already put together a set of countermeasures for untoward eventualities in the Senkaku Islands in conjunction with MOFA, the JDA, the Justice Ministry, the police, the Transport Ministry, and the Maritime Safety Agency (MSA). It had decided in July, when the right-wingers had erected their lighthouse, that they would do their utmost to avoid arrests even if Hong Kong and Taiwanese protesters stormed the area. In October, however, and at the behest of Kajiyama, that policy changed to one of "not foregoing arrests or seizure."

They were having to look very closely, however, at whether they could mobilize the Self-Defense Forces. They decided to step up air surveillance in order to be able to pursue all suspicious vessels. They would deploy the Maritime SDF's sub-spotting plane, the P-3C, and the Air SDF's early warning plane, the E-2C. They would increase the number of P-3C flights above the usual one flight per day.

Should they deploy a Maritime SDF warship? As a result of discussions mainly in the PM's office, it was decided not to deploy one because it would be too provocative. In the end, it was the MSA that was charged with "guarding territorial waters."

The MSA was the maritime equivalent of the police and the fire brigade. Its three main operations were patrol and rescue, piloting, and lighthouse operations. It was created after the war, using the U.S. Coast Guard as the model. Partly for this reason it was placed under the jurisdiction of the transport ministry. Its staff numbered 12,222, and it had 518 patrol boats and 70 aircraft (including helicopters).

The MSA's birth was a complicated story. It was established in 1948, but its main mission at that time was to take over guarding the coast after the breakup of the Imperial Navy, especially controlling smuggling, unlawful entry, and acts of piracy. Since maritime guarding required special skills, however, the MacArthur Command made an exception and allowed a maximum of 10,000 servicemen from the former navy to be hired.

It would have been impossible for amateurs to sweep for the millions of mines the Americans had strewn in the seas around Japan during the war, and a minesweeping unit attached to the second demobilization agency was, in fact, already doing this. This unit was also incorporated into the minesweeping section of the MSA's Safety Bureau.

With the outbreak of the Korean War in the summer of 1950, Japan turned to rearmament. Supreme Commander Douglas MacArthur instructed that the personnel at both the police reserves and the MSA be augmented. The police reserves were the forerunner of today's Ground SDF, while the increase in personnel at the MSA led to the subsequent establishment of the Maritime SDF.

In the fall of 1950, the U.S. Navy requested cooperation from the MSA in minesweeping in the vicinity of the Korean Peninsula. Prime Minister Shigeru Yoshida agreed, and the MSA dispatched minesweepers to Korean waters in October. (During this operation, one of the 20 minesweepers deployed hit a mine, causing one death and 18 injuries. Sakataro Nakatani, the fatality, had worked in the galley. For a long time, both his death and the fact that the minesweepers had been deployed was kept secret. It was not until the fall of 1979 that Nakatani was awarded a posthumous decoration.[103])

Later on when the National Safety Agency was created and the Maritime Guard detached, minesweeping operations were transferred there. The MSA was not part of the military, but unlike other coast guards around the world, it had oceangoing capability.

In fact, in Article 80 of the Self-Defense Forces Law, the prime minister was empowered to place the MSA under his command when a mobilization order had been issued to the SDF and when it was deemed that there was a special need, and to place the director-general of the JDA in command. This presupposes a quasi-military function. Because of this capability, the deployment of MSA patrol boats to protect Japanese tankers from indiscriminate attacks by Iran during the Iran-Iraq War was considered (but not ordered). The MSA also provided protection for the transportation of plutonium from France.

The legal, political, and diplomatic constraints on using the SDF were part of the reason why the MSA ended up substituting for the SDF. Guarding the area around the Senkaku Islands was a perfect job for MSA ships. They were not the military, but they could act as a buffer. As opposed to the protective gray or leaden colors of warships, the patrol boats were painted white. They could be expected to act as a deterrent by showing their presence.

At times of crisis, Hashimoto issued commands directly to the MSA's director-general, Yasutoshi Tsuchisaka. He even mentioned how many patrol boat personnel should be mobilized. As a result, between one-seventh and one-eighth of all the MSA's patrol boats were sent to the vicinity of the Senkaku Islands. So large was the number involved that the MSA decided to cancel its annual review off Haneda. And, in fact, there was no sail-by in 1997.[104] The MSA was afraid they would be held responsible if, during the festivities, a Chinese landing took place.

Territorial Questions/Historical Questions

The suspicions and mistrust in the U.S.-Japan relationship, which the Senkakus threw into sharp relief, highlighted a blind spot inherent in the bilateral security structure. It became apparent that latent (or not so latent) territorial disputes in Sino-Japanese relations (but not in Sino-American relations) could drive a wedge between the United States and Japan. They were dealing with territorial questions and historical questions. China had raised the issue of territorial questions in terms of historical questions.

In the fall of 1996, when Sino-Japanese relations were rocked by this question, once again China invoked the historical question. China took a grave view of Prime Minister Ryutaro Hashimoto visiting Yasukuni Shrine on his birthday, July 29. The fact that the Chinese government, in response to the right-wing group building a lighthouse, claimed "the authorities were inciting right-wing groups" was a very strong indication of its perception that Japan's "militarists" and "authorities" were in league with each other.[105]

China's national news agency, Xinhua, circulated a paper entitled "The Threat Comes from Those Who Advocate the Theory of Threat" (October 17, 1996). It argued, "Slavishly following in the footsteps of the prime minister eleven years ago, Prime Minister Hashimoto paid a visit to Yasukuni Shrine, where the spirits of war criminals are enshrined. Around the same time, the Japanese government used right-wing elements to land on islands in the vicinity of Diaoyu Island, China's innate territory. These activities are an indication of emergent militarist forces in Japan as well as the fact that with its economic prosperity, Japan's prewar illness has once again raised its head, blinding it to the feelings of other peoples and the sovereignty of other countries."[106]

Hashimoto's visit was the first to Yasukuni Shrine since that of Prime Minister Yasuhiro Nakasone in 1985. China started to get suspicious. Is the Hashimoto government trying to change Japanese policy on China?

China's attempt to link territorial questions to historical questions, however, triggered a strong backlash in Japan. Kajiyama's tough stance on the Senkakus, which dated from around early fall, was probably related to this. He recollects feeling at this time that "by rights, it was Japanese territory. Even under the Occupation, [the Senkakus] were on this side of the MacArthur Line. And still they [the Chinese] go on about history and want an apology for everything. Well, it's just not on! Territorial issues are territorial issues. We couldn't let them outflank us. That was how I approached the question."[107]

China was observing closely the differences between the United States and Japan over the Senkakus. China was well aware that territorial and historical issues were capable of straining U.S.-Japan relations. It knew of the Clinton administration's irritation, which was tantamount to saying, "We don't want particular Sino-Japanese problems to trip us up in mending our own relations with China." Japanese efforts to get America's attention by pouting and pinching and saying the United States was lacking in loyalty as an ally were also visible to China.

Taiwan, Okinawa, the Senkakus . . . the islands of the southwest were the most fragile link in the relations among Japan, the United States, and China.

Notes

1. Interview with Yasutomo Mitsui.

2. Ibid.

3. Interview with Ryutaro Hashimoto.

4. Interview with an aide to Ryutaro Hashimoto.

5. Interview with Ryutaro Hashimoto.

6. Ibid.

7. Interview with Masahiro Akiyama.

8. Interview with a senior official at the PM's office. On July 27, 1997, the *Tokyo Shimbun* cited a confidential JDA report as saying that Japan could assist U.S. forces in the event of conflict with China in three ways—refueling U.S. warships, supplying military intelligence, and providing medical treatment to injured American servicemen. The JDA's exploration of the issue was authorized by the PM's office. This testified to the willingness of the Japanese government to prepare for the worst-case scenario. However, the article also quoted a Maritime MSDF officer as saying, "In the event of a Chinese invasion of Taiwan, should the U.S. involve itself militarily there would be a danger of China invading the Yaeyama islands. Yet, as long as the Japanese government remains unable to commit the military to helping Taiwan in cooperation with the U.S., we cannot expect the U.S. to come to help us. . . . It is a serious dilemma." This illustrated the fragile nature of the military and operational construction of the alliance with regard to contingency planning. Even though the military was authorized to map out contingency exercises, it did not mean that the Japanese government had committed itself to such measures. Japan was legally ill-equipped to deal with those eventualities. Guidelines legislation was expected but had not yet been forthcoming. Hashimoto told the author in a conversation much later (January 1999) that he had resolved to push for the maximum measures to provide logistical support (but not combat support) to the United States, even if that meant adopting extrajudicial procedures. He did not, however, share this decision with anybody at the time.

9. Interview with Ryutaro Hashimoto.

10. Yashio Omori, "The Day the Prime Minister's Office Was Shaken," *This Is Yomiuri*, August 1997. (In Japanese.)

11. Interview with a high-ranking SDF officer.

12. Ibid.

13. Ibid.

14. Conversation with a top MOFA official.

15. Interview with a senior MOFA official.

16. Interview with a high-ranking JDA official.

17. Interview with Ryutaro Hashimoto.

18. Interview with a senior White House official.

19. Interview with a White House official.

20. Interview with Rust Deming.

21. Interview with Walter Mondale.

22. Conversation with a senior MOFA official.

23. Interview with a senior DOD official.

24. Interview with Walter Mondale.

25. Interview with a White House official.

26. Ibid.

27. Interview with a top officer at Kadena Air Station.

28. Interview with a high-ranking officer at the Joint Staff Council.

29. Author's conversation with a JDA official.

30. Interview with a high-ranking U.S. Marine officer.

31. Conversations with a high-ranking MOFA official.

32. Interview with a U.S. diplomat stationed in Japan.

33. Interview with Ryutaro Hashimoto.

34. Response to the Standing Committee on Foreign Affairs, House of Representatives, March 13, 1996.

35. Ibid.

36. Yoneo Hirata (New Frontier Party) in the House of Representatives session, March 13, 1996.

37. Hajime Ishii (New Frontier Party) in the House of Representatives session, March 13, 1996.

38. Shinya Izumi (New Frontier Party) in the Standing Committee on Budget, House of Councilors, April 17, 1996.

39. Ryutaro Hashimoto, Standing Committee on Budget, House of Councilors, April 17, 1996.

40. Yukihiko Ikeda, Standing Committee on Foreign Affairs, House of Representatives, February 21, 1996.

41. "U.S. Signals Concern on China's Attitude Toward Taiwan," *Boston Globe*, February 7, 1996, p. 6.

42. Shigeru Sugano (SDP), Standing Committee on Cabinet, House of Councilors, March 15, 1996.

43. Ryozo Kato, director-general of the Asian Affairs Bureau, MOFA, at the Standing Committee on Cabinet, House of Representatives, March 13, 1996.

44. Interview with a senior member of JDA.

45. Interview with a senior White House official.

46. *Sankei Shimbun* (evening edition), June 13, 1996.

47. Interview with a senior DOD official.

48. Interview with Anthony Lake.

49. Interview with Charles Freeman.

50. "China Warned of Japan's Possible Full-Scale Rearmament," *Kyodo News International,* February 16, 1996.

51. Interview with a senior DOD official.

52. Ibid.

53. Ibid.

54. Interview with Rust Deming.

55. Interview with Kurt Campbell.

56. *Asahi Shimbun,* August 18, 1997 (U.S. edition), p. 1.

57. *Asahi Shimbun,* August 15, 1997.

58. Interview with Koichi Kato.

59. Interview with Seiroku Kajiyama.

60. Interview with Yoshio Omori.

61. Federal News Service, October 3, 1996.

62. Ibid.

63. Larry Niksch, "Senkaku (Diaoyu) Islands Dispute: The U.S. Legal Relationship and Obligations," *CRS Report for Congress,* 97-798 F, September 30, 1996, p. 5.

64. "An Asian Mini-Tempest over Mini-Island Group," *New York Times,* September 16, 1996, p. A8.

65. *Asahi Shimbun,* October 3, 1996, p. 4.

66. "Japan Removes Flag Raised by Groups on Disputed Isles," *Kyodo News International,* October 14, 1996.

67. Interview with Yukio Takeuchi.

68. "Statement of the Ministry of Foreign Affairs of the People's Republic of China," December 30, 1971.

69. "The Basic View of the Ministry of Foreign Affairs on the Senkaku Islands," March 8, 1972 (provisional translation).

70. Niksch, "Senkaku Islands Dispute."

71. Ibid.

72. Interview with Yukio Takeuchi.

73. Interview with Walter Mondale.

74. Interview with a White House official.

75. Ibid.

76. Ibid.

77. Ibid.

78. Interview with a senior DOD official.

79. Ibid.

80. Interview with William Perry.

81. Interview with a senior DOD official.

82. *Xinhua News Agency,* September 26, 1996.

83. Author's conversation with a Chinese diplomat.

84. Shingo Nishimura (New Frontier Party), Special Committee on Land Usage Accompanying the Implementation of the Japan-U.S. Security Treaty, House of Representatives, April 8, 1997.

85. "Administrative Reform Key LDP Platform Plank," *Daily Yomiuri,* October 2, 1996, p. 3.

86. Interview with a senior MOFA official.

87. Interview with a senior DOD official.

88. Interview with a DOD official in charge of China affairs.

89. Conversation with a State Department official.

90. Interview with Kurt Campbell.

91. "A Check on U.S. Intervention in the Senkaku Dispute," *Sankei Shimbun,* October 16, 1996.

92. Interview with a U.S. State Department official.

93. Interview with Ryozo Kato.

94. Interviews with Yukio Takeuchi and Hitoshi Tanaka.

95. Interview with a senior MOFA official.

96. Interview with a senior JDA official.

97. Interview with a senior MSDF officer.

98. *JEI Report,* February 28, 1997.

99. Quoted from Koji Kamimura, "A Rush of 'Anti-American' 'Anti-Japanese' Publications in China," *Foresight,* August 1996, p. 30. (In Japanese.)

100. Author's conversation with a Chinese diplomat.

101. *China Youth Daily,* February 15, 1997, p. 8.

102. Interview with Seiroku Kajiyama.

103. Akihiko Tanaka, *Security* (Tokyo: Yomiuri Shimbunsha, 1997), p. 80. (In Japanese.)

104. Interview with Ryutaro Hashimoto.

105. *Asahi Shimbun,* September 17 and October 3, 1996.

106. "The Threat Comes From Those Who Advocate the Theory of Threat," *Xinhua News Agency,* October 17, 1996.

107. Interview with Seiroku Kajiyama.

Chapter Nineteen

The Three-Way Struggle:
United States–Japan–China

"We Haven't Come Here to Listen to Diet Dissembling!"

If the Taiwan Straits crisis of March 1996 had not taken place, perhaps China would not have been as critical of the subsequent strengthening of U.S.-Japan relations. Or perhaps it would have. How many times did the bilateral security authorities ask themselves that question!

China launched a strident campaign following the Joint Security Declaration announced during Clinton's visit to Japan in April. The subsequent guidelines review was also the butt of a fierce attack. While those in charge of bilateral security had expected China to express a certain amount of alarm, they did not imagine it to come out in such force.

A White House official recalled, "We didn't foresee the reaction, particularly from China."[1] A senior Japanese government official echoed this sentiment, saying, "We were a little surprised. It didn't matter who you talked with, they all repeated the same criticism."[2]

In fact, Chinese criticism varied. First, the Chinese argued, the United States' and Japan's security ties had become, or were becoming, a vehicle for containing China. The Chinese were convinced that the United States and Japan were afraid of China emerging as a superpower, saw China as a potential future military power, cultivated the argument that China was a threat, and were promoting policies hostile to China. Strengthening the security ties was a means to that end.

Chi Haotian, the Chinese defense minister, complained that "there are still some people around the world who keep spreading the fallacy of a China threat, arguing that a stronger China will threaten others and become a destabilizing factor in the Asian-Pacific region. I believe these people who spread such rumors have ulterior motives. They are not happy to see China in development and progress." Saying "China has never invaded any country, nor has it stationed a single soldier abroad," he attempted to contrast China's "peace-loving" nature with Japanese and American "aggression."

Another Chinese argument was that the U.S.-Japan security relationship was not fulfilling a stabilizing function in the Asian-Pacific region. Moreover, the military presence of that "foreign interloper," the United States, was a destabilizing factor. This line of argument started to surface in the summer of 1995. During the ASEAN Regional Forum (ARF) held in August of that year, Foreign Minister Qian Qichen said that the United States should withdraw instead of throwing its weight around in the region and always posing as the "Savior of the East."[4] While this was partly an expression of China's irritation over Lee Teng-hui's very recent trip to the United States, it was also a challenge to the U.S. presence itself.

China repeated the line that "it did not recognize the United States as an Asian power."[5] Kui Fulin, deputy chief of general staff in the People's Liberation Army (PLA), repeatedly stated, "The United States should put a stop to its forward deployment in the Asia-Pacific and pull out." While he was not saying "get out right now," he was urging the Americans "to leave in the future."

In April 1997, a spokesman for the Chinese Ministry of Foreign Affairs made an official statement that "the United States should withdraw."[6] William Cohen, U.S. secretary of defense, avoided a direct rebuttal, saying, "Let's take it with a grain of salt."[7] A Chinese diplomat, however, explained "that spokesman's statement reflected the Chinese leadership's view that the U.S. presence would not help stability in the region. It was the first time that position had been voiced and should be seen as a position endorsed by the leadership."[8]

Another fear was that the strengthening of the U.S.-Japan security relationship was threatening to lead to U.S. "domination" and Japanese "militarism." Chinese foreign policy is often regarded as being anti-hegemonic, against the exercise of big power politics, alliances, and spheres of influence.[9] In the same line, Tang Jiaxuan felt that the U.S. deployment of its aircraft carriers during the China-Taiwan crisis was clearly illustrating its doctrine of hegemony.

China was also concerned with the risk of greater Japanese military power. "One of the two U.S. carriers came from Yokosuka. This meant that the U.S.-Japan security relationship had been applied to interfere in China's internal affairs. It was tantamount to Japan hitching a ride on U.S. tanks."[10] "The U.S. needs Japan to be not only a '[rank and file] soldier,' but also a 'general' when it is needed."[11] These types of admonishments were vented by those at the heart of the Chinese military and by think-tank researchers.

Denunciations of the reemergence of Japanese militarism were reiterated throughout this period, but they were not necessarily triggered by what had happened during the showdown between China and Taiwan. China had pointed this out before and took every opportunity to bring this home to the Americans. Time and again, they warned the Americans that they were not sufficiently aware of the risk that strengthening the U.S.-Japan security relationship would increase Japanese militarism. In a series of meetings in August 1997 between Samuel Berger, presidential aide, and Chinese leaders, the Chinese repeated that Japan was militaristic; Japan hadn't changed; Japan was dangerous. One of the members of the American team said, "I have heard 'Yamamoto' at least 10 times from the Chinese."[12] He was referring to Commander Isoroku Yamamoto of the 56th Combined Fleet who led the Japanese in the attack on Pearl Harbor and in the Battle of Midway.

The Chinese also believed that the U.S.-Japan security relationship was expanding from concern with the defense of Japan proper to defense of the region around Japan. This was the strongest of all the criticisms voiced. The Chinese could put up with it if U.S-Japan security was a bilateral defense framework, but it would be a serious matter if it was to be expanded into a defense framework for the whole Asia-Pacific region. They cautioned repeatedly that "the U.S.-Japan security structure must not exceed the bilateral scope." They suspected any such move was aimed at China and were filled with apprehension that the "Japanese vicinity" also included the Spratly Islands in the South China Sea. They even asked precisely that question—were the Spratlys included?—in Sino-Japanese security talks in March 1997.

The Chinese also feared that the United States and Japan would prevent the return of Taiwan to China. Both the United States and Japan might be plotting for a stranglehold on China by keeping Taiwan separate and using it as military and political leverage.

In March 1997, Xiong Guangkai, deputy commander of the PLA, asked the Liberal Democratic Party (LDP) delegation (led by Keizo Obuchi) visiting China, "The Joint Declaration has strengthened U.S.-Japan security cooperation and expanded the scope of Japan's military role. Isn't this strengthening of security aimed at the Korean Peninsula and the Taiwan Straits?"[13]

China's fear, however, was not only that the United States and Japan were plotting to use Taiwan and military leverage against China's emergence as a military power. As a high U.S. government official who had held many talks with the Chinese on this question put it, "They were more afraid that the perception that the U.S. and Japan support Taiwan would lead to political developments in Taiwan."[14]

The Chinese were very nervous about how this strengthening of the U.S.-Japan security relationship affected Taiwan. And they were even more sensitive about the review of the guidelines. China was increasingly frustrated with the Japanese who kept asserting that the "Japanese vicinity," as in "contingencies in the Japanese vicinity," was not a "geographical concept" but a "circumstantial concept." They suspected Japan was keeping this intentionally vague and trying to increase its "deterrent power" vis-à-vis China.

In the March 1997 security talks between China and Japan, they persisted in asking, "What would Japan do if military tensions occurred in the Taiwan Straits? Would U.S.-Japan security be applied or not?" When Hitoshi Tanaka, deputy director of the Ministry of Foreign Affairs' (MOFA) North American Affairs Bureau, replied, "It depends on the case," his Chinese counterpart, Wang Yi, retorted, "We haven't come here to listen to Diet dissembling!"[15]

Reproaching Japan

China reproached Japan from many angles. First it intimated that as a "part of Asia" it expected a different role and behavior from Japan. Touching on Japan's criticism of the Chinese missile firings in the Taiwan Straits, Foreign Minister Qian Qichen told his Japanese counterpart, Yukihiko Ikeda, "Leaving aside the fuss made by the Americans, you're the only other country kicking up a fuss. China is shocked by that."[16]

This was undoubtedly a sly dig at Japan to the effect that of all the neighboring countries of Asia, only Japan was "different"; such a Japan could not even really be called a part of Asia. A Chinese diplomat asked a Japanese friend, "How long does Japan, as an independent state, intend to keep U.S. military bases?"

"It's not only Japan that hosts foreign military bases. Germany, the U.K., and Italy all have U.S. bases."

"Yes, but they're European. They're different from us Asians."[17]

This was Asianism being used to pressure Japan.

The Chinese also made free use of the multilateralist argument. The most typical argument was that "bilateralism is a product of the Cold War; this is the age of multilateralism." China had been secretly lobbying ASEAN to "create some multilateral trust-fostering sea rules on large-scale fleet movements." The Americans were very touchy about this "multilateral framework," which they saw as an attempt to restrict the U.S. fleet's freedom of movement.[18]

Interestingly, China was quick to criticize the U.S.-Japan alliance but never the U.S.-Korea alliance, even though both are products of bilateralism. In other words, the Chinese aim was first and foremost to attack the U.S.-Japan alliance, all the rest of the talk on bilateralism and multilateralism was more or less an afterthought. Nevertheless, it is obvious that the Chinese embarked on this course in order to boost what it deemed to be a growing tendency towards multilateralism within Japan.

Another question China posed was why did Japan want so strongly to team up with the United States, a "foreign interloper"? Was it because

Japan had no confidence in itself? If that was true, such a country was not qualified to assume leadership of the Asian-Pacific region, a veteran Chinese diplomat told his friend, a Japanese journalist.

How can you be so unconcerned about having foreign forces and bases in your own country? Where on earth has the nation of Japan's dignity and pride gone? It would be inconceivable for China! Do the Japanese really think the U.S. military presence has such pure and fine intentions? There must be something wrong with the Japanese if they believe that America is a country with such lofty ideas! "There seem to be some Japanese who see this as a way of stopping Japan from careening off on its own independent course, but we can't possibly work to build a peace structure for Asia with a country that can't trust itself!"[19]

It is clear that whenever China mentioned the withdrawal of the "foreign interloper" from the Asian-Pacific region, it had in mind the growing advocacy within Japan for the withdrawal of the U.S. Marines. By the fall of 1995, there had been no response from the Chinese on Sino-Japanese security talks, which were supposed to be conducted on an annual basis starting in the previous year. That year, 1995, was the 50th anniversary of the end of the war. Another issue was China's nuclear tests. In protest against them, the Japanese government placed a temporary freeze on its aid grants, which China angrily resented.

However, just as the rape incident in Okinawa was making the U.S.-Japan relationship extremely rocky, a positive signal arrived from China. A high-ranking JDA official in charge of setting up the Sino-Japanese security talks revealed, "It was way behind schedule and suddenly, there they were saying let's do it. What's more, it was the Chinese Foreign Ministry that had been in the center of arrangements on their side, but this time it was their Defense Ministry that made the first approach. I got the feeling that they thought the Okinawa rape might do strange things to the U.S.-Japan security relationship."[20]

The Shadow of the Taiwan Straits Crisis

How should this U.S.-Japan security-as-threat position of the Chinese be regarded? The United States came up with many interpretations. It was unmistakably true that U.S. and Japanese criticism of the Chinese missile tests in March 1996 and the deployment of the U.S. carriers had entrenched Chinese attitudes and this stubbornness lay behind the Chinese theory of the U.S.-Japan security threat. Whether consciously or subconsciously, China believed that the U.S.-Japan Security Declaration and the redefinition of the U.S.-Japan security relationship was triggered by the Taiwan Straits crisis of March 1996.

Chinese suspicions that U.S.-Japan security talks had been strengthened by the Taiwan Straits crisis were quite right. However, the

Chinese were wrong to believe that the strengthening of the U.S.-Japan security relationship was brought about by that showdown. The process, in fact, had been set in motion by the Nye Initiative in the fall of 1994. The draft of the U.S.-Japan Joint Security Declaration had already been drawn up in the fall of 1995. Winston Lord, assistant secretary of state, later said, "We had a very good security declaration prepared for Osaka in November of 1995, and of course you remember the president was not able to go due to the budget crisis, and so, therefore, his trip was put off until April. But what people don't understand is that it was already very strong, and it was a big disappointment that we couldn't do it at that point. However, there is no question that the Taiwan Straits crisis in the interval between November and the April meeting served to strengthen that document even more. . . . The point I am trying to make is that, well, a lot of people say we got a strong reaffirmation in April because of the Taiwan Straits crisis, and that is a huge oversimplification."[21]

A senior member of the White House remarked, "There was virtually no connection between the security reaffirmation and the Taiwan Straits crisis. What happened in the Taiwan Straits was a completely separate issue from the process of strengthening the U.S.-Japan security relationship. We also explained that several times to the Chinese."[22]

Masahiro Akiyama, director-general of the JDA's Defense Bureau, commented, "This was a classic case of miscalculation. The proposal for the Joint Security Declaration had already been tabled by February 1995 and the task of reaffirming the security structure was already over by then. In short, it was over before the Taiwan Straits crisis. It just wasn't announced because President Clinton's visit was cancelled."[23]

This doesn't mean, however, that the government did not use the Taiwan Straits crisis to garner domestic support for strengthening the U.S.-Japan security relationship. Both governments, in fact, used the crisis skillfully to that end. Stanley Roth, former presidential aide and senior director of the NSC's East Asian Bureau, noted, "Rather than Gore going to Japan in November 1995 and convincing the American public of the importance of the U.S.-Japan alliance, it was probably far easier for Clinton to go in April 1996 and do the same thing because during this period, China became an issue."[24]

A White House official, who was involved in the Taiwan Straits crisis during the whole period, maintained, "Had it not been for Taiwan, I am not convinced that what occurred in April would have been possible. . . . The Taiwan question very succinctly solidified views on both sides for the viability of the future, at least in the near term, of the relationship."[25]

However, the Americans thought that China's own domestic politics might have made it raise the pitch of its criticism of the U.S.-Japan security relationship. Apprehension over China's actions during the Taiwan Straits crisis spread not only to Japan and the United States but throughout the Asian-Pacific region, leading to a new theory of Chinese threat. The Chinese could not allow the missile tests during the crisis to become a black mark against the leadership which had ordered them. Perhaps that was why the Chinese launched a counteroffensive that it was not China that was a threat but the U.S.-Japanese security relationship.

This was a widely held belief within both the Japanese and the American governments. At the time, a great deal of weight was probably placed on the self-respect of China's military. Prime Minister Ryutaro Hashimoto at one time let slip his feeling that "after the Tiananmen Square incident, the Chinese military were cut off from opportunities for external exchanges and dialogue. That might just be what's behind this round of criticism [against the U.S.-Japan security relationship]."[26]

In other words, he saw the People's Liberation Army as the instigator of this onslaught. Military leaders probably felt they had lost face during the Taiwan Straits crisis and wanted to vent their pent-up frustration. It probably looked to them as if Japan was "blindly following" America's lead. It was not only Hashimoto but also the U.S. authorities who held this view.

Another factor may also have been the power struggle within China. China was in a state of flux. A clear successor to Deng Xiaoping had yet to emerge. For the political leaders, their position on the question of Taiwan had become a touchstone for their suitability to lead. Assessments of the U.S.-Japan security relationship inevitably took place in this light. A senior U.S. government official who accompanied National Security Adviser Anthony Lake to China in July 1996 conjectured that "one has to either conclude that they are not listening and they don't believe us, or that the repetition of this argument has some currency in domestic politics in China that we perhaps don't fully understand." He added, "When the PLA comes up and lectures us about Japan, to a certain degree they are also lecturing their own leadership, saying that we have to make sure that the Americans understand what our policy here is, and this is how we define it."[27]

There were, however, also hints that China wanted the U.S.-Japan security relationship to hold. There were signs that the mainstream Chinese leadership felt they had to be careful not to deny the whole relationship just because of Taiwan. Even in the Sino-Japanese security talks conducted in March 1997, a Chinese participant revealed to one of the Japanese that "we were not attacking Japan just for the sake of attacking. We were raising each point and demanding convincing answers more in a search for material that would be persuasive back home than anything else."[28]

During National Security Adviser Samuel Berger's visit to China in August 1997 as well, the Chinese leadership asked for "more convincing explanations" in a similar kind of "search for material that would be persuasive back home." Premier Li Peng told Berger he was "comfortable . . . we believe that the U.S.-Japan security relationship is your own business. However, there are critics in our country who ask several questions. And we would like to ask you these questions so that we can explain to these critics your answers."[29]

While there was most likely a tactical aspect to this approach—first creating the impression that they were "understanding" and then enlisting the United States to help them handle their domestic "critics" by making some concessions—at the same time the Chinese may well have had a long-term strategic viewpoint of not wishing to destroy the U.S.-Japan security relationship itself.

Such words would seem to indicate that the Chinese leadership had not yet made up its mind about the U.S.-Japan security relationship. Most likely, there were two main positions: It was preferable for the United States to maintain its presence in the Asian-Pacific region, or it should be made to withdraw from the region. A high-ranking official at the Pentagon remarked, "They still haven't decided on their long-term strategy. In the short term, they are asserting that strengthening the U.S.-Japan security relationship represents a threat. By doing this, they are trying to put Japan in a difficult position. In short, this can be seen as a tactical move."[30]

Those Japanese and U.S. policy officials who saw China's criticism of the security relationship as "political and tactical" were in the majority, but there were those who started to consider it "geopolitical and strategic" in nature. China was obviously aiming at holding sway over Asia in the 21st century and saw the United States as an obstacle. Therefore, the first thing it had to do was to jerk Japan into line by undermining the U.S.-Japan security relationship. That would simultaneously fuel regionalism in Asia and make the United States uncomfortable and pave the way for its withdrawal. Those who subscribed to this theory saw the seeds of this kind of geopolitical and strategic thinking in Chinese military circles.

The only catch with this theory was that the trouble the Chinese leadership was having in determining its strategic position on the U.S.-Japan security relationship may have converged on the question of Taiwan, which no one could oppose. While there were many diverse stances on how to tackle China both within Japan and the United States, all sides were beginning to shift in the direction of taking a more realistic approach toward China. The Taiwan Straits crisis undeniably worked to promote this.

One expert saw the U.S. approach to China, which had consisted of an idealistic "engagement and enlargement" in the early days of the Clinton administration, as having been amended to a more realistic stance of coexisting with China as a "nonaggressive power."[31] Japan's approach to China, which had been one of "commercial liberalism" from the 1970s, had also changed to one of "reluctant realism."[32]

Briefing

U.S.-Japan briefing on China was much more frequent and in depth than ever before. A high-ranking U.S. government official was emphatic that "we had never been so open in our briefing of your country in previous bilateral security talks."[33] In the words of former Assistant Secretary of Defense Joseph Nye, Japan and the United States shared the same opinion that "the U.S. security relationship was a matter for the two countries. It was not a matter that a third country could veto, nor could they be permitted to do so."[34] Needless to say, the "third country" here was China.

Both countries also agreed that "extreme caution needed to be exercised when strengthening the U.S. security relationship in a nonthreatening way to China." It was Nye, creator of the Nye Initiative, who made the first briefing trip to China. His visit was "part of Chinese engagement" and was to brief China on the Joint Security Declaration to be announced during Clinton's November 1995 visit to Japan.

A few days before Nye's trip, the Clinton visit was postponed, but Nye still went to China and gave a fairly detailed background briefing. Winston Lord recalled, "We briefed them ahead of [the April 1996 bilateral summit]; we briefed them afterwards; we inserted a statement in the security declaration saying that we wanted constructive relations with China. . . . The Japanese went out of their way to say they were not going to change their constitution and that none of this was inconsistent with their constitution. We went out of our way to say that the Guidelines Review was directed at the Korean contingencies and was not directed at China."[35]

Immediately prior to Clinton's scheduled trip to Japan, the State Department and the Pentagon invited the top people from the Chinese Embassy in Washington over and briefed them in detail. At this time, the Chinese raised three main points: How was Taiwan discussed and how had it been included in the statement; was this new U.S.-Japan security cooperation to take place within the existing framework of the Japanese constitution; and had any changes been made in the mission and role of the U.S.-Japan security relationship?[36]

The Japanese briefed the Chinese in both Tokyo and Beijing. Compared to the briefings by the United States, however, the Japanese briefings were conducted by "briefers of low rank, to be not as good as the U.S., and to be late."[37] The United States was especially successful in creating a good impression with the Chinese through Lake's very detailed briefing in July. Japan's most comprehensive background briefing did not take place until almost one year after the Joint Security Declaration, during the fourth round of Sino-Japanese security talks in March 1997. Eighty percent of the seven-hour-long meeting was devoted to the U.S.-Japan security relationship.[38]

Sino-Japanese security talks had been conducted on an annual basis since 1994 (February 2, 1994; January 13, 1995; January 15, 1996; and March 15, 1997). None had ever been the scene of such intense debate as this. To the Chinese representatives who asserted that Japan and the United States had been prompted by the Taiwan Straits crisis to redefine the U.S.-Japan security relationship and work on a Joint Security Declaration, Masahiro Akiyama, director of the JDA's Defense Bureau, replied, "The reaffirmation is not taking place because of Korea or China. Its single greatest significance for Japan is to reaffirm a solid commitment by both Japan and the United States."[39]

Japan and the United States took the position that the briefings were part of creating "transparent" policy design. The Americans did not only brief the Chinese; they were very forthcoming on the value of fostering mutual trust by ensuring transparency, showing the Chinese around U.S. military facilities and giving them opportunities to talk to officers and men in the field.

This U.S. policy of transparency with China had several aims. The first was the element of deterrence. The Americans didn't use that term with the Chinese but rather "avoiding miscalculations." They would nudge the Chinese towards more realistic responses by having them gain an accurate awareness of America's military level. (Translation: We have incredible weapons like this, so you'd better not do anything foolish!)

The second aim was reciprocity. They expected their military leaders to be shown around China's military installations when they next visited China. (Translation: We showed you ours, so now it's your turn to show us yours!)

The third aim was military cooperation in the future. The Americans took the Chinese to a peacekeeping institute and showed them the peacekeeping operation (PKO) training and classes, sowing the seeds for future Sino-American cooperation in the PKO area. (Translation: If we sweat it out together, we will grow to trust each other; let's think of something.)

And the final aim was showing them American society and the country more broadly. (Translation: This is democracy; pretty good, huh?)

During Defense Minister Chi Haotian's visit to the United States, one of the U.S. officials recounts, "Chi's delegation was all in the bus. He was up in a sedan or a limousine up ahead of us. The delegation, most of it senior generals, were on this bus. So we were driving up the Hud-

son River [and] passed by several small Hudson Valley towns. One of
the generals in front of me, talking in Chinese, said . . . to his colleague,
'All these towns we are passing through, you see all of these American
flags that are hanging out?' And his friend said, 'Yes, so what?' And he
said, 'Well, you know, it's pretty interesting because . . . I had always
thought the Americans were very unpatriotic . . . and don't believe in
their country. In China, you never see flags hanging out from private
homes.' This was just the third day of the visit."[40] The Americans did
not miss even the casual comments.

Later on, both the Americans and Japanese were heard to rue that the
Chinese reaction to the reaffirmation of the U.S.-Japan security relationship might have been quite different if only they had treated China
with a little more care. During his summer 1996 trip to China, Lake provided a fairly lengthy discussion of both the aims and direction of U.S.-
Japan security cooperation, and was told by one of his Chinese
interlocutors, "If you had provided this kind of detailed discussion of
this issue prior to the issuance of the statement, perhaps we wouldn't
have had so many problems with it."[41]

In fact, U.S. government opinion was divided over how much credence should be placed in this kind of remark from the Chinese. There
were limits to how much you could explain. "Then came the March
missile firing exercises. We signed the declaration in April. Now in the
Chinese psyche, with their paranoia, in their minds the timing of that
was clear. . . . It's incorrect, but we can't change that perception because
of the timing."[42] That was how one of the top U.S. China experts saw it.
Many of the people involved in communicating with the Chinese at the
practical level, including this official, knew only too well just how difficult talking policy with them was. The Japanese officials also could say
the same. Sighs laced with pent-up irritation escaped their lips:

"China does not participate in meetings. They come barking through
megaphones."

"It doesn't matter who they're meeting, they just read the same
talking points."

"Their speech is stiff, their attitude is stiff. I wonder if that's for the
benefit of the hawks back home too."

"It's difficult to hold regular meetings with them, so setting up every
meeting is subject to political speculation."

"They have this mentality where they see exchanges as being a favor
China grants to other countries. They call it exchange but they seem to
get a thrill out of forcing people to come."

"They try to set Japan and America against each other, no matter
what the issue. It's like they're still living in the times of Kung Ming!"

"It's exhausting because they're more interested in protocol than
content when it comes to exchange or dialogue."[43]

"Transparency Is Threatening"

Defense officials on both sides of the Pacific were quietly trading horror stories of their experiences in promoting military exchange with China. For example, on his way back from visiting Cuba, a Chinese general stopped off in Japan for a few days. The military attaché at the Chinese Embassy in Tokyo notified Shigeru Sugiyama, chairman of the Joint Staff Council, that "if you wish an audience with him, he is prepared to see you." When Sugiyama replied, "I am not so sure about the expression of 'an audience,' but I will agree to a chat," the military attaché replied, "I didn't think the term was appropriate myself either, but I was instructed to use it from above."[44]

The Americans had been working for six months on preparations for Defense Minister Chi Haotian's visit. Perry had an ambitious list of topics he wished to discuss, including, of course, Taiwan, Japan, and the Middle East. All were confrontational issues, so Perry wanted to get them out of the way in a quiet, small meeting. They would then be able to move into a more relaxed and open session. Perry welcomed Chi warmly when he walked into the room. He said, "You were visiting; what is on your mind?" And then Chi sat down, reached into his briefcase, got out a notebook, put on his glasses, and read a very polemical speech for thirty minutes.[45]

There is another story about Chi Haotian's visit to the United States. The Chinese told the Americans that Chi was not simply minister of defense, but vice-chairman of the Military Commission and a senior member of the inner meeting circle. They made it very clear that they did not want to schedule the visit until they were assured that there would be a meeting with the president.[46] (The meeting took place, but it was orchestrated so that Clinton would just happen to drop by at Anthony Lake's office while he was meeting with Chi Haotian.)

Another story related to Chi's visit concerns who backed it. A Pentagon official said, "First of all, it was not the Chinese push, it was the PLA push. . . . Never once did anybody except for the PLA say that it was imperative that Chi met with Clinton. . . . I believe this was really a PLA push for prestige. . . . Is it that they were somewhat put on the defensive as a result of the Taiwan missile-firing exercises?"[47]

Nevertheless, when the Americans and Chinese started their negotiations on whether a high-level military exchange would take place "once a year" (the U.S. proposal) or "from time to time" (the Chinese proposal), Chi Haotian was not empowered like Perry to negotiate. He had to ask the party Politburo.[48] Americans learned both that overseas trips by military staff were a question for the Politburo and way out of the defense minister's league and that military exchange was a very tricky affair.

At the time of the fourth Sino-Japanese security talks, a separate session for just the defense authorities was scheduled. When the day came, Wang Zaixi, chief of general staff in the PLA General Staff Headquarters, introduced himself, saying, "I came this time because the JDA said they wanted someone important to come; they wanted to talk with someone important." The Japanese were stunned. "Rather than being embarrassed, I was dumbfounded!" said a Japanese participant.[49]

Although China embarked upon the military exchanges, it was apprehensive. They proceeded at a snail-like pace. Both the United States and Japan were dissatisfied that the number of visits to China was lower than the number of visits from China. When Shalikashvili stopped over in Japan en route home from China, he confessed to Japan's top soldiers that "we field three visits to their one."[50]

China was also very dubious about the transparency that America and Japan stressed. In the March 1997 Sino-Japanese security talks, the Chinese came up with a new theory: the transparency threat theory.

"Transparency is not a so-called confidence-building measure."

"It may also be a source of threat."

"America's so-called transparency is a classic example."

"America shows off all its latest weapons; in other words they talk of transparency but are really intimidating us."

"Japan is no exception either. Whether it's the ground, maritime, or air, they all have state-of-the-art weaponry. Japan talks about transparency, but they're actually intimidating us too!"[51]

One instance the Chinese cited was when the Americans showed Chi Haotian around a cutting-edge military technology plant during his trip to the United States. The Chinese asserted that showing something like that was clearly nothing but intimidation.

While the Chinese delegation assumed poker-faced expressions, inwardly they were overwhelmed by the level of U.S. military technology. Chi and his delegation were taken to several state-of-the-art facilities, including Fort Hood in Texas. A senior official at the Pentagon shrugged his shoulders, saying, "It's a kind of no-win situation that you show them nothing and they say you are not being honest; you show them everything and they say it's threatening."[52] He then added, "Chi did [express himself]. . . . We put him in our best tank, the M1-Abrams fighting tank. We took him down to Fort Hood, Texas, and we got him in an armor outfit, a helmet, put him in a tank, and he fired a couple of rounds, hit a target from 2,000 meters. This guy jumped out of the tank . . . talking very expressive Chinese. . . . He jumped out of the tank and jumped down and turned to one of his generals and said, 'That is the best tank I have ever been in!' He said, 'I have been in Russian tanks. They are not anything like that.' And he was delighted."[53]

The same official, a China expert, also expressed concern that "in terms of this great transparency debate that we have with China, again, I am less optimistic that we are going to be able to make much progress. . . . Their approach to transparency is . . . there is this idea in the strategic culture that deception is a critical form in warfare, and where you are strong you show weakness, where you are weak you show strength. And so what they tend to do is show strength of resolve."[54]

The Japanese countered this "art of making yourself invincible" from China head on. In the Sino-Japanese security talks, the Japanese stated "it is rather China which is creating an impression of intimidation. This comes from the lack of transparency." They also said that "China's defense budget is especially ambiguous, so you should be striving to improve transparency by revealing its detailed contents."[55]

On the dispute over territorial rights in the South China Sea, China had shown a willingness to discuss the matter in a multilateral trust-building forum with ASEAN countries. The U.S. State Department's assessment was, however, that China actually had little interest in a multilateral trust-building forum. "Its stance is one of dealing with everything in bilateral frameworks, whether it be with Russia, Indonesia, Japan, or the United States. It may speak of multilateralism, but what China means by that is cutting deals which consist of bilateral give and take. It's really talking about realpolitik."[56]

During this period both Japan and the United States were made keenly aware of just how difficult trust-building with China was. But they realized that the only way to do it was to maintain and improve constant communication and take a brick-by-brick approach comprised of small, daily efforts. In their March security talks with the Chinese, the Japanese came up with a new trick. They distributed a Chinese version of the New Defense Program Outline (NDPO) announced in 1995.

When the Japanese stated that "Japan is defense-oriented and will not become a military power," the Chinese asked, "How can we be sure?" In response, Akiyama said he would like them to take a look at the NDPO of two years ago and handed out copies of the Chinese version. He got the Chinese laughing when he pointed out something in the text, saying, "It's written here—even I have a basic grounding in Chinese writing." He was pointing at the section on defense only, the three nonnuclear principles, and civilian control. "This is one of the fruits of today's discussion. May we tell them back home?"

"With pleasure." For some reason, Akiyama used the English expression.[57]

A Three-Way Struggle

Both Japan and the United States were made aware of their different perceptions of and interests in China through China's challenge against the strengthening of the U.S.-Japan security relationship. It became increasingly more difficult than in the past to manage the trilateral relationship, particularly in light of U.S.-Japan relations. From the U.S. point of view, China seemed to be turning a more hostile eye to Japan than to the United States. "There has been something of a change in China's perspective on Japan over the course of the last few years, and I am not sure I fully understand the dimensions of that."[58] "The attacks on the [U.S.-Japan security] treaty were based on Japan-China history, not anything else . . . mostly on what it might do with respect to Japan's military role, not an attack on the U.S. force presence."[59]

From the Japanese point of view, however, the biggest problem seemed to be that in the long term, China was beginning to have its doubts about U.S. intentions rather than Japanese ones. "Domestic calls for containing China were starting to emerge as well as open hostility towards China. That was what caused Chinese objections to a stronger U.S.-Japan security relationship."[60] "America's awkward diplomacy over Lee Teng-hui's visit to the States and its indecisiveness on China and Taiwan policy increased Chinese mistrust, inviting the attack on the security relationship."[61]

In the United States, people also started asking questions about whether the deterioration in Sino-Japanese relations was Japan's fault or China's. The leading Japan expert of his generation in the United States, Michael Green, noticed that whenever he spoke with U.S. China experts, they all said Japan was in the wrong. When he said "Japan might be to blame, but so is China. It's 50-50," the answer he got was, "No, Japan is 100 percent to blame."[62]

In the larger context, in addition to the sensitive issues of the bilateral system and burden sharing—namely who needed the alliance more, Japan or the United States—a question of responsibility was starting to surface: Who was the principal offender behind China's attacks on the U.S.-Japan security relationship?

Lord's view was that "Japan was increasingly concerned about China's emergence as a superpower and a crisis on the Korean Peninsula, and this strengthened the support of both Japan's leaders and its people at large for a stronger security relationship with the U.S. Despite the demise of the Cold War and the collapse of the Soviet Union, this resulted in making them think that the bilateral alliance was still important."[63]

A White House staff member spoke even more directly on this point. "The emergence and challenge of China raised more serious questions for Japan than America. It is wrong to think that the future of the U.S.-Japan alliance will be difficult. Japan has no other option than to ally itself with the U.S. in order to resist China."[64]

On the Japanese side too there were those who thought "the U.S.-Japan alliance will be shaken to its very roots" if the United States began to view China with hostility. They called for the United States to exercise restraint in its China policy. There was also the danger of what would happen if the U.S. administration truly began to believe that "Japan has no other option." Japan's policymakers were already starting to feel the "Japan passing and the Chinese lens phenomenon that was starting to spread within the U.S. administration."[65] This referred to the U.S. stance of not consulting with Japan but focusing only on China.

Alluding to the danger of the assumption that "Japan had no choice but to rely on the United States" taking on a life of its own, former Prime Minister Yasuhiro Nakasone commented at one time that "a worm can turn." Consequently, there was a strong feeling that Japan should keep some of its options open with regard to China policy. A high-ranking official at the JDA admonished himself, saying, "If America focuses too much on using the redefinition of the U.S.-Japan security relationship to make China more serious, we'll end up with the short end of the stick. We need to be careful."[66]

One of the reasons the JDA leadership failed to jump when Defense Secretary Perry suggested a three-way security dialogue among the United States, Japan, and China was a sense of alarm that the Americans would dominate any three-way talks if Sino-Japanese relations were not improved first. A psychological and diplomatic brake was at work. The Japanese did not want the Americans thinking they would always tag along behind if they used the bilateral alliance as leverage; they didn't want the Americans thinking Japan would do anything for the sake of the alliance.

Prime Minister Ryutaro Hashimoto did not hide these feelings. While stressing the importance of stronger bilateral security ties at the April 1996 summit meeting, he expounded meticulously to Clinton his own stance towards China, namely, "China will not accept the U.S. and Japan consulting jointly with it. We shall work together, but we have to make our own individual efforts over and beyond that."[67]

Hashimoto was thinking that Japan should have its own options in Asia. The Chinese onslaught on the U.S.-Japan alliance had put the countries in the Asian-Pacific region on edge. Only a very few countries had openly supported the U.S. deployment of its carriers. Hashimoto expressed his concern in the Diet at this time over the fact that no Asian country had raised its voice. "I have heard that the number of countries calling for self-restraint by China in accordance with diplomatic rules were only four including Japan, the United States, Australia, and Canada. In a certain sense, this is a very frightening tale, and we need to remember the fact that tensions in the Taiwan Straits did not work in the direction of the international community sending China a message of self-restraint."[68]

Reproaches were also heard to the effect that the United States did not mount a diplomatic offensive to garner support from the ASEAN countries. There were those who believed, rather, that the United States had, in fact, worked specifically to curb any such diplomatic offensive. A Japanese diplomat remarked, "They didn't even tell Japan they were sending the *Nimitz*. They didn't give any information to the other countries of Asia. So, you can't expect anyone to come out in support of U.S. policy even if you asked them to."[69] It is doubtful, however, that ASEAN would have voiced its support even if the United States had launched a diplomatic offensive. ASEAN fears of China were that strong.

Even concerning the U.S.-Japan review of the guidelines, Singapore requested the two "not to provoke China; we want you to be careful not to stir things up."[70] All the countries of Asia without exception supported the U.S.-Japan security relationship. But as long as China was openly objecting to it, the climate was too difficult for ASEAN to come out in open support. Inconsistencies in U.S. and Japanese responses to ASEAN began to stand out.

There was a growing feeling in both Japan and the United States that "ASEAN is just hitching a free ride on the U.S.-Japan security relationship."[71] But when it came to Cambodia and Myanmar, discrepancies in their positions arose easily. One factor was Sino-Japanese rivalry over ASEAN. The U.S. sensitivity and understanding of this left something to be desired, which made it easy for cracks to appear between Japan and the United States. And those cracks encouraged China to induce a split between the United States and Japan.

Throughout this period, the Chinese hinted at "Japanese containment" or the cap-in-the-bottle argument in an attempt to provoke U.S. mistrust towards Japan. They also insinuated to the Japanese that the Americans were showing some interest in that idea in an attempt to increase Japanese mistrust towards the United States. That, at least, was how China watchers in both the Japanese and U.S. governments saw things.

The cap-in-the-bottle argument was capable of igniting Japanese nationalism and shaking the U.S.-Japan security ties. When speaking of Japan on a visit to Washington, Chi Haotian more than once used the phrase, "It would not do to unleash Japan." This was, of course, a reference to the cap in the bottle, and he was just letting the Americans get a whiff of it. Chi even dragged out the story of Wako, thirteenth- to sixteenth-century Japanese pirates. A high-ranking U.S. official testified that "he argued strongly that Japan is an aggressive country, it can't be trusted. They are different."[72]

Saying Japan was "aggressive" and "different" so they "couldn't be trusted" would lead the United States to counter by saying, "We don't think so, but if that is the case, don't you think the U.S.-Japan security relationship is useful in keeping that under control?" In this way the United States was led down the cap-in-the-bottle trail. The Chinese were not completely wrong on this, for this was basically what the United States had in mind. Anthony Lake stated, "There was no question in my mind, and there should be no question in the Chinese mind, that the American presence . . . had contributed to the flourishing of democracy and prosperity and peaceful foreign policies by Japan. . . . I did not imply . . . that we were restraining Japan or anything, but that historically . . . I thought that it did play a role, as it obviously has."[73]

There was a period when the Japanese suspected the Americans were using the argument that "the U.S.-Japan security relationship was a weight to stop Japan from becoming a military power" in an attempt to get the Chinese to accept the significance of the relationship's existence. A high-ranking official at MOFA remarked indignantly, "There were some high-ranking U.S. officials who were whispering to China that the real aim of strengthening U.S.-Japan security ties was to impede any independent Japanese course on defense. I wonder if America realizes just how dangerous that line of argument is!"[74]

U.S. Assistant Secretary of State Winston Lord had this to say on the matter: "The Japanese people themselves and many leaders would say that one of the reasons they support the alliance is so that Japan doesn't have to face tough choices about building up its military, so it's an argument that Japan itself had used. But . . . we were very careful not to lend ourselves to something that could be portrayed as the U.S. playing on fear of Japan to appease China. I can't rule out that some official in some conversation didn't come close to that, but we were quite meticulous about that. . . . Above all, our relations with Japan is what counts, and we didn't want the Chinese playing back to Japan versions of conversations that would cause friction."[75]

During this period the impression could easily be created that bilateral relations would proceed at the cost of relations with the third country. The Japanese government welcomed the fact that the United States had deployed its carriers to protest the Chinese missile-firing exercises, but at the same time it displayed on the domestic front a perception that the Taiwan Straits crisis was a Sino-American bipolar game about who was the most macho. It was not as if there was no discontent over the fact that Japan had been forced to play a losing hand with no way out.

For example, Ikuo Kayahara, a director at the National Institute for Defense Studies, pointed out that during the Taiwan Straits crisis, China used a variety of channels to send the United States the message that "this is first and last an exercise," but there was no such notification for Japan. Japan was left with a bad taste in its mouth that it alone had been shoved into a black box.[76]

The perception of Sino-American bipolarity was quickly taking root both in the United States and China. On learning that a high official at the Chinese Ministry of Foreign Affairs had said "both the United States and China are superpowers, but Japan is only an economic power," a senior Japanese diplomat expressed concern about "the risk of this Chinese animus leading to an eruption of nationalism within Japan."[77]

The move to improve Sino-American relations that began in the fall of 1996 had a subtle effect on U.S.-Japan relations. As reciprocal visits were set up between American and Chinese leaders, there was a growing trend at the White House and the State Department to give China top priority. Around that time, a comment by a high-ranking U.S. government official to the effect that "China is a more natural partner for America than Japan. Why? Because the Chinese market is more open than Japan's" was quoted in the magazine *Business Week*.[78] Masaki Orita, director-general of MOFA's North American Affairs Bureau, mildly expressed Japan's "displeasure" with this comment by asking Lord, his counterpart at the State Department, "What the U.S. government's real intent" was.[79]

The U.S. declaration of neutrality in China and Japan's dispute over the Senkaku (Diaoyu) Islands was also taken this way. In contrast to the Japanese, who wanted to go public with the details of the interim report on the Guidelines Review in June 1997, the United States was reluctant. The Japanese suspected the Americans of backing off because they didn't want to rouse China. Regarding the review of the guidelines, China launched a test of U.S. and Japanese loyalty by focusing on the single issue of whether Taiwan was included in the review. A Chinese military attaché secretly passed on to a Japanese military attaché the information that "Chairman Shalikashvili pledged on his trip to China that Taiwan would be excluded from the review." When the Japanese checked on this with Shalikashvili's side and got a very strong reply that "there is absolutely no truth to that whatsoever," the Japanese just treated it as another example of "China's specialty, playing Japan off against the U.S."[80] Japan and the United States were sensitive to Chinese maneuvers to drive a wedge between them but expected this war of nerves only to escalate in the future.

There is no doubt that U.S.-Japan relations are much more mature and stable than Sino-American or Sino-Japanese relations. Wang Jisi, director of the Institute of North America at the Chinese Academy of Social Sciences, remarked that "U.S.-China ties are the most strained and unstable. As for the Japan-China connection, there seems to be no possibility that the two countries will form a strategic alliance that would make their relations closer than the ties between Japan and the United States. Nor is their bilateral relationship likely to become worse than that between China and the United States." His comment would seem to indicate that China considers not Sino-Japanese but Sino-American relations as "primary contradictions."[81]

Nevertheless, both Japan and the United States were now compelled to check each and every one of their policies towards each other against a screen of "Chinese consideration." This was inevitable as China grew more powerful and its presence increased. It imposed a certain sense of restraint on both the United States and Japan. Japan believed that it was preferable to pursue neither hostility nor a honeymoon but incremental improvements. Japan had been deprived of the opportunity to improve its relations with China in the period of bitter Sino-American confrontation that had lasted from the birth of Communist China until the normalization of Sino-American relations at the start of the 1970s.

There was dissatisfaction within Japan, which sometimes erupted into anti-American criticism. Japan had had its share of leaders like Tanzan Ishibashi, who, although his government was short-lived, had won his way into office campaigning for the restoration of relations with China at the end of the 1950s. Behind this lay a widespread antagonism towards the United States at the popular level for preventing Japan from bettering its relations with China.

Should arguments about the Chinese threat increase in the United States, giving birth to a policy that views China as hostile, Japan would be caught between the two and forced to make an extremely difficult choice. Avoiding just such a situation was also a requirement of Japan's U.S. policy and China policy. The Japanese nightmare was, as always, Sino-American hostility.

On the other hand, Japan had another nightmare: China and the United States going over its head. This was the fear that somewhere beyond Japan's ken, China and the United States would cut a deal that had significant repercussions for Japan. The Japanese had not forgotten the humiliation of Nixon's 1971 visit to China. Henry Kissinger did not hesitate to call Japan's foreign policy "bookkeeper's diplomacy." At that time the United States showed virtually no solicitude towards its ally Japan. The Sato government received only a token notification of this historically momentous about-face a scant three minutes before the announcement. In the end, this brought about the fall of the Sato government, a fact which led to a hard-to-eradicate Japanese mistrust of the United States, especially concerning Sino-American relations.

In the process of developing its China policy in the fall of 1996, the Americans also strained their nerves on this point. Winston Lord, assistant secretary of state, in particular, was one of those who had been personally involved in the U.S. reversal of China policy at the start of the 1970s. "Perhaps it was residual scars from the 1970s with the opening to China and insufficient consultation with Japan, and I am fully sensitive to that. So, knowing this concern . . . we went out of our way to assure Japan [and] to keep them posted on what we were doing with China."[82]

In the summer of 1996, Ambassador Walter Mondale strongly urged the White House to "be very careful that Japan did not feel apprehensive about the normalization of Sino-American relations."[83] A senior member of the White House staff attests that the White House "asked MOFA what was the best way to go about being careful, but at first MOFA just said U.S.-Japan relations are separate from Sino-American relations, so there is no need to worry. But then, two months later they came back to us in a flap saying it was all well and good to improve Sino-American relations but not at the expense of U.S.-Japan relations. The Foreign Ministry probably had underestimated domestic reaction in Japan [over the reciprocal Sino-American summits]."[84]

Clinton listened to Mondale's advice. During the U.S.-Japan summit held in conjunction with the Asia-Pacific Economic Cooperation (APEC) meeting in Manila in November 1996, Clinton reassured Hashimoto on "the decisive difference between the U.S.-Japan relationship and the Sino-American one," remarking that "it seems that there is concern in certain sections of your country that Japan will be left behind by the normalization of Sino-American relations, but there is no need to worry."[85]

China was watching closely developments in the U.S.-Japan relationship. In the process of normalizing Sino-American relations, China found itself compelled by necessity to do something about improving its relations with Japan, the calculation being that China could use this to increase its bargaining power with the United States. Just as the United States was using U.S.-Japan relations as a benchmark for its relationship with China, so too was China using Sino-Japanese relations as a benchmark for its relationship with the United States.

In the fall of 1996, when both Sino-Japanese and U.S.-Japan relations were strained over the Senkaku Islands, a veteran Chinese diplomat told a Japanese journalist that "China is serious about improving its relations with Japan, so it would be to your advantage to respond to that. If Sino-Japanese relations improve, then the U.S. will have to think a little bit before putting pressure on China by using its relations with Japan as leverage."[86]

A triangular diplomatic game had started, heralding the advent of a three-way struggle.

The Holocaust Museum

The United States had the most trouble dealing with historical issues that China raised to criticize Japan. China launched a publicity campaign on the occasion of Chi Haotian's November 1996 visit to the United States. He tried to put Japan on the defensive regarding its invasion of China in the 1930s as well as kindle memories in "the United States, our friend in arms during World War II." In a meeting with top U.S. government officials, Chi spoke from his "own experience as a veteran soldier who had undergone the storm of battle in the first half of this century." He emphasized that "this tragic history had left deep scars on the hearts of the Chinese people," citing the figure of "50 million Chinese who were killed."[87]

To Defense Secretary William Perry, Defense Minister Chi handed over parts of the remains of a U.S. plane flown during World War II, which had just been found in the autonomous district of Guanxi. He concluded a speech at the National Defense University with the following words:

> Before I left for my current visit, I received a book entitled *Pearl Harbor in Pictures* from Admiral Prueher. A famous epigram is inscribed in the book: "Remember Pearl Harbor." Precisely four days ago was the 55th anniversary of the Pearl Harbor incident. World War II bound China and the U.S. together in earnest cooperation against their common enemy. I hope China-U.S. relations today can still reflect the spirit of that sound and positive cooperation.[88]

In the joint meeting between the U.S. National Defense University and the Chinese National Defense University in Beijing in March 1997, one of the attendees revealed that "the Chinese officer used 15 minutes of his allotted hour to badmouth the Japanese. . . . Japan is a sneaky country. They're just using America. He was warning us to make sure we weren't taken in by them."[89]

The United States was apprehensive about China using the historical card to drive a wedge between it and Japan. But, at the same time, Americans were also frustrated that Japan never seemed to be able to come up with an effective way of dealing with historical questions. A high-ranking official at the State Department remarked, "Japan seems to have some problems with China that largely relate to issues of history. . . . Many times . . . they have nothing to do with the U.S. But here are some people who, I think with rather flawed thinking, believe that if the U.S. will simply get into the middle of this, it will lessen the problem for Japan. Now, I don't believe that to be true."[90]

Deputy Chief of General Staff Xiong Guangkai, who accompanied Chi on his trip to the United States in the winter of 1996, was head of Military Intelligence and spoke English. He was a man of the world and had a good sense of humor. The Americans liked him. When they suggested visiting the Korean War Memorial to fill in a couple of blank hours on his schedule, they met with a quick refusal. The Americans thought "he is a very politically correct guy, and the U.S. and China had fought each other. He didn't want a picture of him there."[91]

Instead Xiong said he would like to go to the top of the Washington Monument, but when the Americans pointed out jokingly that "the only problem [is] if we go to the top of the Washington Monument, you are going to be able to see the Korean War Memorial." Xiong saw the humor but said "no." Then, when the Americans suggested going to the Holocaust Museum, he agreed to that. Xiong had been military attaché in West Germany and said he was interested in the Holocaust. At every panel he stopped before, Xiong's lines were always the same. "Terrible. How cruel! But there's no comparison to how cruel the Japanese soldiers were before the war." As they left the museum, Xiong said, "You know, China needs a holocaust museum."[92]

Walter Slocombe briefed Kunihiko Saito, Japanese ambassador to the United States, on the main items that Chi discussed with top Pentagon officials during his trip to the United States. Secretary Perry directly rebutted the main points Chi criticized in the U.S.-Japan security relationship and Japan's future, telling Chi that the alliance was not a threat but one of the main reasons there was no arms buildup in the region, which, in turn, permitted the explosive economic growth in the Asia-Pacific region that China had greatly benefitted from.[93]

After reporting this, Slocombe gave Saito the gist of what Chi Haotian had said about Japan. He added his own evaluation that Chi's image of Japan was probably affected by his personal experiences as a young boy in the war.

Perhaps Slocombe was intentionally trying to soften Chi's harangue on Japan, which he had depicted as a country you couldn't trust. Saito's usually placid, upright face was twisted in pain as he listened. He kept repeating that it was unfair, really unfair. "Japan has always maintained polite dealings with its Asian neighbors. It's not right that they say such things about us and treat us this way!"[94]

The Chinese were not amused by Slocombe giving Saito such a meticulous briefing, and they let the U.S. government know it. The Americans sent back a concise reply: "We believe this to be a trust-building measure. Moreover, Japan and the United States are allies."[95]

Notes

1. Interview with a White House official.

2. Interview with a senior MOFA official.

3. Remarks by Chinese Defense Minister Chi Haotian at the National Defense University, *Federal News Service*, December 10, 1996.

4. "China Warns U.S. Against Maintaining Military Presence in Asia," *Deutsche Presse-Agentur*, July 29, 1995.

5. Ibid.

6. "China Says U.S. Forces Should Get Out of Asia," *Japan Economic Newswire,* April 8, 1997.

7. Jim Mannion, "Cohen Takes China's Objections to U.S. Troops in Asia with a Grain of Salt," *Agence France Presse,* April 9, 1997.

8. Author's conversation with a Chinese diplomat.

9. "When the Power Games Follow the Wealth Games," *Irish Times,* March 16, 1996.

10. Yoshitaka Sasaki, "U.S. Forward Deployment Strategies with China on Its Mind," *Asahi Shimbun* (morning edition), April 18, 1997, p. 4.

11. Zhang Yunling, "The Changing Sino-U.S.-Japanese Relations," paper presented at the international conference on China, the United States, and Japan (Beijing, China, November 1–3, 1996), p. 6.

12. Interview with a member of the U.S. team.

13. Sasaki, "U.S. Forward Deployment Strategies," p. 4.

14. Interview with a senior U.S. administration official.

15. Interview with the Japanese participants.

16. Interview with a senior MOFA official.

17. Author's conversation with a Chinese diplomat.

18. Interview with a senior DOD official.

19. Author's conversation with a Chinese diplomat.

20. Interview with a senior JDA official.

21. Interview with Winston Lord.

22. Interview with a senior White House official.

23. Interview with Masahiro Akiyama.

24. Interview with Stanley Roth.

25. Interview with a White House official.

26. Interview with Ryutaro Hashimoto.

27. Interview with a senior U.S. administration official.

28. Interview with a Japanese participant.

29. Interview with a senior U.S. administration official.

30. Interview with a senior DOD official.

31. Interview with a senior White House official.

32. Michael Green and Benjamin Self, "Japan's Changing China Policy," *Survival,* Summer 1996, p. 36.

33. Interview with Winston Lord.

34. Interview with Joseph Nye.

35. Ibid.

36. Interview with senior State Department and DOD officials.

37. Interview with a senior MOFA official.

38. Interview with a senior JDA official.

39. Interview with Masahiro Akiyama.

40. Interview with a DOD official.

41. Interview with a White House official.

42. Interview with a DOD official.

43. Conversations with U.S. and Japanese defense officials.

44. Interview with Shigeru Sugiyama.

45. Interview with a senior DOD official.

46. Ibid.

47. Ibid.

48. Ibid.

49. Interview with a JDA official.

50. Conversation with a top-level SDF officer.

51. Interview with the Japanese participants.

52. Interview with a DOD official.

53. Ibid.

54. Ibid.

55. Interview with the Japanese participants.

56. Interview with a senior DOD official.

57. Interview with Masahiro Akiyama.

58. Interview with a White House official.

59. Interview with Winston Lord.

60. Interview with a senior MOFA official.

61. Interview with a senior JDA official.

62. Author's conversation with Michael Green.

63. Interview with Winston Lord.

64. Interview with a White House official.

65. Interview with Paul Giarra.

66. Interview with a senior JDA official.

67. Interview with Ryutaro Hashimoto.

68. Ryutaro Hashimoto's reply to the Standing Committee on Budget, House of Councilors, April 15, 1996.

69. Interview with a senior MOFA official.

70. Ibid.

71. Ibid.

72. Interview with a senior U.S. administration official.

73. Interview with Anthony Lake.

74. Interview with a senior MOFA official.

75. Interview with Winston Lord.

76. Interview with Ikuo Kayahara.

77. Interview with a senior MOFA official.

78. Paul Dwyer, "Is Washington Getting Set to Tilt from Tokyo to Beijing?" *Business Week*, October 21, 1996, p. 59.

79. Interview with Masaki Orita.

80. Interview with an SDF officer.

81. Wang Jisi, "Building a Constructive Relationship," in Morton I. Abramowitz, Yoichi Funabashi, and Wang Jisi, *China-Japan-U.S.: Managing the Trilateral Relationship* (Tokyo: Japan Center for International Exchange, 1998), p. 27.

82. Interview with Winston Lord.

83. Interview with Walter Mondale.

84. Interview with a White House official.

85. Interview with a senior MOFA official.

86. Author's conversation with a Chinese diplomat.

87. Interview with a DOD official.

88. Remarks by Chi Haotian at the National Defense University, *Federal News Service*, December 10, 1996.

89. Interview with a senior researcher at the U.S. National Defense University.

90. Interview with a senior State Department official.

91. Interview with a DOD official.

92. Interview with a senior DOD official.

93. Interview with William Perry.

94. Interview with a senior DOD official.

95. Ibid.

Chapter Twenty

The Reverse Pyramid

The Four Challenges

In the three years from 1994 to 1996, the U.S.-Japan alliance faced a fundamental challenge. The year 1994 was ushered in with the breakdown in bilateral economic and trade negotiations at the Hosokawa-Clinton Summit. Economic and trade friction between the two countries ate away at the U.S.-Japan relationship, leading to the American brandishing of numerical targets at the Japanese and trying to force them to accept managed trade on the assumption that Japan was "different." Despite the emergence of "political reformers," Japan was impeded by resistance from poorly competitive but politically strong entrenched vested interests that prevented market-opening measures, structural reform, and administrative reform from becoming a reality. The trade imbalance between Japan and the United States whittled away at the bilateral alliance. The argument that Japan was different started to erode the very core of the alliance, mutual trust.

In the spring and summer of 1994, suspicions of North Korea's nuclear program and calls for U.N. sanctions burst onto the scene. It looked as if the "nightmare" of the Gulf War was about to return on a scale several times larger. "Here are America's youth shedding their blood, but Japan is doing nothing, just offering money!" The alliance could well be destroyed by such a development. The prospect was a chilling one for policy officials.

The fall of 1995 brought the rape of the young Okinawan schoolgirl. A prosperous Japan became much more intolerant of the U.S. bases. The Cold War was over. How long did Japan have to put up with U.S. bases? The statesmen offered no convincing explanation to the populace, nor were they capable of doing so.

Governor Masahide Ota of Okinawa, who had emerged on the scene after the Cold War, appealed repeatedly for the realignment and reduction of the bases, but the government ignored him and the U.S. military paid him virtually no heed. The rape of the twelve-year-old girl was the last straw. The question of the bases rocked the alliance by escalating into an issue not only of peace and land and accidents but of the environment, human rights, women, and regional government. A high-ranking official at the Pentagon sighed, "The question of the bases in Okinawa turned into a vampire." In other words, "It attacked and drew blood."[1]

The Taiwan Straits crisis of March 1996 showed that the future of Sino-American relations would have a decisive impact on the U.S.-Japan alliance. Japan caught a glimpse of the alliance being sucked into the huge, whirling abyss of relations among the United States, Japan, and China.

The U.S.-Japan alliance was facing four overlapping challenges: in economics and trade, the Korean Peninsula, Okinawa, and China.

Just like a film in fast forward, each challenge followed close on the heels of the other, the latest scene being superimposed on the yet-to-fade preceding image. The wheels of history moved forward two or three cogs at a time.

Clearly it was as if the bilateral alliance had abruptly shifted from a "fixed rate" to a "floating rate" regime. It was no longer pegged to the specific threat of the Soviet Union. It had to deal with daily fluctuations generated by unspecific "instabilities." These had to be met quickly in order to uphold the alliance and put it to good use. New political capital had to be injected. If not, the alliance would be downgraded. Both governments started making the necessary reinvestments with the reaffirmation of the U.S.-Japan security relationship, the Joint Security Declaration, Special Action Committee on Okinawa (SACO), and the Guidelines Review.

And yet, the alliance remained fragile. The leaders just didn't seem to be able to come up with a long-term vision on how they should deal with these strange, new challenges. What were they defending? From what? And in what way? Everything suddenly blurred over, creating a gap in their respective perceptions of the alliance.

True, compared with the Cold War era, there is much broader support for U.S.-Japan security ties in Japan. But at the same time that support is also shallower, and it probably is the same in the United States as well.

When considering the bilateral alliance, there was a tendency to overlook the fact that the two countries were the world's leading capitalist nations and that they represented two huge economies often in fierce competition with each other whether they liked it or not. Since the 1970s, their leaders had devoted their greatest political efforts to adjusting their economic and trade relations. This was an important topic for the alliance, but the Cold War made upholding the security ties the top priority.

With the end of the Cold War, this delicate balance fell apart. The wrangle over the joint U.S.-Japan development of the FSX (next-generation fighter) was a precursor of this. Each side regarded the other as an economic rival and tried to modify the alliance accordingly. For Japan, this meant seeing a different United States.

The Clinton administration switched from a policy of trying to contain economic and trade friction to a policy of exposing it. To state the matter simplistically, during the Cold War the economy and trade were subordinated to security. After the Cold War, leaders tried to make security subordinate to economy and trade. The Nye Initiative tried to find a new balance, but ended without being able to identify a point of equilibrium.

The strained U.S.-Japan relationship during the 1994 crisis on the Korean Peninsula was nothing less than dissension over the inherent "one-sidedness" of the alliance. Christian Herter, U.S. secretary of state at the time of the 1960 Security Treaty amendment, described the treaty as having many regulations that were highly unsuitable for an accord between two sovereign states.[2]

On the other hand, a Japanese legislator remarked that in view of the benefits each country derives from the alliance, especially with regard to their interests in the Asian-Pacific region, "while there may be some one-sidedness in the treaty's legalistic terms, the overall security framework is an equal relationship and exists because both countries' judgments are in agreement."[3]

And yet, an alliance that does not require fighting together is a risky thing. The crisis on the Korean Peninsula drove home that point anew.

Okinawa was and still is a sore point in the modern history of U.S.-Japan relations. Even if all the agreements in SACO were implemented, 70 percent of the U.S. military bases in Japan would still be in Okinawa. Should they become permanent fixtures, Okinawa will once again be up in arms.

The decision to return Futenma Air Base and the subsequent difficulties that emerged speak volumes about how serious the problems over the bases are. The provision of the bases is one way of making the alliance more even-sided, and it is also an obligation of the Japanese government under the Security Treaty. They are precisely what makes possible U.S. forward deployment, and in turn its global power. If agreement on the bases could not be reached, the foundations of U.S. global power would be undermined, as would the foundation of the U.S.-Japan alliance.

In the spring of 1996, when the Sobe Communications Site lapsed into a legal vacuum, U.S. Ambassador to Japan Walter Mondale spoke with Vice Minister of Foreign Affairs Sadayuki Hayashi. Mondale asserted that "the U.S. forces have a just right to occupy the bases under the Status of Forces Agreement."

"That goes without saying. That is the Japanese government's obligation."

"Can't the Japanese police stop the sit-ins?"

"That is not legally possible. It would be different if the U.S. military did it, however."

Mondale was lost for words. "I can't possibly report that to my government."[4]

The Hashimoto government exerted a great deal of energy into fulfilling its treaty obligations and not placing the U.S. military in the position of illegally occupying the bases. The task was not a simple one, however. A U.S. official said, "[Okinawa is] like the loose thread in a suit, you know. You don't want to start pulling . . . and [be left] naked."[5]

Despite the efforts of both countries in SACO, the fundamental problems with the bases remain.

The Taiwan Straits crisis was almost a virtual-reality rehearsal. It thrust before Japan its worst choice: Take China or the United States. The U.S.-Japan alliance will continue to be challenged by China in the long term. If the allies prove unable to bring China firmly into the international system, then they should gird themselves for an even more serious challenge from that country. A confrontation over China runs the perilous risk of becoming a clash between civilizations.

When concluding the alliance with Japan, John Foster Dulles stated that the United States was paving the way for Japan to be accepted into the elite Anglo-Saxon Club just as the U.K.-Japan alliance of 1902–1921 had.[6] And Japan had striven admirably to be accepted as a member of that elite club in the postwar era.

Undoubtedly there was a risk that the U.S.-Japan alliance confronting China could have turned into a confrontation between China and the existing order of which Japan and the United States formed the nucleus; in other words, between China and the elite club. There was also the possibility that Japan's relations with Asia would be significantly strained by the fanning of Asian regionalism.

During the Taiwan Straits crisis Prime Minister Ryutaro Hashimoto said the fact that only the four countries of Japan, America, Australia, and Canada had lodged official protests over the Chinese missile-firing exercises was "a very frightening tale."[7] He was referring to the fear that, depending on which way the Chinese moved, it might lead to a split in the Asian-Pacific region.

At the present time, China is not a threat. It does not have great military power. Japan and the United States have no intention of regarding China as hostile. But the alliance has started to make China a potentially divisive issue. Regardless of the meaning each partner decides to impart to its relations with China, maintaining the alliance in the future will be possible only after each has come to terms with that significance. In the light of this and other facts, China will continue to be an issue.

Politics and Geopolitics

During the Cold War, the U.S.-Japan security structure viewed the Soviet Union as the threat. This served to keep U.S.-Japan relations, especially trade friction, in hand and governed relations with other countries in the vicinity. At the very least, that was the clear intention and expectation on the Japanese side.

It could also be said that managing the U.S.-Japan relationship was the single greatest issue in the U.S.-Japan alliance. Hashimoto stated in the Japanese Diet, "I shudder to think of the nature of U.S.-Japan relations should the Japan-U.S. Security Treaty cease to function,"[8] and that was also the feeling of many other Japanese. Should the U.S.-Japan alliance disappear, Japan's greatest immediate problem would be how to maintain relations with the United States. In a word, the U.S.-Japan alliance can be said to be more a product of politics than geopolitics.

Of the three alliances Japan had entered into in its modern history, the U.S.-Japan alliance was unique in this regard. If the Anglo-Japanese alliance at the beginning of the century was a geopolitical calculation and the German-Japan Axis from the 1930s to the 1940s was tactical acrobatics, the postwar alliance with the United States was a political necessity. It was not just a product of the Cold War. For Japan, it could almost be called an existential relationship.

To begin with, the U.S.-Japan alliance had its origins in the history of Japan's defeat at the hands of the United States in the Pacific War. The defeat made creating a new U.S.-Japan relationship possible as well as inevitable. The Peace Treaty and Security Treaty were part of the deal.

Philip Gordon, an expert on European alliance issues, assesses the postwar security relationship between West Germany and France as being "more the product of political intent than dealing with geopolitical realities,"[9] and the same could be said of the U.S.-Japan alliance. The "political intent" of the U.S.-Japan alliance also covered the U.S. bases. While John Foster Dulles scoffed at Japan for forever bending with the wind, saying "Japan acts as if it is in a peaceful green garden no matter how big a storm is brewing internationally,"[10] Japan thought long and hard about whether it should accept the U.S. bases when the process was being set up. It would have no doubt been extremely difficult to create a U.S-Japan relationship if Japan had turned them down.

There had been the possibility that Japan would become a neutral country. During the Occupation, none other than Supreme Commander Douglas MacArthur himself thought that "Japan should become the Switzerland of the Orient."[11] In any event, the U.S.-Japan alliance was born with the bases acting as political collateral. It, in turn, was used as collateral for the Peace Treaty.

During the San Francisco Peace Conference in 1951, after all the delegates signed the peace accord, Shigeru Yoshida was alone at the signing of the U.S.-Japan Security Treaty on the same day at the officers' club of the Sixth Army Headquarters at the Presidio. The signing of the Peace Treaty in the Opera House was bound to be welcomed by the Japanese, but the same could not be said for the Security Treaty. When the people of Okinawa said that the mainland got the fruits, namely the constitution, and they got the bill, namely the Security Treaty, they were only pointing out part of the bitter truth.

It is undeniably true that in the postwar era, the U.S.-Japan alliance has acted as a certain deterrent to trouble between Japan and its neighbors or between those neighbors themselves. Territorial disputes did not become serious crises with the Soviet Union, China, or Korea, but was it really the U.S.-Japan security structure that kept the lid on? The United States mediated the 1965 treaty between Japan and Korea from behind the scenes. Until the start of the 1970s U.S. hostility to China created tension at times between China and Japan. Following the normalization of U.S.-Chinese relations, however, they set up a relationship of strategic cooperation with a view to the Soviet Union.

The U.S.-Japan alliance made a contribution to Japanese peace and stability, improved Japan's relations with the countries of the Asia-Pacific region, and helped Japan make a fresh start on the international stage. This was a huge plus for Japan. It was also a plus for the United States.

Japan's success was a decisive element in fostering democracy in the Asian-Pacific region and creating a climate of economic interdependence, and the U.S.-Japan alliance acted as a foundation for that. The United States was able to function much better as a global power because of the alliance. Japan's defense-only capability and America's offense capability (forward deployment) dovetailed nicely and provided the region with a certain equilibrium and sense of balance.

Nye's vision of the U.S.-Japan alliance in the post–Cold War era as articulated in the Nye Initiative called for maintaining the same complementary structure and developing it further. It was Nye's intention to augment Japan's already unprecedented civilian power. Exposed to the four challenges of 1994 to 1996, however, the U.S.-Japan alliance was affected by a new vector that shifted the emphasis away from its hitherto political nature and made it a more geopolitical factor.

Economics and technology amplified and increased national power and wealth, in the process leading to international tension. Geography and history resisted those forces that could, however, be equally volatile. In the Asian-Pacific region, the emergence of China as a superpower will intensify these kinds of tensions.

The Asian economic miracle (and the subsequent economic melt-down since the summer of 1997), a heightened Asian awareness, and the spread of Asian regionalism have led the Asian countries to redis-cover their neighbors. Relations among these countries are being formed spontaneously, free of externally imposed restraints. They are impacting on the U.S.-Japan relationship, and this multilateralism and regionalism are forcing a redefinition of U.S.-Japan bilateralism.

Japan's role here is significant. It must promote economic consolida-tion and interdependence in the Asian-Pacific region so that a nonex-clusive regionalism can take root. It must develop trust-building measures with each country and create a multilateral, peaceful frame-work. It must create a vehicle for and promote the habit of dialogue among itself, the United States, and China. And the U.S.-Japan alliance must be used to good advantage in promoting these goals.

Fostering multilateralism in the Asian-Pacific region and strengthen-ing the U.S.-Japan partnership are not contradictory. They can be com-plementary as well as mutually reinforcing. Making sure things head in this direction should be precisely the essence of Japanese diplomacy.

The unhappy relations between Japan and other countries in modern history will cast a shadow on the U.S.-Japan relationship. The Sino-Japanese dispute over the Senkaku Islands was tied up with Japan's his-torical issues. The United States hesitated and at times was at a complete loss as to what kind of attitude it should adopt when China criticized and censured Japan over this issue. A high-ranking official at the U.S. State Department called this a "chill" in maintaining the U.S.-Japan security relationship.[12]

Ambivalence and the inadequate education of the Japanese people on these historical issues has made this question a chronic one. It always cre-ates tension in Japan's relations with its neighbors, which, in turn, cools U.S.-Japan relations. Perhaps the United States had started to perceive this as a "burden."[13]

The Secretariat Alliance

The alliance has to answer two questions: Why and how? Why is this partnership necessary? And how will it be maintained and managed? The Joint Security Declaration was an attempt to answer the first question. The Guidelines Review will probably provide one answer to the second. The task of providing the empty "wrapping paper" of an alliance with some "content" has begun. However, the work has concentrated mainly on getting politics to acknowledge and assess the operational and mili-tary requirements. Clarifying further the "active and constructive" role of Japan in diverse areas, as the Higuchi Report put it, should have been a key element of the "how" question, but it did not bear sufficient fruit.

In addition to the diverse multilateral frameworks of the Asian-Pacific region, future cooperation and the roles of Japan and the United States in the United Nations were expected to be a new diplomatic frontier for Japan, but hardly any work was done on the relation between the United Nations and U.S.-Japan security ties. Many issues also remained concerning the quality of policy consultations between Japan and the United States. When asked what was most needed to maintain the bilateral alliance, Rust Deming, deputy chief of mission at the U.S. Embassy in Tokyo, who was always right in the frontlines of Japan policy, replied, "It needs constant consideration, constant reassessment, and constant reaffirmation. It mustn't be a one-time event."[14]

SACO was seen as an endeavor in this area. The Japanese were not quite sure how to go about this, it being "the first time we had consulted with each other, ally to ally," in the words of Nobushige Takamizawa, director of the JDA Defense Operations Division.[15]

Some of the new generation bureaucrats, like Hitoshi Tanaka and Takemasa Moriya, were passionate about realizing an "equal relation of cooperation," not just in words but in practical terms. In Tanaka's case, he secretly hoped to model it on the U.S.-U.K. alliance. "I think there's a mystique to an alliance. It's clear when you look at the U.K. It's established cooperative relations which can have an impact on policies in order to curb U.S. egocentricity, to check their superpower ego, if you like. What Japan needs to create is that kind of friendly check function."[16]

Moriya was aiming at a more equal defense dialogue, backed up by the JDA's military expertise, and more effective bilateral defense cooperation, as well as more genuine consultation on the bases and troop structures. His goal was "bidding farewell to the FSX syndrome, where we don't want to but we cooperate with them for the sake of the alliance, and creating a sound partnership based on national interests."[17]

In both cases, Japan had to be prepared to pay a certain cost in terms of strategy and policy, commitment, information, judgment, and proposals. But what would that be?

Until the Japanese could define that "what," the Americans were not going to give them a second glance, no matter how many "thorough debates or proposals right down to military specifications" or "adjustments" or "consultations" on U.S. troop strength they thrust under their noses. Asking the Americans not to forget to let Japan know what was going on in advance even though Japan was not prepared to participate, contribute, or take any risks was no different from how the bean-counters at the Ministry of Finance's Budget Bureau did things! What was being tested was their willingness and ability to build a partnership.

In the half century since World War II, relations between Japan and the United States became broader and deeper. And yet, the intellectual and political underpinnings of the bilateral partnership are, in fact, frail. Defense Secretary William Perry could not hide his disappointment that the attempt to pursue a more intellectual dialogue with Japan on strategic issues had not succeeded with Japan's director-general of the JDA.

In fact, Deputy Assistant Secretary of Defense Kurt Campbell noted, "For example, people with strategic minds like [Hitoshi] Tanaka or [Takemasa] Moriya challenged us head on. That was sound and very fruitful." Japan had the human resources to do this, and intellectual dialogue during this period did increase. Another successful result was that intellectual and professional dialogue as well as more and deeper cooperation took place between the military in the two countries.

U.S. and Japanese soldiers worked alongside civilians in the Guidelines Review as well. Practical relations in the alliance at a specialist level also started to be built up between the military on both sides. They may well have been the most optimistic about the future of the alliance.

It was not as if there were no problems in this area, however. As the Japanese fiscal deficit caused reductions in the defense budget, criticism over the "compassionate budget" for the U.S. forces began to mount. Additionally, a backlash from the Self-Defense Forces (SDF) as their own budget was threatened by this host nation support was likely to increase. Grumbling could already be heard from the military.

"The U.S. bases in Okinawa have two toilets for every person, but we have to be content with four people to a room!" "SDF air conditioners only kick in at 28 degrees Celsius, but the Americans' start at 25 degrees. In winter, our heaters start when it goes below 20 degrees, but the Americans' start at 21."[18]

Rust Deming noted that "the elite group who ran security in the Cold War are gradually losing control. The fact that it is becoming more and more difficult to handle the Okinawa bases is a reflection of that."[19] Very little work was done on either side on reaffirming or reassessing alliance management, over and above the "high priests" of U.S.-Japan security in the Cold War era.

During this period, both the United States and Japan were undergoing structural shifts in their domestic politics. As long as there was no clear and present threat from an external enemy, the electorate's interest focused on domestic issues; questions closer to home like employment, wages, the environment, education, health, aging, women's rights, and crime surfaced as sharper political issues. And on top of that was the weight of fiscal deficit pressure. There was an urgent need to overhaul and reshuffle the policy priorities of the Cold War era. Both sides were forced to reevaluate what was the most appropriate cost and burden-sharing arrangement for maintaining the alliance.

In a process such as this, both sides may well start looking for a "burdenless partnership." Interest in an alliance with alleviated responsibilities and burdens has surfaced in Japanese advocacy for "stationing during contingency." Motoo Shiina, Independent member of the House of Councilors, ridiculed this concept in the Diet, saying, "Aren't you mistaking the U.S. presence for a pizza delivery service?"[20] but this advocacy for "stationing during contingency" was well received by the generation after Shiina, the so-called me generation of baby boomers.

It was becoming more and more difficult to create a reliable basis for garnering public interest in and support for security. The backdrop here was an ever-widening gap between the security envisioned by these high priests and the security the general public felt they needed in their day-to-day lives.

Certainly, people were more interested in questions closer to home, but this did not mean that they were indifferent to security issues. They were trying to conceive of security in terms of a more familiar "human security"—things like disaster rescue, prevention of harm caused by environmental destruction, protection from terrorism, protection of Japanese nationals overseas, maintaining safety in overseas travel. As they became more exposed to the dangers accompanying overcrowding in cities and the huge jump in the number of Japanese living and traveling abroad, people were trying to think of "security" as an extension of "safety" and "peace of mind." Support for defense (for example, the role, need, and budget for tanks, fighter planes, and mines) that did not respond to these issues fell, while support for large-scale disaster rescue, peacekeeping operation (PKO) deployment, and the rescue of Japanese nationals overseas grew.

Moreover, as Japanese firms have become more globalized, vested interests in protecting investments on a global scale have increased mainly in business circles. The need to respond to greater risk is leading to greater interest in and expectations of the active use of international systems within multilateral and bilateral frameworks and Japan's role therein, rather than to a strengthening of Japan's unilateral defense capabilities.

Nevertheless, not enough work was done on trying to weave this security sense taking root at the citizen level into the overall security concept. Even in the forum for redefining bilateral security, no such pioneering blow was struck. All that could be seen were some faint traces of efforts in that direction in the Guidelines Review.

As a result, interest in strengthening the bilateral alliance at the citizen level remained nominal and the political support base remained weak; the administrative and bureaucratic approach of the foreign policy and defense authority pros dominated the process. British historian Ian H. Nish once described the Anglo-Japanese alliance in the early twentieth century as a "secretariat alliance."[21] The U.S.-Japan alliance has yet to shake off this secretarial aspect.

The Reverse Pyramid

There is no need to be overly pessimistic about the future of the U.S.-Japan alliance. That would be counterproductive. If only because it has become easier for both Japan and the United States to feel it is the victim in the partnership, each needs to be careful to focus not only on the short-term balance sheet. Both can get more than a fair return on their investment if the alliance is useful for their security and if it is managed so as to be of service to long-term regional stability and peace.

Many Japanese tend to think that the U.S.-Japan alliance may not be as important for the United States as it is for Japan, and there is some truth to that observation. As Thomas Foley, former Speaker of the House of Representatives and current U.S. ambassador to Japan, commented, there was the aspect that "the American people have never been asked directly for a yes or no on the alliance with Japan, so they don't show any interest. It's just part of the furniture."[22] In other words, it's a routine, daily thing, so it is taken for granted.

But this point should not be exaggerated. In the U.S. Congress the once-prevalent "free-riding Japan" argument is hardly heard. Furthermore, as the economic and strategic weight of the Asian-Pacific region increases for the United States, there will be a growing awareness that stable relations with Japan are even more important than ever.

Relations with Japan are still given serious weight in U.S. alliance policy, and the U.S.-Japan alliance is given one of the highest priorities of any U.S. alliance. In September 1996, after the United States had staged its reprisal attack on Iraq, the U.S. Defense Intelligence Agency (DIA) invited in the representatives of seven countries for a first briefing: the United Kingdom, Japan, Germany, France, Italy, Canada, and Australia. Japan is at the very least assured of receiving the same treatment as these other U.S. allies.[23]

A high-level official at the Defense Department revealed that "for a global power like America which has alliances with 40 some countries, giving a certain group of countries a special briefing is an extremely delicate question."[24] At least Japan was included in that special briefing group. Should Japan get a permanent seat on the U.N. Security Council, strategic dialogue as a U.S. ally will have to become more planned.

Alliances are always plagued by two fears: entrapment and abandonment. The fear of entrapment was like the libido of Japanese pacifism. As long as you are in an alliance, you can never be totally free of this fear. In the future, however, fear of entrapment and fear of abandonment may merge with each other. This worry is not unique to Japan.

In the United States as well, it is conceivable that the alliance with Japan could induce a growing attitude of "not wanting to get entangled," for example, in a dispute with China. The seeds of that were visible in the dispute over the Senkaku Islands. Alternatively, should Japan's Asian orientation grow, tilting it towards regional multilateralism, or should Sino-Japanese ties become closer, "abandonment" fears of a Japanese drift away from the United States could well surface.

In order to better maintain the alliance, it is important for both sides to ensure even greater transparency than today. In order to better maintain the U.S.-Japan partnership, Japan has to come up with its own security policies, define its own national interests, draw up a strategy to protect those interests, frame the policies, acquire the intelligence, evaluate it, prepare a structure, foster the human talent, and talk with its alliance partner. At such a time, it is crucial that it lets both those at home and abroad know about its capability and its intent. It is in this sense that the coordination of the U.S. *Security Strategy for the East-Asia Pacific Region* (EASR) with Japan's *New Defense Program Outline* during the Nye Initiative, however primitive it seemed, deserved to be praised.

The shared government mechanisms for adjustment and consultation on U.S. troop structure in Japan, including the U.S. Marine Corps, also need to be invigorated. More also needs to be done to make the U.S.-Japan alliance of greater use in regional stability and peace. Transparency should not be a yardstick applied only to China. Japan has done far too little in the past to "know itself," or, more accurately, "to let others know itself," to help others understand what Japan is about, compared with the efforts it has put into "know thy enemy," namely knowing whom it was dealing with. Japan cannot afford to forget its prewar failings of doing virtually nothing to help other countries understand it and wallowing in a sense of victimization that it had been excluded, which led finally to the "no answer required" and "excessive by-the-book" reactive responses that had such a devastating impact on the international order.

Japan needs constantly to inform its alliance partner, the United States, of its plans, and to confirm and exchange ideas. And it needs to ask the same of the United States. That is precisely the way to convince the United States that Japan is its true partner.

Japanese transparency is no less crucial for its neighbors in the Asian-Pacific region. Japan needs always to be aware of the fact that the countries in its vicinity are highly suspicious of it. It cannot forget history. Japan should never delude itself that it has a free hand.

The most important aspect of transparency is civilian control. It is not enough to have the military under civilian control at the Japanese Defense Agency (JDA), treaty control at the Ministry of Foreign Affairs (MOFA), budget control at the Ministry of Finance (MOF), and legal interpretation control at the Cabinet Legislation Office. For better-quality policies, civilian expertise needs a greater voice in the policy decision-making process and in establishing responsibility.

Japan's politicians have leaned towards civilian control in the form of "containing" the military and the role of the SDF by resorting to constitutional arguments and social pressure. They have tended to subcontract that out to civilian bureaucrats. If this could be dubbed a policy of civilian control by "containment," what is required today is a policy of civilian control by "engagement." Even under Japan's prior policy of containment, U.S.-Japan security cooperation and United Nations' peacekeeping operations played the role of engaging Japan's military with international society. The positive aspects of those actions should be lauded and encouraged further. This would also serve to familiarize the Japanese military with Japanese security in terms of an open, internationalist security doctrine aimed at guaranteeing an international system with the U.S.-Japan alliance as its core and a multilateral framework centering on the United Nations, not a unilateral, simplistic, militaristic approach of "specific military requirements."

In the broadest sense, civilian control is none other than using diplomatic power to contain the use of military power. Japan needs to engrave in its mind that poor diplomatic power in the prewar period led it into the vicious circle of relying on its military prowess.

As they work to rebuild the U.S.-Japan alliance, two very key issues for the Japanese are strengthening its diplomatic power and creating a new style of civilian control. Japan needs to consolidate civilian control functions in the Diet and the Cabinet. In particular, it is crucial that the gathering, analysis, and transmission of information be under civilian control.

The information, communications, and mass media revolution has globalized Japan's involvement with the world and its foreign policy coverage. The Japanese people learn and react to events in real time, which has greatly reduced decision time. This will inevitably be another shock for Japan, like Perry's black ships in the nineteenth century, and it is already upon us.

The advent of this era of shorter decision time poses serious questions, especially for Japanese security policy as well as for the nature of civilian control. In a society with a bottom-up style of decision making, where proposals are not directed towards the public good but determined by narrow sectionalism as an extension of the more private domain of smaller units and affiliated sections; in which information becomes a kind of black box because of the manipulation of information caused by the opaque policymaking systems in each bureaucratic organizational "family"; and with weak leadership based on perverted equality and the principle of unanimous consensus, effective foreign policy and security policy cannot be expected to emerge in a timely fashion.

It is easy to poke fun at Prime Minister Ryutaro Hashimoto's information hunger and crisis management responses and his strong inclination towards secrecy, but leaving the policymaking and political culture status quo totally intact also highlighted the figure of a statesman trying to come to terms with a new era.

Centralizing control of information in the Cabinet and the PM's office, raising the transparency of the policymaking process, differentiating between information and policy functions, promoting more professional intelligence gathering and appraisal, switching to a top-down policymaking style, establishing political leadership—all are urgent tasks.

The gravest issue here is bureaucratic sectionalism. Administrative reform must occur to overcome the distortions created by the excessive sectionalism of Japan's bureaucracy, where each organization and section can quite easily develop into a separate fiefdom. If the Japanese suffer from a national disease, it is surely sectionalism.

This, however, is once again nothing more than a manifestation of the absence of political leadership. The political leadership vacuum invites bureaucratic sectionalism and a lord-of-the-manor mentality in each institution. Excessive sectionalism is also fraught with the risk of demolishing civilian control. The poor grasp Japanese politicians have on security issues has forced civilian control by bureaucrats to fill the gap.

The loyalties of the bureaucrats at the JDA, MOFA, MOF, and the Cabinet Legislation Office tend to rest with the organizations they are individually affiliated with. Under such circumstances, the SDF was inclined to deride this kind of bureaucratic civilian control as merely the expression of a power struggle over jurisdiction and influence by the various divisions, ministries, and agencies; in other words, a turf battle, an expression of sectionalisms greedy for more power.

Michita Sakada, director-general of the JDA, stressed the importance of civilian control by the Diet and Cabinet when he disseminated the first defense program outline and the guidelines aimed at creating a new defense concept against the background of détente in the 1970s. Sakada embraced the notion that "without the understanding, support, and cooperation of the Japanese people, the SDF would be of no use no matter how powerful or superbly equipped." That was why he set up a "forum to think about defense" comprising private sector experts and decided to publish a White Paper on Defense every year. He also lobbied for an enhanced National Defense Council in the Cabinet and the establishment of a Standing Committee on Defense in the Diet. There is much that can still be learned from Sakada's thinking and leadership.[25]

In Washington, between 1994 and 1996, the person who thought the most earnestly about the U.S.-Japan alliance and who did his best to strengthen it was Defense Secretary William Perry. Perry was apprehensive about the weak structure of the alliance, how it had no mechanism to protect itself from being rocked by economic and trade issues or the base question in Okinawa. He was also worried about deteriorating Sino-Japanese relations in the security jungle of the Asia-Pacific region and the difficulty of conducting intellectual and strategic dialogue between the United States and Japan. On one occasion, Perry disclosed to his aides, "I feel like the U.S.-Japan alliance has a structure like a reverse pyramid." He carved out the shape in the air. It was an object with substance but was resting on its tiniest, thinnest, riskiest point. Then he added, "There has to be a whole team of people on both sides of the Pacific . . . holding and steadying the pyramid."[26]

Notes

1. Interview with a senior DOD official.

2. U.S. Senate, Foreign Relations Committee, *Treaty of Mutual Cooperation and Security with Japan,* 86th Congress, 2nd Session (June 7, 1960). Quoted in J.W. Dower, *Empire and Aftermath: Yoshida Shigeru and the Japanese Experience, 1878–1954* (Cambridge: Harvard University Press 1979), p. 370.

3. Statement by Kantoku Teruya, member of the House of Councilors, in the Special Committee on Okinawa and Northern Issues, March 15, 1996.

4. Interview with a senior MOFA official.

5. Interview with a senior State Department official.

6. Takeshi Igarashi, *The Formation of Post-War Japan-U.S. Relations* (Tokyo: Kodansha, 1995), p. 248. (In Japanese.)

7. Ryutaro Hashimoto's statement at the Standing Committee on Budget, House of Councilors, April 15, 1996.

8. Ryutaro Hashimoto before the Budget Committee, House of Representatives, February 12, 1997.

9. Philip Gordon, "The Franco-German Security Partnership," in Patrick McCarthy (ed.), *France-Germany 1983–1993: The Struggle to Cooperate* (New York: St. Martin's Press, 1993), p. 156.

10. Akihiko Tanaka, *Security* (Tokyo: Yomiuri Shimbunsha, 1997), p. 46. (In Japanese.)

11. MacArthur maintained this position right up until a month before the outbreak of the Korean War and published it in the May 1950 issue of *Reader's Digest.*

12. Interview with a senior State Department official.

13. Ibid.

14. Interview with Rust Deming.

15. Interview with Nobushige Takamizawa.

16. Interview with Hitoshi Tanaka.

17. Interview with Takemasa Moriya.

18. Interview with high-ranking SDF officials.

19. Interview with Rust Deming.

20. Motoo Shiina before the special committee on land usage accompanying the implementation of the Japan-U.S. Security Treaty, House of Councilors, April 14, 1997.

21. Ian Nish, *The Anglo-Japanese Alliance: The Diplomacy of Two Island Empires 1894–1907* (New York: Athlone Press, 1985), p. 366.

22. Interview with Thomas Foley.

23. Interview with a senior DOD official.

24. Ibid.

25. Tanaka, *Security*, pp. 253–254.

26. Interview with a senior DOD official.

Epilogue

"I'll Be Seeing You"—William Perry at Fort Myers

January 14, 1997.

A retirement ceremony for departing Defense Secretary William Perry was held at Fort Myers. Five people who had worked with him gave farewell speeches. A navy warrant officer thanked Perry, saying, "The Secretary never for a moment forgot the lives of the soldiers, our personal well-being." President Clinton took the dais and expressed his gratitude. "Teddy Roosevelt said that those of us in positions of authority should speak softly and carry a big stick. Bill Perry spoke softly and carried the biggest stick in the world, with great care and effect. I never went to bed worrying about Perry."

Perry then rose to speak. "Four years ago, the United States stood at the crossroads of isolationism or engagement. President Clinton chose to reject isolation and apathy in favor of engagement and action. . . . The history of the United States has always been a repetition of dismantling military power when war ends. It was my conviction that that could not be allowed this time. And it didn't. . . . Four years ago, I faced a choice between leading an easygoing, quiet life or a new challenge. I chose the challenge and am happy today that I did."

Perry was 69 years old.

An air force chorus and a navy brass brand performed "America the Beautiful," followed by "Sunrise, Sunset," "I'll Be Seeing You," "California, Here I Come," and then "Battle Hymn of the Republic." "I'll Be Seeing You" was a standard number that was a huge hit during the Pacific War. Both Frank Sinatra and Joe Stafford had performed it. On that day it was performed by a female soloist from the air force chorus. Perry and his wife, Leonilla, had first heard the number on the evening of their first date. Leonilla was also an official guest at the retirement ceremony.

The ceremony came to a close. There were no tears.

Perry's time in Washington was over. So were trips on VIP planes.

He had driven himself extremely hard in office. The trip at the end of the previous year had been particularly tough. In late November, he traveled to NATO headquarters, Bosnia, Russia, and Saudi Arabia. From

Saudi Arabia, where he was kept waiting two hours by King Fahd, he went on to Japan, landing in Tokyo on the evening of December 2.

Perry was flown from Yokota by helicopter to the Hardy Barracks in Roppongi and taken to the Gaimusho reception house. He was to put the finishing touches on SACO's final report and then fly back to California from Yokota at 2:00 A.M. the next day.

All through the meeting, he couldn't stop yawning despite having drunk coffee steadily on the plane. It was his first meeting with the top Japanese members since the previous September in Washington, when Foreign Minister Yukihiko Ikeda and Director-General of the Defense Agency Hideo Usui had been in Washington for "2+2" talks.

A dinner reception in Director-General Usui's honor had been held at the Smithsonian Castle in the Freer Gallery of Art of the Smithsonian Institution. The cuisine was American: smoked breast of duckling and filet mignon. The wine was an Oregon King Pinot Gris 1994 and a California Chateau Montelena Calistoga Cuvée 1993. The military band played Dixieland jazz, a great favorite of Usui's.

Perry praised Usui and gave a short speech. He said, "We have reaffirmed that Japan and the United States will continue to have a special relationship in the 21st century" and concluded, "A great East and a great West will be bound together by shared interests and concerns." He was quoting the delegation from the Kanrin-maru when they visited New York in 1860. Perry was convinced that it was not ideology, culture, or the Internet but shared economic and military interests and concerns that was the glue of the U.S.-Japan alliance.

Perry presented Usui with a crystal globe of the world from Tiffany's. Now it was Usui's turn to reply. "You dealt with the Okinawan incident with sincerity. You met with Diet members and local parties when they visited Washington. For such thoughtfulness and devotion, I would like to convey my deepest thanks to you this day." He then presented Perry with a framed calligraphy of four Chinese characters, Usui's desk motto, written in his own hand. The interpreter translated them as meaning "protect justice, do not waiver." Perry showed it upside down. When it was pointed out that he had it the wrong way, the ever-meticulous Perry turned it around the right way.

January 23, 1997.

This was Perry's last day at the Pentagon. At 10:00 A.M., Defense Secretary William Cohen was sworn into office. Perry would shortly be coming down to the Mall Gate. Only a short while ago, an e-mail had been sent to the senior staff: "The secretary is leaving soon, so anyone who's free, come down to see him off." About 50 people gathered to say their last good-byes.

They huddled together, the collars on their coats turned up against the cold wind blowing off the bare concrete steps. Perry came out accompanied by chairman of the Joint Chiefs of Staff John Shalikashvili. Everyone burst into applause. Undersecretary Walter Slocombe and Deputy Assistant Secretary Kurt Campbell were also there.

The army team gave an army cheer, "Hurrah!" Perry held up his finger and said, "Just one thing." Then in a loud voice he said, "Hurrah," and disappeared into his car. Everyone exploded with laughter.

Perry had already packed up his house in Virginia. In rare moments of leisure, he would walk the short distance to Mount Vernon, the home and gravesite of George Washington. He would sometimes take with him the book on the Civil War he was reading.

Perry spent that weekend in a hotel and left the following Monday. He would be driving across the continent to home, which was Palo Alto, in northern California. When he was asked by a staff member which route he would be taking, he replied, "To the south," adding, "According to the weather report the south is fine, so I'll take the southern route."

"So This Is How Metternich Did Things"— Kurt Campbell on Etajima Island

March 24, 1997.

The waves at Etajima gently lapped the shore.

Kurt Campbell had landed at the New Kansai International Airport from Seoul, traveled to Hiroshima by bullet train, and overnighted in Kure. He arrived at Etajima early the following morning.

It was still a little early for the cherry blossoms, but the buds were swollen. The cherry trees leading up to the school gate, in front of the auditorium and the reference museum in the quadrangle of the red-bricked students' hall, would soon be in full bloom. The red bricks had been brought all the way from Britain, and the building had been completed in 1894. Campbell was told that this was the first time Japan imported Western bricks.

The Naval Officers' Academy was shifted to Etajima in 1889. Until its closing in December 1945, officer candidates for the Imperial Navy had been trained there. For the following 10 years it was used by the Allies' Occupation offices until it reopened in 1956 as an officers' academy for the SDF. The early risings, the cutter races, the long-distance swimming, the training, all imparted a briskness to the daily activities of the young cadets.

Campbell's discussions with the cadets were enjoyable. They talked about the international situation in the Asian-Pacific region and U.S.

security policy. The cadets' English was good, and they knew a lot about world events.

He was shown around the reference museum. The painting of Mount Fuji by Daikan Yokoyama, a master Japanese painter, was hung there. The spray from the Pacific Ocean flew almost to the top of Fuji. On the far side of the mountain could be seen not clouds but the tumultuous waves of the Sea of Japan in a huge whirlpool. It was Daikan's intuitive rendering of the national crisis of the Sino-Japanese war and the Pacific War.

There was also a snapshot of the Prince of Wales (later the Duke of Windsor) visiting Etajima in 1922. At the beginning of the century, Japan and Britain had formed an alliance, the first ever in Japan's long history. It had served Japan's interests well but lasted only 20 years. The Prince of Wales's visit was a gesture of courtesy by Britain at the termination of the Anglo-Japanese alliance.

As he listened to the explanation, Campbell was deeply moved. What sort of view of Japan did those British officials in charge of the alliance with Japan have back then? How had the two sides communicated? When did the alliance start to go wrong? What was the decisive factor that brought about its end? What were politics like in each country at the time? Campbell had many questions.

The Japanese probably never had a comprehensive strategic dialogue with the Western powers including Britain. Isn't that what led to the demise of the Anglo-Japanese alliance?

When they reached a certain point, Campbell's guide assumed a solemn manner. They were in front of a photograph of Navy Captain Tsutomu Sakuma. Beneath it was his testamentary letter written on rice paper in ink that was now fading. The interpreter translated haltingly.

> It is truly inexcusable that due to my own inadvertence, I have sunk His Majesty's ship, killing all my men. However, the crew performed their duty to a man in a composed manner. Although we may fall for the State, our only regret is that this mistake may have damaged our honorable land's future development of submarines. . . .

The letter then went on to explain in detail how the ship was lost. On April 15, 1911, the sixth submarine out of Kure sank during an exercise. All 14 hands, including the skipper, Captain Sakuma, were lost.

At first, the handwriting is firm and disciplined, but towards the end the letters become bigger and disheveled. People's hearts were moved not only by the details of the accident outlined in Captain Sakuma's letter but also by the evident feelings of the captain and crew as they faced death closing in. Sakuma was 32 years old. Most of the crew were in their 20s.

"At that time, there were many similar accidents with submarines in Europe as well. But the crew were often killed in the crush as they tried to be the first out the escape hatch. Sakuma and his crew, however, manned their posts until the last. I have heard that they were cited as a model case by all the navies at the time," said the tour guide.

Campbell felt something inspirational about the episode. *Why is this moving martial spirit embodied in that Sakuma submarine case? How did it evolve into one of the ugliest forms of militarism, in Japan's actions in World War II? How could it have? What really happened in Japan between the Russo-Japanese War and the Pacific War?*

These thoughts were milling around in Campbell's head as he went outside and glanced across the water to the hilly ridges of Nomi Island.

Nye had gone. Hubbard had moved out as ambassador. Perry was no longer there. Lord had retired. Lake had resigned as well. Although it was the same Clinton administration, the first- and second-term teams felt like completely different governments. Campbell had worked very hard. Now he was starting to think perhaps it was time to return to study and research. There were times he didn't know what to do about the Okinawa bases or when that question would be solved.

Campbell was starting to become a bit of a fatalist. Not a pessimist or an optimist, just a fatalist. Sometimes he found himself thinking, *So this is how Metternich did things.*

He was referring to Klemens Metternich (1773–1859). Held in high respect by Kissinger and others of the realist school, Metternich had been Austria's foreign minister in the first half of the nineteenth century and was largely responsible for the so-called Viennese System that was a framework for international political stability in Europe based on legitimism and balance of power.

Metternich labored extensively to construct a diplomatic framework to sustain the existing European order. Like the U.S.-Japan alliance, European diplomacy during the time of Metternich was an elite preoccupation. After all our labors, are we still vulnerable to a "revolution from the bottom"?

On the afternoon of the same day, Campbell was taken in a small Maritime SDF boat over to the U.S. base at Iwakuni. The sun was shining and it was a beautiful day. In the distance, he could see a Maritime SDF submarine sailing. He filled his lungs with the air. He didn't know why, but at that precise moment he decided that he would stay, he would try to finish what he had begun.

From Iwakuni Campbell took a P³C straight to the U.S. base at Atsugi. From there, he went to LDP headquarters to meet with the general secretary, Koichi Kato. He then rushed over to Narita. He had to be at the three-way talks with Russia, the United States, and Japan in Moscow.

"You Wouldn't Have Any Bourbon, Would You?"—Ryutaro Hashimoto at the White House

April 24, 1997.

Prime Minister Ryutaro Hashimoto was visiting the White House as a state guest. In the car from Andrews Air Force Base en route to the Japanese ambassador's residence, Ambassador Kunihiko Saito informed him that he had just received a message from President Clinton. "The president says that you are probably tired, but if you would like to, he would like to invite you to the White House after dinner for an informal chat. What shall we do?"

Hashimoto okayed it immediately. "I'm drunk today. The situation with the hostages in Peru has been resolved, you know. I feel good. I had some drinks the day before and I drank all the way in the plane, so I'm drunk now."

It was on April 22 that the 24 Japanese hostages held by the Peruvian terrorist group Tupac Amaru had all been safely rescued. Hashimoto was a little tipsy. He always maintained, "I don't eat Japanese food outside Japan. I won't bother you at the residence," but this day he dined at the residence. As a sign of respect for Hashimoto's esthetic or "policy," the staff refrained from serving a Japanese meal. They had ordered special American cuisine from a restaurant in Georgetown, "1789." The embassy's chef, its pride and joy, brought over from the first-class Japanese restaurant *Kicho,* did no business that day.

Some time after 10:00 P.M., Hashimoto went to the White House. Clinton was there to meet him. The treaty banning chemical weapons had just been ratified by Congress, and the president had to be interviewed on television. Telling Hashimoto he would be back as soon as the interview was over, Clinton left the room.

Clinton came back after the interview. "I have something I'd like to show you." The president took Hashimoto to the Oval Office and showed him a photo of the rising sun above the door. It was a photo that the camera-loving Hashimoto had himself taken and signed. He had given it to Clinton at the Santa Monica summit the previous year.

"I always look at it. When I bring leaders from other countries into the Oval Office, they always ask whose work it is. I always tell them Ryu, Ryu." Clinton laughed.

When they were seated on a sofa, Clinton said, "I just got a call from Hillary, who said to tell you that she's in California and she's sorry she won't be able to see you this time, and that we weren't to drink too much together!"

Hashimoto winked when he heard that. "You wouldn't have any bourbon, would you?"

As if checking the request, Clinton replied, "Bourbon is all right, but won't you join me in my favorite Irish whisky today?" He told the waiter to bring some Bushmills.

Bushmills Black Bush was Clinton's favorite. Bushmills was said to be the oldest whisky distillery in the world. When Clinton had received Gerry Adams, the leader of the Irish Sinn Fein party, and Senator Edward Kennedy at the White House on St. Patrick's Day, they had spent much time talking about Irish whisky.

Before Prohibition in the 1920s, Irish whisky had been more popular in the United States than Scotch whisky. After World War I, Ireland became independent of Britain and placed a ban on exports to Britain and all its colonies. The Irish whisky–export industry then collapsed. As a consequence, Scotch whisky supplanted Irish in the American market, and Irish whisky has lagged behind ever since.

Clinton was a political animal. He may have seen an Irish vote in every glass of Irish whisky. Unfortunately, the White House had run out of Bushmills. "Anything then, as long as its Irish whisky."

Clinton's daughter, Chelsea, dropped in to say "hello." She would be studying medicine at Stanford in the fall. It was easy to see how much Clinton cared for her. After giving a brief rundown on herself, standing all the while, Chelsea left the room with a big smile.

The main topic of conversation that night was North Korea. Hashimoto related the various domestic issues involved in sending food assistance to the North. Clinton let his guest speak freely, sticking to the role of listener.

Barely a year had passed since the meeting in Santa Monica. But it seemed longer than that. There was no diffidence to Clinton; he was his own man. And both of them had undergone an electoral baptism. The voters had favored them too.

Times had been toughest about a month after Santa Monica. The injection of public funds into the failing Japanese housing cooperatives was a blow. Hashimoto's ratings slipped to 36 percent in the March polls. Criticism of his "invisibility" found their mark. After the summit in April, however, they bounced back to 53 percent.

Hashimoto poured some more Irish whisky into his tumbler and took another sip. He drank three triples, not doubles. Clinton matched him. It was well past midnight. Hashimoto had to leave.

Outside, the American flag atop the Treasury Department was waving in its spotlight. The night breeze almost seem to shine as it caressed Hashimoto's cheek, then moved on.

Emerging China's Confidence and Pride—
Hitoshi Tanaka in Beijing

June 9, 1997.

Hitoshi Tanaka, deputy director-general of the North American Affairs Bureau at MOFA, was in Beijing. He was there with Kyoji Yanagisawa, defense councillor at the JDA, to brief the Chinese government on the interim report of the Guidelines Review announced the previous day by the governments of Japan and the United States. It was Tanaka's first time in Beijing since 1978. On that occasion, China was just on the verge of its reforms and opening up. Looking out the window of his car at the Beijing landscape, Tanaka thought more of the scars of capitalism than development.

The two Japanese exchanged opinions with the Chinese for some three hours over dinner at the Chinese Ministry of Foreign Affairs' Reception House. Tanaka's counterpart was Wang Yi, director of the Chinese Foreign Ministry's Department of Asian Affairs. He had spoken as the Chinese delegation's representative to the Sino-Japanese security talks in March. He was a sophisticated diplomat fluent in Japanese. He stated officially three "concerns" of the Chinese with the guidelines:

- Why do you have to strengthen the U.S.-Japan security structure now when tensions are easing in the Asian-Pacific region?
- Are you not trying to expand the present scope of the Security Treaty?
- Are you not trying to strengthen the military role of Japan?

Tanaka responded:

- The current security environment is more one of preparing for potential regional disputes rather than large-scale war. The need to deal with this as a security issue is growing, as demonstrated by the nature of the issue and the question of refugees.
- We are trying to clarify the content of what Japan has said it would do in a crisis but has hitherto failed to make clear. In reality, the response Japan takes depends on the nature of the situation.
- No, that is not the case. Japan's defense policies are extremely transparent. There is no change in the three principles of "defense only, nonnuclear, and civilian control."

Wang Yi said, "You're speaking of principles, yes?"

"That is correct. The three principles are that we will not change the rights and obligations of the security treaty; Japanese action will remain within the scope of the constitution; and the foundation in international law."

Regarding Taiwan, the discussion toed the official line even more. Tanaka stated that "the unified government position in the Diet on the Far East mentioned in the Security Treaty is that the vicinity of Japan extending north from the Philippines, including Taiwan and Korea, still pertains and there is no intention of changing this."

The Chinese response was gentlemanly and reasonable, Tanaka thought to himself. *There is also Japan's past history. There is the problem of China's structure too. They are likely to continue to voice concerns in the future. But they will probably go no further than restrained, general remarks.*

Wang Yi revealed that he had just been to the United States for the first time since he had become head of the Asian Bureau and that he had "discussed with the Americans Asian questions." There was a little pride in the way he phrased it. Wang was an expert in the Japanese language but had only started to study English. Without English, it was impossible as a diplomat to move onto a larger stage. (He later went to study in the United States while maintaining his position as bureau head.)

Observing Wang Yi, who seemed the personification of emerging China's confidence and pride, Tanaka could not help but have a foreboding about the advent of an era of Sino-Japanese diplomatic games in the 21st century.

After China, Tanaka flew to Bangkok and Hanoi.

"It must be a big job."

"Thank you very much for coming all this way to brief us. It has been very helpful."

"By the way, I heard you've just been to China. What was the Chinese reaction?"

No matter where he went, the same question was posed. There was a marked reticence towards China everywhere.

Just as I thought, it's the U.S.-Japan-China age. The countries of Southeast Asia are holding their breath as they watch every move the three of us make.

Tanaka had been determined to achieve a review of the guidelines from the day he was appointed deputy director-general of the North American Affairs Bureau. During his time as director of the Policy Coordination Division in the Foreign Policy Bureau, he had run straight into the North Korean nuclear suspicion and U.N. economic sanctions. As he ran around MOFA coordinating responses, he suffered a deep sense of helplessness. With things as they stood, Japan would not even be able to arrange a satisfactory rescue of its own nationals in the case of a contingency on the Korean Peninsula. *I'm begging you. If something happens, this country will go under!*

He used that experience to drive himself on towards a review of the guidelines. In January 1996, when he met Deputy Assistant Secretary Kurt Campbell in San Francisco, Tanaka took Campbell somewhat aback by arguing forcefully for "having to finish the guidelines." Campbell had never heard this kind of strong resolve from the Japanese before.

Looking back, Tanaka was grateful that they had not forced a review of the guidelines in 1994. *If we had done it then, it would have provoked the North Koreans and may have irrevocably changed the course of history.*

The return of the Okinawan bases, the offshore heliport, U.S. Marine cutbacks. . . . It would be a falsehood to say that he had not been discouraged and saddened during this period. He had experienced the limits of a bureaucrat.

Tanaka also felt he had misread the situation more than once. One time was the call for cutbacks in the U.S. Marines in the spring of 1997. He may just have misread the turning of the tide in the U.S. administration.

But the eddies of domestic politics were even more transient. He was acutely aware that there were many who supported the U.S.-Japan alliance verbally, but the nature of their support seemed very flimsy. "Right now, you find nationalism lurking just below the surface of any debate in Japan. The people who are the keenest on protecting the U.S.-Japan security relationship are probably becoming the most liberal of the day."

"At the Risk of Going Against Your Word, Sir"—Masahide Ota at the Okinawa Prefectural Seat

The governor's office at the Okinawa Prefectural Seat, April 12, 1997.

Hidehiko Kuwataka (counselor, the governor's office) came into the room. He said, "You have a call from the prime minister." Governor Masahide Ota was in a meeting with Tatsuo Matayoshi, director, and Masaaki Aguni, director-general, of the Executive Office of the Governor, respectively. For some reason, Matayoshi looked at his watch. It was 6:05 P.M.

Ota checked the two, who were starting to leave the room, with a "you two listen too." Ota picked up the receiver. Of course, only Ota could hear the voice on the other end of the line. Ryutaro Hashimoto's voice was upbeat. "We may be able to get back Futenma. I'm scheduled to see Ambassador Mondale right after this. We're to work out the final details. It's extremely difficult, but we might pull it off. I want you to agree to a relocation within the prefecture. I'd like your cooperation on that point."

Ota was surprised by this sudden turn of events. But he countered, "I will cooperate as much as possible. However, I don't know the details and even with cooperation, there are things we can and can't do."

"Mondale will be here in any minute. I'll settle the matter with him as the representative of the Japanese government. I'm thinking of something removable for the relocation site."

"You may well say that, sir, but I don't know what it is about and in the light of this issue's importance, I would like to leave my decision until it has been put to our regular top-three meeting or some similar forum."

"I'm here deciding things on the spot without making concessions to anyone and I'm running a coalition government! I'd like you to do the same." Ota could tell that Hashimoto was miffed.

"At the risk of going against your word, sir, there are things we can cooperate on and things we cannot."

Hashimoto hung up, saying, "I'll call you back when it's over."

Ota could not grasp on the spur of the moment what Hashimoto meant by "relocation." *Where does he intend to relocate? How can he expect me to cooperate if I don't know what he's talking about! And what was all that "removable" business about? What does "removable" mean? I don't know where they're taking it, and what about the runway? How big a runway are they thinking about?*

Hashimoto offered no clear explanation. Ota was troubled. That night, Hashimoto called Ota one more time. This was the phone call in which Hashimoto, after informing Ota of Futenma's return, had asked him to thank Ambassador Mondale directly.

Hashimoto had dialed himself because he thought it would be tactless to have someone connect him. So Ota's assistants were thrown off balance when they answered the phone and suddenly heard, "Is the governor there? It's Hashimoto speaking."

All well and good if Ota was there, but it hurt them just to think of what to say if he wasn't. Total panic would break out if Counselor Kuwataka was out of the office as well.

June 23, 1997.

As was usual, Ota hosted a memorial service for the fallen in the Battle of Okinawa at the Mabuni Cornerstone of Peace. He then visited the Teachers' College Strong Boys Monument and prayed for the souls of the students who had died in the war. Every year, except when he was studying in the United States, Ota has performed the same rite. This year, once again he was to give a speech. The moment he saw the names inscribed on the monument as he bent to lay the wreath he had brought himself, he was struck dumb.

Antsu Aragaki

Seigo Shinjo

Eika Miyara

They had all been his friends at the Teachers' College. Antsu, like him, had come from an outlying island. That was one reason why they had hit it off. He had been the only son of the village head on Iheyajima. In those days they were not allowed to have girlfriends, but he already had a fiancée. They would all strain their ears to catch every word Antsu said when he started off with "now, the female of the species . . . ."

Seigo had loved music. He played the violin and his elder brother was a musician. Seigo was drafted into the "shock troops." When he left for battle that day, he left his rice and dried bonito with Ota, who had been injured at Mabuni and couldn't move. That food had kept Ota alive.

And Eika, who was brilliant. He and Ota had always been class captains of different classes. They boarded in the same dorm and were good friends. Eika was studying English and always said he was going to go to the Tokyo University of Literature and Science. In Shuri, he would sneak in at night and speak to the U.S. POWs in English, bringing water and food. He came back one night having been caught by the Military Police and beaten with the stock of their rifles and kicked in the face until he couldn't open his eyes.

They had all fallen in their teens.

Fifty years had passed. Here I am, alive. I was able to have a family. They sent me to America as well. And yet, they died without music, without English, without families, without any of the joys of life. I have worked like a mad thing to get where I am. And still I haven't been able to live up to their expectations.

Ota was remembering the words of one of the younger girls at the Teachers' College. "The survivors of the Lily Troop have built a memorial museum and collected all the photos, but the boys have done nothing; they haven't even collected photos." He could not tell what his feelings were: penitence, remorse, chagrin, or sorrow.

The edges of the names started to blur, and as the tears flowed, a character here, a character there found their way into his heart.

Persons Interviewed

Japan

Masahiro Akiyama	Director-General, Bureau of Defense Policy, Japan Defense Agency (JDA)
Hiroyasu Ando	Secretary for the Prime Minister
Yuji Dochin	Staff Member, General Affairs Division, Secretariat of the Minister of State for Defense, JDA
Kenji Eda	Political Secretary for the Prime Minister
Seishiro Eto	Former Minister of State, Director-General of the Defense Agency
Ichiro Fujisaki	Minister, Japanese Embassy in the United States
Masayuki Fujisawa	Chief Counselor, Defense Facilities Administration Agency
Takeo Fukuchi	Former Chief of Staff, Maritime Self-Defense Force (MSDF)
Sadajiro Furukawa	Deputy Cabinet Secretary
Masaharu Gotoda	Former Lower House Diet Member, Liberal Democratic Party (LDP)
Ryutaro Hashimoto	Prime Minister
Tsutomu Hata	Former Prime Minister
Motoaki Hatake	Special Research Staff, Research Office, Upper House Cabinet Committee
Hirokazu Hayashi	Secretary for the Prime Minister
Junji Hayashi	Former Administrative Vice-Minister, Ministry of Transport
Sadayuki Hayashi	Vice Minister for Foreign Affairs
Hiroshi Hirabayashi	Chief Cabinet Counselor for External Affairs, Prime Minister's Office
Hiroshi Hashimoto	Press Secretary and Director-General for the Press and Public Relations, Ministry of Foreign Affairs (MOFA)
Katsuei Hirasawa	Lower House Diet Member, LDP
Akira Hiyoshi	Former Administrative Vice-Minister of State for Defense
Morihiro Hosokawa	Former Prime Minister
Noboru Hoshuyama	Former Director-General, Defense Facilities Administration Agency

Yukihiko Ikeda	Minister of Foreign Affairs
Hisao Ikeuchi	Policy Counselor, Social Democratic Party (SDP)
Takashi Imai	President, New Nippon Steel Company
Nobuo Ishihara	Former Deputy Cabinet Secretary
Koichi Isobe	Lt. Colonel, Japanese Self-Defense Forces, Ministry of Defense
Shigeru Ito	Lower House Diet Member, SDP
Yoshiyuki Jibiki	Director of Facilities and Planning Section, Facilities Department, Defense Facilities Administration Agency
Seiroku Kajiyama	Cabinet Secretary
Koichi Kato	Lower House Diet Member, General Secretary, LDP
Ryozo Kato	Director-General of the Asian Affairs Bureau, MOFA
Katsuaki Katori	Counselor to the Cabinet
Chikao Kawai	Private Secretary to the Minister for Foreign Affairs
Tsutomu Kawara	Lower House Diet Member; Chairman, Research Commission on Security, Policy Research Council, LDP
Ikuo Kayahara	Director, Second Research Department, National Institute for Defense Studies
Yoshitaka Kinoshita	General Manager, Oppama Site Office, Technological Research Association, Megafloat Project
Yoji Koda	Head of Planning and Programs Division, MSDF
Mitsukuni Komatsu	Head of Very-Large-Scale Floating General Systems Research Center
Masaharu Kono	Director of the First North American Affairs Division, MOFA
Yohei Kono	Minister of Foreign Affairs
Wataru Kubo	Lower House Diet Member, SDP
Masahiro Kunimi	Director, Defense Intelligence HQ, Joint Staff Council
Masafumi Kunugi	Head of the Central Officer Candidate School, MSDF
Tetsuo Kuroe	Deputy Director, Secretariat of the Minister of State for Defense, Bureau of Defense Policy, JDA
Hideyuki Maeshima	Lower House Diet Member, SDP
Yasutomo Mitsui	Former Head of the Cabinet Security Office

Takemasa Moriya	Councillor, Bureau of Defense, JDA
Masuo Morodomi	Director-General, Defense Facilities Administration Agency, JDA
Ken Moroi	Advisory Board Member, Chichibu-Onoda Company
Koji Muraki	Chief of Staff, Air Self-Defense Force (ASDF)
Tomiichi Murayama	Former Prime Minister
Ryuichi Nagao	Professor, University of Tokyo
Yoshitoku Nagasaki	Head of the First Technology Institute, MSDF
Yasuhiro Nakasone	Former Prime Minister
Kazuya Natsukawa	Chief of Staff, MSDF
Masanori Nishi	Director, Maritime Weapons Section, Bureau of Equipment, JDA
Yasunori Nishi	Deputy Chairman, Iwo Jima Association
Michio Nishida	Head of the Fourth Section, First Research Center, National Institute for Defense Studies, Bureau of Defense
Tetsuya Nishimoto	Former Chairman, Joint Staff Council
Fukushiro Nukaga	Lower House Diet Member, Vice-Chairman of the Research Commission on Security, Policy Research Council, LDP
Kazuo Ofuru	Director, Defense Policy Division, Bureau of Defense Policy, JDA
Yukio Okamoto	Special Adviser to the Prime Minister on Okinawa Affairs
Keiji Omori	President, National Institute for Defense Studies, JDA
Yoshio Omori	Former Head of Cabinet Research and Information Office
Masaki Orita	Director-General of the North American Affairs Bureau, MOFA
Masao Ota	Counselor, Japanese Embassy in the United States
Kunihiko Saito	Ambassador to the United States
Ken Sato	Director-General, Bureau of Finance, JDA
Shigekazu Sato	Director of the China and Mongolia Division, MOFA
Takafumi Sato	Budget Officer, Budget Bureau, Ministry of Finance (MOF)
Masayoshi Shinbo	Director, Ships Division, Bureau of Equipment, JDA
Kazuhiro Sugita	Head of Cabinet Research and Information Office

Shigeru Sugiyama	Chairman, Joint Staff Council
Hiroshi Tada	Former Administrative Vice Minister, Ministry of Health and Welfare
Nobushige Takamizawa	Director, Defense Operations Division, Defense Policy Bureau, Bureau of Defense, JDA
Norimoto Takano	Deputy Director-General of the North American Affairs Bureau, MOFA
Keizo Takemi	Upper House Diet Member, LDP
Masayoshi Takemura	Former Finance Minister
Noboru Takeshita	Former Prime Minister
Sumio Takeichi	Executive Vice President, Mitsubishi International Corp.
Yo Takeuchi	Director of First Funds Division, Financial Bureau, MOF
Yukio Takeuchi	Minister Plenipotentiary, Japanese Embassy in the United States
Tokuichiro Tamazawa	Former Minister of State, Director-General of the Defense Agency
Minoru Tamba	Deputy Minister for Foreign Affairs
Shigenobu Tamura	Special Researcher, Policy Research Council, LDP
Hitoshi Tanaka	Deputy Director-General of the North American Affairs Bureau, MOFA
Hideshi Tokuchi	Special Assistant to the Director-General, Bureau of Defense Policy, JDA
Ryubun Tsuboi	Former Head of the Cabinet Security Office
Kosuke Uehara	Lower House Diet Member, SDP
Kazuyoshi Umemoto	Director of U.S.-Japan Treaty Division, North American Affairs Bureau, MOFA
Jiro Ushio	President of Ushio Denki Company; Chairman of Japan Association of Corporate Executives (Keizai Doyukai)
Hideo Usui	Minister of State, Director-General of the Defense Agency
Masatake Wakabayashi	Professor, University of Tokyo
Akio Watanabe	Professor, Aoyama Gakuin University
Kazuhiko Watanabe	Megafloat Technology Research Union
Makoto Watanabe	Imperial Household Agency Chamberlain
Noboru Yamaguchi	Deputy Chief, Defense Planning Division, Ground Self-Defense Forces, (GSDF)
Tadamichi Yamamoto	Director of the First North American Affairs Division, MOFA
Yasumasa Yamamoto	Vice-Admiral, Commander of Yokosuka District

Taku Yamasaki   Lower House Diet Member; Chairman of
                       the Policy Research Council, LDP
Chisato Yamauchi   Defense Intelligence Officer for Security
                       Policy, Defense Intelligence Head-
                       quarters, Joint Staff Council
Shunji Yanai   Vice Minister for Foreign Affairs

Okinawa

Nagayoshi Arazaki   Head of Planning Office, Yonaguni-cho
Shoichi Chibana   Operator/Owner of a local supermarket in
                       Yomitan Village, Okinawa
Hideki Harashima   Special Minister Plenipotentiary for Oki-
                       nawan Affairs, MOFA
Tetsuya Higa   Mayor of Nago City
Keiichi Inamine   President, Ryuseki Corporation
Seizo Irinaka   Mayor of Yonaguni-cho
Hideo Kuwataka   Counselor, Executive Office of the Governor,
                       Okinawa Prefecture
Tatsuo Matayoshi   Policy Adviser to the Governor, Okinawa
                       Prefecture
Daisuke Matsunaga   Special Assistant to the Coordination Of-
                       ficer, Okinawa Liaison Office, MOFA
Tokujitsu Miyagi   Mayor of Kadena-cho
Masao Nakachi   Okinawa Prefecture Advisor in the United
                       States
Masahide Ota   Governor, Okinawa Prefecture
Akira Sakima   Chairman, Naha Chamber of Commerce
                       and Industry; Chairman, Ryukyu Bank
Takehiko Shimaguchi   Director, Defense Facilities Administration
                       Bureau of Naha
Suzuyo Takazato   Council Member, Naha City Council
Choko Takayama   Deputy Mayor of Naha
Seiken Toharu   Mayor of Ginowan City
Fumihiko Yamada   Counselor, Executive Office of the Governor,
                       Okinawa Prefecture
Masanori Yoshimoto   Vice-Governor, Okinawa Prefecture

United States

Michael Armacost   Former Ambassador to Japan
Richard Armitage   Former Assistant Secretary of Defense
James Auer   Former Director of Japan Desk, Department
                       of defense (DOD)
John Baker   Commander 18th Wing, Kadena Air Base
Andrew Bennett   Assistant Professor, Georgetown University

Doug Bereuter	Chairman, House Committee on International Relations, Subcommittee on the Asia Pacific (R-Neb.)
Melba Boling	Secretary for the Secretary of Defense
William Breer	Staff Member, Policy and Planning Staff, Department of State; Former Minister in the U.S. Embassy in Japan
Richard Bush	Advanced Analyst, National Intelligence Council
Benjamin Caetano	Governor of Hawaii
Kurt Campbell	Deputy Assistant Secretary of Defense
William Cohen	Senator (R-Maine)
Patrick Cronin	Institute for National Strategic Studies, National Defense University
Rust Deming	Deputy Chief of Mission, the U.S. Embassy in Japan
Richard Douglas	Staff Member, Japan Country Desk, DOD
Chuck Downs	Deputy Director, Regional Affairs and Congressional Relations, Asian and Pacific Region, DOD
Charles Dyke	Former Commander of U.S. Forces in Japan
Gayle Von Eckartsburg	Staff Member, Japan Country Desk, DOD
Karl Eikenberry	Director of China Desk, DOD
Thomas Foley	Former Speaker of the House of Representatives
Carl Ford	Former Deputy Assistant Secretary of Defense
Charles Freeman	Former Assistant Secretary of Defense
Paul Giarra	Director of Japan Desk, DOD
Paul Godwin	Professor, National War College
Michael Green	Analyst, Institute for Defense Analysis
Robert Hall	Special Assistant to the Secretary of Defense
Dennis Hejlik	Colonel, U.S. Marine Corps (Ret.)
Brig. Gen. Tom Hobbins	Commander 18th Wing, Kadena Air Base
Thomas Hubbard	Deputy Assistant Secretary of State
Charles Kartman	Deputy Assistant Secretary of State
Sandra Kristoff	Senior Director, East Asian Bureau, National Security Council (NSC)
Charles Krulak	Commandant of the Marine Corps
Victor Krulak	General, Marine Corps (Ret.)
Anthony Lake	National Security Adviser, NSC

Mark Lambert	Japan Country Desk Officer, Department of State
James Lilley	Former U.S. Ambassador to China
Thomas Linn	Chief Officer for Strategic Concepts, Marine Corps
Winston Lord	Assistant Secretary of State
Mike Mansfield	Former Ambassador to Japan
John McCain	Senator (R-Ariz.)
Michael McDevitt	General, Marine Corps (Ret.)
Eric McVadon	Admiral, U.S. Navy (Ret.)
Frank Meeks	Head of Domino's Pizza Washington Business Center
Richard Meyers	Commander of U.S. Forces in Japan
Walter Mondale	Ambassador to Japan
Joseph Nye	Assistant Secretary of Defense
Aloysius O'Neill	Consul-General, U.S. Consulate in Naha
William Owens	Vice-Admiral, U.S. Navy
Douglas Paal	Former Senior Director, East Asian Bureau, NSC
Torkel Patterson	Former Director, East Asian Bureau, NSC
William Pendley	Former Deputy Assistant Secretary of Defense
William Perry	Secretary of Defense
Michael Powell	Former Staff Member of the Office of Secretary of Defense
Charles Pritchard	Director, East Asian Bureau, NSC
Robert Reis, Jr.	Director, Office of Japanese Affairs, Department of State
Alan Romberg	Deputy Head of the Policy and Planning Staff, Department of State
Stanley Roth	Senior Director, East Asian Bureau, NSC
Robin Sakoda	Director of Japan Desk, DOD
Brent Scowcroft	Former National Security Adviser
Joseph Sestuk	Director, Arms Control and Defense Policy Bureau, NSC
David Shear	Chief of Political-Military Affairs Section, U.S. Embassy in Japan
Walter Slocombe	Undersecretary of Defense
James Steinberg	Chief of Policy and Planning Staff, Department of State
John Steinbrunner	Researcher Fellow, Brookings Institution
Robert Suettinger	Director, East Asian Bureau, NSC
Ezra Vogel	Advanced Analyst, National Intelligence Council (NIC)

Kent Wiedermann	Deputy Assistant Secretary of State
James Woolsey	Former Director of the Central Intelligence Agency (CIA)
William Wright	Director, Asian and Pacific Affairs Region, DOD

Others

José Ebro	Press Officer, Philippines Embassy in the United States
Gong Ro-Myung	Former Minister of Foreign Affairs, Republic of Korea (ROK)
Han Seung-Joo	Former Minister of Foreign Affairs, ROK
Yoo Chong Ha	Former Senior Secretary for National Security and Foreign Affairs, Presidential Secretariat, ROK; Minister of Foreign Affairs, ROK

Titles are those at the time of interviews.
The list does not include those officials—mainly from China and Taiwan—who requested anonymity.

Abbreviations and Acronyms

ACSA	Agreement Concerning Reciprocal Provision of Logistic Support, Supplies, and Services
APEC	Asia-Pacific Economic Cooperation
ASDF	Air Self-Defense Force (Japan)
ASEM	Asia-Europe Meeting
CIA	Central Intelligence Agency
CINCPAC	Commander-in-Chief, Pacific Command
CLB	Cabinet Legislative Bureau
CRIO	Cabinet Research and Information Office
CSO	Cabinet Security Office
DFAA	Defense Facilities Administration Agency
DIA	Defense Intelligence Agency
DMZ	Demilitarized Zone (Korea)
DOD	Department of Defense
DPP	Democratic Progressive Party (Taiwan)
EASR	East Asia Strategic Report
EASI	East Asia Strategy Initiative
FSX	next-generation fighter (aircraft)
GSDF	Ground Self-Defense Force (Japan)
IAEA	International Atomic Energy Agency
IDA	Institute for Defense Analysis
III MEF	Third Marine Expeditionary Force
IISS	International Institute for Strategic Studies
INSS	Institute for National Strategic Studies
ISA	International Security Agency
JDA	Japanese Defense Agency
JDIH	Japan Defense Intelligence Headquarters
JIIA	Japan Institute for International Affairs
JSP	Japan Socialist Party
KEDO	Korean Energy Development Organization
KMT	Kuomintang
LDP	Liberal Democratic Party
MFN	most-favored nation
MITI	Ministry of International Trade and Industry (Japan)
MHW	Ministry of Health and Welfare (Japan)
MOB	mobile offshore base
MOF	Ministry of Finance (Japan)
MOFA	Ministry of Foreign Affairs (Japan)

MPF	Maritime Pre-Positioning Force
MSA	Maritime Safety Agency (Japan)
MSDF	Maritime Self-Defense Force (Japan)
NDPO	National Defense Program Outline
NDU	National Defense University
NEC	National Economic Council
NIC	National Intelligence Council
NPA	National Police Agency (Japan)
NPT	Non-proliferation Treaty
NSA	National Security Agency
NSC	National Security Council
PKF	peacekeeping forces
PKO	peacekeeping operation
PLA	People's Liberation Army (China)
POAC	Pentagon Athletic Club
QDR	Quadrennial Defense Review
QIP	quick installation platform
SACO	Special Action Committee on Okinawa
SBF	sea-based facility
SCC	U.S.-Japan Security Consultation Committee
SDF	Self-Defense Forces
SLOC	sea lines of communication
SDP	Social Democratic Party
SOFA	Status of Forces Agreement
TMD	theater missile defense
31 MEU	31st Marine Expeditionary Unit
USTR	U.S. Trade Representative
WTO	World Trade Organization

Index

About the Author

Yoichi Funabashi, columnist and chief diplomatic correspondent of *Asahi Shimbun* and a contributing editor of *Foreign Policy*, is a leading journalist in the area of Japanese foreign policy. He served as correspondent for *Asahi Shimbun* in Beijing (1980–81) and Washington (1984–87) and as American General Bureau Chief (1993–97). He was awarded the Japan Press Award, known as Japan's Pulitzer Prize, in 1994 for his columns on foreign policy, and his articles for *Foreign Affairs* and *Foreign Policy* won the Ishibashi Tanzan Prize in 1992. In 1985 he received the Vaughn-Ueda Prize for his reporting on international affairs.

Mr. Funabashi's other books include *Neibu: Inside China* (1983); *U.S.-Japan Economic Entanglement: The Inside Story* (1987); *Managing the Dollar: From the Plaza to the Louvre* (1998, winner of the Yoshino Sakuzo Prize); *A Design for a New Course of Japan's Foreign Policy* (1993); and *Asia-Pacific Fusion: Japan's Role in APEC* (1995, winner of the Mainichi Shimbun Asia Pacific Grand Prix Award).

He obtained his doctorate from Keio University in 1992 and his bachelor's degree from Tokyo University in 1968. He was a Neiman Fellow at Harvard University (1975–76) and an Ushiba Fellow at the Institute for International Economics (1987).